# *Electrical Networks and Circuits*



**B.S. Manke**

*Formerly Prof. of Electrical Engineering*
*Maulana Azad National Institute of Technology*
*Bhopal, (M.P.)*

**KHANNA PUBLISHERS**

Operational Office
4575/15, Onkar House, Ground Floor,
Darya Ganj, New Delhi 110 002
*Phones* : 011-23243042, 011-23243043 & Mob. 9811541460
*E-mail* : contactus@khannapublishers.in

*Published by :*
Romesh Chander Khanna & Vineet Khanna
*for* **KHANNA PUBLISHERS**
2-B, Nath Market, Nai Sarak
Delhi- 110 006 (India)

**Website : www.khannapublishers.in**



*Hologram & Description*

To all readers of our books, from yourself if being defrauded by pirates to prevent, please make sure that there is an Hologram on the cover of our books with the below specifications. If you find any book without Hologram and Description, please mail us at **contactus@khannapublishers.in**

Thanking you

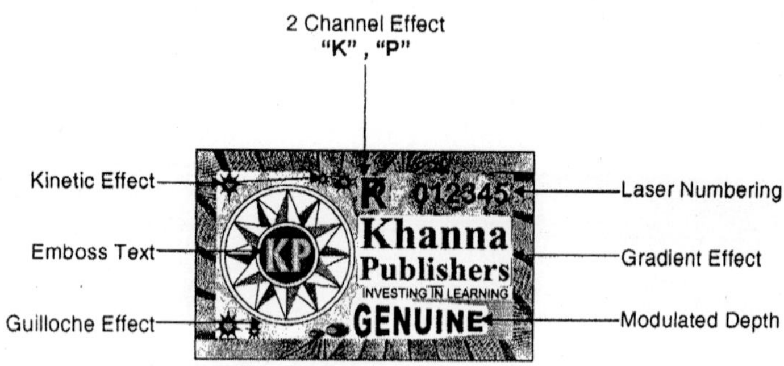


**ISBN No. 978-81-7409-247-2**

***First Edition : 2010***

***Price :* ₹ 249.00**

# *Preface to the First Edition*

The book provides a basic approach for the development of fundamental concepts and insight into the subject matter. The text dealt in the book gives contents in a simplified sequential manner. The theoretical explanation is supported by graded examples. The answers to the numerical problems are provided, to enable students to verify the results.

The book is written as introductory course in the subject Electrical Networks/Circuits and it is assumed that the students using this book have the knowledge of Basic Electrical Engineering.

The book meets the requirements of undergraduate students of Electrical, Electronics, Instrumentation Control and Computer Science branch in the subject Networks/Circuits. The book is also useful for professional and competitive examinations.

—B.S. Manke

# *About the Author*

**B.S. Manke,** graduated in Electrical Engineering from Madhav Institute of Technology and Science, Gwalior in 1962 and completed postgraduation in Electrical Engineering in 1964 from College of Engineering, Pune, where he was awarded Senior Fellowship from 1962 to 1965 under Technical Teachers Training Programme of Government of India.

He joined Maulana Azad National Institute of Technology, Bhopal, as a Lecturer in Electrical Engineering Department in 1965, and was promoted to the post of Asstt. Prof. and Prof. in 1974 and 1991 respectively. He also served as the Head of Electrical Engineering Department from 1994 to 1996 in the same institution.

Besides teaching control systems at undergraduate and postgraduate levels for about four decades, Prof. Manke has been teaching basic courses in Electrical Engineering and Electrical Network Theory.

On attaining age of superannuation Prof. Manke retired from service in January 2002.

Prof. B.S. Manke had written books with the following titles.

1. Linear Control Systems.
2. Control System Design.

# Contents

# 1

# INTRODUCTION

## 1.1 ELECTRIC CURRENT

The transfer of electrons constitute a flow of current in a conductor. The electron has a charge of $1.602 \times 10^{-19}$ coulomb and by convention this charge is assumed to be negative.

As the electric current is rate of flow of positive charges, the positive direction of electric current in a conductor is opposite to that of the flow of electrons.

The flow of electric current in a conductor is thus,

$$i = \frac{dq}{dt}$$

where $i$ : current (ampere)

$q$ : charge (coulomb)

and $t$ : time (second)

The charge of an electron is $1.602 \times 10^{-19}$ coulomb, hence, one coulomb of charge contains $1 / 11.602 \times 10^{-19} = 6.25 \times 10^{18}$ electrons. A current of one ampere flows, if the movement of charge across the cross-section of a conductor is at the rate of one coulomb per second. The direction of the current is considered to be a flow of positive charge and an arrow used to indicate the current flow.

The flow of electric current in a conductor is due to application of the electrical voltage across, the conductor. The electrical voltage across the conductor is termed as electromotive force and its unit is volt. The pressure voltage (potential difference) across a conductor allows a flow of current in it.

## 1.2 POTENTIAL DIFFERENCE

The potential difference between two points in an electric circuit is given by the work done for transferring a unit positive charge from one point to another. The unit of potential difference is volt. To have a potential difference of one volt, the work done 1 joule is required to transfer a unit positive charge from one point to another. The current flows from higher potential to lower potential.

The electromotive force (*e.m.f.*) is the potential difference between terminals of the electrical energy source (battery/generator), when the source is not delivering current.

The potential difference is expressed in terms of energy per unit charge. Thus, $V = \frac{W}{Q}$

or $\quad v = \frac{dw}{dq}$

$W$ : Energy in joules
$Q$ : Charge in coulombs
$V$ : Voltage in volts.

## 1.3 ELECTRIC POWER AND ENERGY

### POWER

Power is the rate at which the energy is consumed. Thus,

$$p = \frac{dw}{dt}$$

The electrical power is the product of voltage and current as given below,

$$p = \frac{dw}{dq} \cdot \frac{dq}{dt}$$

$$\because \quad \frac{dw}{dq} = v \text{ and } \frac{dq}{dt} = i$$

$$\therefore \quad p = v\, i$$

The power at any instant is given by the product of voltage and current. For time-invariant voltage and current.

$$P = V\, I$$

The unit of power is watt.

When the power consumed is less than one watt the same is expressed in fraction of watt *i.e.* milliwatt (mW), microwatt $\mu W$ as in electronic and communication networks. For electrical power circuits the power is expressed in kilowatt kW and megawatt MW

$$1 \text{ mW} = 10^{-3} \text{ watt}$$

$$1 \text{ }\mu\text{W} = 10^{-6} \text{ watt}$$

$$1 \text{ kW} = 10^{3} \text{ watt}$$

$$1 \text{ MW} = 10^{6} \text{ watt}$$

### Energy

Electrical Power $p = v\, i$

$$\because \quad p = \frac{dw}{dt}$$

$$\therefore \quad \frac{dw}{dt} = v\, i$$

On integrating both sides

$$\int d\,w = \int v\, i\, dt$$

$\therefore$ Electrical energy

$$W = \int v\, i\, dt$$

The unit of electrical energy is watt-secs. Thus joule = watt-sec.

For d.c. circuits

$$P = VI$$

$$\because \quad V = IR$$

$$\therefore \quad P = I^2 R$$

Also $\because$ $\quad I = \dfrac{V}{R}$

$$\therefore \quad P = \frac{V^2}{R}$$

$$W = Pt = VIt \qquad \text{watt–sec}$$

or $\quad W = I^2\; Rt \qquad$ watt–sec

or $\quad W = \dfrac{V^2}{R} t \qquad$ watt–sec

For large energy consumption, the energy is expressed as

$$1 \text{ kWh} = 10^3 \text{ watt–hour}$$

$$1 \text{ MWh} = 10^6 \text{ watt–hour}$$

## 1.4 OHM'S LAW

The fundamental law in electrical engineering is Ohm's law which states:

"The electric current flowing in a conductor is directly proportional to the voltage applied across its terminals." *i.e.*

$$i \propto v$$

The constant of proportionality is $\dfrac{1}{R}$. Therefore,

$$i = \frac{1}{R.}\; v$$

or $$i = \nu R$$

$R$ is known as the resistance of the conductor through which the current ($i$) is flowing due to the application of voltage ($\nu$) across it.

The resistance of a conductor offers opposition to the flow of current. The unit of resistance is ohm ($\Omega$).

The reciprocal $\left(\frac{1}{R}\right)$ of the resistance is known as conductance $G$. The unit of conductance is mho $\mho$. In terms of conductance the Ohm's law is written as:

$$i = G\nu$$

or $$\nu = \frac{1}{G} \cdot i$$

## 1.5 CIRCUIT ELEMENTS AND NETWORK

The voltage, source, current source and resistor ($R$), inductor ($L$), capacitor ($C$) are the elements of an electrical network. The network is termed as a circuit, if it has at least one closed path through its elements. Thus, every circuit is a network but all networks may not be a circuit as shown in Fig. 1.5.1 and 1.5.2.

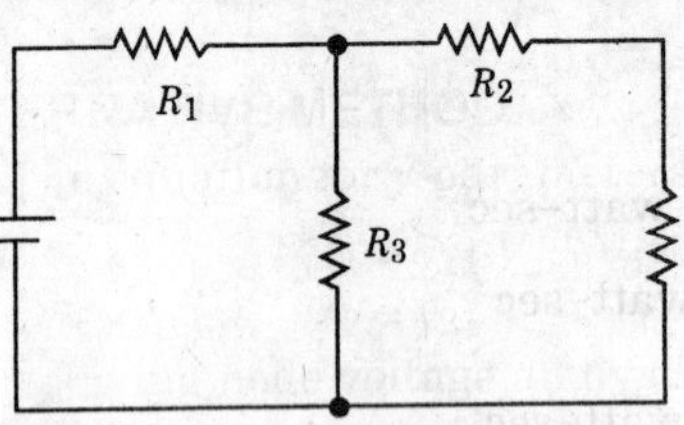

Fig. 1.5.1: This network is a circuit.

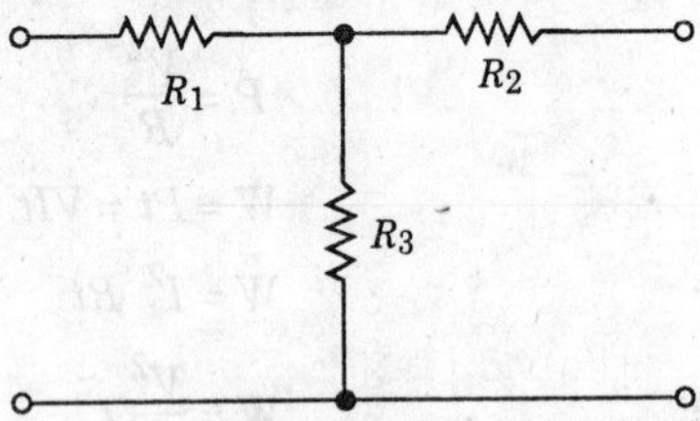

Fig. 1.5.2: This network is not a circuit.

The relationship of the current through an element to the voltage across it classifies the element as follows:

1. The element across which the voltage is proportional to the current through it, is called a resistor
$$\nu = R\,i$$
and power $$p = \nu\,i$$
2. The element across which the voltage is proportional to time derivative of the current flowing through it, is called an inductor
$$\nu = L\frac{di}{dt}$$
and the energy stored in the inductor is
$$W_L = \frac{1}{2} L\,i^2$$

The unit of inductance $L$ of the inductor is henry ($H$).

3. The element across which the voltage is proportional to time integral of the current through it, is called a capacitor.

$$v = \frac{1}{C}\int i dt$$

and the energy stored in the capacitor is

$$w_C = \frac{1}{2} C v^2$$

The unit of capacitance $C$ of the capacitor is farad ($F$).

The resistor, inductor and capacitor are two terminal elements.

## 1.6 KIRCHHOFF'S LAWS

The equation relating the voltages and currents in term of resistance ($R$) of the resistor, inductance ($L$) of the inductor, capacitance ($C$) of the capacitor are formulated on the basis of Kirchhoff's laws as stated below:

1. Kirchhoff's Current Law (*KCL*)

"The algebraic sum of all currents at a node (junction) in an electric circuit is zero at any instant".

2. "Kirchhoff's Voltage Law (*KVL*)

The algebraic sum of all voltages around a closed path in an electric circuit is zero at any instant".

An electrical network is formed by appropriate connection of circuit elements. The elements are resistor, inductor and capacitor. These elements are passive as they consume or store electrical energy. The elements such as voltage and current sources are active elements *i.e.* they supply electrical energy.

The analysis of an electrical network/circuit enables to determine

(*i*) the voltage (potential difference) across various elements
(*ii*) the current flowing through various elements.

## 1.7 VOLTAGE DROP AND CURRENT THROUGH A RESISTOR, INDUCTOR AND CAPACITOR

The voltage and current are usually functions of time denoted by lower-case letters $v$ and $i$ respectively. The upper-case letters $V$ and $I$ refer to voltage and current which are time-invariant *i.e.* d.c. quantities and also *r.m.s.* values in a.c. circuits.

The circuit elements symbols are shown in Fig. 1.7.1.

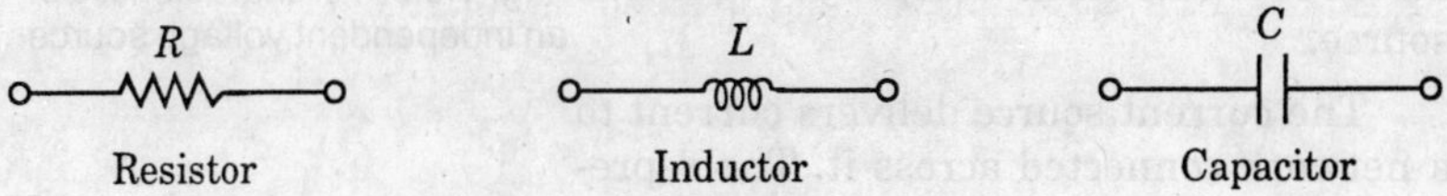


Fig. 1.7.1. Circuit element symbols.

While formulating equations based on Kirchhoff's voltage law, the algebraic summation of the following terms is used:

$$Ri, L\frac{di}{dt} \text{ and } \frac{1}{C}\int i\,dt$$

These terms represent voltage drops across resistor, inductor and capacitor respectively.

Similarly, while formulating equations based on Kirchhoff's current law, the algebraic summation of the following terms is used:

$$\frac{v}{R} \text{ or } G\,v, \frac{1}{L}\int v\,dt \text{ and } C\frac{d\,v}{dt}$$

These terms represent current flowing through the resistor, inductor and capacitor respectively.

## 1.8 SOURCES OF ELECTRICAL ENERGY

The electrical energy source wherein the voltage is completely independent of the current delivered from it is known as independent voltage source.

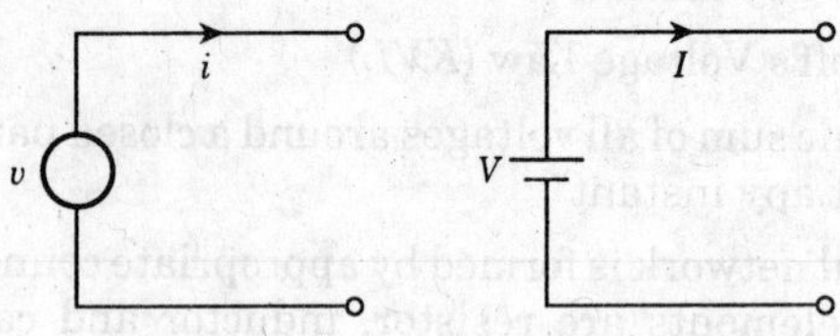


(a) (b)

Fig. 1.8.1. Independent voltage source.

**1. The Voltage Source:** The generator type independent voltage source which has a constant terminal voltage is shown in Fig. 1.8.1 (*a*).

If the source is a battery, the independent voltage source is represented as shown in Fig. 1.8.1 (*b*).

The v-*i* characteristic of an independent voltage is shown in Fig. 1.8.2. The voltage of the independent voltage source is constant whatever may be the current drawn from it.

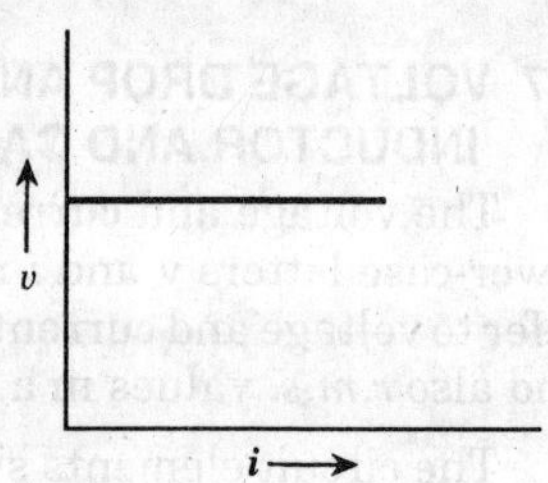


Fig. 1.8.2. v-*i* characteristic of an independent voltage source.

**2. The Current Source:** The energy source wherein the current delivered is completely independent of the voltage across it is known as independent current source.

The current source delivers current to a network connected across it. The representation of an independent current source is shown in Fig. 1.8.3(*a*).

If the source supplies a direct current the representation is shown in Fig. 1.8.3(*b*).

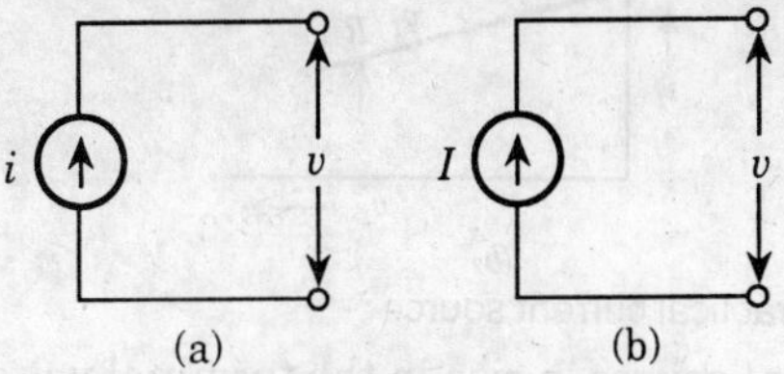

Fig. 1.8.3. Independent current source.

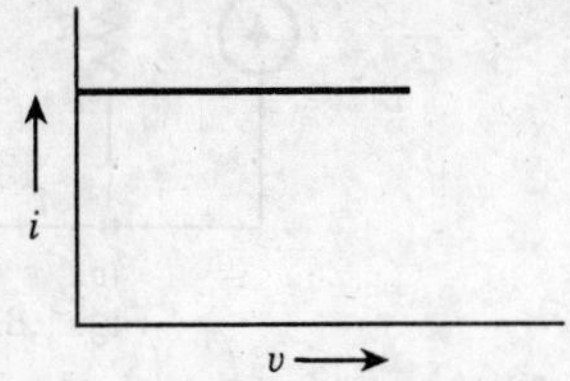

Fig.1.8.4 $v$-$i$ characteristic of an independent current source.

The $v$-$i$ characteristic at the terminals of an independent current source is shown in Fig. 1.8.4.

The current supplied by the independent current source is constant whatever may be the voltage across it.

The sources of electrical energy described above are ideal sources because the value of source quantity is not affected in any way be the network configuration connected across its terminals. However, a practical energy source has an internal resistance associated with it.

**3. Practical Voltage Source:** In case of a practical voltage source, its internal resistance $R$ is connected in series, Fig. 1.8.5(*a*).

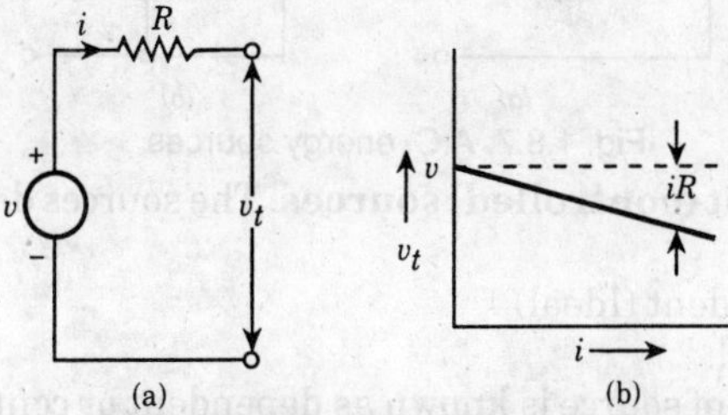

Fig. 1.8.5. Practical voltage source.

The voltage $v_t$ at the terminals of a practical voltage source is

$$v_t = v - iR$$

The voltage at the terminals of a practical voltage source falls with the current drawn from the source, because the voltage drop ($iR$) appears across the internal resistance ($R$). The $v$–$i$ characteristic at the terminals of a practical voltage source is shown in Fig. 1.8.5(*b*).

**4. Practical Current Source:** The practical current source has an internal resistance ($R$), which is placed in parallel at its terminals Fig. 1.8.6(*a*).

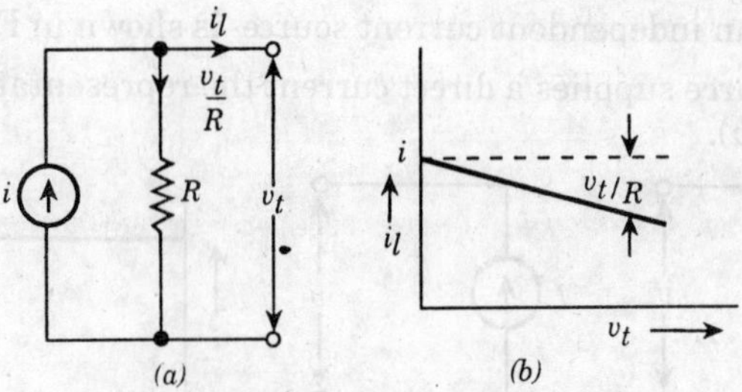

Fig. 1.8.6 Practical current source

In case of a practical current source, a rise in the terminal voltage ($v_t$) increases the current ($v_t/R$) in the internal resistance. Hence, the load current ($i_l$) decreases as per equation given below:

$$i_l = i - \frac{v_t}{R}$$

The v-*i* characteristic at the terminals of a current source is shown in Fig. 1.8.6.(*b*).

The symbolic representation of a.c. voltage source and current source is shown in Fig.1.8.7(*a*) and (*b*) respectively.

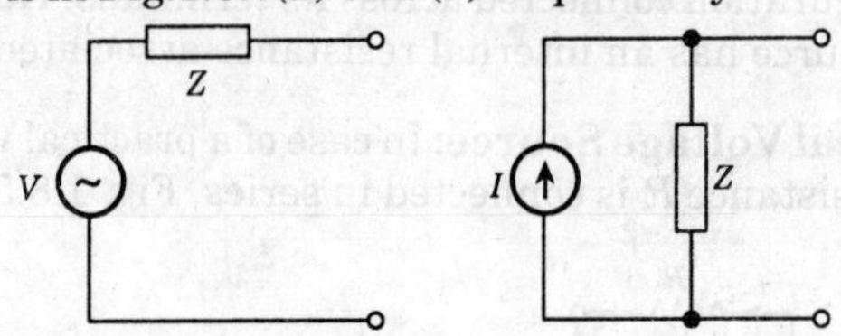

Fig. 1.8.7. A.C. energy sources

**5. Dependent (controlled) sources**: The sources described above are:-

(*i*) Independent (Ideal)
(*ii*) Practical.

Another type of source is known as dependent or controlled source, wherein the value of the source depends on the voltage or current at some other location say *x* in the network connected across the terminals of such a source, such sources are represented by a diamond shaped symbol as shown in Fig. 1.8.8(*a*) and (*b*).

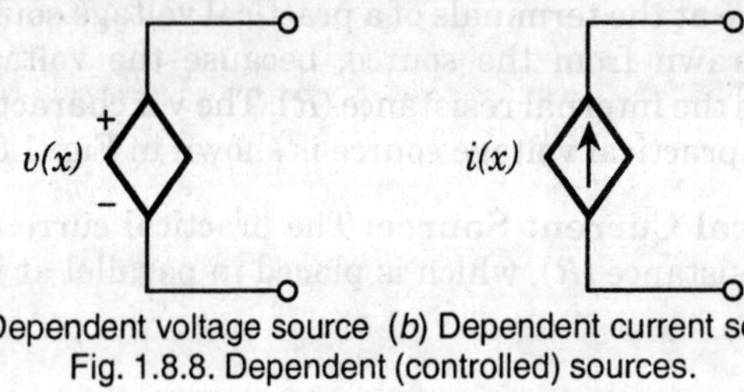

(*a*) Dependent voltage source (*b*) Dependent current source.
Fig. 1.8.8. Dependent (controlled) sources.

## 1.9 SOURCE TRANSFORMATION

For formulating network equation it is some times required to convert a voltage/current source into an equivalent current/voltage source. The two sources are said to be equivalent, if their effect is same.

The equivalence of voltage source and current source is derived below:

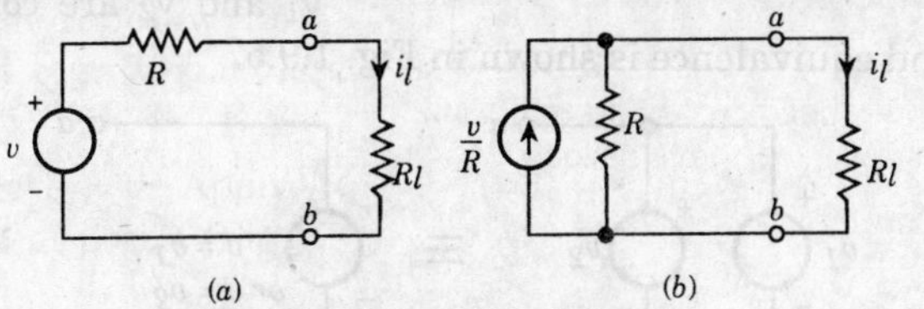

Fig. 1.9.1 Source transformation.

As shown in Fig. 1.9.1($a$), a practical voltage source $v$ having internal resistance $R$ is connected across terminals $a$-$b$ to a load resistance $R_l$. The current flowing through the load resistance $R_l$ is

$$i_l = \frac{v}{R + R_l}$$

If the voltage source is converted to a current source of value $v/R$ with a parallel internal resistance $R$, the circuit across terminals $a$-$b$ is obtained as shown in Fig. 1.9.1($b$). The current flowing through the load resistance $R_l$ is

$$i_l = \frac{v}{R} \cdot \frac{R}{R + R_l}$$

or

$$i_l = \frac{v}{R + R_l}$$

Hence, the voltage source and current source shown in Fig. 1.9.1 ($a$) and 1.9.1 ($b$) are equivalent. The symbolic equivalence representation is shown in Fig. 1.9.2.

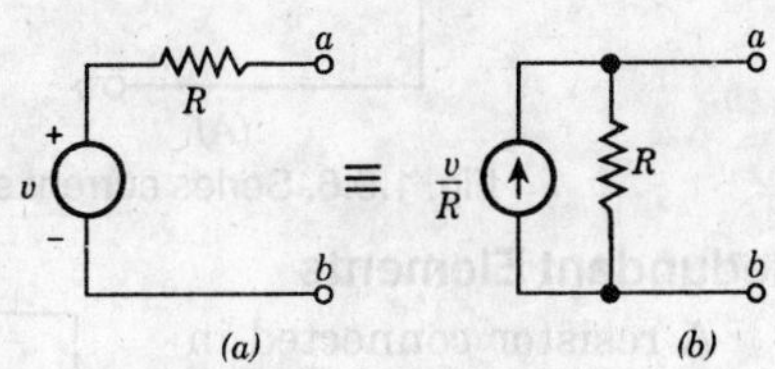

Fig. 1.9.2. Equivalence of voltage-current source.

The controlled voltage/current source can be transformed into an equivalent current/voltage source. As the value of controlled source depend on the controlling signals, these signals should not be altered during the process of transformation.

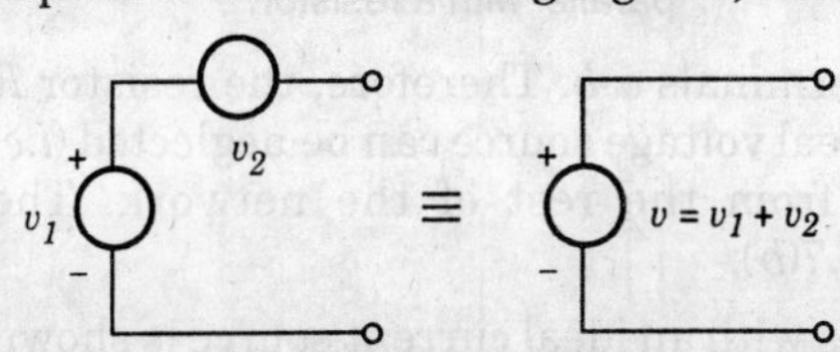

Fig. 1.9.3 Voltages in series.

**Source Equivalence :** As shown in Fig. 1.9.3, two voltages $v_1$ and $v_2$ are connected in series with additive polarity. The single source equivalence is $v = v_1 + v_2$

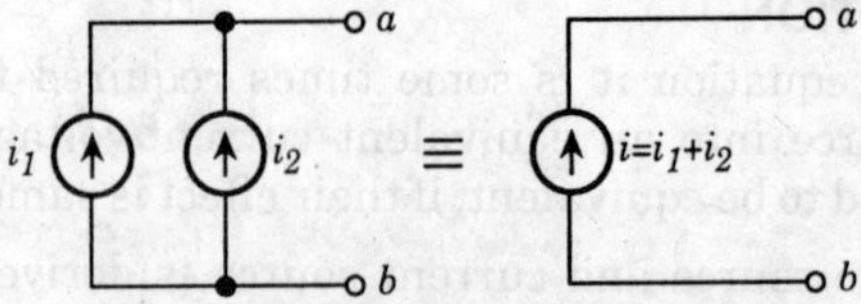


Fig. 1.9.4 Parallel current sources.

The two current sources $i_1$ and $i_2$ are connected is parallel (Fig. 1.9.4), the single source equivalence is $i = i_1 + i_2$

The two voltage sources $v_1$ and $v_2$ are connected in parallel and equivalence is shown in Fig. 1.9.5.

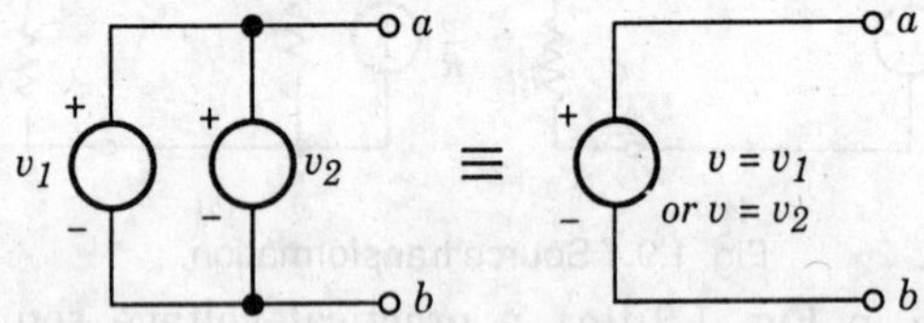


Fig. 1.9.5. Voltage sources in parallel (valid for $v_1 = v_2$).

It should be noted that parallel combination of two voltages is possible only if, they have identical values *i.e.* $v_1 = v_2$.

The connection of two current sources in series is shown in Fig. 1.9.6., the equivalence is possible if they have identical values.

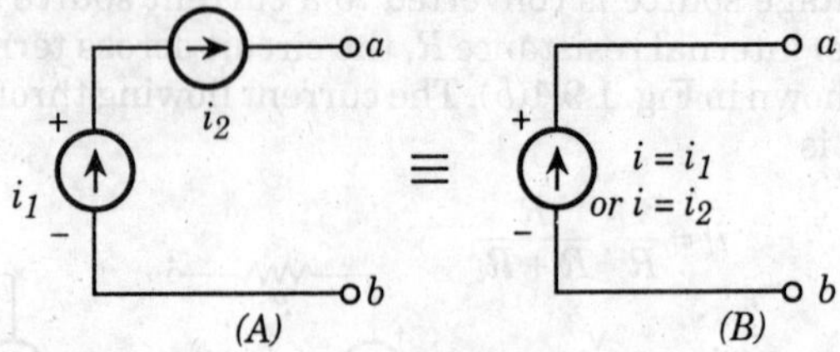


Fig. 1.9.6. Series current sources (valid for $i_1 = i_2$).

## Redundant Elements

A resistor connected in parallel with an ideal voltage source is shown in Fig. 1.9.7 (*a*).

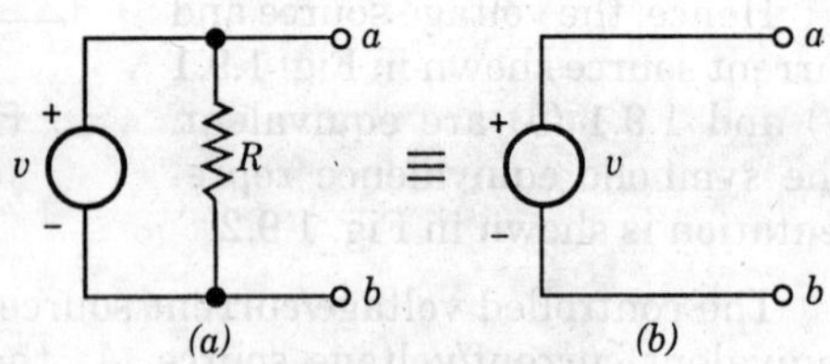


Fig. 1.9.7 Ideal voltage source in parallel with a resistor.

As the voltage across the terminals *a*-*b* is v, the resistor *R* is no longer needed in calculation for the network connected across the terminals *a*-*b*. Therefore, the resistor *R* connected in parallel with the ideal voltage source can be neglected (*i.e.* replaced by an open-circuit) from the rest of the network. The equivalence is shown in Fig. 1.9.7(*b*).

A resistor connected in series with an ideal current source is shown in Fig. 1.9.8. (*a*). This resistor is not affecting the current supplied by the source, as such the same may be deleted (*i.e.* replaced by a short circuit) from the network connected across terminals $a$-$b$. The equivalence is shown in Fig. 1.9.8($b$).

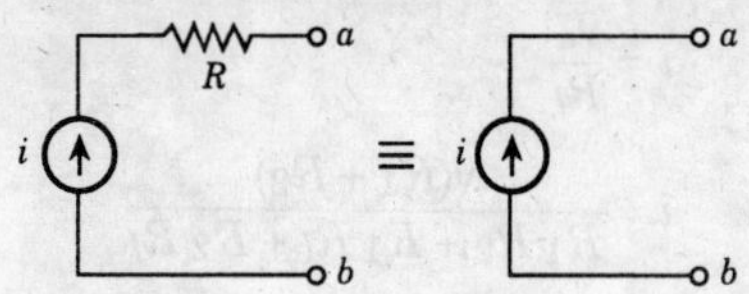


Fig. 1.9.8. Ideal current source in series with a resistor.

## 1.10 SOURCE SHIFTING

The transformation of practical voltage source to current source and vice-versa requires that a single resistor be in series with a voltage source, and in parallel with a current source. The source shifting technique is used so that the voltage source gets a series resistor or a current source a parallel resistor.

The two examples given below explain the process of source shifting.

1. The networks shown in Fig. 1.10.1 ($a$) and 1.10.1 ($b$) are equivalent.

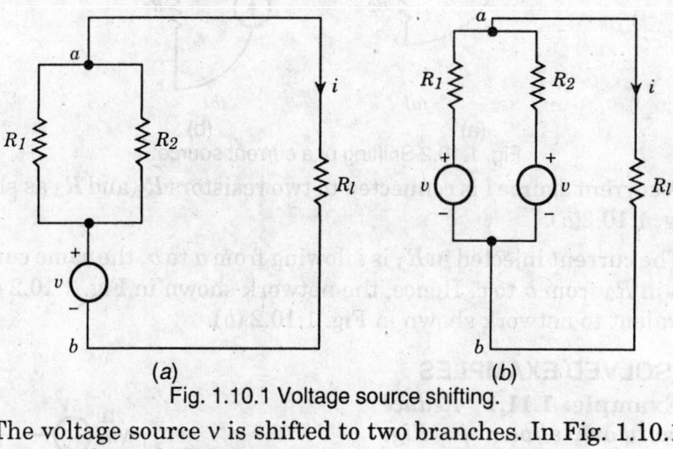


Fig. 1.10.1 Voltage source shifting.

The voltage source ν is shifted to two branches. In Fig. 1.10.1 ($a$), The current through $R_l$ is

$$i = \frac{\nu}{\dfrac{R_1 R_2}{R_1 + R_2} + R_l} = \frac{\nu(R_1 + R_2)}{R_1 R_2 + R_1 R_l + R_2 R_l}$$

In Fig. 1.10.1 ($b$), apply $KCL$ at junction a

$$i - i, - i_2 = 0$$

$$\therefore \quad \frac{\nu_a}{R_l} - \frac{\nu - \nu_a}{R_2} - \frac{\nu - \nu_a}{R_2} = 0$$

Solving above equation:

$$v_a = \frac{v(R_1 + R_2)R_l}{R_1 R_2 + R_1 R_l + R_2 R_l}$$

$$\because \quad i = \frac{v_a}{R_l}$$

$$\therefore \quad i = \frac{v(R_1 + R_2)}{R_1 R_2 + R_1 R_l + R_2 R_l}$$

Thus, the current $i$ in the resistance $R_l$ in Fig. 1.10.1(*a*) and 1.10.1(*b*) is same, the equivalence between network shown in Fig. 1.10.1(*a*) and 1.10.1(*b*) is established.

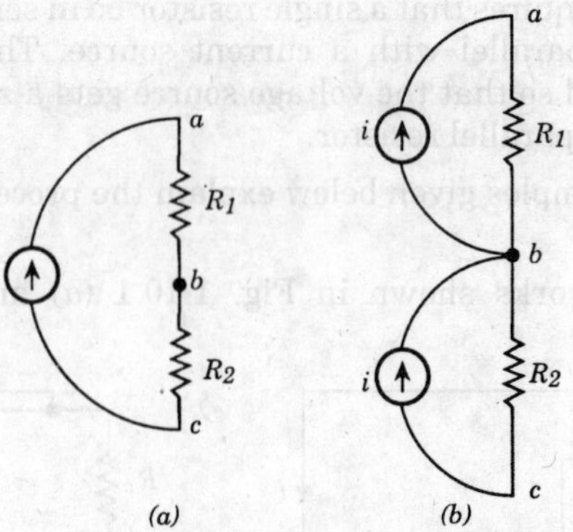


(a) (b)

Fig. 1.10.2 Shifting of a current source.

A current source $i$ is connected to two resistors $R_1$ and $R_2$ as shown in Fig. 1.10.2(*a*).

The current injected in $R_1$ is $i$ flowing from $a$ to $b$, the same current flows in $R_2$ from $b$ to $c$. Hence, the network shown in Fig. 1.10.2 (*a*) is equivalent to network shown in Fig. 1.10.2 (*b*).

## 1.11 SOLVED EXAMPLES

**Example: 1.11.1** *Reduce the network shown in Fig. 1.11.1. to a single voltage sources.*

**Solution**: Convert 5V, 2V and 8V voltage source in to equivalent current source to get Fig. 1.11.1 (*a*).

(*i*) Add 3 A and 4 A current sources (parallel)

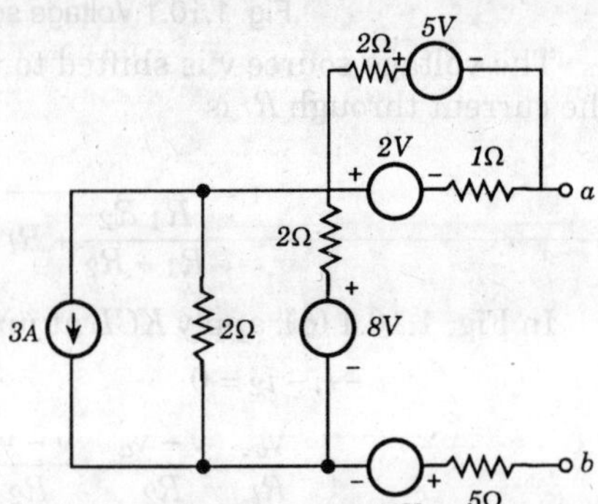


Fig. 1.11.1 Network for example 1.11.1.

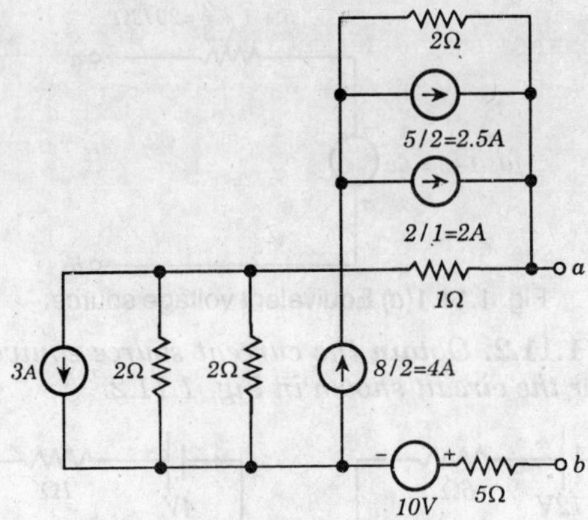


Fig. 1.11.1.(*a*) Reduction of Fig. 1.11.1.

(*ii*) Add 2.5 A and 2 A current sources (parallel) to obtain Fig. 1.11.1 (*b*).

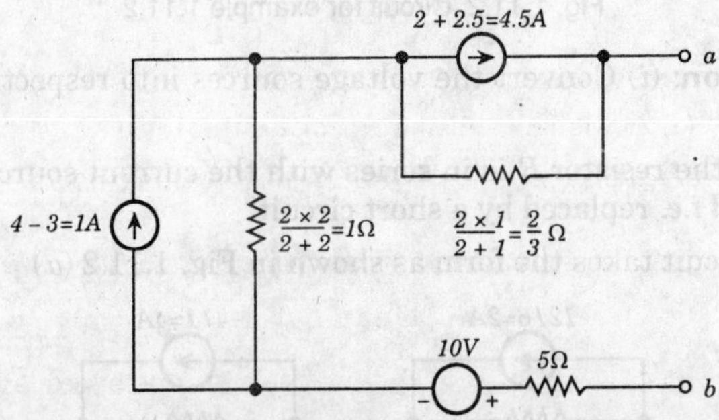


Fig. 1.11.1(*b*) Reduction of Fig. 1.11.1(*a*).

Convert 1A and 4.5 A current source into respective equivalent voltage source as shown in Fig. 1.11.1(*c*).

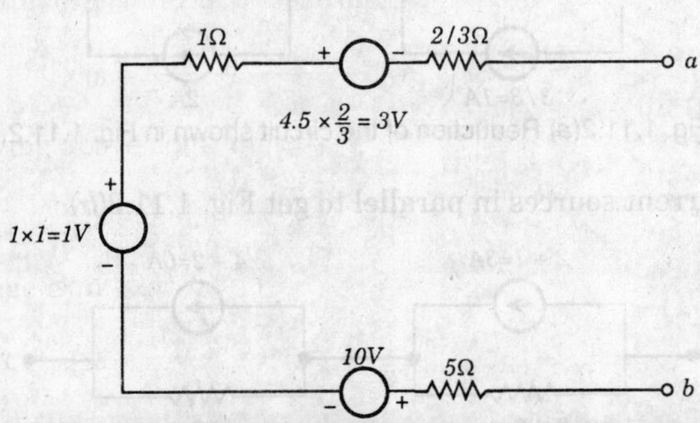


Fig. 1.11.1(*c*) Reduction of fig.1.11.1(*b*).

The equivalent voltage source for the network [Fig.1.11.1(*c*)] is shown in Fig. 1.11.1 (*d*). **Ans.**

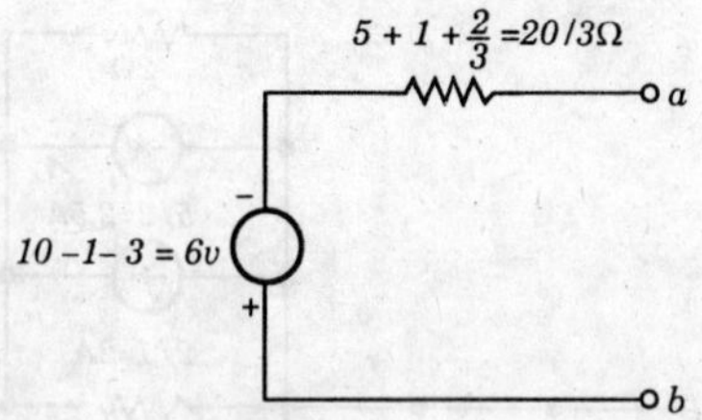


Fig. 1.11.1(*d*) Equivalent voltage source.

**Example: 1.11.2.** *Obtain the current source equivalence between terminals x-y for the circuit shown in Fig. 1.11.2.*

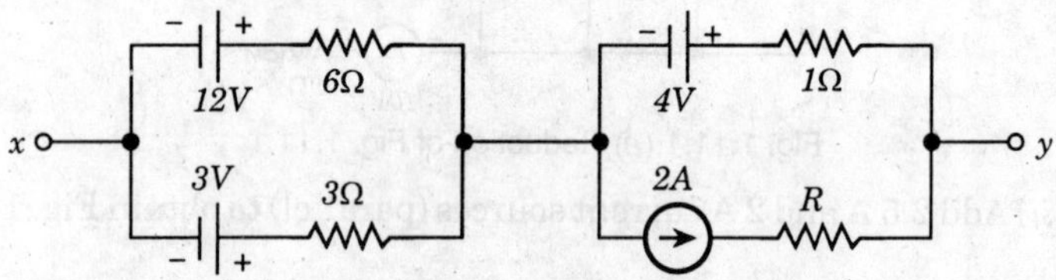


Fig. 1.11.2. Circuit for example 1.11.2.

**Solution**: (*i*) Convert the voltage sources into respective current sources.

(*ii*) As the resistor $R$ is in series with the current source the same is neglected *i.e.* replaced by a short circuit.

The circuit takes the form as shown in Fig. 1.11.2 (*a*)

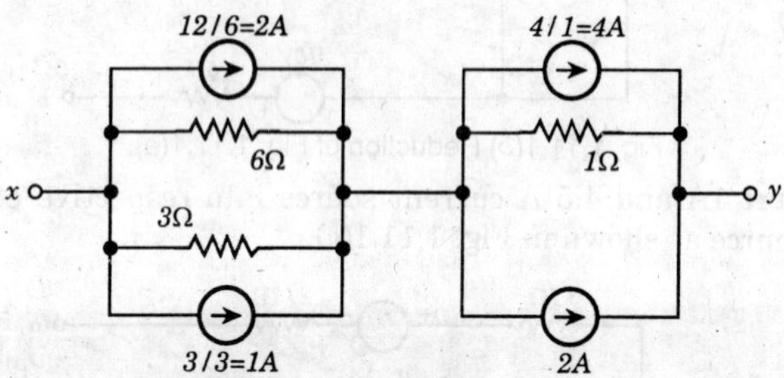


Fig. 1.11.2(*a*) Reduction of the circuit shown in Fig. 1.11.2.

Add current sources in parallel to get Fig. 1.11.2(*b*)

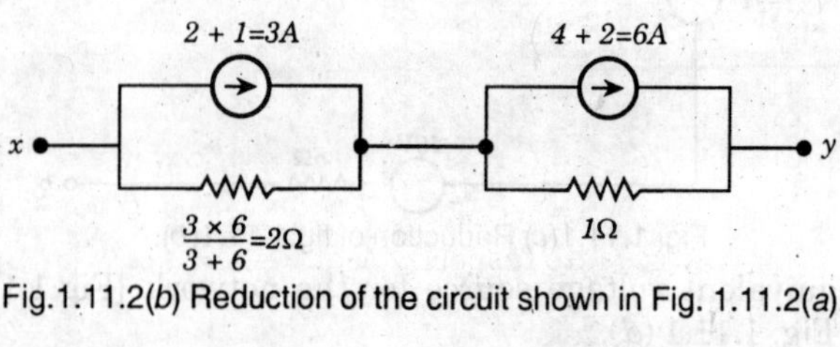


Fig.1.11.2(*b*) Reduction of the circuit shown in Fig. 1.11.2(*a*).

Convert the current sources into respective equivalent voltage sources as shown in Fig. 1.11.2($c$)

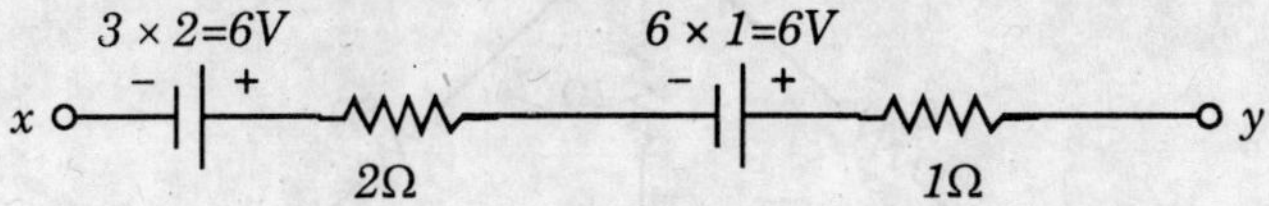


Fig.1.11.2($c$) Reduction of circuit shown in Fig.1.11.2($b$)

The equivalent circuit for Fig.1.11.2(c) is shown in Fig.1.11.2($d$).

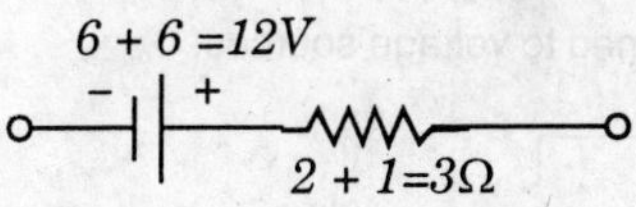


Fig. 1.11.2($d$) Equivalence of Fig. 1.11.2(c)

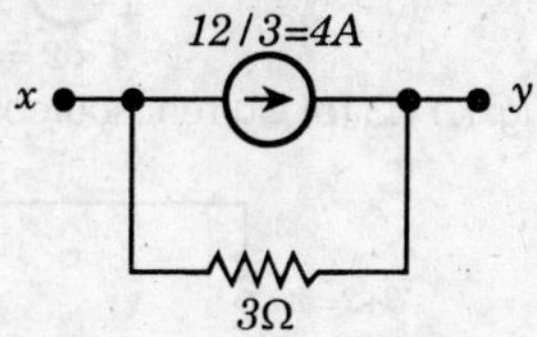


Fig.1.11.2($e$) Equivalent current source.

The equivalent current source is shown in Fig.1.11.2($e$) **Ans.**

**Example** : 1.11.3. *Obtain the single voltage source at terminals a-b for the network shown in Fig. 1.11.3*

**Solution:** Shift the 4 A current source Fig. 1.10.3 ($a$)

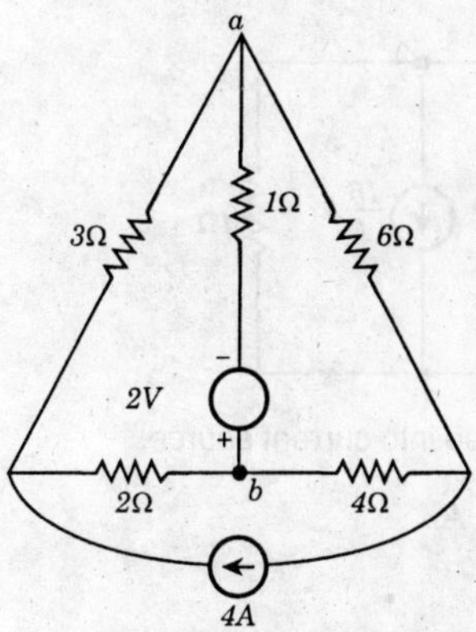


Fig.1.11.3 Network for example 1.11.3.

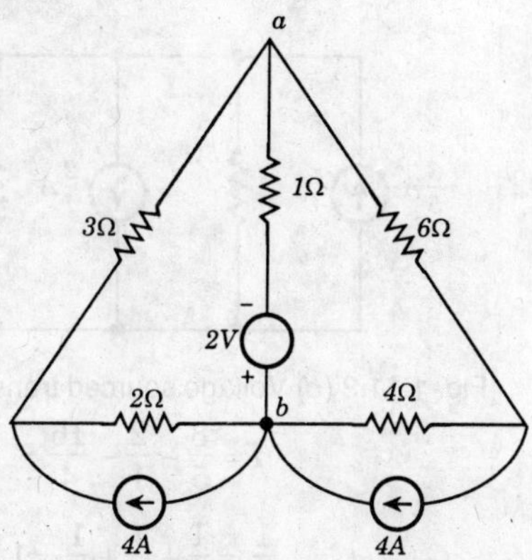


Fig.1.11.3($a$) Shifting of $A$ current source.

Transform the current sources into equivalent voltage sources as shown in Fig. 1.11.3.($b$).

Rearrange circuit shown in Fig. 1.11.3 ($b$) as shown below in Fig. 1.11.3($c$).

Transform voltage sources into respective equivalent current sources Fig. 1.11.3($d$)

Add current sources in parallel

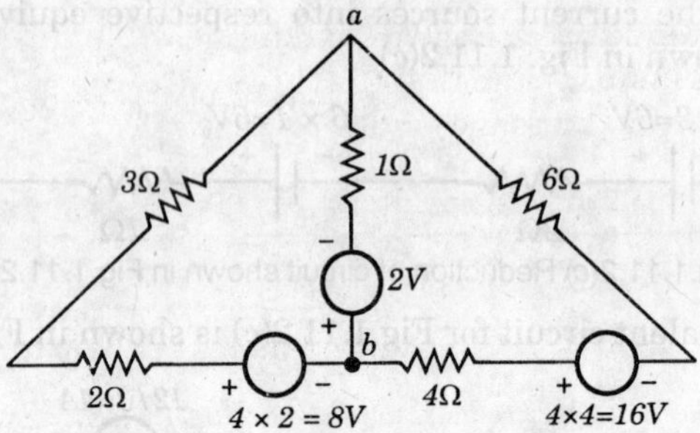

Fig.1.11.3 (*b*) Current sources transformed to voltage sources.

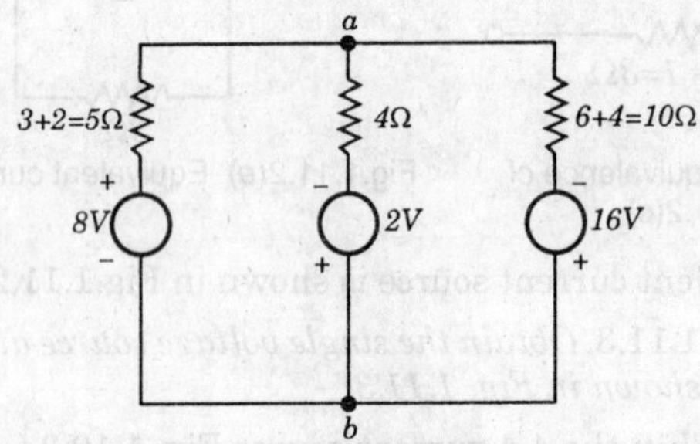

Fig.1.11.3 (*c*) Rearrangement of Fig.1.11.3 (*b*)

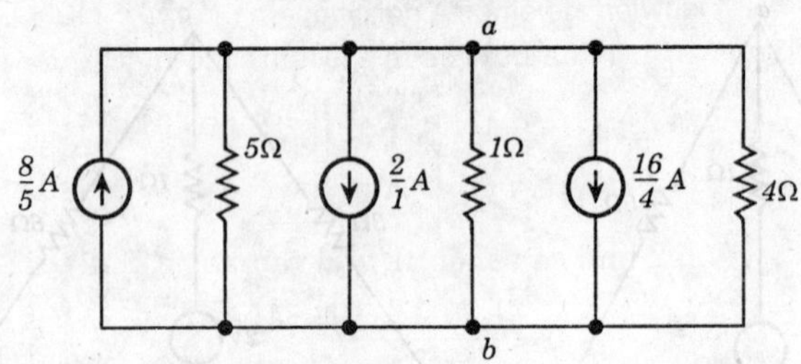

Fig. 1.11.3 (*d*) Voltage sourced transformed into current source.

$$I = \frac{8}{5} - \frac{2}{1} - \frac{16}{4} = -4.4 \text{ A}$$

$$\frac{1}{R} = \frac{1}{5} + \frac{1}{1} + \frac{1}{4} = 1.45$$

$$\therefore \quad R = \frac{1}{1.45} = 0.689\Omega$$

The equivalent current source is shown in Fig. 1.11.3 (*e*)

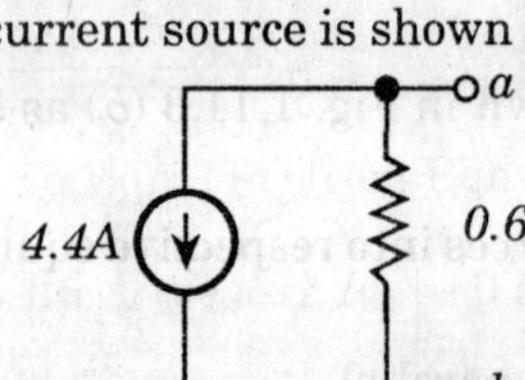

Fig.1.11.3(*e*) Current equivalent source.

The single voltage source network is shown in Fig. 1.11.3 (*f*)

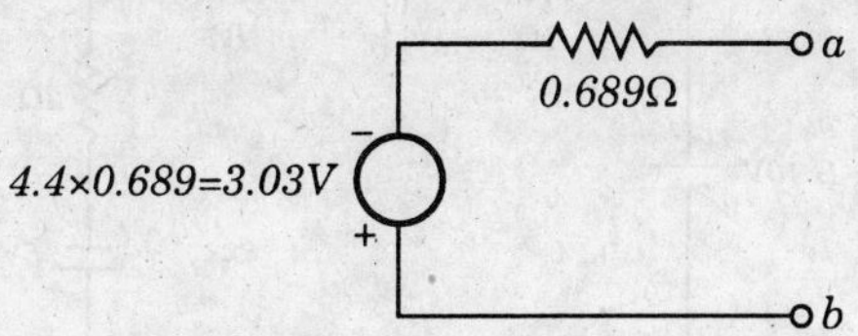


Fig.1.11.3(*f*) Single voltage source equivalence. **Ans.**

**Example: 1.11.4.** *Determine the equivalent current source for the network shown below.*

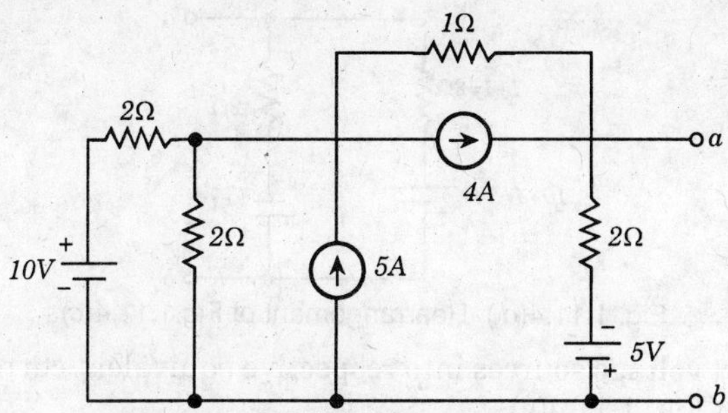


Fig.1.11.4 Network for example 1.11.4.

**Solution**: Transform,

(*i*) 10 *V* voltage source into equivalent current source.

(*ii*) 4 *A* current source into equivalent voltage source.

The transformed network is shown in Fig. 1.11.4(*a*)

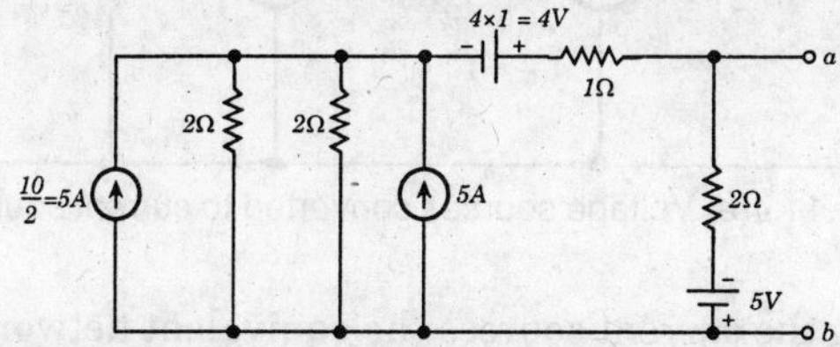


Fig.1.11.4(*a*) Transformation of 10 *V* and 4 *A* source.

Add parallel current sources as shown in Fig.1.11.4(*b*)

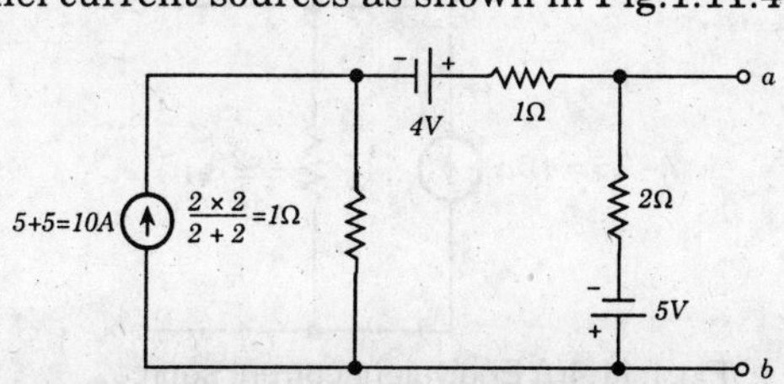


Fig. 1.11.4(*b*) Addition of current sources.

Convert 10 A current source into equivalent voltages source as shown in Fig. 1.11.4(*c*)

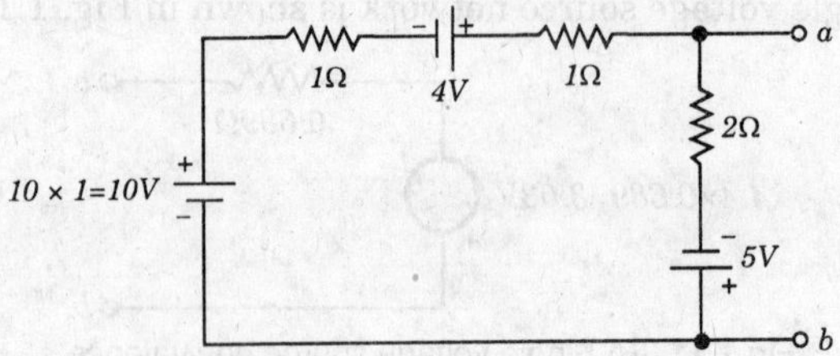


Fig. 1.11.4(*c*) 10 *A* current source converted to equivalent voltage source.

Rearrange network as shown in Fig. 1.11.4(*d*)

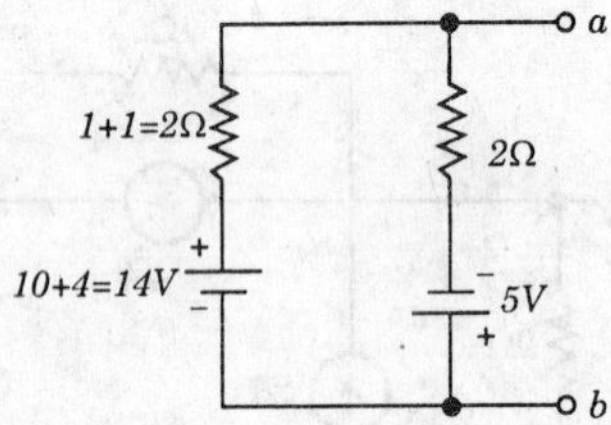


Fig. 1.11.4(*d*) Rearrangement of Fig.1.11.4(*c*)

Convert voltage sources into respective equivalent current sources as shown in Fig. 1.11.4(*e*)

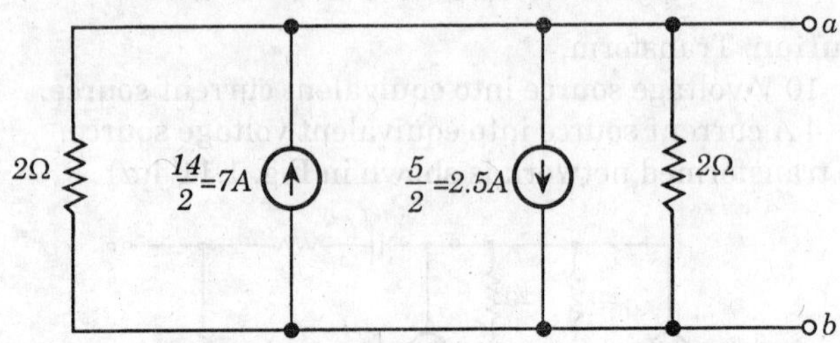


Fig. 1.11.4(*e*) Voltage sources converted to current sources.

On adding the current sources the equivalent network is shown in Fig. 1.11.4(*f*).

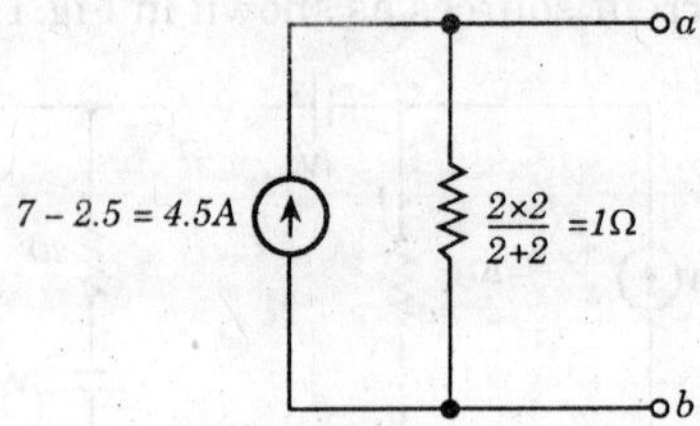


Fig.1.11.4(*f*) Equivalent current source. **Ans.**

## PROBLEMS

**1.1.** For the network shown below determine the single voltage source equivalent between terminals *a*-*b*.

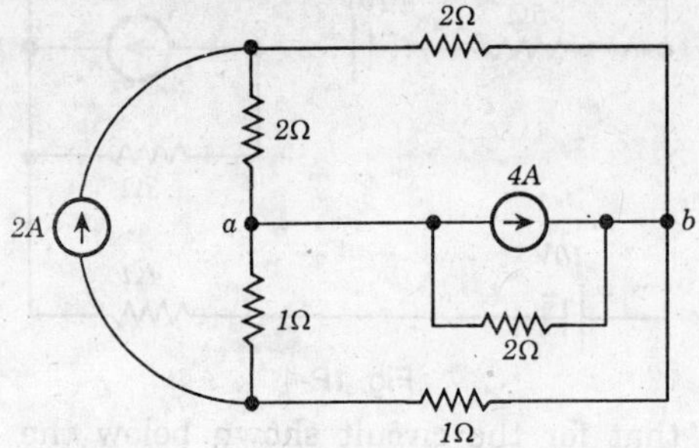

Fig. 1P-1

( **Ans** . 3.2 V, 0.8 Ω )

**1.2.** Determine single current source equivalent between terminals *a*-*b* of the network given :

( **Ans**. 3A, 1.25Ω )

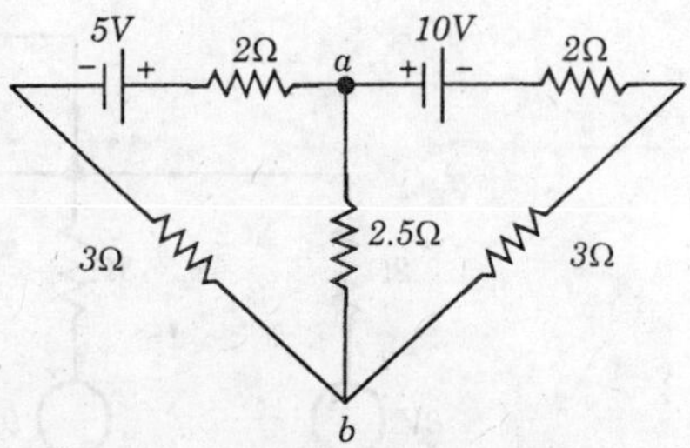

Fig. 1P-2

**1.3.** Use source transformation to obtain current source equivalent at *a*-*b* in the network given below:

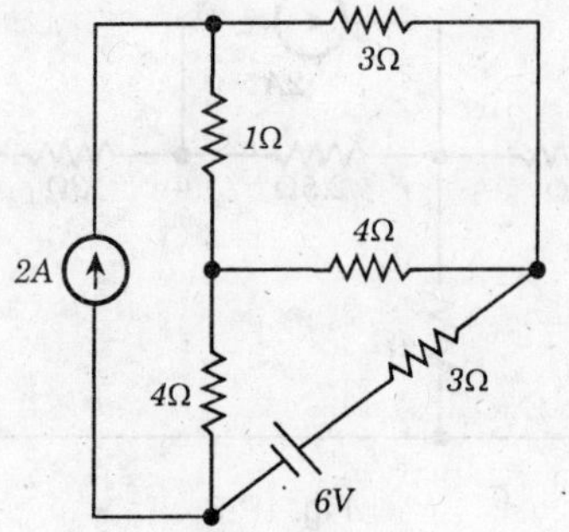

Fig. 1P-3

( **Ans.** 3.5 A, 2Ω )

**1.4.** Determine $V_{eq}$ and $R_{eq}$ between terminals *a*-*b* for the network given below.

( **Ans**. 20 V, 8/3 Ω )

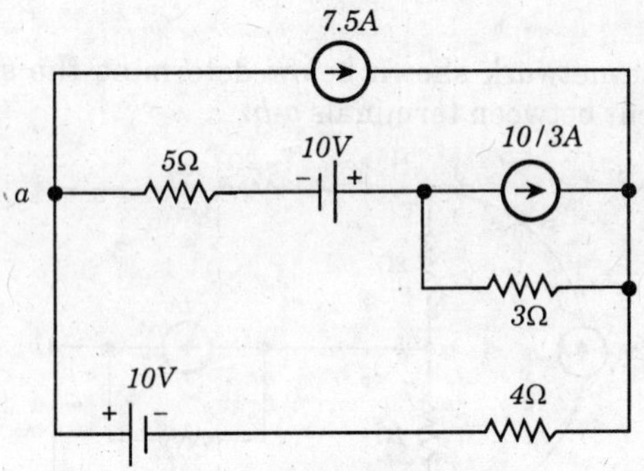


Fig. 1P-4

**1.5**. Show that for the circuit shown below the equivalence is $V_{ab} = 15.06V$, $R_{ab} = 2.311\Omega$

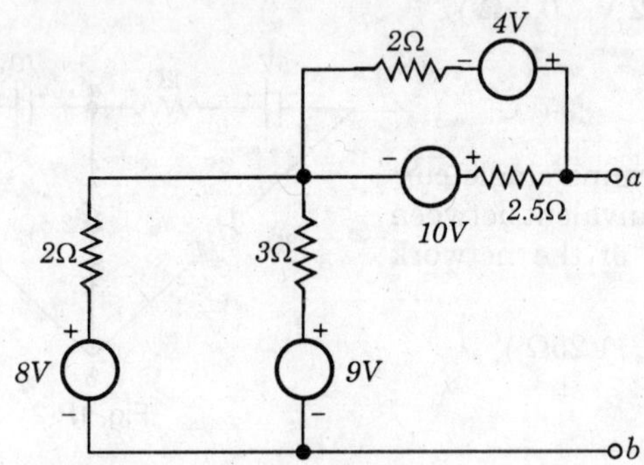


Fig. 1P-5

**1.6.** Determine the current source equivalence at $a$-$b$

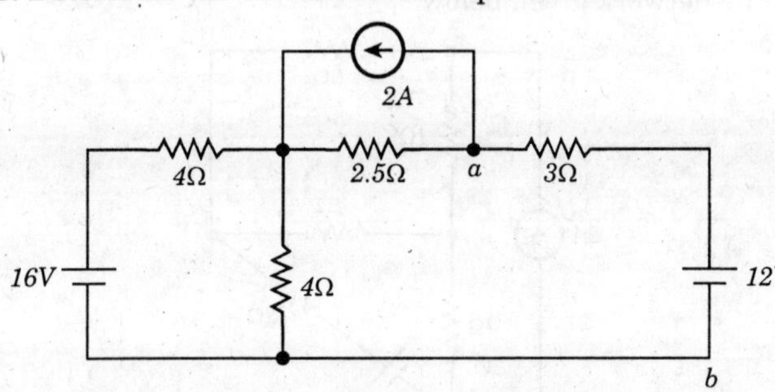


Fig. 1P-6

( **Ans**. 4.66 A, 1.8Ω )

**1.7.** For the network shown below obtain voltage source equivalence at $a$-$b$.

( **Ans**. 3.05 V, 5.295Ω )

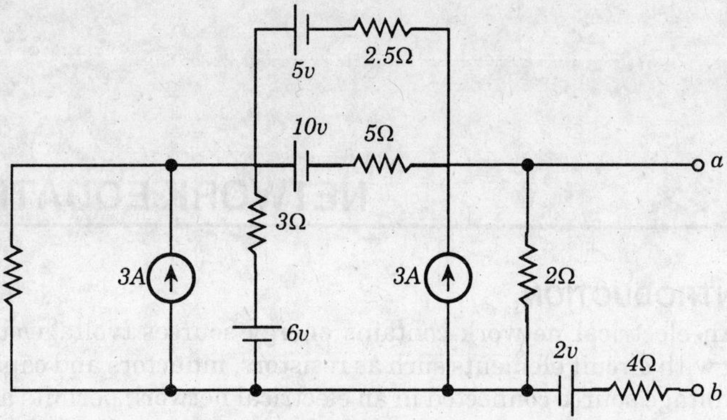


Fig. 1P-7.

**1.8.** Apply source transformation method to determine the current through 9 Ω resistor connected across the terminals *a-b* in the network shown below.

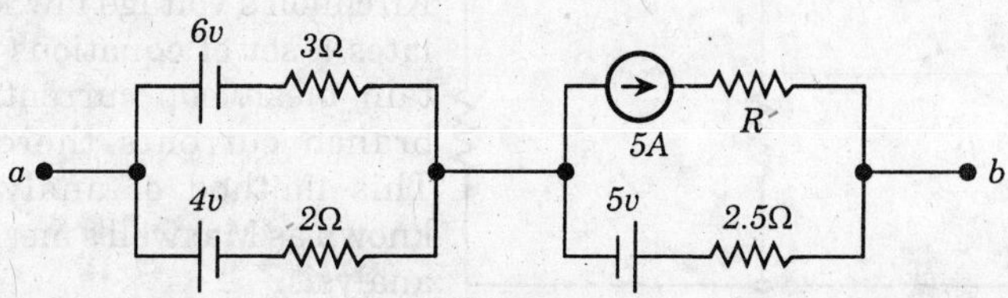


Fig. 1P-8.

( **Ans.** 1 A flowing from *b* to *a* )

# 2

# NETWORK EQUATIONS

## 2.1 INTRODUCTION

An electrical network contains energy sources (voltage/current), along with circuit elements such as resistors, inductors and capacitors. The voltage source connected in an electrical network permits a flow of electric current in the branches with the respective voltage drops. The application of electrical network analysis determines the current in branches and the voltage drops across the branches.

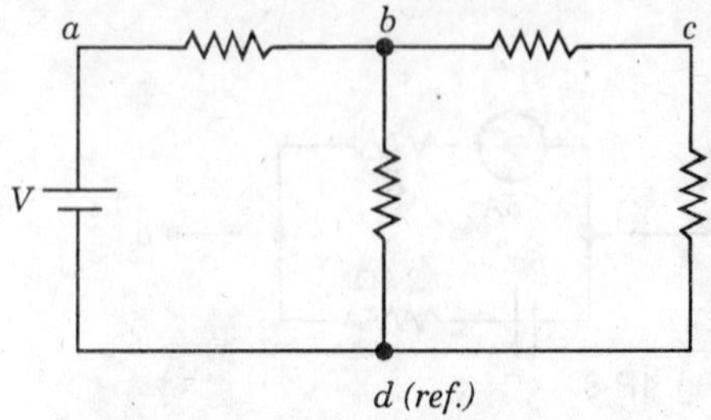

Fig. 2.1.1 Nodes and branches.

The application of Kirchhoff's voltage law formulates a set of equations to obtain mesh/loop currents and branch currents therefrom. This method of analysis is known as Maxwell's mesh/loop analysis.

The application of Kirchhoff's current law formulates a set of equations to obtain node voltages with respect to a reference node. This method of analysis is known as node voltage analysis.

### Node and Branch

The junction point of two or more end terminals of a network element is called a node. The node *w.r.t.* which the voltages of remaining nodes of a network are measured is known as reference node.

The network element connected between two nodes is known as branch.

In Fig. 2.1.1, *a, b* and *c* are nodes and *d* is considered as reference node. The branches are *a b, b c, b d* and *c d* and the source *V* is connected between nodes *a* and *d*.

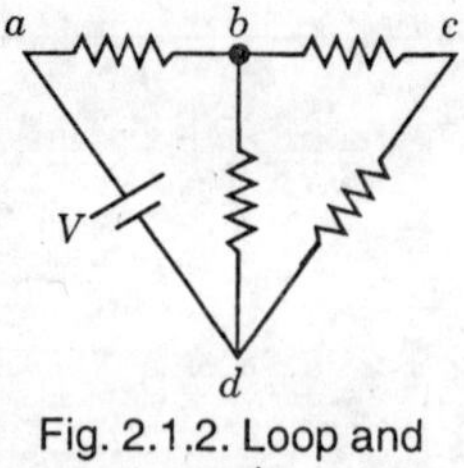

Fig. 2.1.2. Loop and mesh.

### Loop and Mesh

The loop is formed by a closed path through network elements. As shown in Fig. 2.1.2, the closed path *a-b-c-d-a* forms a loop. Similarly, the two other loops are *a-b-d-a* and *b-c-d-b*, these two loops are not having any other loop inside, it is known as a mesh. Thus, the closed path *a-b-d-a* and *b-c-d-b* are meshes. The closed path *a-b-c-d-a* is a loop.

## 2.2 NETWORK EQUATIONS

In an electrical passive element, the current flows from a higher potential terminal (+) to a lower potential (–). Thus, in the direction of current flow a voltage drop is experienced. While formulating equation for an electrical network/circuit, the voltage drop is assigned a positive sign and hence, the voltage rise a negative sign.

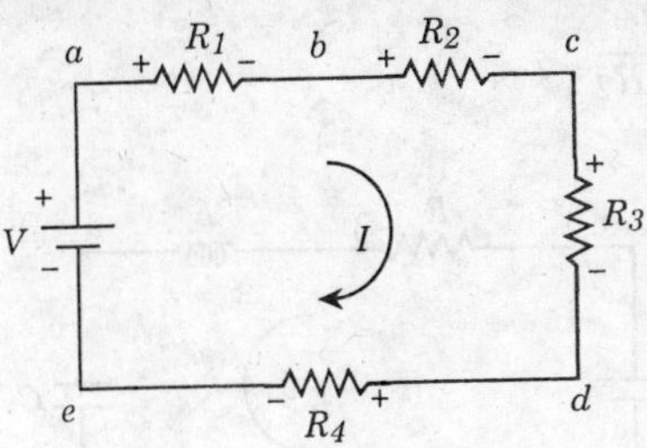


Fig. 2.2.1 Series circuit.

### Series circuit

The equation relating the voltage and current based on Kirchhoff's Voltage Law (KVL) is formulated for a series circuit [Fig. 2.2.1] consisting of resistor elements and a voltage source. The direction of the loop current flowing along the periphery of the closed path is assumed to be clockwise. The selection of the current direction is arbitrary.

The closed path considered is *a-b-c-d-e-a*. As the circuit is connected in series, the current flowing in all elements is $I$.

The voltage drop across $R_1$ (from $a$ to $b$) = $R_1 I$
The voltage drop across $R_2$ (from $b$ to $c$) = $R_2 I$
The voltage drop across $R_3$ (from $c$ to $d$) = $R_3 I$
The voltage drop across $R_4$ (from $d$ to $e$) = $R_4 I$
The voltage rise (from $e$ to $a$) = $V$.

As per KVL, the algebraic sum of voltage drops and voltage rises is equal to zero. Therefore,

$$R_1 I + R_2 I + R_3 I + R_4 I - V = 0$$

or

$$R_1 I + R_2 I + R_3 I + R_4 I = V$$

As per above equation,

$$\frac{V}{I} = R_1 + R_2 + R_3 + R_4$$

Therefore, for a series connection

$$R_{eq} = R_1 + R_2 + R_3 + \ldots$$

### Voltage Division in a Two Branch Series Circuit

Fig. 2.2.2 shows two resistors in series connected to a voltage $V$, the current flowing in the circuit is

Fig. 2.2.2. Voltage division

$$I = \frac{V}{R_1 + R_2}$$

The voltages across resistors are

$$V_1 = I R_1 = \frac{V R_1}{R_1 + R_2}$$

and $$V_2 = I R_2 = \frac{V R_2}{R_1 + R_2}$$

### *RLC* Series Circuit

In the circuit shown (Fig. 2.2.3), the elements resistor ($R$), inductor ($L$) and capacitor ($C$) are connected in series across a voltage source ($V$).

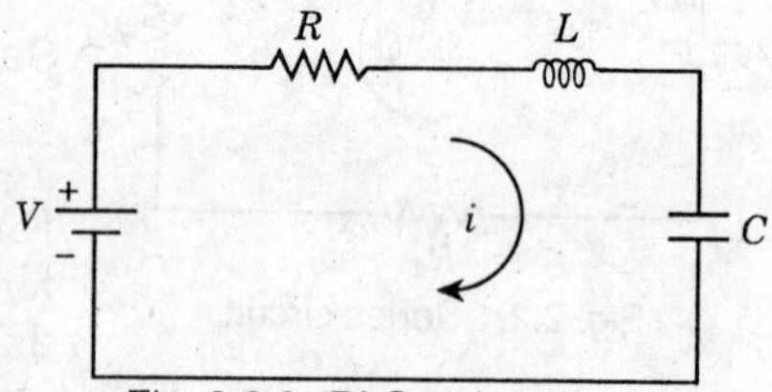

Fig. 2.2.3. *RLC* series circuit.

The equation relating voltage and current $i$ is formulated below:

The voltage drop across the resistor ($R$) = $Ri$

The voltage drop across the inductor ($L$) = $L\frac{di}{dt}$

The voltage drop across the capacitor ($C$) = $\frac{1}{C}\int idt$

The voltage rise across the source = $V$

As per *KVL*, the equation relating $V$ and $i$ is given below:

$$Ri + L\frac{di}{dt} + \frac{1}{C}\int i\,dt - V = 0$$

or $$Ri + L\frac{di}{dt} + \frac{1}{C}\int i\,dt = V$$

(The current is time-variant, therefore lower case letter $i$ is used)

### Parallel Circuit

A circuit consisting of three resistors $R_1$, $R_2$ and $R_3$ in parallel is shown in Fig. 2.2.4. The equation relating voltage and the currents $I$, $I_1$, $I_2$ and $I_3$ is formulated as per Kirchhoff's current law (*KCL*).

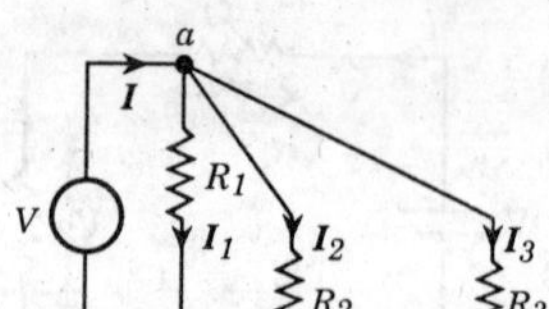

Fig. 2.2.4. Parallel Circuit.

At the junction (node) "$a$", the converging current is assigned a negative sign and diverging current positive sign. The choice of sign mentioned above is arbitrary.

The current through $R_1 : I_1 = \dfrac{V}{R_1}$

The current through $R_2 : I_2 = \dfrac{V}{R_2}$

The current through $R_3 : I_3 = \dfrac{V}{R_3}$

The current supplied by the source : $I$

Applying *KCL* at the junction (node) "*a*", following equation is obtained.

$$I_1 + I_2 + I_3 - I = 0$$

or
$$I = I_1 + I_2 + I_3$$
$$= \frac{V}{R_1} + \frac{V}{R_2} + \frac{V}{R_3}$$
$$\therefore \quad \frac{I}{V} = \frac{1}{R_1} + \frac{1}{R_2} + \frac{1}{R_3}$$
$$\because \quad \frac{I}{V} = \frac{1}{R_{eq}}$$

Therefore, for a parallel circuit

$$\frac{1}{R_{eq}} = \frac{1}{R_1} + \frac{1}{R_2} + \text{---------}$$

## Current Division in a Two Branch Parallel Circuit

Fig. 2.2.5 shows a two branch parallel circuit containing resistors, connected across a voltage source $V$.

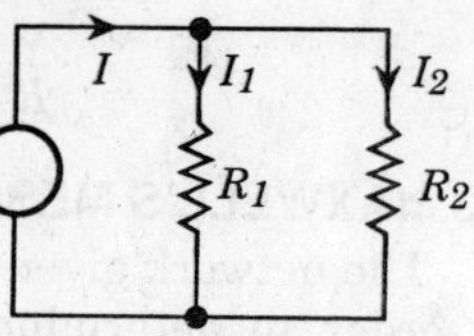

Fig. 2.2.5. Current division

The equivalent resistance of the parallel branch is determined as

$$\frac{1}{R_{eq}} = \frac{1}{R_1} + \frac{1}{R_2}$$
$$\therefore \quad R_{eq} = \frac{R_1 R_2}{R_1 + R_2}$$

The current supplied by the source is

$$I = \frac{V}{R_{eq}}$$

or
$$I = \frac{V(R_1 + R_2)}{R_1 R_2}$$

Also,
$$I_1 = \frac{V}{R_1}$$

On dividing $$\frac{I_1}{I} = \frac{R_2}{R_1 + R_2}$$

$\therefore$ $$I_1 = \frac{IR_2}{R_1 + R_2}$$

Similarly, $$I_2 = \frac{IR_1}{R_1 + R_2}$$

### *RLC* Parallel Circuit

In the circuit shown [Fig. 2.2.6], three elements resistor ($R$), inductor ($L$) and capacitor ($C$) are connected in parallel across a source voltage v on application.

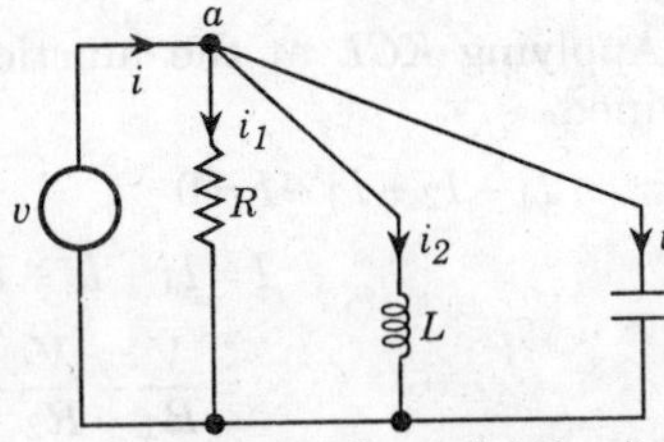

Fig. 2.2.6. *RLC* parallel circuit.

The current through the resistor ($R$): $i_1 = \frac{v}{R}$

The current through the inductor ($L$): $i_2 = \frac{1}{L}\int v\,dt$

The current through the capacitor ($C$) : $i_3 = C\frac{dv}{dt}$

The current supplied by the source : $i$

Applying $KCL$ at node "$a$" following equation is obtained:

$$i_1 + i_2 + i_3 - i = 0$$

or $$\frac{v}{R} + \frac{1}{L}\int v\,dt + \frac{c\,dv}{dt} = i$$

## 2.3 MAXWELL'S MESH CURRENT ANALYSIS

The network given (Fig. 2.3.1) contains resistors in five branches. In order to determine branch currents $I_{ab}$, $I_{bc}$, $I_{cd}$, $I_{ce}$, and $I_{be}$ five simultaneous equations are to be formulated.

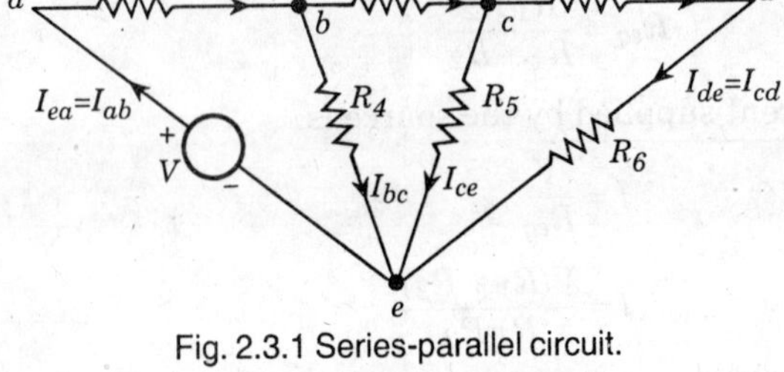

Fig. 2.3.1 Series-parallel circuit.

It is observed that there are three meshes *i.e.* *a-b-e-a*, *b-c-e-b* and *c-d-e-c*.

As per the procedure proposed by Maxwell, the five branch currents $I_{ab}$, $I_{bc}$, $I_{cd}$, $I_{be}$, and $I_{ce}$ can be determined by solving three simultaneous equations because there are three meshes.

As indicated in Fig. 2.3.2, hypothetical mesh currents $I_1$, $I_2$ and $I_3$ are assumed to flow only around the periphery of meshes 1 (*a-b-e-a*) 2 (*b-c-e-b*) and 3 (*c-d-e-c*) respectively. The clockwise direction of mesh current is assumed which is arbitrary. The relation between the branch currents and mesh currents is given below:

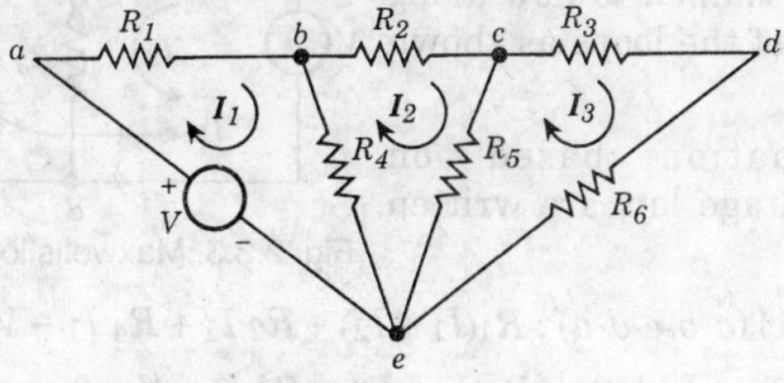


Fig. 2.3.2 Mesh current analysis.

$$I_{ab} = I_1$$

$$I_{bc} = I_2$$

$$I_{cd} = I_3$$

$$I_{be} = I_1 - I_2$$

$$I_{ce} = I_2 - I_3$$

It is concluded that five branch currents can be determined in terms of the unknown mesh currents $I_1$, $I_2$ and $I_3$.

The branch containing $R_4$ is common to meshes 1 and 2. The effective current flowing in this branch is $(I_1 - I_2)$ in the direction of $I_1$.

Similarly, the current flowing in $R_5$ is $(I_2 - I_3)$ in the direction of $I_2$.

Applying Kirchhoff's voltage law to the network shown in Fig. 2.3.2, following Maxwell's equations are obtained:

Mesh no. 1 : $R_1 I_1 + R_4 (I_1 - I_2) - V = 0$

Mesh no. 2 : $R_2 I_2 + R_5 (I_2 - I_3) + R_4 (I_2 - I_1) = 0$

Mesh no. 3 : $R_3 I_3 + R_6 I_3 + R_5 (I_3 - I_2) = 0$

On rearranging,

$$(R_1 + R_4) I_1 - R_4 I_2 = V$$

$$- R_4 I_1 + (R_2 + R_4 + R_5) I_2 - R_5 I_3 = 0$$

$$- R_5 I_2 + (R_3 + R_5 + R_6) I_3 = 0$$

(upper case letter may be used for branch current and lower case letter for mesh/loop current).

$$\begin{bmatrix} R_1+R_4 & -R_4 & 0 \\ -R_4 & R_2+R_4+R_5 & -R_5 \\ 0 & -R_5 & R_3+R_5+R_6 \end{bmatrix}\begin{bmatrix} I_1 \\ I_2 \\ I_3 \end{bmatrix}=\begin{bmatrix} v \\ 0 \\ 0 \end{bmatrix}$$

### Maxwells Loop Equations

The procedure given above can also be used for formulating Maxwell's loop equations. The loop currents are assumed to flow along the periphery of the loops as shown in Fig. 2.3.3.

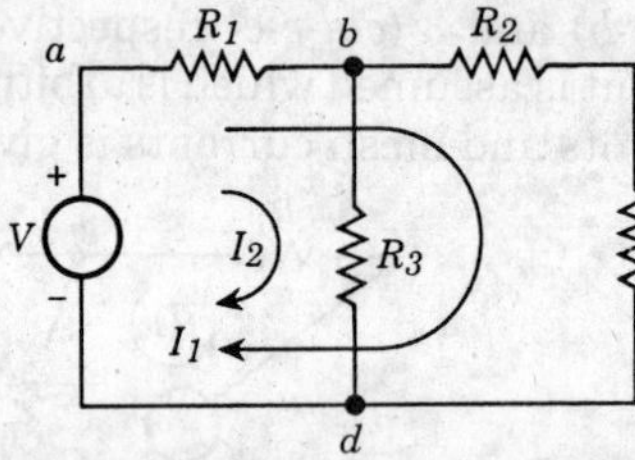

Fig. 2.3.3. Maxwells loop equations.

The equation based on Kirchhoff's voltage law are written below:

Loop no. (1) (*a-b-c-d-a*) : $R_1(I_1+I_2)+R_2\,I_1+R_4\,I_1-V=0$

Loop no. (2) (*a-b-d-a*) : $R_1(I_1+I_2)+R_3\,I_2-V=0$

On rearranging,

$$(R_1+R_2+R_4)\,I_1+R_1\,I_2=V$$

$$R_1\,I_1+(R_1+R_3)\,I_2=V$$

$$\begin{bmatrix} R_1+R_2+R_4 & R_1 \\ R_1 & R_1+R_3 \end{bmatrix}\begin{bmatrix} I_1 \\ I_2 \end{bmatrix}=\begin{bmatrix} V \\ V \end{bmatrix}$$

The relation between the branch currents and loop currents is given below:

$$I_{ab}=I_1+I_2$$

$$I_{bc}=I_{cd}=I_1$$

$$I_{bd}=I_2$$

Maxwell's equations can be written on the basis of mesh or loop. However, it is convenient to write Maxwell's equation on mesh basis for network solutions.

### Super Mesh

In the network shown in Fig. 2.3.4, the current source $I$ is shared by two adjacent meshes.

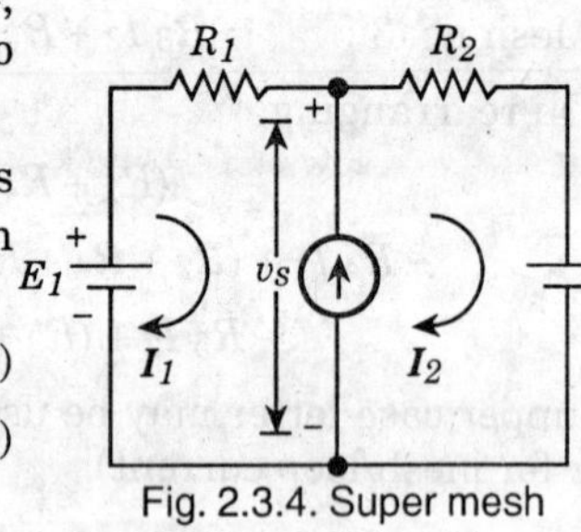

Fig. 2.3.4. Super mesh

Let the voltage $V_s$ appear across the current source. Maxwell's mesh equations are given below:

Mesh no. 1 : $R_1\,I_1+V_s-E_1=0$ ...(1)

Mesh no. 2 : $R_2\,I_2+E_2-V_s=0$ ...(2)

Adding Eqns. (1) and (2)

$$R_1 I_1 + R_2 I_2 + E_2 - E_1 = 0 \quad ...(3)$$

In view of Eqn. (3), a closed path consisting of elements $R_1$, $R_2$, $E_2$ and $E_1$ is formed. This closed path is termed as super mesh.

By inspection,

$$I_1 - I_2 = I \quad ...(4)$$

Using Eqns. (3) and (4), the unknown mesh currents $I_1$ and $I_2$ can be determined.

## 2.4 NODE VOLTAGE ANALYSIS

The node voltage analysis is used to determine the node voltage in an electrical network by applying Kirchhoff's current law. The node voltage is the potential of a given node *w.r.t.* selected reference node. The reference node is considered to be at zero potential. Hence, the node voltage is a node-pair voltage between the given node and reference node.

In the node voltage analysis principal nodes are taken into consideration and usually the node which is at zero potential is a reference node.

With reference to Fig. 2.4.1. "$a$" and "$b$" are principal nodes (junction of more than two branches other them reference node) and "$c$" the reference node.

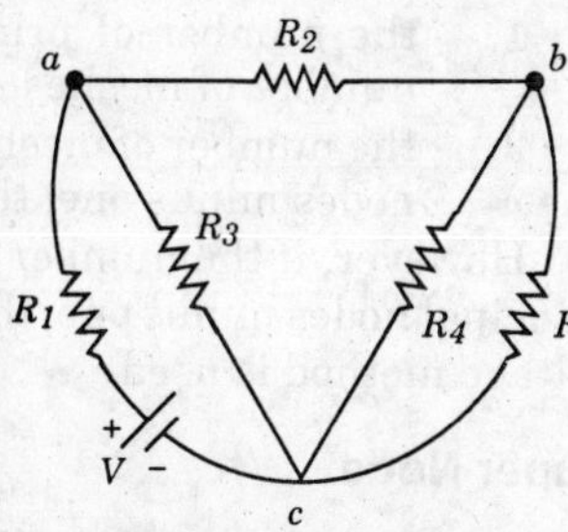

Fig. 2.4.1. Node analysis

If the voltages of nodes are $V_a$ and $V_b$ are determined, the branch currents can be determined as follows:

The current through $R_1 : I_1 = \dfrac{V_a - V}{R_1}$, flowing from node "$a$" to "$c$".

The current through $R_2 : I_2 = \dfrac{V_a - V_b}{R_2}$, flowing from node "$a$" to "$b$".

The current through $R_3 : I_3 = \dfrac{V_a - 0}{R_3}$, flowing from node "$a$" to "$c$".

The current through $R_4 : I_4 = \dfrac{V_b - 0}{R_4}$, flowing from node "$b$" to "$c$".

The current through $R_5 : I_5 = \dfrac{V_b - 0}{R_5}$, flowing from node "$b$" to "$c$".

Applying Kirchhoff's current law following equations are obtained,

$$\text{At node } (a): \quad \frac{V_a - V}{R_1} + \frac{V_a - V_b}{R_2} + \frac{V_a - 0}{R_3} = 0$$

At node $(b)$ : $\dfrac{V_b - V_a}{R_2} + \dfrac{V_b - 0}{R_4} + \dfrac{V_b - 0}{R_5} = 0$

On rearranging $\begin{bmatrix} \dfrac{1}{R_1} + \dfrac{1}{R_2} + \dfrac{1}{R_3} & -\dfrac{1}{R_2} \\ -\dfrac{1}{R_2} & \dfrac{1}{R_2} + \dfrac{1}{R_4} + \dfrac{1}{R_5} \end{bmatrix} \begin{bmatrix} V_a \\ V_b \end{bmatrix} = \begin{bmatrix} \dfrac{V}{R_1} \\ 0 \end{bmatrix}$

While writing the node equations based on Kirchhoff's current law, the currents diverging from the nodes are considered positive and this choice is arbitrary.

The number of node voltage equation = $N$–1 where $N$ is the number of principal nodes including reference node.

For the solution of electrical networks it convenient that the number of equations solved be minimum. Thus, if

1. the number of principal nodes minus one is less than the number of meshes, the node voltage method is used.
2. the number of meshes/loops is less than the number principal nodes minus one, the mesh/loop current method is used.

However, if the number of meshes/loops is equal to the number of principal nodes minus one, then either mesh/loop current or super node voltage method is used.

### Super Node

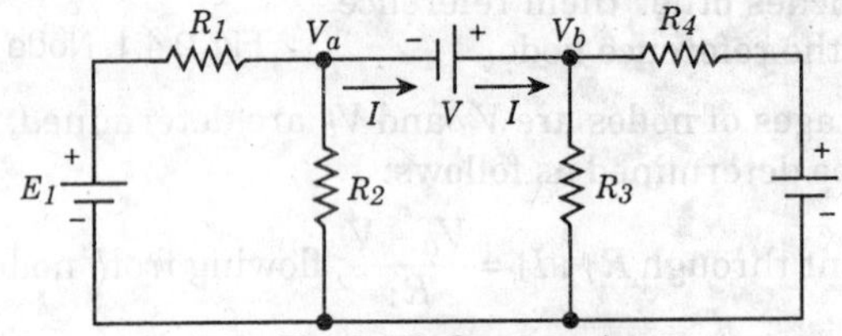

Fig. 2.4.2. Super node

In the network shown (Fig. 2.4.2), the voltage source $V$ is connected between two adjacent nodes "$a$" and "$b$".

Let the current from node "$a$" to '$b$" be $I$. the voltage equations are formulated below:

At node $(a)$ $\dfrac{V_a - E_1}{R_1} + I + \dfrac{V_a}{R_2} = 0$

At node $(b)$ $\dfrac{V_b}{R_3} + \dfrac{V_b - E_2}{R_4} - I = 0$

On adding above equations,

$$\frac{V_a - E_1}{R_1} + \frac{V_a}{R_2} + \frac{V_b}{R_3} + \frac{V_b - E_2}{R_4} = 0 \quad ...(1)$$

The adjacent nodes connected through a voltage source are termed as super nodes.

By inspection, $V_b - V_a = V$ ...(2)

Solving Eqns. (1) and (2), the unknown node voltages $V_a$ and $V_a$ can be determined.

## 2.5 SOLVED EXAMPLES

**Example 2.5.1.** *Write mesh current equations for the network (Fig. 2.5.1) given below:*

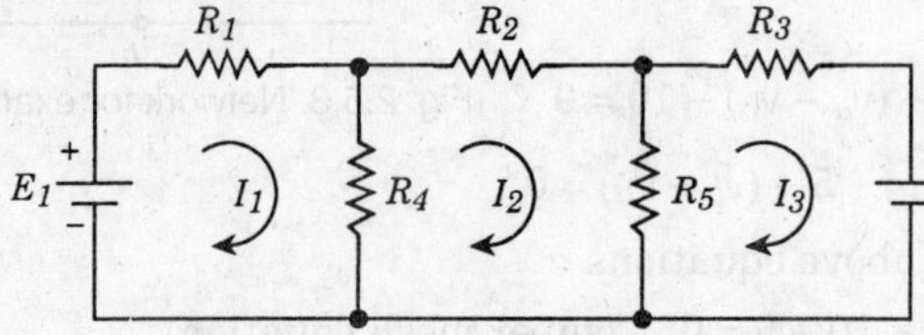


Fig. 2.5.1 Network for example 2.5.1.

**Solution:**

Mesh 1 : $I_1 R_1 + (I_1 - I_2) R_4 - E_1 = 0$

Mesh 2 : $I_2 R_2 + (I_2 - I_3) R_5 + (I_2 - I_1) R_4 = 0$

Mesh 3 : $I_3 R_3 + E_2 + (I_2 - I_3) R_5 = 0$

In matrix form above equations takes the form as below:

$$\begin{bmatrix} (R_1 + R_4) & -R_4 & 0 \\ -R_5 & (R_2 + R_4 + R_5) & -R_5 \\ & -R_5 & (R_3 + R_5) \end{bmatrix} \begin{bmatrix} I_1 \\ I_2 \\ I_3 \end{bmatrix} \begin{bmatrix} E_1 \\ 0 \\ -E_2 \end{bmatrix} \quad \textbf{Ans.}$$

**Example 2.5.2:** *Select mesh currents and write mesh equations for the circuit given below:*

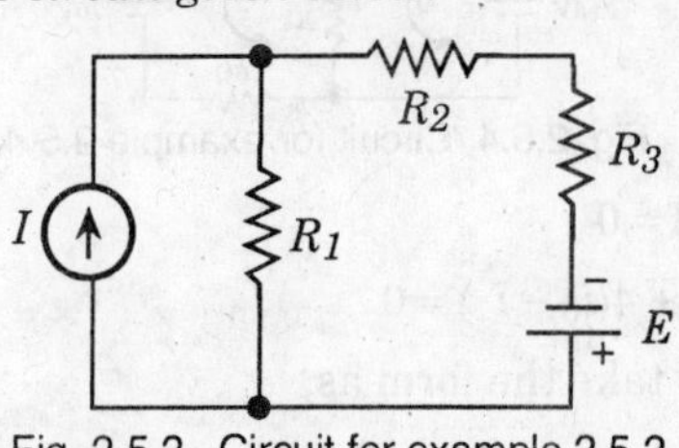


Fig. 2.5.2. Circuit for example 2.5.2.

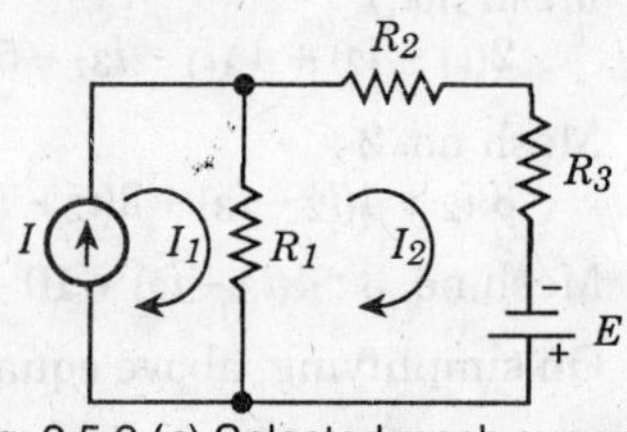


Fig. 2.5.2 (*a*) Selected mesh currents.

**Solution:** Mesh currents $I_1$ and $I_2$ are selected as shown in Fig. 2.5. 2(*a*).

The mesh current equations w.r.t. Fig. 2.5.2 (*a*) are written below:

Mesh 1 : $I_1 = I$

Mesh 2 : $(I_2 - I_1) R_1 + I_2 R_2 + I_2 R_3 - E = 0$

or

$$\begin{bmatrix} 0 & 1 \\ -R_1 & (R_1 + R_2 + R_3) \end{bmatrix} \begin{bmatrix} I_1 \\ I_2 \end{bmatrix} = \begin{bmatrix} I \\ E \end{bmatrix} \quad \textbf{Ans.}$$

**Example 2.5.3:** *Apply mesh current analysis to determine currents $i_1$ and $i_2$ for the network shown in Fig. 2.5.3.*

**Solution :** The voltage drop across the current source is $(v_a - v_b)$.

The mesh current equations are written below:

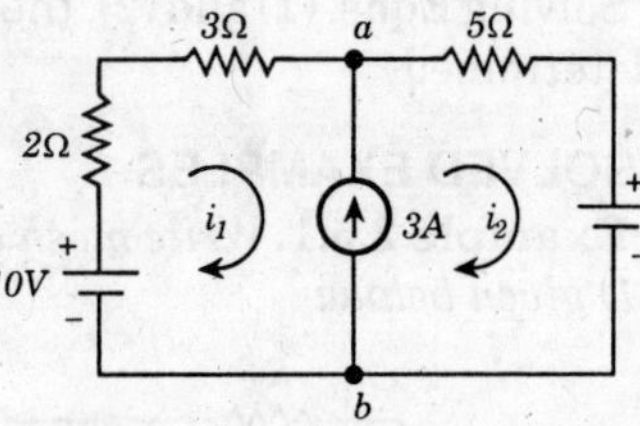


Fig. 2.5.3. Network for example 2.5.3.

Mesh 1 :

$$2\,i_1 + 3\,i_1 + (v_a - v_b) - 10 = 0$$

Mesh 2 : $5\,i_2 + 5 + (v_b - v_a) = 0$

On adding above equations

$$5\,i_1 + 5\,i_2 - 10 + 5 = 0 \quad \text{(super mesh equation)}$$

or $$i_1 + i_2 = 1$$

Also, $$i_2 - i_1 = 3$$

Solving above equations

$$i_1 = -1\text{ A}$$

and $$i_2 = 2\text{ A}$$ **Ans.**

**Example 2.5.4:** *Determine the current through 6 Ω resistor in the network shown below:*

**Solution :** The mesh current equations are written below:

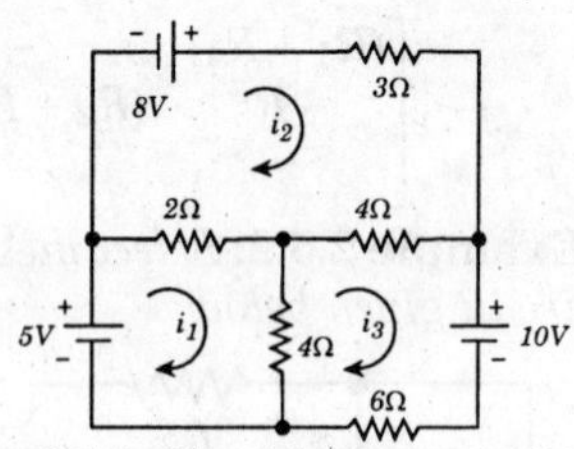


Fig. 2.5.4 Circuit for example 2.5.4.

Mesh no. 1 :

$$2(i_1 - i_2) + 4\,(i_1 - i_3) - 5 = 0$$

Mesh no. 2 :

$$3\,i_2 + 4(i_2 - i_3) + 2(i_2 - i_1) - 8 = 0$$

Mesh no. 3 : $4(i_3 - i_2) + 10 + 6\,i_3 + 4(i_3 - i_1) = 0$

On simplifying, above equations take the form as,

$$6\,i_1 - 2\,i_2 - 4\,i_3 = 5$$

$$-2\,i_1 + 9\,i_1 - 4\,i_3 = 8$$

$$-4\,i_1 - 4\,i_2 + 14\,i_3 = -10$$

Determinant form of the above equation is given below,

$$\begin{vmatrix} 6 & -2 & -4 \\ -2 & 9 & -4 \\ -4 & -4 & 14 \end{vmatrix} \begin{vmatrix} i_1 \\ i_2 \\ i_3 \end{vmatrix} = \begin{vmatrix} 5 \\ 8 \\ -10 \end{vmatrix}$$

$$\therefore \quad i_3 = \frac{\begin{vmatrix} 6 & 2 & 5 \\ -2 & 9 & 8 \\ -4 & -4 & -10 \end{vmatrix}}{\begin{vmatrix} 6 & -2 & -4 \\ -2 & 9 & -4 \\ -4 & -4 & 14 \end{vmatrix}} = \frac{-24}{396} = -0.06$$

$i_3 = -0.06$ A **Ans.**

**Example 2.5.5:** *Determine the current supplied by the voltage source, the network is shown in Fig. 2.5.5.*

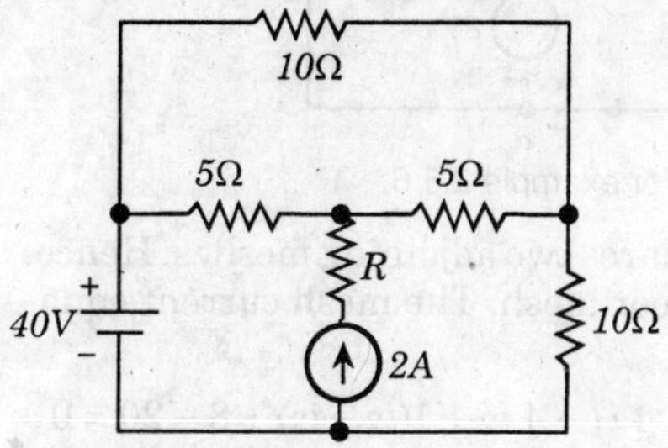


Fig. 2.5.5 Network for example 2.5.5

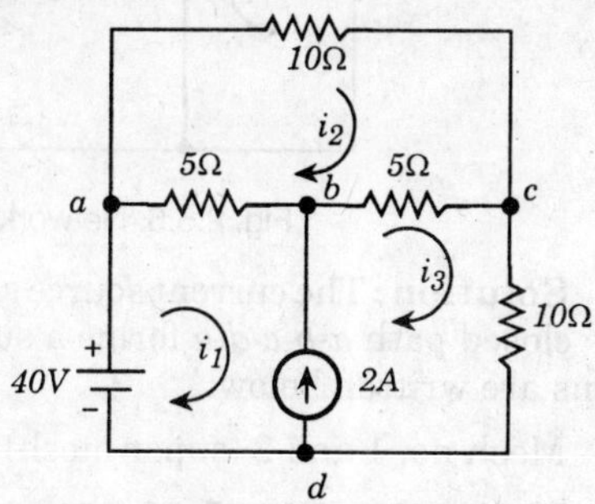


Fig. 2.5.5(*a*) Mesh currents selected

**Solution:** The resistance $R$ in series with current source can be deleted *i.e.* replaced by short circuit. The mesh currents are selected as shown in Fig. 2.5.5(*a*).

The current source is shared by adjoining meshes and the super mesh is formed as *a-b-c-d-a*. The mesh equation are written below:

Super mesh *a-b-c-d-a* : $5(i_1 - i_2) + 5(i_3 - i_2) + 10\, i_3 - 40 = 0$

Mesh *a-b-c-a* : $10\, i_2 + 5(i_2 - i_3) + 5(i_2 - i_1) = 0$

Simplifying above equations,

$$5\, i_1 - 10\, i_2 + 15\, i_3 = 40 \quad \text{...(1)}$$

and $$-5\, i_1 + 20\, i_2 - 5\, i_3 = 0 \quad \text{...(2)}$$

Multiply Eqn. (1) by 2

$$10\, i_1 - 20\, i_2 + 30\, i_3 = 80 \quad \text{...(3)}$$

Add Eqns. (2) and (3)

$$5\, i_1 + 25\, i_3 = 80 \quad \text{...(4)}$$

As per Fig. 2.5.5 (*a*)

$$i_3 - i_1 = 2 \quad \text{...(5)}$$

Substitute for $i_3$ in Eqn. (4) from (5)

$\therefore\ 5\, i_1 + 25(i_1 + 2) = 80$

$\therefore \quad 30\, i_1 = 30$

and $\quad i_1 = 1$ **Ans.**

**Example 2.5.6:** *With the choice of mesh current given in Fig. 2.5.6, determine* $i_1$, $i_2$ and $i_3$.

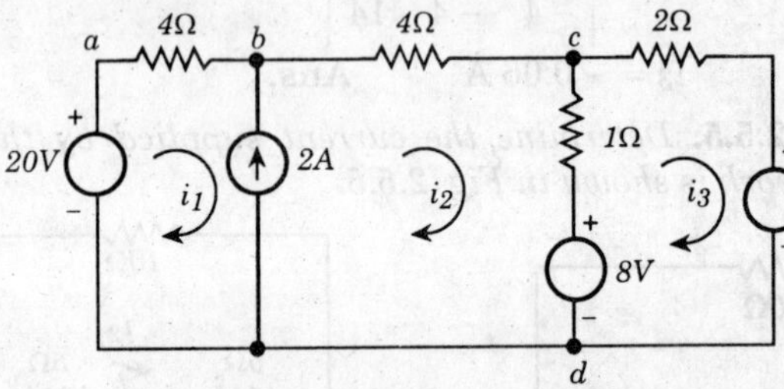


Fig. 2.5.6. Network for example 2.5.6.

**Solution :** The current source shares two adjoining meshes. Hence, the closed path *a-b-c-d-a* forms a super mesh. The mesh current equations are written below:

Mesh no. 1 and 2 (super mesh) : $4\, i_1 + 4\, i_2 + 1(i_2 - i_3) + 8 - 20 = 0$

Mesh no. 3 : $2\, i_3 + 5 - 8 + 1(i_3 - i_2) = 0$

On simplification above two equations take the form

$$4\, i_1 + 5\, i_2 - i_3 = 12 \quad \text{...(1)}$$

and

$$-\, i_2 + 3\, i_3 = 3 \quad \text{...(2)}$$

Also, the current source is shared by mesh no. 1 and 2.

$$\therefore \quad i_2 - i_1 = 2 \quad \text{...(3)}$$

Substitute for $i_1$ in Eqn. (1) from (3)

$$\therefore \quad 4(i_2 - 2) + 5\, i_2 - i_3 = 12$$

or

$$9 i_2 - i_3 = 20 \quad \text{...(4)}$$

Eqns. (4) and (2) are written in determinant form as below :

$$\begin{vmatrix} 9 & -1 \\ -1 & 3 \end{vmatrix} \begin{vmatrix} i_2 \\ i_3 \end{vmatrix} = \begin{vmatrix} 20 \\ 3 \end{vmatrix}$$

$$i_2 = \frac{\begin{vmatrix} 9 & 20 \\ -1 & 3 \end{vmatrix}}{\begin{vmatrix} 9 & -1 \\ -1 & 3 \end{vmatrix}} = \frac{27 + 20}{27 - 1} = \frac{47}{26}$$

$$i_2 = \frac{47}{26} = 1.80\, A \quad \textbf{Ans.}$$

$$i_3 = \frac{\begin{vmatrix} 20 & -1 \\ 3 & 3 \end{vmatrix}}{\begin{vmatrix} 9 & -1 \\ -1 & 3 \end{vmatrix}} = \frac{60+3}{27-1} = \frac{63}{26}$$

$$i_3 = \frac{63}{26} = 2.42\,A \qquad \textbf{Ans.}$$

$\because$ $\quad i_2 - i_1 = 2$

$\therefore$ $\quad i_1 = i_2 - 2$

or $\quad i_1 = (1.80 - 2) = -\,0.2\,A \qquad$ **Ans.**

**Example 2.5.7:** *Apply mesh current analysis to determine the branch currents in the network given below:*

**Solution :** The mesh current equations are written as

Mesh no. 1 : $\quad i_1 = 5\,A$

Mesh no. 2 : $\quad 4\,i_2 + 4(i_2 - i_3) = 0$

On simplification, $\quad 8\,i_2 - 4\,i_3 = 0 \qquad$ ...(1)

Mesh no. 3 : $\quad 4(i_3 - i_2) + 1(i_3 - i_4) + 5(i_3 - 5) = 0$

On simplification, $\quad -\,4\,i_2 + 10\,i_3 - i_4 = 25 \qquad$ ...(2)

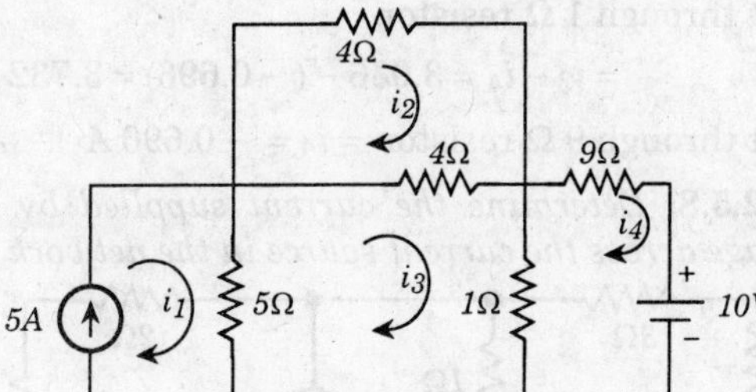


Fig. 2.5.7. Network for example 2.5.7.

Mesh no. 4 : $\quad 9\,i_4 + 10 + 1(i_4 - i_3) = 0$

On simplification $\quad -\,i_3 + 10\,i_4 = -\,10 \qquad$ ...(3)

Eqns. (1), (2) & (3) can be written in determinant form as

$$\begin{vmatrix} 8 & -4 & 0 \\ -4 & 10 & -1 \\ 0 & -1 & 10 \end{vmatrix} \begin{vmatrix} i_2 \\ i_3 \\ i_4 \end{vmatrix} = \begin{vmatrix} 0 \\ 25 \\ -10 \end{vmatrix}$$

$$i_2 = \frac{\begin{vmatrix} 0 & -4 & 0 \\ 25 & 10 & -1 \\ -10 & -1 & 10 \end{vmatrix}}{\begin{vmatrix} 8 & -4 & 0 \\ -4 & 10 & -1 \\ 0 & -1 & 10 \end{vmatrix}} = \frac{120}{79},$$

$$i_3 = \frac{\begin{vmatrix} 8 & 0 & 0 \\ -4 & 25 & -1 \\ 0 & -10 & 10 \end{vmatrix}}{\begin{vmatrix} 8 & -4 & 0 \\ -4 & 10 & -1 \\ 0 & -1 & 10 \end{vmatrix}} = \frac{240}{79}$$

$$i_4 = \frac{\begin{vmatrix} 8 & -4 & 0 \\ -4 & 10 & 25 \\ 0 & -1 & -10 \end{vmatrix}}{\begin{vmatrix} 8 & -4 & 0 \\ -4 & 10 & -1 \\ 0 & -1 & 10 \end{vmatrix}} = \frac{-55}{79}$$

$$\therefore \; i_2 = \frac{120}{79} = 1.518\,A, \; i_3 = \frac{240}{79} = 3.036\,A, \; i_4 = -\frac{55}{79} = -0.696\,A$$

The current through 5 Ω resistor $= i_1 - i_3 = 5 - 3.036 = 1.964\,A$

The current through 4 Ω resistor $= i_2 = 1.518$

The current through 4 Ω resistor

$$= i_2 - i_3 = 1.518 - 3.036 = -1.518\,A$$

The current through 1 Ω resistor

$$= i_3 - i_4 = 3.036 - (-0.696) = 3.732\,A$$

The current through 9 Ω resistor $= i_4 = -0.696\,A$ **Ans.**

**Example 2.5.8:** *Determine the current supplied by the voltage source and voltage across the current source in the network shown.*

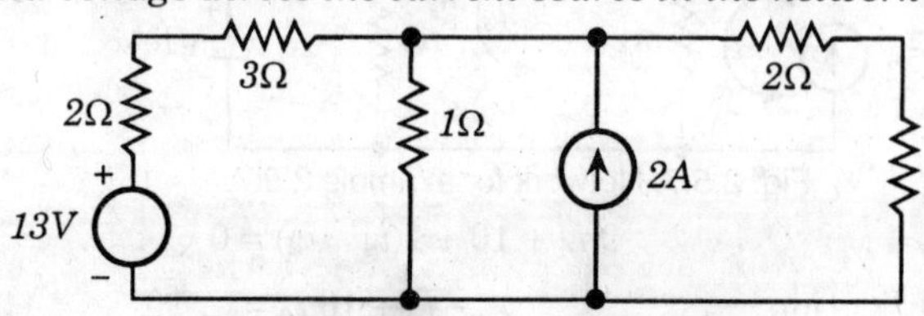


Fig. 2.5.8. Network for example 2.5.8.

**Solution :** The mesh currents are selected as shown in Fig. 2.5.8 (*a*)

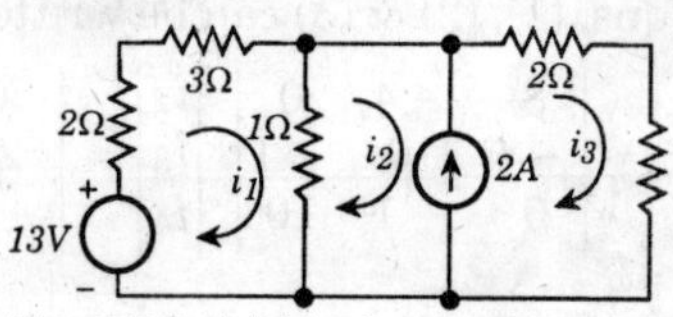


Fig. 2.5.8. (*a*) Mesh currents selected for the network

The mesh equations are written below:

Mesh no. 1:

$$2\,i_1 + 3\,i_1 + 1(i_1 - i_2) - 13 = 0$$

On simplification,

$$6\,i_1 - i_2 = 13 \qquad ...(1)$$

Mesh no. 2 & 3 supermesh :

$$1(i_2 - i_1) + 2\,i_3 + 1\,i_3 = 0$$

On simplification,

$$-i_1 + i_2 + 3\,i_3 = 0 \qquad ...(2)$$

The current source is shared by mesh no. 2 and 3.

Hence, $$i_3 - i_2 = 2 \qquad ...(3)$$

Substitute for $i_3$ in Eqn. (2) from Eqn. (3)

$$\therefore \quad -i_1 + i_2 + 3(2 + i_2) = 0 \qquad ..(4)$$

Eqns. (1) and (4) can be written in determinant form as

$$\begin{vmatrix} 6 & -1 \\ -1 & 4 \end{vmatrix} \begin{vmatrix} i_1 \\ i_2 \end{vmatrix} = \begin{vmatrix} 13 \\ -6 \end{vmatrix}$$

$$\therefore \quad i_1 = \frac{\begin{vmatrix} 13 & -1 \\ -6 & 4 \end{vmatrix}}{\begin{vmatrix} 6 & -1 \\ -1 & 4 \end{vmatrix}} = \frac{46}{23} = 2.0\ \text{A}$$

and $$i_2 = \frac{\begin{vmatrix} 6 & 13 \\ -1 & -6 \end{vmatrix}}{\begin{vmatrix} 6 & -1 \\ -1 & 4 \end{vmatrix}} = \frac{-23}{23} = -1.0\ \text{A}$$

$$\therefore \quad i_3 = i_2 + 2 = (-1) + 2 = 1.0\ \text{A}$$

The current supplied by the voltage source, $i_1 = 2.0\,A$

The voltage across the current source

$$= (2 + 1)\,i_3 = 3 \times 1 = 3\ \text{V} \qquad \textbf{Ans.}$$

**Example 2.5.9:** *Use mesh analysis to determine the branch currents in the network given below:*

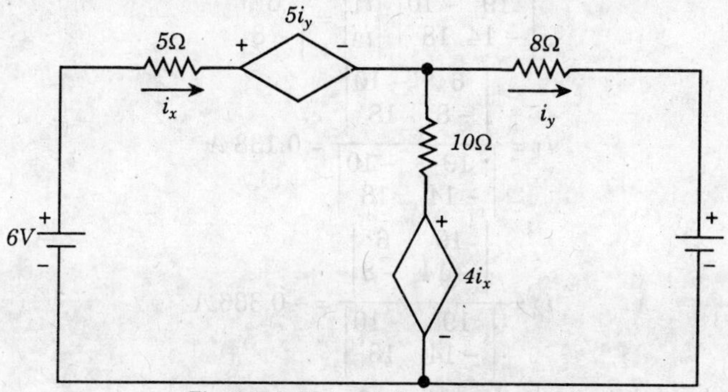


Fig. 2.5.9. Network for example 2.5.9

**Solution :** Select the direction of mesh currents as shown in Fig. 2.5.9 (*a*)

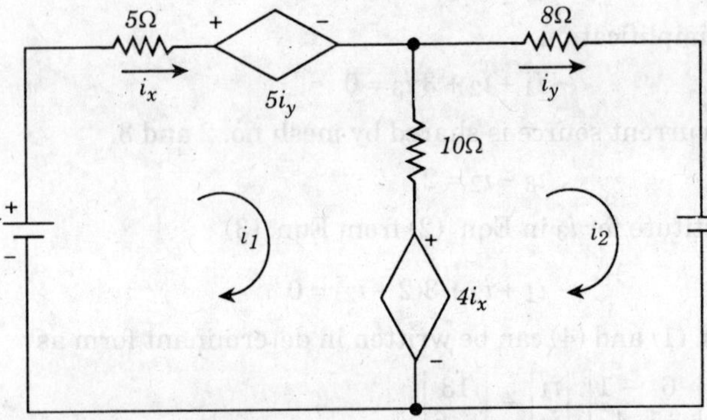


Fig. 2.5.9. (*a*) Selection of mesh currents for example 2.5.9.

The mesh current equation are written below:

Mesh no. (1) : $5\,i_1 + 5\,i_y + 10(i_1 - i_2) + 4\,i_x - 6 = 0$

Mesh no. (2) : $8\,i_2 + 8 - 4\,i_x + 10(i_2 - i_1) = 0$

Also $i_x = i_1$

and $i_y = i_2$

Substituting the values of $i_x$ and $i_y$ in respective equations as above, following equations are obtained

$$5\,i_1 + 5\,i_2 + 10(i_1 - i_2) + 4\,i_1 - 6 = 0$$

and $$8\,i_2 + 8 - 4\,i_1 + 10\,(i_2 - i_1) = 0$$

On simplification,

$$19\,i_1 - 10\,i_2 = 6$$

and $$14\,i_1 + 18\,i_2 = -8$$

Above equations are written in determinant form as

$$\begin{vmatrix} 19 & -10 \\ -14 & 18 \end{vmatrix} \begin{vmatrix} i_1 \\ i_2 \end{vmatrix} = \begin{vmatrix} 6 \\ -8 \end{vmatrix}$$

$\therefore$ $$i_1 = \frac{\begin{vmatrix} 6 & -10 \\ -8 & 18 \end{vmatrix}}{\begin{vmatrix} 19 & -10 \\ -14 & 18 \end{vmatrix}} = 0.138\,A$$

and $$i_2 = \frac{\begin{vmatrix} 19 & 6 \\ -14 & -8 \end{vmatrix}}{\begin{vmatrix} 19 & -10 \\ -14 & 18 \end{vmatrix}} = -\,0.336\,A$$

The branch currents are

$$i_1 = 0.138\ A$$
$$i_2 = -0.366\ A$$

and $i_1 - i_2 = 0.138 - (-0.336)$

$= 0.474$ A (in the dirn.of $i_1$) **Ans.**

**Example 2.5.10 :** *Determine $v_x$ in the network shown below.*

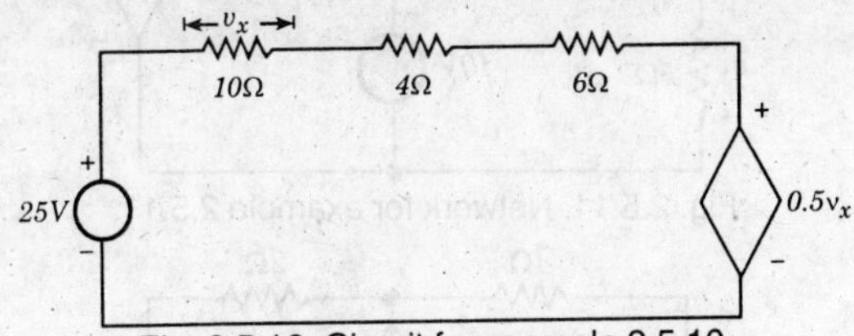


Fig. 2.5.10. Circuit for example 2.5.10.

**Solution :** Consider loop current as shown in Fig. 2.5.10 ($a$).

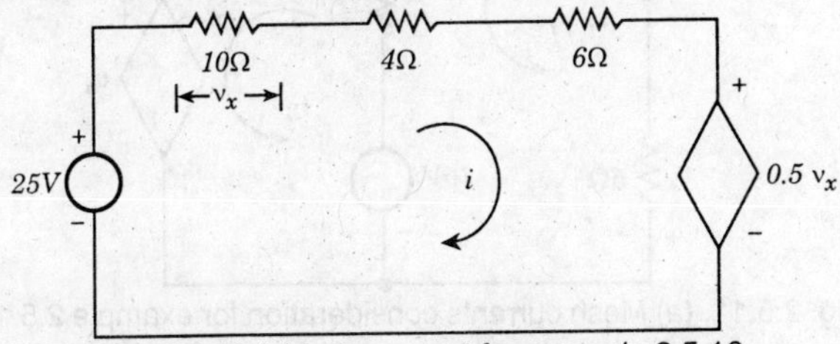


Fig. 2.5.10.($a$) loop current for example 2.5.10.

Applying Kirchhoff's voltage law,

$$10\,i + 4\,i + 6\,i + 0.5\,v_x - 25 = 0$$

$\because$ $v_x = 10\,i$

$\therefore$ $10\,i + 4\,i + 6\,i + 0.5(10\,i) - 25 = 0$

$\therefore$ $25\,i = 25$

$$i = 1\,A$$

and $v_x = 10\,i = 10 \times 1 = 10\ V$ **Ans.**

**Example 2.5.11:** *Determine the current i flowing in 5 Ω resistance in the network shown in Fig.2.5.11.*

**Solution:** Mesh currents are considered as shown in Fig. 2.5.11.($a$)

Apply Kirchhoff's voltage law to the network shown in Fig. 2.5.11($a$).

Mesh no. 1 : $4\,i_1 + 5(i_1 - i_2) + 10 + 5\,i_1 - 20 = 0$ ...(1)

Mesh no. 2 : $2\,i_2 + v_x - 10 + 5(i_2 - i_1) = 0$ ...(2)

put $v_x = 5\,i_1$ in Eqn. (2)

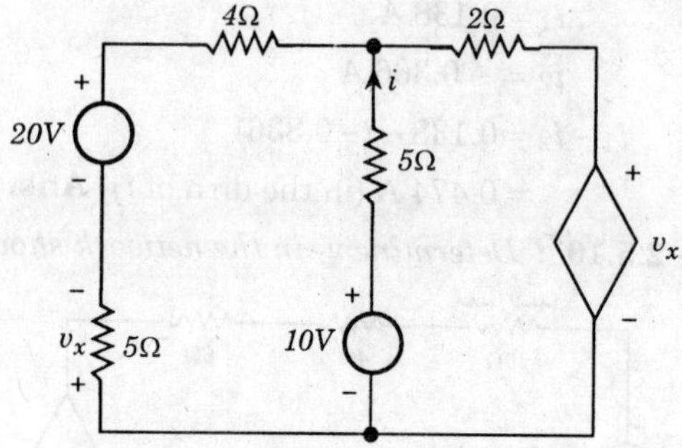


Fig. 2.5.11. Network for example 2.5.11.

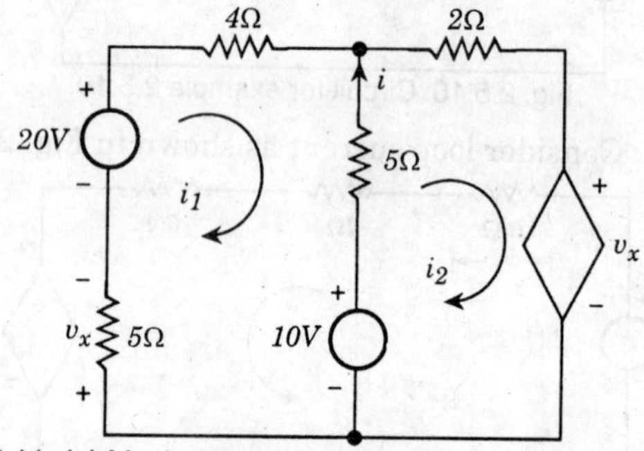


Fig. 2.5.11. (*a*) Mesh currents consideration for example 2.5.11.

$\therefore$ $$2\,i_2 + 5\,i_1 - 10 + 5(i_2 - i_1) = 0 \qquad ...(3)$$

On simplifying Eqns. (1) and (3)

$$14\,i_1 - 5\,i_2 = 10$$

and $$7\,i_2 = 10$$

Solving above equations.

$$i_2 = \frac{10}{7} = 1.428 \text{ A} \text{ and } i_1 = \frac{120}{7 \times 14} = 1.224 \text{ A}$$

$$i = i_2 - i_1 = 1.428 - 1.224 = 0.204 \text{ A} \qquad \textbf{Ans.}$$

**Example 2.5.12:** *Determine* $V_b$ and $V_c$ *using node voltage analysis the network is shown in Fig. 2.5.12.*

**Solution :** It is noted that $V_a = 10$ V

The node-voltage equations are written below:

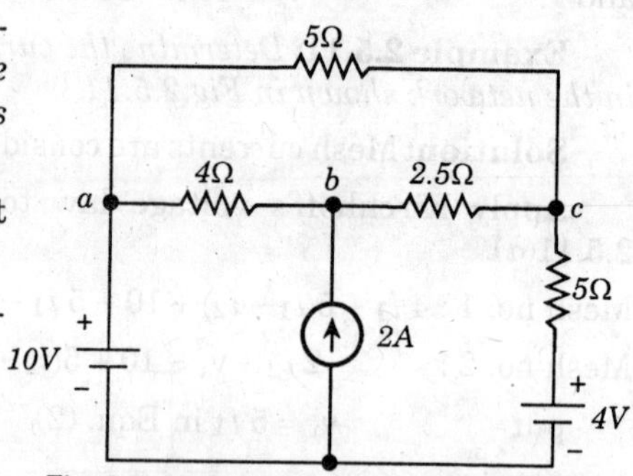


Fig. 2.5.12. Network for example 2.5.12.

At node (b) : $\frac{V_b - 10}{4} + \frac{V_b - V_c}{2.5} - 2 = 0$

At node (c) : $\frac{V_b - V_b}{2.5} + \frac{V_c - 10}{5} + \frac{V_c - 4}{5} = 0$

Above equations can be arranged in determinant form as

$$\begin{vmatrix} \frac{1}{4}+\frac{1}{2.5} & -\frac{1}{2.5} \\ -\frac{1}{2.5} & \frac{1}{2.5}+\frac{1}{5}+\frac{1}{5} \end{vmatrix} \begin{vmatrix} V_b \\ V_c \end{vmatrix} = \begin{vmatrix} \frac{10}{4}+2 \\ \frac{10}{5}+\frac{4}{5} \end{vmatrix}$$

or
$$\begin{vmatrix} 0.65 & -0.4 \\ -0.4 & 0.8 \end{vmatrix} \begin{vmatrix} V_b \\ V_c \end{vmatrix} = \begin{vmatrix} 4.5 \\ 2.8 \end{vmatrix}$$

$$\therefore \quad V_b = \frac{\begin{vmatrix} 4.5 & -0.4 \\ 2.8 & 0.8 \end{vmatrix}}{\begin{vmatrix} 0.65 & -0.45 \\ -0.4 & 0.8 \end{vmatrix}} = \frac{4.5 \times 0.8 - [2.8 \times (-0.4)]}{0.65 \times 0.8 - (-0.4)(-0.4)} = 13.11 \text{ V}$$

and
$$V_c = \frac{\begin{vmatrix} 0.65 & 4.5 \\ -0.4 & 2.8 \end{vmatrix}}{\begin{vmatrix} 0.65 & -0.4 \\ -0.4 & 0.8 \end{vmatrix}} = \frac{0.65 \times 2.8 - 4.5 \times (-0.4)}{0.65 \times 0.8 - (-0.4)(-0.4)} = 10.05 \text{ V}$$

$V_b = 13.11\ V$

$V_c = 10.05$ V **Ans.**

**Example 2.5.13.** *Apply node voltage analysis to determine* $V_1$, $V_2$ and $V_3$ *for the network shown in Fig. 2.5.13.*

**Solution:** Applying Kirchhoff's current law, node voltage equation are developed below:

At node 1 : $\frac{V_1 - 5}{10} + \frac{V_1 - V_2}{5} + \frac{V_1 - V_2}{5} + \frac{V_1}{4} = 0$

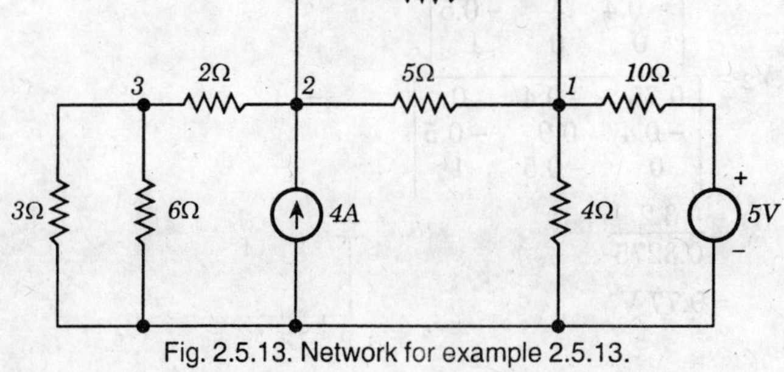


Fig. 2.5.13. Network for example 2.5.13.

At node 2 : $\frac{V_2 - V_1}{5} + \frac{V_2 - V_1}{5} + \frac{V_2 - V_3}{2} - 4 = 0$

At node 3 : $\frac{V_3 - V_2}{2} + \frac{V_3}{6} + \frac{V_3}{9} = 0$

Above equations can be arranged in determinant form as

$$\begin{vmatrix} \frac{1}{10}+\frac{1}{5}+\frac{1}{5} & -\frac{1}{2}-\frac{1}{2} & 0 \\ -\frac{1}{5}-\frac{1}{5} & \frac{1}{5}+\frac{1}{5}+\frac{1}{2} & -\frac{1}{2} \\ 0 & -\frac{1}{2} & \frac{1}{3}+\frac{1}{6}+\frac{1}{2} \end{vmatrix} \begin{vmatrix} V_1 \\ V_2 \\ V_3 \end{vmatrix} = \begin{vmatrix} 0.5 \\ 4 \\ 0 \end{vmatrix}$$

or

$$\begin{vmatrix} 0.75 & -0.4 & 0 \\ -0.4 & 0.9 & -0.5 \\ 0 & -0.5 & 1 \end{vmatrix} \begin{vmatrix} V_1 \\ V_2 \\ V_3 \end{vmatrix} = \begin{vmatrix} 0.5 \\ 4 \\ 0 \end{vmatrix}$$

$$\therefore\ V_1 = \frac{\begin{vmatrix} 0.5 & -0.4 & 0 \\ 4 & 0.9 & -0.5 \\ 0 & -0.5 & 1 \end{vmatrix}}{\begin{vmatrix} 0.75 & -0.4 & 0 \\ -0.4 & 0.9 & -0.5 \\ 0 & -0.5 & 1 \end{vmatrix}}$$

$$= \frac{0.5 \begin{vmatrix} 0.9 & -0.5 \\ -0.5 & 1 \end{vmatrix} - (-0.4) \begin{vmatrix} 4 & -0.5 \\ 0 & 1 \end{vmatrix} + 0 \begin{vmatrix} 4 & 0.9 \\ 0 & -0.5 \end{vmatrix}}{0.75 \begin{vmatrix} 0.9 & -0.5 \\ -0.5 & 1 \end{vmatrix} - (-0.4) \begin{vmatrix} -0.4 & -0.5 \\ 0 & 1 \end{vmatrix} + 0 \begin{vmatrix} -0.4 & 0.9 \\ 0 & -0.5 \end{vmatrix}}$$

$$= \frac{0.5\,[0.9 \times 1 - (-0.5)(-0.5)] + 0.4\,[4 \times 1 + 0 \times (-0.5)] + 0}{0.75\,[0.9 \times 1 - (-0.5)(-0.5)] + 0.4\,[(-0.4 \times 1) + 0 \times (-0.5)] + 0}$$

$$= \frac{1.925}{0.3275}$$

$$= 5.87 \text{ V}$$

$$V_2 = \frac{\begin{vmatrix} 0.75 & 0.5 & 0 \\ -0.4 & 4 & -0.5 \\ 0 & 0 & 1 \end{vmatrix}}{\begin{vmatrix} 0.75 & -0.4 & 0 \\ -0.4 & 0.9 & -0.5 \\ 0 & -0.5 & 1 \end{vmatrix}}$$

$$= \frac{3.2}{0.3275}$$

$$= 9.77 \text{ V}$$

$$V_3 = \frac{\begin{vmatrix} 0.75 & -0.4 & 0.5 \\ -0.4 & 0.9 & 4 \\ 0 & -0.5 & 0 \end{vmatrix}}{\begin{vmatrix} 0.75 & -0.4 & 0 \\ -0.4 & 0.9 & -0.5 \\ 0 & -0.5 & 1 \end{vmatrix}} = \frac{1.61}{0.3275} = 4.88 \text{ V}$$

$$V_1 = 5.87 \text{ V}, \; V_2 = 9.77 \text{ V}$$

and $V_3 = 4.88$ V **Ans.**

**Example 2.5.14:** *Using nodal method, find the node voltages* $V_b$, $V_c$ and $I_{bc}$ *for the network shown below:*

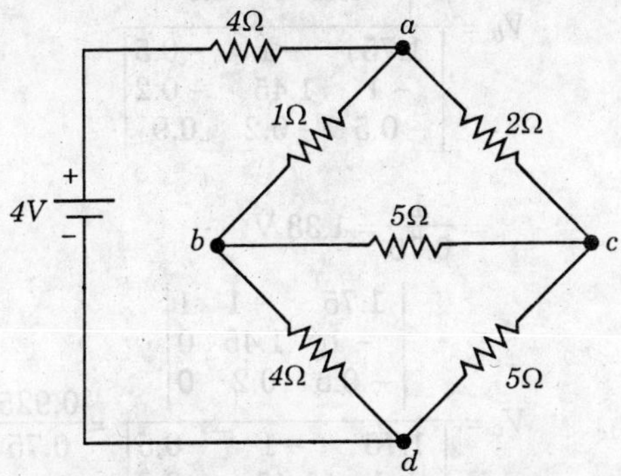


Fig. 2.5.14. Network for example 2.5.14.

**Solution :** Applying Kirchhoff's current law

At node $a$ : $\dfrac{V_a - 4}{4} + \dfrac{V_a - V_b}{1} + \dfrac{V_a - V_c}{2} = 0$

At node $b$ : $\dfrac{V_b - V_a}{1} + \dfrac{V_b - 0}{4} + \dfrac{V_b - V_c}{5} = 0$

At node $c$ : $\dfrac{V_c - V_a}{2} + \dfrac{V_c - V_b}{5} + \dfrac{V_c - 0}{5} = 0$

Above equations can be arranged in determinant form as

$$\begin{vmatrix} \frac{1}{4}+\frac{1}{1}+\frac{1}{2} & -1 & -\frac{1}{2} \\ -1 & \frac{1}{1}+\frac{1}{4}+\frac{1}{5} & -\frac{1}{5} \\ -\frac{1}{2} & -\frac{1}{5} & \frac{1}{2}+\frac{1}{5}+\frac{1}{5} \end{vmatrix} \begin{vmatrix} V_a \\ V_b \\ V_c \end{vmatrix} = \begin{vmatrix} 4/4 \\ 0 \\ 0 \end{vmatrix}$$

or

$$\begin{vmatrix} 1.75 & -1 & -0.5 \\ -1 & 1.45 & -0.2 \\ -0.5 & -0.2 & 0.9 \end{vmatrix} \begin{vmatrix} V_a \\ V_b \\ V_c \end{vmatrix} = \begin{vmatrix} 1 \\ 0 \\ 0 \end{vmatrix}$$

$$\therefore \quad V_a = \frac{\begin{vmatrix} 1 & -1 & -0.5 \\ 0 & 1.45 & -0.2 \\ 0 & -0.2 & 0.9 \end{vmatrix}}{\begin{vmatrix} 1.75 & -1 & -0.5 \\ -1 & 1.45 & -0.2 \\ -0.5 & -0.2 & 0.9 \end{vmatrix}}$$

$$= \frac{1.26}{0.75} = 1.68 \text{ V}$$

$$V_b = \frac{\begin{vmatrix} 1.75 & 1 & -0.5 \\ -1 & 0 & -0.2 \\ -0.5 & 0 & 0.9 \end{vmatrix}}{\begin{vmatrix} 1.75 & -1 & -0.5 \\ -1 & 1.45 & -0.2 \\ -0.5 & -0.2 & 0.9 \end{vmatrix}}$$

$$= \frac{1}{0.75} = 1.33 \text{ V}$$

$$V_c = \frac{\begin{vmatrix} 1.75 & -1 & 1 \\ -1 & 1.45 & 0 \\ -0.5 & 0.2 & 0 \end{vmatrix}}{\begin{vmatrix} 1.75 & -1 & -0.5 \\ -1 & 1.45 & -0.2 \\ -0.5 & -0.2 & 0.9 \end{vmatrix}} = \frac{0.925}{0.75} = 1.23 \text{ V}$$

$$V_a = 1.68 \ V$$

$$V_b = 1.33 \ V$$

$$V_c = 1.23 \ V$$

$$I_{bc} = \frac{V_b - V_c}{5} = \frac{1.33 - 1.23}{5}$$

$$= 0.02 \text{ A} \qquad \textbf{Ans.}$$

**Example 2.5.15:** *Determine node voltages* $V_1$ and $V_2$. *Calculate current through* 10 Ω *resistor.*

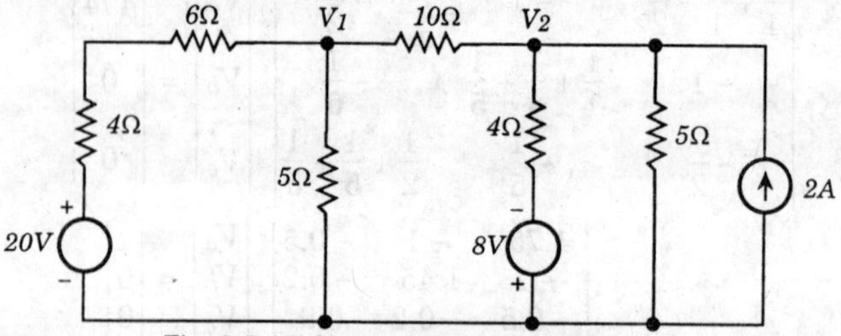


Fig. 2.5.15: Network for example 2.5.15.

**Solution :** Applying node voltage analysis.

At node 1 : $\dfrac{V_1 - 20}{6+4} + \dfrac{V_1}{5} + \dfrac{V_1 - V_2}{10} = 0$

At node 2 : $\dfrac{V_2 - V_1}{10} + \dfrac{V_2 + 8}{4} + \dfrac{V_2}{5} - 2 = 0$

On rearranging above equations,

$$\left(\frac{1}{6+4} + \frac{1}{5} + \frac{1}{10}\right) V_1 - \frac{V_2}{10} = 2$$

$$-\frac{V_1}{10} + \left(\frac{1}{10} + \frac{1}{4} + \frac{1}{5}\right) V_2 = 0$$

Above equations can be written in determinant form as

$$\begin{vmatrix} \frac{1}{10} + \frac{1}{5} + \frac{1}{10} & -\frac{1}{10} \\ -\frac{1}{10} & \frac{1}{10} + \frac{1}{4} + \frac{1}{5} \end{vmatrix} \begin{vmatrix} V_1 \\ V_2 \end{vmatrix} = \begin{vmatrix} 2 \\ 0 \end{vmatrix}$$

or

$$\begin{vmatrix} 0.3 & -0.1 \\ -0.1 & 0.55 \end{vmatrix} \begin{vmatrix} V_1 \\ V_2 \end{vmatrix} = \begin{vmatrix} 2 \\ 0 \end{vmatrix}$$

$$V_1 = \frac{\begin{vmatrix} 2 & -0.1 \\ 0 & 0.55 \end{vmatrix}}{\begin{vmatrix} 0.3 & -0.1 \\ -0.1 & 0.55 \end{vmatrix}} = 7.09\ V \text{ and } V_2 = \frac{\begin{vmatrix} 0.3 & 2 \\ -0.1 & 0 \end{vmatrix}}{\begin{vmatrix} 0.3 & -0.1 \\ -0.1 & 0.55 \end{vmatrix}} = 1.29\text{ V} \quad \textbf{Ans.}$$

The current through 10 Ω resistor

$$= \frac{V_1 - V_2}{10} = \frac{7.09 - 1.29}{10} = 0.58\text{ A} \qquad \textbf{Ans.}$$

**Example 2.5.16.** *In the network given below, determinant* $V_a$ and $V_b$.

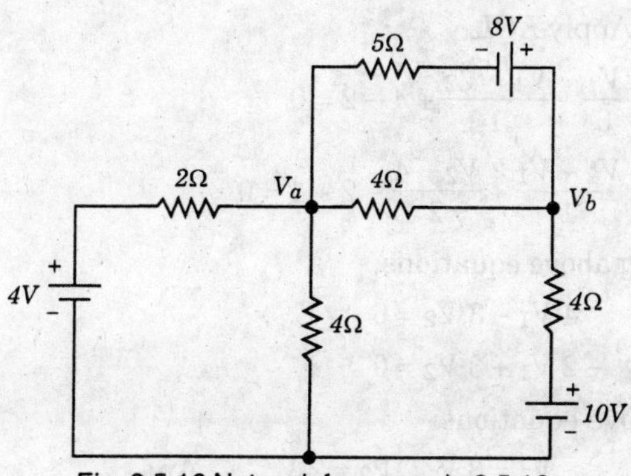


Fig. 2.5.16 Network for example 2.5.16.

**Solution :** The node equations are written below:

At node (*a*) : $\frac{V_a - 4}{2} + \frac{V_a - V_b}{4} + \frac{V_a}{4} + \frac{(V_a + 8) - V_b}{5} = 0$

At node (*b*) : $\frac{V_b - 10}{4} + \frac{V_b - V_a}{4} + \frac{(V_b - 8) - V_a}{5} = 0$

On rearranging above equations.

$$\left(\frac{1}{2} + \frac{1}{4} + \frac{1}{4} + \frac{1}{5}\right) V_a - \left(\frac{1}{4} + \frac{1}{5}\right) V_b = \frac{4}{2} - \frac{8}{5}$$

$$-\left(\frac{1}{4} + \frac{1}{5}\right) V_a + \left(\frac{1}{4} + \frac{1}{4} + \frac{1}{5}\right) V_b = \frac{10}{4} - \frac{8}{5}$$

or

$$1.2\ V_a - 0.45\ V_b = 0.4$$

$$-\ 0.45\ V_a + 0.7\ V_b = 4.1$$

Solving above equations

$$V_a = \frac{10}{3}\ V$$

$$V_b = 8.0\ \text{V} \qquad \textbf{Ans.}$$

**Example 2.5.17.** *Write the node voltage equations and determine* $V_1$ and $V_2$.

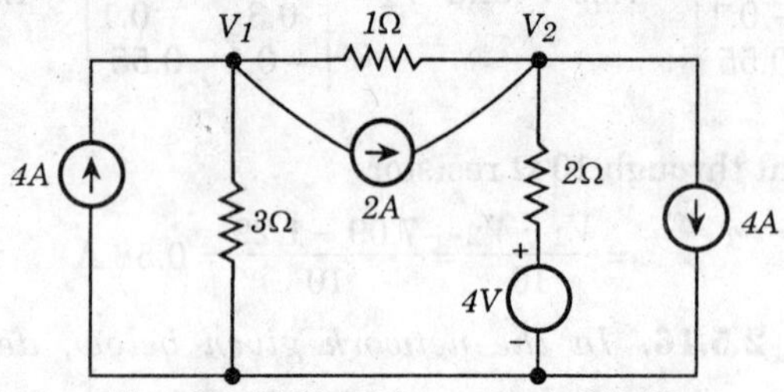


Fig. 2.5.17 Circuit for example 2.5.17.

**Solution:** Apply *KCL*,

At node 1 : $\frac{V_1}{3} + \frac{V_1 - V_2}{1} + 4 - 2 = 0$

At node 2 : $\frac{V_2 - V_1}{1} + \frac{V_2 - 4}{2} - 2 + 4 = 0$

Simplifying above equations,

$$4\ V_1 - 3\ V_2 = 6$$

and

$$-\ 2\ V_1 + 3\ V_2 = 0$$

Solving above equations

$$V_1 = 3\ V\ ;\ V_2 = 2\ V \qquad \textbf{Ans.}$$

**Example 2.5.18:** *Determine* $V_1$, $V_2$ and $V_3$ *shown in Fig. 2.5.18 given below:*

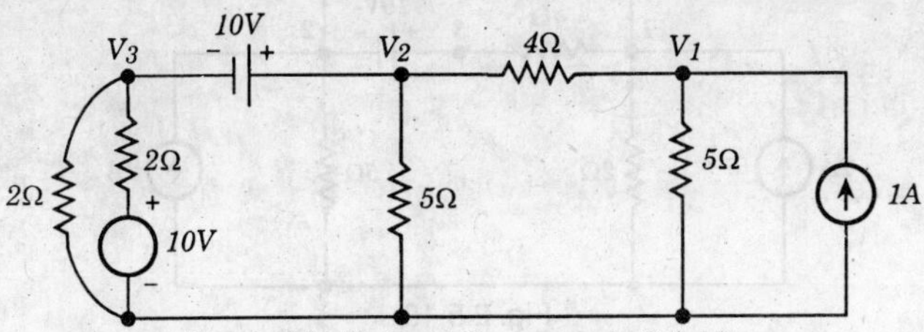


Fig. 2.5.18 Network for example 2.5.18.

**Solution:** The nodes (2) and (3) are super nodes. As per node voltage analysis.

At node 1 : $\dfrac{V_1}{5} + \dfrac{V_1 - V_2}{4} - 1 = 0$

At node (2) and (3) (Super nodes) :

$$\frac{V_2}{5} + \frac{V_2 - V_1}{4} + \frac{V_3 - 10}{2} + \frac{V_3}{2} = 0$$

On simplification,

$$\left(\frac{1}{5} + \frac{1}{4}\right) V_1 - \frac{1}{4} V_2 = 1$$

$$-\frac{V_1}{4} + \left(\frac{1}{5} + \frac{1}{4}\right) V_2 + \left(\frac{1}{2} + \frac{1}{2}\right) V_3 = 5$$

or $$0.45\ V_1 - 0.25\ V_2 = 1 \qquad \text{...(1)}$$

$$-\ 0.25V_1 + 0.45\ V_2 + V_3 = 5 \qquad \text{...(2)}$$

It is noted that $V_2 - V_3 = 10$ ...(3)

Substitute for $V_3$ in Eqn. (2) from Eqn. (3) to get

$$-\ 0.25V_1 + 1.45V_2 = 15 \qquad \text{...(4)}$$

Solving Eqns. (1) and (4)

$$V_1 = 8.81 \text{ V},$$

$$V_2 = 11.86 \text{ V}$$

$$V_3 = V_2 - 10$$

$$= 11.86 - 10$$

$$= 1.86 \text{ V}$$ **Ans.**

**Example 2.5.19:** *Determine* $V_1$, $V_2$ *and current through* 4 Ω *resistor.*

**Solution :** The nodes (2) and (3) can be considered as super nodes.

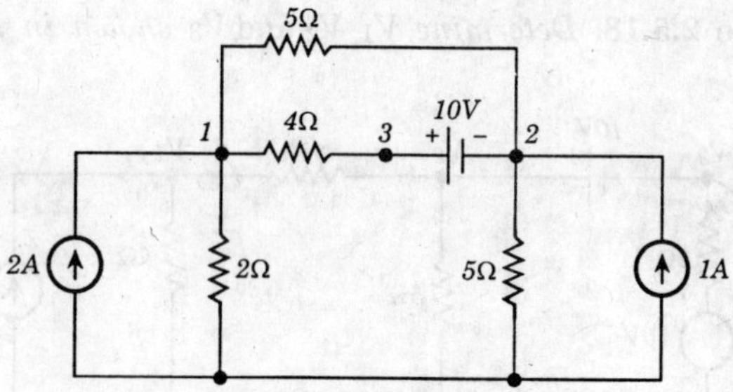


Fig. 2.5.19

The nodal equations are written below:

At node 1 : $\frac{V_1}{2} + \frac{V_1 - V_3}{4} + \frac{V_1 - V_2}{5} - 2 = 0$

At node (2) and (3) (super nodes) :

$$\frac{V_2 - V_1}{5} + \frac{V_2}{5} - 1 + \frac{V_3 - V_1}{4} = 0$$

On rearranging above equations,

$$\left(\frac{1}{2} + \frac{1}{4} + \frac{1}{5}\right) V_1 - \frac{V_2}{5} - \frac{V_3}{4} = 2$$

$$-\left(\frac{1}{5} + \frac{1}{4}\right) V_1 + \left(\frac{1}{5} + \frac{1}{5}\right) V_2 + \frac{V_3}{4} = 1$$

or $$0.95\ V_1 - 0.2\ V_2 - 0.25\ V_3 = 2 \qquad ...(1)$$

$$-0.45\ V_1 + V_2 + 0.25\ V_3 = 1 \qquad ...(2)$$

Also, $$V_3 - V_2 = 10 \qquad ...(3)$$

Eliminate $V_3$ from Eqns.(1) & (2) using Eqn. (3)

∴ $$0.95\ V_1 - 0.2\ V_2 - 0.25\ (V_2 + 10) = 2$$

$$-0.45\ V_1 + V_2 + 0.25(V_2 + 10) = 1$$

or $$0.95\ V_1 - 0.45\ V_1 = 4.5$$

$$-0.41\ V_1 + 1.25\ V_2 = -1.5$$

The determinant form of above equations is given below:

$$\begin{vmatrix} 0.95 & -0.45 \\ -0.45 & 1.25 \end{vmatrix} \begin{vmatrix} V_1 \\ V_2 \end{vmatrix} = \begin{vmatrix} 4.5 \\ -1.5 \end{vmatrix}$$

∴ $$V_1 = \frac{\begin{vmatrix} 4.5 & -0.45 \\ -1.5 & 1.25 \end{vmatrix}}{\begin{vmatrix} 0.95 & -0.45 \\ -0.45 & 1.25 \end{vmatrix}} = \frac{4.95}{0.98} = 5.02 \text{ V}$$ **Ans.**

$$V_2 = \frac{\begin{vmatrix} 0.95 & 4.5 \\ -0.45 & -1.5 \end{vmatrix}}{\begin{vmatrix} 0.95 & -0.45 \\ -0.45 & 1.25 \end{vmatrix}} = \frac{0.6}{0.985} = 0.609 \text{ V} \quad \textbf{Ans.}$$

$\because \qquad V_3 - V_2 = 10$

$\therefore \qquad V_3 = 10 + V_2 = 10 + 0.609 = 10.609 \text{ V}$

The current through 4 Ω resistor,

$$I = \frac{V_3 - V_1}{4} = \frac{10.609 - 5.02}{4} = \frac{5.589}{4}$$

$$= 1.397 \text{ A} \quad \textbf{Ans.}$$

**Example 2.5.20:** *In the circuit shown in figure given below determine $I_{ab}$.*

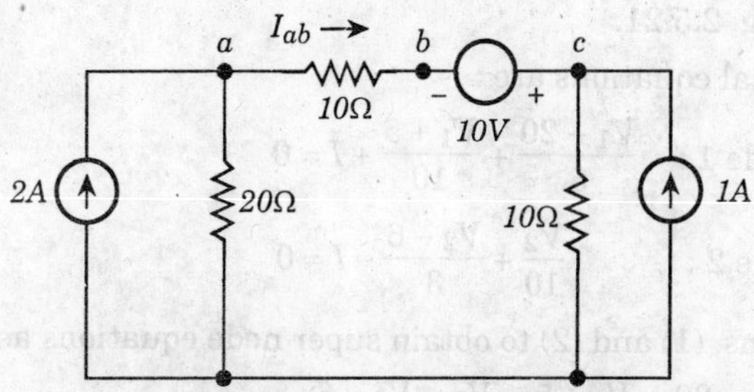


Fig. 2.5.20. Circuit for example 2.5.20.

**Solution** : As the voltage source is connected between nodes $b$ and $c$, these two nodes can be considered as super nodes.

Writing nodal equations

At node $a$ : $\qquad \dfrac{V_a}{20} - \dfrac{V_a - V_b}{2} - 2 = 0 \qquad$ ...(1)

At node $b$ and $c$ (super nodes) : $\qquad \dfrac{V_b - V_a}{10} + \dfrac{V_c}{10} - 1 = 0 \qquad$ ...(2)

Also, $\qquad V_c - V_b = 10 \qquad$ ...(3)

Substitute $V_c = V_b + 10$ in Eqn (2) and on simplification following equation are obtained,

From Eqn.(1) $3\,V_a - 2\,V_b = 40 \qquad$ ...(4)

From Eqn.(2) $-V_a + 2\,V_b = 0 \qquad$ ...(5)

Solving Eqns. (4) and (5)

$$V_a = 20 \text{ V}$$

and $\qquad V_b = 10 \text{ V}$

$$I_{ab} = \frac{V_a - V_b}{10} = \frac{20 - 10}{10} = 1.0 \text{ A} \qquad \textbf{Ans.}$$

**Example 2.5.21:** *Determine the node voltages* $V_1$ and $V_2$ *for the network shown in Fig. 2.5.21.*

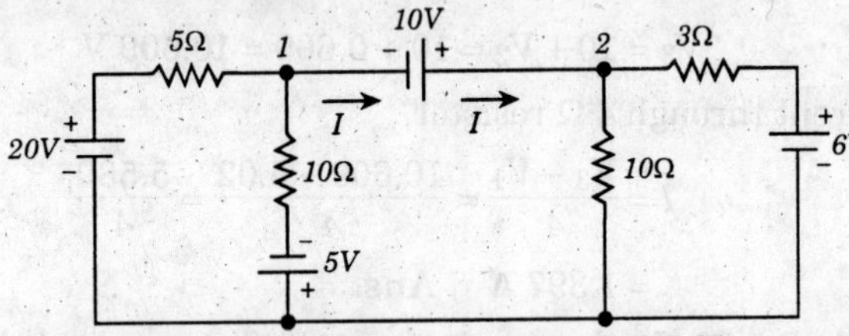


Fig. 2.5.21. Network for example 2.5.21.

**Solution :** Let the current flowing through 10 $V$ source be $I$ as shown in Fig. 2.5.21.

The nodal equations are :

At node 1 : $\dfrac{V_1 - 20}{5} + \dfrac{V_1 + 5}{10} + I = 0$ ...(1)

At node 2 : $\dfrac{V_2}{10} + \dfrac{V_2 - 6}{3} - I = 0$ ...(2)

Add Eqns. (1) and (2) to obtain super node equations as:

$$\frac{V_1 - 20}{5} + \frac{V_1 + 5}{10} + \frac{V_2}{10} + \frac{V_2 - 6}{3} = 0 \text{ (super node equation)}$$

Simplifying above equation,

$0.3\ V_1 + 0.433\ V_2 = 1.5$ ...(3)

Also, $V_2 - V_1 = 10$ ...(4)

or $\begin{vmatrix} 0.3 & 0.433 \\ -1 & 1 \end{vmatrix} \begin{vmatrix} V_1 \\ V_2 \end{vmatrix} = \begin{vmatrix} 1.5 \\ 10 \end{vmatrix}$

$$V_1 = \frac{\begin{vmatrix} 1.5 & 0.433 \\ 10 & 1 \end{vmatrix}}{\begin{vmatrix} 0.3 & 0.4333 \\ 10 & 1 \end{vmatrix}}$$

$$= \frac{-2.83}{-4.03} = 0.7 \text{ V}$$

$$V_2 = \frac{\begin{vmatrix} 0.3 & 1.5 \\ -1 & 10 \end{vmatrix}}{\begin{vmatrix} 0.3 & 0.433 \\ 10 & 1 \end{vmatrix}} = \frac{4.5}{-4.03} = -1.11 \text{ V}$$

$V_1 = 0.7$ V, $V_2 = -1.11$ V **Ans.**

**Example 2.5.22:** *Apply node voltage analysis to determine* $V_1$, $V_2$, $V_3$ and $V_4$.

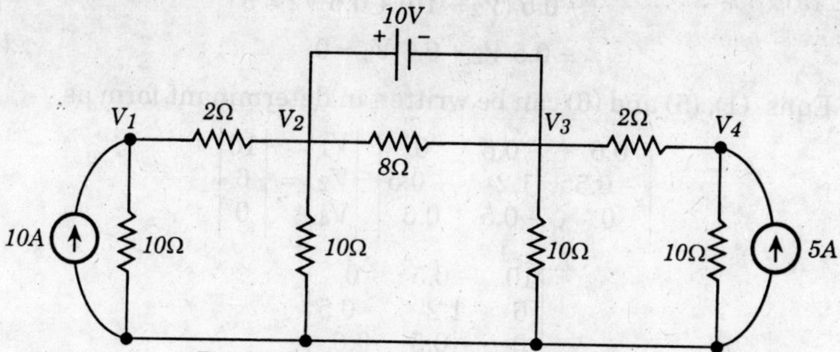


Fig. 2.5.22 Network for example 2.5.22.

**Solution :** The 8 Ω resistor is across the 10V voltage source, therefore, the same is not considered in the network (*i.e.* replaced by an open circuit) as shown in Fig. 2.5.22(*a*).

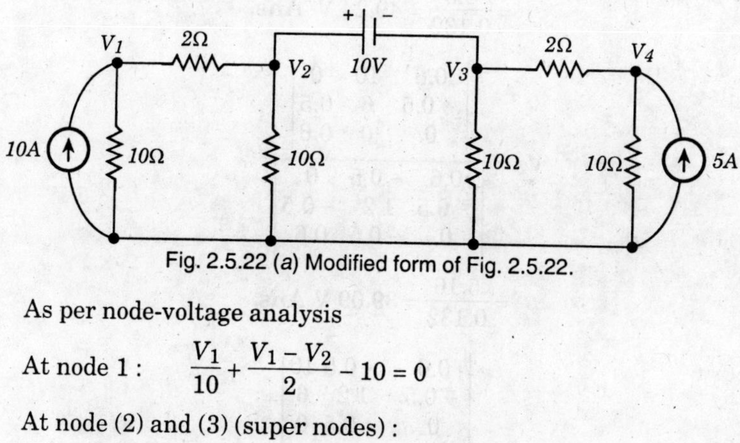


Fig. 2.5.22 (*a*) Modified form of Fig. 2.5.22.

As per node-voltage analysis

At node 1 : $\frac{V_1}{10} + \frac{V_1 - V_2}{2} - 10 = 0$

At node (2) and (3) (super nodes) :

$$\frac{V_2 - V_1}{2} + \frac{V_2}{10} + \frac{V_3}{10} + \frac{V_3 - V_4}{2} = 0$$

At node 4 : $\frac{V_4 - V_3}{2} + \frac{V_4}{10} - 5 = 0$

Above equations are simplified as below,

$$0.6\, V_1 - 0.5\, V_2 = 10 \quad \text{...(1)}$$

$$-0.5\, V_1 + 0.6\, V_2 + 0.6\, V_3 - 0.5\, V_4 = 0 \quad \text{...(2)}$$

$$0.5\, V_3 + 0.6\, V_4 = 5 \quad \text{...(3)}$$

$$\therefore \quad V_2 - V_3 = 10 \quad \text{...(4)}$$

Using Eqn. (4), substitute for $V_3$ in Eqn. (2) and (3)

$$\therefore \quad -0.5\,V_1 + 0.6\,V_2 + 0.6(V_2 - 10) - 0.5\,V_4 = 0$$

or $$0.5\,V_1 + 1.2\,V_2 - 0.5\,V_4 = 6 \quad \text{...(5)}$$

and $$-0.5\,(V_2 - 10) + 0.6\,V_4 = 5$$

or $$-0.5\,V_2 + 0.6\,V_4 = 0 \quad \text{...(6)}$$

Eqns. (1), (5) and (6) can be written in determinant form as

$$\begin{vmatrix} 0.6 & -0.5 & 0 \\ -0.5 & 1.2 & -0.5 \\ 0 & -0.5 & 0.6 \end{vmatrix} \begin{vmatrix} V_1 \\ V_2 \\ V_4 \end{vmatrix} = \begin{vmatrix} 10 \\ 6 \\ 0 \end{vmatrix}$$

$$\therefore \quad V_1 = \frac{\begin{vmatrix} 10 & -0.5 & 0 \\ 6 & 1.2 & -0.5 \\ 0 & -0.5 & 0.6 \end{vmatrix}}{\begin{vmatrix} 0.6 & -0.5 & 0 \\ -0.5 & 1.2 & -0.5 \\ 0 & -0.5 & 0.6 \end{vmatrix}}$$

$$= \frac{6.5}{0.132} = 49.24\text{ V} \quad \textbf{Ans.}$$

$$V_2 = \frac{\begin{vmatrix} 0.6 & 10 & 0 \\ -0.5 & 6 & 0.5 \\ 0 & 0 & 0.6 \end{vmatrix}}{\begin{vmatrix} 0.6 & -0.5 & 0 \\ -0.5 & 1.2 & -0.5 \\ 0 & -0.5 & 0.6 \end{vmatrix}}$$

$$= \frac{5.16}{0.132} = 39.09\text{ V} \quad \textbf{Ans.}$$

$$V_4 = \frac{\begin{vmatrix} 0.6 & -0.5 & 10 \\ -0.5 & 1.2 & 6 \\ 0 & -0.5 & 0 \end{vmatrix}}{\begin{vmatrix} 0.6 & -0.5 & 0 \\ -0.5 & 1.2 & -0.5 \\ 0 & -0.5 & 0.6 \end{vmatrix}}$$

$$= \frac{4.3}{0.132}$$

$$= 32.57\text{ V} \quad \textbf{Ans.}$$

$$V_3 = V_2 - 10$$

$$= 39.09 - 10$$

$$= 29.09\text{ V} \quad \textbf{Ans.}$$

**Example 2.5.23.** *Determine the node voltages $V_1$, $V_2$ and the current flowing through 4 Ω resistor.*

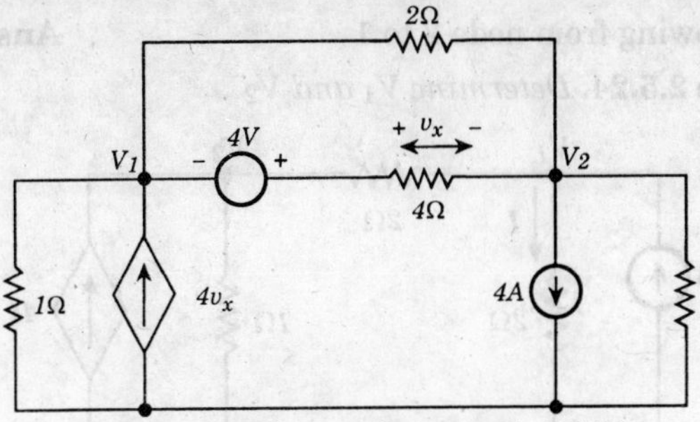


Fig. 2.5.23. Network for example 2.5.23.

**Solution** : Apply Kirchhoff's current law,

At node 1 : $\frac{V_1}{1} - 4\,v_x + \frac{V_1 - V_2}{2} + \frac{(V_1 + 4) - V_2}{4} = 0$ ...(1)

At node 2 : $\frac{V_2 - V_1}{2} + 4 + \frac{V_2}{1} + \frac{(V_2 - 4) - V_1}{4} = 0$ ...(2)

Also, $(V_1 + 4) - v_x = V_2$

$\therefore$ $v_x = (V_1 + 4) - V_2$ ...(3)

Substitute for $v_x$ in Eqn. (1) from (3) to get,

$$\frac{V_1}{1} - 4\,[\,(V_1 + 4) - V_2\,] + \frac{V_1 - V_2}{2} + \frac{(V_1 + 4) - V_2}{4} = 0$$

On simplification,

$$-2.25\,V_1 + 3.25\,V_2 = 15 \quad ...(4)$$

On simplification, Eqn.(2) takes the form,

$$-0.75\,V_1 + 1.75\,V_2 = -3 \quad ...(5)$$

Eqns. (4) and (5) can be written in determinant form as

$$\begin{vmatrix} -2.25 & 3.25 \\ -0.75 & 1.75 \end{vmatrix} \begin{vmatrix} V_1 \\ V_2 \end{vmatrix} = \begin{vmatrix} 15 \\ -3 \end{vmatrix}$$

$$\therefore \quad V_1 = \frac{\begin{vmatrix} 15 & 3.25 \\ -3 & 1.75 \end{vmatrix}}{\begin{vmatrix} -2.25 & 3.25 \\ -0.75 & 1.75 \end{vmatrix}} = \frac{36}{-1.5} = -24\ V,$$

$$V_2 = \frac{\begin{vmatrix} -2.25 & 15 \\ -0.75 & -3 \end{vmatrix}}{\begin{vmatrix} -2.25 & 3.25 \\ -0.75 & 1.75 \end{vmatrix}} = \frac{18}{-1.5} = -12\ \text{V} \qquad \textbf{Ans.}$$

$$v_x = (V_1 + 4) - V_2 = (-24 + 4) - (-12) = -8 \text{ V}$$

The current through 4 Ω resistor $= \dfrac{v_x}{4} = -\dfrac{8}{4} = -2 \text{ A}$

*i.e.* 2 A flowing from node 2 to 1 **Ans.**

**Example 2.5.24.** *Determine $V_1$ and $V_2$*

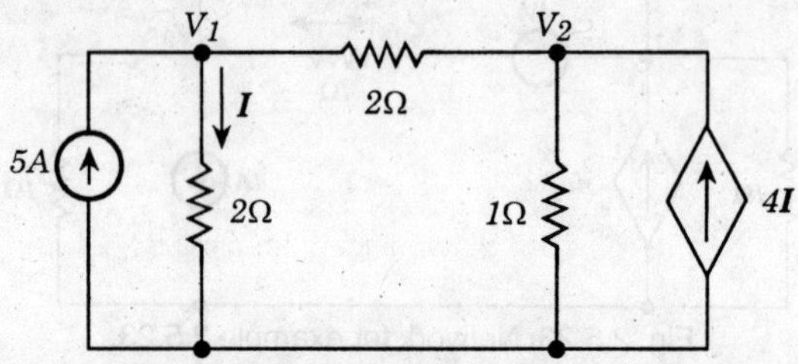


Fig. 2.5.24. Circuit for example 2.5.24.

**Solution :** Applying Kirchhoff's current law

At node 1 : $$\frac{V_1}{2} - 5 + \frac{V_1 - V_2}{2} = 0 \quad ...(1)$$

At node 2 : $$\frac{V_2}{1} - \frac{V_2 - V_1}{2} - 4I = 0 \quad ...(2)$$

$$I = \frac{V_1}{2} \quad ...(3)$$

Substitute Eqn.(3) in (2) to obtain.

$$\frac{V_2}{1} + \frac{V_2 - V_1}{2} - \frac{4V_1}{2} = 0 \quad ...(4)$$

On simplifying Eqns. (1) and (4)

$$V_1 - 0.5\,V_2 = 5 \quad ...(5)$$

$$-2.5\,V_1 + 1.5\,V_2 = 0 \quad ...(6)$$

or $$\begin{vmatrix} 1 & -0.5 \\ -2.5 & 1.5 \end{vmatrix} \begin{vmatrix} V_1 \\ V_2 \end{vmatrix} = \begin{vmatrix} 5 \\ 0 \end{vmatrix}$$

$$\therefore \quad V_1 = \frac{\begin{vmatrix} 5 & -0.5 \\ 0 & 1.5 \end{vmatrix}}{\begin{vmatrix} 1 & -0.5 \\ -2.5 & 1.5 \end{vmatrix}} = \frac{7.5}{0.25} = 30 \text{ V},$$

$$V_2 = \frac{\begin{vmatrix} 1 & 5 \\ -2.5 & 0 \end{vmatrix}}{\begin{vmatrix} 1 & -0.5 \\ -2.5 & 1.5 \end{vmatrix}} = \frac{12.5}{0.25}$$

$$= 50 \text{ V}$$ **Ans.**

**Example 2.5.25 :** *Determine the current, $I_2$ in the network given below:*

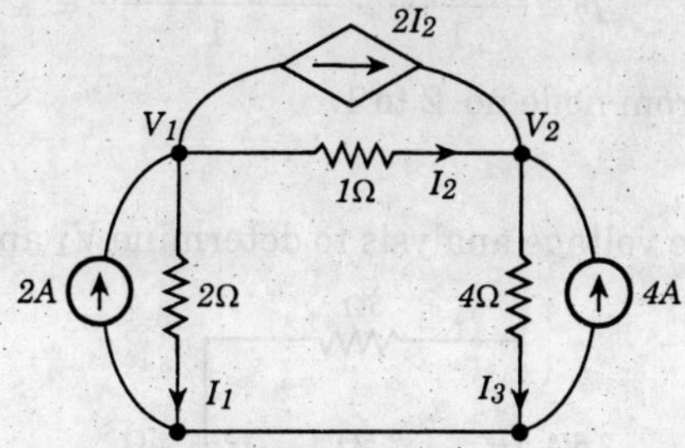


Fig. 2.5.25. Network for example 2.5.25.

**Solution :** Apply node analysis,

At node 1 : $\frac{V_1}{2} + \frac{V_1 - V_2}{1} - 2 + 2\,I_2 = 0$

At node 2 :

$$\frac{V_2}{4} + \frac{V_2 - V_1}{1} - 4 - 2\,I_2 = 0$$

$$\because \qquad I_2 = \frac{V_1 - V_2}{1}$$

Substituting the value of $I_2$ in node voltage equations following equations are obtained:

$$\frac{V_1}{2} + \frac{V_1 - V_2}{1} - 2 + 2\,\frac{(V_1 - V_2)}{1} = 0$$

$$\frac{V_2}{4} + \frac{V_2 - V_1}{1} - 4 - 2\,\frac{(V_1 - V_2)}{1} = 0$$

On simplifying above equations

$$3.5\,V_1 - 4\,V_s = 2$$

$$-3\,V_1 + 3.25\,V_2 = 4$$

$$\begin{vmatrix} 3.5 & -4 \\ -3 & 3.25 \end{vmatrix} \begin{vmatrix} V_1 \\ V_2 \end{vmatrix} = \begin{vmatrix} 2 \\ 4 \end{vmatrix}$$

$$\therefore \qquad V_1 = \frac{\begin{vmatrix} 2 & -4 \\ 4 & 3.25 \end{vmatrix}}{\begin{vmatrix} 3.5 & -4 \\ -3 & 3.25 \end{vmatrix}} = \frac{22.5}{-0.625} = -36\text{ V},$$

$$V_2 = \frac{\begin{vmatrix} 3.5 & 2 \\ -3 & 4 \end{vmatrix}}{\begin{vmatrix} 3.5 & -4 \\ -3 & 3.25 \end{vmatrix}} = \frac{20}{-0.625} = 32\text{ V}$$

$$I_2 = \frac{V_1 - V_2}{1} = \frac{-36-(-32)}{1} = -4 \text{ A} \qquad \textbf{Ans.}$$

*i.e.* flowing from node no. 2 to 1.

## PROBLEMS

**2.1.** Use node voltage analysis to determine $V_1$ and $V_2$

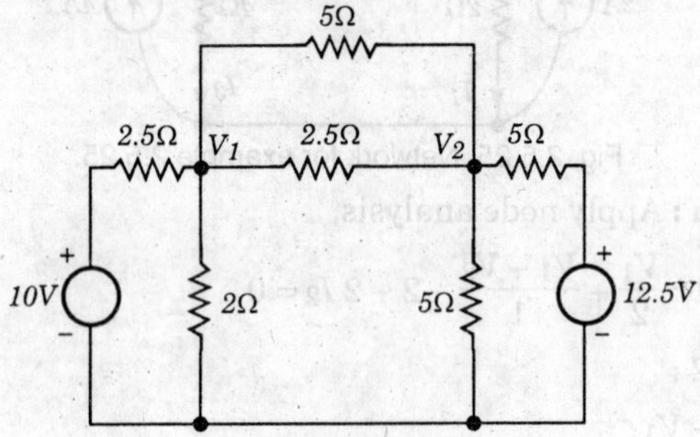


Fig. 2P-1

(**Ans.** $V_1 = 4.82$ V, $V_2 = 5.39$ V)

**2.2.** Determine $V_1$ and $V_2$ in the network given below.

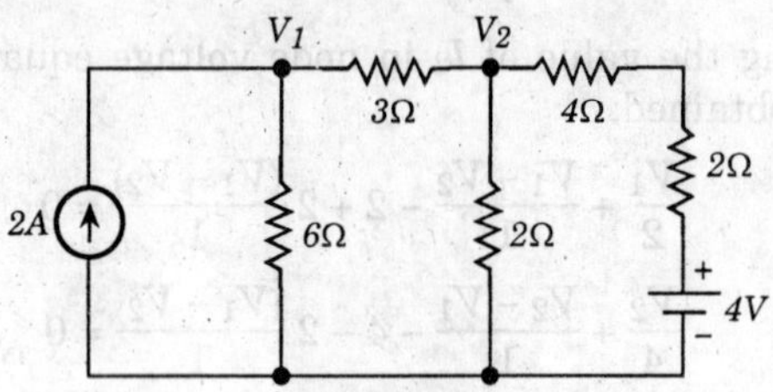


Fig. 2P-2

(**Ans.** $V_1 = 5.71$ V, $V_2 = 2.57$ V)

**2.3.** Determine the node voltages $v_a$, $v_b$ and power delivered by 5 V source.

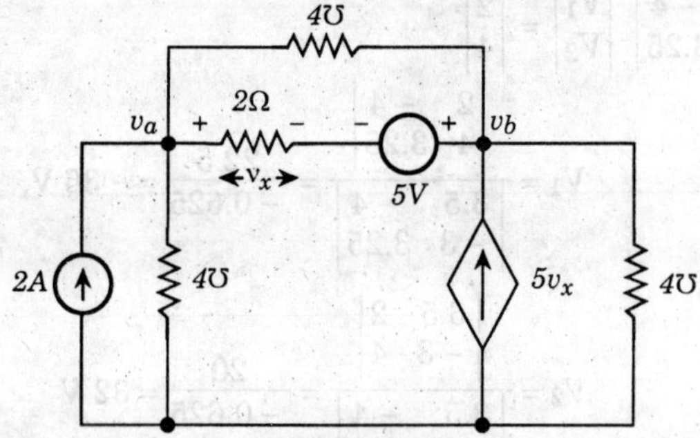


Fig. 2P-3

(**Ans.** $v_a = 2.11$ V, $v_b = 4.85$ V, $P = 2.6$ W)

**2.4.** Select mesh currents and write Maxwell's mesh current equations.

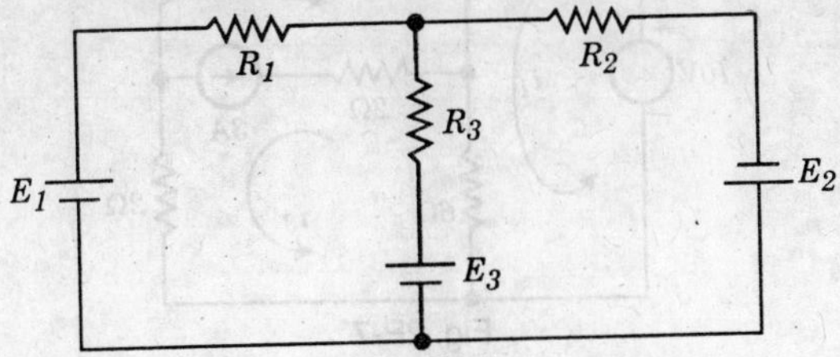


Fig. 2P-4

**2.5.** Select mesh currents, write Maxwell's mesh current equations and determine $V_a$

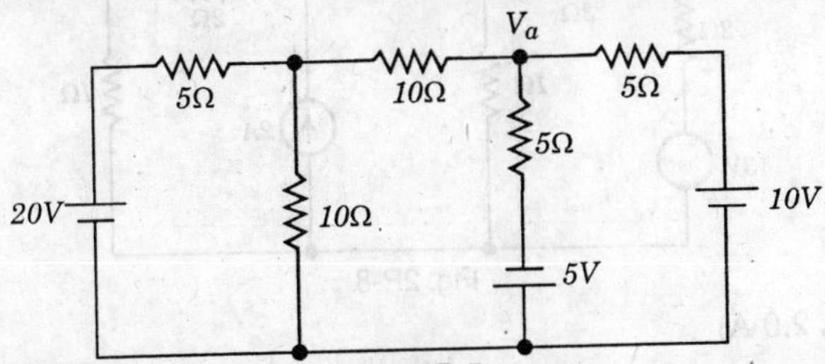


Fig. 2P-5

(**Ans.** $V_a = 0.79$ V)

**2.6.** Determine the current $I$ either by mesh current or node voltage analysis.

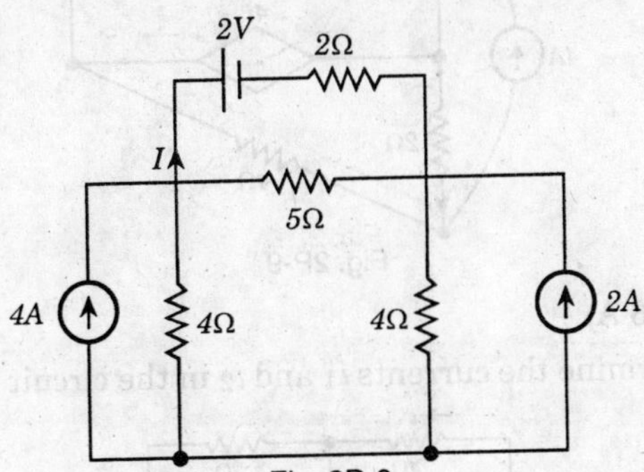


Fig. 2P-6

(**Ans.** $I_a = 0.212$ A)

**2.7.** Apply Maxwell's mesh current analysis to determine the current $i_1$ supplied by the source.

(**Ans.** $i_1 = 1.939$ A)

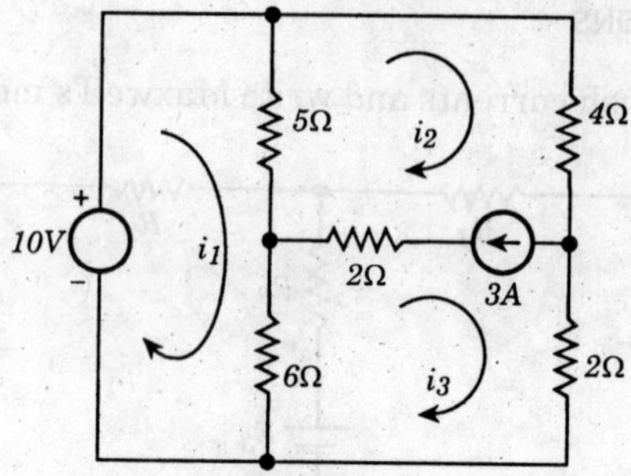


Fig. 2P-7

**2.8 .** Determine the current through 3 Ω resistor. Use mesh current analysis and verify the answer by nodal analysis.

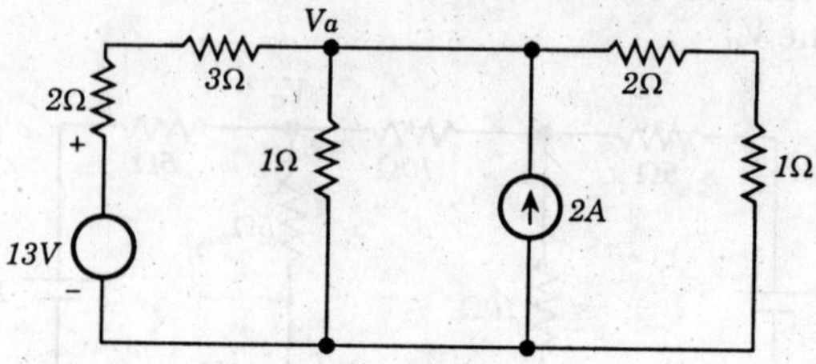


Fig. 2P-8

(**Ans.** 2.0 A)

**2.9 .** In the network shown below determine the current through 5 Ω resistor.

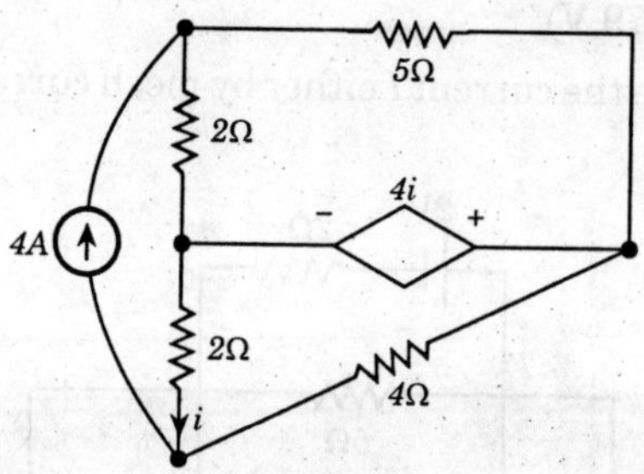


Fig. 2P-9

(**Ans.** 0.228 A)

**2.10.** Determine the currents $i_1$ and $i_2$ in the circuit given below.

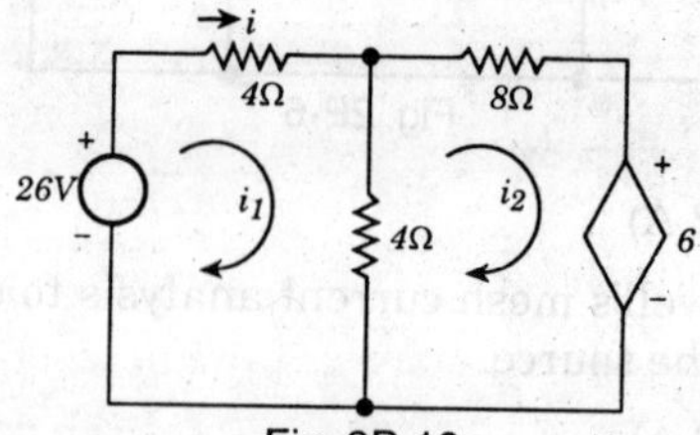


Fig. 2P-10

( **Ans.** $i_1 = 3$ A, $i_2 = 0.5$ A )

**2.11.** Determine the equivalent resistance at terminals $a$-$b$

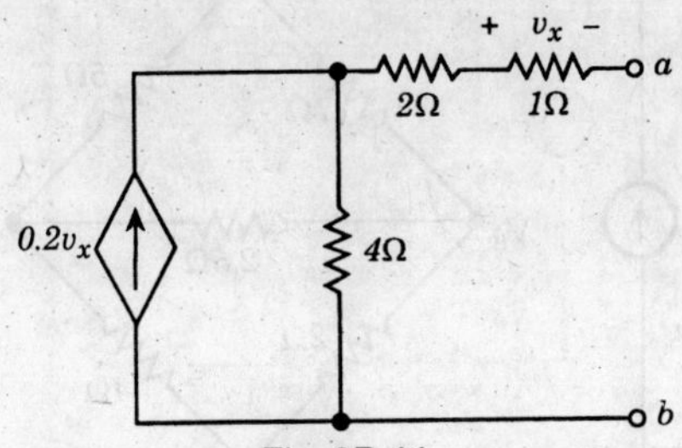


Fig. 2P-11

( **Ans.** 7.8 Ω)

**2.12.** Determine the value of $i_a$ in the network given below

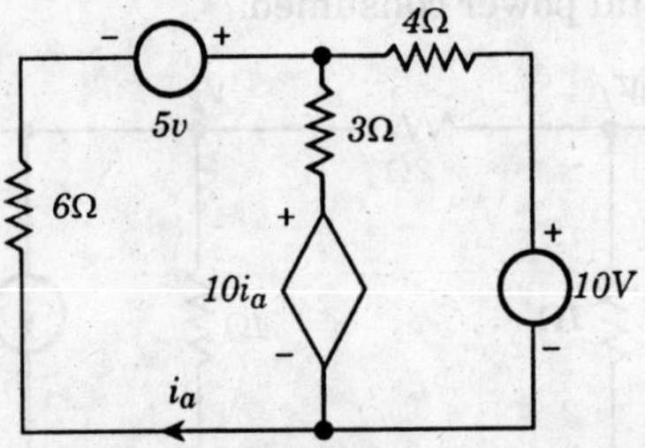


Fig. 2P-12

( **Ans.** $i_a$ = 5/42A )

**2.13.** Determine $V_a$, $V_b$ and $V_c$ in the network shown below.

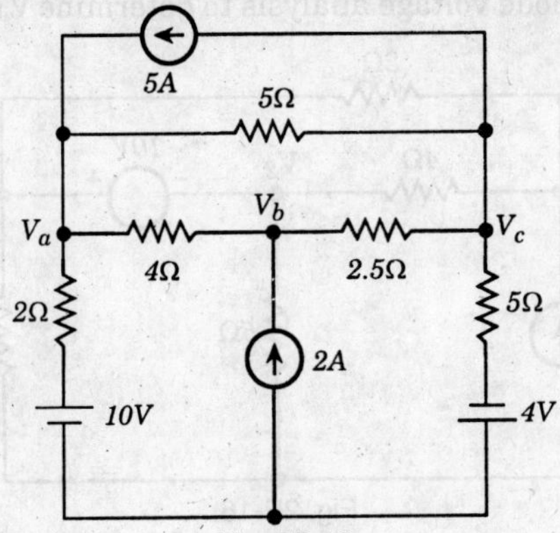


Fig. 2P-13

( **Ans.** $V_a$ = 12.504 V, $V_b$ = 7.725 V and $V_c$ = − 0.261 V)

**2.14.** Write node voltage equations and determine $v_1$, $v_2$ and $v_3$

( **Ans.** $V_1$ = 8.818 V, $V_2$ = 5.636 V and $V_3$ = 4.727 V)

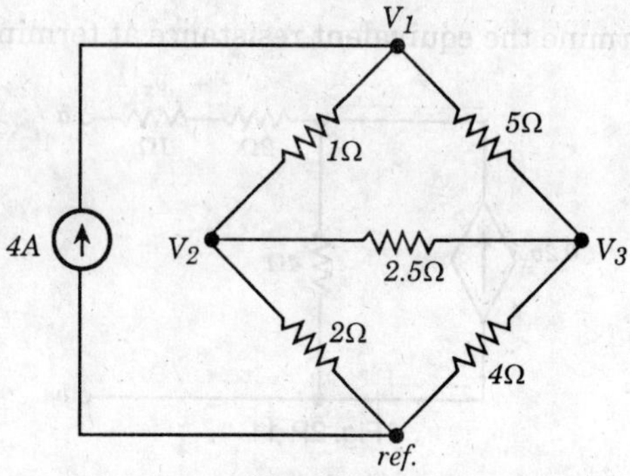


Fig. 2P-14

**2.15.** With reference to circuit shown in figure given below determine $V_1$, $V_2$ and total power consumed.

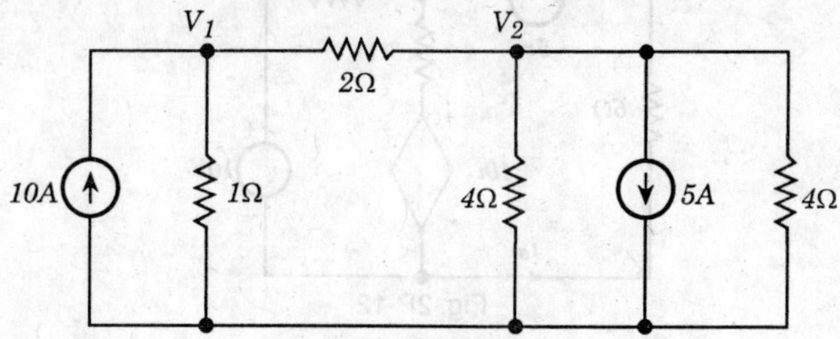


Fig. 2P-15

( **Ans.** $V_1 = 6$ V, $V_2 = -2$ V, P = 70 W)

**2.16.** Apply node voltage analysis to determine $V_1$, $V_2$ and $V_3$

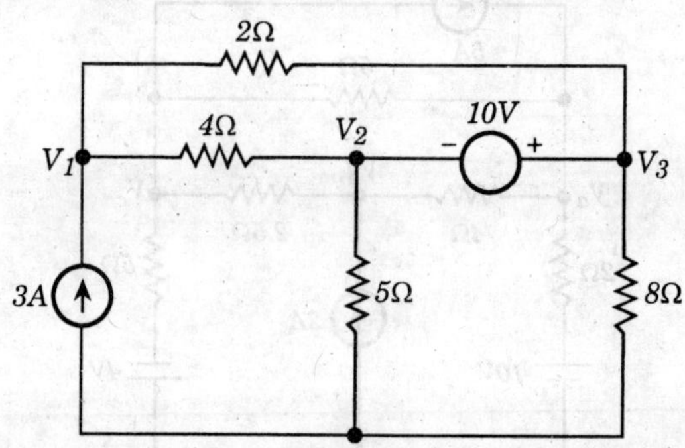


Fig. 2P-16

( **Ans.** $V_1 = 16.05$ V, $V_2 = 5.384$ V and $V_3 = 15.384$ V)

**2.17.** In the network given below determine the node voltages $V_1$ and $V_2$

( **Ans.** $V_1 = 13.07$ V, $V_2 = 9.23$ V)

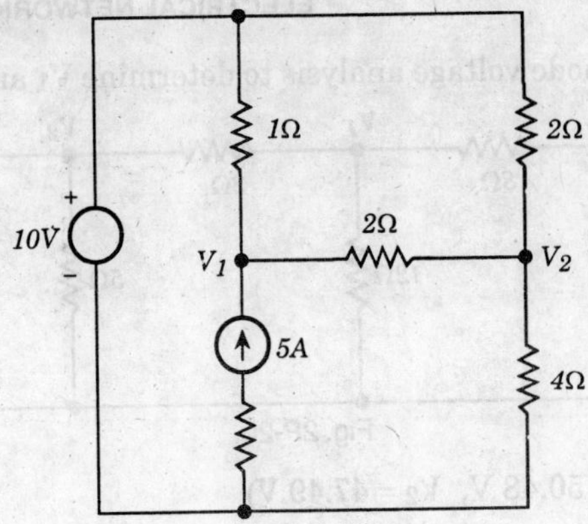


Fig. 2P-17

**2.18.** Apply node voltage analysis to determine $V_1$ and $V_2$

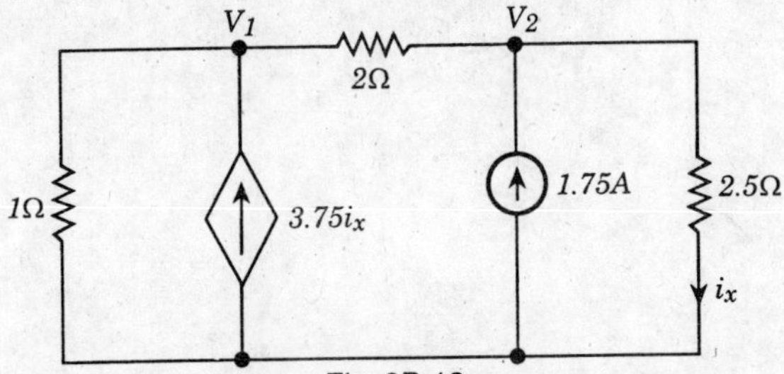


Fig. 2P-18

( **Ans.** $V_1 = 10$ V, $V_2 = 7.5$ V)

**2.19.** In the network shown below determine $i_1$

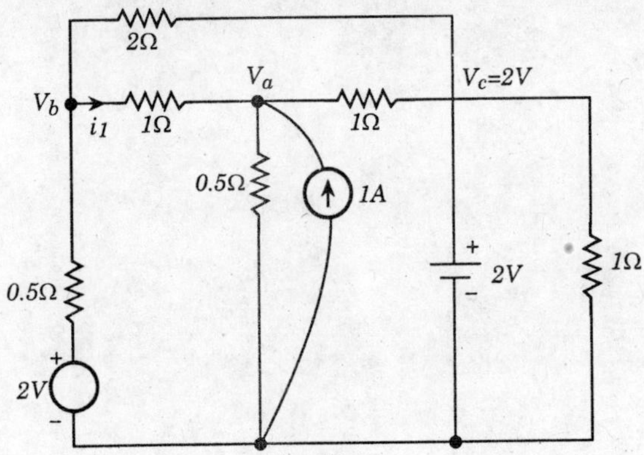


Fig. 2P-19

( **Ans.** $i_1 = 0.538$ A)

**2.20.** Use node voltage analysis to determine $V_1$ and $V_2$

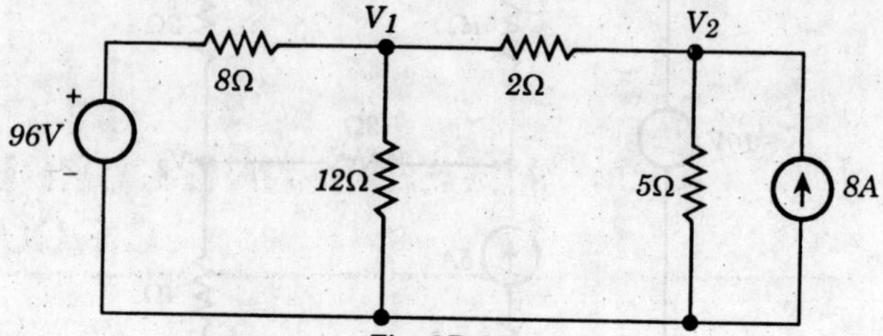


Fig. 2P-20.

( **Ans.** $V_1 = 50.48$ V, $V_2 = 47.49$ V)

# 3

# ALTERNATING CURRENT CIRCUITS

## 3.1. SINUSOIDAL VOLTAGE WAVEFORM

A time-variant voltage $v$ is applied to a circuit, then the current $i$ flowing in the circuit is also time-variant. The instantaneous power is the product of voltage and current at any instant of time *i.e.*

$$p = vi$$

The sinusoidal a.c. voltage source is given by an expression as below:

$$v = V_m \sin \omega t$$

where, $v$ : instantaneous value of the voltage.

$V_m$ : maximum value of the voltage.

$\omega$ : frequency (radian/second)

Time period $\quad T = \dfrac{2\pi}{\omega}$

$\therefore \quad f = \dfrac{1}{T} = \dfrac{\omega}{2\pi}$

$f$ : frequency (Hz)

Hence, $\quad \omega = 2\pi f$

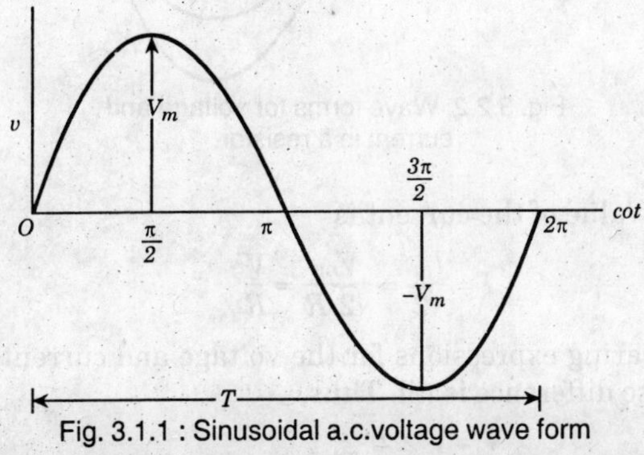


Fig. 3.1.1 : Sinusoidal a.c.voltage wave form

The variation of sinusoidal a.c. voltage is shown in Fig. 3.1.1.

The root mean square (*rms*) value or the effective value of the sinusoidal a.c. voltage is

$$V = \frac{V_m}{\sqrt{2}}$$

## 3.2. A.C. VOLTAGE APPLIED TO A RESISTOR

An a.c. voltage source

$$v = V_m \sin \omega t \qquad ...(1)$$

is connected to a resistor as shown in Fig. 3.2.1.

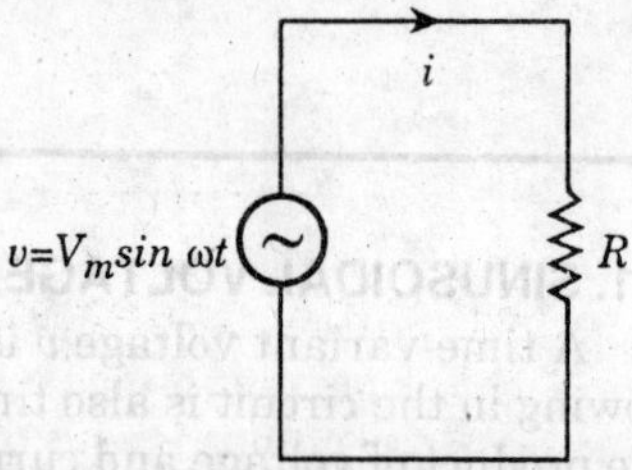

Fig. 3.2.1. A.C. voltage connected to a resistor.

As per Ohm's law, the current flowing through the resistor is

$$i = \frac{v}{R}$$

$$= \frac{V_m}{R} \sin \omega t$$

or

$$i = I_m \sin\omega t \qquad ...(2)$$

where, $I_m = \frac{V_m}{R}$ (The maximum value of the current)

The variation of voltage and current in a resistor is shown in Fig. 3.2.2.

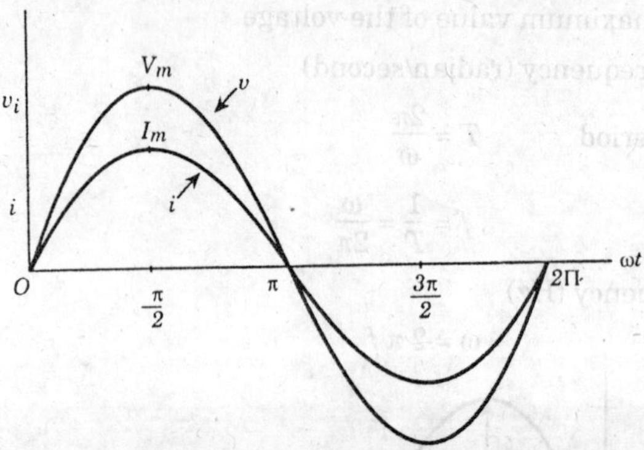

Fig. 3.2.2. Wave forms for voltage and current in a resistor.

The *rms* value of the current is

$$I = \frac{I_m}{\sqrt{2}} = \frac{V_m}{\sqrt{2}\,R} = \frac{V}{R}$$

On comparing expressions for the voltage and current, it is noted that the phase difference is nil. Thus,

$$\mathbf{V} = V \angle 0°$$

and

$$\mathbf{I} = I \angle 0°$$

The phasor diagram considering voltage phasor as reference is shown in Fig. 3.2.3.

The instantaneous power is given by

$$p = v\, i$$
$$= V_m \sin \omega t\, I_m \sin\omega t$$
$$= V_m I_m \sin^2\omega t$$
$$= V_m I_m \frac{(1 - \cos 2\omega t)}{2}$$
$$= \frac{V_m}{\sqrt{2}} \frac{I_m}{\sqrt{2}} - \frac{V_m}{\sqrt{2}} \frac{I_m}{\sqrt{2}} \cos 2\, \omega t$$
$$= V I - V I \cos 2\omega t$$

The term $V I \cos\omega t$ is a sinusoidal function and its average value over a time period $T$ is zero.

The term $V I$ is time-invarient and its average value is $V I$. Therefore the average power consumed in a resistor is

$$P = V I$$

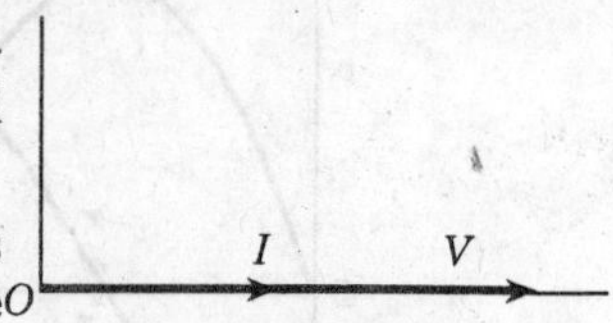


Fig. 3.2.3. Phasor diagram : a.c. voltage applied to a resistor.

## 3.3. A.C. VOLTAGE APPLIED TO AN INDUCTOR

An a.c. voltage source

$$v = V_m \sin\omega t \quad ...(1)$$

is connected to an inductor as shown in Fig. 3.3.1. The applied voltage $v$ is related to current $i$ flowing in the inductor as

$$i = \frac{1}{L} \int v dt$$

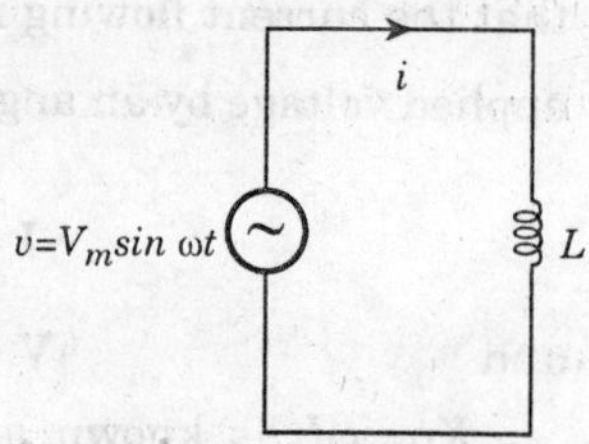


Fig. 3.3.1. A.C. Voltage applied to an inductor

$\because$ $$v = V_m \sin \omega t$$

$\therefore$ $$i = \frac{1}{L} \int V_m \sin \omega t$$
$$= \frac{V_m}{\omega L} (- \cos \omega t)$$
$$= \frac{V_m}{\omega L} \sin \left(\omega t - \frac{\pi}{2}\right) \quad ...(2)$$

or $$i = I_m \sin \left(\omega t - \frac{\pi}{2}\right)$$

---

Bold faced upper case letter denotes a phasor quantity.

Normal upper - case letter denotes $RMS$ value.

where, $$I_m = \frac{V_m}{\omega L}$$

$$\therefore \quad \frac{I_m}{\sqrt{2}} = \frac{V_m}{\sqrt{2}\,\omega L}$$

$$\because \quad I = \frac{I_m}{\sqrt{2}} \text{ and } V = \frac{V_m}{\sqrt{2}}$$

$$\therefore \quad I = \frac{V}{\omega L}$$

The variation of the applied voltage $v$ and current $i$ flowing in an inductor is shown in Fig. 3.3.2.

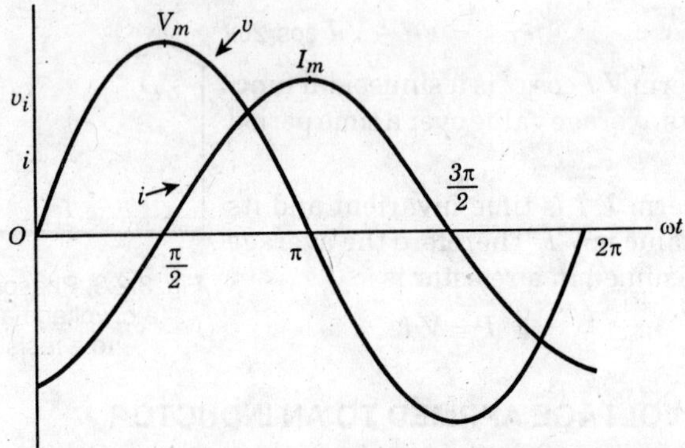


Fig. 3.3.2. Waveforms for voltage and current in an inductor.

On comparing the expressions for the voltage and current it is noted that the current flowing in an inductor lags the applied voltage by an angle $\frac{\pi}{2}$ rad. Therefore,

$$\mathbf{I} = \frac{V}{\omega L} \angle -\frac{\pi}{2}$$

and $$\mathbf{V} = V \angle 0$$

$X_L = \omega L$ is known as inductive reactance, expressed in ohm.

In rectangular form $\mathbf{X_L} = j\,X_L$

In polar form $\mathbf{X_L} = X_L \angle \frac{\pi}{2}$

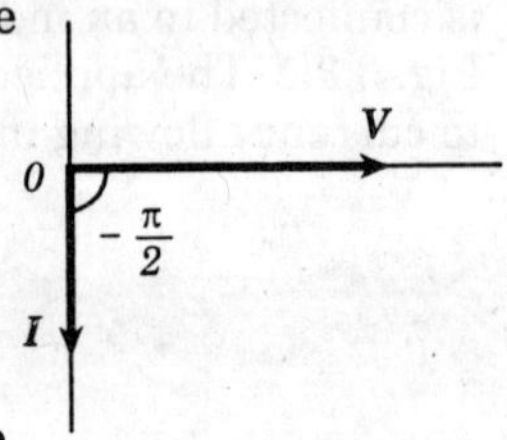


Fig. 3.3.3. Phasor diagram: a.c. voltage applied to an inductor.

The phasor diagram is shown in Fig. 3.3.3.

The instantaneous power is given by

$$p = v\,i$$

$$= V_m \sin\omega t \; I_m \sin\left(\omega t - \frac{\pi}{2}\right)$$

$$= V_m I_m \sin\omega t\,(-\cos\omega t)$$

$$= -V_m I_m \sin\omega t \cos\omega t = -V_m I_m \frac{\sin 2\omega t}{2}$$

$$= -\frac{V_m}{\sqrt{2}}\frac{I_m}{\sqrt{2}} \sin 2\omega t = -VI \sin 2\omega t$$

The above expression for the instaneous power is sinusoidal and its average value over a time period $T$ is zero. Thus, average power

$$P = 0$$

## 3.4 A.C. VOLTAGE APPLIED TO A CAPACITOR

An a.c. voltage $\qquad v = V_m \sin \omega t \qquad$ ...(1)

is connected to a capacitor as shown in Fig. 3.4.1. The applied voltage $v$ is related to current $i$ flowing in the capacitor as

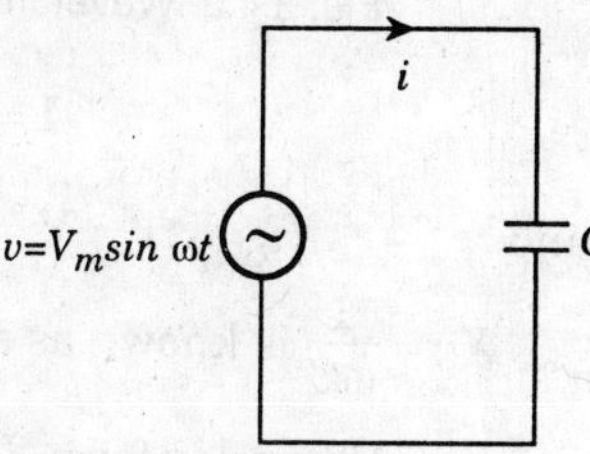

Fig. 3.4.1. A.C. voltage applied to a capacitor.

$$i = C\frac{dv}{dt}$$

$\because \qquad v = V_m \sin\omega t$

$\therefore \qquad i = C\dfrac{d}{dt}(V_m \sin\omega t)$

$$= \omega C V_m \cos \omega t$$

$$= \frac{V_m}{(1/\omega C)} \sin\left(\omega t + \frac{\pi}{2}\right)$$

or $\qquad I = I_m \sin\left(\omega t + \dfrac{\pi}{2}\right) \qquad$ ...(2)

where, $\qquad I_m = \dfrac{V_m}{(1/\omega C)}$

$\therefore \qquad \dfrac{I_m}{\sqrt{2}} = \dfrac{V_m}{\sqrt{2}\,(1/\omega C)}$

$\because \qquad \dfrac{I_m}{\sqrt{2}} = I$ and $\dfrac{V_m}{\sqrt{2}} = V$

$\therefore \qquad I = \dfrac{V}{(1/\omega C)}$

The variation of the applied voltage and current in capacitor is shown in Fig. 3.4.2.

On comparing expressions for the voltage and current it is noted that the current flowing in a capacitor leads the applied voltage by an angle $\frac{\pi}{2}$ rad. Therefore,

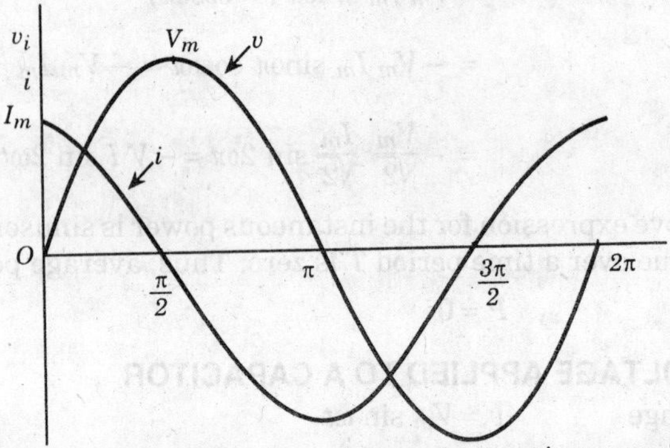


Fig. 3.4.2. Waveforms for voltage and current in a capacitor.

$$\mathbf{I} = \frac{V}{1/\omega C} \angle \frac{\pi}{2}$$

and
$$\mathbf{V} = V \angle 0$$

$X_C = \dfrac{1}{\omega C}$ is known as capacitive reactance expressed in ohm.

In rectangular form $\mathbf{X}_C = -j\, X_C$

In polar form $\mathbf{X}_C = X_C \angle -\dfrac{\pi}{2}$

The phasor diagram considering voltage phasor as reference is shown in Fig. 3.4.3.

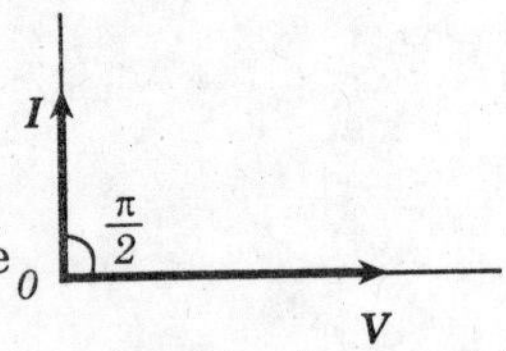


Fig. 3.4.3. Phasor diagram a.c. voltage applied to a capacitor

The instantaneous power is given by

$$p = v\, i$$

$$= V_m \sin\omega t \sin\left(\omega t + \frac{\pi}{2}\right)$$

$$= V_m\, I_m \frac{\sin 2\omega t}{2}$$

$$= \frac{V_m}{\sqrt{2}} \frac{I_m}{\sqrt{2}} \sin 2\omega t = V I \sin 2\,\omega t$$

The above expression for instantaneous power is sinusoidal and its average value over a time period $T$ is zero. Therefore, average power

$$P = 0$$

## 3.5. RL SERIES CIRCUIT

A circuit consisting of a resistor $R$ and inductor $L$ in series is connected to an a.c. voltage source $\mathbf{V}$ as shown in Fig. 3.5.1.

The frequency of the a.c. supply voltage is ω. The inductive reactance is $X_L = \omega L$

As the resistor $R$ and inductor $L$ are connected in series, they carry the same current **I**.

The voltage drop across the resistor is $\mathbf{I}R$. The current **I** in the inductor lags the voltage drop $\mathbf{I}\,X_L$ by an angle $-\frac{\pi}{2}$ rad. ( – 90°).

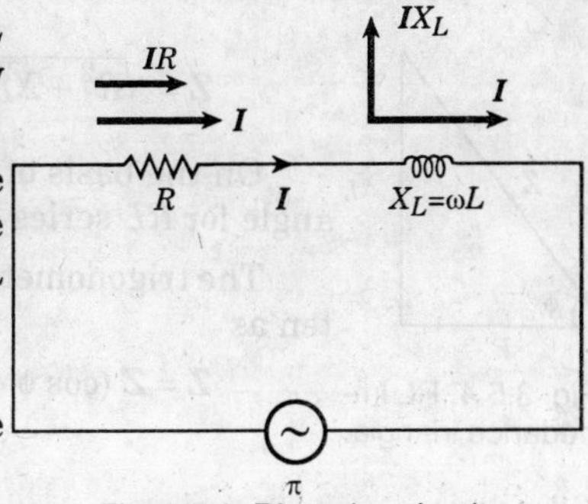


Fig. 3.5.1. RL series circuit.

Applying Kirchhoff's voltage law,

$$\mathbf{V} = \mathbf{I}\,R + \mathbf{I}\,X_L$$

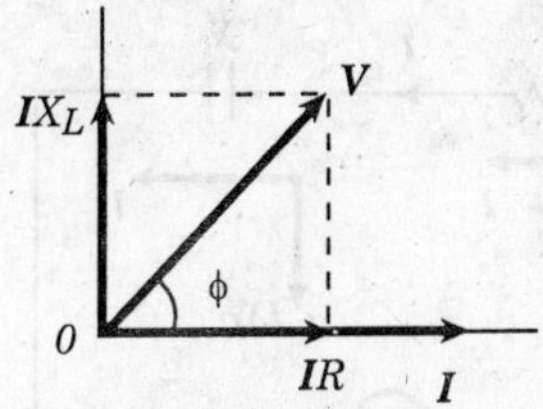


Fig. 3.5.2. Phasor diagram for RL series circuit

The corresponding phasor diagram, considering the current phasor **I** as reference is shown in Fig. 3.5.2.

As per phasor diagram shown,

$$V^2 = (I\,R)^2 + (I\,X_L)^2$$

$$\therefore\ I = \frac{V}{\sqrt{R^2 + X_L^2}}$$

$Z = \sqrt{R^2 + X_L^2}$ is known as impedance and the unit is ohm.

In polar form $\mathbf{Z} = Z \angle \phi$, where $\phi = \tan^{-1}\frac{X_L}{R}$

Considering **V** as a reference phasor, the phasor diagram takes the form as shown in Fig. 3.5.3.

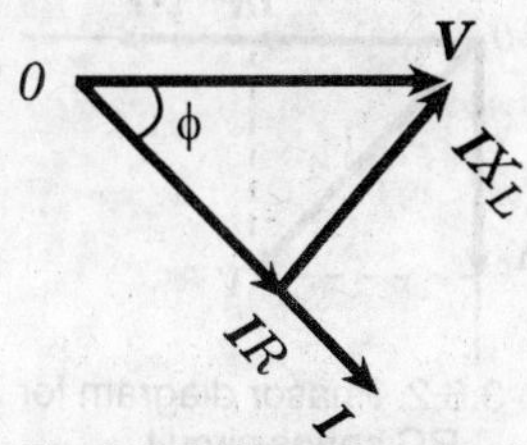


Fig. 3.5.3. RL series circuit phasor diagram: **V** as reference phasor.

As per phasor diagram (Fig. 3.5.3),

$$\mathbf{I} = \frac{\mathbf{V}}{\mathbf{Z}} = \frac{V \angle 0°}{Z \angle \phi}$$

$$\therefore\ \mathbf{I} = \frac{V}{Z} \angle -\phi\ ,\quad \phi = \tan^{-1}\frac{X_L}{R}$$

The current phasor **I** lags the voltage phasor **V** by an angle $-\phi$.

In rectangular form, the impedance **Z** ($RL$ series circuit) is written as,

$$\mathbf{Z} = R + j\,X_L$$

(The operator $j$ rotates the phasor by an angle of $\frac{\pi}{2}$ rad in counter-clockwise direction)

The equivalent polar form for the impedance $\mathbf{Z} = R + j\,X_L$ is

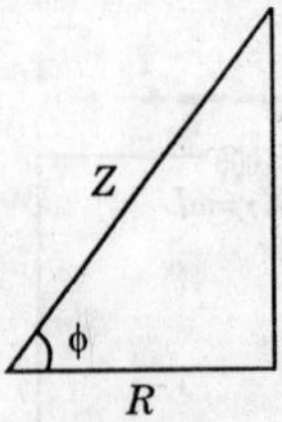

Fig. 3.5.4. RL Impedance triangle.

$$\mathbf{Z} = \sqrt{R^2 + X_L^2} \angle \phi , \quad \phi = \tan^{-1} \frac{X_L}{R}$$

On the basis of above relation, the impedance triangle for *RL* series circuit is shown in Fig. 3.5.4.

The trigonometric form of *RL* impedance **Z** is written as

$$\mathbf{Z} = Z (\cos \phi + j \sin \phi)$$

## 3.6. RC SERIES CIRCUIT

A series circuit consisting of a resistor *R* and capacitance *C* is connected to an a.c. voltage source **V** as shown in Fig. 3.6.1.

The frequency of the a.c. supply voltage is ω. The capacitive reactance is $X_c = \frac{1}{\omega c}$.

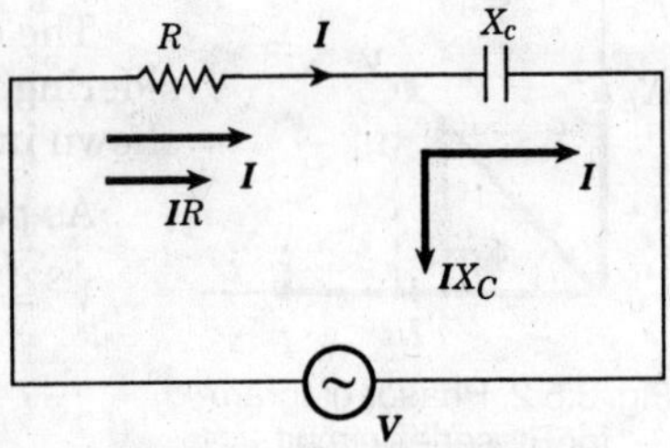

Fig. 3.6.1. RC Series Circuit

As the resistor *R* and the capacitor are connected in series, they carry the same current **I**.

The voltage drop across the resistor is **I** *R*, in phase with current **I**.

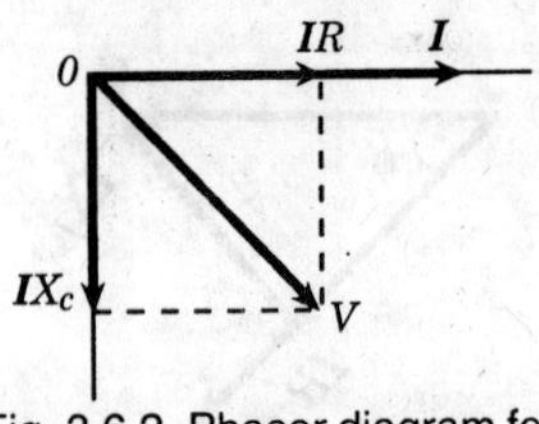

Fig. 3.6.2. Phasor diagram for RC series circuit.

The current **I** in the capacitor leads the voltage drop **I** $X_C$ by an angle $\frac{\pi}{2}$ rad. ( + 90°).

Applying Kirchhoff's voltage law,

$$\mathbf{V} = \mathbf{I}\,R + \mathbf{I}\,X_c$$

The corresponding phasor diagram, considering the current phasor **I** as reference is shown in Fig. 3.6.2.

As per phasor diagram shown above,

$$V^2 = (I\,R)^2 + (I\,X_c)^2$$

$$\therefore \qquad I = \frac{V}{\sqrt{R^2 + X_c^2}}$$

$Z = \sqrt{R^2 + X_c^2}$ is known a impedance and the unit is ohm.

In polar form

$$\mathbf{Z} = Z \angle - \phi, \text{ where } \phi = \tan^{-1} \frac{X_c}{R}$$

Considering **V** as reference phasor, the phasor diagram takes the form as shown in Fig. 3.6.3.

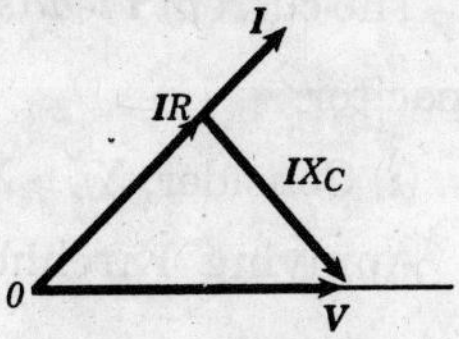


Fig. 3.6.3. RC series circuit phasor diagram : V as reference phasor.

As per phasor diagram (Fig. 3.6.3.),

$$\mathbf{I} = \frac{\mathbf{V}}{\mathbf{Z}} = \frac{V \angle 0°}{Z \angle -\phi}, \quad \phi = \tan^{-1}\frac{X_c}{R}$$

The current Phasor **I** leads the voltage phasor **V** by an angle $\phi$

In rectangular form, the impedance **Z** (*RC* series circuit) is written as,

$$\mathbf{Z} = R - j\,X_c$$

The equivalent polar form for the impedance $\mathbf{Z} = R - j\,X_c$ is

$$\mathbf{Z} = \sqrt{R^2 + X_c^2}\ \angle -\phi,$$

$$\phi = \tan^{-1}\frac{X_c}{R}$$

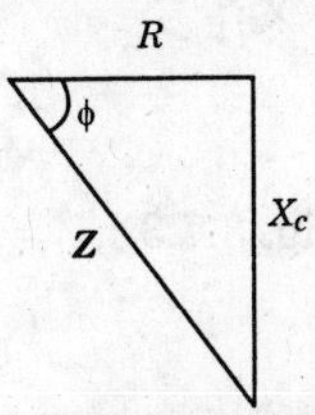


Fig. 3.6.4. RC impedance triangle

On the basis of above relation, the impedance triangle for *RC* series circuit is shown in Fig. 3.6.4.

The trigonometric form of *RC* impedance is written as

$$\mathbf{Z} = Z\,(\cos\phi - j\,\sin\phi)$$

## 3.7 RLC SERIES CIRCUIT

A series circuit consisting of a resistor *R*, inductor *L* and capacitance *C* is connected to an a.c. voltage source **V** as shown in Fig. 3.7.1.

The frequency of the a.c. supply voltage is $\omega$.

(*i*) The inductive reactance of inductor is, $X_L = \omega L$

(*ii*) The capacitive reactance of capacitor is,

$$X_c = \frac{1}{\omega C}$$

As the resistor *R*, inductor *L* and capacitor are in series, they carry the same current **I**.

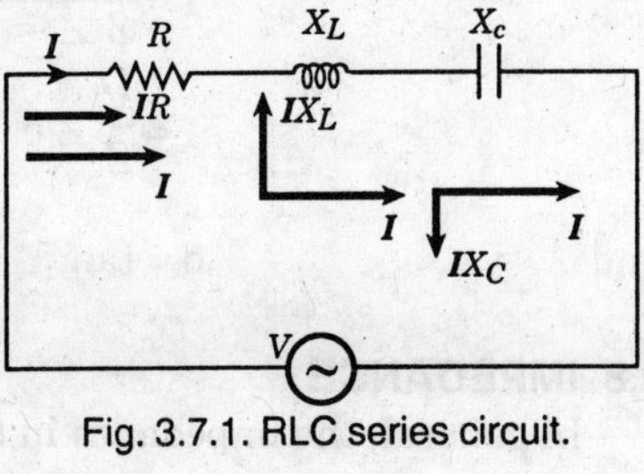


Fig. 3.7.1. RLC series circuit.

The voltage drop across the resistor is **I***R*, *in phase* with the current **I**.

The current **I** *lags* by an angle $\frac{\pi}{2}$ rad. w.r.t. voltage drop across **I** $X_L$ across the inductor.

The current **I** *leads* by an angle $\frac{\pi}{2}$ *w.r.t.* voltage drop **I** $X_c$ across the capacitor.

(*i*) Consider, $X_L > X_c$.

Applying Kirchhoff's voltage law,

$$\mathbf{V} = \mathbf{I}\,R + \mathbf{I}\,(X_L - X_c)$$

The corresponding phasor diagram considering current phasor as reference is shown in Fig. 3.7.2.

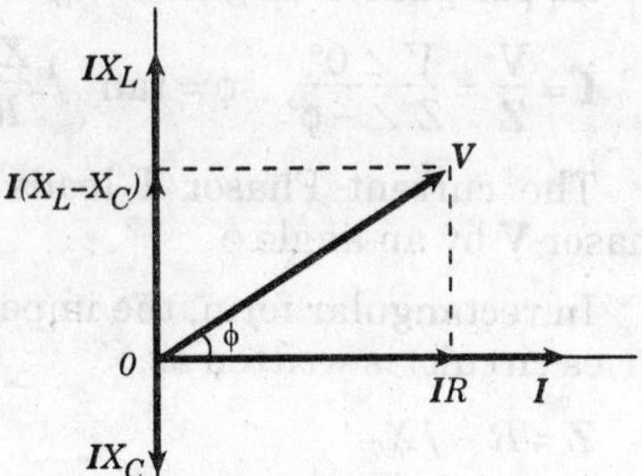

Fig. 3.7.2. Phasor diagram RLC series circuit ($X_L > X_c$)

Considering **V** as reference phasor, the phasor diagram takes the form as shown in Fig. 3.7.3.

It is noted that the current phasor lags behind the voltage phasor by an angle $\phi$.

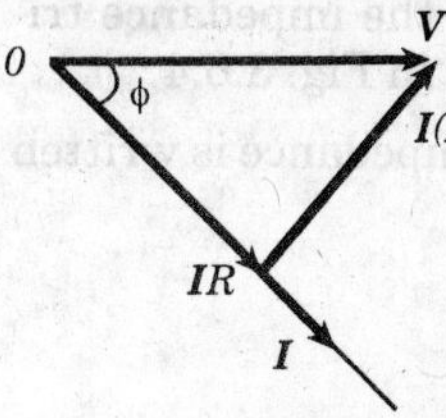

Fig. 3.7.3. Phasor diagram, RLC series circuit, **V** reference ($X_L > X_c$)

As per phasor diagram (Fig. 3.7.3.),

$$\mathbf{I} = \frac{V\angle 0°}{Z\angle\phi} = \frac{V}{Z}\angle -\phi$$

where $Z = \sqrt{R^2 + (X_L - X_c)^2}$

and

$$\phi = \tan^{-1}\frac{(X_L - X_c)}{R}$$

(*ii*) Consider $X_c > X_L$ :

The phasor diagram is shown in Fig. 3.7.4.

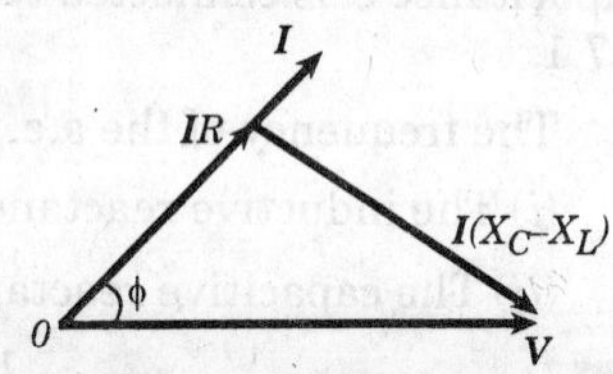

Fig. 3.7.4. Phasor diagram RLC series circuit, *V* reference ($X_c > X_L$)

As per phasor diagram (Fig. 3.7.4.)

$$\mathbf{I} = \frac{V\angle 0°}{Z\angle -\phi}$$

$$= \frac{V}{Z}\angle\phi \quad \text{where } Z = \sqrt{R^2 + (X_C - X_L)^2}$$

and

$$\phi = \tan^{-1}\frac{(X_c - X_L)}{R}$$

## 3.8. IMPEDANCE

In general, the impedance in trignometric form is denoted as

$$\mathbf{Z} = R \pm jX$$

The magnitude is given by

$$Z = \sqrt{R^2 + X^2}$$

and phase angle $\phi = \tan^{-1} \frac{\pm X}{R}$

In polar form,

$$\mathbf{Z} = Z \angle \pm \phi$$

+ sign indicates inductive reactance.

– sign indicates capacitive reactance.

### Impedances Connected in Series.

The equivalent impedance of impedances connected in series is given by

$$\mathbf{Z}_{eq} = \mathbf{Z}_1 + \mathbf{Z}_2 + \mathbf{Z}_3 + - - - - - - + \mathbf{Z}_n$$

### Voltage Division in a Two Branch Series Circuit

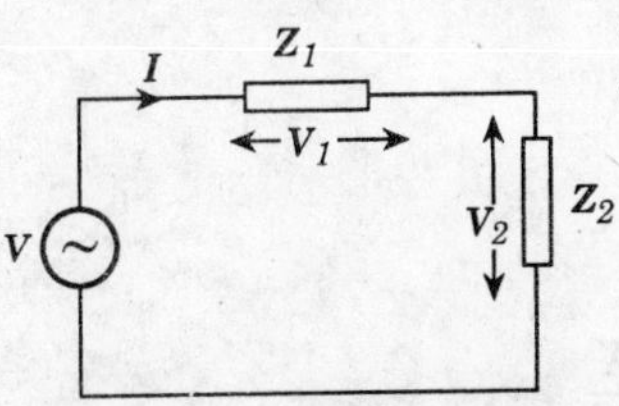

Fig. 3.8.1 Voltage division

Fig. 3.8.1 shows two impedances in series connected to a voltage source **V**, the current flowing in the circuit is

$$\mathbf{I} = \frac{\mathbf{V}}{\mathbf{Z}_1 + \mathbf{Z}_2}$$

The voltages across impedances are

$$\mathbf{V}_1 = \mathbf{I}\,\mathbf{Z}_1 = \frac{\mathbf{V}\,\mathbf{Z}_1}{\mathbf{Z}_1 + \mathbf{Z}_2}$$

and

$$\mathbf{V}_2 = \mathbf{I}\,\mathbf{Z}_2 = \frac{\mathbf{V}\,\mathbf{Z}_2}{\mathbf{Z}_1 + \mathbf{Z}_2}$$

### Impedances Connected in Parallel

The equivalent impedance of impedances connected in parallel is given by

$$\frac{1}{\mathbf{Z}_{eq}} = \frac{1}{\mathbf{Z}_1} + \frac{1}{\mathbf{Z}_2} + \frac{1}{\mathbf{Z}_3} + - - - - + \frac{1}{\mathbf{Z}_n}$$

### Current Division in a Two Branch Parallel Circuit

Fig. 3.8.2 shows a two branch parallel circuit containing impedances, connected across a voltage **V**.

The equivalent impedance of the parallel branch is determined as

$$\frac{1}{\mathbf{Z}_{eq}} = \frac{1}{\mathbf{Z}_1} + \frac{1}{\mathbf{Z}_2}$$

$$\therefore \quad \mathbf{Z}_{eq} = \frac{\mathbf{Z}_1 \mathbf{Z}_2}{\mathbf{Z}_1 + \mathbf{Z}_2}$$

The current supplied by the source is

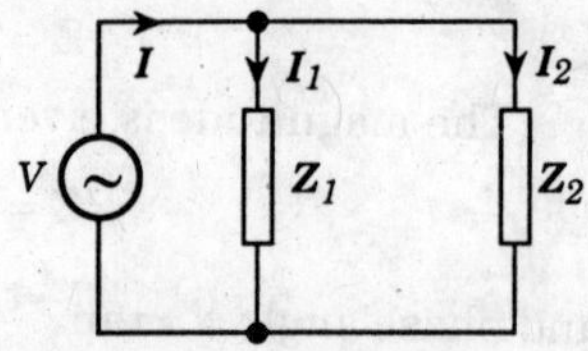

Fig. 3.8.2. Current division.

$$\mathbf{I} = \frac{\mathbf{V}}{\mathbf{Z}_{eq}}$$

or
$$\mathbf{I} = \frac{\mathbf{V}(\mathbf{Z}_1 + \mathbf{Z}_2)}{\mathbf{Z}_1 \mathbf{Z}_2}$$

Also,
$$\mathbf{I}_1 = \frac{\mathbf{V}}{\mathbf{Z}_1}$$

On dividing
$$\frac{\mathbf{I}_1}{\mathbf{I}} = \frac{\mathbf{Z}_2}{\mathbf{Z}_1 + \mathbf{Z}_2}$$

$\therefore$
$$\mathbf{I}_1 = \frac{\mathbf{I}\,\mathbf{Z}_2}{\mathbf{Z}_1 + \mathbf{Z}_2}$$

Similarly,
$$\mathbf{I}_2 = \frac{\mathbf{I}\,\mathbf{Z}_1}{\mathbf{Z}_1 + \mathbf{Z}_2}$$

## 3.9. ADMITTANCE, CONDUCTANCE AND SUSCEPTANCE

The reciprocal of impedance is termed as admittance and denoted as **Y**. The unit of admittance is mho.

$$\mathbf{Y} = \frac{1}{\mathbf{Z}}$$

$\because$
$$\mathbf{Z} = R \pm jX$$

$\therefore$
$$\mathbf{Y} = \frac{1}{R \pm jX} = \frac{R \mp jX}{R^2 + X^2}$$

or
$$\mathbf{Y} = \frac{R}{R_2 + X^2} \mp \frac{jX}{R^2 + X^2} = G \mp jB$$

where,
$$G = \frac{R}{R^2 + X^2} \quad \text{is termed as conductance}$$

$$B = \frac{X}{R^2 + X^2} \quad \text{is termed as susceptance}$$

– sing before $j$ indicates inductive susceptance

+ sign before $j$ indicates capacitive susceptance

For the parallel connection,

$$\mathbf{Y}_{eq} = \mathbf{Y}_1 + \mathbf{Y}_2 + \mathbf{Y}_3 + ----+ \mathbf{Y}_n$$

## 3.10. POWER RELATION IN A.C. CIRCUIT

A sinusoidal voltage $v = V_m \sin \omega t$ is applied to an impedance $\mathbf{Z} \angle \pm \phi$. The instantaneous current flowing in the impedance is given by

$$i = \frac{V_m}{Z} \sin(\omega t \mp \phi)$$

or
$$i = I_m \sin(\omega t \mp \phi)$$

where, (*i*) $I_m = \frac{V_m}{Z}$

(*ii*) $\phi$ is the angle between the voltage phasor and current phasor

$-\phi$ for lagging current phasor w.r.t. voltage phasor.

$+\phi$ for leading current phasor w.r.t. voltage phasor.

The instantaneous power is given by

$$p = v\, i$$
$$= V_m \sin\omega t\, I_m \sin(\omega t \mp \phi)$$
$$= V_m I_m \sin\omega t \sin(\omega t \mp \phi)$$
$$= V_m I_m \frac{[\cos\phi - \cos(2\omega t \mp \phi)]}{2}$$
$$= \frac{V_m}{\sqrt{2}} \cdot \frac{I_m}{\sqrt{2}} \cos\phi - \frac{V_m}{\sqrt{2}} \cdot \frac{I_m}{\sqrt{2}} \cos(2\omega t \mp \phi)$$
$$= V I \cos\phi - V I \cos(2\omega t \mp \phi)$$

The term $VI \cos(2\omega t \mp \phi)$ is sinusoidal and hence, its average value over a time period $T$ is zero.

The term $VI \cos\phi$ is time-in variant therefore, its average value is $VI \cos\phi$. The average value of the power in a.c. circuit is

$$P = V I \cos\phi$$

(The angle $\phi$ is valid between $\pm \frac{\pi}{2}$)

### Power Factor

The term $\cos\phi$ is known as power factor. The power factor is lagging in case the current lags the voltage and leading when the current leads the voltage.

### Active Power

The average power $P$ is also termed as active power.

Active power : $P = VI \cos\phi$, the unit is $W$ (watt).

Apparent power : $S = VI$, the unit is $VA$ (Volt-Ampere)

Reactive power : $Q = VI \sin\phi$, the unit is $VA_r$ (Volt-Ampere reactive)

The complex power is given by $\mathbf{V}\,\mathbf{I}^*$

Average power $P = R_e\, \mathbf{V}\,\mathbf{I}^*$

Apparent power $S$ = Absolute value (magnitude) of $\mathbf{V}\,\mathbf{I}^*$

Reactive Power $Q = I_{mj}\,\mathbf{V}\,\mathbf{I}^*$ + for lagging p.f. – for leading p.f.

Power factor $= \dfrac{P}{S}$

## 3.11. MAXWELL'S MESH CURRENT ANALYSIS/NODE VOLTAGE ANALYSIS APPLIED TO A.C. CIRCUITS

Maxwell's mesh current analysis/Node voltage analysis described earlier refers to d.c. circuits containing resistors. The a.c. circuits under steady state conditions can also be solved using Maxwell's mesh current/node voltage analysis with slight modifications.

The polarity of a sinusoidal voltage and current change in a periodic time. At a particular instant the a.c. voltage/current is either positive or negative. The sinusoidal voltages and currents are represented by a phasor. The mathematical computation of voltage/current is performed as per phasor rules.

The impedance is a complex quantity represented in the following form.

(*i*) $\mathbf{Z} = R + jX$ rectangular form

(*ii*) $\mathbf{Z} = Z \angle \phi$ polar form

where $Z = \sqrt{R^2 + Z^2}$ and $\phi = \tan^{-1}\left(\dfrac{X}{R}\right)$

The voltage across any passive element is given by the product of impedance and current both expressed in complex form

The division of voltage across any passive element by the impedance in complex form gives the current.

### 3.11.1. A.C. Circuit: Maxwell's Mesh Current Analysis

An a.c. network containing three meshes is shown in Fig. 3.11.1. The a.c. voltage sources are $\mathbf{V_1}$ and $\mathbf{V_2}$.

The arrow-head at the voltage source indicates the instantaneous polarily. The direction of mesh currents $\mathbf{I_1}$, $\mathbf{I_2}$ and $\mathbf{I_3}$ is selected clockwise. This selection is arbitrary.

Mesh current equations based on Kirchhoff's voltage law are written below.

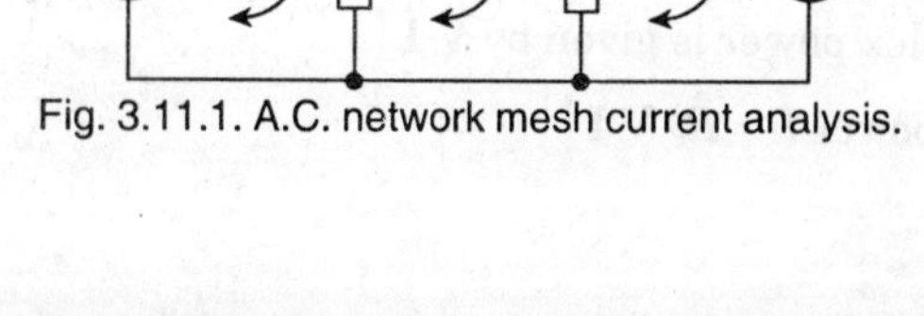


Fig. 3.11.1. A.C. network mesh current analysis.

Mesh no. 1 : $I_1 Z_1 + (I_1 - I_2) Z_2 - V_1 = 0$

Mesh no. 2 : $I_2 Z_3 + (I_2 - I_3) Z_4 + (I_2 - I_1) Z_2 = 0$

Mesh no. 3 : $I_3 Z_5 + V_2 + (I_3 - I_2) Z_4 = 0$

On rearranging in matrix form above set of equations can be written as below.

$$\begin{bmatrix} Z_1 + Z_2 & -Z_2 & 0 \\ -Z_2 & Z_2 + Z_3 + Z_4 & -Z_4 \\ 0 & -Z_4 & Z_4 + Z_5 \end{bmatrix} \begin{bmatrix} I_1 \\ I_2 \\ I_3 \end{bmatrix} = \begin{bmatrix} V_1 \\ 0 \\ -V_2 \end{bmatrix}$$

For a network containing three meshes a set of Maxwell's mesh current equations can be written in matrix form as below.

$$\begin{bmatrix} Z_{11} & \pm Z_{12} & \pm Z_{13} \\ \pm Z_{21} & Z_{22} & \pm Z_{23} \\ \pm Z_{31} & \pm Z_{32} & Z_{33} \end{bmatrix} \begin{bmatrix} I_1 \\ I_2 \\ I_3 \end{bmatrix} \begin{bmatrix} V_1 \\ V_2 \\ V_3 \end{bmatrix}$$

Thus, the Ohm's law can be written in matrix as

$$[Z]\,[I] = [V]$$

where [Z] = impedance matrix (in general)

The impedance matrix can also be denoted as $[Z_m]$ mesh impedance matrix or $[Z_l]$ loop impedance matrix.

The Maxwell's mesh current equations can also be written by inspection identifying,

1. The self impedance $Z_{11}$ of mesh no. 1 which consists of the sum of all impedances wherein the current $I_1$ flows. $Z_{22}$, $Z_{33}$ are the self impedances of mesh nos. 1 and 2 respectively.
2. The impedance $Z_{12} = Z_{21}$ is the sum of impedances shared by mesh nos. 1 and 2. positive sign is placed if the mesh currents $I_1$ and $I_2$ flow through $Z_{12}$ in same direction. Negative sign for opposing currents.

Similarly, $Z_{13} = Z_{31}$, $Z_{23} = Z_{32}$ are the sums of impedances shared by respective meshes.

3. The source of voltages $V_1$, $V_2$, $V_3$ are the sums of voltages around respective meshes.
4. $I_1$, $I_2$ and $I_3$ are the respective unknown mesh currents.

The unknown mesh currents $I_1$, $I_2$ and $I_3$ are determined by solving the matrix form of mesh current equations. Thus

$$I_1 = V_1 \left(\frac{\Delta_{11}}{\Delta_z}\right) + V_2 \left(\frac{\Delta_{21}}{\Delta_z}\right) + V_3 \left(\frac{\Delta_{31}}{\Delta_z}\right)$$

$$\mathbf{I_2} = \mathbf{V_1}\left(\frac{\Delta_{12}}{\Delta_z}\right) + \mathbf{V_2}\left(\frac{\Delta_{22}}{\Delta_z}\right) + \mathbf{V_3}\left(\frac{\Delta_{32}}{\Delta_z}\right)$$

$$\mathbf{I_3} = \mathbf{V}_1\left(\frac{\Delta_{13}}{\Delta_z}\right) + \mathbf{V}_2\left(\frac{\Delta_{23}}{\Delta_z}\right) + \mathbf{V}_3\left(\frac{\Delta_{33}}{\Delta_z}\right)$$

where $\Delta_z = |\mathbf{Z}|$

and $\Delta_{11}, \Delta_{22}, \Delta_{33}$; $\Delta_{12}, \Delta_{21}$; $\Delta_{23}, \Delta_{32}$; $\Delta_{31}, \Delta_{13}$ — corresponding co-factors.

For the case $\mathbf{V_2} = \mathbf{V_3} = 0$, *i.e.* only $\mathbf{V_1}$ applied in mesh no. 1. The current $\mathbf{I_1}$ is given by

$$\mathbf{I_1} = \mathbf{V_1}\frac{\Delta_{11}}{\Delta_z}$$

**Input (Driving Point) Impedance.**

$$\underset{\text{(input)}}{\mathbf{Z_1}} = \frac{\mathbf{V_1}}{\mathbf{I_1}} = \frac{\Delta_z}{\Delta_{11}}$$

$\mathbf{Z_1}$ is called input (driving-point) impedance.

The input (driving-point) impedance is the ratio of voltage and current at the specified terminals with all other remaining voltage sources set to zero (*i.e.* sources replaced by their internal impedances).

**Transfer Impedance**

The transfer impedance is the ratio of driving voltage in one mesh to the resulting current in another mesh with all the sources in other meshes are set to zero.

For example, in a three mesh network

$$\mathbf{I}_2 = \mathbf{V_1}\left(\frac{\Delta_{12}}{\Delta_z}\right) + \mathbf{V_2}\left(\frac{\Delta_{22}}{\Delta_z}\right) + \mathbf{V_3}\left(\frac{\Delta_{32}}{\Delta_z}\right)$$

setting source voltages $\mathbf{V}_2$ and $\mathbf{V_3}$ to zero

$$\mathbf{I_2} = \mathbf{V_1}\left(\frac{\Delta_{12}}{\Delta_z}\right)$$

The transfer impedance from mesh no. 1 to 2 is given by

$$\underset{\text{(transfer)}}{\mathbf{Z_{12}}} = \frac{\mathbf{V_1}}{\mathbf{I_2}} = \frac{\Delta_z}{\Delta_{12}}$$

where $\Delta_{12}$ is the corresponding cofactor of $\Delta_z$

Similarly
$$\underset{\text{(transfer)}}{\mathbf{Z_{13}}} = \frac{\mathbf{V_1}}{\mathbf{I_3}} = \frac{\Delta_z}{\Delta_{13}}$$

In general $$Z_{pq} = \frac{V_p}{I_q} = \frac{\Delta_z}{\Delta_{pq}}$$

### 3.11.2. A.C Circuit : Node Voltage Analysis

An a.c. circuit consisting of three principal nodes is shown in Fig. 3.11.2.

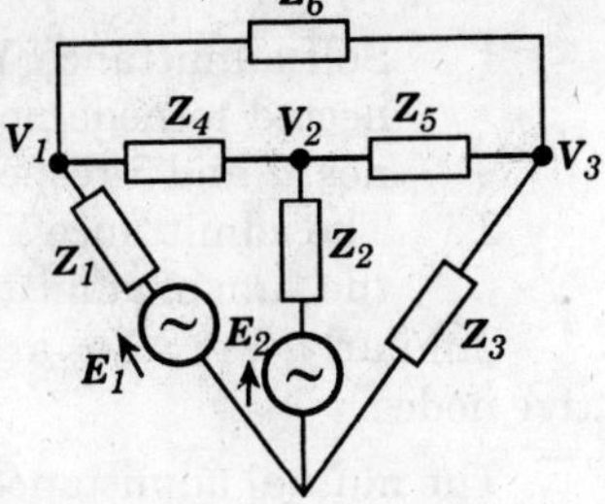

Fig. 3.11.2. A.C. circuit node voltage analysis.

Applying Kirchhoff's current law the node voltage equations are written below,

Node no 1 :

$$\frac{V_1 - E_1}{Z_1} + \frac{V_1 - V_2}{Z_4} + \frac{V_1 - V_3}{Z_6} = 0$$

Node no 2 :

$$\frac{V_2 - E_2}{Z_2} + \frac{V_2 - V_1}{Z_4} + \frac{V_2 - V_3}{Z_5} = 0$$

Node no 3 : $$\frac{V_3 - 0}{Z_3} + \frac{V_3 - V_2}{Z_5} + \frac{V_3 - V_1}{Z_6} = 0$$

On rearranging, above set of equations can be written in matrix form as below,

$$\begin{bmatrix} \frac{1}{Z_1} + \frac{1}{Z_4} + \frac{1}{Z_6} & -\frac{1}{Z_4} & -\frac{1}{Z_6} \\ -\frac{1}{Z_4} & \frac{1}{Z_2} + \frac{1}{Z_4} + \frac{1}{Z_5} & -\frac{1}{Z_5} \\ -\frac{1}{Z_6} & -\frac{1}{Z_5} & \frac{1}{Z_3} + \frac{1}{Z_5} + \frac{1}{Z_6} \end{bmatrix} \begin{bmatrix} V_1 \\ V_2 \\ V_3 \end{bmatrix} = \begin{bmatrix} I_1 \\ I_2 \\ 0 \end{bmatrix}$$

where $I_1 = \frac{E_1}{Z_1}$ ; $I_2 = \frac{E_2}{Z_2}$

Since, admittance $Y = \frac{1}{Z}$

$$\therefore \quad \begin{bmatrix} Y_1 + Y_4 + Y_6 & -Y_4 & -Y_6 \\ -Y_4 & Y_2 + Y_4 + Y_5 & -Y_5 \\ -Y_6 & -Y_5 & Y_3 + Y_5 + Y_6 \end{bmatrix} \begin{bmatrix} V_1 \\ V_2 \\ V_3 \end{bmatrix} = \begin{bmatrix} I_1 \\ I_2 \\ 0 \end{bmatrix}$$

For a network consisting of three principal nodes a set a node voltage equation can be written in matrix as below,

$$\begin{bmatrix} Y_{11} & Y_{12} & Y_{13} \\ Y_{21} & Y_{22} & Y_{23} \\ Y_{31} & Y_{32} & Y_{33} \end{bmatrix} \begin{bmatrix} V_1 \\ V_2 \\ V_3 \end{bmatrix} = \begin{bmatrix} I_1 \\ I_2 \\ I_3 \end{bmatrix}$$

The node voltages are related to source currents as

$$[Y]\,[V] = [I]$$

where $[Y]$ = Node admittance matrix

The node voltage equations can also be written by inspection indentifying

1. Self admittance $\mathbf{Y_{11}}$ which consists of all admittances connected to node no. 1. $\mathbf{Y_{22}}, \mathbf{Y_{33}}$ are self admittances at node nos. 2 and 3 respectively.
2. The admittance $\mathbf{Y_{12}} = \mathbf{Y_{21}}$ is the mutual admittance given by the sum of admittances shared by node nos. 1 and 2.

Similarly, $\mathbf{Y_{13}} = \mathbf{Y_{31}}$ are the sum of admittances shared by respective nodes.

The mutual admittances have a negative sign.

3. The source currents $\mathbf{I_1}$, $\mathbf{I_2}$ and $\mathbf{I_3}$ are the sum of current sources at the respective nodes.
4. $\mathbf{V_1}$, $\mathbf{V_2}$ and $\mathbf{V_3}$ are unknown node voltages w.r.t. reference node.

The unknown voltage $\mathbf{V_1}$, $\mathbf{V_2}$ and $\mathbf{V_3}$ are determined by solving the matrix form of node voltage equations. Thus,

$$\mathbf{V_1} = \mathbf{I_1}\left(\frac{\Delta_{11}}{\Delta_y}\right) + \mathbf{I_2}\left(\frac{\Delta_{21}}{\Delta_y}\right) + \mathbf{I_3}\left(\frac{\Delta_{31}}{\Delta_y}\right)$$

$$\mathbf{V_2} = \mathbf{I_1}\left(\frac{\Delta_{12}}{\Delta_y}\right) + \mathbf{I_2}\left(\frac{\Delta_{22}}{\Delta_y}\right) + \mathbf{I_3}\left(\frac{\Delta_{32}}{\Delta_y}\right)$$

$$\mathbf{V_3} = \mathbf{I_1}\left(\frac{\Delta_{13}}{\Delta_y}\right) + \mathbf{I_2}\left(\frac{\Delta_{23}}{\Delta_y}\right) + \mathbf{I_3}\left(\frac{\Delta_{33}}{\Delta_y}\right)$$

where $\Delta_y = |\mathbf{Y}|$

and $\Delta_{11}, \Delta_{22}, \Delta_{23}$
$\Delta_{12}, \Delta_{21}$
$\Delta_{23}, \Delta_{32}$
$\Delta_{31}, \Delta_{13}$ Corresponding co–factors.

For the case $\mathbf{I_2} = \mathbf{I_3} = 0$ *i.e.* only the source current $\mathbf{I_1}$ injected at node no. 1. The voltage $\mathbf{V_1}$ is given by $\mathbf{V_1} = \mathbf{I_1}\left(\frac{\Delta_{11}}{\Delta_y}\right)$

### Input (driving point) admittance

$$\mathbf{Y_1} = \frac{\mathbf{I_1}}{\mathbf{V_1}} = \frac{\Delta_y}{\Delta_{11}}$$

### Transfer Admittance

The driving current at one node in a network results in voltages at all other nodes w.r.t. the reference node. The transfer admittance is the ratio of the driving current at one node to the resulting voltage at another node with all other current sources set to zero.

For example, in a three node network (excluding reference node)

$$\mathbf{V_2} = \mathbf{I_1}\left(\frac{\Delta_{12}}{\Delta_y}\right) + \mathbf{I_2}\left(\frac{\Delta_{22}}{\Delta_y}\right) + \mathbf{I_3}\left(\frac{\Delta_{32}}{\Delta_y}\right)$$

Setting source currents $\mathbf{I_2}$ and $\mathbf{I_3}$ to zero

$$\mathbf{V_2} = \mathbf{I_1}\left(\frac{\Delta_{12}}{\Delta_y}\right)$$

The transfer admittance from node no 1 to 2 is given by

$$\underset{\text{(transfer)}}{\mathbf{Y}_{12}} = \frac{\mathbf{I_1}}{\mathbf{V_2}} = \frac{\Delta_y}{\Delta_{12}}$$

where $\Delta_{12}$ is the corresponding cofactor of $\Delta_z$

Similarly $$\underset{\text{(transfer)}}{\mathbf{Y_{13}}} = \frac{\mathbf{I_1}}{\mathbf{V_3}} = \frac{\Delta_y}{\Delta_{13}}$$

In general $$\mathbf{Y_{pq}} = \frac{\mathbf{I_p}}{\mathbf{V_q}} = \frac{\Delta_y}{\Delta_{pq}}$$

(**Note:** The return path for the driving current source is through the reference node.)

## 3.12. SOLVED EXAMPLES

**Example 3.12.1.** *A series circuit given below is connected to 200V a.c. supply. Determine the current, power factor and voltage drops $V_1$, $V_2$. Draw the phasor diagram.*

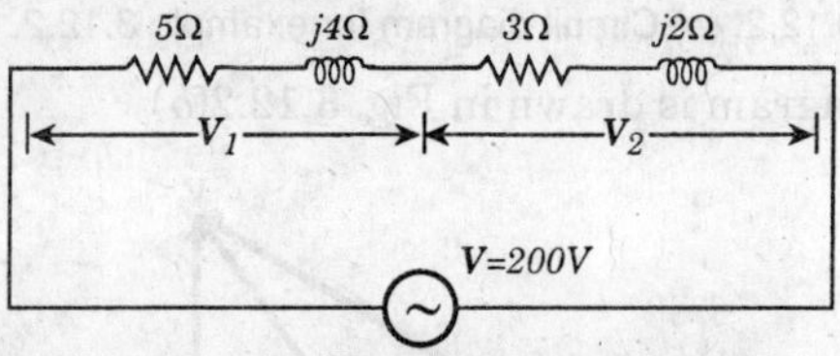


Fig. 3.12.1 (*a*) Circuit for example 3.12.1.

**Solution:** $\mathbf{Z_{eq}} = \mathbf{Z_1} + \mathbf{Z_2}$

$$= (5 + j\,4) + (3 + j\,2)$$

$$= (8 + j\,6) = \sqrt{8^2 + 6^2}\,\angle\tan^{-1}\frac{6}{8}$$

$$= 10 \angle 36.86°$$

$$\mathbf{I} = \frac{\mathbf{V}}{\mathbf{Z}} = \frac{200\angle 0°}{10\angle 36.86°}$$

$$= 20\angle -36.86°,\ I = 20A\ \textbf{Ans.}$$

power factor = $\cos\phi = \cos 36.86°$

$$= 0.8 \text{ lag} \quad \textbf{Ans.}$$

$$\mathbf{V_1 = I\, Z_1} = 20\angle -36.86° \times (5 + j\,4)$$

$$= 20\angle -36.86° \times \sqrt{5^2 + 4^2}\ \angle \tan^{-1} 4/5$$

$$= 20\angle -36.86° \times 6.4\angle 38.65°$$

$$= 128\angle 1.79°,\ V_1 = 128V \quad \textbf{Ans.}$$

$$\mathbf{V_2 = I\, Z_2} = 20\angle -36.86° \times (3 + j\,2)$$

$$= 20\angle -36.86° \times \sqrt{3^2 + 2^2}\ \angle \tan^{-1} 2/3$$

$$= 20\angle -36.86° \times 3.6\angle 33.69°$$

$$= 72\angle -3.17°,\ V_2 = 72\ V \quad \textbf{Ans.}$$

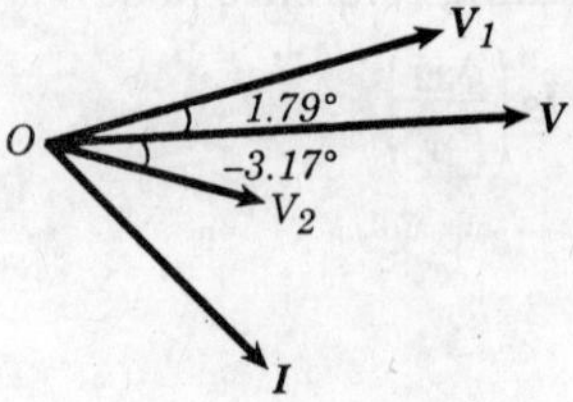

Fig. 3.12.1. (*b*) Phasor diagram

**Example 3.12.2.** *A series circuit consists of a pure resistance and an inductive coil is connected across an a.c. supply voltage. The current drawn by the circuit is 5A. The voltage drops across the resistance and inductive coil are 300V and 200V respectively. The power factor of the coil is 0.8.*

*Determine the supply voltage and total power factor.*

**Solution:** As per the data given the circuit diagram is drawn in Fig. 3.12.2(*a*)

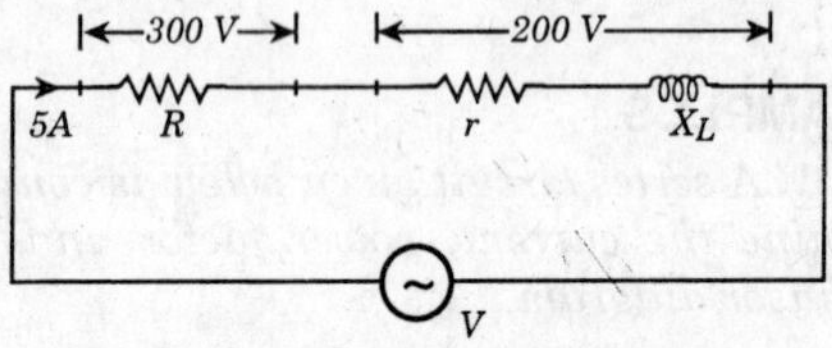

Fig. 3.12.2. (*a*) Circuit diagram for example 3.12.2.

The phasor diagram is drawn in Fig. 3.12.2(*b*)

Fig. 3.12.2. (*b*) Phasor diagram for example 3.12.2.

$$I\,R = 300, \quad \therefore\ R = \frac{300}{5} = 60\ \Omega$$

$$Z_{coil} = \frac{V_{coil}}{I} = \frac{200}{5} = 40\ \Omega$$

$$\cos \phi_{coil} = \frac{r}{Z_{coil}} = \frac{r}{40}, \therefore\ 0.8 = \frac{r}{40}, r = 0.8 \times 40 = 32\Omega$$

$$\sin\phi_{coil} = \frac{X_L}{Z_{coil}}, \therefore 0.6 = \frac{X_L}{40}, X_L = 0.6 \times 40 = 24\Omega$$

From phasor diagram,

$$V^2 = (I\,R + I\,r)^2 + (I\,X_L)^2$$

$$= (5 \times 60 + 5 \times 32)^2 + (5 \times 24)^2 = 22.6 \times 10^4$$

$$\therefore \quad V = \sqrt{22.6 \times 10^4} = 475.3V \textbf{ Ans.}$$

$$Z_{total} = \sqrt{(R + r)^2 + (X_L)^2} = \sqrt{(60 + 32)^2 + (24)^2}$$

$$= 95\ \Omega$$

$$\cos\phi_{total} = \frac{R + r}{Z_{total}}$$

$$= \frac{60 + 32}{95} = 0.968 \textbf{ Ans.}$$

**Example 3.12.3.** *An impedance of* 200∠– 30° *ohm is connected to 400V, 100 Hz. supply. Find (a)* Resistance, Reactance and capacitance (*b*) current (*c*) power consumed.

**Solution:** $\mathbf{Z} = Z\,(\cos\phi + j\sin\phi)$

$$\because \quad \phi = -30°$$

$$\therefore \quad \mathbf{Z} = 200\,[\cos(-30°) + j\sin(-30°)]$$

$$= 200\,(0.866 - j\,0.5) = 173.2 - j\,100$$

$$\therefore \quad R = 173.2\ \Omega \quad \textbf{Ans.}$$

$$X_c = 100\ \Omega \quad \textbf{Ans.}$$

$$X_c = \frac{1}{\omega C}$$

$$\therefore \quad C = \frac{1}{X_c\,\omega} = \frac{1}{100 \times 2\pi \times 100}$$

$$= \frac{10^6}{100 \times 2\,\pi \times 100}\ \mu f = 15.9\ \mu f$$

$$\mathbf{I} = \frac{\mathbf{V}}{\mathbf{Z}} = \frac{400 \angle 0°}{200 \angle -30°} = 2 \angle 30°$$

$$I = 2\,A \quad \textbf{Ans.}$$

$$P = I^2 R = 2^2 \times 173.2$$

$$= 692.8\ \text{W} \quad \textbf{Ans.}$$

**Example 3.12.4.** *Determine the current supplied by the voltage source and power supplied.*

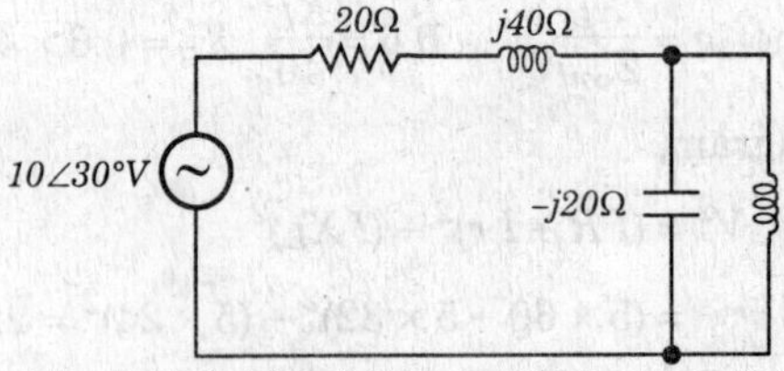


Fig. 3.12.4. Circuit diagram for example 3.12.4.

**Solution :**

$$\mathbf{Z_1} = 20 + j\,40$$

$$\mathbf{Z_2} = \frac{-j\,20 \times j\,60}{-j\,20 + j\,60} = \frac{1200}{j\,40} = -j\,30$$

$$\mathbf{Z_{eq}} = \mathbf{Z_1} + \mathbf{Z_2} = (20 + j\,40) + (-j\,30) = 20 + j\,10$$

$$\mathbf{I} = \frac{\mathbf{V}}{\mathbf{Z_{eq}}} = \frac{10 \angle 30°}{20 + j\,10} = \frac{10 \angle 30°}{\sqrt{20^2 + 10^2} \angle \tan^{-1}\frac{10}{2}}$$

$$= \frac{10 \angle 30°}{10\sqrt{5} \angle 26.56} = \frac{1}{\sqrt{5}} \angle 30° - 26.56°$$

$$= \frac{1}{\sqrt{5}} \angle 3.44°,\ I = \frac{1}{\sqrt{5}} A \quad \textbf{Ans.}$$

$$\phi = (30° - 3.44°) = 26.56° \text{ lag.}$$

$$P = V I \cos \phi$$

$$= 10 \times \frac{1}{\sqrt{5}} \times \cos 26.56°$$

$$= 10 \times \frac{1}{\sqrt{5}} \times 0.894 = 3.99 \text{ W} \quad \textbf{Ans.}$$

**Example 3.12.5.** *A 30Ω resistor is connected in parallel with an inductor. The combination take a current of 10A from a 240V, 60 Hz supply. Determine the frequency, if the current drawn at 240 V is 16 A.*

**Solution:** 1. $f_1 = 60$ Hz

The circuit diagram is shown in Fig. 3.12.5. (*a*)

$$\mathbf{I} = \mathbf{I_1} + j\,\mathbf{I}_2$$

$$I_1 = \frac{240\angle 0°}{30\angle 0°} = 8A$$

$$I^2 = I_1^2 + I_2^2$$

$$\therefore \quad 10^2 = 8^2 + I_2^2$$

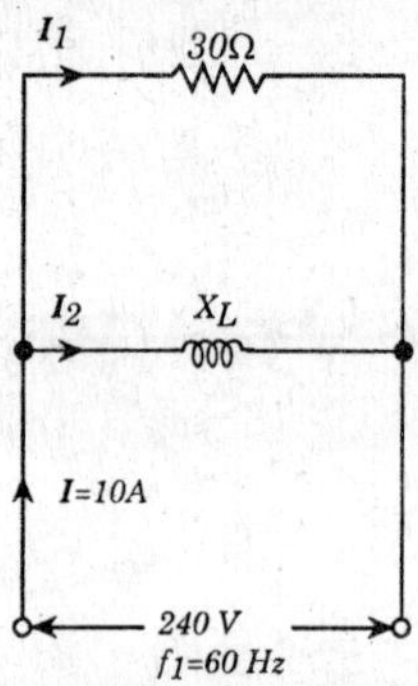


Fig. 3.12.5. (*a*) $f_1 = 60$ Hz

$$I_2^2 = 10^2 - 8^2$$

$$\therefore \quad I_2 = 6A$$

$$X_L = \frac{V}{I_2} = \frac{240}{6} = 40\Omega$$

(2) $f_2$ The circuit diagram is shown in Fig. 3.12.5 (*b*).

$$\mathbf{I}' = \mathbf{I}'_1 + j\,\mathbf{I}'_2$$

$$\mathbf{I}'_1 = \frac{240\angle 0°}{30\angle 0°} = 8\ A$$

$$(I')^2 = (I'_1)^2 + (I'_2)^2$$

$$16^2 = 8^2 + (I'_2)^2$$

$$\therefore \quad (I'_2)^2 = 16^2 - 8^2$$

$$\therefore \quad I'_2 = 13.85\ A$$

$$X_L' = \frac{V}{I_2}$$

$$= \frac{240}{13.85} = 17.32\ \Omega$$

$$\frac{X_L}{X'_L} = \frac{f_1}{f_2}$$

$$\therefore \quad f_2 = \frac{X'_L f_1}{X_L}$$

$$= \frac{17.32 \times 60}{40} = 25.98 \text{ Hz} \quad \textbf{Ans.}$$

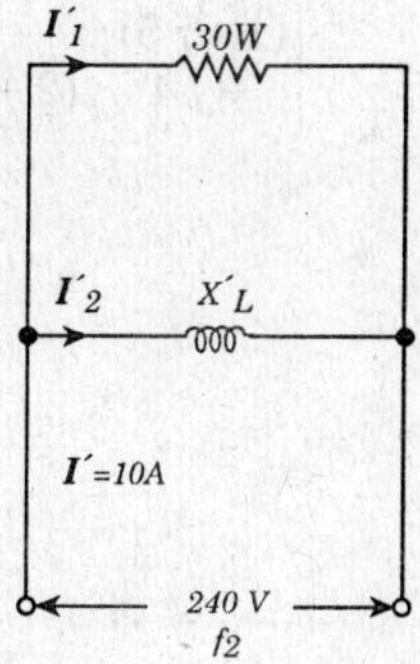

Fig. 3.12.5 (*b*) $f_2$

**Example 3.12.6.** *Determine the currents* $\mathbf{I_1}$, $\mathbf{I_2}$ and $\mathbf{I_3}$ *in the network given below.*

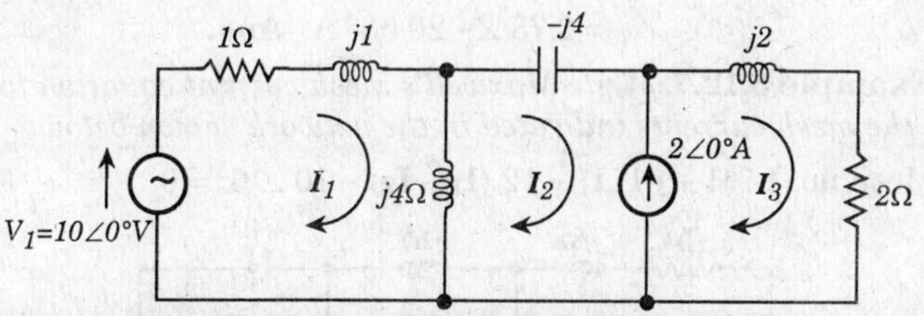

Fig. 3.12.6. Circuit diagram for example 3.12.6.

**Solution.**

Mesh no. 1 : $(1 + j\,1)\,\mathbf{I_1} + j\,4\,(\mathbf{I_1} - \mathbf{I_2}) - 10 \angle 0° = 0$ ...(1)

Mesh no. 2 and 3 (Supermesh) :

$$-j\,4\,\mathbf{I}_2 + (j\,2+2)\,\mathbf{I}_3 + j\,4\,(\mathbf{I}_2 - \mathbf{I}_1) = 0 \qquad ...(2)$$

$$\mathbf{I}_3 - \mathbf{I}_2 = 2\angle 0° \qquad ...(3)$$

substituting for $\mathbf{I}_3$ in Eqn. (2) from Eqn. (3) and simplifying following equation is obtained,

$$-j\,4\mathbf{I}_1 + j\,(2+j\,2)\,\mathbf{I}_2 = -\,2\angle 0° \qquad ...(4)$$

Eqns. (1) and (4) can be written as below,

$$\begin{vmatrix} (1+j\,5) & -j\,4 \\ -j\,4 & (2+j\,2) \end{vmatrix} \begin{vmatrix} \mathbf{I}_1 \\ \mathbf{I}_2 \end{vmatrix} = \begin{vmatrix} 10\angle 0° \\ -2\angle 0° \end{vmatrix}$$

$$\mathbf{I}_1 = \frac{\begin{vmatrix} (10\angle 0°) & -j\,4 \\ -2\angle 0° & (2+j\,2) \end{vmatrix}}{\begin{vmatrix} 1+j\,5 & -j\,4 \\ -j4 & 2-j\,2 \end{vmatrix}}$$

$$= \frac{2+j\,12}{-\,24+j\,12} = \frac{28.32\angle 30.96°}{26.83\angle 180° - 26.56°}$$

$$= 0.869\angle -\,122.44° \text{ A} \quad \textbf{Ans.}$$

$$\mathbf{I}_2 = \frac{\begin{vmatrix} (1+j\,5 & 10\angle 0° \\ -j\,4 & -2\angle 0° \end{vmatrix}}{\begin{vmatrix} 1+j\,5 & -j\,4 \\ -j4 & 2+j\,2 \end{vmatrix}}$$

$$= \frac{-\,2+j\,30}{26.83\angle 180° - 26.56°}$$

$$= \frac{30.06\angle 180° - 86.18°}{26.83\angle 153.44°}$$

$$= 1.12\angle -\,59.62° \text{ A} \quad \textbf{Ans.}$$

$$\mathbf{I}_3 = 2\angle 0° + \mathbf{I}_2 = 2 + 1.12\angle -\,59.62°$$

$$= 2 + 1.12(\cos 59.12° - j\sin 59.62°)$$

$$= 2 + 0.566 - j\,0.961 = 2.566 - j\,0.961$$

$$= 2.73\angle -\,20.53° \text{ A} \quad \textbf{Ans.}$$

**Example 3.12.7.** *Write Maxwell's mesh current equation to determine the mesh currents indicated in the network shown below.*

Mesh no. 1 : $(1+j\,1)\,\mathbf{I}_1 - j\,2\,(\mathbf{I}_1 - \mathbf{I}_2) - 10\angle 0° = 0$

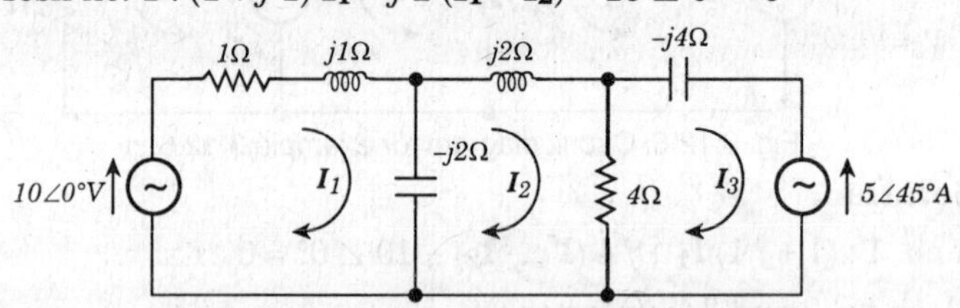


Fig. 3.12.7. Circuit diagram for example 3.12.7.

Mesh no. 2 : $j2\,\mathbf{I_2} + 4(\mathbf{I_2} - \mathbf{I_3}) - j2(\mathbf{I_2} - \mathbf{I_1}) = 0$

Mesh no. 3 : $-j4\,\mathbf{I_3} + 5\angle 45° + 4(\mathbf{I_3} - \mathbf{I_2}) = 0$

$$\therefore \begin{vmatrix} (1-j1) & j2 & 0 \\ j2 & 4 & -4 \\ 0 & -4 & (4-j4) \end{vmatrix} \begin{vmatrix} \mathbf{I_1} \\ \mathbf{I_2} \\ \mathbf{I_3} \end{vmatrix} = \begin{vmatrix} 10\angle 0° \\ 0 \\ -5\angle 45° \end{vmatrix}$$

$$\mathbf{I_1} = \frac{\begin{vmatrix} 10\angle 0° & j2 & 0 \\ 0 & 4 & -4 \\ -5\angle 45° & -4 & (4-j4) \end{vmatrix}}{\begin{vmatrix} (1-j1) & j2 & 0 \\ j2 & 4 & -4 \\ 0 & -4 & (4-j4) \end{vmatrix}}$$

$$= \frac{-134.7\angle 77.83°}{-j32} = \frac{134.7\angle 77.83°}{32\angle 90°}$$

$$= 4.2\angle -12.17° \text{ A} \quad \textbf{Ans.}$$

$$\mathbf{I_2} = \frac{\begin{vmatrix} 1-j1 & 10\angle 0° & 0 \\ j2 & 0 & -4 \\ 0 & -5\angle 45° & (4-j4) \end{vmatrix}}{\begin{vmatrix} (1-j1) & j2 & 0 \\ j2 & 4 & -4 \\ 0 & -4 & (4-j4) \end{vmatrix}}$$

$$= \frac{-134.7\angle 36.54°}{-j32}$$

$$= \frac{134.7\angle 36.54°}{32\angle 90°}$$

$$= 4.2\angle -53.46° \text{ A} \quad \textbf{Ans.}$$

$$\mathbf{I_3} = \frac{\begin{vmatrix} (1-j1) & j2 & 10\angle 0° \\ j2 & 4 & 0 \\ 0 & -4 & -5\angle 45° \end{vmatrix}}{\begin{vmatrix} (1-j1) & j2 & 0 \\ j2 & 4 & -4 \\ 0 & -4 & (4-j4) \end{vmatrix}}$$

$$= \frac{-84.85\angle 70.53}{-j32} = \frac{84.85\angle 70.53°}{32\angle 90°}$$

$$= 2.65\angle -19.47° \text{ A} \quad \textbf{Ans.}$$

**Example 3.12.8.** *Determine the current flowing through 1 Ω resistance.*

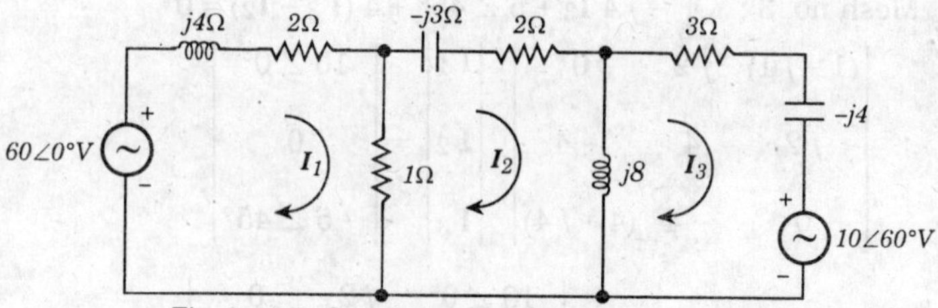


Fig. 3.12.8. Circuit diagram for example 3.12.8.

**Solution:** Apply *KVL*, mesh current equations are written below.

Mesh no. 1 : $(j\,4 + 2)\,\mathbf{I}_1 + 1\,(\mathbf{I}_1 - \mathbf{I}_2) - 60 \angle 0° = 0$

Mesh no. 2 : $(-j\,3 + 2)\,\mathbf{I}_2 + j\,8\,(\mathbf{I}_2 - \mathbf{I}_3) + 1\,(\mathbf{I}_2 - \mathbf{I}_1) = 0$

Mesh no. 3 : $(3 - j\,4)\,\mathbf{I}_3 + 10 \angle 60° + j\,8\,(\mathbf{I}_3 - \mathbf{I}_2) = 0$

Above set of equations can be written in the form as below

$$\begin{vmatrix} (3+j\,4) & -1 & 0 \\ -1 & (3+j\,5) & -j\,8 \\ 0 & -j\,8 & (3+j\,4) \end{vmatrix} \begin{vmatrix} \mathbf{I}_1 \\ \mathbf{I}_2 \\ \mathbf{I}_3 \end{vmatrix} = \begin{vmatrix} 60 \angle 0° \\ 0 \\ -10 \angle 60° \end{vmatrix}$$

$$\therefore \qquad \mathbf{I}_1 = \frac{\begin{vmatrix} (60 \angle 0°) & -1 & 0 \\ 0 & (3+j\,5) & -j\,8 \\ -10 \angle 60° & -j\,8 & (3+j\,4) \end{vmatrix}}{\begin{vmatrix} (3+j\,4) & -1 & 0 \\ -1 & (3+j\,5) & -j\,8 \\ 0 & -j\,8 & (3+j\,4) \end{vmatrix}}$$

$$= \frac{3249.28 + j\,1580}{48 + j\,289} = \frac{3612.8 \angle 25.93°}{292.9 \angle 80.56°}$$

$$\therefore \qquad \mathbf{I}_1 = 12.33 \angle -54.63°\ A$$

$$\mathbf{I}_2 = \frac{\begin{vmatrix} (3+j\,4) & 60 \angle 0° & 0 \\ -1 & 0 & -j\,8 \\ 0 & -10 \angle 60° & (3+j\,4) \end{vmatrix}}{\begin{vmatrix} (3+j\,4) & -1 & 0 \\ -1 & (3+j\,5) & -j\,8 \\ 0 & -j\,8 & (3+j\,4) \end{vmatrix}}$$

$$= \frac{547.84 + j\,397.12}{292.9 \angle 80.56°} = \frac{676.46 \angle 35.9°}{292.9 \angle 80.56°}$$

$$\therefore \qquad \mathbf{I}_2 = 2.3 \angle -44.66°$$

The current flowing through 1 Ω resistance is

$$\mathbf{I_1} - \mathbf{I_2} = 12.33 \angle -54.63° - 2.3 \angle -44.66°$$

$$= 12.33 (\cos 54.63° - j \sin 54.63°)$$

$$- 2.3 (\cos 44.66° - j \sin 44.66°)$$

$$= 12.33 (0.578 - j\, 0.815) - 2.3 (0.711 - j0.702)$$

$$= 7.12 - j\, 10.4 - 1.63 + j\, 1.61 = 5.49 - j\, 8.43$$

$$= \sqrt{5.49^2 + 8.43^2} \angle - \tan^{-1} \frac{8.43}{5.49}$$

$$= 10.06 \angle -56.92°$$

$I$ (through 1 Ω resistance) = 10.06 A **Ans.**

**Example 3.12.9.** *A network is shown in Fig. 3.12.9. Determine the current supplied by 12 V source.*

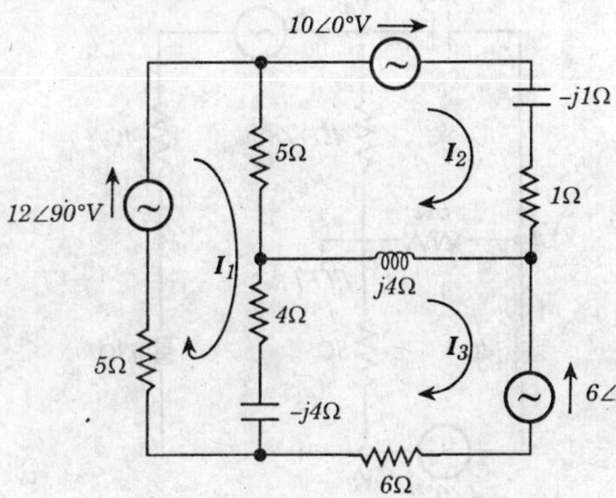


Fig. 3.12.9 Network for example 3.12.9

**Solution:** Mesh equations are formed below.

Mesh no. 1 $5(\mathbf{I_1} - \mathbf{I_2}) + (4 - j\,4)(\mathbf{I_1} - \mathbf{I_3}) + 5\,\mathbf{I_1} - 12 \angle 90° = 0$

Mesh no. 2 $(1 - j\,1)\mathbf{I_2} + j\,4\,(\mathbf{I_2} - \mathbf{I_3}) + 5\,(\mathbf{I_2} - \mathbf{I_1}) - 10 \angle 0° = 0$

Mesh no. 3 $j\,4(\mathbf{I_3} - \mathbf{I_2}) + 6 \angle 30° + 6\,\mathbf{I_3} + (4 - j\,4)(\mathbf{I_3} - \mathbf{I_1}) = 0$

The set of above equations can be written in the following form:

$$\begin{vmatrix} (14 - j\,4) & -5 & -(4 - j\,4) \\ -5 & (6 + j\,3) & -j\,4 \\ -(4 - j\,4) & -j\,4 & 10 \end{vmatrix} \begin{vmatrix} \mathbf{I_1} \\ \mathbf{I_2} \\ \mathbf{I_3} \end{vmatrix} = \begin{vmatrix} 12 \angle 90° \\ 10 \angle 0° \\ -6 \angle 30° \end{vmatrix}$$

The current supplied by 12*V* source,

$$\mathbf{I_1} = \frac{\begin{vmatrix} (12 \angle 90°) & -5 & -(4-j\,4) \\ 10 \angle 0° & (6+j\,3) & -j\,4 \\ -6 \angle 30° & -j\,4 & 10 \end{vmatrix}}{\begin{vmatrix} 14-j\,4 & -5 & -(4-j\,4) \\ -5 & (6+j\,3) & -j\,4 \\ -(4-j\,4) & -j\,4 & 10 \end{vmatrix}}$$

$$= \frac{150.33 + j\,882.9}{6.77.6 + j\,148}$$

$$= \frac{895.6 \angle 80.33°}{693.5 \angle 12.32°}$$

$$= 1.29 \angle 68.01° \text{ A} \quad \textbf{Ans.}$$

$$\mathbf{I_1} = 1.29 \text{ A} \quad \textbf{Ans.}$$

**Example 3.12.10.** *Determine the node voltage $V_1$ in the network shown in Fig. 3.12.10.*

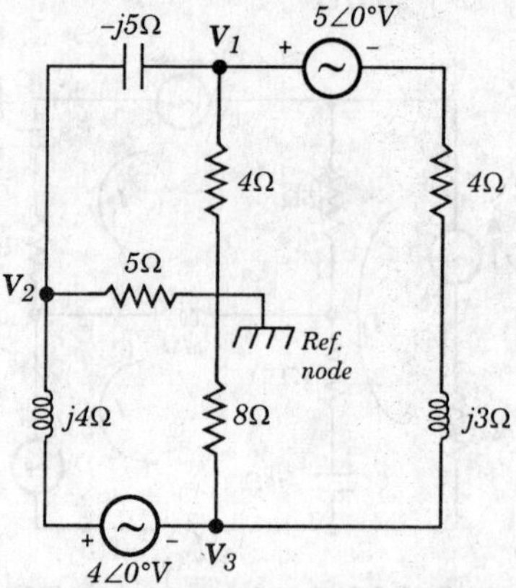


Fig. 3.12.10. Network for example 3.12.10.

**Solution:** The node voltage equations are formed as below.

At node no. 1: $$\frac{\mathbf{V_1} - \mathbf{V_2}}{-j\,5} + \frac{\mathbf{V_1}}{4} + \frac{(\mathbf{V_1} - 5 \angle 0°) - \mathbf{V_3}}{4 + j\,3} = 0$$

At node no. 2: $$\frac{(\mathbf{V_2} - 4 \angle 0°) - \mathbf{V_3}}{j\,4} + \frac{\mathbf{V_2}}{5} + \frac{\mathbf{V_2} - \mathbf{V_1}}{-j\,5} = 0$$

At node no. 3: $$\frac{(\mathbf{V_3} + 4 \angle 0°) - \mathbf{V_2}}{j\,4} + \frac{\mathbf{V_3}}{8} + \frac{(\mathbf{V_3} + 5 \angle 0°) - \mathbf{V_1}}{4 + j\,3} = 0$$

Above set of equations is rearranged as below,

$$\left(\frac{1}{-j\,5} + \frac{1}{4} + \frac{1}{4+j\,3}\right)\mathbf{V_1} - \frac{1}{(-j\,5)}\mathbf{V_2} - \left(\frac{1}{4+j\,3}\right)\mathbf{V_3} = \frac{5 \angle 0°}{4+j\,3}$$

$$-\left(\frac{1}{-j\,5}\right)\mathbf{V_1} + \left(\frac{1}{j\,4} + \frac{1}{5} + \frac{1}{-j\,5}\right)\mathbf{V_2} - \left(\frac{1}{j\,4}\right)\mathbf{V_3} = \frac{4 \angle 0°}{j\,4}$$

$$-\left(\frac{1}{4+j3}\right)\mathbf{V_1}-\left(\frac{1}{-j4}\right)\mathbf{V_2}+\left(\frac{1}{j4}+\frac{1}{8}+\frac{1}{4+j3}\right)\mathbf{V_3}$$

$$=\frac{-5\angle 0°}{4+j3}-\frac{4\angle 0°}{j4}$$

On simplifying,

$$\left[\begin{array}{l} (j\,0.2+0.25+0.16-j\,12)\mathbf{V_1}-j\,0.2\,\mathbf{V_2}-(0.16-j\,0.12)\,\mathbf{V_3} \\ \qquad =5\,(0.16-j\,0.12) \\ -j\,0.2\mathbf{V_1}+(-j\,0.25+0.2+j\,0.2)\,\mathbf{V_2}+j\,0.25\mathbf{V}_3=-j\,1 \\ -(0.16-j\,0.12)\mathbf{V}_1+j\,0.25\,\mathbf{V}_2+(-j\,0.25+0.125+0.16-j\,0.12)\,\mathbf{V_3} \\ \qquad =-(0.16-j\,0.12)+j\,1 \end{array}\right.$$

$$\text{or}\left[\begin{array}{l} (0.41+j\,0.08)\,\mathbf{V_1}-j\,0.2\,\mathbf{V}_2-(0.16-j\,0.12)\,\mathbf{V_3}=(0.8-j\,0.6) \\ -j\,0.2\,\mathbf{V_1}+(0.2-j\,0.05)\,\mathbf{V_2}+j\,0.25\,\mathbf{V}_3=-j\,1 \\ -(0.16-j\,0.12)\,\mathbf{V_1}+j\,0.25\,\mathbf{V}_2+(0.285-j\,0.37)\,\mathbf{V_3} \\ =(-0.8+j\,1.6) \end{array}\right.$$

In determinant form above equations can be written as,

$$\begin{vmatrix} 0.41+j\,0.08 & -j\,0.2 & -(0.16-j\,0.12) \\ -j\,0.2 & (0.2-j\,0.05) & j\,0.25 \\ -(0.16-j\,0.12) & j\,0.25 & (0.285-j\,0.37) \end{vmatrix}\begin{vmatrix}\mathbf{V_1}\\ \mathbf{V_2}\\ \mathbf{V_3}\end{vmatrix}$$

$$=\begin{vmatrix}(0.8-j\,0.6)\\ -j\,1\\ (-0.8+j\,1.6)\end{vmatrix}$$

$$\therefore \qquad \mathbf{V_1}=\frac{\begin{vmatrix} (0.8-j\,0.6) & -j\,0.2 & -(0.16-j\,0.12) \\ -j\,1 & (0.2-j\,0.05) & j\,0.25 \\ (-0.8-j\,1.6) & j\,0.25 & (0.285-j\,0.37) \end{vmatrix}}{\begin{vmatrix} 0.41+j\,0.08 & -j\,0.2 & -(0.16-j\,0.12) \\ -j\,0.2 & (0.2-j\,0.05) & j\,0.25 \\ -(0.16-j\,0.12) & j\,0.25 & (0.285-j\,0.37) \end{vmatrix}}$$

$$=\frac{0.0352-j\,0.1152}{0.0427-j\,0.0227}$$

$$=\frac{0.12\angle -73°}{0.0482\angle -27.9°}=2.48\angle -45.1°$$

$$V_1=2.48\ V\ \textbf{Ans.}$$

**Example 3.12.11.** *Determine the voltages $V_1$ and $V_2$ in the network shown (Fig. 3.12.11)*

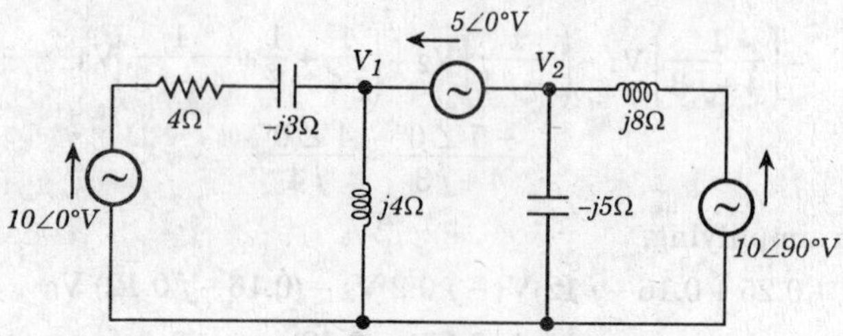


Fig. 3.12.11

**Solution:** The node nos. 1 and 2 are super nodes. The node voltage equation is formed below,

At node nos 1 & 2 (super nodes)

$$\frac{\mathbf{V}_1 - 10\angle 0°}{4 - j\,3} + \frac{\mathbf{V}_1}{j\,4} + \frac{\mathbf{V}_2}{-j\,5} + \frac{\mathbf{V}_2 - 10\angle 90°}{j\,8} \qquad ...(1)$$

Also, $\mathbf{V}_2 - \mathbf{V}_1 = 5\angle 0°$

On rearranging, Eqn. (1) takes the following form,

$$\left(\frac{1}{4 - j\,3} + \frac{1}{j\,4}\right)\mathbf{V}_1 + \left(\frac{1}{-j\,5} + \frac{1}{j\,8}\right)\mathbf{V}_2 = \frac{10\angle 0°}{4 - j3} + \frac{10\angle 90°}{j\,8}$$

or $$(0.16 + j0.12 - j\,0.25)\,\mathbf{V}_1 + (j\,0.2 - j\,0.125)\,\mathbf{V}_2$$

$$= 10\,(0.16 + j\,12) + \frac{j\,10}{j\,8}$$

or $(0.16 - j\,0.13)\,\mathbf{V}_1 + j\,0.075\,\mathbf{V}_2 = (2.85 + j\,1.2)$ ...(2)

$\because \quad \mathbf{V}_2 - \mathbf{V}_1 = 5\angle 0°$

$\therefore \quad \mathbf{V}_2 = \mathbf{V}_1 + 5\angle 0°$ ...(3)

Substituting for $\mathbf{V}_2$ in Eqn. (2) from (3),

$$(0.16 - j\,0.13)\,\mathbf{V}_1 + j\,0.075(\mathbf{V}_1 + 5\angle 0°) = (2.85 + j\,1.2)$$

or $$(0.16 - j\,0.13 + j\,0.075)\,\mathbf{V}_1 + j\,0.075 \times 5 = (2.85 + j\,1.2)$$

or $$(0.16 - j\,0.055)\,\mathbf{V}_1 = 2.85 + j\,0.825$$

$$\therefore \quad \mathbf{V}_1 = \frac{2.85 + j\,0.825}{0.16 - j\,0.055} = \frac{2.96\angle 16.14°}{0.169\angle -18.97°}$$

$$= 17.51\angle 35.11°$$

$$\mathbf{V}_2 = \mathbf{V}_1 + 5\angle 0° = 17.51\angle 35.11° + 5\angle 0°$$

$$= 17.51\,(\cos 35.11° + j\sin 35.11°) + 5$$

$$= 17.51(0.818 + j\,0.575) + 5 = 19.32 + j\,10.06$$

$$= 21.78\angle 27.5°$$

$V_1 = 17.51$ V, $V_2 = 21.78$ V **Ans.**

**Example 3.12.12.** *Write nodal equations and express them in matrix form.*

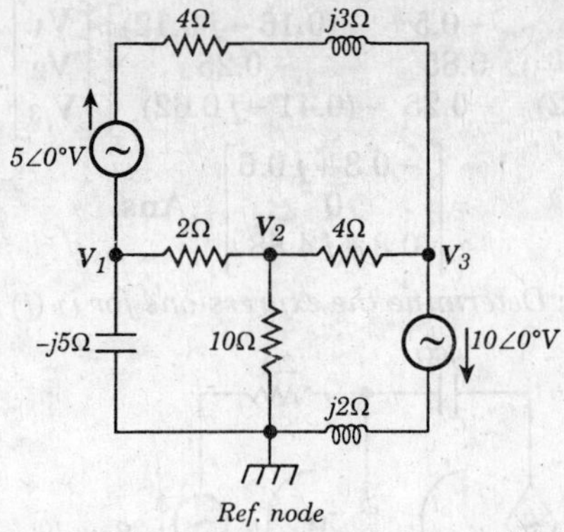


Fig. 3.12.12. Network for example 3.12.12.

**Solution:** The node voltage equation at node nos 1, 2 and 3 are written below.

At node no. 1: $$\frac{(\mathbf{V_1} + 5\angle 0°) - \mathbf{V_3}}{4 + j3} + \frac{\mathbf{V_1} - \mathbf{V_2}}{2} + \frac{\mathbf{V_1}}{-j5} = 0$$

At node no. 2: $$\frac{\mathbf{V_2} - \mathbf{V_1}}{2} + \frac{\mathbf{V_2}}{10} + \frac{\mathbf{V_2} - \mathbf{V_3}}{4} = 0$$

At node no. 3: $$\frac{(\mathbf{V_3} - 5\angle 0°) - \mathbf{V_1}}{4 + j3} + \frac{\mathbf{V_3} - \mathbf{V_2}}{4} + \frac{\mathbf{V_3} + 10\angle 0°}{j2} = 0$$

On rearranging, above set of equations take the following form,

$$\left(\frac{1}{4+j3} + \frac{1}{2} + \frac{1}{-j5}\right)\mathbf{V_1} - \frac{1}{2}\mathbf{V_2} - \left(\frac{1}{4+j3}\right)\mathbf{V_3} = -\frac{5\angle 0°}{4+j3}$$

$$-\frac{1}{2}\mathbf{V_1} + \left(\frac{1}{2} + \frac{1}{10} + \frac{1}{4}\right)\mathbf{V_2} - \frac{1}{4}\mathbf{V_3} = 0$$

$$-\frac{1}{(4+j3)}\mathbf{V_1} - \frac{1}{4}\mathbf{V_2} + \left(\frac{1}{4+j3} + \frac{1}{4} + \frac{1}{j2}\right)\mathbf{V_3} = \frac{5\angle 0°}{4+j3} - \frac{10\angle 0°}{j2}$$

On simplification above set of equations can be written as,

$$(0.16 - j\,0.12 + 0.5 + j\,0.2)\,\mathbf{V_1} - 0.5\,\mathbf{V_2} - (0.16 - j\,0.12)\,\mathbf{V_3}$$
$$= -0.5\,(0.16 - j\,0.12)$$
$$-0.5\,\mathbf{V_1} + (0.5 + 0.1 + 0.25)\,\mathbf{V_2} - 0.25\,\mathbf{V_3} = 0$$
$$-(0.16 - j\,0.12)\,\mathbf{V_1} - 0.25\,\mathbf{V_2} + (0.16 - j\,0.12 + 0.25 - j\,0.5)\,\mathbf{V_3}$$
$$= 5\,(0.16 - j\,0.12) + j\,0.5$$

$$(0.66 + j\,0.08)\,\mathbf{V_1} - 0.5\,\mathbf{V_2} - (0.16 - j\,0.12)\,\mathbf{V_3} = -0.8 + j\,0.6$$

or $$-0.5\,\mathbf{V_1} + 0.85\,\mathbf{V_2} - 0.25\,\mathbf{V_3} = 0$$

$$-(0.16 - j\,0.12)\,\mathbf{V_1} - 0.25\,\mathbf{V_2} + (0.41 - j\,0.62)\,\mathbf{V_3} = 0.8 + j\,4.88$$

The matrix form is given below,

$$\begin{bmatrix} (0.66+0.08) & -0.5 & -(0.16-j\,0.12) \\ -0.5 & 0.85 & -0.25 \\ -(0.16-j\,0.12) & -0.25 & (0.41-j\,0.62) \end{bmatrix} \begin{bmatrix} \mathbf{V_1} \\ \mathbf{V_2} \\ \mathbf{V_3} \end{bmatrix} = \begin{bmatrix} -0.8+j\,0.6 \\ 0 \\ 0.8+j\,4.88 \end{bmatrix} \quad \textbf{Ans.}$$

**Example 3.12.13:** *Determine the expressions for* $i_1(t)$ and $i_2(t)$

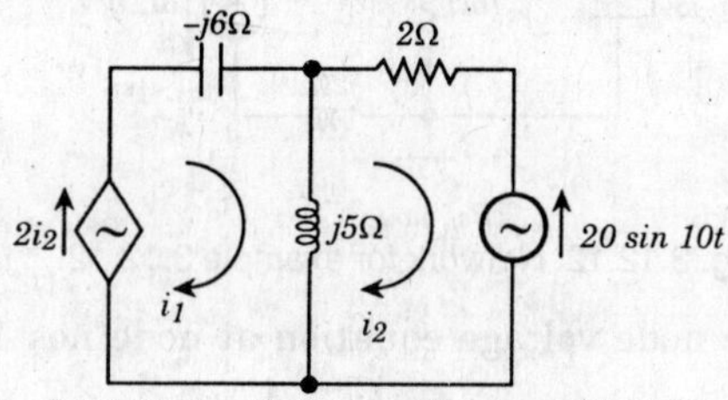


Fig. 3.12.13 circuit diagram for example 3.12.13.

**Solution:** The *RMS* value of the voltage $= \dfrac{20}{\sqrt{2}}\,V$

Applying *KVL*

Mesh no. 1 : $\quad -j\,6\,\mathbf{I_1} + j\,5\,(\mathbf{I_1} - \mathbf{I_2}) - 2\,\mathbf{I_2} = 0$

Mesh no. 2 : $\quad 2\,\mathbf{I_2} + \dfrac{20}{\sqrt{2}} + j\,5\,(\mathbf{I_2} - \mathbf{I_1}) = 0$

On simplification, above equations are written as below:

$$-j\,\mathbf{I_1} - (2 + j\,5)\,\mathbf{I_2} = 0$$

$$-j\,5\,\mathbf{I_1} + (2 + j\,5)\,\mathbf{I_2} = -\frac{20}{\sqrt{2}}$$

or

$$\begin{vmatrix} -j\,1 & -(2+j\,5) \\ -j\,5 & (2+j\,5) \end{vmatrix} \begin{vmatrix} \mathbf{I_1} \\ \mathbf{I_2} \end{vmatrix} = \begin{vmatrix} 0 \\ -\dfrac{20}{\sqrt{2}} \end{vmatrix}$$

$$\mathbf{I_1} = \frac{\begin{vmatrix} 0 & -(2+j\,5) \\ -20/\sqrt{2} & (2+j\,5) \end{vmatrix}}{\begin{vmatrix} -j\,1 & -(2+j\,5) \\ -j\,5 & (2+j\,5) \end{vmatrix}}$$

$$= \frac{-(20/\sqrt{2})\,(2+j\,5)}{30 - j\,12}$$

$$= \frac{-14.14\,\sqrt{2^2+5^2}\,\angle \tan^{-1} 5/2}{\sqrt{30^2+12^2}\,\angle \tan^{-1} -12/30}$$

$$= \frac{-2.35 \angle 68.19}{32.31 \angle -21.8} = 2.35 \angle 89.99$$

$$\mathbf{I_2} = \frac{\begin{vmatrix} -j\,1 & 0 \\ -j\,5 & -20\sqrt{2} \end{vmatrix}}{\begin{vmatrix} -j\,1 & -(2+j\,5) \\ -j\,5 & (2+j\,5) \end{vmatrix}}$$

$$= \frac{j\,20/\sqrt{2}}{32.31 \angle -21.8°}$$

$$= \frac{14.14 \angle 90°}{32.31 \angle -21.8°} = 0.437 \angle 111.8°$$

$$i_1(t) = -I_{1m} \sin(10t + 89.99°) = -2.35\sqrt{2} \sin(10t + 89.99°)$$

$$i_2(t) = I_{2m} \sin(10t + 111.8°) = 0.437\sqrt{2} \sin(10t + 111.8°)$$ **Ans.**

**Example 3.12.14.** *In the circuit given below determine the voltage drop across (i) resistance (ii) inductor (iii) capacitor.*

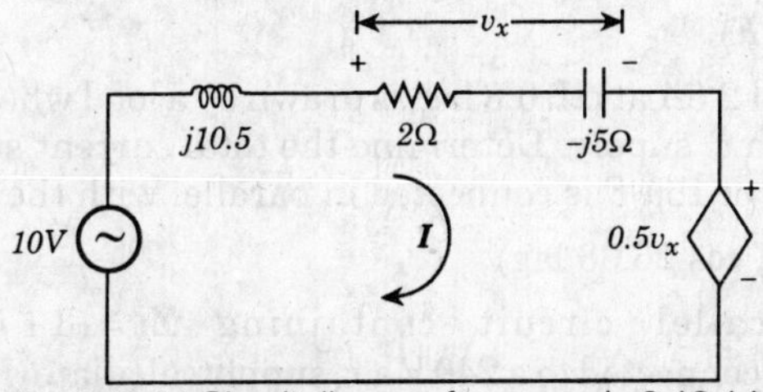


Fig. 3.12.14 Circuit diagram for example 3.12.14.

**Solution:** Applying *KVL*

$$j\,10.5\,\mathbf{I} + 2\,\mathbf{I} - j\,5\,\mathbf{I} + 0.5\,v_x - 10 = 0$$

or $$(2 + j\,5.5)\,\mathbf{I} + 0.5\,v_x = 10$$

$\because$ $$v_x = (2 - j\,5)\,\mathbf{I}$$

$$\therefore\ (2 + j\,5.5)\,\mathbf{I} + 0.5\,(2 - j\,5)\,\mathbf{I} = 10$$

or $$(3 + j\,3)\,\mathbf{I} = 10$$

$\therefore$ $$\mathbf{I} = \frac{10}{3 + j\,3}$$

$$= \frac{10}{\sqrt{2^2 + 3^2} \angle \tan^{-1} 3/3} = 2.35 \angle -45°$$

$\therefore$ $$I = 2.35$$

$$V_R = 2.35 \times 2 = 4.7 \text{ V}$$

$$V_L = 2.35 \times 2 = 24.65 \text{ V}$$

$$V_c = 2.35 \times 5 = 11.75 \text{ V}$$ **Ans.**

## PROBLEMS

**3.1.** A series circuit consists of a 80Ω resistor, 0.636 H inductor and a capacitor. The supply voltage is 240V, 60 Hz. The current flowing in the circuit is $3\angle 0°$ *A*. Calculate (*a*) the value of the capacitance (*b*) the voltage across inductor (*c*) power consumed.

[**Ans.** (*a*) 11.06μ *F* (*b*) 1719.1*V* (*c*) 720 *W*]

**3.2.** The series circuit is shown in Fig. 3P-1. Determine the value of capacitance.

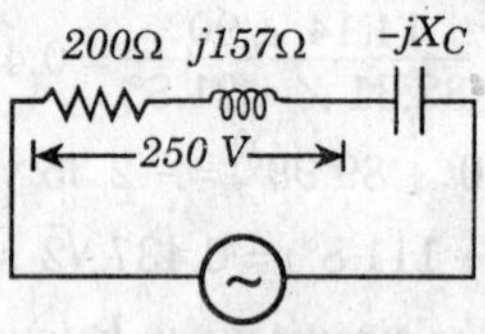


Fig. 3P-1

(**Ans.** 89.2 μ *F*)

**3.3.** A current 2.5*A* at p.f. 0.8 lag, is drawn by a load when connected to 250 V, 50 Hz. a.c. supply. Determine the total current supplied and p.f. if a capacitor of 16μ F is connected in parallel with the load.

(**Ans.** 1.76 A, cos 26.38 lag)

**3.4.** A parallel circuit containing $\mathbf{Z_1} = (3 + j\,4)\ \Omega$ and $\mathbf{Z_2} = (8 - j\,6)\ \Omega$ is connected to a 240 *V* a.c. supply calculate (*i*) the branch currents and total current. (*ii*) the phase difference of the total current w.r.t. supply voltage (*iii*) power consumed.

(**Ans.** $I_1 = 48$ A, $I_2 = 24$ A, $I_t = 53.66$ A and $P = 11520$ W)

**3.5.** Write loop equations, determine the current supplied by the voltage source and the voltage across the capacitor.

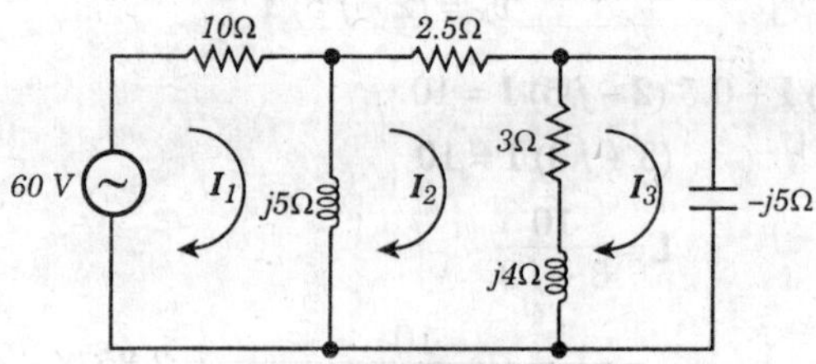


Fig. 3P-2

(**Ans.** $I_1 = 4.56 \angle 19.58°$ A, $V_c = 17.45 \angle 37.91°$ V)

**3.6.** Determine the current supplied by the 10V source. Fig. 3P-3

(**Ans.** $1.74 \angle -47.79°$ A)

**3.7.** Determine the current through $j4\ \Omega$ reactance. Fig. 3P-4

(**Ans.** $1.06 \angle -51.5°$ A)

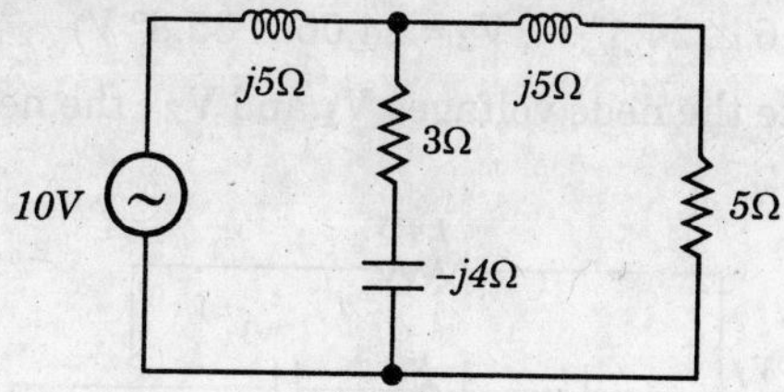


Fig. 3P-3

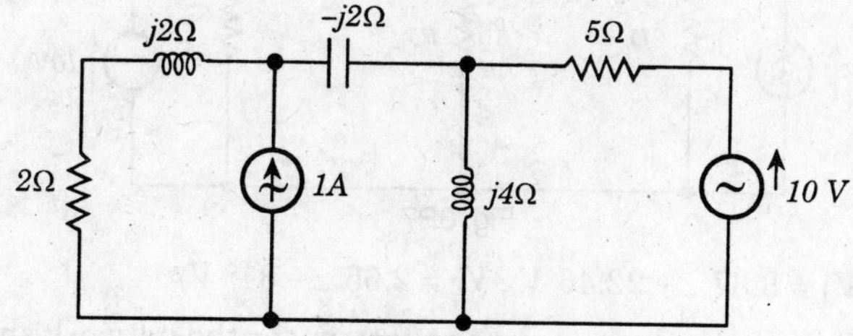


Fig. 3P-4

**3.8.** The selected mesh currents are given in network shown in Fig. 3P-5. Write mesh current equations and calculate $\mathbf{I}_2$.

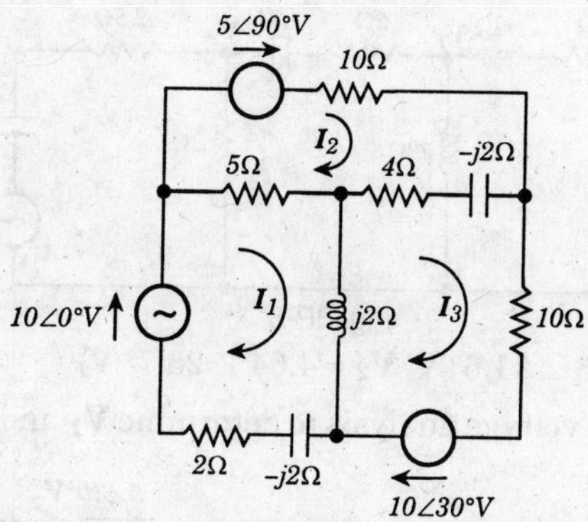


Fig. 3P-5

(**Ans.** $\mathbf{I}_2 = 0.82 \angle 41.05°$ A)

**3.9.** Determine the node voltages $\mathbf{V}_1$ and $\mathbf{V}_2$ in the network shown (Fig. 3P-6).

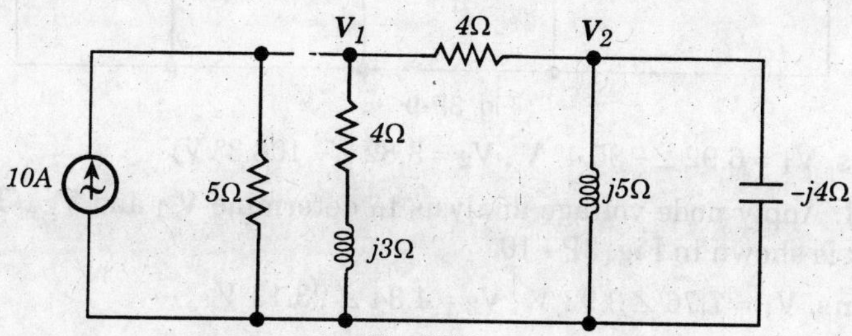


Fig. 3P-6

(**Ans.** $V_1 = 24.6 \angle 24.4°$ V, $V_2 = 24.06 \angle 35.8°$ V)

**3.10.** Calculate the node voltages $\mathbf{V_1}$ and $\mathbf{V_2}$, the network is given in Fig. 3P-7.

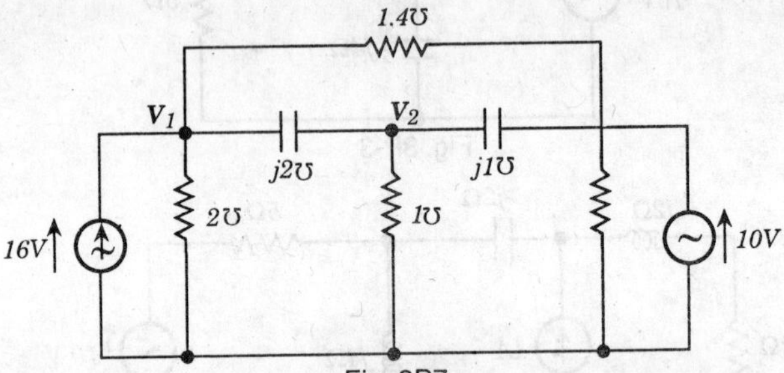


Fig. 3P7

(**Ans.** $V_1 = 8.37 \angle -22.46°$V, $V_2 = 2.65 \angle -31°$ V)

**3.11.** (*i*) Write the loop current equations for the network shown in Fig. 3P-8. (*ii*) Determine the node voltages $\mathbf{V_1}$ and $\mathbf{V_2}$ using node voltage analysis.

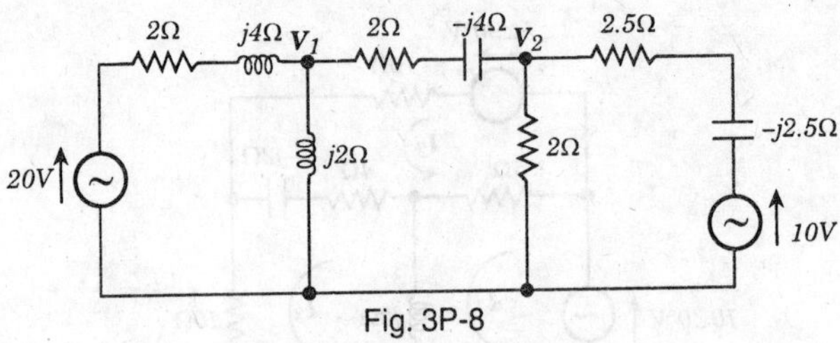


Fig. 3P-8

(**Ans.** $\mathbf{V_1} = 6.56 \angle 11.6°$ V, $\mathbf{V_2} = 4.64 \angle 28.7°$ V)

**3.12.** Use node voltage analysis to determine $\mathbf{V_1}$ and $\mathbf{V_2}$ (Fig. 3P-9)

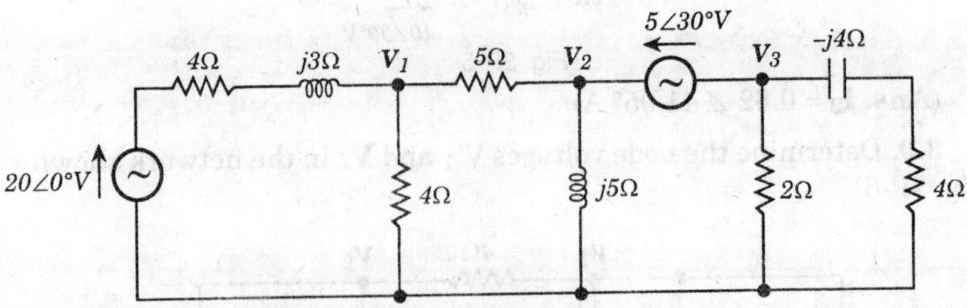


Fig. 3P-9

(**Ans.** $\mathbf{V_1} = 6.92 \angle -35.4°$ V, $\mathbf{V_2} = 3.82 \angle -108.3°$ V)

**3.13.** Apply node voltage analysis to determine $\mathbf{V_1}$ and $\mathbf{V_2}$. The network is shown in Fig. 3P - 10.

**Ans.** $\mathbf{V_1} = 7.76 \angle 3.92°$V, $\mathbf{V_2} = 4.34 \angle 23.13°$V

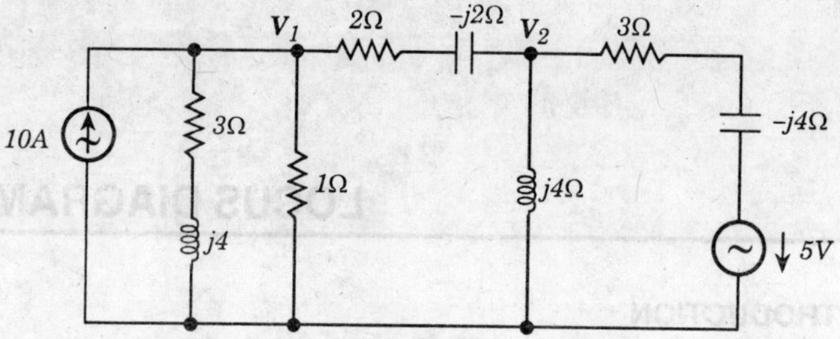


Fig. 3P-10

**3.14.** Determine the voltage across the capacitor.

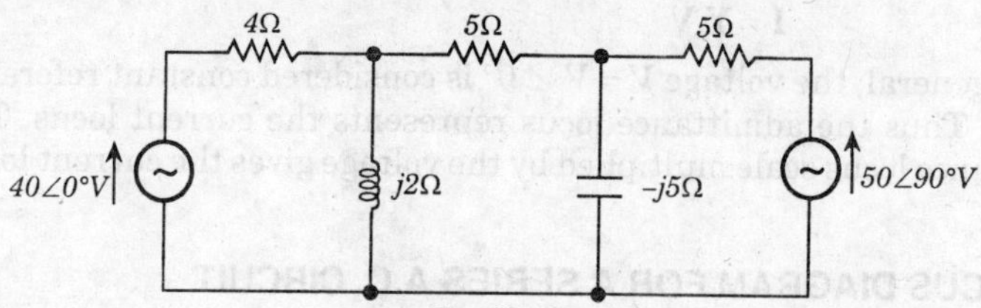


Fig. 3P-11

(**Ans.** 31.5 ∠ 57.35°V)

**3.15.** Determine the equivalent impedance between terminals $a - b$.

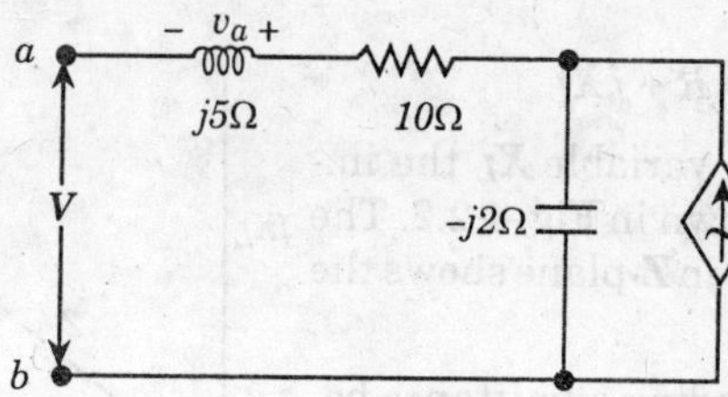


Fig. 3P-12

(**Ans.** $\mathbf{Z_{eq}} = j\,3.0\ \Omega$)

# 4

# LOCUS DIAGRAMS

## 4.1 INTRODUCTION

The admittance locus diagram helps in analysing circuits which have one variable element

$$\mathbf{I} = \mathbf{Y}\,\mathbf{V}$$

In general, the voltage $\mathbf{V} = V \angle 0°$ is considered constant reference phasor. Thus the admittance locus represents the current locus. The admittance locus scale multiplied by the voltage gives the current locus scale.

## 4.2 LOCUS DIAGRAM FOR A SERIES A.C. CIRCUIT

1. A.C. series circuit: Fixed $R$ and variable $X_L$

Fig. 4.2.1. Fixed $R$ and variable $X_L$

A series a.c. circuit with fixed resistance $R$ and variable inductive reactance $X_L$ is shown in Fig. 4.2.1.

$$\because \qquad \mathbf{Z} = R + jX_L$$

With fixed $R$ and variable $X_L$ the impedance **Z**-locus is shown in Fig. 4.2.2. The line parallel to $X_L$ axis in **Z**-plane shows the locus of **Z.**

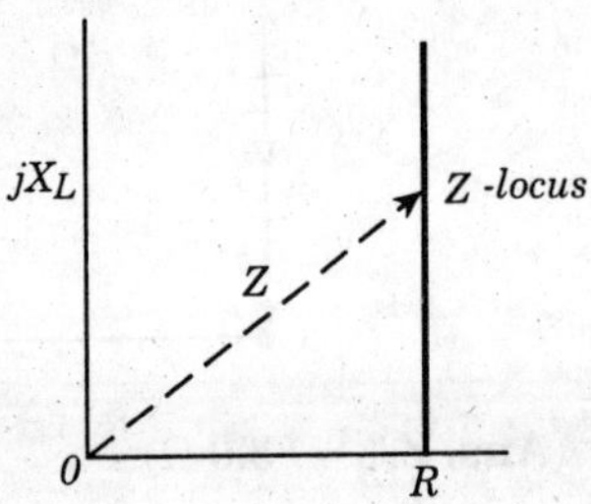


Fig. 4.2.2. **Z** locus (fixed $R$, variable $X_L$)

Let, the corresponding admittance be

$$\mathbf{Y} = G + jB$$

$$\therefore \qquad \mathbf{Z} = \frac{1}{\mathbf{Y}} = \frac{1}{G + jB}$$

or

$$\mathbf{Z} = \frac{G}{G^2 + B^2} - \frac{jB}{G^2 + B^2} \qquad ...(1)$$

Also,

$$\mathbf{Z} = R + jX_L \qquad ...(2)$$

Equating real parts of Eqns. (1) and (2)

$$R = \frac{G}{G^2 + B^2}$$

$$\therefore \quad G^2 - \frac{G}{R} + B^2 = 0$$

Add $\dfrac{1}{(2R)^2}$ on both sides to get

$$G^2 - \frac{G}{R} + \frac{1}{(2\,R)^2} + B^2 = \frac{1}{(2\,R)^2}$$

$$\therefore \qquad \left(G - \frac{1}{2\,R}\right)^2 + B^2 = \frac{1}{(2\,R)^2} \qquad \text{...(3)}$$

(*i*) For a series *RL* circuit with fixed resistance *R* and variable inductive reactance $X_L$ from *O* to ∞, the impedance **Z** locus is a straight line in **Z**-plane (Fig. 4.2.2.)

(*ii*) As per Eqn. (3) the corresponding locus of admittance **Y** is a semi circle in **Y**-plane having radius (1/2*R*) and centre $\dfrac{1}{2R}$, 0. The said semi circle is located in the fourth quadrant of **Y**-plane because the admittance phase angle varies from 0 to $-\pi/2$ as $X_L$ varied from 0 to ∞.

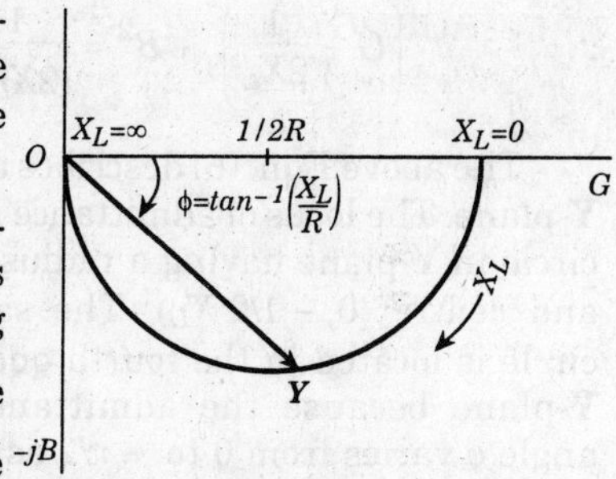


Fig. 4.2.3. **Y**-locus for fixed *R* and variable $X_L$

2. A.C. series circuit : Fixed $X_L$ variable *R*

Fig. 4.2.4. Fixed $X_L$ and variable R.

A series a.c. circuit with fixed inductive reactance $X_L$ and variable resistance *R* is shown in Fig. 4.2.4.

$$\because \qquad \mathbf{Z} = R + j\,X_L$$

with fixed $X_L$ and variable *R*, the impedance **Z**-locus is shown in Fig. 4.2.5. The line parallel to *R*-axis in **Z**-plane shows the locus of **Z**.

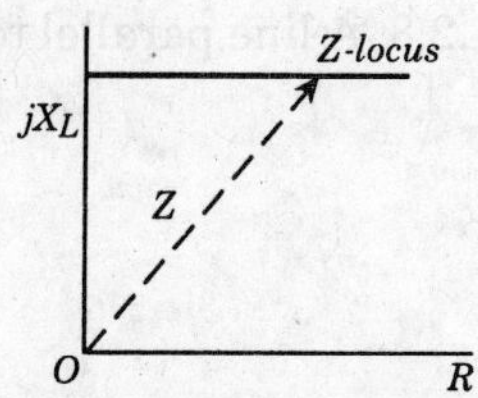


Fig. 4.2.5. **Z**-locus (fixed

Let, corresponding admittance be

$$\mathbf{Y} = G + j\,B$$

$$\therefore \qquad \mathbf{Z} = \frac{1}{\mathbf{Y}} = \frac{1}{G + j\,B}$$

or
$$\mathbf{Z} = \frac{G}{G^2 + B^2} - \frac{j\,B}{G^2 + B^2} \qquad \text{...(4)}$$

Also
$$\mathbf{Z} = R + j\,X_L \qquad \text{...(5)}$$

Equating imaginary parts of Eqns. (4) and (5)

$$X_L = -\frac{B}{G^2 + B^2}$$

or
$$G^2 + \frac{B}{X_L} + B^2 = 0$$

Add $(1/2X_L)$ on both sides to get

$$G^2 + \frac{B}{X_L} + \frac{1}{(2X_L)} + B^2 = \frac{1}{(2X_L)^2}$$

$$\therefore \quad \left(G + \frac{1}{2X_L}\right)^2 + B^2 = \frac{1}{(2X_L)^2} \quad ...(6)$$

The above Eqn. (6) describes a circle in **Y**-plane. The locus of admittance is a semi-circle in **Y**-plane having a radius ( $1/2\,X_L$) and centre ($0, -1/2\,X_L$). The said semi-circle is located in the fourth quadrant of **Y**-plane because the admittance phase angle $\phi$ varies from 0 to $-\pi/2$ as $R$ varied from $\infty$ to 0. The **Y**-locus is shown in Fig. 4.2.6.

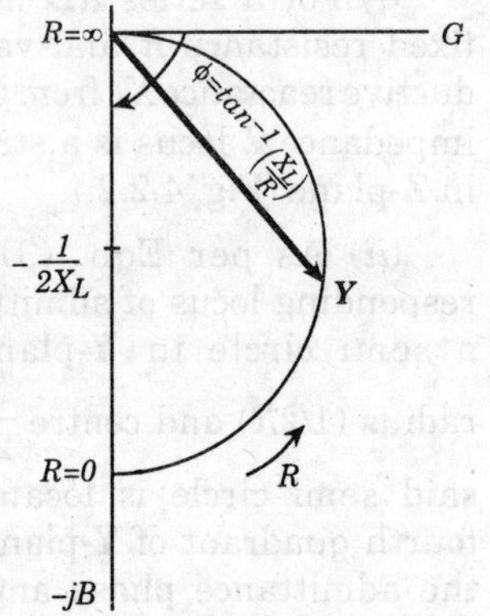


Fig. 4.2.6. **Y**-locus (fixed $X_L$ and variable R)

3. A.C. series $RC$ circuit : Fixed $R$ and variable $X_c$

A series $R$ $C$ circuit with fixed resistance $R$ and variable capacitive reactance $X_c$ is shown in Fig. 4.2.7.

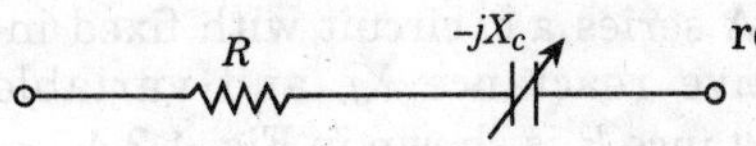


Fig. 4.2.7. Fixed $R$ and variable $X_c$

$$\because \mathbf{Z} = R - j\,X_C$$

With fixed $R$ and variable $X_C$, the impedance **Z** - locus is shown in Fig. 4.2.8. A line parallel to $-jX_c-$ axis is **Z**-plane shows the locus of **Z**.

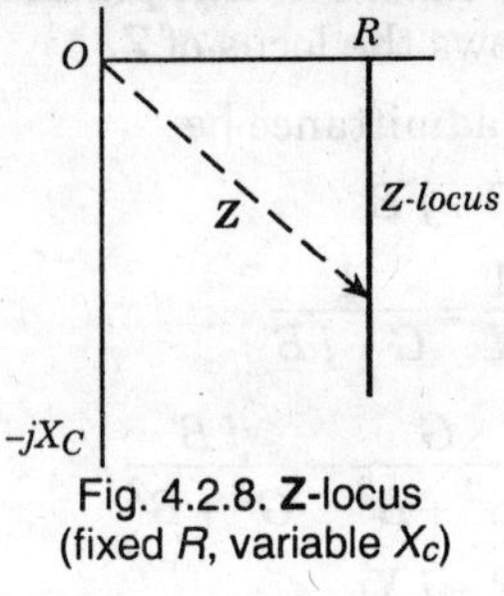


Fig. 4.2.8. **Z**-locus (fixed $R$, variable $X_C$)

Let, the corresponding admittance be

$$\mathbf{Y} = G + j\,B$$

$$\mathbf{Z} = \frac{1}{\mathbf{Y}} = \frac{G}{G^2 + B^2} - \frac{jB}{G^2 + B^2} \qquad \text{...(7)}$$

Also $$\mathbf{Z} = R - j X_c \qquad \text{...(8)}$$

Equating real parts of Eqns. (7) and (8)

$$R = \frac{G}{G^2 + B^2}$$

$$\therefore \quad G^2 - \frac{G}{R} + B^2 = 0$$

Adding $1/(2R)^2$ on both sides

$$G^2 - \frac{G}{R} + \frac{1}{(2R)^2} + B^2 = \frac{1}{(2R)^2}$$

$$\therefore \quad \left(G - \frac{1}{2R}\right)^2 + B^2 = \frac{1}{(2R)^2} \qquad \text{...(9)}$$

The Eqn. (9) describes a circle in **Y**-plane. The locus of admittance is a semicircle of radius $1/2R$ and centre $(1/2R, 0)$. The said semicircle is located in first quadrant of **Y**-plane because the admittance phase angle varies from 0 to $\pi/2$ as $X_c$ is carried from 0 to $\infty$. The **Y**-locus is shown in Fig. 4.2.9.

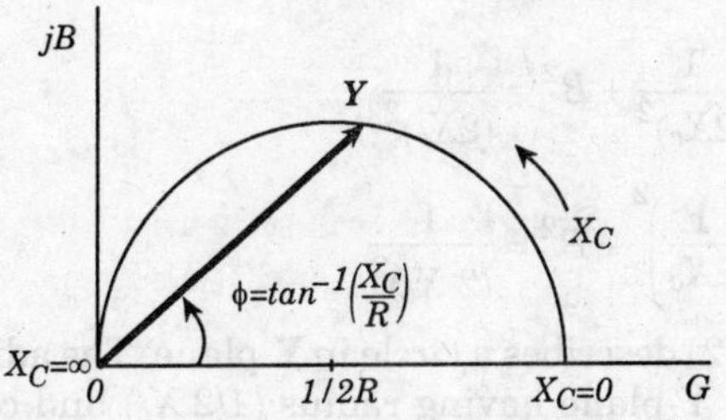


Fig. 4.2.9. Y-locus (Fixed $R$ and variable $X_c$)

4. A.C. series circuit : Fixed $X_c$ and variable $R$

A series $RC$ circuit with fixed capacitive reactance $X_c$ and variable resistance $R$ is shown in Fig. 4.2.10.

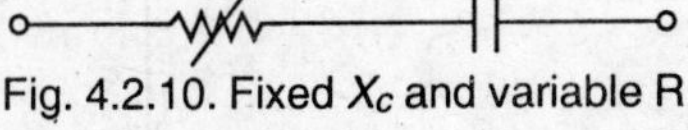


Fig. 4.2.10. Fixed $X_c$ and variable R

With fixed $X_c$ and variable $R$, the impedance **Z** locus is shown in Fig. 4.2.11. A line parallel to $R$-axis in **Z**-plane shows the locus of **Z**.

Let, the corresponding admittance be

$$\mathbf{Y} = G + j B$$

$$\mathbf{Z} = \frac{1}{\mathbf{Y}} = \frac{1}{G + j B}$$

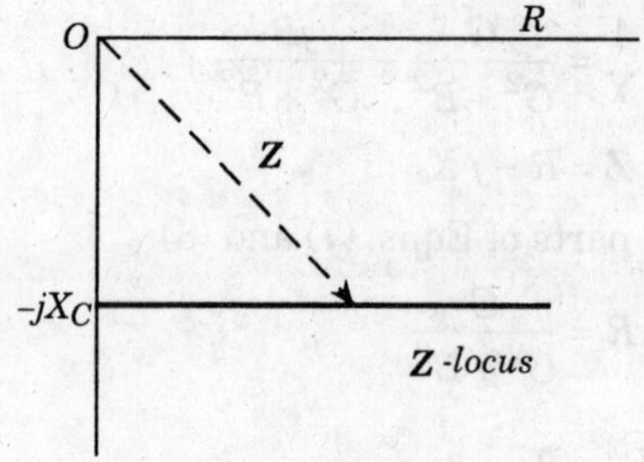


Fig. 4.2.11. **Z**-locus (fixed $X_c$, variable $R$)

$$= \frac{G}{G^2 + B^2} - \frac{jB}{G^2 + B^2} \qquad ...(10)$$

Also $$\mathbf{Z} = R - j\,X_c \qquad ...(11)$$

Equating imaginary parts of Eqns. (10) and (11)

$$X_c = \frac{B}{G^2 + B^2}$$

$$\therefore\ G^2 - \frac{B}{X_c} + B^2 = 0$$

Add $\frac{1}{(2X_c)^2}$ on both sides to get

$$G^2 - \frac{B}{X_c} + \frac{1}{(2X_c)^2} + B^2 = \frac{1}{(2X_c)^2}$$

or $$\left(G - \frac{1}{2X_c}\right)^2 + B^2 = \frac{1}{(2\,X_c)^2} \qquad ...(12)$$

The Eqn. (12) describes a circle in **Y**-plane. The admittance locus is a semi circle in **Y**-plane having radius ($1/2\,X_c$) and centre ($0$, $1/2\,X_c$).

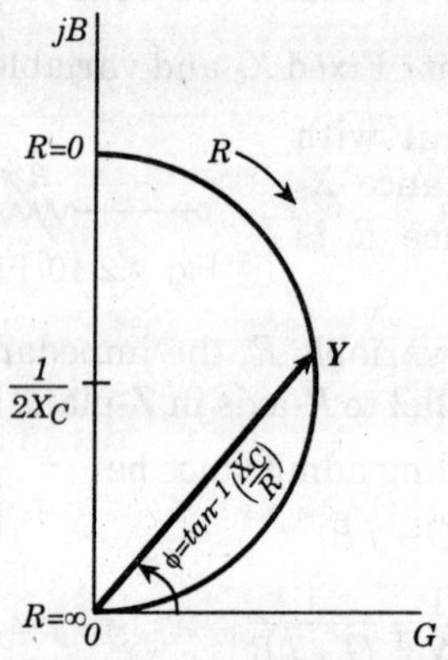


Fig. 4.2.12. **Y**-locus (fixed $X_c$, variable $R$)

The said semi circle is located is first quadrant of **Y**-plane because the admittance phase angle $\phi$ varies from 0 to $\pi/2$ as $R$ changes from $\infty$ to 0. They **Y**-locus is shown in Fig. 4.2.12.

## 4.3 LOCUS DIAGRAM FOR PARALLEL CIRCUITS

(1) A two branch parallel circuit is shown in Fig. 4.3.1 wherein the elements in $R_L\,X_L$ branch are fixed.

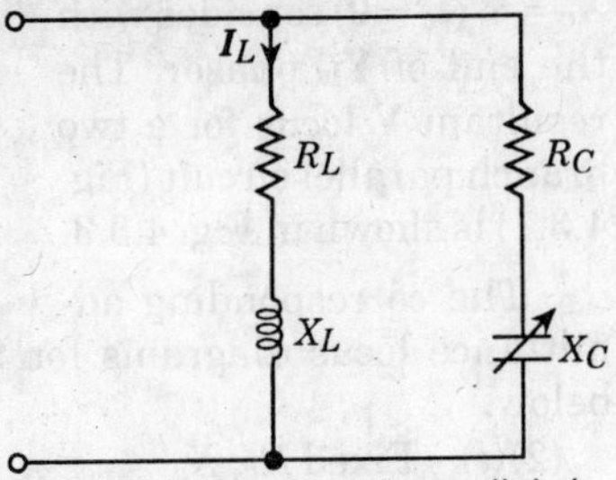

Fig. 4.3.1. Two branch parallel circuit, $X_c$ variable

The circuit is connected to a sinusoidal constant voltage. The value of elements $R_L$ and $X_L$ is fixed. The admittance of the fixed branch is given by

$$\mathbf{Y_L} = \frac{1}{R_L + jX_L}$$

$$= G_L - jB_L$$

where $$G_L = \frac{R_L}{R_L^2 + X_L^2}$$

and $$B_L = \frac{X_L}{R_L^2 + X_L^2}$$

The admittance $\mathbf{Y_L}$ is shown by a phasor in Fig. 4.3.2.

The locus diagram for the branch containing fixed $R_c$ with variable $X_c$ is shown in Fig. 4.3.2. (broken lines)

The locus diagram for the total admittance $\mathbf{Y} = \mathbf{Y}_L + \mathbf{Y}_C$ is drawn by the phasor addition of fixed branch admittance $\mathbf{Y}_L$ and variable

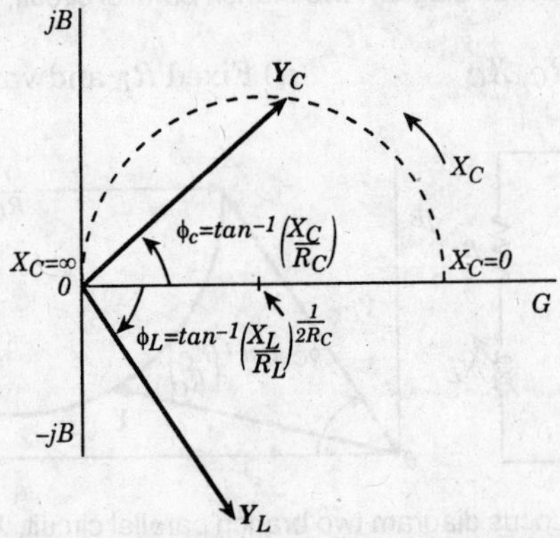

4.3.2. Locus diagram, addition of fixed and variable branch admittance

---

**Note : Supply frequency is kept at a constant value.**
$X_L$, $X_C$ are varied by changing value of inductance L, capacitance $C$.

branch admittance $\mathbf{Y}_C$. The semicircle locus of variable admittance $\mathbf{Y}_C$ is shifted such that the point corresponding to $X_c = \infty$ $(I_c = 0)$ concides with the end of $\mathbf{Y_L}$ phasor. The resultant $\mathbf{Y}$ locus for a two branch parallel circuit (Fig. 4.3.1) is shown in Fig. 4.3.3.

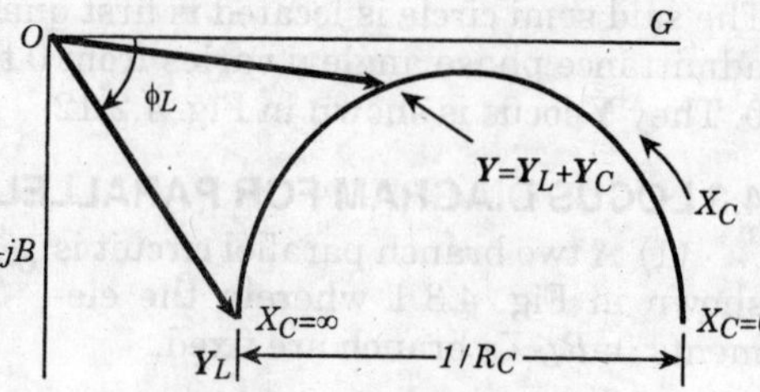


Fig. 4.3.3. Locus diagram, two branch parallel circuit $X_c$ variable.

The corresponding admittance locus diagrams for two branch parallel circuits are shown below.

(2)(*i*) Fixed $R_c$, $X_c$ (*ii*) Fixed $X_L$ and variable $R_L$

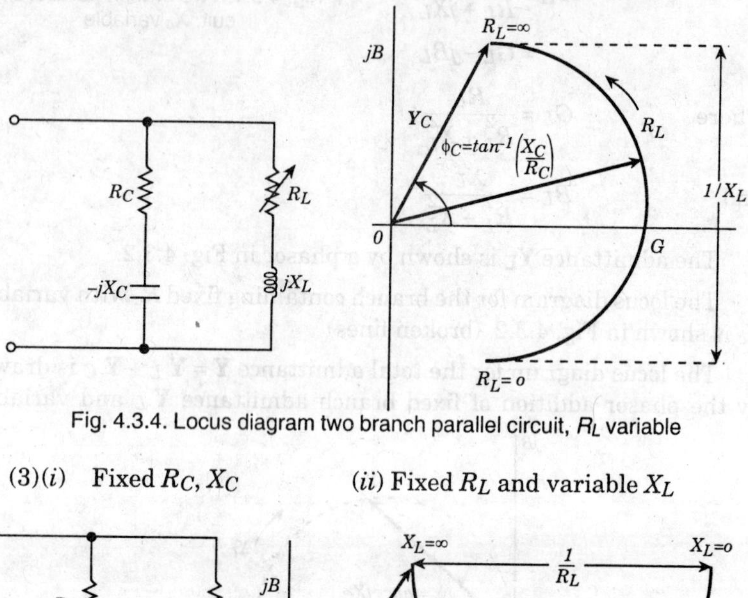


Fig. 4.3.4. Locus diagram two branch parallel circuit, $R_L$ variable

(3)(*i*) Fixed $R_C$, $X_C$ (*ii*) Fixed $R_L$ and variable $X_L$

Fig. 4.3.5. Locus diagram two branch parallel circuit, $X_L$ variable.

(4)(*i*) Fixed $R_L$, $X_L$ (*ii*) Fixed $X_c$, variable $R_c$

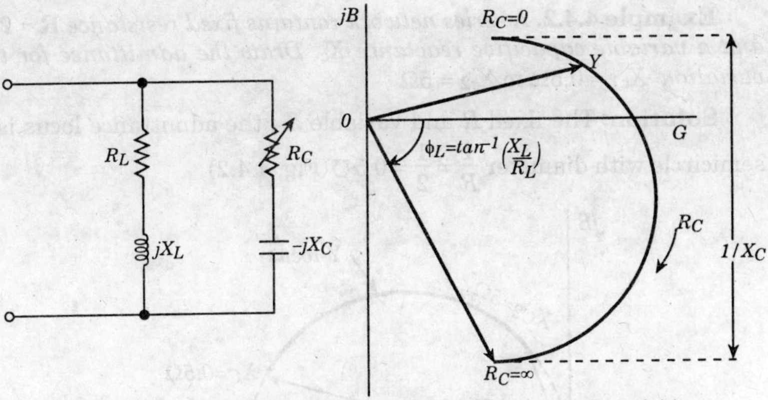


Fig. 4.3.6. Locus diagram two branch parallel circuit, $R_c$ variable.

## 4.4. SOLVED EXAMPLES

**Example 4.4.1.** *Draw the locus diagram. Determine the current if the p.f. is 0.866 lag. The series RL circuit is shown in Fig. 4.4.1.*

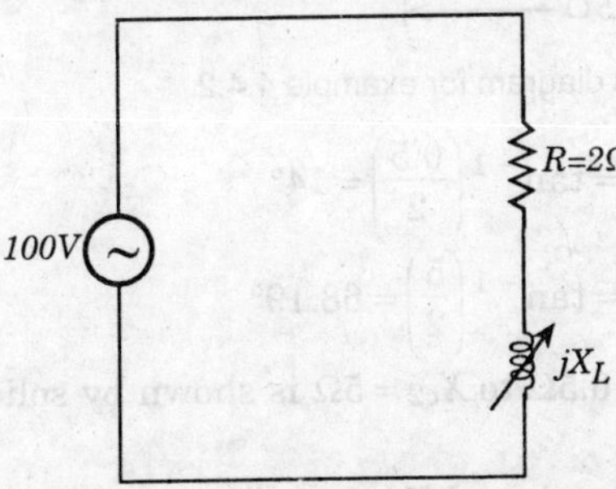


Fig. 4.4.1 Circuit for example 4.4.1.

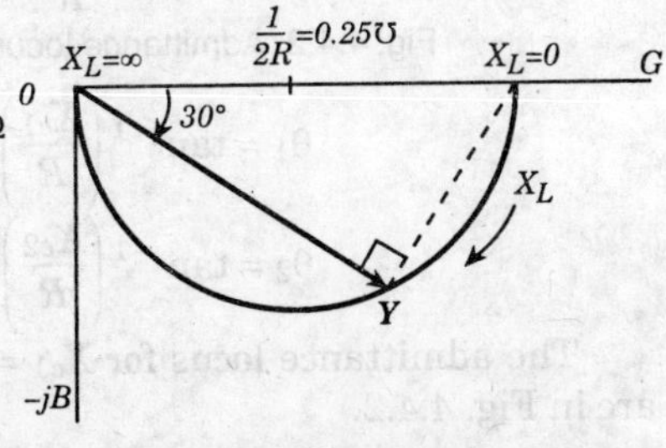


Fig. 4.4.1. (*a*) Admittance Locus diagram for example 4.11.1.

**Solution.** The admittance locus diagram is a semicircle [Fig. 4.4.1 (*a*)] having radius $\left(\frac{1}{2R}, 0\right)$

$\because$ p.f = 0.866,

$$\cos\phi = 0.866,$$

$$\phi = \cos^{-1} 0.866 = 30° \text{ Lagging}$$

Admittance $\mathbf{Y} = (0.25 + 0.25) \cos 30°$

$$= \frac{0.5 \times \sqrt{3}}{2} = 0.25\sqrt{3}\,\Omega$$

$$I = YV$$

$$= 0.25\sqrt{3} \times 100$$

$$= 25\sqrt{3} \text{ A} \qquad \textbf{Ans.}$$

**Example 4.4.2.** *A series network contains fixed resistance* **R** = 2 Ω *and a variable capacitive reactance* $X_c$. *Draw the admittance for the variation* $X_{c1} = 0.5\Omega$ *to* $X_{c2} = 5\Omega$

**Solution:** The fixed $R$ and variable $X_c$, the admittance locus is a semicircle with diameter $\frac{1}{R} = \frac{1}{2} = 0.5$ ℧ (Fig. 4.4.2)

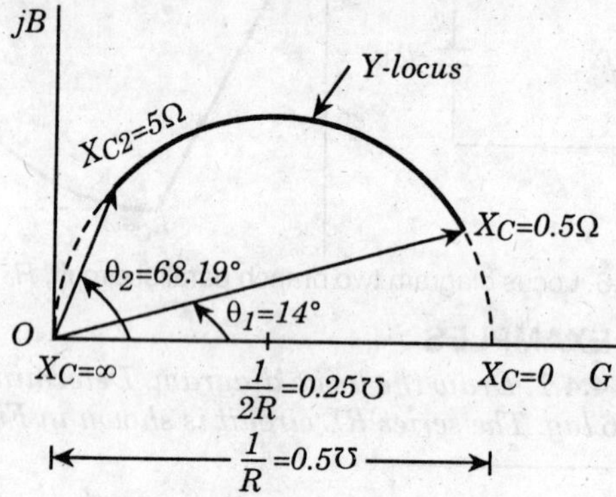


Fig. 4.4.2. Admittance locus diagram for example 4.4.2.

$$\theta_1 = \tan^{-1}\left(\frac{X_{c1}}{R}\right) = \tan^{-1}\left(\frac{0.5}{2}\right) = 14°$$

$$\theta_2 = \tan^{-1}\left(\frac{X_{c2}}{R}\right) = \tan^{-1}\left(\frac{5}{2}\right) = 68.19°$$

The admittance locus for $X_{c1} = 0.5\Omega$ to $X_{c2} = 5\Omega$ is shown by solid arc in Fig. 4.4.2.

**Example 4.4.3.** *Determine the value of* $X_L$ *such that the overall current is drawn at unity p.f. in the network given (Fig. 4.4.3.)*

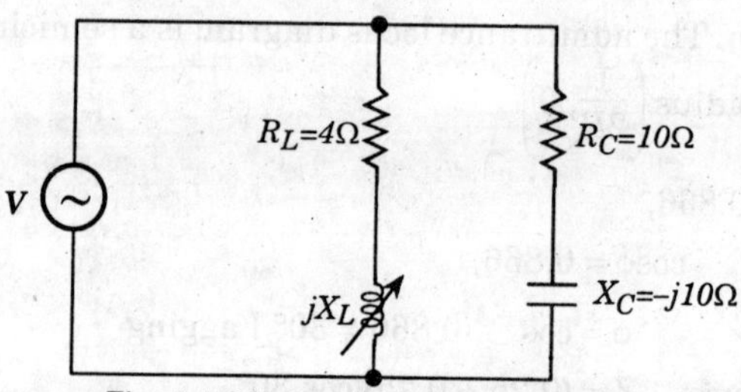


Fig. 4.4.3 Network for example 4.4.3

**Solution**: The fixed branch admittance $\mathbf{Y_c} = \frac{1}{10 - j10} = 0.5\sqrt{2}\ \angle 45°$ ℧. The variable branch has fixed $R_L = 4\Omega$ and variable $X_L$. The admittance locus of this branch is a semi circle with diameter $\frac{1}{R_L} = \frac{1}{4} = 0.25$ ℧ as shown in Fig. 4.4.3($a$).

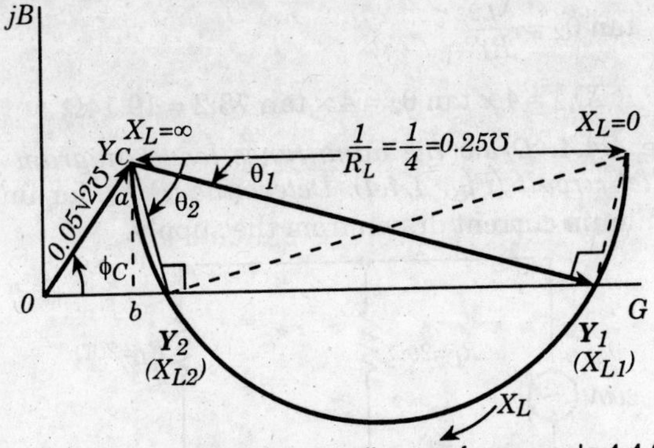


Fig. 4.4.3(a) Admittance locus diagram for example 4.4.3

For unity power factor the locus intersects $G$-axis at $\mathbf{Y}_1$ and $\mathbf{Y}_2$. The corresponding inductive reactances are $X_{L1}$ and $X_{L2}$.

According to locus diagram.

$$ab = Y_c \sin \phi_c = 0.05\sqrt{2} \times \frac{1}{\sqrt{2}} = 0.05 \quad ...(1)$$

Also $\quad ab = Y_1 \sin \theta_1$

$\therefore \quad Y_1 = 0.25 \cos \theta_1$

$\therefore \quad ab = 0.25 \cos \theta_1 \sin \theta_1 \quad ...(2)$

Equating (1) and (2)

$$0.05 = 0.25 \sin \theta_1 \cos \theta_1$$

or $\quad 0.2 = \sin \theta_1 \cos \theta_1$

or $\quad 0.4 = 2 \sin \theta_1 \cos\theta_1$

$\therefore \quad \sin 2\theta_1 = 0.4$

$$2\theta_1 = \sin^{-1} 0.4 = 23.57°$$

$\therefore \quad \theta_1 = 11.78°$

$$\tan \theta_1 = \frac{X_{L1}}{R_L}$$

$\therefore \quad \tan \theta_1 = \frac{X_{L1}}{4}$

$$X_{L1} = 4 \times \tan 11.78° = 4 \times 0.208 = 0.803\ \Omega$$ **Ans.**

$$2\theta_2 = 180° - 2\theta_1 = 180° - 2 \times 11.78° = 156.4°$$

$\therefore \quad \theta_2 = \frac{156.4}{2} = 78.2°$

$$\tan \theta_2 = \frac{X_{L2}}{R_L}$$

$$X_{L2} = 4 \times \tan \theta_2 = 4 \times \tan 78.2 = 19.14\Omega \qquad \textbf{Ans.}$$

**Example 4.4.4.** *Draw the admittance locus diagram for a two branch parallel circuit (Fig. 4.4.4). Determine (i) $X_L$ for unity power factor (ii)* minimum current drawn from the supply.

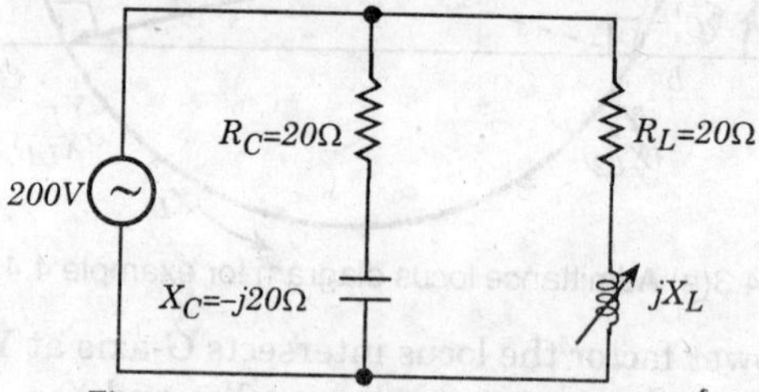


Fig. 4.4.4. Network for example 4.4.4.

**Solution:** The admittance of fixed branch

$$\mathbf{Y}_c = \frac{1}{20 - j20} = 0.025\sqrt{2}\angle 45° \,℧$$

The variable branch $R_c = 20\ \Omega$ and variable $X_L$. The diameter of the semicircle $\frac{1}{R_c} = \frac{1}{20} = 0.05℧$ [Fig. 4.4.4 (*a*)]. The admittance locus is shown in Fig. 4.4.4 (*a*).

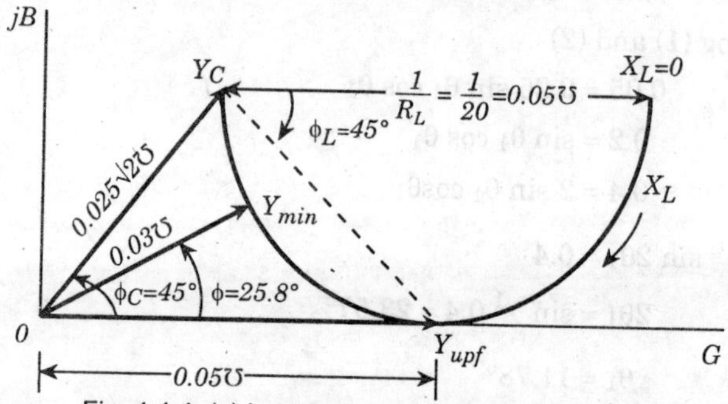


Fig. 4.4.4. (*a*) Locus diagram for example 4.4.4.

To have a unity power factor the admittance locus intersects *G*-axis at $\mathbf{Y}_{u.p.f.}$

(*i*) $\mathbf{Y}_{upf} = (0.025 + 0.025) = 0.05\ ℧$ (measured on the locus)

$$\tan^{-1} \phi_L = \frac{X_L}{R_L}$$

$$\therefore \quad \tan^{-1} 45° = \frac{X_L}{20},\ X_L = 20\ \Omega \qquad \textbf{Ans.}$$

For minimum current

$$Y_{min} = 0.03\ \mho \quad \text{(measured on the locus)}$$

(ii) $I_{min} = Y_{min} \times V = 0.03 \times 200 = 6.0$ A **Ans.**

p.f. at minimum current = cos 25.8° leading = 0.9 leading

**Example 4.4.5:** *Determine the value of $R_L$ such that the overall leading power factor is 0.809 for the circuit given in Fig. 4.4.5.*

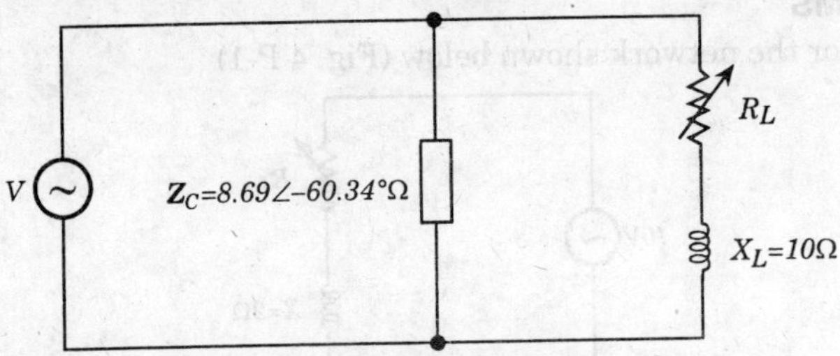


Fig. 4.4.5. Circuit for example 4.4.5.

**Solution:** $\mathbf{Y_C} = \frac{1}{\mathbf{Z_c}} = \frac{1}{8.69\angle -60.34°} = 0.115 \angle 60.34°\ \Omega$

$$\theta = \tan^{-1} 0.809 = 36°$$

For the variable branch inductive reactance (fixed) $X_L = 10\Omega$ and variable $R_L$.

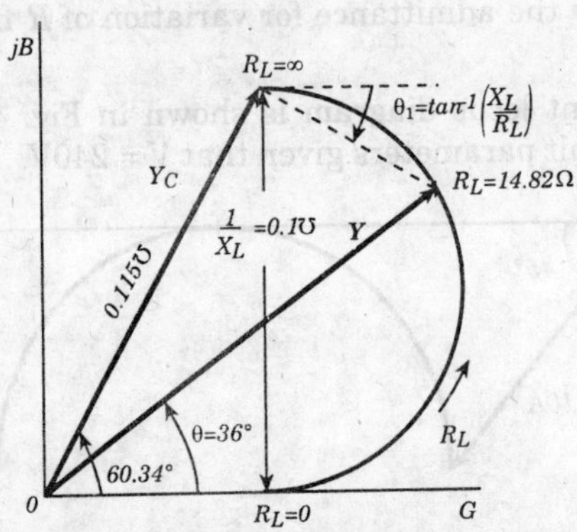


Fig. 4.4.5 (*a*) Admittance locus for example 4.4.5.

The diameter of semicircle is $\frac{1}{X_L} = \frac{1}{10} = 0.1\ \mho$

The admittance locus is shown in Fig. 4.4.5 (*a*).

$$\theta_1 = 34° \quad \text{(measured on the locus)}$$

$$\tan\theta_1 = \frac{X_L}{R_L}$$

$$\therefore \qquad \tan 34^\circ = \frac{10}{R_L}$$

$$\therefore \qquad R_L = \frac{10}{\tan 34^\circ}$$

$$= \frac{10}{0.674}$$

$$= 14.82\ \Omega \qquad \textbf{Ans.}$$

## PROBLEMS

**4.1.** For the network shown below (Fig. 4 P-1)

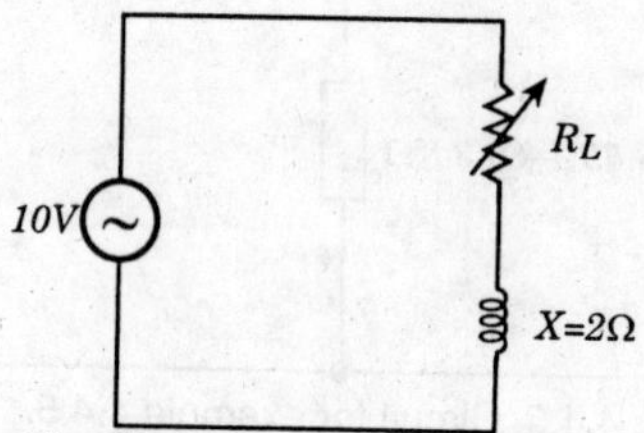


Fig. 4P-1 circuit for problem 4.1

(*i*) Draw the admittance locus

(*ii*) Determine the admittance and current drawn such that the power consumed is 25W.

(**Ans.** $0.5\sqrt{2}\Omega$, $5/\sqrt{2}A$)

**4.2.** A series circuit consists of a fixed reactance $X_L = 5\ \Omega$ and resistance R. Draw the admittance for variation of $R$ from $R = 4\ \Omega$ to $R = 20\ \Omega$

**4.3.** The current locus diagram is shown in Fig. 4P-2. Find the corresponding circuit parameters given that $V = 240V$.

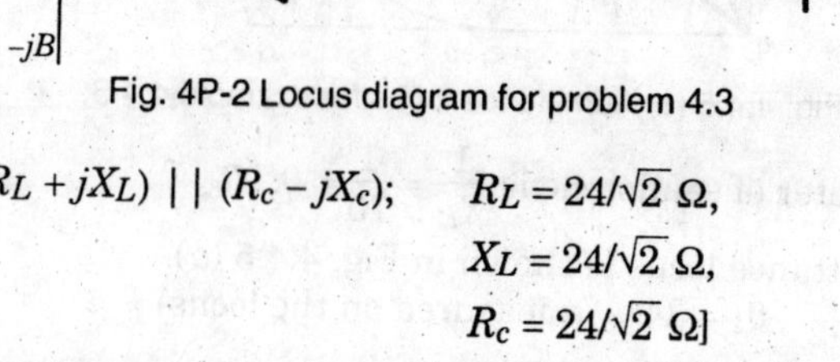


Fig. 4P-2 Locus diagram for problem 4.3

[**Ans**: $(R_L + jX_L) \mid\mid (R_c - jX_c)$; $R_L = 24/\sqrt{2}\ \Omega$,

$X_L = 24/\sqrt{2}\ \Omega$,

$R_c = 24/\sqrt{2}\ \Omega$]

**4.4.** The admittance locus is shown in Fig. 4P-3. Determine the circuit parameters.

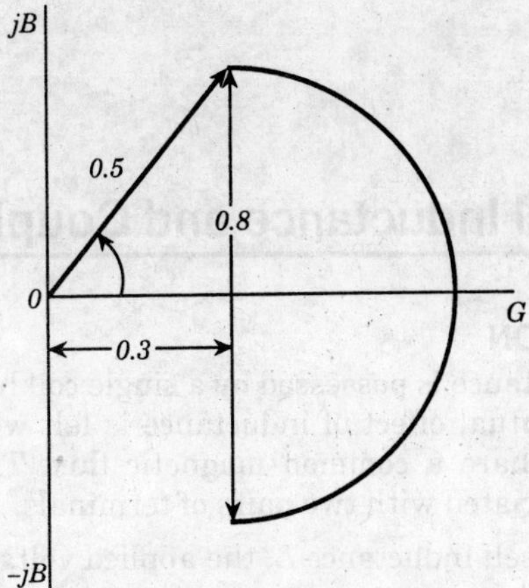


Fig. 4P-3 Locus diagram for problem 4.4

[**Ans**: $(R_c - jX_c) \mid\mid (R_L + jX_L)$

$R_c = 1.2\ \Omega$, $X_c = 1.6\ \Omega$,

$X_L = 1.2\ \Omega$]

**4.5.** A two branch parallel circuit is shown in Fig. 4P-4. Draw the admittance locus and determine the capacitive reactance to have a unity power factor.

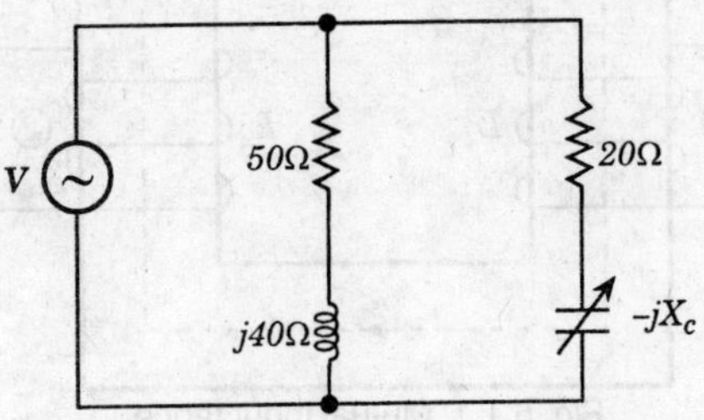


Fig. 4P-4. Circuit for problem 4.5

(**Ans**: $X_{c1} = 4.08\ \Omega$,

$X_{c2} = 98.64\ \Omega$)

# 5

# Mutual Inductance and Coupled Circuits

## 5.1 INTRODUCTION

The self inductance is possessed by a single coil having one pair of terminals. The mutual effect of inductance is felt when two or more inductance coils share a common magnetic flux. Thus, the mutual inductance is associated with two pairs of terminals.

In the case of self inductance $L$, the applied voltage $v$ is related to current $i$ as below,

$$v = L\frac{di}{dt}$$

Fig. 5.1.1 shows two coils (1) and (2) share a common path for the magnetic flux $\phi$.

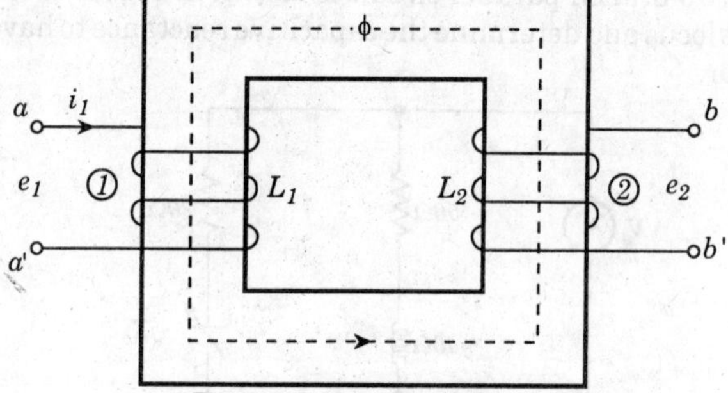


Fig. 5.1.1. Mutual Inductance

The time varying magnetic flux $\phi$ established by the current $i_1$ in coil (1) is shared by coil (2). The induced *e.m.f.* $e_2$ in coil (2) is proportional to the rate of change of current $\frac{di_1}{dt}$ in coil (1), *i.e.*

$$e_2 = M_{21}\frac{di_1}{dt}$$

where $M_{21}$ is the coefficient of mutual inductance between coil (1) and (2) indicating the effect of coil (1) on (2).

Similarly, the rate of change of current $\frac{di_2}{dt}$ in coil (2) produce mutually induced e.m.f. $e_1$ in coil (1), *i.e.*

$$e_1 = M_{12}\frac{di_2}{dt}$$

$$M = M_{12} = M_{21}$$

The magnitude of the mutually induced *e.m.f.* depends on the coefficient of mutual inductance $M$. The unit of $M$ is henry.

The direction of mutually induced e.m.f. depends on the relative winding sense (direction) of mutally coupled coils sharing a common magnetic flux. The mutually induced e.m.f in an inductor may be +ive (voltage drop) or –ive (voltage rise) as per the magnetic fluxes produced by coupled coils are adding or opposing.

## 5.2 DOT CONVENTION

The dot convention described below is used for identifying the direction of mutually induced e.m.f. The terminals having same polarity are marked with a dot (•).

Fig. 5.2.1 shows a magnetic core wound with two coils. As seen from the top end, the coil (1) is wound in clockwise direction and coil (2) anticlockwise.

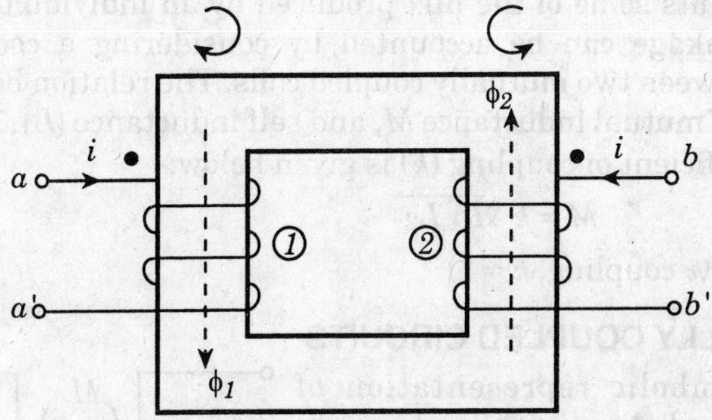


Fig. 5.2.1. Dot convention (magnetic fluxes adding)

1. The current $i$ entering at terminal "α" in coil (1) flows in the clockwise direction. Hence, as per *RH* thumb rule, the flux $\phi_1$ is directed downwards.
2. The current entering at terminal "$b$" in coil (2) flows in anticlockwise direction. Hence, as per *RH* thumb rule, the flux $\phi_2$ is directed upwards.

The two fluxes $\phi_1$ and $\phi_2$ are additive. Therefore, terminals "$a$" and "$b$" have the same polarity and identified by placing a dot (•) on the same.

(The terminals $a'$ and $b'$ also have the same polarity. The dot (•) can be placed either on $a$ and $b$ or $a'$ and $b'$.)

Fig. 5.2.2 shows two coils sharing a common magnetic flux path. The coils are wound such that they produce opposing magnetic fluxes. The currents entering terminals "$a$" and "$b$" produce magnetic fluxes

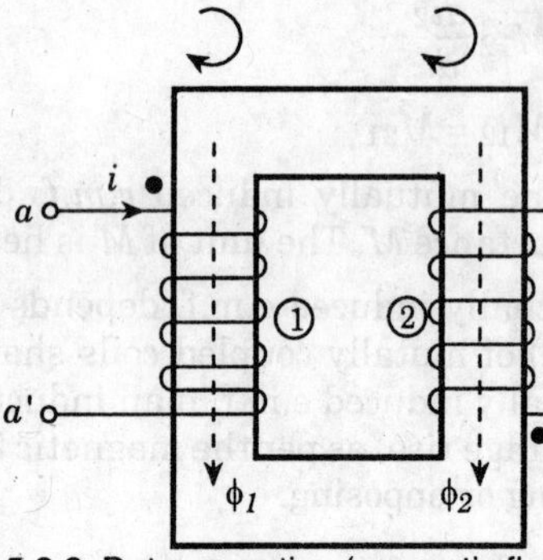

Fig. 5.2.2. Dot convention (magnetic fluxes opposing)

$\phi_1$ and $\phi_2$ respectively which are opposing each other. There terminals $a$ and $b'$ having same polarity are marked with a dot (•).

### Coefficient of Coupling

In the case of mutual inductance, it is assumed that the flux produced by one coil links completely with another coil. In practical coupled circuits some of the flux produced by an individual coil leaks and this leakage can be accounted by considering a coefficient of coupling between two mutually coupled coils. The relation between the coefficient of mutual inductance $M$, and self inductance ($L_1$, $L_2$) of each coil and coefficient of coupling ($k$) is given below:-

$$M = k\sqrt{L_1 L_2}$$

(For 100% coupling, $k = 1$)

## 5.3 MUTUALLY COUPLED CIRCUITS

The symbolic representation of mutually coupled network is shown in Fig. 5.3.1.

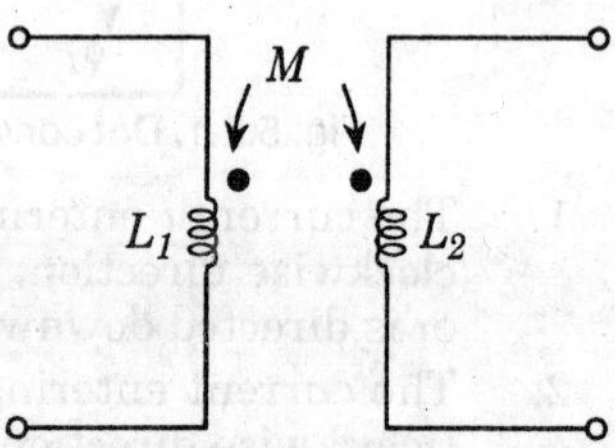

Fig. 5.3.1. Mutually coupled network

The polarity of mutually induced *e.m.f.* is decided as below.

1. In mutually coupled inductors, if both the dots have entering/leaving currents, then a +*ive* sign is placed prior to $M$, *i.e.* $M$ has the same sign as that of voltage drop due to current flowing in the respective inductor.
2. If one of the dots has entering current while other leaving current, the a –ive sign is placed prior to $M$, *i.e.* $M$ has a opposite sign as that of voltage drop due to current flowing in the respective inductor.

The application of dot convention for writing Kirchhoff's law equations for a mutually coupled network shown in Fig. 5.3.2 is given below:

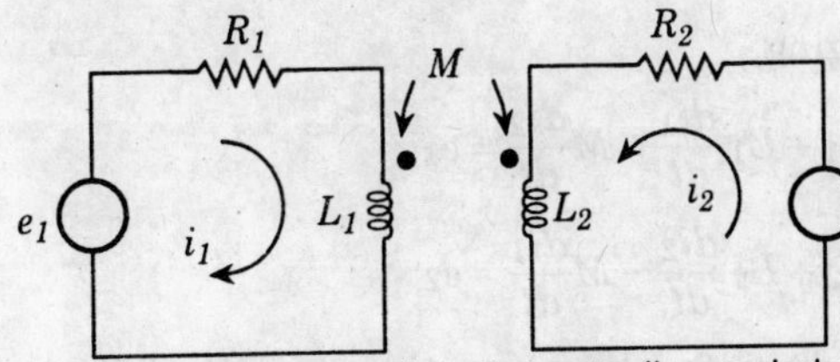


Fig. 5.3.2. Network equations for mutually coupled circuit (entering current at dots).

The currents $i_1$ and $i_2$ are entering the dots, therefore, the coeff. of mutual inductance, is $+M$. As per Kirchhoff's voltage law the network equation are,

$$\text{Loop no. 1} : R_1 i_1 + L_1 \frac{di_1}{dt} + M \frac{di_2}{dt} - e_1 = 0$$

$$\text{Loop no. 2} : R_2 i_2 + L_2 \frac{di_2}{dt} + M \frac{di_1}{dt} - e_2 = 0$$

On rearranging,

$$R_1 i_1 + L_1 \frac{di_1}{dt} + M \frac{di_1}{dt} = e_1$$

$$R_2 i_2 + L_2 \frac{di_2}{dt} + M \frac{di_1}{dt} = e_2$$

For a.c. steady state above equations take the following form :

$$R_1 I_1 + j\omega L_1 I_1 + j\omega M I_2 = E_1$$

$$R_2 I_2 + j\omega L_2 I_2 + j\omega M I_1 = E_2$$

In Fig. 5.3.3, the current $i$, enters the dot and the current $i_2$ leaves the dot. Hence, the coeff. of mutual inductance is $-M$

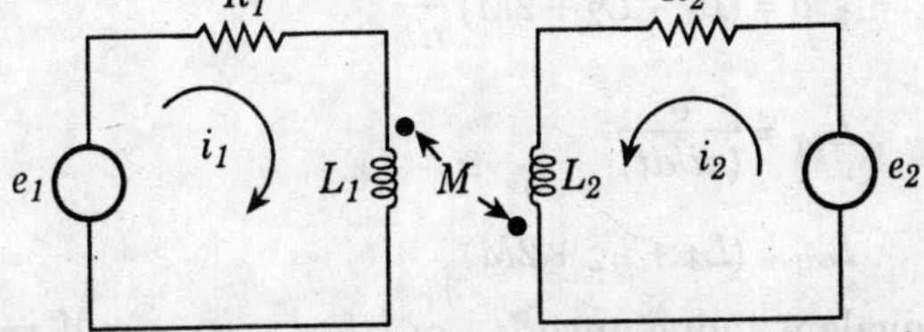


Fig. 5.3.3. Network equations for mutually coupled circuit (current $i_1$ enters the dot and current $i_2$ leaves the dot.)

The network equations based on Kirchhoff's voltage law are written below.

$$\text{Loop no. 1} : R_1 i_1 + L_1 \frac{di_1}{dt} - M \frac{di_2}{dt} - e_1 = 0$$

$$\text{Loop no. 2} : R_2 i_2 + L_2 \frac{di_1}{dt} - M \frac{di_1}{dt} - e_2 = 0$$

On rearranging,

$$R_1 i_1 + L_1 \frac{di_1}{dt} - M\frac{di_2}{dt} = e_1$$

$$R_2 i_2 + L_2 \frac{di_2}{dt} - M\frac{di_1}{dt} = e_2$$

For *a.c.* steady state, above equations take the following form,

$$R_1 I_1 + j\,\omega\, L_1 I_1 - j\,\omega\, M\, I_2 = E_1$$

$$R_2 I_2 + j\,\omega\, L_2 I_2 - j\,\omega\, M\, I_1 = E_2$$

## 5.4 SERIES CONNECTION OF MUTUALLY COUPLED COILS

(*i*) Fig. 5.4.1 shows two inductively coupled coils connected in series with polarity indicated by dots.

The self inductances of coils are $L_1$ and $L_2$ respectively. The current $i$ enters the dots. Hence, the coeff. of mutual inductance is $+M$ (adding fluxes).

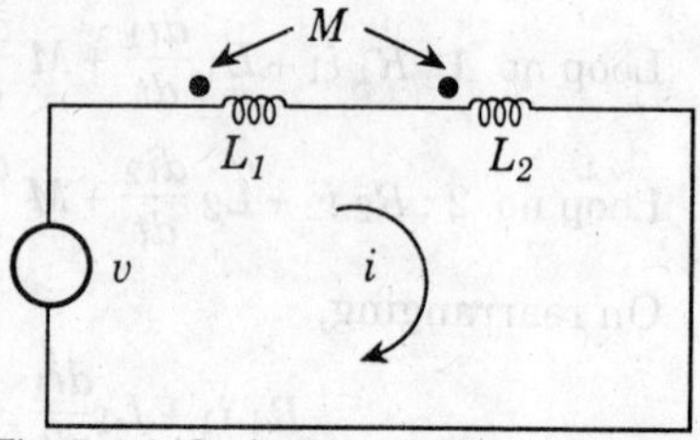

Fig. 5.4.1. Series connection of coupled coils (adding fluxes)

The series connection of the coils is connected to a supply voltage $v$, the current $i$ flows in the coils. Applying Kirchhoff's voltage law,

$$v = L_1 \frac{di}{dt} + L_2 \frac{di}{dt} + \underbrace{M \frac{di}{dt}}_{\text{effect of } L_1 \text{ on } L_2} + \underbrace{M\frac{di}{dt}}_{\text{effect of } L_2 \text{ on } L_1}$$

On rearranging,

$$v = (L_1 + L_2 + 2M)\,\frac{di}{dt}$$

$$\therefore \qquad L_{eq} = \frac{v}{(di/dt)}$$

$$\therefore \qquad L_{eq} = (L_1 + L_2 + 2M)$$

(The equivalent inductance $L_{eq}$ of the series coupled coils as shown in Fig. 5.4.1 is more than the sum of self inductance of individual coils. This series connection is cumulative coupled.)

(*ii*) Fig. 5.4.2 shows two inductively coupled coils connected in series with polarity indicated by dots.

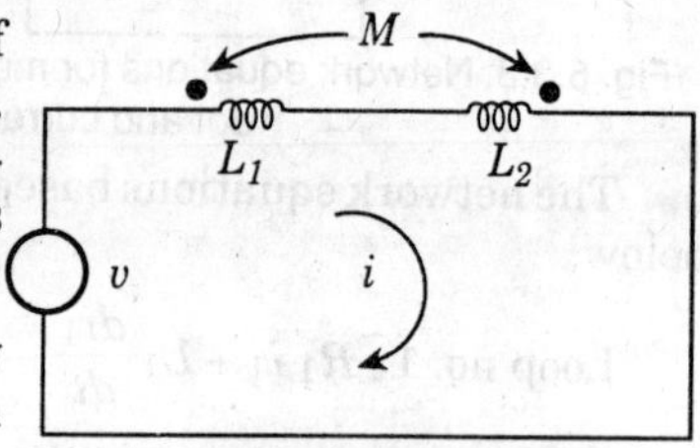

Fig. 5.4.2. Series connections of mutually coupled coils (opposing fluxes).

The two coils are connected such that the current in one coil enters the dot while in other leaves the dot. This produces opposing fluxes. Hence the coeff. of mutual inductance is $-M$.

The series connection of the coils is connected to a supply voltage $v$, the current $i$ flows in the coils. Applying Kirchhoff's current law.

$$v = L_1 \frac{di}{dt} + L_2 \frac{di}{dt} - M \frac{di}{dt} - M \frac{di}{dt}$$

On rearranging,

$$v = (L_1 + L_2 - 2M) \frac{di}{dt}$$

$$\because \quad L_{eq} = \frac{v}{(di/dt)}$$

$$\therefore \quad L_{eq} = L_1 + L_2 - 2M$$

(The equivalent inductance $L_{eq}$ of the series coupled coils as shown in Fig. 5.4.2 is less than the sum of self inductances of individual coils. This series connection is differential coupled.)

## 5.5 PARALLEL CONNECTION OF MUTUALLY COUPLED COILS

A parallel circuit consisting of two inductively coupled coils with polarities indicated by dots is shown in Fig. 5.5.1.

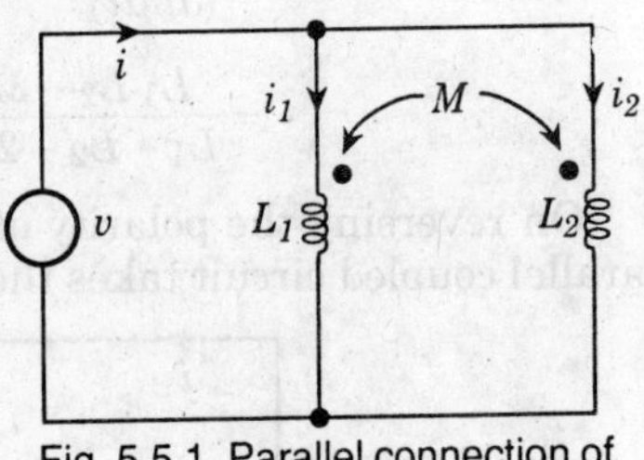

Fig. 5.5.1. Parallel connection of coupled coils (Adding flux)

The self inductances of coils are $L_1$ and $L_2$ respectively. The voltage applied to the combination is $v$, the total current drawn is $i = i_1 + i_2$ where $i_1$ and $i_2$ are branch currents.

Applying Kirchhoff's voltage law following loop equations are written,

$$\text{Loop no. 1}: v = L_1 \frac{di_1}{dt} + M \frac{di_2}{dt}$$

$$\text{Loop no. 2}: v = L_2 \frac{di_2}{dt} + M \frac{di_1}{dt}$$

+ sign is prefixed to $M$ as the currents $i_1$ and $i_2$ are entering respective dots.

On rearranging above equations are arranged as

$$\begin{vmatrix} L_1 & M \\ M & L_2 \end{vmatrix} \begin{vmatrix} \frac{di_1}{dt} \\ \frac{di_2}{dt} \end{vmatrix} = \begin{vmatrix} v \\ v \end{vmatrix}$$

$$\therefore \qquad \frac{di_1}{dt} = \frac{\begin{vmatrix} v & M \\ v & L_2 \end{vmatrix}}{\begin{vmatrix} L_1 & M \\ M & L_2 \end{vmatrix}} = \frac{v\,(L_2 - M)}{L_1 L_2 - M^2}$$

and
$$\frac{di_2}{dt} = \frac{\begin{vmatrix} L_1 & v \\ M & v \end{vmatrix}}{\begin{vmatrix} L_1 & M \\ M & L_2 \end{vmatrix}} = \frac{v\,(L_1 - M)}{L_1 L_2 - M^2}$$

$$\because \qquad i = i_1 + i_2$$

$$\therefore \qquad \frac{di}{dt} = \frac{di_1}{dt} + \frac{di_2}{dt}$$

or
$$\frac{di}{dt} = \frac{v\,(L_2 - M)}{L_1 L_2 - M^2} + \frac{v\,(L_1 - M)}{L_1 L_2 - M^2}$$

or
$$\frac{di}{dt} = \frac{v\,(L_1 + L_2 - 2M)}{L_1 L_2 - M^2}$$

$$L_{eq} = \frac{v}{(di/dt)}$$

$$= \frac{L_1 L_2 - M^2}{L_1 + L_2 - 2\,M} \quad \text{(cumulative coupled)}$$

On reversing the polarity of one of the the coils in Fig. 5.5.1, the parallel coupled circuit takes the form as shown in Fig. 5.5.2.

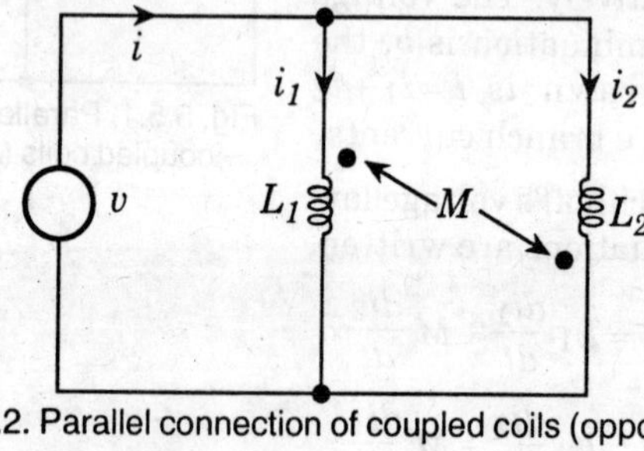


Fig. 5.5.2. Parallel connection of coupled coils (opposing flux)

Applying Kirchhoff's voltage law, following equations are written,

Loop no. 1 : $v = L_1 \dfrac{di_1}{dt} - M \dfrac{di_2}{dt}$

Loop no. 2 : $v = L_2 \dfrac{di_2}{dt} - M \dfrac{di_1}{dt}$

– sign is prefixed to $M$, as the current $i_1$ is entering the dot while $i_2$ leaves the dot.

On rearranging above equations

$$\begin{vmatrix} L_1 & -M \\ -M & L_2 \end{vmatrix} \begin{vmatrix} \frac{di_1}{dt} \\ \frac{di_2}{dt} \end{vmatrix} = \begin{vmatrix} v \\ v \end{vmatrix}$$

$$\therefore \quad \frac{di_1}{dt} = \frac{\begin{vmatrix} v & -M \\ v & L_2 \end{vmatrix}}{\begin{vmatrix} L_1 & -M \\ -M & L_2 \end{vmatrix}} = \frac{v\,(L_2 + M)}{L_1 L_2 - M^2}$$

and
$$\frac{di_2}{dt} = \frac{\begin{vmatrix} L_1 & v \\ -M & v \end{vmatrix}}{\begin{vmatrix} L_1 & -M \\ -M & L_2 \end{vmatrix}} = \frac{v\,(L_1 + M)}{L_1 L_2 - M^2}$$

$$\because \quad i = i_1 + i_2$$

$$\therefore \quad \frac{di}{dt} = \frac{di_1}{dt} + \frac{di_2}{dt}$$

or
$$\frac{di}{dt} = \frac{v\,(L_2 + M)}{L_1 L_2 - M^2} + \frac{v\,(L_1 + M)}{L_1 L_2 - M^2}$$

or
$$\frac{di}{dt} = \frac{v\,(L_1 + L_2 + 2M)}{L_1 L_2 - M_2}$$

$$L_{eq} = \frac{v}{(di/dt)} = \frac{L_1 L_2 - M^2}{L_1 + L_2 + 2\,M} \quad \text{(differential coupled)}$$

## 5.6 CONDUCTIVELY COUPLED EQUIVALENT CIRCUIT

An inductively coupled circuit is shown in Fig. 5.6.1.

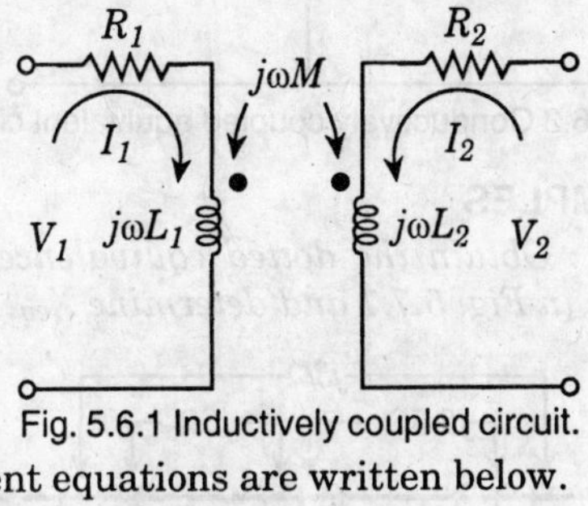


Fig. 5.6.1 Inductively coupled circuit.

The loop current equations are written below.

$$R_1\,\mathbf{I}_1 + j\,\omega\,L_1\,\mathbf{I}_1 + j\,\omega\,M\,\mathbf{I}_2 = \mathbf{V}_1$$

$$R_2\,\mathbf{I}_2 + j\,\omega\,L_2\,\mathbf{I}_2 + j\,\omega\,M\,\mathbf{I}_1 = \mathbf{V}_2$$

+ sign is prefixed to $M$ as the currents $I_1$ and $I_2$ are entering the respective dots.

On rearranging above set of equations,

$$\begin{bmatrix} R_1 + j\,\omega\,L_1 & j\,\omega\,M \\ j\,\omega\,M & R_2 + j\,\omega\,L_2 \end{bmatrix} \begin{bmatrix} \mathbf{I}_1 \\ \mathbf{I}_2 \end{bmatrix} = \begin{bmatrix} \mathbf{V}_1 \\ \mathbf{V}_2 \end{bmatrix}$$

Let, the equivalent conductively coupled circuit be as shown in Fig. 5.6.2.

The corresponding loop current equations are

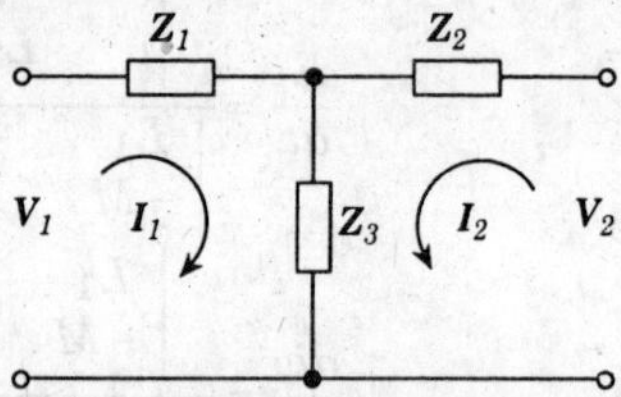

Fig. 5.6.2. Conductively coupled circuit.

$$\begin{bmatrix} \mathbf{Z}_1 + \mathbf{Z}_3 & \mathbf{Z}_3 \\ \mathbf{Z}_3 & \mathbf{Z}_2 + \mathbf{Z}_3 \end{bmatrix} \begin{bmatrix} \mathbf{I}_1 \\ \mathbf{I}_2 \end{bmatrix} = \begin{bmatrix} \mathbf{V}_1 \\ \mathbf{V}_2 \end{bmatrix}$$

On comparing,

(*i*) $$\mathbf{Z}_1 + \mathbf{Z}_3 = R_1 + j\,\omega\,L_1$$

and $$\mathbf{Z}_3 = j\,\omega\,M$$

$\therefore$ $$\mathbf{Z}_1 = R_1 + j\,\omega\,(L_1 - M)\ldots(L_1 > M)$$

(*ii*) $$\mathbf{Z}_2 + \mathbf{Z}_3 = R_2 + j\,\omega\,L_2$$

$\therefore$ $$\mathbf{Z}_2 = R_2 + j\,\omega\,(L_2 - M)\ldots(L_2 > M)$$

The conductively coupled equivalent circuit for Fig. 5.6.1 is shown in Fig. 5.6.3 below,

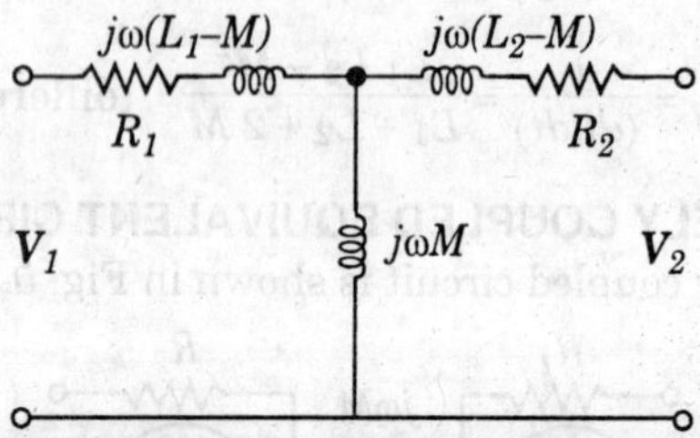

Fig. 5.6.3 Conductively coupled equivalent circuit.

## 5.7 SOLVED EXAMPLES

**Example 5.7.1:** *Obtain the dotted equivalence for the mutually coupled coils shown in Fig. 5.7.1 and determine $X_{eq}$*

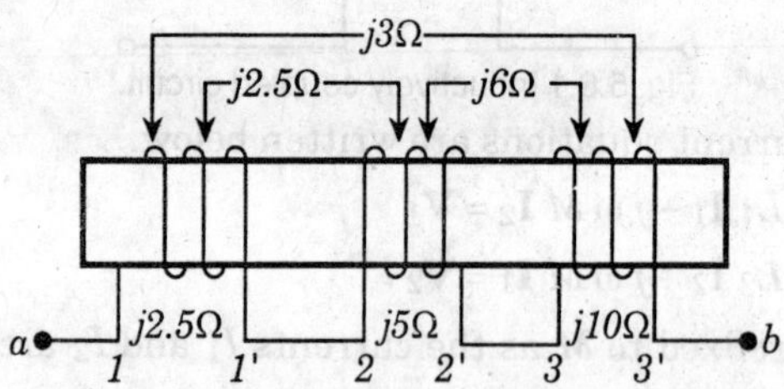

Fig. 5.7.1. Coil arrangement for example 5.7.1

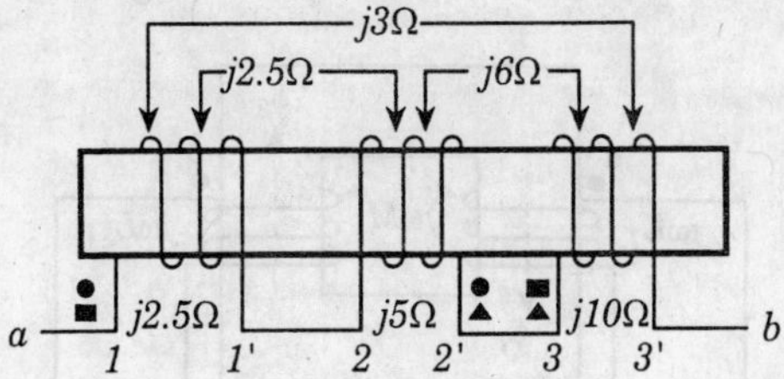


Fig. 5.7.1 (*a*) Coil arrangement with dot placement.

1. Coil nos. 1 and 2 are wound in opposite directions, produce opposing fluxes. Hence, terminals 1 and 2′ have same polarity (•).
2. Coil nos. 2 and 3 are wound in opposite directions, produce opposing fluxes. Hence, terminals 2′ and 3 have same polarity (Δ).
3. Coil nos. 3 and 1 are wound in same direction produce adding fluxes. Hence, terminals 3 and 1 have the same polarity (■).

The coil are connected in series. The equivalent reactance $X_{ab}$ is determined below.

$$j\,X_{eq} = (j\,2.5 + j\,5 + 10) - j\,2 \times 2.5 - j\,2 \times 6 + j\,2 \times 3$$

or $$X_{eq} = 6.5\ \Omega \quad \textbf{Ans.}$$

**Example 5.7.2.** *For the arrangement shown in Fig. 5.7.2 obtain the dotted equivalent circuit and write the mesh current equations.*

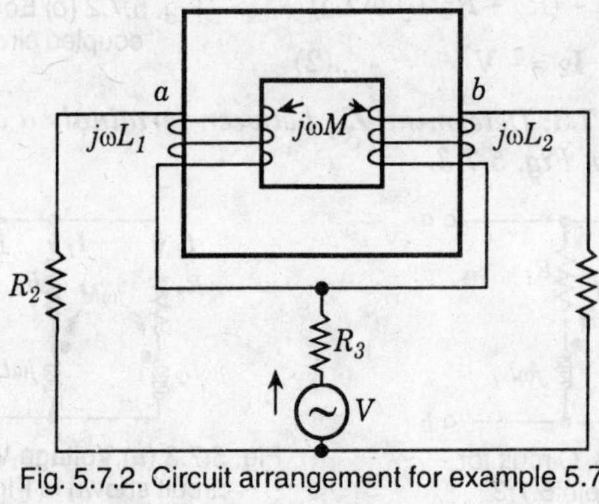


Fig. 5.7.2. Circuit arrangement for example 5.7.2

**Solution:** On entering the current at the terminals *a* and *b* in coils 1 and 2 respectively, the fluxes produced are additive.

Therefore, the terminals *a* and *b* have the same polarity (•).as shown in Fig. 5.7.2 (*a*).

The equivalent coupled circuit is shown in Fig. 5.7.2 (*b*) with selected mesh currents.

Mesh current equations for the circuit (Fig. 5.7.2*b*) are written below,

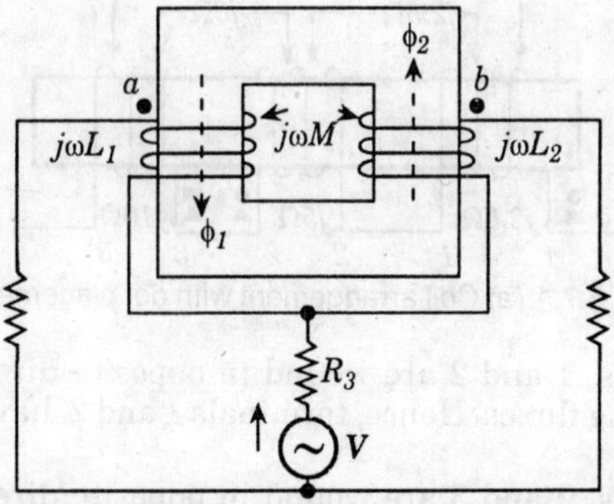

Fig. 5.7.2 (*a*) Circuit arrangement with dot placement.

Mesh no .1 : $R_1\,\mathbf{I}_1 - \mathbf{V} + R_3 +$

$(\mathbf{I}_1 - \mathbf{I}_2) + j\,\omega L_1 \mathbf{I}_1 - j\,\omega\,M\,\mathbf{I}_2 = 0$

Mesh no. 2 : $R_2\,\mathbf{I}_2 + j\,\omega\,L_2\,\mathbf{I}_2$

$+ R_3\,(\mathbf{I}_2 - \mathbf{I}_1) + \mathbf{V} - j\,\omega\,M\,\mathbf{I}_1 = 0$

On rearranging,

$(R_1 + R_3 + j\,\omega\,L_1)\,\mathbf{I}_1$

$-\,(R_3 + j\,\omega\,M)\,\mathbf{I}_2 = \mathbf{V}$ ...(1)

$-\,(R_3 + j\,\omega\,M)\,\mathbf{I}_1 + (R_2 + R_3 + j\,\omega\,L_2)$

$\mathbf{I}_2 = -\,\mathbf{V}$ ...(2)

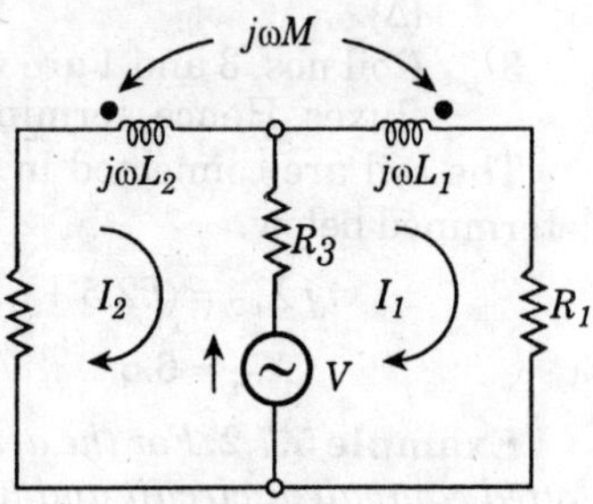

Fig. 5.7.2 (*b*) Equivalent coupled circuit.

**Example 5.7.3:** *Determine* $\mathbf{Z}_{eq}$ *between terminals a and b for the network shown in Fig. 5.7.3.*

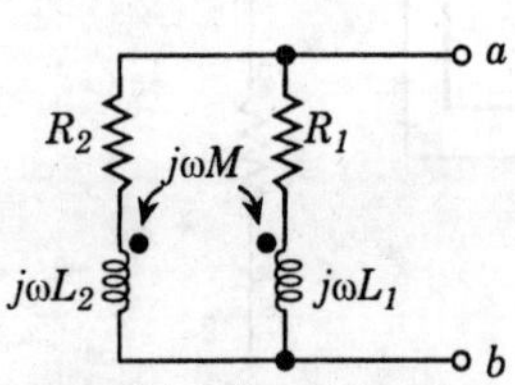

Fig. 5.7.3. Circuit for example 5.7.3

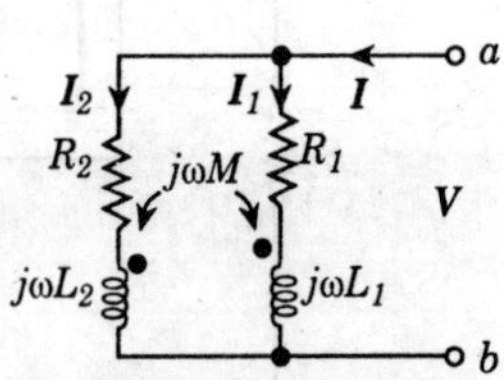

Fig. 5.7.3 (*a*) Voltage **V** applied to circuit shown in FIg. 5.7.3.

**Solution:** Apply voltage **V** at terminals *a* and *b*, the total current drawn by the circuit is **I** *and branch currents* $\mathbf{I}_1$ and $\mathbf{I}_2$.

The loop current equations are written below,

$R_1\,\mathbf{I}_1 + j\,\omega\,L_1\,\mathbf{I}_1 + j\,\omega\,M\,\mathbf{I}_2 = \mathbf{V}$

$R_2\,\mathbf{I}_2 + j\,\omega\,L_2\,\mathbf{I}_2 + j\,\omega\,M\,\mathbf{I}_1 = \mathbf{V}$

+ sign is prefixed to $M$, as the branch currents $\mathbf{I_1}$ and $\mathbf{I_2}$ are entering the respective dots.

On rearranging, mesh currents equations can be represented in determinant form as,

$$\begin{vmatrix} R_1 + j\omega L_1 & j\omega M \\ j\omega M & R_2 + j\omega L_2 \end{vmatrix} \begin{vmatrix} \mathbf{I_1} \\ \mathbf{I_2} \end{vmatrix} = \begin{vmatrix} \mathbf{V} \\ \mathbf{V} \end{vmatrix}$$

put $\mathbf{Z_1} = R_1 + j\omega L_1$

$\mathbf{Z_2} = R_2 + j\omega L_2$

and $\mathbf{Z}_m = j\omega \mathbf{M}$

$$\therefore \quad \begin{vmatrix} \mathbf{Z_1} & \mathbf{Z}_m \\ \mathbf{Z}_m & \mathbf{Z_2} \end{vmatrix} \begin{vmatrix} \mathbf{I_1} \\ \mathbf{I_2} \end{vmatrix} = \begin{vmatrix} \mathbf{V} \\ \mathbf{V} \end{vmatrix}$$

$$\mathbf{I_1} = \frac{\begin{vmatrix} \mathbf{V} & \mathbf{Z}_m \\ \mathbf{V} & \mathbf{Z_2} \end{vmatrix}}{\begin{vmatrix} \mathbf{Z_1} & \mathbf{Z}_m \\ \mathbf{Z}m & \mathbf{Z_2} \end{vmatrix}}, \quad \mathbf{I_2} = \frac{\begin{vmatrix} \mathbf{Z_1} & \mathbf{V} \\ \mathbf{Z}_m & \mathbf{V} \end{vmatrix}}{\begin{vmatrix} \mathbf{Z_1} & \mathbf{Z}_m \\ \mathbf{Z}_m & \mathbf{Z_2} \end{vmatrix}}$$

$$= \frac{\mathbf{V}(\mathbf{Z_2} - \mathbf{Z}_m)}{\mathbf{Z_1}\mathbf{Z_2} - \mathbf{Z}_m^2} \qquad = \frac{\mathbf{V}(\mathbf{Z_1} - \mathbf{Z}_m)}{\mathbf{Z_1}\mathbf{Z_2} - \mathbf{Z}_m^2}$$

$$\therefore \quad \mathbf{I_1} + \mathbf{I_2} = \frac{\mathbf{V}(\mathbf{Z_1} + \mathbf{Z_2} - 2\,\mathbf{Z}_m)}{\mathbf{Z_1}\mathbf{Z_2} - \mathbf{Z}_m^2}$$

$$\because \quad \mathbf{I} = \mathbf{I_1} + \mathbf{I_2}$$

$$\therefore \quad \mathbf{I} = \frac{\mathbf{V}(\mathbf{Z_1} + \mathbf{Z_2} - 2\,\mathbf{Z}_m)}{\mathbf{Z_1}\mathbf{Z_2} - \mathbf{Z}_m^2}$$

$$\mathbf{Z}_{ab} = \frac{\mathbf{V}}{\mathbf{I}} = \frac{\mathbf{Z_1}\mathbf{Z_2} - \mathbf{Z}_m^2}{\mathbf{Z_1} + \mathbf{Z_2} - 2\,\mathbf{Z}_m} \quad \textbf{Ans.}$$

**Example 5.7.4.** *A mutually coupled circuit is shown in Fig. 5.7.4. Write Maxwell's mesh current equations.*

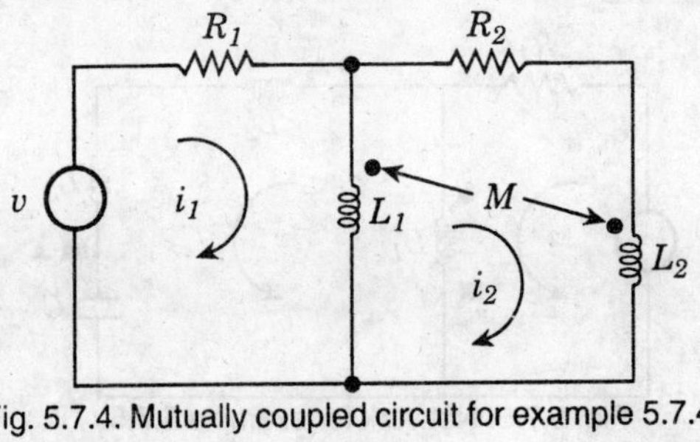


Fig. 5.7.4. Mutually coupled circuit for example 5.7.4.

**Solution:** The effect of mutual inductance is as follows:

Mesh no. 1. **Effect of $L_2$ on $L_1$**

The current $(i_1 - i_2)$ enters the dot (•) in $L_1$.

The current $i_2$ enters the dot (•) in $L_2$.

Therefore, $+M_{12}\dfrac{di_2}{dt}$ is the effect of $L_2$ on $L_1$.

Maxwell's mesh current equation for mesh no. 1 is written below:

$$R_1 i_1 + L_1\frac{d}{dt}(i_1 - i_2) + M_{12}\frac{di_2}{dt} - v = 0 \quad ...(1)$$

Mesh no. 2. (*a*) **Effect of $L_1$ on $L_2$**

The current $(i_2 - i_1)$ leaves dot (•) in $L_1$.

The current $i_2$ enters the dot (•) in $L_2$.

Therefore, $-M_{21}\dfrac{d}{dt}(i_2 - i_1)$ is the effect of $L_1$ on $L_2$.

(*b*) **Effect of $L_2$ on $L_1$**

The current $i_2$ enters the dot (•) in $L_2$.

The current $(i_2 - i_1)$ leaves the dot (•) in $L_1$.

Therefore, $-M_{12}\dfrac{di_2}{dt}$ is the effect of $L_2$ on $L_1$.

Maxwell's mesh current equation for mesh no. 2 is written below:

$$R_2 i_2 + L_2\frac{di_2}{dt} + L_1\frac{d}{dt}(i_2 - i_1) - M_{21}\frac{d}{dt}(i_2 - i_1) - M_{12}\frac{di_2}{dt} = 0 \quad ...(2)$$

On rearranging Eqns. (1) and (2)

$$R_1 i_1 + L_1\frac{d}{dt}(i_1 - i_2) + M_{12}\frac{di_2}{dt} = v$$

and $R_2 i_2 + L_2\dfrac{di_2}{dt} + L_1\dfrac{d}{dt}(i_2 - i_1) - M_{21}\dfrac{d}{dt}(i_2 - i_1) - M_{12}\dfrac{di_2}{dt} = 0$ **Ans.**

**Example 5.7.5:** *Write Maxwell's mesh current equations, the network is shown in Fig. 5.7.5.* ($M_{12} = M_{21}$, $M_{23} = M_{32}$ and $M_{31} = M_{13}$)

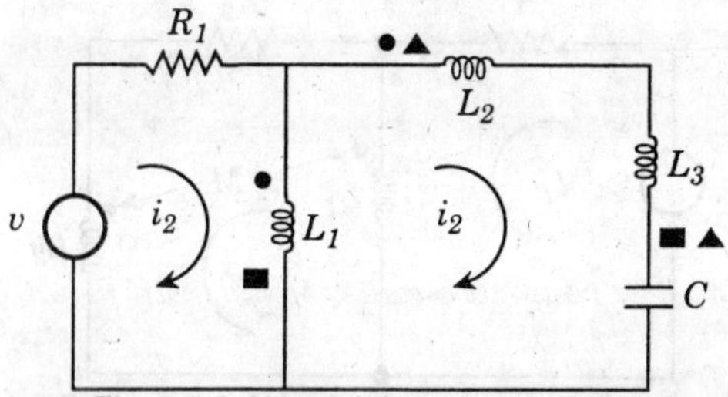


Fig. 5.7.5. Network for example 5.7.5.

**Solution:** (*a*) In mesh no. (1), mutual effect of $L_2$ on $L_1$ ($M_{12}$) and that of $L_3$ on $L_1$ ($M_{13}$) is to be considered.

(*b*) In mesh no. (2), the following mutual effects are to be considered.

(1) effect of $L_2$ on $L_1$ ($M_{12}$)
(2) effect of $L_3$ on $L_1$ ($M_{13}$)
(3) effect of $L_3$ on $L_2$ ($M_{23}$)
(4) effect of $L_1$ on $L_2$ ($M_{21}$)
(5) effect of $L_1$ on $L_3$ ($M_{31}$)
(6) effect of $L_2$ on $L_3$ ($M_{32}$)

Mesh no. 1 :

$$R_1 i_1 + L_1 \frac{d}{dt}(i_1 - i_2) + M_{12}\frac{di_2}{dt} + M_{13}\frac{di_2}{dt} - v = 0 \qquad ...(1)$$

$M_{12}\frac{di_2}{dt}$ ↓ $i_2$ enters □ at $L_2$, $(i_1 - i_2)$ enters □ at $L_1$,

$M_{13}\frac{di_2}{dt}$ ↓ $i_2$ leaves □ at $L_3$, $(i_1 - i_2)$ leaves □ *at* $L_1$

Mesh no. 2 :

$$L_1\frac{d}{dt}(i_2 - i_1) + L_2\frac{di_2}{dt} + L_3\frac{di_2}{dt} + \frac{1}{C}\int i_2\,dt - M_{12}\frac{di_2}{dt}$$

$- M_{12}\frac{di_2}{dt}$ ↓ $i_2$ enters• at $L_2$, $(i_2 - i_1)$ leaves• at $L_1$

$$- M_{13}\frac{di_2}{dt} \qquad - M_{23}\frac{di_2}{dt} \qquad - M_{21}\frac{d}{dt}(i_2 - i_1)$$

$- M_{13}\frac{di_2}{dt}$ ↓ $i_2$ leaves□ at $L_3$, $(i_2 - i_1)$ enters□ at $L_1$

$- M_{23}\frac{di_2}{dt}$ ↓ $i_2$ leavesΔ at $L_3$, $i_2$ entersΔ at $L_2$

$- M_{21}\frac{d}{dt}(i_2 - i_1)$ ↓ $(i_2 - i_1)$ leaves• at $L_1$, $i_2$ enters• at $L_2$

$$- M_{31}\frac{d}{dt}(i_2 - i_1) \qquad - M_{32}\frac{di_2}{dt} \qquad = 0 \qquad ...(2)$$

$- M_{31}\frac{d}{dt}(i_2 - i_1)$ ↓ $(i_2 - i_1)$ enters□ at $L_1$, $i_2$ leaves□ at $L_3$

$- M_{32}\frac{di_2}{dt}$ ↓ $i_2$ leavesΔ at $L_3$, $i_2$ entersΔ at $L_2$

On rearranging Eqns. (1) and (2),

$$R_1 i_1 + L_1\frac{di}{dt}(i_1 - i_2) + M_{12}\frac{di_2}{dt} + M_{13}\frac{di_2}{dt} = v$$

and $$L_1\frac{d}{dt}(i_2 - i_1) + L_2\frac{di_2}{dt} + L_3\frac{di_2}{dt} + \frac{1}{C}\int idt - M_{12}\frac{di_2}{dt} - M_{13}\frac{di_2}{dt}$$

$$- M_{23}\frac{di_2}{dt} - M_{21}\frac{d}{dt}(i_2 - i_1) - M_{31}\frac{d}{dt}(i_2 - i_1) - M_{23}\frac{di_2}{dt} = 0 \qquad \textbf{Ans.}$$

**Example 5.7.6:** *The coupled circuit is shown in Fig. 5.7.6. Determine* $\mathbf{V}_2$ *such that* $\mathbf{I}_1 = 0$.

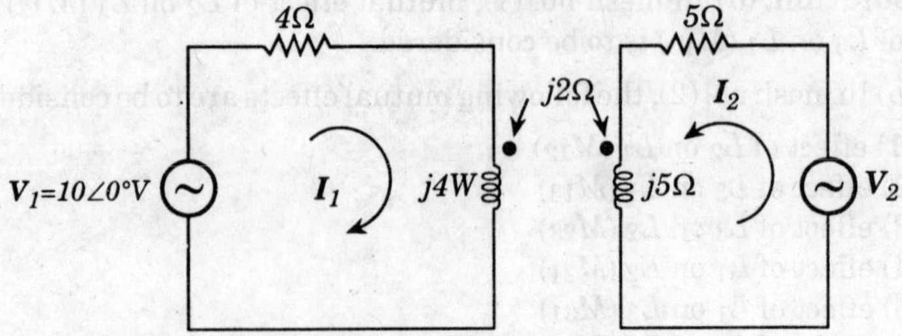


Fig. 5.7.6. Network for example 5.7.6.

**Solution:** The mesh current equations are written below,

$$(4 + j\,4)\,\mathbf{I_1} + j\,2\,\mathbf{I_2} = 10 \angle 0°$$

$$j\,2\,\mathbf{I_1} + (5 + j\,5)\,\mathbf{I_2} = \mathbf{V_2}$$

or
$$\begin{vmatrix} 4 + j\,4 & j\,2 \\ j\,2 & 5 + j\,5 \end{vmatrix} \begin{vmatrix} \mathbf{I_1} \\ \mathbf{I_2} \end{vmatrix} = \begin{vmatrix} 10 \angle 0° \\ \mathbf{V_2} \end{vmatrix}$$

$\therefore$
$$\mathbf{I_1} = \frac{\begin{vmatrix} 10 \angle 0° & j\,2 \\ \mathbf{V_2} & 5 + j\,5 \end{vmatrix}}{\begin{vmatrix} 4 + j\,4 & j\,2 \\ j\,2 & 5 + j\,5 \end{vmatrix}}$$

$\because$ $\mathbf{I_1} = 0$

$\therefore$
$$\begin{vmatrix} 10 \angle 0° & j\,2 \\ \mathbf{V_2} & 5 + j\,5 \end{vmatrix} = 0$$

or
$$10 \angle 0° \times (5 + j\,5) - j\,2\mathbf{V_2} = 0$$

$\therefore$
$$\mathbf{V_2} = \frac{10 \times 5\sqrt{2} \angle 45°}{j\,2}$$

$$= \frac{50\sqrt{2} \angle 45°}{2 \angle 90°}$$

$\therefore$
$$\mathbf{V_2} = 25\sqrt{2} \angle -45° \quad \textbf{Ans.}$$

**Example 5.7.7:** *The coupled circuit is shown in Fig. 5.7.7. (i) Determine the current in 6 Ω resistor (ii) obtain conductively coupled circuit.*

**Solution:** (*i*)
$$k = \frac{M}{\sqrt{L_1 L_2}}$$

$\therefore$
$$M = k\sqrt{L_1 L_2}$$

$$= 0.5\sqrt{2 \times 8} = 2$$

or
$$j\,\omega\,M = j\,1 \times 2 = j\,2\,\Omega$$

The mesh current equations are,

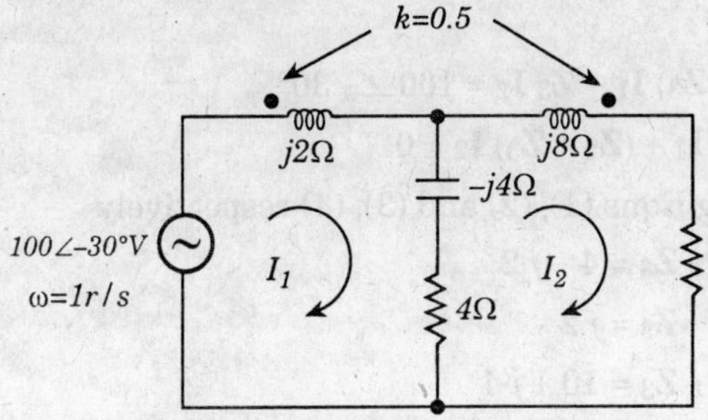


Fig. 5.7.7. Circuit for example 5.7.7.

Mesh no. 1 : $(j\,2 + 4 - j\,4)\,\mathbf{I_1} - j\,2\,\mathbf{I_2} = 100\angle-30°$

Mesh no. 2 : $(4 - j\,4 + j\,8 + 6)\,\mathbf{I_1} - j\,2\,\mathbf{I_2} = 0$

or $(4 - j\,2)\,\mathbf{I_1} - j\,2\,\mathbf{I_2} = 100\angle-30°$ ...(1)

and $-j\,2\,\mathbf{I_1} + (10 + j\,4)\,\mathbf{I_2} = 0$ ...(2)

The current $\mathbf{I_1}$ is entering and $\mathbf{I_2}$ leaving the respective dots. Hence, –sign is prefixed to mutual inductance $j\,2\,\Omega$.

On rearranging above equations

$$\begin{vmatrix} 4-j\,2 & -j\,2 \\ -j\,2 & 10+j\,4 \end{vmatrix} \begin{vmatrix} \mathbf{I_1} \\ \mathbf{I_2} \end{vmatrix} = \begin{vmatrix} 100\angle-30° \\ 0 \end{vmatrix}$$

$$\therefore \qquad \mathbf{I_2} = \frac{\begin{vmatrix} 4-j\,2 & 100\angle-30° \\ -j\,2 & 0 \end{vmatrix}}{\begin{vmatrix} 4-j\,2 & -j\,2 \\ -j\,2 & 10+j\,4 \end{vmatrix}}$$

$$= \frac{+j\,2 \times 100\angle-30°}{(4-j\,2)(10+j\,4) - (-j\,2)(-j\,2)}$$

$$= \frac{2\angle 90° \times 100\angle-30°}{52.08\angle-4.33°} = \frac{200\angle 60°}{52.08° - 4.33°}$$

$$= 3.84\angle 64.33°$$

$\therefore$ $I_2 = 3.84$ A. **Ans.**

(*ii*) Let, the conductively coupled circuit corresponding to Eqn. (1) and (2) be as shown in Fig. 5.7.7 (*a*).

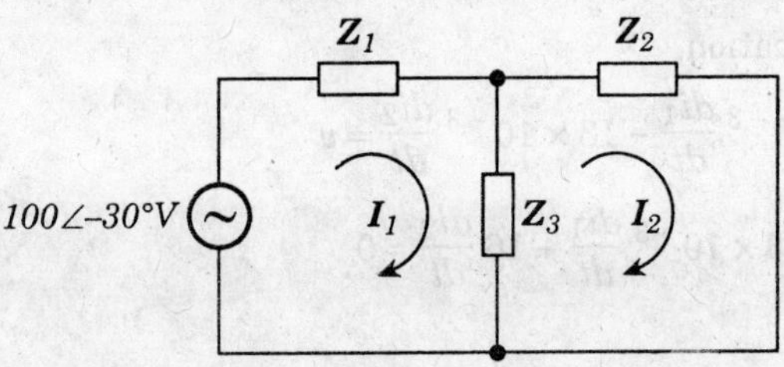


Fig. 5.7.7 (*a*) Conductively coupled equivalent circuit.

The mesh current equations for the conductively coupled circuit are written below,

$$(\mathbf{Z_1} + \mathbf{Z_3})\,\mathbf{I_1} - \mathbf{Z_3}\,\mathbf{I_2} = 100 \angle -30° \qquad ...(3)$$

$$-\mathbf{Z_3}\,\mathbf{I_1} + (\mathbf{Z_2} + \mathbf{Z_3})\,\mathbf{I_2} = 0 \qquad ...(4)$$

On comparing Eqns.(1), (2) and (3), (4) respectively

$$\mathbf{Z_1} + \mathbf{Z_3} = 4 - j\,2$$

$$\mathbf{Z_3} = j\,2$$

$$\mathbf{Z_2} + \mathbf{Z_3} = 10 + j\,4$$

$$\therefore \quad \mathbf{Z_1} = (4 - j\,4)\,\Omega$$

$$\mathbf{Z_2} = (10 + j\,2)\,\Omega$$

$$\mathbf{Z_3} = j\,2\,\Omega \qquad \textbf{Ans.}$$

**Example 5.7.8:** *Determine the equivalent inductance $L_{eq}$ between terminals a and b for the network shown in Fig. 5.7.8.$L_1$ =* 4mH

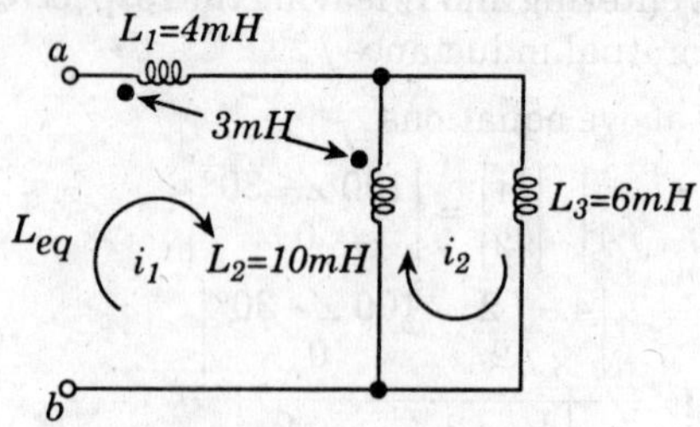


Fig. 5.7.8. Network for example 5.7.8.

**Solution:** On applying voltage $v$ across the terminals $a$ and $b$, the mesh current equations are written below,

$$\text{Mesh no. 1}: 4 \times 10^{-3}\frac{di_1}{dt} + 10 \times 10^{-3}\frac{d}{dt}(i_1 - i_2) + 3 \times 10^{-3}\frac{di_1}{dt}$$

$$+ 3 \times 10^{-3}\frac{d}{dt}(i_1 - i_2) = v$$

Mesh no. 2 :

$$6 \times 10^{-3}\frac{di_2}{dt} + 10 \times 10^{-3}\frac{d}{dt}(i_2 - i_1) - 3 \times 10^{-3}\frac{di_1}{dt} = 0$$

On simplification,

$$20 \times 10^{-3}\frac{di_1}{dt} - 13 \times 10^{-3}\frac{di_2}{dt} = v$$

$$-13 \times 10^{-3}\frac{di_1}{dt} + 16\frac{di_2}{dt} = 0$$

or
$$\begin{vmatrix} 20\times 10^{-3} & -13\times 10^{-3} \\ -13\times 10^{-3} & 16\times 10^{-3} \end{vmatrix} \begin{vmatrix} di_1/dt \\ di_2/dt \end{vmatrix} = \begin{vmatrix} v \\ 0 \end{vmatrix}$$

$$\therefore \quad \frac{di_1}{dt} = \frac{\begin{vmatrix} v & -13\times 10^{-3} \\ 0 & 16\times 10^{-3} \end{vmatrix}}{\begin{vmatrix} 20\times 10^{-3} & -13\times 10^{-3} \\ -13\times 10^{-3} & 16\times 10^{-3} \end{vmatrix}}$$

$$= \frac{v\times 16\times 10^{-3}}{(20\times 10^{-3})(16\times 10^{-3}) - (13\times 10^{-3})(13\times 10^{-3})}$$

$$= \frac{v\ 16\times 10^{-3}}{151\times 10^{-6}}$$

$$L_{eq} = \frac{v}{\dfrac{di_1}{dt}} = \frac{151\times 10^{-3}}{16} = 9.437\times 10^{-3}\ \text{H}$$

or
$$L_{eq} = 9.437\ \text{mH} \quad \textbf{Ans.}$$

**Example 5.7.9.** *Determine the current $I_1$ and $I_2$ in the coupled network shown in Fig. 5.7.9.*

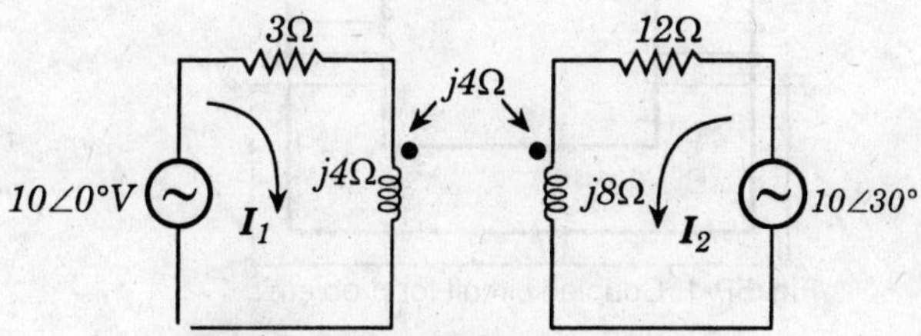


Fig. 5.7.9. Network for example 5.7.9

**Solution:** Applying Kirchhoff's voltage law, mesh current equations are written below,

Mesh no 1 : $(3 + j\,4)\,\mathbf{I}_1 + j\,4\mathbf{I}_2 - 10 \angle 0° = 0$

Mesh no 2 : $j\,4\,\mathbf{I}_1 + (12 + j\,8)\,\mathbf{I}_2 - 10 \angle 30° = 0$

On rearranging,

$$\begin{vmatrix} (3+j\,4) & j\,4 \\ j\,4 & (12+j\,8) \end{vmatrix} \begin{vmatrix} \mathbf{I}_1 \\ \mathbf{I}_2 \end{vmatrix} = \begin{vmatrix} 10\angle 0° \\ 10\angle 30° \end{vmatrix}$$

$$\therefore \quad \mathbf{I}_1 = \frac{\begin{vmatrix} 10\angle 0° & j\,4 \\ 10\angle 30° & 12+j\,8 \end{vmatrix}}{\begin{vmatrix} (3+j\,4) & j\,4 \\ j\,4 & (12+j\,8) \end{vmatrix}}$$

$$= \frac{140 + j\,45.36}{24.62 + j\,71.52} = \frac{147.16 \angle 17.95°}{75.63 \angle 71°}$$

$$= 1.94 \angle -53.05°$$

and
$$\mathbf{I}_2 = \frac{\begin{vmatrix} (3 + j\,4) & 10 \\ j\,4 & 10 \angle 30° \end{vmatrix}}{\begin{vmatrix} (3 + j\,4) & j\,4 \\ j\,4 & (12 + j\,8) \end{vmatrix}}$$

$$= \frac{5.98 + j\,9.6}{24.62 + j\,71.52} = \frac{11.31 \angle 58.08°}{75.63 \angle 71°}$$

$$= 0.149 \angle -12.92°$$

$$I_1 = 1.94 \text{ A}$$

$$I_2 = 0.149 \text{ A} \quad \textbf{Ans.}$$

## PROBLEMS

**5.1.** Draw the dotted equivalence at terminals 1-3 for the coupled circuit shown in Fig. 5P-1.

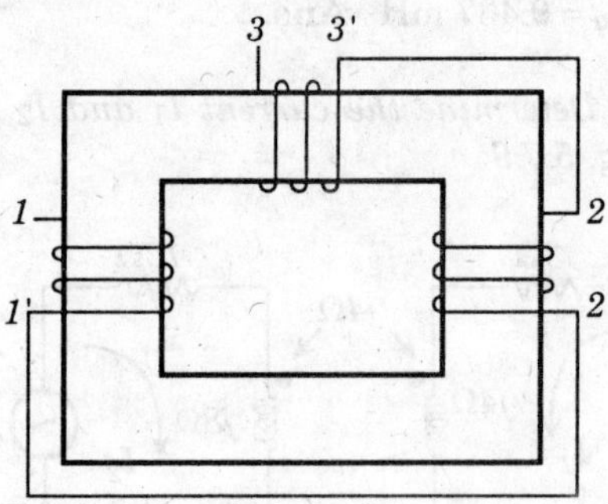

Fig. 5P-1. Coupled circuit for problem 5.1.

**5.2.** In the coupled network given below (Fig. 5P-2) determine the current supplied by the source voltage.

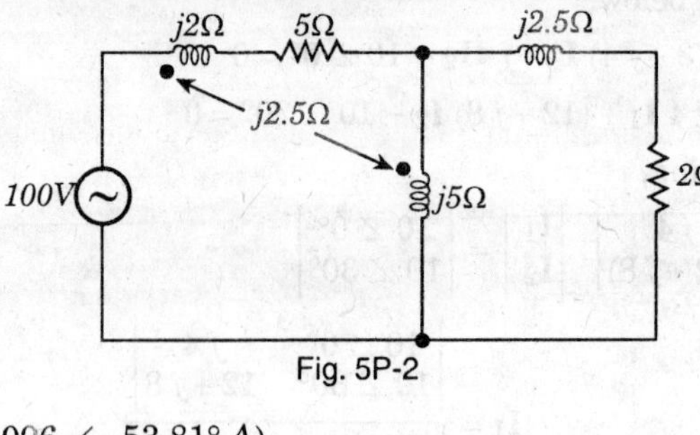

Fig. 5P-2

(**Ans.** $3.096 \angle -53.81°\ A$)

**5.3.** Determine the equivalent impedance between terminals $a - b$ in Fig. 5P-3.

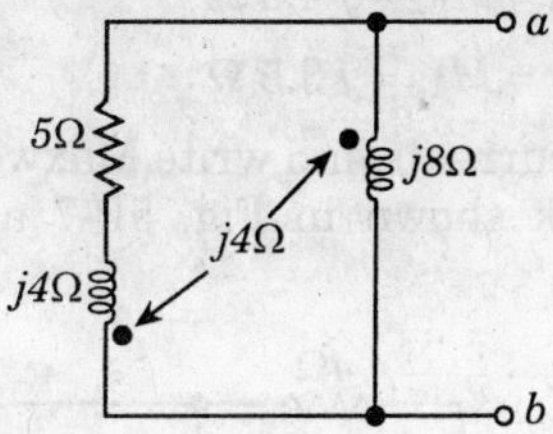


Fig. 5P-3

(**Ans.** $2.09 \angle 35.85° \ \Omega$)

**5.4.** Determine $L_{eq}$ for the coupled network shown in Fig. 5P-4.

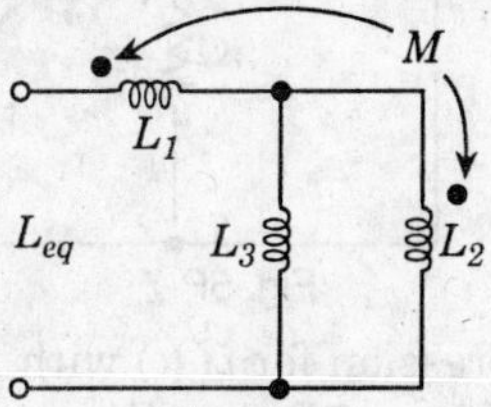


Fig. 5P-4

$$\left( \textbf{Ans. } L_{eq} = \frac{L_1 L_2 + L_2 L_3 + L_1 L_3 + 2 M L_3 - M^2}{L_2 + L_3} \right)$$

**5.5.** Determine $\mathbf{Z}_{eq}$ for the network (Fig. 5P-5)

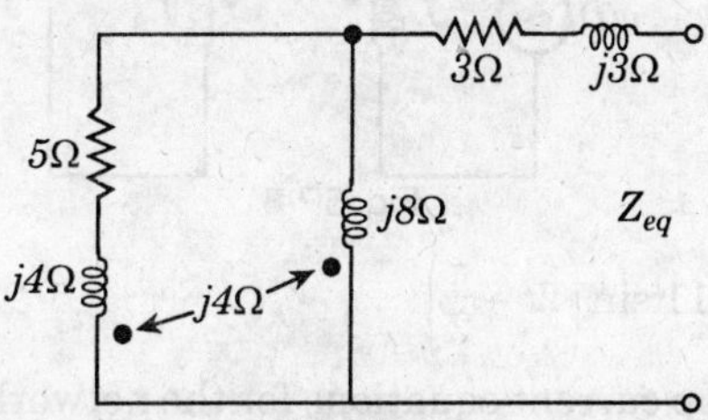


Fig. 5P-5

(**Ans.** $\mathbf{Z}_{eq} = 10.65 \angle 62.33° \ \Omega$)

**5.6.** Write mesh current equations for the given network (Fig. 5P-6).

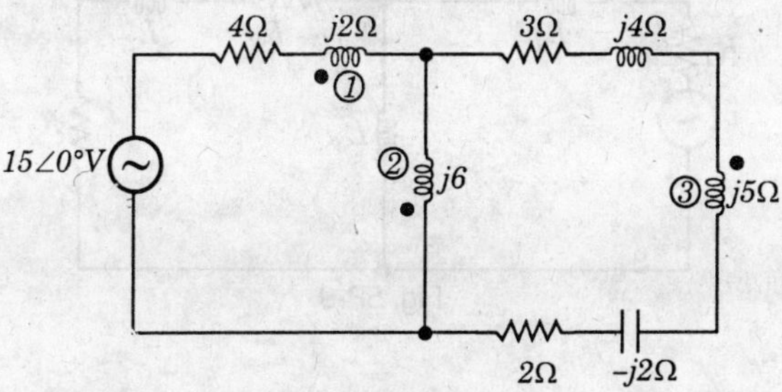


Fig. 5P-6

$$M_{12} = M_{21} = j\,2.5\ \Omega$$

$$M_{23} = M_{32} = j\,4.5\ \Omega$$

$$M_{31} = M_{13} = j\,3.5\ \Omega$$

**5.7.** Select mesh currents and write Maxwell's mesh current equations for the network shown in Fig. 5P-7 and obtain conductively coupled circuit.

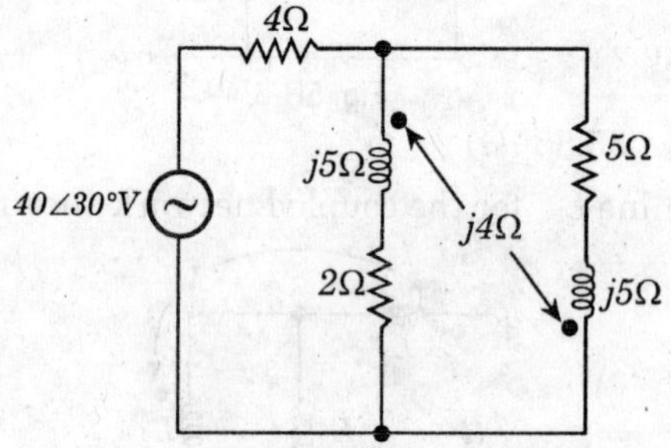


Fig. 5P-7

**5.8.** Determine expression for $i_1(t)$ with reference to coupled network shown in Fig. 5P-8. Given that $v(t) = 2\sqrt{2}\sin 2t$, $L_1 = 0.5H$, $L_2 = 0.4H$ and $M = 0.25H$.

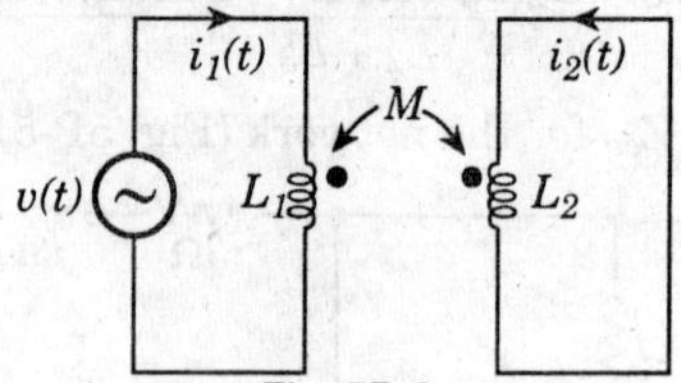


Fig. 5P-8

**Ans.** $i(t) = 4.11\sin\left(2t - \frac{\pi}{2}\right)$

**5.9.** Write loop current equations for the network given below (Fig. 5P-9).

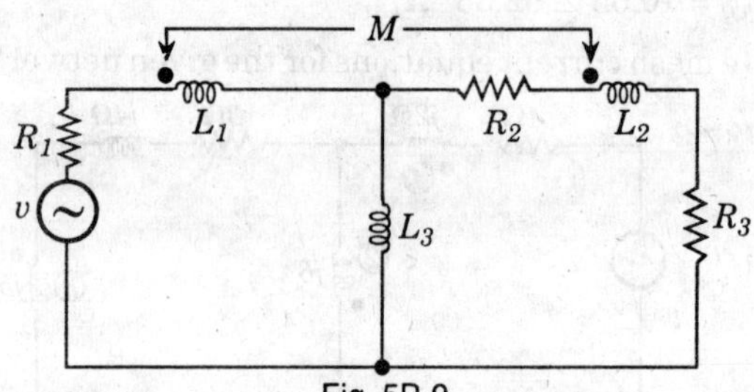


Fig. 5P-9

# 6

# RESONANCE IN A.C. CIRCUITS

## 6.1 INTRODUCTION

An electric circuit consisting of elements such as resistor, inductor and capacitor connected to a sinusoidal voltage of variable frequency is said to be in resonance at a particular frequency, if it draws the current at unity power factor, *i.e.* the current drawn and the applied voltage are in phase. This is possible, if the imaginary part of the complex impedance/admittance of the circuit equals zero. The two types of resonance are (*i*) series resonance and (*ii*) parallel resonance.

## 6.2 SERIES RESONANCE

The circuit shown in Fig. 6.2.1 consists of a resistance $R$, inductive reactance $X_L$ and capacitive reactance $X_c$ connected in series is supplied by a sinusoidal voltage **V** having variable frequency.

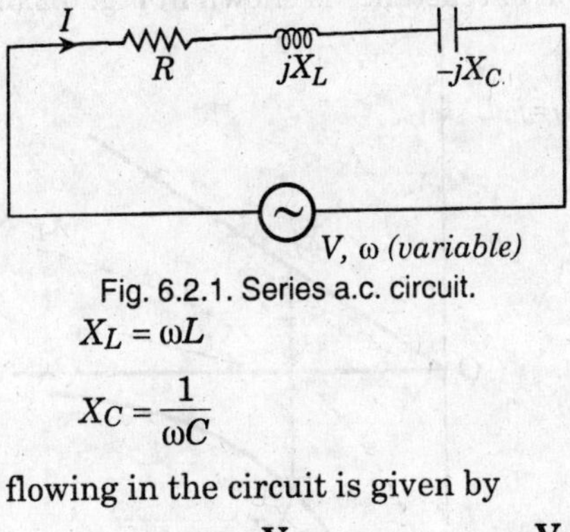


Fig. 6.2.1. Series a.c. circuit.

$$X_L = \omega L$$

and $$X_C = \frac{1}{\omega C}$$

The current flowing in the circuit is given by

$$\mathbf{I} = \frac{\mathbf{V}}{R + j(X_L - X_C)} = \frac{\mathbf{V}}{R + j\left(\omega L - \dfrac{1}{\omega C}\right)}$$

The inductive reactance $X_L = \omega L$ is directly proportional to frequency $\omega$ and the capacitive reactance $X_c = 1/\omega c$ inversely proportional to $\omega$.

The frequency at which

| $X_L$ | = | $X_c$ |
|---|---|---|
| (Inductive reactance) | | (Capacitive reactance) |

is known as resonant frequency, denoted as $\omega_0$. Thus,

$$\omega_0 L = \frac{1}{\omega_0 C}$$

$$\therefore \quad \omega_0 = \frac{1}{\sqrt{LC}}$$

or $$f_0 = \frac{1}{2\pi\sqrt{LC}}$$

The current $\mathbf{I_0}$ drawn by the series circuit (Fig. 6.2.2) at resonant frequency $\omega_0$ is given by

$$\mathbf{I_0} = \frac{\mathbf{V}}{R}$$

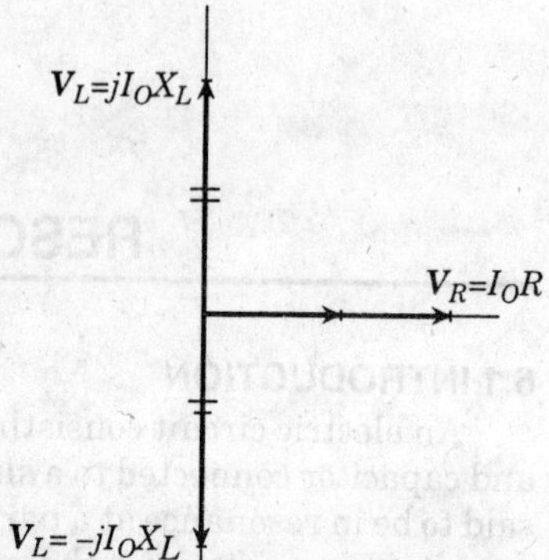

Fig. 6.2.2. Phasor diagram: Series-resonant circuit.

Since, the reactance at the resonant frequency $\omega_0$ is zero, the current phasor $\mathbf{I_0}$ is in phase with the applied voltage phasor $\mathbf{V}$. Thus, the p.f. of the series circuit at resonance is unity.

The phasor diagram for a series-resonant circuit is shown in Fig. 6.2.2.

The variation of reactance is shown in Fig. 6.2.3.

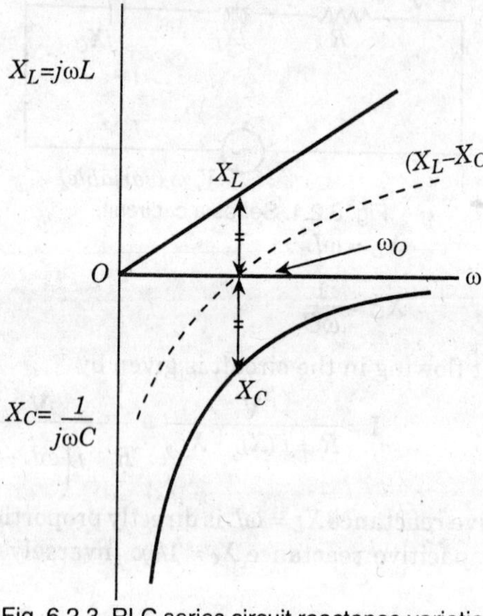

Fig. 6.2.3. RLC series circuit reactance variation

For $\omega < \omega_0$, $X_L < X_C$ (leading p.f.)

For $\omega = 0$, $X_L = X_C$ (unity p.f.)

For $\omega > \omega_0$, $X_C < X_L$ (lagging p.f.)

With reference to Fig. 6.2.1, the complex form of impedance is given by

$$\mathbf{Z} = R + j\left(\omega L - \frac{1}{\omega c}\right)$$

and

$$\underset{(\text{magnitude})}{Z} = \left[R^2 + \left(\omega L - \frac{1}{\omega C}\right)^2\right]^{1/2}$$

The variation of Z as per above equation is shown in Fig. 6.2.4.

Since, $\omega_0 L = \dfrac{1}{\omega_0 C}$ the impedance at resonant frequency $\omega_0$ is

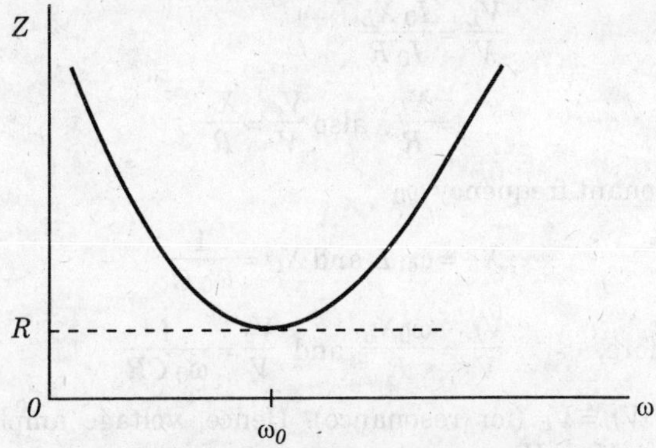


Fig. 6.2.4. Impedance variation.

$$Z = R$$

The current flowing in a series resonant circuit is given by

$$I = \frac{V}{Z} = \frac{V}{\sqrt{R^2 + \left(\omega L - \dfrac{1}{\omega C}\right)}}$$

On increasing the frequency $\omega$, the current $I$ increases till $\omega = \omega_0$. The maximum current $I_0$ flows when the frequency reaches a value $\omega_0$ and

$$I_0 = \frac{V}{R}$$

Further increase in the value of $\omega$ for $\omega > \omega_0$ the current $I$ decreases.

It is noted that the current variation is more selective for a lower value

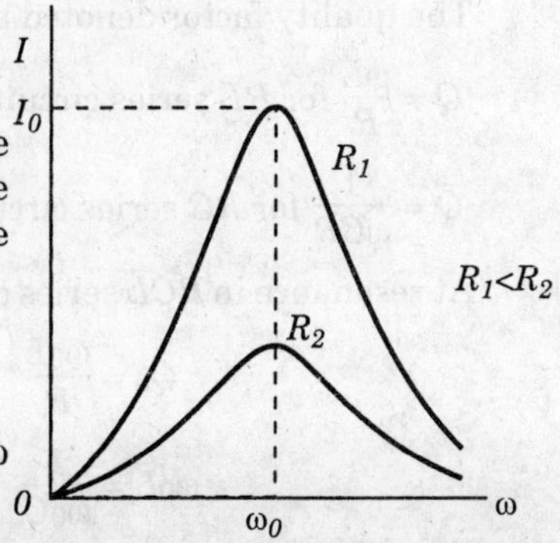


Fig. 6.2.5. Current variation in series resonant circuit

of $R$. Increasing the value of $R$ makes the series resonant circuit less selective.

The current $I$ has the same value for two values of $\omega$, one for $\omega < \omega_0$ and other $\omega > \omega_0$.

### Voltage Magnification

In a series circuit, at resonant frequency $\omega_0$ the voltages across the inductor, capacitor and resistor are $V_L = I_0 X_L$, $V_C = I_0 X_C$ and $V_R = I_0 R$ respectively.

As $$V_L = V_c \mid_{\omega_0}$$

Therefore, applied voltage $V = I_0 R$

Hence, $$\frac{V_L}{V} = \frac{I_0 X_L}{I_0 R}$$

$$= \frac{X_L}{R}, \text{ also } \frac{V_c}{V} = \frac{X_c}{R}$$

At resonant frequency $\omega_0$

$$X_L = \omega_0 L \text{ and } X_C = \frac{1}{\omega_0 C}$$

Therefore, $$\frac{V_L}{V} = \frac{\omega_0 X_L}{R} \text{ and } \frac{V_c}{V} = \frac{1}{\omega_0 CR}$$

Since, $V_L = V_c$ (for resonance). Hence, voltage amplification at resonance is $\frac{V_L}{V} = \frac{V_c}{V}$.

$$\therefore \quad \frac{V_L}{V} = \frac{\omega_0 L}{R} = \frac{1}{\omega_0 C R}$$

## 6.3 QUALITY FACTOR (FIGURE OF MERIT)

The quality factor denoted as $Q$ is given by

$Q = \frac{\omega L}{R}$ for $RL$ series circuit.

$Q = \frac{1}{\omega CR}$ for $RC$ series circuit.

At resonance in $RCL$ series circuit the quality factor is given below.

$$Q_0 = \frac{\omega_0 L}{R}$$

$$\because \quad \omega_0 L = \frac{1}{\omega_0 C}$$

$$\therefore \quad Q_0 = \frac{1}{\omega_0 CR} \text{ also.}$$

The relation for the quality factor $Q$ can also be obtained as per energy considerations. The derivation is given below.

$$Q = 2\pi\left(\frac{\text{Maximum energy stored}}{\text{Energy dissipated per cycle}}\right)$$

### 1. *RL* series circuit

With reference to *RL* series circuit (Fig. 6.3.1.)

(*i*) The maximum energy stored in inductor

$$= \frac{1}{2} L I_{max}^2$$

(*ii*) Energy dissipated/cycle in resistor $= I^2 R / f$

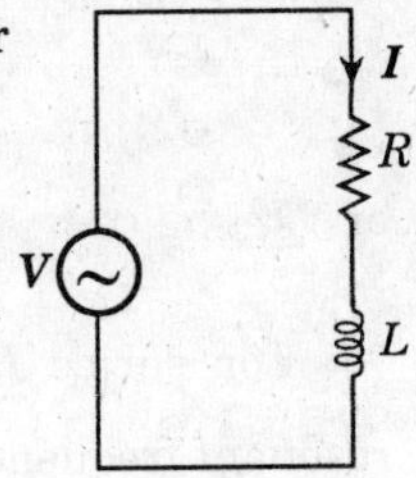


Fig. 6.3.1. R.L series circuit.

$$\therefore \quad Q = 2\pi\left(\frac{\frac{1}{2} L I^2 \max}{I^2 R / f}\right)$$

$$\because \quad I_{max} = I\sqrt{2}$$

$$\therefore \quad Q = 2\pi f\left(\frac{\frac{1}{2} L I^2 \times 2}{I^2 R}\right)$$

$$\because \quad \omega = 2\pi f$$

$$\therefore \quad Q = \frac{\omega L}{R}$$

### 2. *RC* series circuit

With reference to *RC* series circuit (Fig. 6.3.2.)

(*i*) The maximum energy stored in capacitor

$$= \frac{1}{2} C V_{cm}^2$$

(*ii*) Energy dissipated/cycle in resistor $= I^2 R / f$

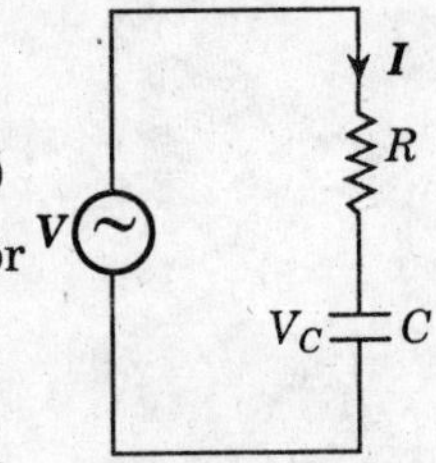


Fig. 6.3.1. R.C series circuit.

$$\therefore \quad Q = 2\pi\left(\frac{\frac{1}{2} C V_{cmax}^2}{I^2 R / f}\right)$$

$$\because \quad I_{max} = \frac{V_{cmax}}{1/\omega C}$$

$$\therefore \quad V_{c\,max} = \frac{I_{max}}{\omega C}$$

$$= \frac{I\sqrt{2}}{\omega C}$$

$$\therefore \qquad Q = 2\pi \left( \frac{\frac{1}{2} C \frac{I^2 \times 2}{\omega^2 C^2}}{I^2 R / f} \right)$$

or
$$Q = 2\pi f \left( \frac{1}{\omega^2 CR} \right)$$

$$\because \qquad \omega = 2\pi f$$

$$\therefore \qquad Q = \omega \left( \frac{1}{\omega^2 CR} \right)$$

or
$$Q = \frac{1}{\omega\, CR}$$

For series *R.L.C.* resonant circuit $\omega_0 L = \frac{1}{\omega_0 C}$. Therefore, at resonant frequency $\omega_0$

$$Q_0 = \frac{\omega_0 L}{R} = \frac{1}{\omega_0 CR}$$

## 6.3.1 Frequency for Maximum Voltage Across a Capacitor.

A series *RLC* circuit when connected to an a.c supply voltage *V* the voltage across the capacitor is given by

$$V_c = I X_c$$

$$\because \qquad X_c = \frac{1}{\omega C} \quad \text{and} \quad I = \frac{V}{\sqrt{R^2 + \left( \omega L - \frac{1}{\omega C} \right)^2}}$$

$$\therefore \qquad V_c = \frac{V}{\omega C \sqrt{R^2 + \left( \omega L - \frac{1}{\omega C} \right)^2}}$$

$$= \frac{V}{\left[ R^2 C^2 \omega^2 + \omega^2 C^2 \left( \omega L - \frac{1}{\omega C} \right)^2 \right]^{1/2}}$$

$$= \frac{V}{\left[ R^2 C^2 \omega^2 \left( \omega^2 L C - 1 \right)^2 \right]^{1/2}}$$

or
$$V_c = \frac{V}{(R^2 C^2 \omega^2 + \omega^4 L^2 C^2 - 2\omega^2 LC - 1)^{1/2}}$$

To determine the frequency $\omega_c$ for the maximum voltage across the capacitor, put $dV_C / d\omega = 0$ and solve for $\omega$.

$$\frac{dV_c}{d\omega} = \frac{[V(R^2C^2\omega^2 + \omega^4L^2C^2 - 2\omega^2LC)^{\frac{1}{2}} \times 0 - 1/2\,(R^2C^2\omega^2 + \omega^4L^2C^2 - 2\omega^2LC)^{-1/2}\,(2R^2C^2\omega + 4\omega^3L^2C^2 - 4\omega LC)]}{[(R^2C^2\omega^2 + \omega^4L^2C^2 - 2\omega^2LC - 1)]}$$

Equating above experssion to zero

$$-\frac{1}{2}(2R^2C^2\omega + 4\omega^3L^2C^2 - 4\omega LC) = 0$$

or
$$R^2C^2 + 2\omega^2L^2C^2 - 2LC = 0$$

or
$$2\omega^2L^2C^2 = 2LC - R^2C^2$$

$\therefore$
$$\omega^2 = \frac{1}{LC} - \frac{R^2}{2L^2}$$

Hence ,
$$\omega_c = \sqrt{\frac{1}{LC} - \frac{R^2}{2L^2}}$$

$\therefore$
$$V_{c\max} = \frac{V / \omega_c C}{\sqrt{R^2 + \left(\omega_c L - \frac{1}{\omega c C}\right)}}$$

### 6.3.2. Frequency for Maximum Voltage Across an Inductor.

A series *RLC* circuit when counected to an *a.c.* supply voltage *V*, the voltage across the inductor is given by

$$V_L = I X_L$$

$\because$
$$X_L = \omega L$$

and
$$I = \frac{V}{\sqrt{R^2 + \left(\omega L - \frac{1}{\omega}C\right)^2}}$$

$\therefore$
$$V_L = \frac{V\omega L}{\left[R_2 + \left(\omega L - \frac{1}{\omega C}\right)^2\right]^{\frac{1}{2}}}$$

or
$$V_L = \frac{V\omega L}{\left(R^2 + \omega^2L^2 - 2\frac{L}{C} + \frac{1}{\omega^2C^2}\right)^{\frac{1}{2}}}$$

To determine the frequency for the maximum voltage across the inductor, put $dV_L/d\omega = 0$ and solve for $\omega$

$$\frac{dV_L}{d\omega} = \frac{[(R^2 + \omega^2L^2 - 2L/C + 1/\omega^2C^2)^{1/2}\, V.1.L - V\,\omega L\,.\,1/2\,(R^2 + \omega^2 L^2 - 2\,L/C + 1/\omega^2C^2)^{-1/2}\,(2\,\omega\,L^2 - 2/\omega^3C^2)]}{[(R^2 + \omega^2L^2 - 2\,L/C + 1/\omega^2C^2)]}$$

$$\therefore \quad [(R^2 + \omega^2L^2 - 2L/C + 1/\omega^2C^2)^{1/2} - \frac{\omega}{2}(R^2 + \omega^2L^2 - 2L/C + 1/\omega^2C^2)^{-\frac{1}{2}}(2\omega L^2 - 2/\omega^2C^2)] = 0$$

or $\quad 2\,(R^2 + \omega^2L^2 - 2L/C + 1/\omega^2C^2) - (2\omega L^2 - 2/\omega^2C^2) = 0$

or $\quad (R^2 + \omega^2L^2 - 2L/C + 1/\omega^2C^2) - (\omega^2L^2 - 1/\omega^2C^2) = 0$

or $$R^2 - 2\frac{L}{C} + \frac{2}{\omega^2C^2} = 0$$

$$\therefore \quad \frac{2}{\omega^2C^2} = \frac{2L}{C} - R^2$$

$$\therefore \quad \omega^2 = \frac{1}{LC - \frac{R^2C^2}{2}}$$

Hence , $$\omega_L = \frac{1}{\sqrt{\left(LC - \frac{R^2C^2}{2}\right)}}$$

$$\therefore \quad V_{L\,max} = \frac{V\omega_L L}{\sqrt{R^2 + \left(\omega_L L - \frac{1}{\omega_L C}\right)}}$$

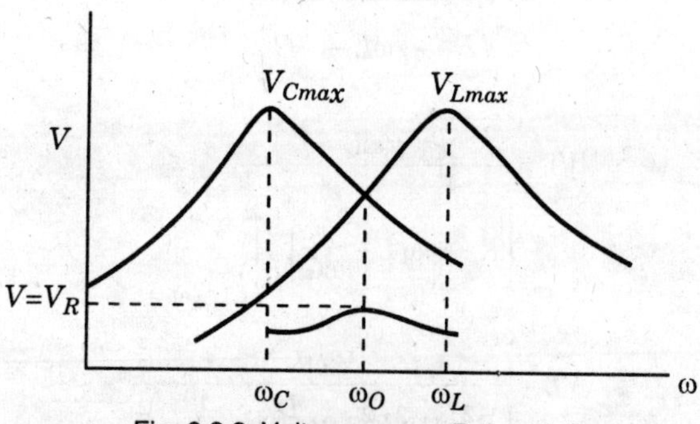


Fig. 6.3.3 Voltage across *R*, *L* and *C*

## 6.4. SELECTIVITY AND BANDWIDTH

The response curve shown in Fig. 6.4.1 indicates the selectivity of a seres resonant circuit. The selectivity of a resonant circuit gives the

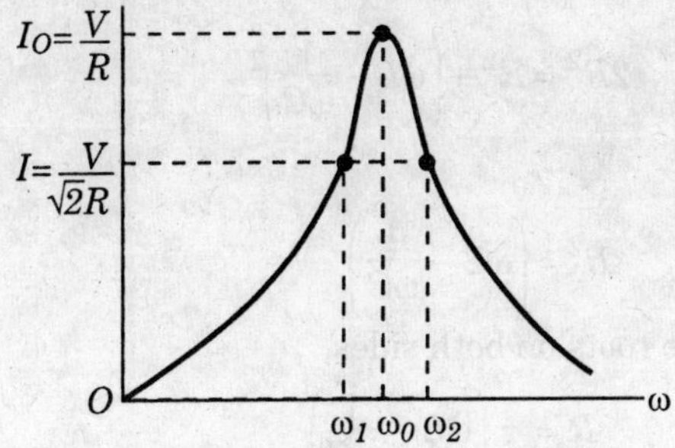


Fig. 6.4.1 Selectivity and Bandwidth.

response to a certain range of frequencies. A sharp response represents better selectivity while a flat response poor selectivity.

The measure of selectivity is the band-width. The band width is a frequency range for which the response falls to a value $I_0/\sqrt{2}$ where $I_0 = \frac{V}{R}$, *i.e.* the current flowing in a series resonant circuit at resonant frequency $\omega_0$. The frequency at which this occurs is known as half power frequency. There are two half power frequencies, the lower $\omega_1$ and upper $\omega_2$

### Determination Of Half Power Frequencies.

For any frequency ω,

$$I = \frac{V}{\sqrt{R^2 + \left(\omega L - \frac{1}{\omega c}\right)^2}}$$

For resonance frequency $\omega = \omega_0$ , $\omega_0 L = \frac{1}{\omega_0 C}$ ,

$$\therefore \qquad I_0 = \frac{V}{R}$$

At half power frequencies $\omega_1$, $\omega_2$ (Fig. 6.4.1),

$$I = \frac{I_0}{\sqrt{2}} = \frac{V}{(\sqrt{2})\,R}$$

$$\therefore \qquad \frac{V}{(\sqrt{2})\,R} = \frac{V}{\sqrt{R^2 + \left(\omega L - \frac{1}{\omega C}\right)^2}}\Bigg|_{\omega = \omega_1,\, \omega_2}$$

or
$$(\sqrt{2})\,R = \sqrt{R^2 + (\omega L - \frac{1}{\omega C})^2}$$

Squaring both sides,

$$2R^2 = R^2 + \left(\omega L - \frac{1}{\omega C}\right)^2$$

$$\therefore \quad R^2 = \left(\omega L - \frac{1}{\omega C}\right)^2$$

Taking square roots on both sides,

$$R = \pm\left(\omega L - \frac{1}{\omega C}\right)$$

Simplifying, $\pm(\omega^2 LC - 1) - \omega RC = 0$

The two possible solutions of the above equation are

1. Consider + sign before the term $(\omega^2 LC - 1)$

$$\therefore \quad \omega^2 LC - \omega RC - 1 = 0$$

Solving above equation

$$\omega = \frac{RC \pm \sqrt{R^2C^2 + 4LC}}{2LC}$$

$$\therefore \quad \omega = \frac{R}{2L} \pm \sqrt{\left(\frac{R^2}{4L^2} + \frac{1}{LC}\right)}$$

As the frequency ω is + ive number, to obtain upper half frequency delete – sign before the term $\sqrt{\left(\frac{R^2}{4L^2} + \frac{1}{LC}\right)}$

$$\therefore \quad \omega_2 = \frac{R}{2L} + \sqrt{\left(\frac{R^2}{4L^2} + \frac{1}{LC}\right)}$$

2. Consider – sign before the term $(\omega^2 LC - 1)$

$\therefore - \omega^2 LC - \omega RC + 1 = 0$

Solving above equation,

$$\omega = \frac{RC \pm \sqrt{R^2C^2 + 4LC}}{-2LC}$$

$$\therefore \quad \omega = -\frac{R}{2L} \pm \sqrt{\left(\frac{R^2}{4L^2} + \frac{1}{LC}\right)}$$

As the frequency ω is a +ive number, delete –sign before the term $\sqrt{\left(\frac{R^2}{4L^2} + \frac{1}{LC}\right)}$.

$$\therefore \qquad \omega_1 = -\frac{R}{2L} + \sqrt{\left(\frac{R^2}{4L^2} + \frac{1}{LC}\right)}$$

$$\omega_1 \omega_2 = \left(-\frac{R}{2L} + \sqrt{\frac{R^2}{4L^2} + \frac{1}{LC}}\right)\left(\frac{R}{2L} + \sqrt{\frac{R^2}{4L^2} + \frac{1}{LC}}\right)$$

$$= \frac{1}{LC}$$

$$\therefore \qquad \omega_0^2 = \frac{1}{LC}$$

$$\therefore \qquad \omega_0^2 = \omega_1 \omega_2$$

or

$$\omega_0 = \sqrt{\omega_1 \omega_2}$$

Thus, the resonant frequency $\omega_0$ is the geometric mean of the lower half power frequency $\omega_1$ and upper half frequency $\omega_2$

The range of frequency $(\omega_2 - \omega_1)$ is known as bandwidth,

$$\therefore \qquad \omega_2 - \omega_1 = \left(\frac{R}{2L} + \sqrt{\frac{R^2}{4L^2} + \frac{1}{LC}}\right) - \left(-\frac{R}{2L} + \sqrt{\frac{R^2}{4L^2} + \frac{1}{LC}}\right)$$

$$= \frac{R}{L}$$

$\therefore$ Bandwidth : $\omega_2 - \omega_1 = \dfrac{R}{L}$

On dividing both sides by $\omega_0$,

$$\frac{\omega_2 - \omega_1}{\omega_0} = \frac{R}{\omega_0 R}$$

The term $Q_0 = \dfrac{\omega_0 L}{R}$, the quality factor at resonance is also the property of a series resonant circuit.

$$\therefore \qquad \frac{\omega_2 - \omega_1}{\omega_0} = \frac{1}{Q_0}$$

For small bandwidth *i.e.* better selectivity, the value of $Q_0$ should be higher.

For large bandwidth *i.e.* poor selectivity, the value of $Q_0$ should be lower.

The bandwidth is inversely proportional to $Q$ factor.

## 6.5 PARALLEL RESONANCE

1. Three branch parallel circuit.

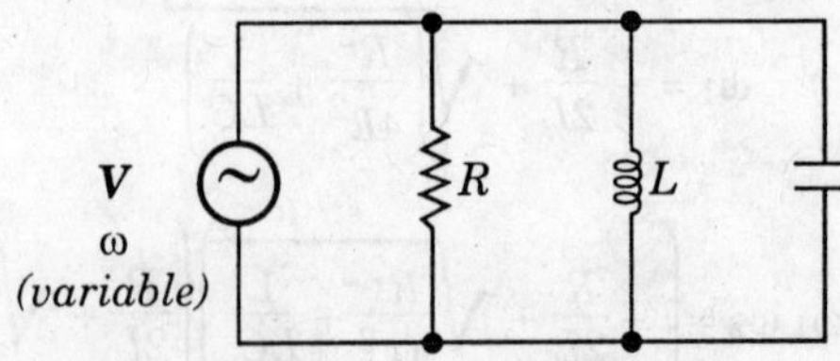

Fig. 6.5.1. *RLC* parallel circuit.

A three branch parallel circuit consisting of resistor $R$, inductor $L$ and capacitor $C$ as shown in Fig. 6.5.1 is connected to a sinusoidal variable frequency voltage **V**

The total admittance of the circuit is

$$\mathbf{Y} = G + j\,(B_C - B_L)$$

where, $G = \dfrac{1}{R}$ conductance.

$B_C = \omega C$ capacitive susceptance.

and $B_L = \dfrac{1}{\omega L}$ inductive susceptance.

The resonant frequency for a parallel circuit is denoted as $\omega_{ar}$ (antiresonance). This is to distinguish it from the series resonant frequency $\omega_0$. At resonance as well as antiresonance the power factor is always unity. Hence, the susceptance (imaginary part of complex admittance) is equated to zero to obtain the antiresonant frequency $\omega_{ar}$.

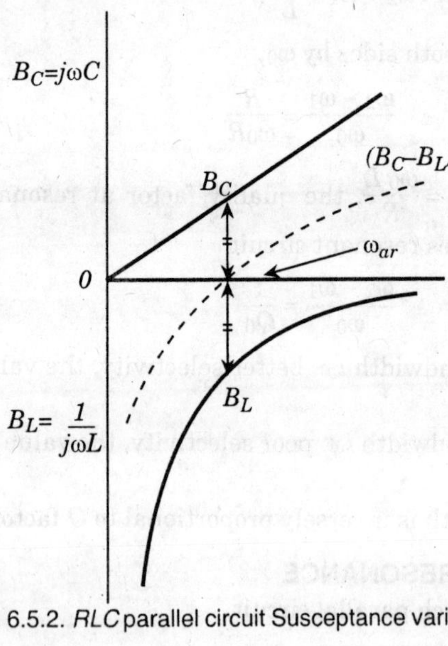

Fig. 6.5.2. *RLC* parallel circuit Susceptance variation.

$$\therefore \qquad B_C - B_L = 0$$

$$\therefore \qquad B_C = \omega c \text{ and } B_L = \frac{1}{\omega L}$$

$$\therefore \qquad \omega C - \frac{1}{\omega L} = 0$$

At antiresonance $\omega = \omega_{ar}$

$$\therefore \qquad \omega_{ar} C - \frac{1}{\omega_{ar} L} = 0$$

$$\therefore \qquad \omega_{ar} = \frac{1}{\sqrt{LC}}$$

The variation of capacitive reactance $B_C = \omega C$ and inductive susceptance $B_L = \dfrac{1}{\omega L}$ with frequency $\omega$ is shown in Fig. 6.5.2.

At $\omega = \omega_{ar}$, $\omega_{ar} C$ equals $1/\omega_{ar} L$ and the equivalent susceptance is zero

For $\omega < \omega_{ar}$ susceptance is inductive

and $\omega > \omega_{ar}$ susceptance is capacitive

The complex admittance of the *RLC* parallel circuit is given by

$$\mathbf{Y} = G + j\left(\omega C - \frac{1}{\omega L}\right)$$

and the magnitude $Y = \sqrt{G^2 + \left(\omega C - \dfrac{1}{\omega L}\right)}$

The variation of admittance (magnitude) with frequency is shown in Fig. 6.5.3

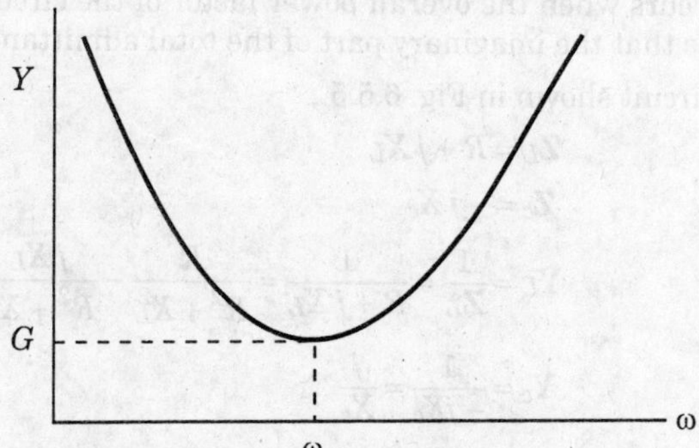


Fig. 6.5.3. Admittance variation.

The corresponding variation of impedance $\left(Z = \dfrac{1}{Y}\right)$ of the parallel *RLC* circuit is shown in Fig. 6.5.4.

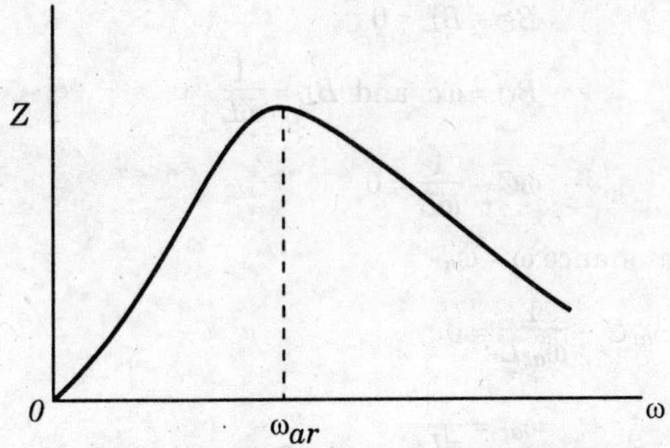


Fig. 6.5.4. Impedance variation : parallel *RLC* circuit.

At antiresonant frequency $\omega_{ar}$, the impedance of a parallel *RLC* circuit is high and as such the current drawn from the supply is minimum. Therefore, a parallel resonant circuit is called a "rejector circuit."

At resonant frequency $\omega_0$, a series resonant circuit draws maximum current from the supply. Therefore, a series resonant circuit is called an "acceptor circuit."

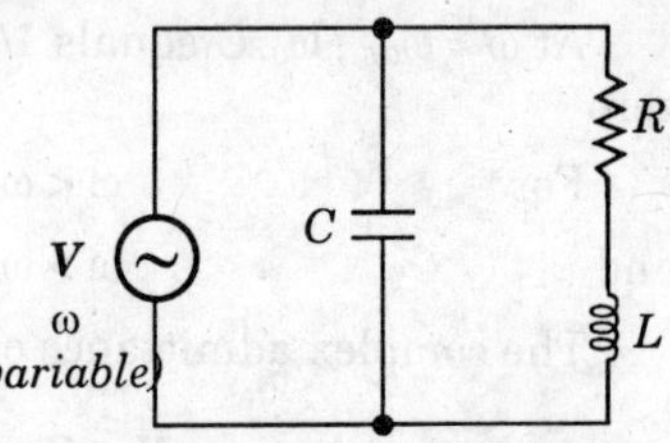


Fig. 6.5.5. Tow branch parallel circuit with capacitor in one branch.

2.(*a*) A two branch parallel circuit connected to a sinusoidal variable frequency supply voltage **V** as shown in Fig. 6.5.5.

One branch cantains an inductive coil having inductance $L$ and inherent resistance $R$, the other branch has a loss less capacitor $C$. The resonance occurs when the overall power factor of the circuit is unity. This requires that the imaginary part of the total admittance is zero.

As per circuit shown in Fig. 6.5.5.,

$$\mathbf{Z}_L = R + jX_L$$

and
$$\mathbf{Z}_c = -jX_c$$

$$\mathbf{Y}_L = \frac{1}{\mathbf{Z}_L} = \frac{1}{R + jX_L} = \frac{R}{R^2 + X_L^2} - \frac{jX_L}{R^2 + X_L^2}$$

and
$$\mathbf{Y}_c = \frac{1}{-jX_c} = \frac{j}{X_c}$$

Total admittance

$$\mathbf{Y} = \mathbf{Y}_L + \mathbf{Y}_c$$

$$= \frac{R}{R^2 + X_L^2} - \frac{jX_L}{R^2 + X_L^2} + \frac{j}{X_C}$$

$$= \frac{R}{R^2 + X_L^2} + j\left(\frac{1}{X_C} - \frac{X_L}{R^2 + X_L^2}\right)$$

At antiresonant frequency $\omega_{ar}$, the imaginary part of the admittance **Y** is zero.

$$\therefore j\left(\frac{1}{X_C} - \frac{X_L}{R^2 + X_L^2}\right) = 0$$

$$\therefore \quad \frac{1}{X_C} = \frac{X_L}{R^2 + X_L^2}$$

$$\therefore \quad X_C = \frac{1}{\omega_{ar}C} \text{ and } X_L = \omega_{ar}L$$

$$\therefore \quad \omega_{ar} C = \frac{\omega_{ar} L}{R^2 + \omega_{ar}^2 L^2}$$

or $$R^2 + \omega_{ar}^2 L^2 = \frac{L}{C}$$

$$\therefore \quad \omega_{ar}^2 = \frac{1}{LC} - \frac{R^2}{L^2}$$

Taking square root on both sides and considering + value of $\omega_{ar}$.

$$\omega_{ar} = \sqrt{\frac{1}{LC} - \frac{R^2}{L^2}}$$

$\omega_{ar}$ is the anti resonant frequency for the two branch parallel circuit shown in Fig. 6.5.5. As the frequency $\omega_{ar}$ is a real quantity, the condition for the antiresonance of a parallel circuit is

$$\frac{R^2}{L^2} < \frac{1}{LC}$$

The circuit shown in Fig. 6.5.5. is a practical circuit applicable to parallel resonance.

### Dynamic Resistance

The total admittance of the circuit shown in Fig. 6.5.5. is

$$\mathbf{Y} = \frac{R}{R^2 + X_L^2} - j\left(\frac{1}{X_c} - \frac{X_L}{R^2 + X_L^2}\right)$$

At resonance, $$\left(\frac{1}{X_C} - \frac{X_L}{R^2 + X_L^2}\right) = 0$$

$$\therefore \quad Y_{ar} = \frac{R}{R^2 + X_L^2} \text{ and } Z_{ar} = \frac{R^2 + X_{20}L^2}{R} = \frac{R^2 + \omega_{ar}^2 L^2}{R}$$

$$\therefore \quad R^2 + \omega_{ar}^2 L^2 = \frac{L}{C}$$

$$\therefore \quad Z_{ar} = \frac{L}{RC}$$

which is resistive and known as dynamic resistance of a parallel resonant circuit. For low values of $R$, the dynamic resistance $Z_{ar}$ becomes large and as such the current drawn from the supply is minimum.

## 6.6 BANDWIDTH : PARALLEL RESONANT CIRCUIT.

For the parallel resonant circuit shown in Fig. 6.6.1,

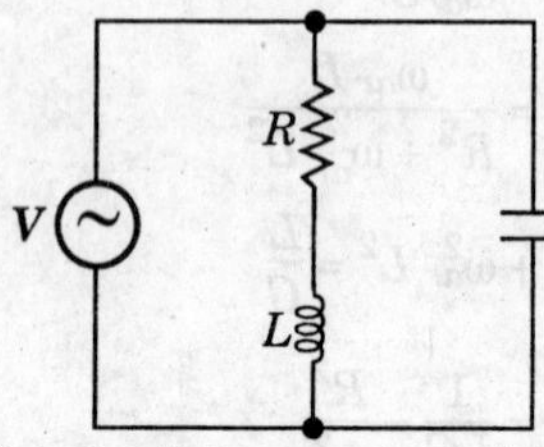


Fig. 6.6.1 Parallel resonant circuit : bandwidth.

$$\mathbf{Z}_L = R + j X_L\,, \quad \mathbf{Y}_L = \frac{R - jX_L}{R^2 + X_L^2} = \frac{R}{R^2 + X_L^2} - \frac{j X_L}{R^2 + X_L^2}$$

$$\mathbf{Z}_c = -jX_c\,, \quad \mathbf{Y}_C = j / X_C$$

Total admittance

$$\mathbf{Y} = \mathbf{Y}_L + \mathbf{Y}_C = \frac{R}{R^2 + X_L^2} + j\left(\frac{1}{X_c} - \frac{X_L}{R^2 + X_L^2}\right)$$

$$= G + j\left(\frac{1}{X_C} - \frac{X_L}{R^2 + X_L^2}\right)$$

$$\because \quad X_L = \omega L \text{ and } X_C = \frac{1}{\omega C}$$

$$\therefore \quad \mathbf{Y} = G + j\left(\omega C - \frac{\omega L}{R^2 + \omega^2 L^2}\right)$$

Since, $R << \omega^2 L^2$, neglect $R$ in comparison to $\omega^2 L^2$

$$\therefore \quad \mathbf{Y} = G + j\left(\omega C - \frac{1}{\omega L}\right) \quad \text{to a fair approximation.}$$

and

$$Y = \sqrt{G^2 + \left(\omega C - \frac{1}{\omega L}\right)^2}$$

The effective impedance of a parallel resonant circuit at $\omega = \omega_{ar}$ is $Z_{ar}$ and this being a maximum impedance. However, the effective impedance of a parallel resonant circuit decreases for $\omega < \omega_{ar}$ as well as

$\omega > \omega_{ar}$ . At half power frequencies $\omega_1$ and $\omega_2$ the effective impedance falls to $Z_{ar}/\sqrt{2}$.

The variation of effective impedance of a parallel resonant circuit is shown in Fig. 6.6.2.

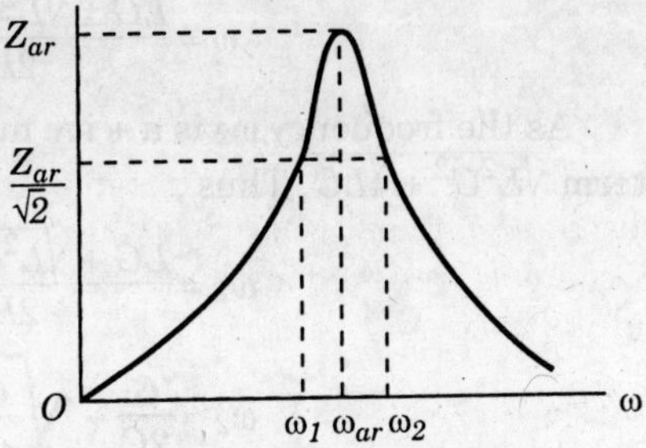


Fig. 6.6.2 Impedance curve : parallel circuit.

At any frequency ω,

$$Z = \frac{1}{\sqrt{G^2 + \left(\omega C - \frac{1}{\omega L}\right)^2}}$$

Since, at

$$\omega = \omega_{ar}, \quad \left(\omega C - \frac{1}{\omega L}\right) = 0$$

$$\therefore \quad Z_{ar} = \frac{1}{G}$$

At half power frequencies the impedance falls to

$$\frac{Z_{ar}}{\sqrt{2}} = \frac{1}{(\sqrt{2})G}$$

$$\therefore \quad \frac{1}{(\sqrt{2})G} = \frac{1}{\sqrt{G^2 + \left(\omega C - \frac{1}{\omega L}\right)^2}} \quad \Big| \; \omega = \omega_{ar}$$

or $$\sqrt{G^2 + \left(\omega C - \frac{1}{\omega L}\right)^2} = (\sqrt{2})G$$

Squaring both sides

$$G^2 + \left(\omega C - \frac{1}{\omega L}\right)^2 = 2G^2$$

or $$G^2 = \left(\omega C - \frac{1}{\omega L}\right)^2$$

$$\therefore \quad G = \pm\left(\omega C - \frac{1}{\omega L}\right)$$

or $$\pm\frac{(\omega^2 LC - 1)}{\omega L} = G$$

or $$\pm(\omega^2 LC - 1) = \omega L G$$

(*i*) To determine upper half power frequency $\omega_2$, consider + sign before the term $(\omega^2 LC - 1)$ and solve for ω.

$$\therefore \quad \omega^2 LC - \omega LG - 1 = 0$$

on solving above equation,

$$\omega = \frac{LG \pm \sqrt{L^2G^2 + 4LC}}{2LC}$$

As the frequency $\omega_2$ is a + ive number, delete – ive sign before the term $\sqrt{L^2G^2 + 4LC}$. Thus ,

$$\omega_2 = \frac{LG + \sqrt{L^2G^2 + 4LC}}{2LC}$$

$$\therefore \quad \omega_2 = \frac{G}{2C} + \sqrt{\frac{G^2}{4C^2} + \frac{1}{LC}}$$

(*ii*) To determine lower half power frequency $\omega_1$ consider – sign before the term $(\omega^2 LC - 1)$ and solve for $\omega$

$$\therefore \quad - \omega^2 LC + 1 - \omega LG = 0$$

or

$$\omega^2 LC + \omega LG - 1 = 0$$

$$\therefore \quad \omega_1 = \frac{- LG \pm \sqrt{L^2G^2 + 4LC}}{2LC}$$

As the frequency $\omega_1$ is a + number, delete – sign before the term $\sqrt{L^2G^2 + 4LC}$.

$$\therefore \quad \omega_1 = - \frac{G}{2C} + \sqrt{\frac{G^2}{4C^2} + \frac{1}{LC}}$$

For a parallel resonant circuit, the range of frequency $(\omega_2 - \omega_1)$ is the bandwidth as determined below,

$$\omega_2 - \omega_1 = \left(\frac{G}{2C} + \sqrt{\frac{G^2}{4^2C^2} + \frac{1}{LC}}\right) - \left(- \frac{G}{2C} + \sqrt{\frac{G^2}{4C^2} + \frac{1}{LC}}\right)$$

$$= \frac{G}{C}, \qquad \left(G = \frac{R}{R^2 + XL^2}\right)$$

On dividing both sides by $\omega_{ar}$

$$\frac{\omega_2 - \omega_1}{\omega_{ar}} = \frac{G}{\omega_{ar} C}$$

## 6.7 GENERAL CASE : PARALLEL CIRCUIT WITH RESISTORS IN *L* AND *C* BRANCHES

A parallel circuit containing an inductor $L$ in series with a resistor $R_L$ and a capacitance $C$ in series with a resistor $R_c$ is shown in Fig. 6.7.1.

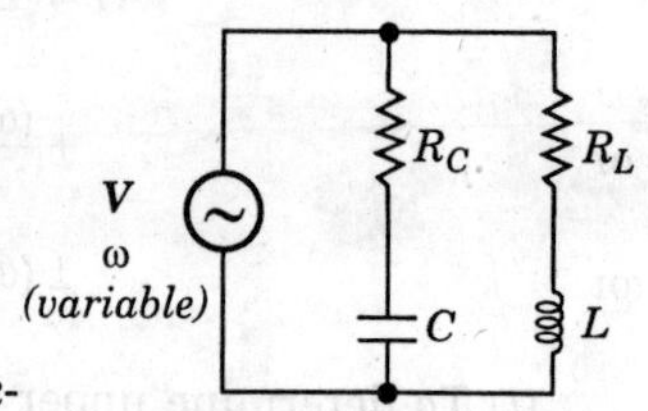


Fig. 6.7.1 Parallel resonant circuit : General case.

The parallel circuit shown in Fig. 6.7.1 is connected to a sinusoidal voltage **V** of variable frequency. The resonance (anti resonance) occurs when the overall power factor of the circuit is unity. This requires that the imaginary part (susceptance) of the total admittance is zero.

(*i*) The impedance of inductive branch :

$$\mathbf{Z}_L = R_L + j\,X_L\,,\quad \mathbf{X}_L = j\,\omega L$$

(*ii*) The impedance of capacitive branch :

$$\mathbf{Z}_C = R_C - j\,X_C\,,\quad \mathbf{X}_C = \frac{1}{j\,\omega C}$$

The corresponding admittances are ,

$$\mathbf{Y}_L = \frac{1}{R_L + j\,X_L} = \frac{R_L}{R_L^2 + X_L^2} - \frac{j\,X_L}{R_L^2 + X_L^2} = G_L - j\,B_L$$

and

$$\mathbf{Y}_C = \frac{1}{R_C - j\,X_C} = \frac{R_C}{R_C^2 + X_C^2} + \frac{j\,X_C}{R_C^2 + X_C^2} = G_C + j\,B_C$$

The symbol $G$ stands for conductance and $B$ for susecptance. The total admittance

$$\mathbf{Y} = \mathbf{Y}_L + \mathbf{Y}_C = (G_L + G_C) - j\,(B_C - B_L)$$

At the resonance the imaginary part of the admittance equals zero

$$\therefore \quad (B_C - B_L) = 0$$

or

$$B_C = B_L$$

Hence,

$$\frac{X_C}{R_C^2 + X_C^2} = \frac{X_L}{R_L^2 + X_L^2}$$

At the resonance of a parallel circuit, the antiresonant frequency is denoted as $\omega_{ar}$. Thus,

$$\frac{1/\omega_{ar} C}{R_C^2 + 1/\omega_{ar}^2 C^2} = \frac{\omega_{ar} L}{R_L^2 + \omega_{ar}^2 L^2}$$

or

$$\omega_{ar}^2\left(R_C^2 - \frac{L}{C}\right) = \frac{1}{LC}\left(R_L^2 - \frac{L}{C}\right)$$

$$\therefore \quad \omega_{ar} = \frac{1}{\sqrt{LC}}\sqrt{\frac{R_L^2 - (L/C)}{R_C^2 - (L/C)}}$$

If $R_L^2 = R_C^2 = \dfrac{L}{C}$ The parallel circuit of Fig. 6.7.1 resonates at all frequencies.

## SOLVED EXAMPLES

**Examples 6.8.1** *On application of voltage V = 120 sin (400 t) V to a series RLC circuit, the current flowing is i = 3 sin (400 t – 45°) The* *value of inductance is 0.25H. Determine (i) the value of R and C (ii) Resonant frequency.*

**Solution :** $Z = \frac{120}{3} = 40\ \Omega$

$\because \quad \phi = 45° \ lag.$

$$\mathbf{Z} = 40 \angle 45° = 40 \cos 45° + j\ 40 \sin 45°$$

$$= \frac{40}{\sqrt{2}} + j\frac{40}{\sqrt{2}}$$

$\therefore \quad X = \frac{40}{\sqrt{2}}, \quad X_L = \omega L = 400 \times 0.25 = 100\ \Omega$

$\therefore \quad X = X_L - X_C$

$\therefore \quad \frac{40}{\sqrt{2}} = 100 - X_C$

or $\quad X_C = 100 - \frac{40}{\sqrt{2}} = 71.71\ \Omega$

$$X_C = \frac{1}{\omega C}$$

$\therefore \quad C = \frac{1}{\omega X_C} = \frac{1}{400 \times 71.71} = 2.5 \times 13.9 \times 10^{-6}\ \text{F}$

or $\quad C = 2.5 \times 13.9 = 34.75\ \mu\text{F}$ **Ans.**

Resonant frequency

$$\omega_0 = \frac{1}{\sqrt{LC}} = \frac{1}{\sqrt{0.25 \times 34.75 \times 10^{-6}}}$$

$$= \frac{10^3}{\sqrt{0.25 \times 34.75}}$$

$$= 339.2 \text{ r/s} \quad \textbf{Ans.}$$

**Example : 6.8.2** *A coil and a capacitor are connected in series to a 230V, 50 Hz. supply. The circuit resonates at 50 Hz. At resonance the current flowing in the series combination is 0.46 A and the voltage across the capacitor is 322V. Determine the resistance, inductance, Q-factor of the coil, bandwidth and half power frequencies.*

**Solution :** At resonance

1. $\quad I_0 = \frac{V}{R}$

$\therefore \quad R = \frac{V}{I_0} = \frac{230}{0.46}$

$$= 500\ \Omega \quad \textbf{Ans.}$$

2. $$V_L = V_C,$$

$$\therefore \quad V_L = 322V$$

$$V_L = I_0 X_L$$

$$\therefore \quad X_L = \frac{V_L}{I_0} = \frac{322}{0.46} = 700\Omega$$

$$L = \frac{X_L}{\omega_0} = \frac{700}{314} = 2.229 \text{ H} \qquad \textbf{Ans.}$$

$$Q_0 = \frac{\omega_0 L}{R} = \frac{314 \times 2.229}{500} = 1.39$$

Bandwidth, $\omega_2 - \omega_1 = \frac{R}{L} = \frac{500}{2.229} = 224.3$ r/s

or $$f_2 - f_1 = \frac{224.3}{2\pi} = 35.69 \text{ Hz} \qquad \textbf{Ans.}$$

Lower half power frequency,

$$\omega_1 = -\frac{R}{2L} + \sqrt{\frac{1}{LC} + \frac{R^2}{4L^2}}$$

$$\because \quad \frac{1}{LC} = \omega_0^2 \text{ and } \omega_0 = 314 \text{ r/s (given)}$$

$$\therefore \quad \omega_1 = -\frac{500}{2 \times 2.229} + \sqrt{314^2 + \frac{500^2}{4 \times 2.229^2}}$$

$$= 179.05 \text{ r/s}$$

$$f_1 = \frac{179.055}{2\pi} = 28.49 \text{ Hz} \qquad \textbf{Ans.}$$

Upper half power frequency,

$$\omega_2 = \frac{R}{2L} + \sqrt{\frac{1}{LC} + \frac{R^2}{4L^2}}$$

$$= \frac{500}{2 \times 2.229} + \sqrt{314^2 + \frac{500^2}{4L^2}} = 403.35 \text{ r/s}$$

$$f_2 = \frac{403.35}{2\pi} = 64.18 \text{ Hz} \qquad \textbf{Ans.}$$

**Example 6.8.3.** *A capacitor 18, μ F is connected in parallel with a coil having resistance 8 Ω and inductance 0.5H. Determine the frequency of resonance and bandwidth.*

**Solution :** The frequency of resonance for a parallel circuit,

$$\omega_{ar} = \sqrt{\frac{1}{LC} - \frac{R^2}{L^2}}$$

$$= \sqrt{\frac{1}{0.5 \times 18 \times 10^{-6}} - \frac{8^2}{0.5^2}} = \sqrt{110855}$$

or $$\omega_{ar} = 332.9 \text{ r/s} \quad \textbf{Ans.}$$

Bandwidth,

$$\omega_2 - \omega_1 = \frac{G}{C}, \text{ where } G = \frac{R}{R^2 + X_L^2}$$

$$X_L = \omega_{ar} L$$

$$\therefore \quad \omega_2 - \omega_1 = \frac{R}{(R^2 + X_L^2)\, C}$$

$$= \frac{8}{(8^2 + 332.9^2 \times 0.5^2)\, 18 \times 10^{-6}}$$

$$= \frac{2.88}{18} \times 10^2 = 16 \text{ r/s}$$

or $$f_2 - f_1 = \frac{16}{2\pi} = 2.54 \text{ Hz} \qquad \textbf{Ans.}$$

**Example 6.8.4** *Determine the resonant frequency and the current drawn by the circuit (Fig. 6.8.4) and the current in inductive branch.*

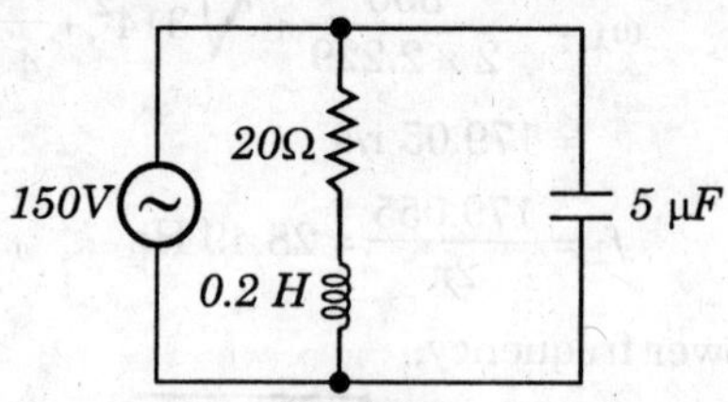


Fig. 6.8.4.

**Solution :** $$\omega_{ar} = \sqrt{\frac{1}{LC} - \frac{R^2}{L^2}}$$

$$= \sqrt{\frac{1}{0.2 \times 5 \times 10^{-6}} - \frac{20^2}{0.2^2}}$$

$$= 999.4 \text{ r/s} \quad \textbf{Ans.}$$

Dynamic resistance.

$$Z_{ar} = \frac{L}{CR} = \frac{0.2}{5 \times 10^{-6} \times 20} = 2000\ \Omega$$

$$I = \frac{V}{Z_{ar}} = \frac{150}{2000} = 0.075 \text{ A}$$

$$I_L = \frac{V}{\sqrt{R_L^2 + X_L^2}} = \frac{150}{\sqrt{20^2 + (0.2 \times 999.4)^2}}$$

$$= \frac{150}{\sqrt{400^2 + 199.8^2}} = \frac{150}{200.7}$$

$$= 0.747 \text{ A.} \quad \textbf{Ans.}$$

**Example : 6.8.5** *Determine the value of capacitive reactance $X_C$ such the parallel circuit (Fig. 6.8.5) resonates*

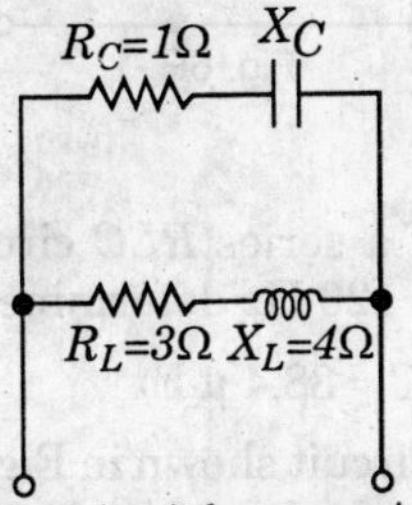


Fig. 6.8.5 circuit for example 6.8.5

**Solution :**

$$\mathbf{Y}_c = \frac{1}{1 - jX_C} = \frac{1 + jX_C}{1^2 + X_C^2}$$

$$= \frac{1}{1 + X_C{}^2} + \frac{jX_C}{1 + X_C^2}$$

$$\mathbf{Y}_L = \frac{1}{3 + j4} = \frac{3 - j4}{3^2 + 4^2}$$

$$= \frac{3}{25} - \frac{j4}{25}$$

Total admittance, $\mathbf{Y} = \mathbf{Y}_L + \mathbf{Y}_C$

$$= \left(\frac{3}{25} - \frac{j4}{25}\right) + \left(\frac{1}{1 + X_c^2} + \frac{jX_c}{1 + X_c^2}\right)$$

$$= \left(\frac{3}{25} + \frac{1}{1 + X_c^2}\right) + j\left(\frac{X_c}{1 + X_c^2} - \frac{4}{25}\right)$$

For resonance the imaginary part of the admittance is zero *i.e.*,

$$\frac{X_C}{1 + X_C^2} - \frac{4}{25} = 0$$

$$\therefore \quad -X_C^2 + 25X_C - 4 = 0$$

Solving above equation,

$$X_C = 24.83\Omega, \ 0.165\ \Omega \qquad \textbf{Ans.}$$

## PROBLEMS

**6.1** Determine the limiting value of $R_C$ for the resonance. The network is shown in Fig. 6P-1

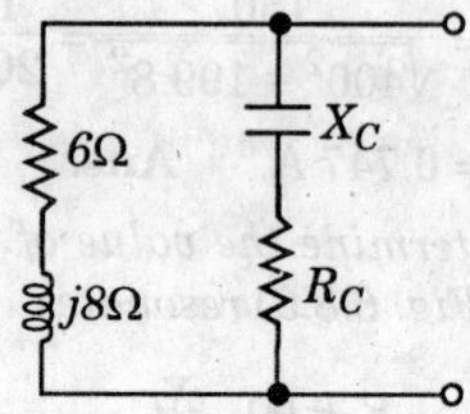


Fig. 6P -1

(**Ans.** $R_c \leq 3.125\ \Omega$)

**6.2** The bandwidth of a series *RLC* circuit is to be 80 Hz. If the resistance is 10Ω and $\omega_r$ = 120 Hz determine the values of *L* and *C*

(**Ans.** $L = 0.0198\text{H}$ , $C = 88.4\ \mu\ \text{F}$)

**6.3** With reference to circuit shown in Fig. 6P.2 the supply frequency is varied till the capacitor voltage reaches a maximum value.

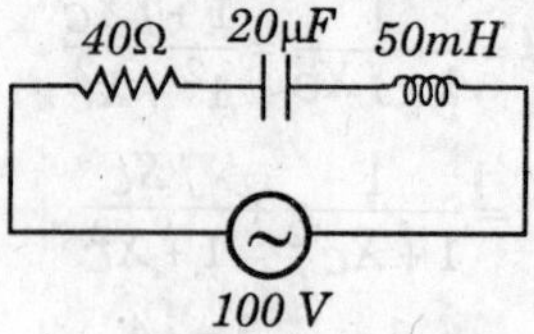


Fig. 6P-2

(*i*) Determine the frequency and the maximum voltage mentioned above.

(*ii*) Resonant frequency.

[**Ans.** (*i*) $\omega_c = 824.6$ r/s, $V_{c\ max} = 136.35\ V$ (*ii*) $\omega_0 = 10^3$ r/s.]

**6.4** Calculate the resonant frequency for a series *RLC* circuit having $R = 40\Omega$, $L = 0.075$ H and $C = 25\mu$ F. The circuit is connected to a sinusoidal variable frequency supply having a voltage 120 V.

Determine (*i*) Frequency for $V_{c\ max}$.

(*ii*) Frequency for $V_{L\ max}$.

[**Ans** : $f_0 = 116.18$ Hz (*i*) 99.47 Hz (*ii*) 135.6 Hz]

**6.5** Determine the resonant frequency, *Q* factor, half-power frequencies and maximum current drawn for a series circuit consisting $R = 800\Omega$, $L = 75$ mH and $C = 25p$ F. The circuit is connected to a 200 *V* variable frequency supply.

(**Ans** : $f_0 = 116.18$ kHz , $f_2 = 117.09$ kHz ,

$f_1 = 115.39$ kHz , $I_0 = 0.25$A)

**6.6** Determine the half-power frequencies for *RLC* series circuit having given

$R = 10\Omega$ , $L = 0.5$ mH and $C = 0.5\ \mu$ F.

(**Ans** : $f_1 = 0.859 \times 10^4$ Hz $\quad f_2 = 1.777 \times 10^4$ Hz)

**6.7** Determine the value of $L$ and $C$ parameters of a series *RLC* circuit to have a bandwidth 60 Hz. Given that $R = 5\Omega$ and resonant frequency 400 Hz.

(**Ans** : $L = 0.0132$ H , $C = 11.93\ \mu$ F.)

**6.8** The resonant frequency for the network shown in Fig. 6P.3 is 600 Hz. Find the value of $C$.

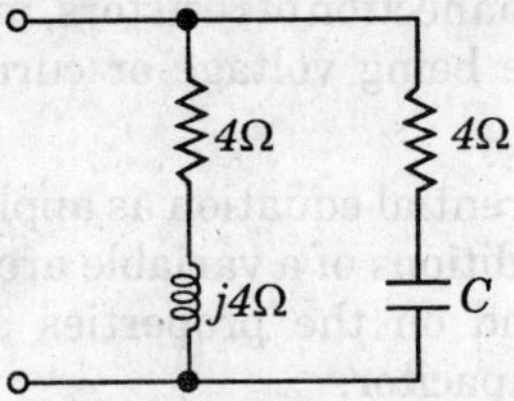


Fig. 6P.3

(**Ans** : $C = 66.27\ \mu$ F.)

# 7
# Differential Equations and Solution of Electrical Networks

## 7.1 INTRODUCTION

The differential equations used in electrical network analysis are formulated as per interconnection of resistors, inductors and capacitors. The dependent variable being voltage or current and time as independent variable.

On solving the differential equation as applied to eletrical network equation, the initial conditions of a variable are to be determined. The initial conditions depend on the properties of circuit elements *i.e.* resistor, inductor and capacitor.

## 7.2 DIFFERENTIAL EQUATIONS

The highest order of a derivative in a differential equation gives its order.

$$a_0 \frac{di}{dt} + a_1 i = v \text{ : first order differential equation}$$

$$a_0 \frac{d^2i}{dt^2} + a_1 \frac{di}{dt} + a_2 i = v \text{ : second order differential equations}$$

$a_0$ , $a_1$ , $a_2$ are constants.

The equations given above are non-homogeneous. If the dependent variable and all its derivatives are of first degree the differential equation is said to be linear.

If the derivatives in a differential equation are total *i.e* not partial, the differential in called ordinary differential equation

An electrical circuit consisting of resistors, inductors and capacitors and sources is considered to form ordinary-linear differential equation with constant coefficients.

### 7.2.1 Solution of a First Order Differential Equation

A first order differential equation with constant coefficients is given below,

$$\frac{di}{dt} + Pi = Q$$

where $P$ is a constant and $Q$ may be constant or a function of independent variable (time). To solve above differential equation multiply the same by the integrating factor $e^{Pt}$. Thus,

$$e^{Pt} \frac{di}{dt} + e^{Pt} P i = e^{Pt} Q$$

The derivative of a product is given by

$$\frac{d}{dt}(uv) = u \frac{dv}{dt} + v \frac{du}{dt}$$

Let, $$u = i$$

and $$v = e^{Pt}$$

$$\therefore \quad \frac{d}{dt}(i\, e^{Pt}) = iPe^{Pt} + e^{Pt} \frac{di}{dt}$$

or $$\frac{d}{dt}(i\, e^{Pt}) = \left(\frac{di}{dt} + P\, i\right) e^{Pt}$$

$$\because \quad \frac{di}{dt} + P\, i = \text{Q}$$

$$\therefore \quad \frac{d}{dt}(i\, e^{Pt}) = e^{Pt}\, Q$$

On integrating both sides,

$$i\, e^{Pt} = \int e^{Pt}\, Q\, dt + k$$

where $k$ is the constant of integration. The solution is given by

$$i = e^{-Pt} \int e^{Pt} Q + k\, e^{-Pt}$$

The first term on the *RHS* of the solution is known as particular solution and second complementary function.

An electrical network contains energy storage elements (inductor and capacitor) leads to formation of a differential equation. The two parts of the solution of a differential equation are particular solution and complementary function. The complementary function is the transient response vanishing with time and particular solution refers to steady state response. Thus, the complete solution is

$$i = i_{ss} + i_p$$

## 7.3 TIME RESPONSE

### 7.3.1 Time Response of a Series *RL* Circuit Connected to a d.c. Voltage Source

A series *RL* circuit is switched on to a d.c. voltage $V$ as shown in Fig. 7.3.1

Applying Kischhoff's voltage law,

$$R\,i + L\frac{di}{dt} = V$$

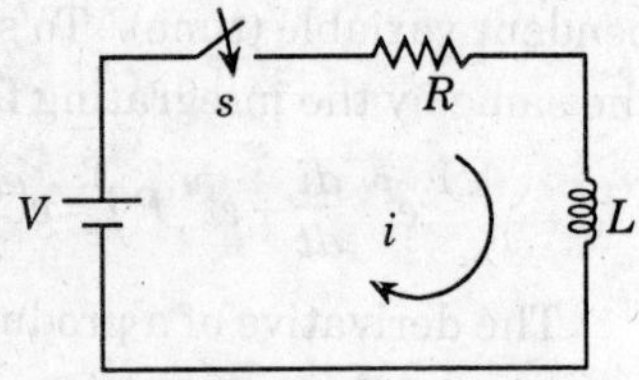


Fig. 7.3.1 Series RL circuit connected to a d.c. supply.

The first order differential equation given above is non-homogeneous.

On rearranging,

$$\frac{di}{dt} + \frac{R}{L}i = \frac{V}{L}$$

The integrating factor is $e^{(R/L)\,t}$

The solution of the above differential equation is given below :

$$i = e^{-(R/L)\,t}\int \frac{V}{L}\,e^{R/Lt}\,dt + k\,e^{-(R/L)\,t}$$

On evaluating the integral

$$i = e^{-(R/L)t}\,\frac{V}{L}\cdot\frac{L}{R}\,e^{(R/L)t} + k\,e^{-(R/L)t}$$

On simplification,

$$i = \frac{V}{R} + k\,e^{-RLt}$$

The integration constant $k$ is to be determined from the knowledge of initial condition prevailing in the network. It is known that at the instant of closing the switch

"S" *i.e.* at $t = 0$, $i(0) = 0$

$$\because \qquad i\,(0) = \frac{V}{R} + ke^{-(R/L)\times 0}$$

$$\therefore \qquad 0 = \frac{V}{R} + k$$

Hence, $$k = -\frac{V}{R}$$

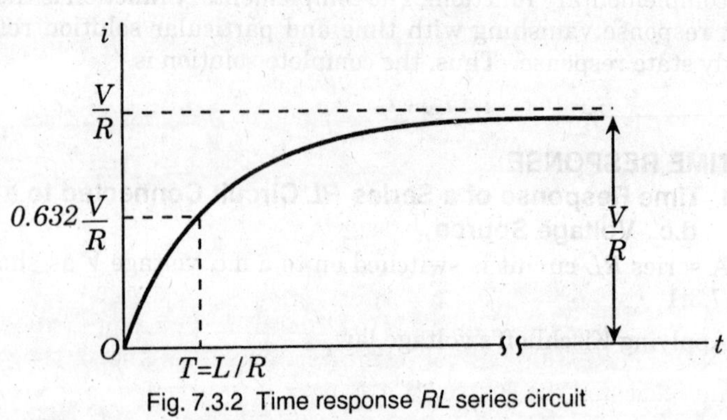


Fig. 7.3.2 Time response *RL* series circuit

Therefore, the particular solution is

$$i = \frac{V}{R} - \frac{V}{R} e^{-\frac{R}{L}t}$$

or $$i = \frac{V}{R}(1 - e^{-R/Lt})$$

### 7.3.2 Time Response of a Series *RC* Circuit Connected to a d.c. voltage Source.

A series *RC* circuit is switched on to a d.c. voltage *V* as shown in Fig. 7.3.3.

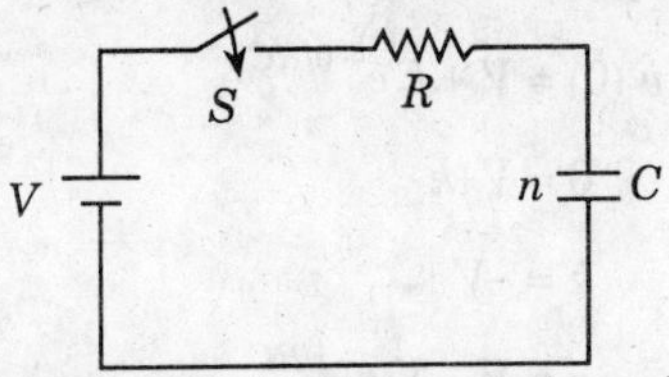


Fig. 7.3.3 Series *RC* circuit connected to a d.c. supply.

The voltage across the capacitor is $v$. Applying Kirchhoff's voltage low

$$R\,i + v = V$$

$$\because \quad i = C\frac{dv}{dt}$$

$$\therefore \quad RC\frac{dv}{dt} + v = V$$

The first order differential equation given above is non - homogeneous.

On rearranging.

$$\frac{dv}{dt} + \frac{1}{RC}v = \frac{V}{RC}$$

The integrating factor is $e^{\frac{t}{RC}}$

The solution of above differential equation is

$$v = e^{-t/RC}\int e^{t/RC}\frac{V}{RC}\,dt + k\,e^{-t/RC}$$

On evaluating the integral.

$$v = e^{-tRC}\frac{1}{RC}\,.\,RC\,e^{t/RC}\,V + k\,e^{-t/RC}$$

On simplification, $v = V + k\,e^{-t/RC}$

The integration constant $k$ is to be determined from the knowledge of initial condition prevailing in the network. It is known that at the instant of closing the switch "S" *i.e.* at $t = 0 \quad v(0) = 0$

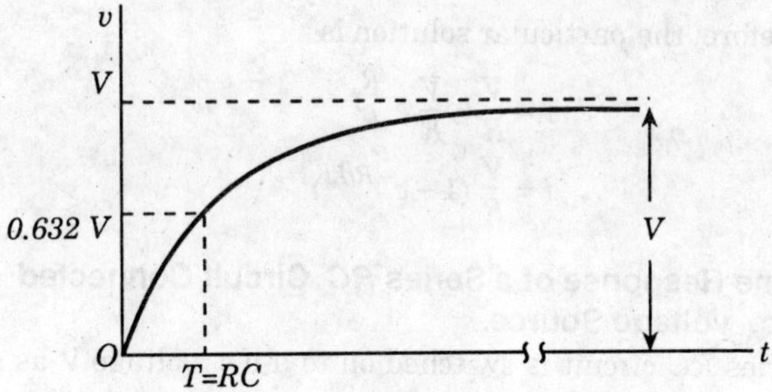


Fig. 7.3.4 Time response $RC$ series circuit.

$$\because \quad v(0) = V + k e^{-0/RC}$$

$$\therefore \quad 0 = V + k$$

$$\therefore \quad k = -V$$

$$\therefore \quad v = V - V e^{-t/RC}$$

or
$$v = V(1 - e^{-t/RC})$$

## 7.4 SOLUTION OF A SECOND ORDER DIFFERENTIAL EQUATION

The homogeneous form of a second order differential equation with constant coefficients is given below.

$$a_0 \frac{d^2 i}{dt^2} + a_1 \frac{di}{dt} + a_2 i = 0 \qquad ...(1)$$

If the above equation is to be satisfied the, second derivative, first derivative and the solution each multiplied by the respective coefficients when added equals zero. Let the solution be of the form,

$$i = k e^{mt}$$

where $k$ and $m$ are constants. Therefore,

$$\frac{di}{dt} = k\, m\, e^{mt}$$

and
$$\frac{d^2}{dt^2} = k\, m^2 e^{mt}$$

Substituting in Eqn.(1)

$$a_0 k m^2 e^{mt} + a_1 k m e^{mt} + a_2 k m^2 e^{mt} = 0$$

or
$$k e^{mt} (a_0 m^2 + a_1 m + a_2) = 0$$

If $ke^{mt}$ is the solution of Eqn. (1), then

$$a_0 m^2 + a_1 m + a_2 = 0$$

Above equation is known as auxiliary equation or characteristic equation. The roots of the auxiliary equation are

$$m_1, m_2 = \frac{-a_1 \pm \sqrt{a_1^2 - 4a_0 a_2}}{2a_0}$$

Thus, the two possible solutions of Eqn. (1) are

$$i_1 = k_1 e^{m_1 t}$$

and $$i_2 = k_2 e^{m_2 t}$$

The solution of Eqn. (1) is also the sum of two solutions given above. Thus,

$$a_0 \frac{d^2}{dt^2}(i_1 + i_2) + a_1 \frac{d}{dt}(i_1 + i_2) + a_2 (i_1 + i_2) = 0$$

or $$\left(a_0 \frac{d^2 i_1}{dt^2} + a_1 \frac{di_1}{dt} + a_2 i_1\right) + \left(a_0 \frac{d^2 i_2}{dt^2} + a_1 \frac{di_2}{dt} + a_2 i_2\right) = 0$$

The general solution of a second order homogeneous differential equation is given by

$$i = k_1 e^{m_1} + k_2 e^{m_2 t}$$

The roots $m_1, m_2$ of the auxiliary equation depend on the value of equation coefficients as below,

$m_1, m_2$ are *real* , if $a_1^2 > 4 a_0 a_2$

$m_1, m_2$ are real and equal, if $a_1^2 = 4a_0 a_2$

$m_1, m_2$ are complex conjugate, if $a_1^2 < 4 a_0 a_2$

### 7.4.1 Time Response of a Series *RLC* Circuit connected to a d.c voltage source.

A series *RLC* circuit is switched on to a d.c. voltage *V* is shown in Fig. 7.4.1.

On application of Kirchhoff's voltage law

$$R i + L \frac{di}{dt} + \frac{1}{C}\int i \, dt = V$$

On differentiation

$$R \frac{di}{dt} + L \frac{d^2 i}{dt^2} + \frac{i}{C} = \frac{dV}{dt}$$

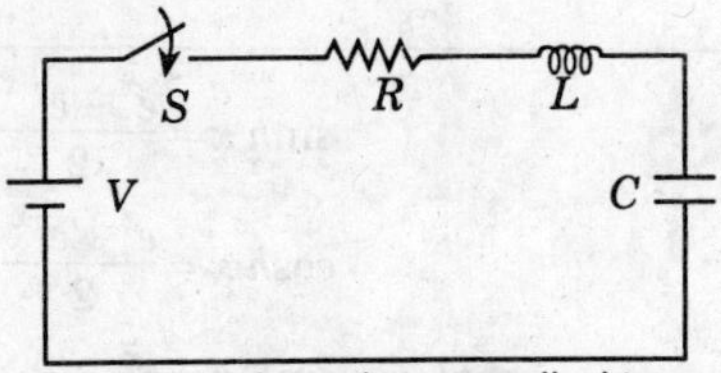

Fig. 7.4.1 *d.c.* voltage applied to a series *RLC* circuit.

Rearranging above equation

$$\frac{d^2 i}{dt^2} + \frac{R}{L}\frac{di}{dt} + \frac{i}{LC} = \frac{1}{L}\frac{dV}{dt}$$

As the source voltage is d.c., $\frac{dV}{dt} = 0$

$$\therefore \quad \frac{d^2i}{dt^2} + \frac{R}{L}\frac{di}{dt} + \frac{i}{LC} = 0$$

The differential equation given above is homogeneous with constant coeffs. and its auxiliary equation given below,

$$m^2 + \frac{R}{L} m + \frac{1}{LC} = 0$$

The auxiliary equation given above is written in the form as below,

$$m^2 + 2\,\xi\,\omega_n\, m + \omega^2 n = 0$$

where, $$2\,\xi\,\omega_n = \frac{R}{L}$$

and $$\omega_n = \frac{1}{\sqrt{LC}}$$

The roots of the auxiliary equation are

$$m_1, m_2 = -\,\xi\,\omega_n \pm \omega_n\sqrt{\xi^2 - 1}$$

Positive values of $\xi$ and $\omega_n$ are to be considered.

(*i*) $\xi > 1$ over damped response

The general solution of a second order homogeneous differential equation is given below.

$$i\,(t) = k_1\, e^{m_1 t} + k_2\, e^{m_2 t}$$

$$\therefore \quad i\,(t) = k_1\, e^{(-\xi\,\omega_n + \omega_n\sqrt{\xi^2 - 1})\,t} + k_2\, e^{(-\xi\,\omega_n\sqrt{\xi^2\, l})t}\,{}^{*}$$

$$= e^{-\xi\omega_m t}\,[k_1 \cosh\,(\omega_m\sqrt{\xi^2 - 1})\,t$$

$$+ k_1 \sinh\,(\omega_m\sqrt{\xi^2 - 1})t$$

$$+ k_2 \cosh\,(\omega_n\sqrt{\xi^2 - 1})\,t - k_2 \sinh\,(\omega_n\sqrt{\xi^2 - 1})t]$$

$$= e^{-\xi\omega_m t}\,[(k_1 + k_2)\cosh\,(\omega_n\sqrt{\xi^2 - 1})\,t$$

$$+ (k_1 - k_2)\sinh\,(\omega_n\sqrt{\xi^2 - 1})\,t]$$

---

$$^{*} \quad \sinh x = \frac{e^x - e^{-x}}{2} = \frac{e^x}{2} - \frac{e^{-x}}{2}$$

$$\cosh x = \frac{e^x + e^{-x}}{2} = \frac{e^x}{2} + \frac{e^{-x}}{2}$$

$$\therefore \quad \cosh x + \sinh x = e^x$$

$$\cosh x - \sinh x = e^{-x}$$

put $\quad (k_1 + k_2) = k_3$ and $(k_1 - k_2) = k_4$

$$\therefore \quad i(t) = e^{-\xi\omega_n t}\,[k_3 \cosh(\omega_n \sqrt{\xi^2 - 1})\, t$$

$$+ k_4 \sinh(\omega_n \sqrt{\xi^2 - 1})\, t] : \text{General solution}$$

$$\text{At } t = 0,\ i(0) = 0,\ \cosh(\omega_m \sqrt{\xi^2 - 1}) \times 0 \to 1$$

and $\quad \sinh(\omega_n \sqrt{\xi^2 - 1}) \times 0 \to 0$

$$\therefore \quad 0 = e^{-\xi\omega_n \times 0}\, k_3 \times 1$$

$$\therefore \quad k_3 = 0$$

Hence, $\quad i(t) = e^{-\xi\omega_n t} k_4 \sinh(\omega_n \sqrt{\xi^2 - 1})\, t$

and $\quad \dfrac{di(t)}{dt} = k_4\,[e^{-\xi\omega_n} (\omega_n \sqrt{\xi^2 - 1}) \cosh(\omega_n \sqrt{\xi^2 - 1})\, t$

$$+ \sinh(\omega_n \sqrt{\xi^2 - 1})\, t\,(-\xi\omega_n)\, e^{-\xi\omega_n t}]$$

$$\text{At } t \to 0 \quad \cosh(\omega_n \sqrt{\xi^2 - 1} \times 0 \to 1$$

$$\sinh(\omega_n \sqrt{\xi^2 - 1} \times 0 \to 0 \text{ and } e^{-\xi\omega_n \times 0} \to 1$$

$$\therefore \quad \frac{di(0)}{dt} = k_4 \times 1 \times (\omega_n \sqrt{\xi^2 - 1}) \times 1$$

The integro-differential equation for the

is $R\,i + L\dfrac{di}{dt} + \dfrac{1}{C}\displaystyle\int i\,dt = V$

$$\text{At } t = 0,\ i(0) = 0$$

$$v_c(0) = 0, \text{ because } \frac{1}{C}\int i(0)\,dt = 0$$

$$\therefore \quad L\frac{di(0)}{dt} = V - R\,i(0) + \frac{1}{C}\int i(0)\,dt$$

$$= V - 0 - 0$$

Hence, $\quad \dfrac{di(0)}{dt} = \dfrac{V}{L}$

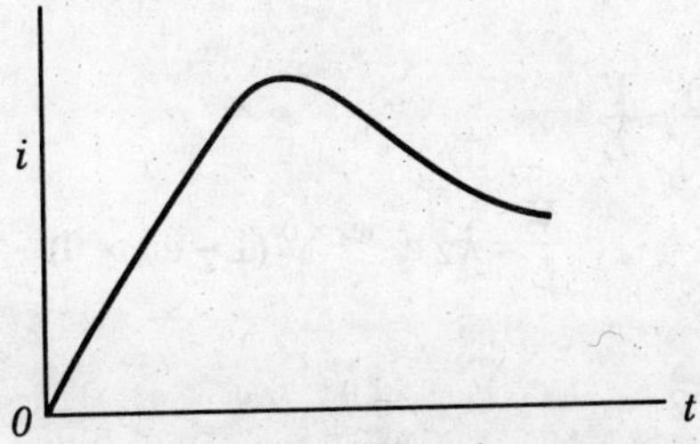


Fig. 7.4.2 Over damped response

$$\therefore \qquad \frac{V}{L} = k_4\, \omega_n \sqrt{\xi^2 - 1}$$

or
$$k_4 = \frac{V}{\omega_n L \sqrt{\xi^2 - 1}}$$

and
$$i(t) = \frac{V}{\omega_n \sqrt{\xi^2 - 1}}\, e^{-\xi \omega_n t} \sinh\left(\omega_n \sqrt{\xi^2 - 1}\right) t$$

(*ii*) $\xi = 1$ critically damped response.

The two roots of the auxiliary equation are

$$m = m_1 = m_2 = -\omega_n$$

The general solution is given below.

$$i(t) = k_1 e^{mt} + k_2\, t\, e^{m_1 t}$$

or
$$i(t) = (k_1 + k_2 t)\, e^{-\omega_n t}$$

At $t = 0 \quad i(0) = 0$

$$\therefore \qquad 0 = (k_1 + k_2 \times 0)\, e^{-\omega_n \times 0}$$

Hence, $k_1 = 0$

$$\therefore \qquad i(t) = k_2\, t\, e^{-\omega_n t}$$

and
$$\frac{di(t)}{dt} = k_2 \left[t(-\omega_n)\, e^{-\omega_n t} + e^{-\omega_n t} \times 1\right]$$

$$= k_2\, e^{-\omega_n t} (1 - \omega_n t)$$

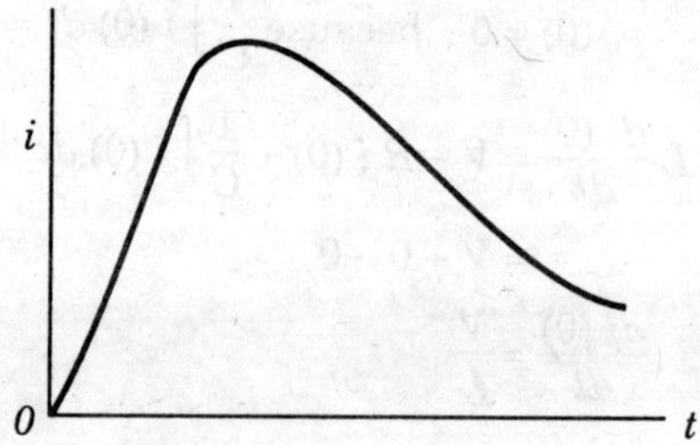


Fig. 7.4.3 Critically damped response

At $t = 0$, $\dfrac{di(0)}{dt} = \dfrac{V}{L}$

$$\therefore \qquad \frac{V}{L} = k_2\, e^{-\omega_n \times 0} (1 - \omega_n \times 0)$$

Hence, $k_2 = \dfrac{V}{L}$

Thus, the solution is

$$i(t) = \frac{V}{L} t\, e^{-\omega_n t}$$

(*iii*) $\xi < 1$ Under damped response.

The two roots of the auxiliary equation are

$$m_1, m_2 = -\xi\omega_n \pm j\omega_n\sqrt{1-\xi^2}$$

The general form of the solution is given below

$$i(t) = k_1 e^{m_1 t} + k_2 e^{m_2 t}$$

$$= k_1 e^{(-\xi\omega_n + j\omega_n\sqrt{1-\xi^2})t} + k_2 e^{(-\xi\omega_n - j\omega_n\sqrt{1-\xi^2})t}$$

$$= e^{-\xi\omega_n t}[k_1 e^{(j\omega_n\sqrt{1-\xi^2})t} + k_2 e^{(-j\omega_n\sqrt{1-\xi^2})t}$$

$$= e^{-\xi\omega_n t}[k_1 \cos \omega_n \sqrt{1-\xi^2} t + j k_1 \sin \omega_n \sqrt{1-\xi^2}$$

$$+ k_2 \cos \omega_n \sqrt{1-\xi^2} t - j k_2 \sin \omega_n \sqrt{1-\xi^2} t]$$

$$= e^{-\xi\omega_n t}[(k_1 + k_2)\cos \omega_n \sqrt{1-\xi^2} t$$

$$+ j(k_1 - k_2)\sin \omega_n \sqrt{1-\xi^2} t)]$$

Put $(k_1 + k_2) = k_3$ and $(k_1 - k_2) = k_4$

$$\therefore\; i(t) = e^{-\xi\omega_n t}(k_3 \cos \omega_n \sqrt{1-\xi^2} t + j k_4 \sin \omega_n \sqrt{1-\xi^2} t)$$

At $t = 0,\; i(0) = 0$

$$\therefore\quad 0 = e^{-\xi\omega_n \times 0}\,.\,[(k_3 \cos \omega_n \sqrt{1-\xi^2} \times 0)$$

$$+ (j k_4 \sin \omega_n \sqrt{1-\xi^2} \times 0)]$$

or $\quad 0 = 1\,(k_3 \times 1 + j k_4 \times 0)$

$\therefore\quad k_3 = 0$

Hence, $\quad i(t) = e^{-\xi\omega_n t}\,.\,j k_4 \sin \omega_n \sqrt{1-\xi^2}\, t$

$$\frac{di(t)}{dt} = j k_4 [(e^{-\xi\omega_n t}\omega_n \sqrt{1-\xi^2} \cos \omega_n \sqrt{1-\xi^2} t)$$

$$+ (\sin \omega_n \sqrt{1-\xi^2} t)(-\xi\omega_n) e^{-\xi\omega_n t}]$$

At $\quad t = 0$

$$\frac{d\,i(0)}{dt} = j k_4 [(e^{-\xi\omega_n \times 0}\omega_n \sqrt{1-\xi^2} \cos \omega_n \sqrt{1-\xi^2} \times 0)$$

$$+ (\sin \omega_n \sqrt{1-\xi^2} \times 0)(-\xi\omega_n) e^{-\xi\omega_n \times 0}]$$

As $\quad t \to 0$

$$\cos \omega_n \sqrt{1-\xi^2} \times 0 \to 1$$

and $\quad \sin \omega_n \sqrt{1-\xi^2} \times 0 \to 0,\; e^{-\xi\,\omega_n \times 0} = 1$

$\therefore \quad \frac{di(0)}{dt} = j\,k_4\,\omega_n\sqrt{1-\xi^2}$

$\because \quad \frac{di(0)}{dt} = \frac{V}{L}$

$\therefore \quad k_4 = \frac{V}{j\,\omega_n L\sqrt{1-\xi^2}}$

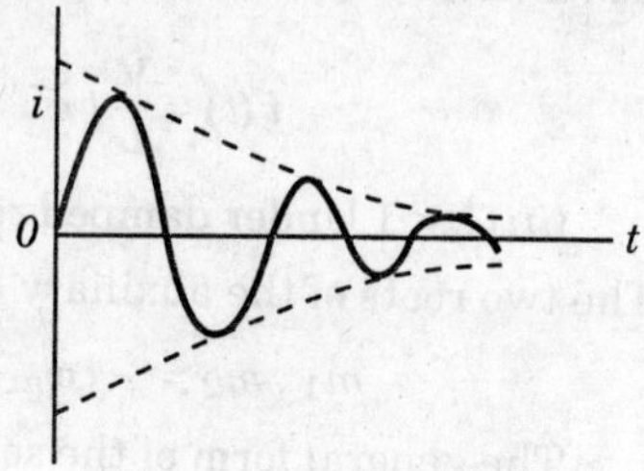


Fig. 7.4.4 Under damped response.

Therefore,

$$i(t) = e^{-\xi\omega_n t}\frac{jV}{j\omega_n L\sqrt{1-\xi^2}}\sin\omega_n\sqrt{1-\xi^2}\,t$$

or $$i(t) = \frac{V}{\omega_n L\sqrt{1-\xi^2}}e^{-\xi\,\omega_n t}\sin\omega_n\sqrt{1-\xi^2}\,t$$

(*iv*) $\xi = 0$ *Oscillatory* response

$\because \quad \xi = 0$

The two roots of auxiliary equation are

$$m_1, m_2 = \pm\, j\,\omega_n$$

The general form of the solution is give below

$$i(t) = k_1 e^{j\,\omega_n t} + k_2\,e^{-j\,\omega_n t}$$

$$= k_1(\cos\omega_n t + j\sin\omega_n t) + k_2(\cos\omega_n t - j\sin\omega_n t)$$

$$= (k_1 + k_2)\cos\omega_n t + j(k_1 - k_2)\sin\omega_n t$$

Put $(k_1 + k_2) = k_3$ and $(k_1 - k_2) = k_4$

$\therefore \quad i(t) = k_3\cos\omega_n t + j\,k_4\sin\omega_n t$

At $\quad t = 0 \quad i(0) = 0$

$\therefore \quad 0 = k_3\cos\omega_n \times 0 + j\,k_4\sin\omega_n \times 0$

or $\quad 0 = k_3 \times 1 + j\,k_4 \times 0$

$$k_3 = 0$$

$\therefore \quad i(t) = j\,k_4\sin\omega_n t$

$$\frac{di(t)}{dt} = j\,k_4\,\omega_n\cos\omega_n t$$

$\therefore \quad \frac{di(0)}{dt} = j\,k_4\,\omega_n\cos\omega_n \times 0$

or $\quad \frac{di(0)}{dt} = j\,k_4\,\omega_n \times 1$

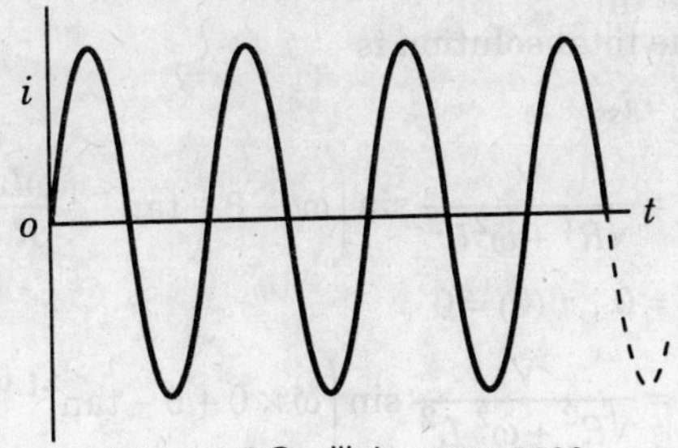


Fig. 7.4.5 Oscillatory response

$$\therefore \quad \frac{di\,(0)}{dt} = \frac{V}{L}$$

$$\therefore \quad \frac{V}{L} = j\, k_4\, \omega_n$$

and $$k_4 = \frac{V}{j\, \omega_n\, L}$$

$$\therefore \quad i(t) = j\, \frac{V}{j\, \omega_n\, L} \sin \omega_n\, t$$

or $$i(t) = \frac{V}{\omega_n\, L} \sin \omega_n\, t$$

### 7.4.2 Time Response of a Series *RL* Circuit Connected to a Sinusoidal Voltage Source

A series $RL$ circuit is shown in Fig. 7.4.6 is connected to a sinusoidal voltage $v = V_m \sin(\omega t + \theta)$.

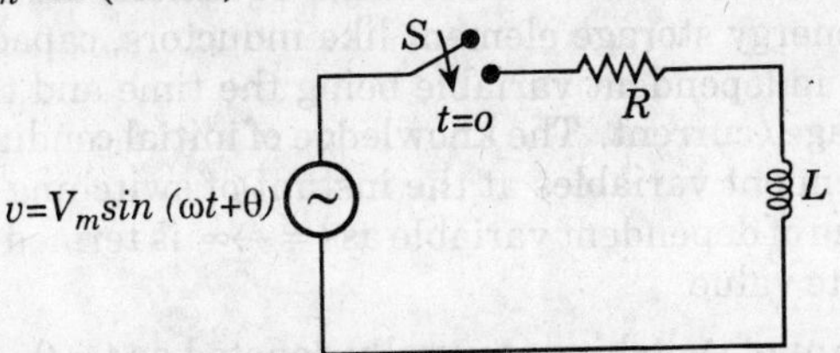


Fig. 7.4.6 *R L* series circuit connected to sinusoidal voltage source.

The switch $S$ is closed at $t = 0$. As per a.c. circuit analysis the steady state current flowing in the circuit is

$$i_{ss} = \frac{V}{\sqrt{R^2 + \omega^2 L^2}} \sin\left(\omega t + \theta - \tan^{-1}\frac{\omega L}{R}\right)$$

where $$V = \frac{V_m}{\sqrt{2}}$$

The transient part of the current is given by the complementary function as below

$$i_c = k\, e^{-(R/L)\,t}$$

Therefore, the total solution is

$$i = i_{ss} + i_c$$

or $$i = \frac{V}{\sqrt{R^2 + \omega^2 L^2}} \sin\left(\omega t + \theta - \tan^{-1}\frac{\omega L}{R}\right) + k\,e^{-\frac{R}{L}t}$$

At $t = 0$, $i(0) = 0$

$$\therefore \quad 0 = \frac{V}{\sqrt{R^2 + \omega^2 L^2}} \sin\left(\omega \times 0 + \theta - \tan^{-1}\frac{\omega L}{R}\right) + k\,e^{-\frac{R}{L}\times 0}$$

$$\therefore \quad k = -\frac{V}{\sqrt{R^2 + \omega^2 L^2}} \sin\left(\theta - \tan^{-1}\frac{\omega L}{R}\right)$$

Thus, $$i = \frac{V}{\sqrt{R^2 + \omega^2 L^2}} \sin\left(\omega t + \theta - \tan^{-1}\frac{\omega L}{R}\right) - \frac{V}{\sqrt{R^2 + \omega^2 L^2}} \sin\left(\theta - \tan^{-1}\frac{\omega L}{R}\right) e^{-(R/L)\,t}$$

If the switch $S$ is closed such that $\left(\theta - \tan^{-1}\frac{\omega L}{R}\right) = 0$

or $$\theta = \tan^{-1}\frac{\omega L}{R}.$$

The transient disappears and the response is transient free.

## 7.5 INITIAL CONDITIONS

In an electrical network differential equations are formed due to presence of energy storage element like inductors, capacitors or both, where in the independent variable being the time and the dependent variable voltage / current. The knowledge of initial conditions gives the value of dependent variables at the instant of switching ($t = 0$). However, the value of dependent variable as $t = \rightarrow\infty$ is termed as final value or steady state value.

The instant of switching is usually denoted as $t = 0$. It is assumed that the switch operates in zero time but for convenience, the time just before the switch operation is denoted as $t = 0^-$ and just after $t = 0^+$.

Thus, the concerned dependent variables just before the switch operation are denoted as $v(0^-)$, $i(0^-)$ and just after as $v(0^+)$, $i(0^+)$ etc.

The state of a network prior to switching operation decide the initial condition of variables. The current, voltage and their time derivatives in an inductor, capacitor determine the initial conditions in a network.

The initial conditions for resistor, inductor and capacitor at the instant of switching are determined below.

### 7.5.1 Resistor

A resistor $R$ connected through a switch $S$ to a d.c. voltage $V$ is shown in Fig. 7.5.1

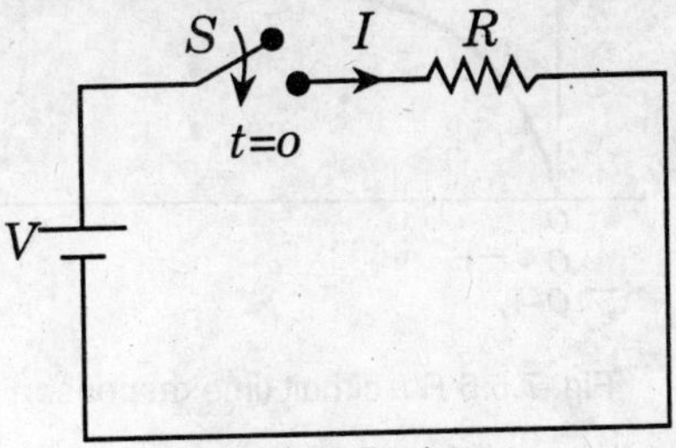

Fig. 7.5.1 Resistor (switch closed at $t = 0$)

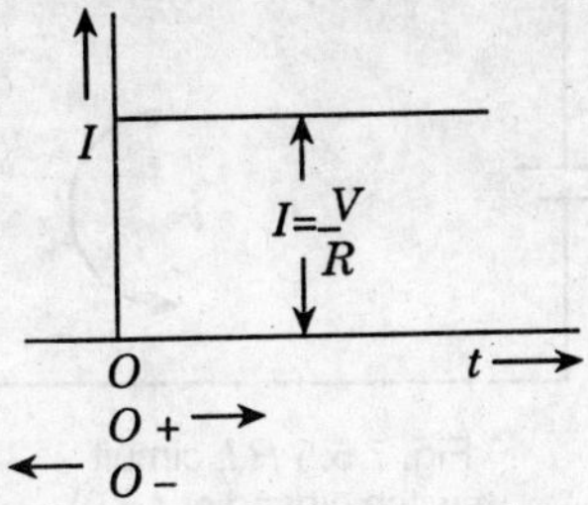

Fig. 7.5.2 current $I = \frac{V}{R}$

The open position of the switch does not allow the flow of current through $R$ *i.e* $I = 0$. This is the situation for $t = 0^-$. At $t = 0$ the switch is closed and a current $I = \frac{V}{R}$ flows through $R$ for all the time. The initial condition for the current is $I(0^-) = 0$ and on closing the switch

$$I(0^+) = \frac{V}{R}$$

Thus, $I(0^-) \neq I(0^+)$

The circuit shown in Fig 7.5.3 refers to opening of a switch.

The switch $S$ is already closed. Prior to opening the switch the current through $R$ is $I = \frac{V}{R}$.

The switch is opened at $t = 0$ and the current flowing through $R$ is zero

Thus, $I(0^-) \neq I(0^+)$

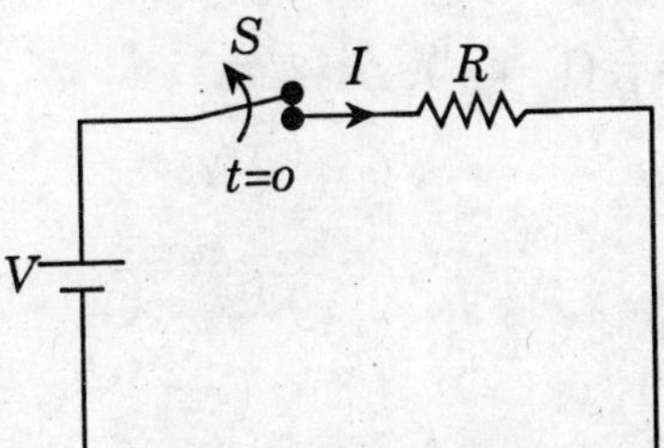

Fig. 7.5.3 Resistor (switch opened at $t = 0$)

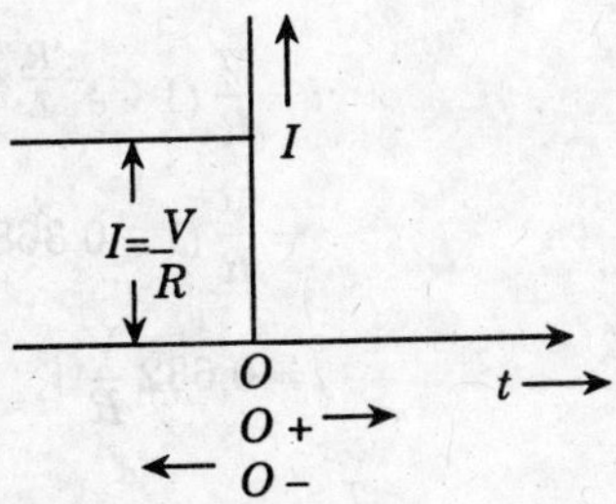

Fig. 7.5.4 $I = 0$ for $t < 0$

### 7.5.2 Inductor

The combination of a resistor and inductor in series is connected through switch $S$ to a d.c. voltage source as shown in Fig 7.5.5.. At $t =$ 0 the switch $S$ is closed.

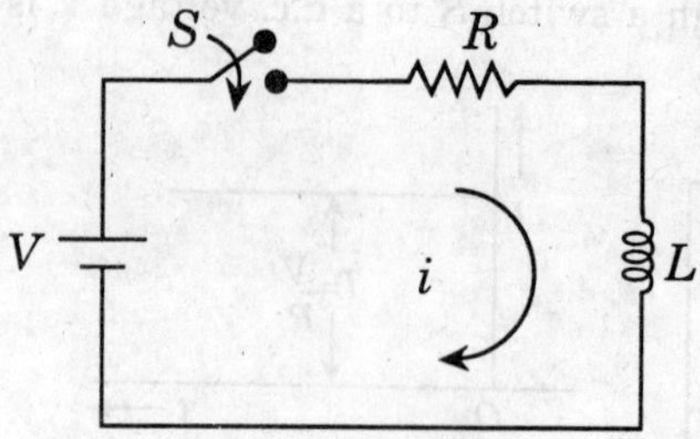


Fig. 7.5.5 $R\,L$ circuit (switch closed at $t = 0$)

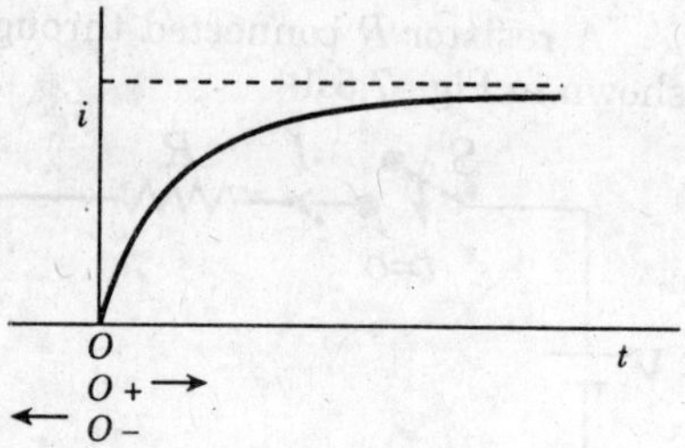


Fig. 7.5.6 $R\,L$ circuit time response.

Applying Kirchhoff's voltage law

$$R\,i + L\frac{di}{dt} = L$$

The solution of first order differential equation given above is

$$i = \frac{V}{R}(1 - e^{-(R/L)\,t})$$

The time response (variation of current w.r.t. time) of a series $RL$ circuit subjected to a d.c. voltage $V$ (excitation) is given by the relation mentioned above (Fig. 7.5.6.)

The steady state response $i_{ss}$ *i.e* $t \to \infty$ is determined below.

$$i_{ss} = \frac{V}{R}(1 - e^{-R/L \times \infty})$$

$$\therefore \quad i_{ss} = \frac{V}{R}$$

$$\text{At} \quad t = \frac{L}{R}$$

$$i = \frac{V}{R}\left(1 - e^{-\frac{R}{L}\times\frac{L}{R}}\right) = \frac{V}{R}(1 - e^{-1})$$

$$= \frac{V}{R}(1 - 0.368)$$

$$\text{or} \quad i = 0.632\,\frac{V}{R}\Big|_{t = \frac{L}{R}}$$

The ratio $\frac{L}{R}$ is termed as time constant of a series $RL$ circuit and denoted as $T = \frac{L}{R}$

In one time constant the current $i$ reaches 63.2% of the steady state value.

At $t = 4T$, The response reaches a value as determined below.

$$i = \frac{V}{R}(1 - e^{-(R/L) \times 4\,L/R}) = \frac{V}{R}(1 - e^{-4})$$

$$\cong \frac{V}{R}(1 - 0.02)$$

or $$i \cong 0.98\frac{V}{R}\bigg|_{t=4T}$$

The time constant indicates the speed of time response, the lower value of time constant gives a fast response while higher value results in a slow response.

The time response is divided into two parts

(i) From $t = 0$ to $t = 4T$ the transiont response

(ii) Beyond $t = 4T$ it is considered that steady state is reached

As per time response expression,

$$i = \frac{V}{R}(1 - e^{-(R/L)\,t})$$

it is noted that

1. at $t = 0^-$ (switch open), $i\,(0^-) = 0$
2. at $t = 0^+$ (switch just closed), $i\,(0^+) = 0$
3. as $t \to \infty$ (switch still closed), $i_{ss} = \frac{V}{R}$

Therefore, for the inductor

$$i\,(0^-) = i(0^+)$$

Thus for the current rise in an inductor the current can not change instantaneously.

Since, $i\,(0^+) = 0$, the inductor behaves like an open circuit.

Further, $i_{ss} = \frac{V}{R}$, the inductor behaves like a short circuit as $t \to \infty$

The steady state current flowing through the inductor stores the energy in it.

If the source voltage is disconnect and external short circuit is applied to *RL* series circuit (Fig. 7.5.7), The energy stored in inductor is dissipated in the resistor till the current reaches a zero value.

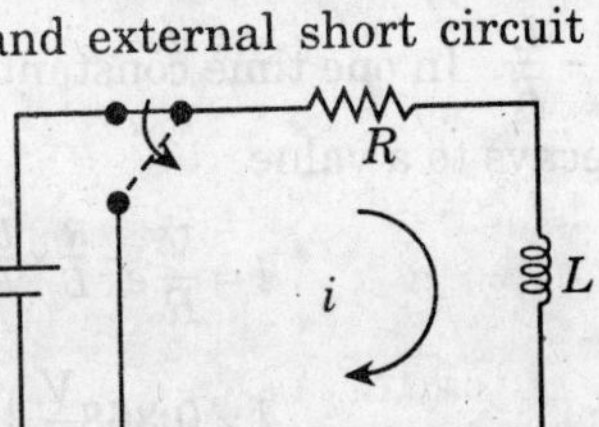

Fig. 7.5.7 *R L* circuit current decay

The expression for the current decay mentioned above deverived below.

The switch $S$ is held at position (1) for a long time, so that $i_{ss} = \frac{V}{R}$

At $t = 0$, the switch $S$ is moved at position (2) applying short circuit at the terminals of series $RL$ combination. Therefore, Applying Kirchhoff's voltage law

$$R\,i + L\frac{di}{dt} = 0$$

*separating* the variables,

$$\frac{di}{i} = -\frac{R}{L}\,dt$$

On integrating both sides,

$\log_e i = -\frac{R}{L}t + k$, where $k$ is the constant of integration

At $\quad t = 0 \quad i = \frac{V}{R}$

$$\therefore \quad \log_e\left(\frac{V}{R}\right) = -\frac{R}{L}\times 0 + k$$

or $$k = \log_e\left(\frac{V}{R}\right)$$

$$\therefore \quad \log_e i = -\frac{R}{L}t + \log_e\left(\frac{V}{R}\right)$$

or $$\log_e\left(\frac{i}{V/R}\right) = -\frac{R}{L}t$$

or $$\frac{i}{V/R} = e^{-\frac{R}{L}t}$$

Thus, the time response expression for the current decay in a series $RL$ circuit is given below

$$i = \frac{V}{R}e^{-R/L\,t}$$

The variation of current w.r.t. time is shown in Fig. 7.5.8.

The time constant of the circuit is $T = \frac{L}{R}$. In one time constant the current decays to a value

$$i = \frac{V}{R}e^{-\frac{R}{L}\times\frac{L}{R}} = \frac{V}{R}e^{-1}$$

or $$i = 0.368\frac{V}{R}\Big|_{t=\frac{L}{R}}$$

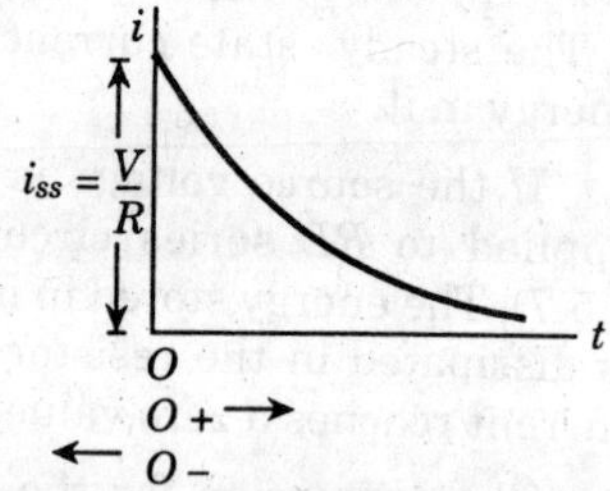

Fig. 7.5.8 Time response current decay (R L).

At $t = (0^-)$ , $i(0^-) = i_{ss} = \dfrac{V}{R}$

Further, at $t = (0^+)$ , $i\,(0^+) = \dfrac{V}{R}$, $\left[ i\,(0^+) = \dfrac{V}{R} e^{-\frac{R}{L} \times 0} = \dfrac{V}{R} \right]$

Hence, $i\,(0^-) = i\,(0^+)$

Thus, for the current decay is an inductor also the current can not change instantaneously.

In general, the current in an inductor can not change instantaneously.

### 7.5.3 Capacitor

The combination of a resistor and capacitor in series connected through a switch to a d.c. supply voltage $V$ is shown in Fig. 7.5.9.

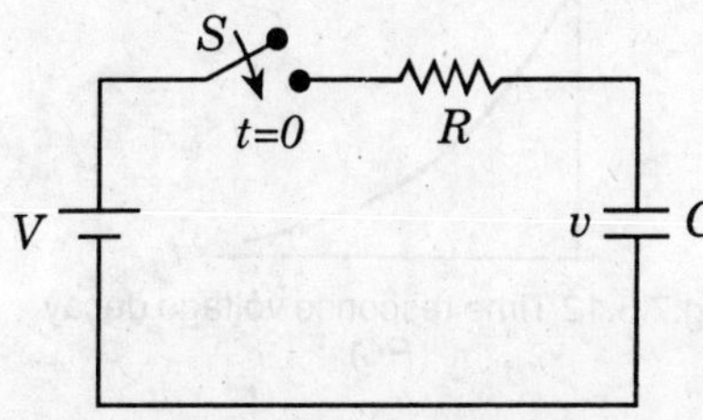


Fig. 7.5.9 $RC$ circuit switch closed at $t = 0$

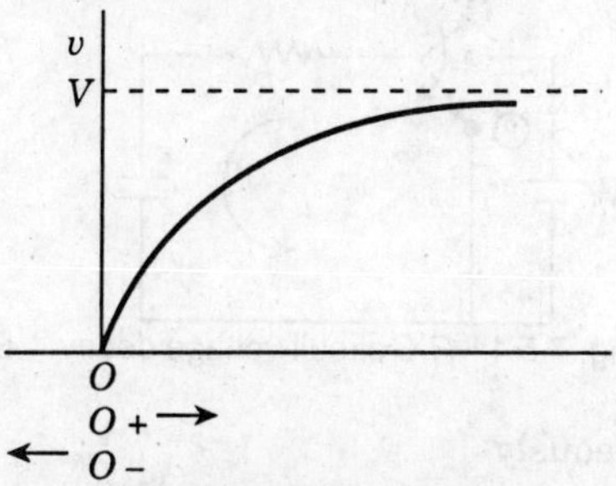


Fig. 7.5.10 Time response $RC$ circuit

The switch is closed at $t = 0$. The instantaneous voltage across the capacitor is considered as $v$.

Applying Kirchhoff's voltage law,

$$R\,i + v = V$$

$$\because \qquad i = C\frac{dv}{dt}$$

$$RC\frac{dv}{dt} + v = V$$

or
$$\frac{dv}{dt} + \frac{v}{RC} = \frac{V}{RC}$$

The solution of the first order differential equation

$$v = V\,(1 - e^{-t/RC})$$

The time response (variation of the capacitor voltage w.r.t. time) of a $RC$ series circuit is shown in Fig. 7.5.10. The time constant of a series $RC$ circuit is $T = RC$

On switching , a d.c. voltage the rise in the capacitor voltage is due to the charging of a capacitor. As $t \to \infty$, $v(\infty) \to V$ and the current flowing in the series $RC$ circuit reaches a zero value.

In one time constant the capacitor voltage reaches a value of 63.2% of $V$

It is noted that.

at $t = (0^-)$ (switch open) $v(0^-) = 0$

at $t = (0^+)$ (switch closed) $v(0^+) = 0$

$\therefore \quad v(0^-) = v(0^+)$

Therefore, The voltage across the capacitor can not change instan-

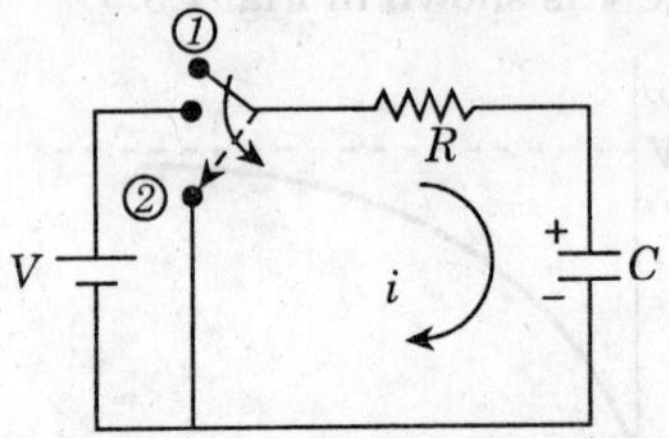


Fig. 7.5.11 $RC$ circuit voltage decay

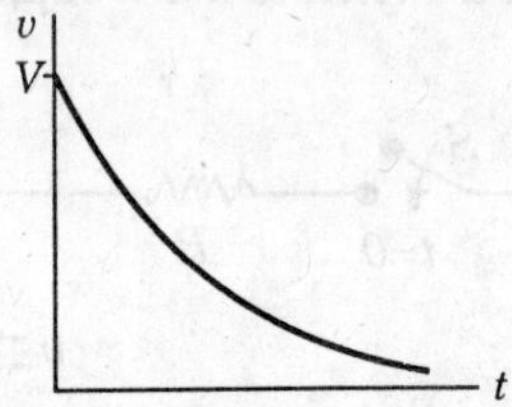


Fig.7.5.12 Time response voltage decay ($RC$)

taneously

The expression for the current flowing in a series $RC$ circuit (Fig. 7.5.10) is determined below.

$$\therefore \quad i = C\frac{dv}{dt}$$

$$i = C\frac{d}{dt}\left\{\left(V - e^{-t/RC}\right)\right\} = CV\frac{d}{dt}(1 - e^{-tRC})$$

$$= -CV\frac{d}{dt}e^{-t/RC}) = -CV\left(-\frac{1}{RC}e^{-t/RC}\right)$$

or
$$i = \frac{V}{R}e^{-\frac{t}{RC}}$$

At $t = (0^+)$, $i(0^+) = \frac{V}{R}$, the capacitor behaves as short circuit

As $t \to \infty$, $i(\infty) \to 0$ , the capacitor behaves as open circuit

A d.c. voltage $V$ connected to a combination of a resistor and capacitor through a switch $S$ held at position (1) for a long time (Fig. 7.5.11) so that the capacitor is fully charged to supply voltage $V$.

The switch is moved to position (2) at $t = 0$. The final condition for $v$ at position (1) is the initial condition for switch position (2).

For switch at position (2), the Kirchhoff's voltage law equation is written below.

$$Ri + v = 0$$

where, $v$ is the instantaneous value of capacitor voltage.

$$\because \quad i = C\frac{v}{dt}$$

$$\therefore \quad RC\frac{dv}{dt} + v = 0$$

Separating the variables,

$$\frac{dv}{v} = \frac{-dt}{RC}$$

On integrating both sides,

$$\log_e v = -\frac{t}{RC} + k$$

where, $k$ is the constant of integration

At $t = 0 \quad v = V$

$$\therefore \quad \log_e v = -\frac{o}{RC} + k$$

and $$k = \log_e V$$

$$\therefore \quad \log_e v = -\frac{t}{RC} + \log_e V$$

or $$\log_e\left(\frac{v}{V}\right) = -\frac{t}{RC}$$

and $$v = V e^{-\frac{t}{RC}}$$

At $t=0^-$ (switch in position 1 for a long time) $v(0^-) = V$

At $t = 0^+$ (switch in position 2) $v(0^+) = V$

Thus, $v(0^-) = v(0^+)$

The voltage across the capacitor can not change instantaneously.

The current supplied by the charged capacitor $C$ when dischared through resistor $R$ is determined below:

$$i = C\frac{dv}{dt}$$

$$\therefore \; i = C\frac{d}{dt}(V e^{-t/RC}) = -\frac{C V e^{-t/RC}}{RC} = -\frac{V}{R}e^{-t/RC}$$

The results obtained above are applied for the determination of initial condition in electrical network during switching operations.

## Initial State and Final State for *RLC* Elements

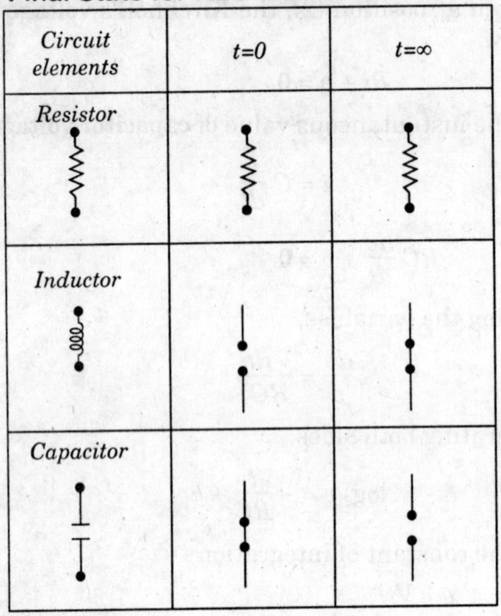


## 7.6 SOLVED EXAMPLES

**Example . 7.6.1** *Determine the expression for v on switching at t = 0. The capacitor has an initial voltage 2 V.*

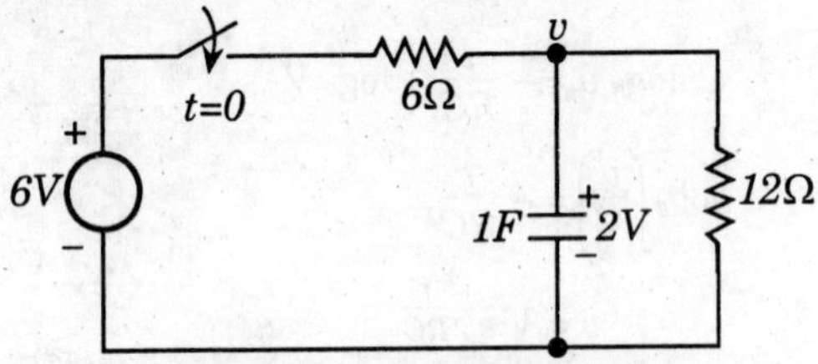


Fig. 7.6.1 Network for example 7.6.1

**Solution.** On switching at $t = 0$, apply *KCL*

$$\therefore \qquad \frac{v-6}{6} + 1\frac{dv}{dt} + \frac{v}{12} = 0$$

On rearranging, $$\frac{dv}{dt} + \frac{v}{4} = 1$$

Separating the variables, $$\frac{dv}{1 - \frac{v}{4}} = dt$$

Integrating on both sides, $$\frac{\log_e\left(\frac{1-v}{4}\right)}{-\frac{1}{4}} = t + k$$

At $t = 0^+$ , $v(0^+) = 2V$ (given)

$$\therefore \quad \frac{\log_e\left(1 - \frac{2}{4}\right)}{-\frac{1}{4}} = 0 + k$$

$$\therefore \quad k = -4 \log_e\left(\frac{1}{2}\right)$$

$$\therefore \quad \frac{\log_e\left(1 - \frac{v}{4}\right)}{-\frac{1}{4}} = t - 4 \log_e\left(\frac{1}{2}\right)$$

or
$$\log_e\left[\frac{\left(1 - \frac{v}{4}\right)}{½}\right] = -\frac{t}{4}$$

$$\therefore \quad 1 - \frac{v}{4} = \frac{1}{2} e^{-\frac{t}{4}}$$

$$\therefore \quad v = 4 - 2\, e^{-\frac{t}{4}} \qquad \textbf{Ans.}$$

**Example : 7.6.2** *The network shown in Fig. 7.6.2 remains in relaxed state with switch S open. At t = 0 the switch is closed determine the expression for v.*

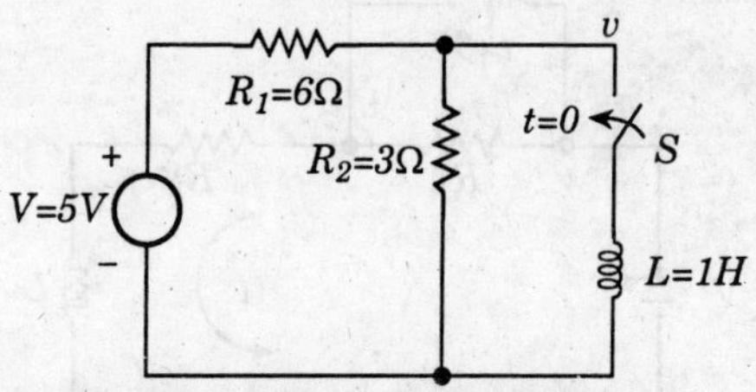


Fig. 7.6.2 Network for example 7.6.2.

**Solution :** At $t = 0$, apply $KCL$

$$\frac{v - V}{R_1} + \frac{v}{R_2} + \frac{1}{L}\int v\, dt = 0$$

or
$$\left(\frac{1}{R_1} + \frac{1}{R_2}\right) v + \frac{1}{L}\int v\, dt = \frac{V}{R_1}$$

Differentiate

$$\left(\frac{1}{R_1} + \frac{1}{R_2}\right)\frac{dv}{dt} + \frac{v}{L} = 0$$

$$\therefore \quad \left(\frac{1}{6} + \frac{1}{3}\right)\frac{dv}{dt} + \frac{v}{1} = 0$$

or $$\frac{dv}{dt} + 2v = 0$$

Separating variables. $$\frac{dv}{v} = -2dt$$

On integrating both sides.

$$\log_e v = -2t + k$$

At $t = 0$ (inductor o/c), $v(0) = 5 \times \frac{6}{6+3} = \frac{10}{3} V$

$$\therefore \quad \log_e \left(\frac{10}{3}\right) = -2 \times 0 + k$$

$$\therefore \quad k = \log_e \left(\frac{10}{3}\right)$$

$$\therefore \quad \log_e v = -2t + \log_e \left(\frac{10}{3}\right)$$

$$\log_e \left(\frac{v}{10/3}\right) = -2t$$

or $$v = \frac{10}{3} e^{-2t}$$ **Ans.**

**Example : 7.6.3** *In the network shown (Fig. 7.6.3) the switch S is closed at t = 0. Determine the variation of current i.*

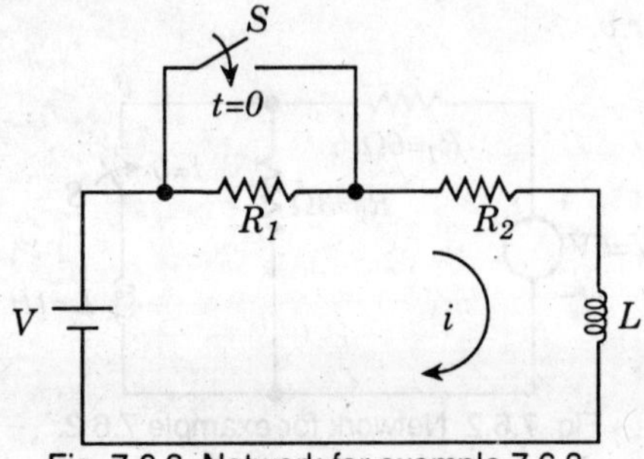


Fig. 7.6.3 Network for example 7.6.3.

**Solution :** At $t = o^-$ (switch $S$ open), the network is relaxed

$$\therefore \quad i(0^-) = \frac{V}{R_1 + R_2}, \quad \text{(inductor L, s/c)}$$

At $t = 0^+$ (switch $S$ closed)

$$R_2 i + L \frac{di}{dt} = V$$

Separating variables $$\frac{di}{V - R_2 i} = \frac{1}{L} dt$$

Integrating both sides

$$\frac{\log_e (V - R_2\, i)}{-R_2} = \frac{t}{L} + k$$

At $$t = 0^-, \quad i\,(0^-) = \frac{V}{R_1 + R_2}$$

$$\therefore \quad \frac{\log_e\left(V - R_2 \dfrac{V}{R_1 + R_2}\right)}{-R_2} = \frac{o}{L} + k\ ,$$

$$\therefore \quad k = \frac{\log_e\left(\dfrac{VR_1}{R_1 + R_2}\right)}{-R_2}$$

$$\therefore \quad \frac{\log_e( V - R_2\, i\,)}{-R_2} = \frac{t}{L} + \frac{\log_e\left(\dfrac{VR_1}{R_1 + R_2}\right)}{-R_2}$$

or $$\log_e\left(\frac{V - R_2\, i}{VR_1/R_1 + R_2}\right) = -\frac{R_2\, t}{L}$$

$$\therefore \quad V - R_2\, i = \frac{VR_1}{R_1 + R_2}\, e^{-R_2/L\, t}$$

$$i = \frac{V}{R_2}\left(1 - \frac{R_1}{R_1 + R_2}\, e^{-R_2/L\, t}\right) \quad \textbf{Ans.}$$

**Example . 7.6.4** *The switches* $S_1$ and $S_2$ *closed at t = 0. Determine the expression for* $v_c$

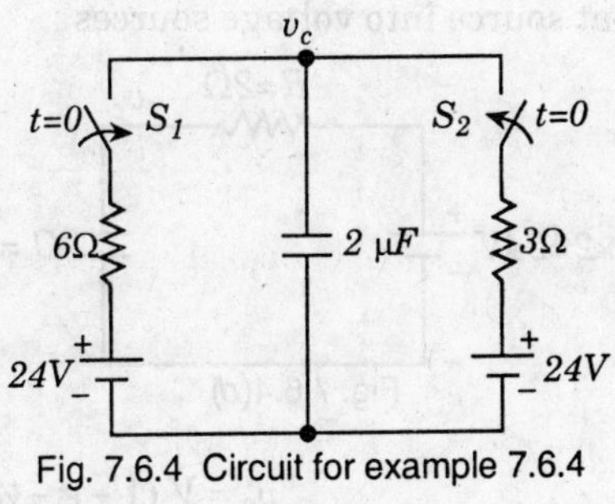


Fig. 7.6.4 Circuit for example 7.6.4

**Solution .** At $t = 0^-$ , $v_c\,(0^-) = 0$

$\therefore$ At $t = 0^+$ , $v_c\,(0^+) = 0$, because capacitor voltage cannot change instantaneously.

For $t \geq 0^+$, the circuit takes the forum as shown in Fig.7.6.4($a$).

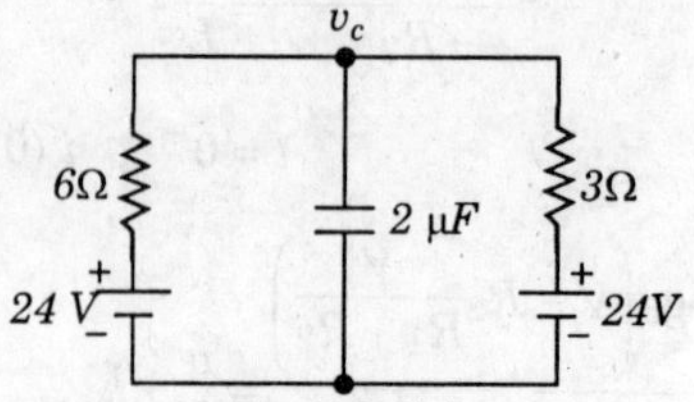


Fig. 7.6.4($a$)

Convert voltage sources into current sources [Fig.7.6.4($b$)]

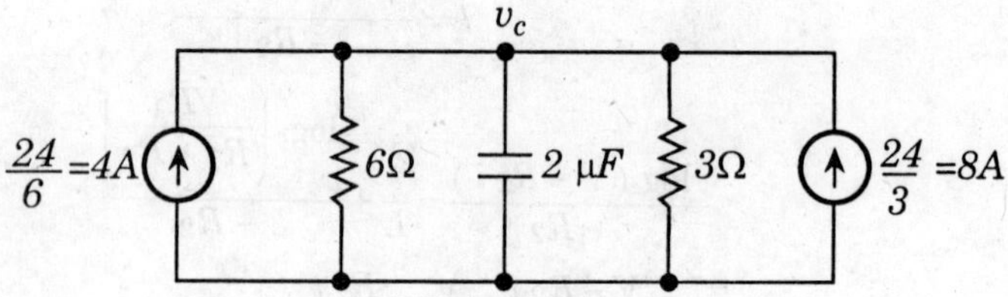


Fig. 7.6.4($b$)

The equivalence of Fig. 7.6.4($b$) is shown in Fig. 7.6.4($c$)

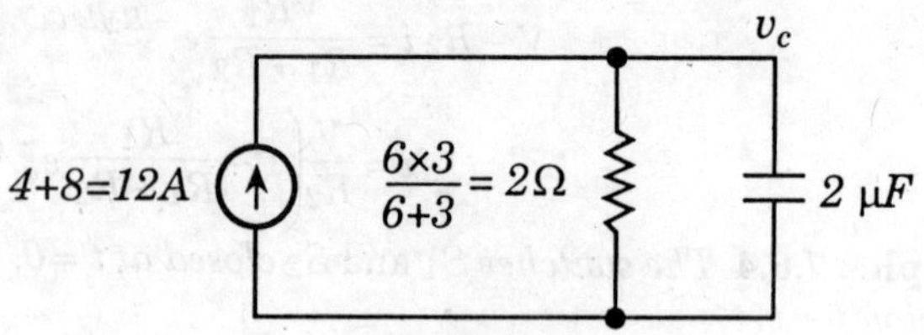


Fig. 7.6.4($c$)

Convert current source into voltage sources

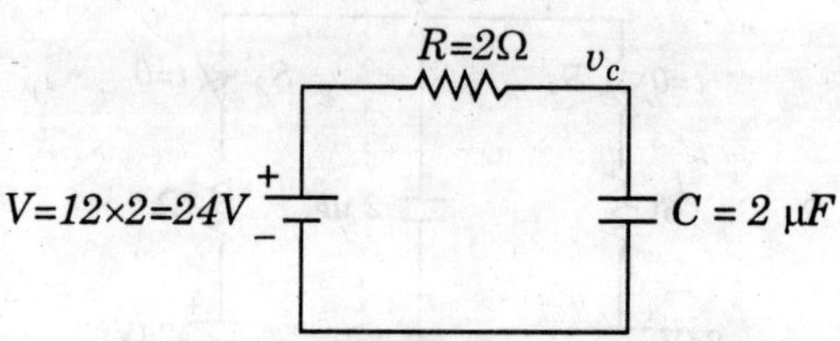


Fig. 7.6.4($d$)

$$v_c = V(1 - e^{-t/RC})$$

or $$v_c = 24\left(1 - e^{-\frac{t}{4\times10^{-6}}}\right)$$ **Ans.**

**Example : 7.6.5** *The switch is kept in position (1) for a long time, then at t = 0 changed to position (2). Determine the current i.*

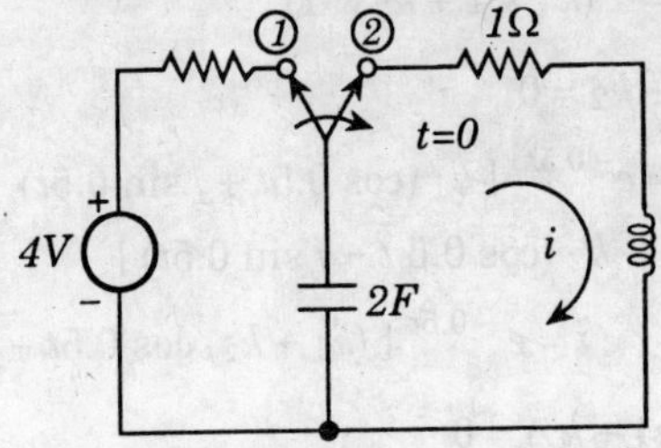


Fig. 7.6.5 circuit for example 7.6.5

**Solution :** Initial condition are determined below.

At $t = 0^-$ (switch at (1))

$$i\,(0^-) = 0$$

$$\therefore \quad i\,(0^-) = i\,(0^+) = 0 \quad \text{(In inductor)}$$

$$v_c\,(0^-) = 4V$$

$$v_c\,(0^-) = v_c\,(0+)$$

$$= 4V \quad \text{(Across capacitor)}$$

At switch position (2), the circuit is shown in Fig. 7.6.5($a$)

The $KVL$ equation (general) is written below

$$1\,i + 1\frac{di}{dt} + \frac{1}{2}\int i\,dt = 0$$

Differentiate above equation,

$$\therefore \frac{d^2i}{dt^2} + \frac{di}{dt} + \frac{i}{2} = 0$$

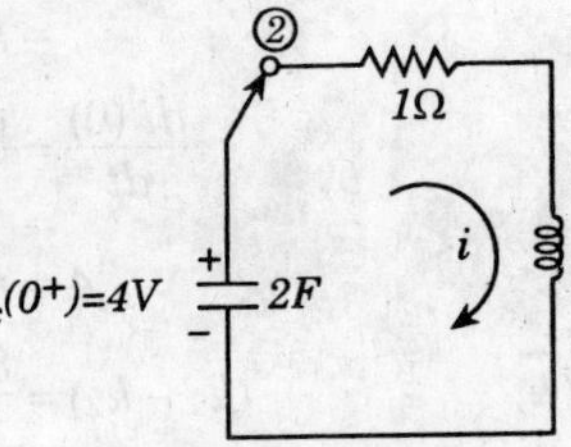


Fig. 7.6.5($a$) circuit at $t = 0^+$

The auxiliary equation is

$$m^2 + m + 0.5 = 0$$

The roots of the above equation are

$$m_1\,,\, m_2 = \frac{-1 \pm \sqrt{1 - 4 \times 0.5}}{2} = -0.5 \pm j0.5$$

The solution is given by

$$i = k_1\, e^{m_1 t} + k_2\, e^{m_2 t}$$

or $$i = k_1\, e^{(-0.5 + j0.5)t} + k_2\, e^{(-0.5 - j0.5)\,t}$$

or $$i = e^{-0.5t}\,(k_1\, e^{j\,0.5t} + k_2\, e^{-j0.5t})$$

$$\therefore \quad i\,(0) = e^{-0.5 \times 0}\,(k_1\, e^{j0.5 \times 0} + k_2\, e^{-j\,0.5 \times 0})$$

$$\because \quad i\,(0) = 0$$

$$\therefore \quad 0 = 1\,(k_1 \times 1 + k_2 \times 1)$$

$$\therefore \quad k_1 + k_2 = 0$$

$$i = e^{-0.5t}\,[\,k_1\,(\cos 0.5t + j\sin 0.5t) + k_2\,(\cos 0.5\,t - j\sin 0.5t)\,]$$

or
$$i = e^{-0.5t}\,[\,(k_1 + k_2)\cos 0.5t + j(k_1 - k_2)\sin 0.5t\,]$$

$$\because \quad (k_1 + k_2) = 0$$

$$\therefore \quad i = e^{-0.5t}\,.\,j\,(k_1 - k_2)\sin 0.5t$$

Differentiate above equation,

$$\frac{di}{dt} = e^{-0.5t}\,[\,j\,(k_1 - k_2) \times 0.5\cos 0.5t\,] + [\,j\,(k_1 - k_2)\sin 0.5t\,(-0.5)e^{-0.5t}]$$

$$\therefore \quad \frac{di(0)}{dt} = e^{-0.5\times 0}\,[\,j\,(k_1 - k_2) \times 0.5\cos 0.5 \times 0] + [\,j\,(k_1 - k_2)\sin 0.5 \times 0\,(-0.5)e^{-0.5\times 0}]$$

$$= 1\,[\,j\,(k_1 - k_2) \times 0.5 \times 1] + [\,j\,(k_1 - k_2) \times 0\,(-0.5)1\,]$$

$$= j\,0.5\,(k_1 - k_2)$$

$$\therefore \quad \frac{di\,(0)}{dt} = \frac{v_c\,(0)}{L} = \frac{V}{L} = \frac{4}{1} = 4\text{ A/s}$$

$$\therefore \quad 4 = j\,0.5\,(k_1 - k_2)$$

$$(k_1 - k_2) = \frac{8}{j}$$

and
$$i = 8e^{-0.5t}\sin 0.5t \qquad \textbf{Ans.}$$

**Example . 7.6.6** *In the network shown (Fig. 7.6.6) prior to closing the switch the capacitor is charged to a voltage $V_0$ and the current through the inductor is zero. The switch is closed at $t = 0$. Determine the expression for $v$.*

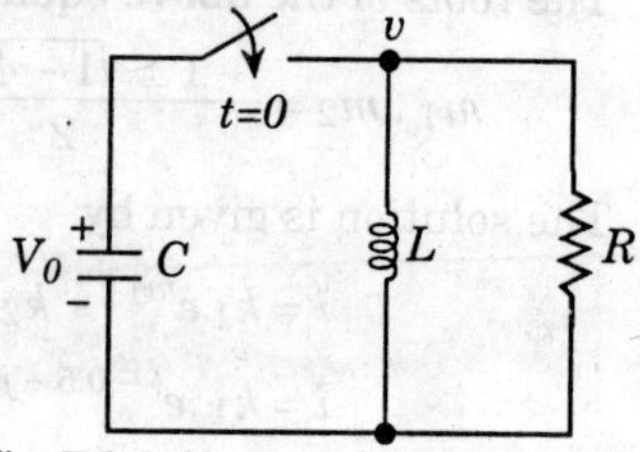


Fig. 7.6.6 Network for example 7.66

**Solution :** Applying *KCL*

$$C\frac{dv}{dt} + \frac{v}{R} + \frac{1}{L}\int v\,dt = 0$$

On differentiating

$$\frac{d^2v}{dt^2} + \frac{1}{RC}\frac{dv}{dt} + \frac{v}{LC} = 0 \quad ..(1)$$

The auxiliary equation for the differential Eqn(1) is given as

$$m^2 + \frac{m}{RC} + \frac{1}{LC} = 0$$

Let $m_1 . m_2$ be two roots of the auxiliary equation.

Thus, the solution of Eqn.(1) is

$$v = k_1 e^{m_1 t} + k_2 e^{m_2 t} \quad ...(2)$$

At $t = 0$ $\quad v(0) = V$

$$v(0) = k_1 e^{m_1 \times 0} + k_2 e^{m_2 \times 0}$$

or $$v(0) = k_1 \times 1 + k_2 \times 1$$

$\therefore$ $$(k_1 + k_2) = V \quad ...(3)$$

Differentiate Eqn.(2)

$\therefore$ $$\frac{dv}{dt} = k_1 m_1 e^{m_1 t} + k_2 m_2 e^{m_2 t} \quad ...(4)$$

$\because$ At $t = 0$,

the voltage across the inductor $\frac{1}{L}\int v dt = 0.$

Thus $$\frac{dv(0)}{dt} = -\frac{v(0)}{RC}$$

$$= -\frac{V_o}{RC}$$

Substituting in Eqn.(4)

$\therefore$ $$-\frac{V_0}{RC} = k_1 m_1 e^{m_1 \times 0} + k_2 m_2 e^{m_2 \times 0}$$

$$= k_1 m_1 \times 1 + k_2 m_2 \times 1$$

or $$k_1 m_1 + k_2 m_2 = -\frac{V}{RC} \quad ...(5)$$

Substitute for $k_2$ in Eqn. (5) from Eqn.(3) to get

$$-\frac{V}{RC} = k_1 m_1 + (V - k_1) m_2$$

$\therefore$ $$k_1 = \frac{V\left(\frac{1}{RC} + m_2\right)}{m_2 - m_1}$$

$$k_2 = V - k_1$$

or $$k_2 = V - \frac{V\left(\frac{1}{RC} + m_2\right)}{m_2 - m_1} = \frac{V(m_1 RC + 1)}{m_1 - m_2}$$

$$\therefore \quad v = \frac{V\left(\frac{1}{RC} + m_2\right)}{m_2 - m_1} e^{m_1 t} + \frac{V(m_1 RC + 1)}{m_1 - m_2} e^{m_2 t} \quad \textbf{Ans.}$$

**Example . 7.6.7** *In the network shown (Fig. 7.6.7) the switch is held at terminal (1) for a long time, then moved to terminal (2). Determine* $i(0^+)$, $\frac{di(0^+)}{dt}$ and $\frac{d^2 i(0^+)}{dt^2}$

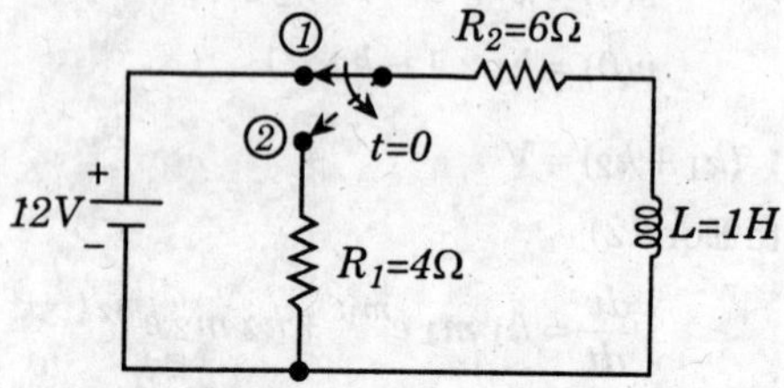


Fig. 7.6.7 Network for example 7.6.7

**Solution .** At $t = 0$ , the network takes the form as shown in Fig. 7.6.7(*a*)

The general *KVL* equation is written below

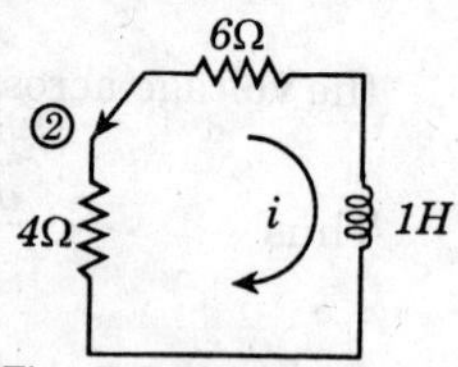


Fig. 7.6.7(*a*) Network at $t = 0$

$$4i + 6i + L\frac{di}{dt} = 0$$

or $$10i + \frac{di}{dt} = 0 \ldots(1)$$

$$i(0^-) = \frac{12}{6} = 2A$$

[current through $L$ with switch at (1)]

$$i(0^+) = i(0^-) = 2\text{A} \quad \ldots\textbf{Ans.}$$

At $t = 0^+$

$$10\, i(0^+) + \frac{di(0^+)}{dt} = 0$$

$$\therefore \quad \frac{di(0^+)}{dt} = -10\, i(0^+) = -10 \times 2 = -20 \text{ A/s} \quad \textbf{Ans.}$$

Differentiate Eqn.(1) : $10\frac{di}{dt} + \frac{d^2 i}{dt^2} = 0$

At $t = 0^+$

$$10\frac{di(0^+)}{dt} + \frac{d^2i(0^+)}{dt^2} = 0$$

$$\therefore \quad \frac{d^2i(0^+)}{dt^2} = -10\frac{di(0^+)}{dt} = -10 \times (-20)$$

$$= 200 \text{ A/s}^2 \quad \text{...Ans.}$$

**Example . 7.6.8** *The switch K is kept at position (a) till the steady state condition is reached. At t = 0 The switch is shifted to position (b). Determine* $i(0^+)$, $\frac{di(0^+)}{dt}$ and $\frac{d^2i(0^+)}{dt^2}$.

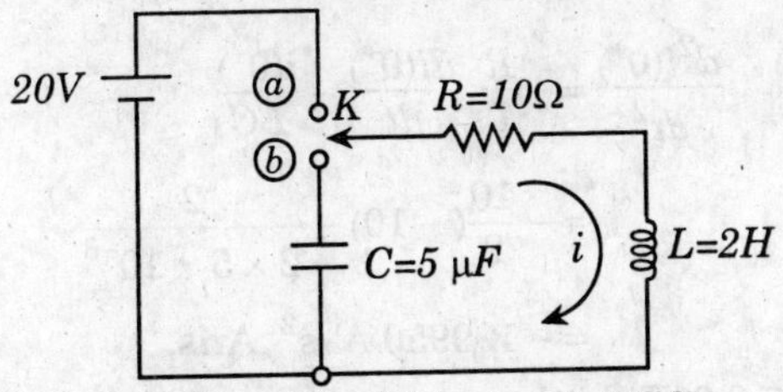


Fig. 7.6.8 Circuit for example 7.6.8

**Solution .** At $t = 0^-$ [switch at (1)]

$$i\,(0^-) = \frac{20}{10} = 2 \text{ A flowing in inductor}$$

$$\therefore \quad i(0^+)\, i\,(0^-) = 2 \text{ A} \quad \text{...Ans.}$$

$$v_c\,(0^-) = 0 \text{ voltage across capacitor}$$

$$v_c\,(0^-) = v_c\,(0^+) = 0$$

At $t = 0^+$ The circuit takes the form as shown in Fig. 7.6.8(*a*)

The general *KVL* equation is written below

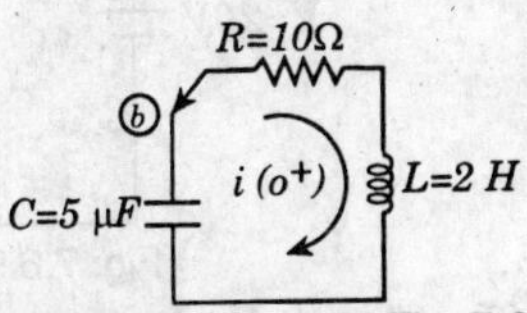


Fig.7.6.8(*a*) circuit in Fig. 7.6.8 at $t = 0^+$

$$R\,i + L\frac{di}{dt} + \frac{1}{C}\int idt = 0 \quad \text{...(1)}$$

At $t = 0^+$

$$R\,i(0^+) + L\frac{di(0^+)}{dt} + \frac{1}{C}\int i(0^+)dt = 0$$

$$\because \quad v_c\,(0^+) = \frac{1}{C}\int i(0^+)dt = 0$$

$$\therefore \quad R\,i(0^+) + L\frac{di(0^+)}{dt} + 0 = 0$$

$$\frac{di(0^+)}{dt} = -\frac{R}{L}\, i\,(0^+)$$

$$= -\frac{10}{2} \times 2 = -10 \text{ A/s} \quad \textbf{Ans.}$$

Differntiate Eqn. (1)

$$R\frac{di}{dt} + L\frac{d^2 i}{dt^2} + \frac{i}{C} = 0$$

$$\text{At } t = 0^+, \quad R\frac{di(0^+)}{dt} + L\frac{d^2\, i(0^+)}{dt^2} + \frac{i(0^+)}{c} = 0$$

$$\therefore \quad \frac{d^2 i(0^+)}{dt^2} = -\frac{R}{L}\frac{di(0^+)}{dt} - \frac{i(0^+)}{LC}$$

$$\therefore \quad = -\frac{10}{2}(-10) - \frac{2}{2 \times 5 \times 10^{-6}}$$

$$= -199950 \text{ A/s}^2 \quad \textbf{Ans.}$$

**Example . 7.6.9** *Find the value of*

*(i),* $i\,(0^+)$, $\frac{di\,(0^+)}{dt}$ *and* $\frac{d^2 i\,(0^+)}{dt^2}$ *(ii)* $v_c\,(0^+)$ *and* $\frac{dv_c\,(0^+)}{dt}$

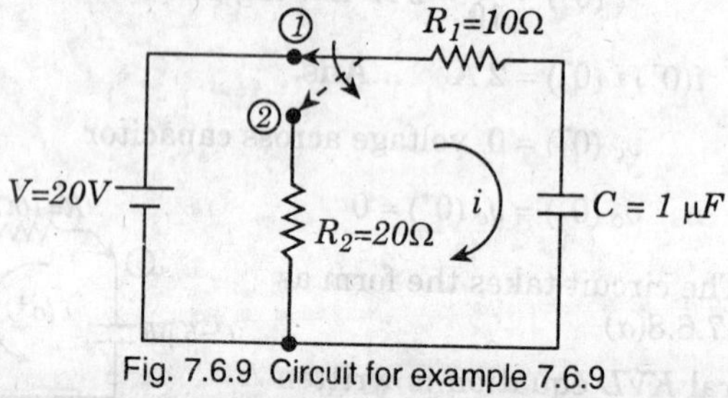


Fig. 7.6.9 Circuit for example 7.6.9

*The circuit is shown in Fig. 7.6.9. At switch position (1) the circuit is relaxed then moved to position (2) at t = 0.*

**Solution.** At switch position (1),

$$t = (0^-),\ v_C\,(0^-) = 20V,$$

$\therefore\ v_C\,(0^+) = 20V.$ **Ans.**

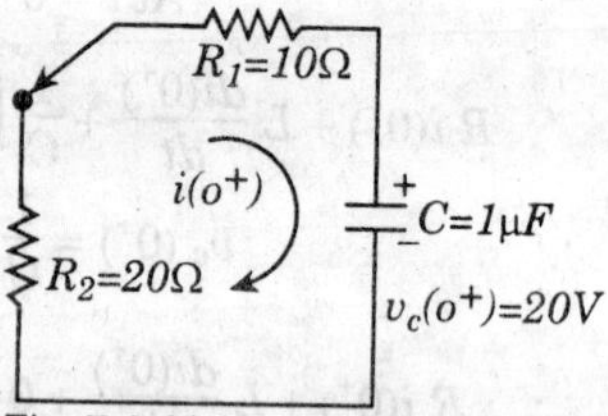


Fig. 7.6.9(*a*) circuit for example 7.6.9 at $t = (0^+)$.

At $t = 0^+$. The circuit is drawn in Fig. 7.6.9(*a*)

The general *KVL* equation is written below

$$(R_1 + R_2)\, i + \frac{1}{C}\int i dt = 0$$

On differentiation

$$(R_1 + R_2)\frac{di}{dt} + \frac{i}{C} = 0$$

$$\frac{di}{dt} = \frac{-i}{C\,(R_1 + R_2)} \qquad ...(1)$$

At $t = 0^+$

[$i\ (0^+)$ direction shown clockwise, charged capacitor sends current in opposite direction.]

$$i\ (0^+) = -\frac{v_c\ (0^+)}{R_1 + R_2} = -\frac{20}{10 + 20} = -\frac{2}{3}\ \text{A}$$

$$\frac{di\ (0^{+})}{dt} = \frac{-\,i(0^{+})}{C(10 + 20)} = \frac{-\,(-\,2/3)}{1 \times 10^{-6} \times 30}$$

$$= 2.22 \times 10^4\ \text{A/s} \quad \textbf{Ans.}$$

Differentiate Eqn. (1)

$$\frac{d^2i}{dt^2} = -\frac{1}{C(R_1 + R_2)} \cdot \frac{di}{dt}$$

At $t = 0^+$

$$\frac{d^2i\ (0^+)}{dt^2} = -\frac{1}{1 \times 10^{-6}(10 + 20)}\ \frac{di(0^+)}{dt}$$

$$= -\frac{10^6}{30}(2.22 \times 10^4)$$

$$= -\,7.4 \times 10^8\ \text{A/s}^2\ ...\textbf{Ans.}$$

$$i = C\frac{dv}{dt}$$

$$i\ (0^+) = C\,\frac{dv\ (0^+)}{dt}$$

$$\therefore \quad \frac{dv\ (0^+)}{dt} = \frac{i\ (0^+)}{C} = \frac{-\,2/3}{1 \times 10^{-6}} = -\frac{2}{3} \times 10^6\ \text{V/s} \quad \textbf{Ans.}$$

**Example 7.6.10** *For the network shown in Fig. 7.6.10 the switch is closed at t = 0. Determine*

$$i_1(0^{+}),\ i_2\ (0^+),\ \frac{di_1\ (0^+)}{dt},\ \frac{di_2(0^+)}{dt},\ \frac{d^2\ i_1(0^+)}{dt^2} \text{ and } \frac{d^2i_2\ (0^+)}{dt^2}.$$

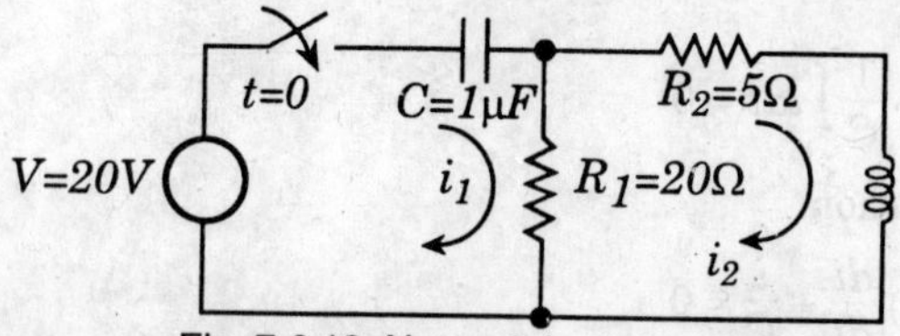


Fig. 7.6.10 Network for example 7.6.10

**Solution :** At $t = 0^+$, The capacitor acts as s/c and inductor o/c. The network takes the form as shown in Fig. 7.6.10(*a*)

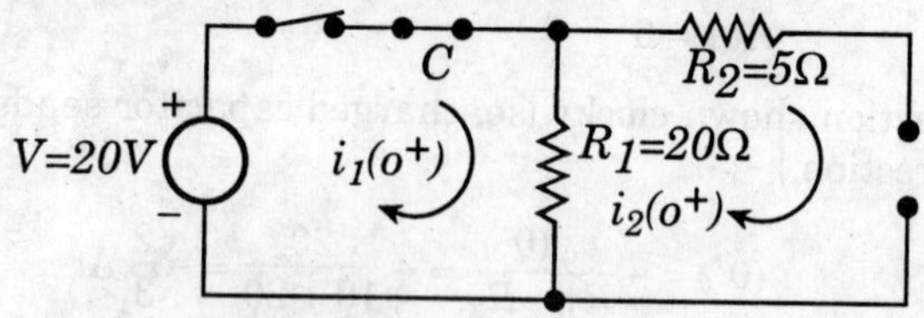


Fig. 7.6.10(*a*) Network in Fig. 7.6.10 at $t = 0^+$.

$$i_1\,(0^+) = \frac{V}{R_1} = \frac{20}{20} = 1 \text{ A} \qquad \text{...}\textbf{Ans.}$$

$$i_2\,(0^+) = 0$$

General *KVL* equation for mesh (2) (Fig. 7.6.10) is written below.

$$R_2\,i_2 + L\,\frac{di_2}{dt} + R_1(i_2 - i_1) = 0 \qquad \text{...(1)}$$

On rearranging $\quad \dfrac{di_2}{dt} = -\dfrac{R_2}{L}\,i_2 - \dfrac{R_1}{L}\,i_2 + \dfrac{R_1}{L}\,i_1$

At $t = 0^+$,

$$\frac{di_2\,(0^+)}{dt} = -\frac{R_2}{L}\,i_2(0^+) - \frac{R_1}{L}\,i_2\,(0^+) + \frac{R_1}{L}\,i_1(0)$$

$$= -0 - 0 + \frac{R_1}{L}\,i_1(0)$$

$$\therefore \quad \frac{di_2(0^+)}{dt} = \frac{R_1}{L}\,i_1(0^+) = \frac{20}{4} \times 1 = 5 \text{ A/s} \;\text{...}\textbf{Ans.}$$

General *KVL* equation for mesh (1) (Fig 7.6.10) is written below.

$$\frac{1}{C}\int i_1 dt + R_1\,(i_1 - i_2) = V$$

Differentiate $\dfrac{i_1}{C} + R_1\,\dfrac{di_1}{dt} - R_1\,\dfrac{di_2}{dt} = 0 \qquad \text{...(2)}$

At $t = 0^+$

$$\frac{i_1\,(0^+)}{C} + R_1\,\frac{di_1(0^+)}{dt} - R_1\,\frac{di_2(0^+)}{dt} = 0$$

$$\therefore \quad \frac{1}{1\times 10^{-6}} + 20\frac{di_1(0^+)}{dt} - 20 \times 5 = 0$$

$$\therefore \quad \frac{di_1(0^+)}{dt} = \frac{100 - 10^6}{20}$$

$$= (5 - 5 \times 10^4) \text{ A/s} \qquad \textbf{...Ans.}$$

Differentiate Eqn. (1)

$$R_2 \frac{di_2}{dt} + L\frac{d^2 i_2}{dt_2} + R_1 \frac{d}{dt}(i_2 - i_1) = 0$$

On rearranging

$$\frac{d^2 i_2}{dt^2} = -\frac{R_2}{L}\frac{di_2}{dt} - \frac{R_1}{L}\frac{di_2}{dt} + \frac{R_1}{L}\frac{di_1}{dt}$$

$$= \left(-\frac{R_1}{L} - \frac{R_2}{L}\right)\frac{di_2}{dt} + \frac{R_1}{L}\frac{di_1}{dt}$$

$$= \left(-\frac{5}{4} - \frac{20}{4}\right) \times 5 + \frac{5}{4}(5 - 5 \times 10^4)$$

$$= -\frac{100}{4} + 5 \times 10^4$$

$$= -(25 + 5 \times 10^4) \text{ A/s}^2 \textbf{ ...Ans.}$$

Differentiate Eqn. (2)

$$\frac{1}{C}\frac{di_1}{dt} + R_1\frac{d^2 i_1}{dt^2} - R_1\frac{d^2 i_2}{dt^2} = 0$$

On rearranging

$$\frac{d^2 i_1}{dt^2} = \frac{d^2 i_2}{dt^2} - \frac{1}{R_1 C}\frac{di_1}{dt} \qquad \textbf{...Ans.}$$

**Example. 7.6.11** *In the network (Fig. 7.6.11) the switch is opened at t = 0. Determine* $v(0^+)$, $\frac{dv(0^+)}{dt}$ *and* $\frac{d^2v(0^+)}{dt^2}$.

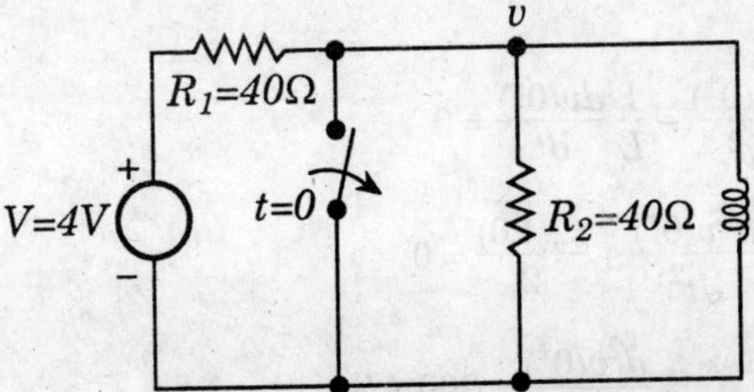


Fig. 7.6.11. Network for example 7.6.11.

**Solution.** At $t = 0^+$, the network is shown in Fig. 7.6.11(*a*)

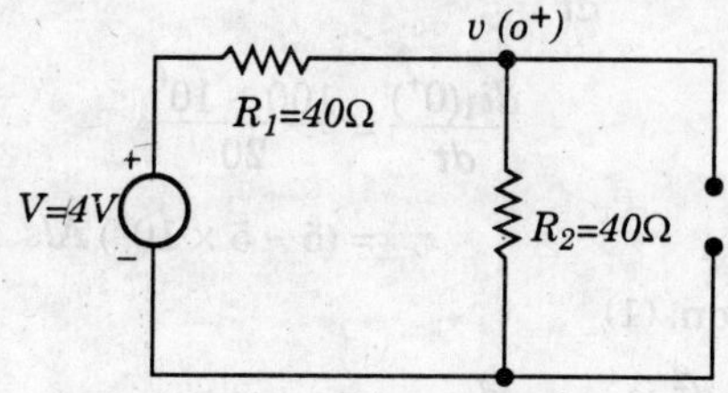


Fig. 7.6.11(*a*) Network for example 7.6.11 at $t = 0^+$

$$v(0^+) = 4 \times \frac{40}{40+40} = 2V \qquad \text{...Ans.}$$

With switch open general *KCL* equation is

$$\frac{v - V}{R_1} + \frac{v}{R_2} + \frac{1}{L}\int v dt = 0$$

or
$$\left(\frac{1}{R_1} + \frac{1}{R_2}\right) v + \frac{1}{L}\int v dt = \frac{V}{R_1} \qquad \text{...(1)}$$

Differentiate Eqn. (1)

$$\left(\frac{1}{R_1} + \frac{1}{R_2}\right) \frac{dv}{dt} + \frac{v}{L} = 0 \qquad \text{...(2)}$$

At $t = 0^+$,

$$\left(\frac{1}{R_1} + \frac{1}{R_2}\right) \frac{dv(0^+)}{dt} + \frac{v(0^+)}{L} = 0,$$

$$\therefore \quad \left(\frac{1}{40} + \frac{1}{40}\right) \frac{dv(0^+)}{dt} + \frac{2}{2} = 0$$

or
$$\frac{dv\,(0^+)}{dt} = -\,20 \text{ V/s} \qquad \text{...Ans.}$$

Differentiate Eqn.(2)

$$\left(\frac{1}{R_1} + \frac{1}{R_2}\right) \frac{d^2v}{dt^2} + \frac{1}{L}\frac{dv}{dt} = 0$$

At $t = 0^+$

$$\left(\frac{1}{R_1} + \frac{1}{R_2}\right) \frac{d^2v(0^+)}{dt^2} + \frac{1}{L}\frac{dv(0^+)}{dt} = 0$$

$$\therefore \quad \left(\frac{1}{40} + \frac{1}{40}\right) \frac{d^2v(0^+)}{dt^2} + \frac{(-20)}{2} = 0$$

$$\therefore \quad \frac{d^2v(0^+)}{dt^2} = 200 \text{ A/s}^2 \qquad \text{...Ans.}$$

**Example : 7.6.12** *The switch K is closed at $t = 0^+$. Determine $v_2(0^+)$. The network is shown in Fig. 7.6.12*

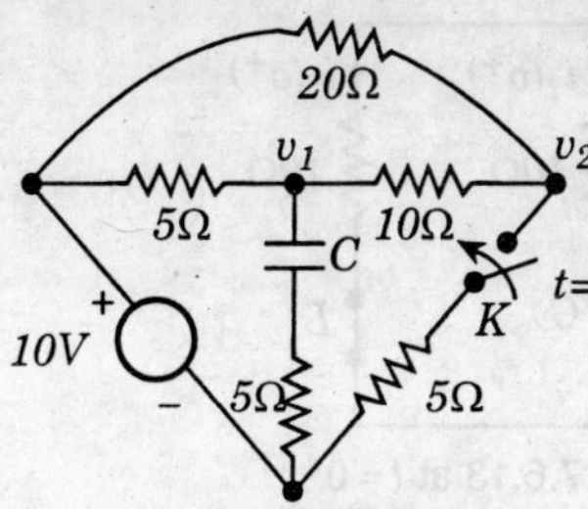


Fig. 7.6.12 Network for example 7.6.12

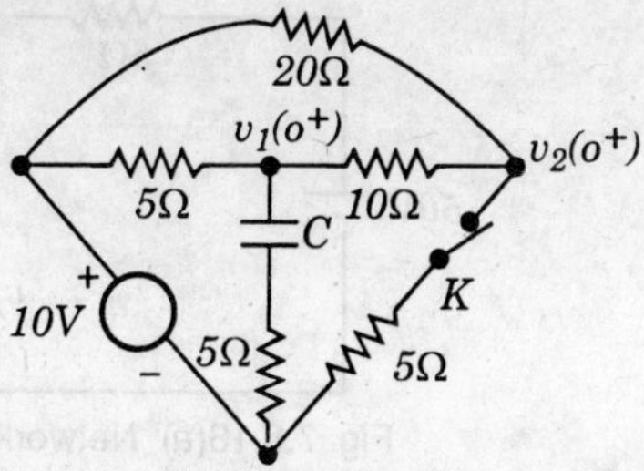


Fig. 7.6.12(*a*) Network in Fig. 7.6.12 at $t = 0^+$

**Solution :** At $t = 0^-$ (switch $K$ open)

$v_1(0^-) = v_c(0^-) = 10V, \quad \therefore \; v_c\,(0^+) = 10V$

At $t = 0^+$ (switch $K$ close), the network is drawn in Fig. 7.6.12(a),

At node 2, *KCL* equation is

$$\frac{v_2(0^+) - v_1(0^+)}{10} + \frac{v_2(0^+) - 10}{20} + \frac{v_2(0^+)}{5} = 0$$

$$\therefore \qquad \left(\frac{1}{10} + \frac{1}{20} + \frac{1}{5}\right) v_2(0^+) = \frac{v_1(0^+)}{10} + \frac{10}{20}$$

or

$$0.35\, v_2\,(0^+) = \frac{v_1(0^+)}{10} + \frac{1}{2}$$

$$\because \qquad v_1(0^+) = 10\ V$$

$$\therefore \qquad 0.35\, v_2\,(0^+) = \frac{10}{10} + \frac{1}{2} = 1.5$$

$$\therefore \qquad v_2\,(0^+) = \frac{1.5}{0.35} = 4.28\ \text{V}$$ **...Ans.**

**Example. 7.6.13** *The switch is closed at $t = 0$. Determine $i_1(0^+)$, $i_2(0^+)$ and $\frac{di_2(0^+)}{dt}$. The network is shown in Fig. 7.6.13*

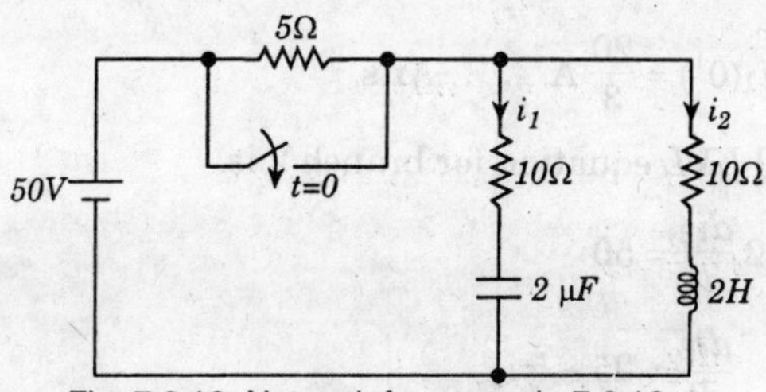


Fig. 7.6.13 Network for example 7.6.13

**Solution :** At $t = 0^-$ (switch open) the network is shown in Fig. 7.6.13(*a*)

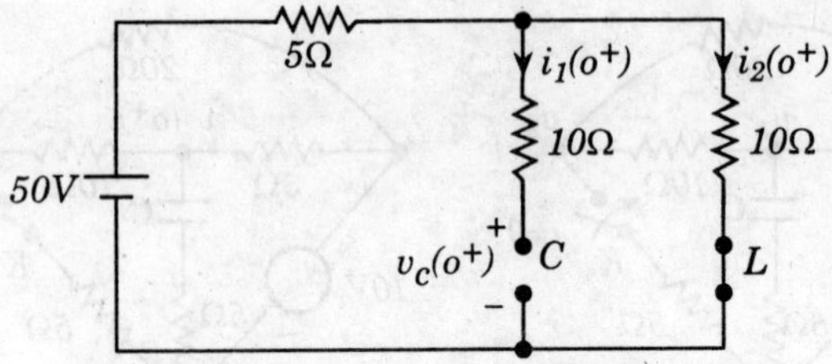


Fig. 7.6.13(*a*) Network in Fig. 7.6.13 at $t = 0^-$

$i_2(0^-) = 50/(5 + 10) = 10/3$ A (flowing through the inductor),

$$i_2(0^+) = i_2(0^-) = \frac{10}{3} \text{ A.} \quad \text{...Ans.}$$

$v_c(0^-) = (50 \times 5)/(5 + 10) = 50/3$ V (across capacitor),

$v_c(0^+) = v_c(0^-) = 50/3$ V.

At $t = 0^+$ the network is shown in Fig. 7.6.13(*b*)

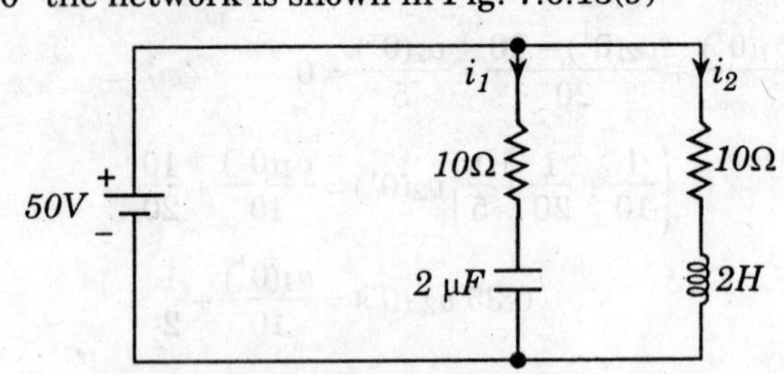


Fig. 7.6.13(*b*) Network in Fig. 7.6.13 at $t = 0^+$

The general *KVL* equation for branch 1 is

$$10\, i_1 + \frac{1}{2 \times 10^{-6}} \int i_1 dt = 50$$

At $t = 0^+$, $v_c(0^+) = \frac{50}{3} V$, therefore $\frac{1}{2 \times 10^{-6}} \int i_1(0^+) dt = \frac{50}{3}$ V

Thus $\quad 10\, i_1(0^+) + \left(+\frac{50}{3}\right) = 50,$

$$\therefore \quad i_1(0^+) = \frac{20}{3} \text{ A} \quad \text{...Ans.}$$

The general *KVL* equation for branch 2 is

$$10\, i_2 + 2\frac{di_2}{dt} = 50$$

or

$$\frac{di_2}{dt} = 25 - 5\, i_2$$

At $t = 0^+$

$$\frac{di_2(0^+)}{dt} = 25 - 5\,i_2\,(0^+) = 25 - \frac{5 \times 10}{3} = 8.34 \text{ A/s}^2 \quad \textbf{...Ans.}$$

## PROBLEMS

**7.1** The switch is closed at $t = 0$ (Fig. 7P-1). Determine expression for the current through inductor.

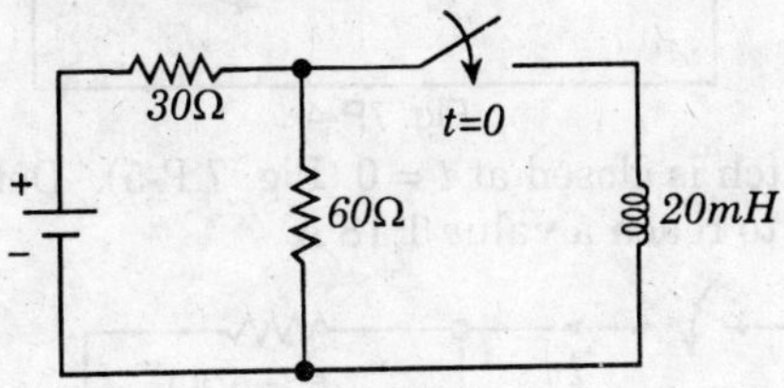


Fig. 7P-1

**Ans.** $i = 2\,(1 - e^{-1000\,t})$.

**7.2** In Fig. 7P-2 the capacitor is initially charged to a voltage $V_0$. The switch is closed at $t = 0$. Find the voltage $\vartheta$

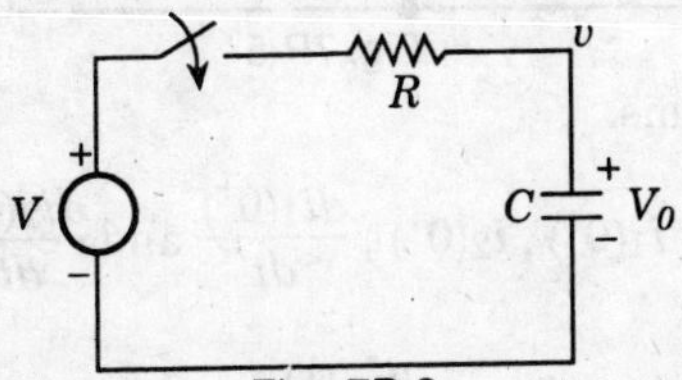


Fig. 7P-2

**Ans.** $v = V - (V - V_0)\,e^{-t/RC}$.

**7.3** The switches, $S_1$ and $S_2$ are closed at $t = 0$. Determine $i$.

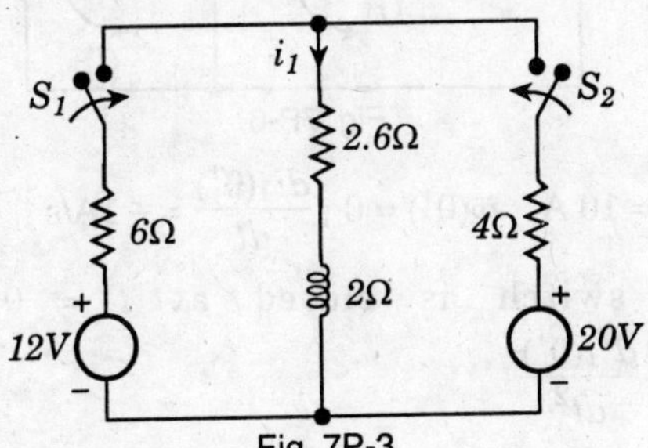


Fig. 7P-3

**Ans.** $i = 3.36(1 - e^{-2.5\,t})$.

**7.4** Determine expression for the current $i$ if the switch is closed at $t = 0$. Fig. 7P-4

$$\textbf{Ans.} \quad i = \left(1 + \frac{e^{-8t}}{2}\right).$$

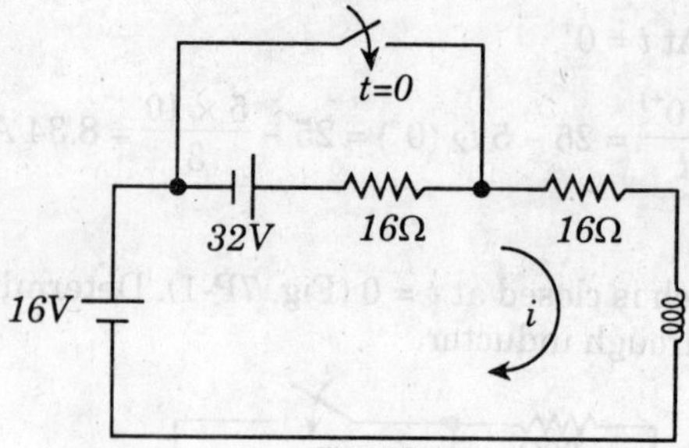


Fig. 7P-4

**7.5** The switch is closed at $t = 0$ (Fig. 7.P-5). Determine the time for the current $i$ to reach a value 1.18 A

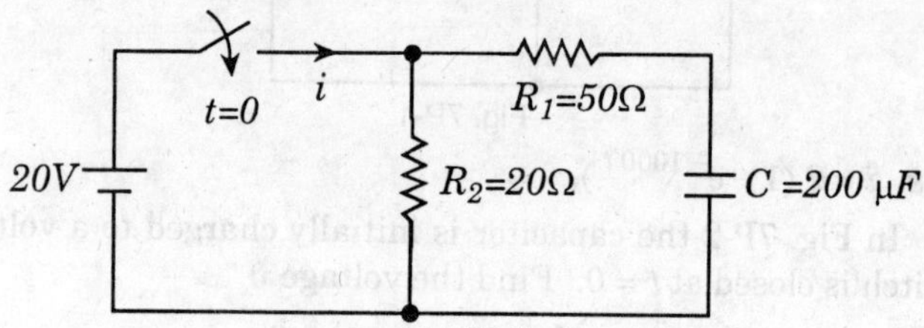


Fig. 7P-5

**Ans.** $t = 0.798$ ms.

**7.6** Determine $i_1(0^+)$, $i_2(0^+)$, $\frac{di_1(0^+)}{dt}$ and $\frac{di_2(0^+)}{dt}$. The network is shown in Fig. 7P-6.

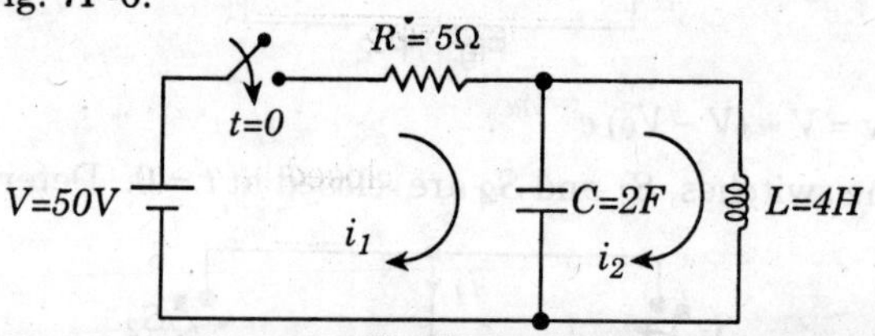


Fig. 7P-6

**Ans.** $i_1(0^+) = 10$ A, $i_2(0^+) = 0$, $\frac{di_1(0^+)}{dt} = -1$A/s, $\frac{di_2(0^+)}{dt} = 0$

**7.7** The switch is closed at $t = 0$. Determine $i(0^+)$, $\frac{di(0^+)}{dt}$ and $\frac{d^2i(0^+)}{dt^2}$

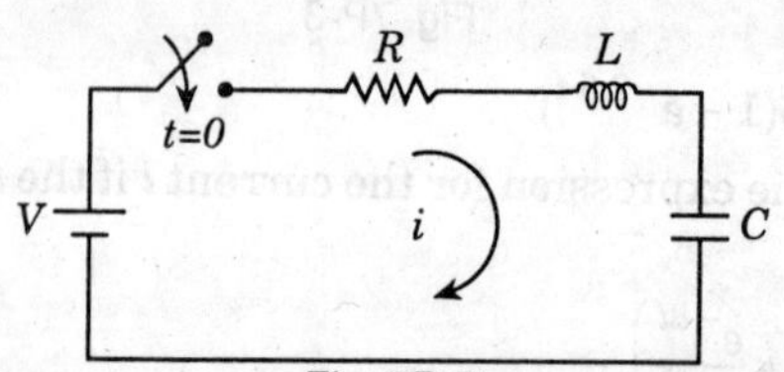


Fig. 7P-7

**Ans.** $i(0^+) = 0\ ,\ \dfrac{di(0^+)}{dt} = \dfrac{V}{L}$ A/s , $\dfrac{d^2i(0^+)}{dt^2} = -\dfrac{R^V}{L^2}$ A/s$^2$.

**7.8** The switch is opened at $t = 0$. Determine

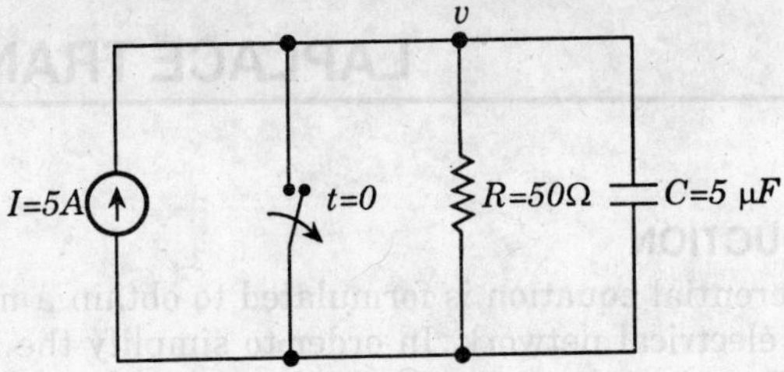


Fig. 7P-8

$v(0^+)\ ,\ \dfrac{dv(0^+)}{dt}$ and $\dfrac{d^2v(0^+)}{dt^2}$

**Ans.** $v(0^+) = 0\ ,\ \dfrac{dv(0^+)}{dt} = 10^6$ V/s , $\dfrac{d^2v(0^+)}{dt^2} = -\,4 \times 10^9$ V/s$^2$

**7.9** The switch is opened at $t = 0$. Determine $\dfrac{dv_s(0^+)}{dt}$.

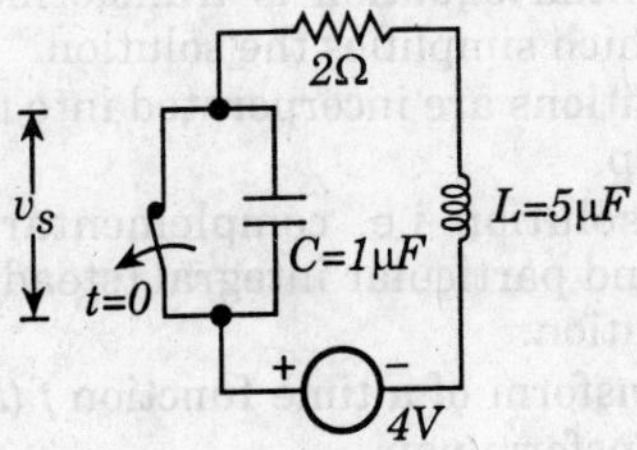


Fig. 7P-9

**Ans.** $\dfrac{dv_s(0^+)}{dt} = 2 \times 10^6$ V/s

**7.10** The switch is closed at $t = 0$. Determine $v_1\,(0^+)$ .

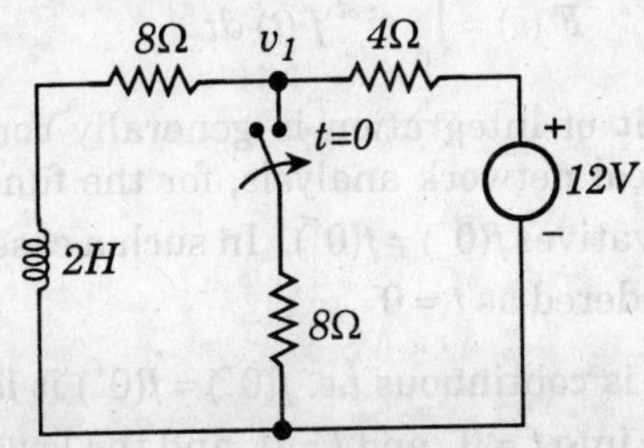


Fig 7P-10

**Ans.** $v_1\,(0^+) = \dfrac{16}{3}$ V

# 8

# LAPLACE TRANSFORM

## 8.1 INTRODUCTION

The differential equation is formulated to obtain a mathemetical model of an electrical network. In order to simplify the solution of a differential equation, the same is transformed into an algebraic form by using Laplace transform technique. In the case of a differential equation for electrical network, the independant variable is time. The Laplace transform transforms a time-domain differential equation into a frequency domain equation where in the independent variable is a complex frequency variable $s = \sigma + j\,\omega$ and the transformed equation being an algebraic equation.

The advantages of the Laplace transformation are,

1. The differential equation is transformed into an algebraic equation which simplifies the solution.
2. Initial conditions are incorporated into the problem as one of the first step.
3. The total solution i.e. complementary function (natural response) and particular integral (steady state) are obtained in one operation.

The Laplace transform of a time function $f(t)$ is denoted as $F(s)$ and constitutes a transform pair.

$$f(t) \leftrightarrow F(s)$$

If $f(t)$ is a continuous function of time for all $t \geq 0$, then the Laplace transform of $f(t)$ is given by

$$F(s) = \int_0^\infty e^{-st} f(t)\, dt$$

The lower limit of integration is generally considered as $t = 0$. However in electrical network analysis, for the function like impulse and its higher derivatives $f(0^-) \neq f(0^+)$. In such a case the lower limit of integration is considered as $t = 0^-$

If the function is continuous *i.e.* $f(0^-) = f(0^+)$ it is not necessary to sub-divide the time into $t = 0^-$ and $t = 0^+$ and the lower limit of integration can be considered as $t = 0$

$F(s)$ is called the Laplace transform of $f(t)$ and denoted as

$$F(s) = £\,[f(t)]$$

The notation £ read as "Laplace transform of" ... The time function $f(t)$ multiplied by $e^{-st}$ is integrated *w.r.t.* time winthin limits $t = 0^-$ and $t = \infty$ to obtain its Laplace transform. The independent variable for the Laplace transform $F(s)$ is the complex variable $s = \sigma + j\,\omega$ where $\sigma$ and $\omega$ are real and imaginary parts respectively. The condition given below is to be satisfied by the time function $f(t)$ to have its Laplace transform.

$$\int_{0^-}^{\infty} |f(t)|\, e^{-\sigma_1 t} dt < \infty \quad \text{...for real positive value of } \sigma_1$$

The inverse Laplace transform is given by.

$$f(t) = £^{-1} F(s) = \frac{1}{2\pi j} \int_{\sigma_1 - j\infty}^{\sigma_1 + j\infty} F(s)\, e^{st}\, ds.$$

The notation $£^{-1}$ is read as "inverse Laplace transform of"...

It may not be always necessary to determine the inverse Laplace transform of $F(s)$ evaluating the integral mentioned above. However, on the derivation of Laplace transform of the time function $f(t)$, corresponding pairs of $f(t)$ and $F(s)$ are formed and tabulated for reference.

## 8.2 DERIVATION OF LAPLACE TRANSFORM

**1. Laplace Transform Of $f(t) = e^{at}$, $t \geq 0$**

$$£[e^{at}] = \int_{0-}^{\infty} e^{at} e^{-st} dt$$

$$= \int_{0^-}^{\infty} e^{(a-s)t}\, dt$$

$$= \frac{1}{s-a}$$

As the inverse Laplace transform is denoted as $£^{-1}$, Therefore, the inverse Laplace transform of $F(s) = \dfrac{1}{s-a}$ is $f(t) = e^{at}$. Hence,

$$£^{-1} \frac{1}{s-a} = f(t),\ t \geq 0$$

**2. Unit Step Function**

The Unit step function is defined as

$$u(t) = f(t) = 1 \quad ; \ t \geq 0$$

$$= 0 \quad ; \ t < 0$$

In the case of a battery of voltage $V = 1\ V$ connected to a circuit can be considered as a unit step function $u(t)$ meaning that the battery is switched on to the circuit at $t = 0$.

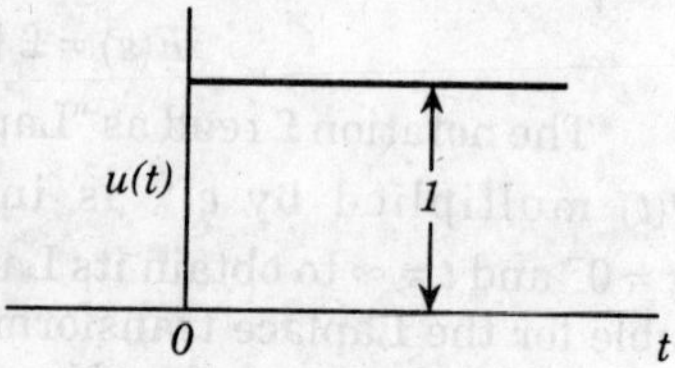

Fig. 8.2.1 Unit step function

The Laplace transform of the unit step function is determined below,

$$£\ u(t) = \int_{0^-}^{\infty} 1 \,.\, e^{-st}\, dt \quad ; \quad t \geq 0$$

$$= -\frac{1}{s} e^{-st} \Big|_{0^-}^{\infty} = \frac{1}{s}$$

The inverse Laplace transform of $F(s) = \frac{1}{s}$ is

$$£^{-1} \frac{1}{s} = u\ (t)$$

**3. Laplace Transform of sin $\omega t$ and cos $\omega t$.**

Put $a = j\,\omega$ in $f(t) = e^{at}$

$$\therefore \quad f(t) = e^{j\omega t}$$

$$\therefore \quad £\ e^{j\omega t} = \frac{1}{s - j\omega}$$

$$\because \quad e^{j\omega t} = \cos \omega t + j \sin \omega t$$

$$\therefore \quad £(\cos \omega t + j \sin \omega t) = \frac{1}{s - j\omega} = \frac{s + j\,\omega}{s^2 + \omega^2}$$

Separating into real and imaginary parts

$$£\ \cos \omega t = \frac{s}{s^2 + \omega^2}$$

$$£\ \sin \omega t = \frac{\omega}{s^2 + \omega^2}$$

and

$$£^{-1} \frac{s}{s^2 + \omega^2} = \cos \omega t$$

$$£^{-1} \frac{\omega}{s^2 + \omega^2} = \sin \omega t$$

**4. Laplace Transform of $e^{-\alpha t}$ sin $\omega t$ and $e^{-\alpha t}$ cos $\omega t$.**

Put $a = (-\alpha + j\,\omega)$ in $f(t) = e^{at}$ $\quad t \geq 0$

$$\therefore \quad f(t) = e^{(-\alpha + j\omega)t}$$

$$\therefore \quad £\, e^{(-\alpha + j\omega)t} = \frac{1}{s-(-\alpha+j\omega)} = \frac{1}{(s+\alpha)-j\omega}$$

$$\because \quad e^{(-\alpha+j\omega)t} = e^{-\alpha t}\cos\omega t + j\,e^{-\alpha t}\sin\omega t$$

$$\therefore \; £\,(e^{-\alpha t}\cos\omega t + je^{-\alpha t}\sin\omega t) = \frac{1}{(s+\alpha)-j\omega} = \frac{(s+\alpha)+j\omega}{(s+\alpha)^2+\omega^2}$$

Separating into real and imaginary part,

$$£\, e^{-\alpha t}\cos\omega t = \frac{(s+\alpha)}{(s+\alpha)^2+\omega^2}$$

$$£\, e^{-\alpha t}\sin\omega t = \frac{\omega}{(s+\alpha)^2+\omega^2}$$

and $$£^{-1}\frac{(s+\alpha)}{(s+\alpha)^2+\omega^2} = e^{-\alpha t}\cos\omega t$$

$$£^{-1}\frac{\omega}{(s+\alpha)^2+\omega^2} = e^{-\alpha t}\sin\omega t$$

5. Put $a = 1$ in $f(t) = e^{at}, \quad t \geq 0$

$$\therefore \quad f(t) = e^t$$

$$\therefore \quad £(e^t) = \frac{1}{s-1}$$

$$\because \quad e^t = 1 + t + \frac{t^2}{2!} + \frac{t^3}{3!} + ----$$

and $$\frac{1}{s-1} = \frac{1}{s} + \frac{1}{s^2} + \frac{1}{s^3} + -----$$

On comparing the term

$$£\,1 = \frac{1}{s}, \quad £\,t = \frac{1}{s^2}, \quad £\,\frac{t^2}{2!} = \frac{1}{s^3}, ----- £\frac{t^n}{n!} = \frac{1}{s^n}$$

**Table of Laplace transform pairs**

| *S. No.* | *f(t)* | *F (s) = L [ f (t) ]* |
|---|---|---|
| 1. | $\delta(t)$ unit impulse at $t = 0$ | $1$ |
| 2. | $u$ (t) unit step at $t = 0$ | $\frac{1}{s}$ |
| 3. | $u(t-T)$ unit step at $t = T$ | $\frac{1}{s}e^{-sT}$ |

| | | |
|---|---|---|
| 4. | $t$ | $\frac{1}{s^2}$ |
| 5. | $\frac{t^2}{2}$ | $\frac{1}{s^3}$ |
| 6. | $t^n$ | $\frac{n!}{s^{n+1}}$ |
| 7. | $e^{-at}$ | $\frac{1}{s+a}$ |
| 8. | $e^{at}$ | $\frac{1}{s-a}$ |
| 9. | $te^{-at}$ | $\frac{1}{(s+a)^2}$ |
| 10. | $te^{at}$ | $\frac{1}{(s-a)^2}$ |
| 11. | $t^n e^{-at}$ | $\frac{n!}{(s+a)^{n+1}}$ |
| 12. | $\sin \omega t$ | $\frac{\omega}{s^2+\omega^2}$ |
| 13. | $\cos \omega t$ | $\frac{s}{s^2+\omega^2}$ |
| 14. | $e^{-\alpha t}\sin \omega t$ | $\frac{\omega}{(s+\alpha)^2+\omega^2}$ |
| 15. | $e^{-\alpha t}\cos \omega t$ | $\frac{(s+\alpha)}{(s+\alpha)^2+\omega^2}$ |
| 16. | $\sinh \alpha t$ | $\frac{\alpha}{s^2-\alpha^2}$ |
| 17. | $\cosh \alpha t$ | $\frac{s}{s^2-\alpha^2}$ |

### 6. Laplace Transform of Shifted Function

The time function $f(t)$ showm in Fig. 8.2.2($a$) exists for $t \geq 0$.

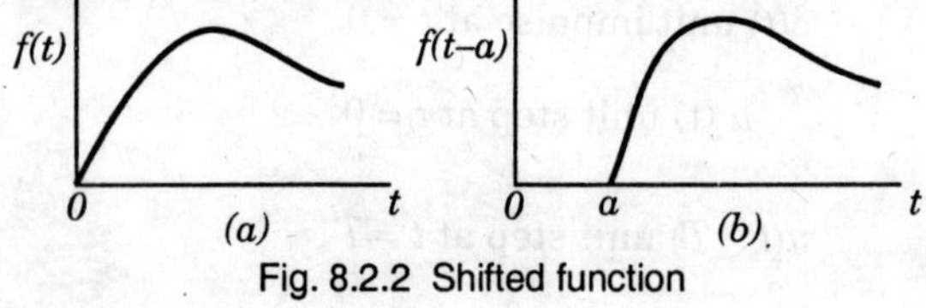


Fig. 8.2.2 Shifted function

This function shifted to start from the instant $t = a$ is known as shifted function [Fig. 8.2.2(*b*)] and denoted as $f(t - a)$ which exists for time $t \geq 0$.

$$£ f(t-a) = \int_{0^-}^{\infty} f(t-a)\, e^{-st}\, dt$$

Put $$t' = t - a$$

$$\therefore \quad £ f(t-a) = \int_{0^-}^{\infty} f(t')\, e^{-s(t'+a)}\, dt'$$

$$= e^{-as} \int_{0^-}^{\infty} f(t')\, e^{-st'}\, dt' = e^{-as} F(s)$$

Hence, $$£ f(t-a) = e^{-as} F(s)$$

## 8.3 LAPLACE TRANSFORM THEOREMS

Basic theorems of Laplace transform are given below.

**1. Laplace Transform Of Linear Combination.**

$$£[a\, f_1(t) + b\, f_2(t)] = a\, F_1(s) + b\, F_2(s)$$

Where, $f_1(t)$ and $f_2(t)$ are time functions and $a$, $b$ are constants

**2. Laplace Transform Of Derivative Function**

If the Laplace transform the funtions $f(t)$ is $F(s)$, Then

(*i*) $$£ \frac{d f(t)}{dt} = [sF(s) - f(0^-)]$$

(*ii*) $$£ \frac{d^2 f(t)}{dt^2} = [s^2 F(s) - s\, f(0^-) - f'(0^-)]$$

(*iii*) $$£ \frac{d^3 f(t)}{dt^3} = [s^3 F(s) - s^2 f(0^-) - s\, f'(0^-) - f''(0^-)]$$

where, $f(0^-)$, $f'(0^-)$, $f'(0^-)$. are The values of

$$f(t), \ \frac{d f(t)}{dt}, \ \frac{d^2 f(t)}{dt^2} \ ----- \ \text{at } t = 0^-$$

**3. Laplace Transform of Integral Function**

If the Laplace transform of $f(t)$ is $F(s)$, then

(*i*) $$£ \int f(t) dt = \left[\frac{F(s)}{s} + \frac{f^{-1}(0^-)}{s}\right]$$

(*ii*) $$£ \int\int f(t)\, dt = \left[\frac{F(s)}{s^2} + \frac{f^{-1}(0^-)}{s^2} + \frac{f^{-2}(0^-)}{s}\right]$$

(iii) $\pounds \int\int\int f(t)\,dt = \left[\frac{F(s)}{s^3} + \frac{f^{-1}(0^-)}{s^3} + \frac{f^{-2}(0^-)}{s^2} + \frac{f^{-3}(0^-)}{s}\right]$

where, $f^{-1}(0^-)$, $f^{-2}(0^-)$, $f^{-3}(0^-)$ ..... are The values of $\int f(t)$, $\int\int f(t)$, $\int\int\int f(t)$.. at $t = 0^-$

The time function $f(t)$ to be integrated between limits $-\infty$ to $t$ can be divided into two parts as below

$$\int_{-\infty}^{t} f(t)\,dt = \int_{-\infty}^{0} f(t)\,dt + \int_{0}^{t} f(t)\,dt.$$

The first term on the *RHS* *i.e.* $\int_{-\infty}^{0} f(t)\,dt$ being a constant which accounts for The initial condition, *e.g.* in an electrical network

(*i*) The inductor current

$$i_L(0) = \frac{1}{L}\int_{-\infty}^{0} v\,dt = \frac{\psi(0)}{L} \quad : \psi(0) = \text{flux linkages at } t = 0$$

(*ii*) The capacitor voltage

$$v_c(0) = \frac{1}{C}\int_{-\infty}^{0} i\,dt = \frac{q(0)}{C} \quad : q(0) \text{ electric charge at } t = 0$$

**4. If The Laplace Transform of $f(t)$ is $F(s)$, Then**

$$\pounds\,[t^n f(t)] = (-1)^n \frac{d^n F(s)}{d s^n}$$

**5. Initial Value Theorem.**

If $f(t)$ and $F(s)$ are Laplace transformable, then

$$\lim_{t \to 0} f(t) = \lim_{s \to \infty} s\,F(s)$$

or

$$f(0) = \lim_{s \to \infty} sF(s)$$

**6. Final Value Theorem.**

If $f(t)$ and $F(s)$ are Laplace transformable, then

$$\lim_{t \to \infty} f(t) = \lim_{s \to 0} s\,F(s)$$

or

$$f(\infty) = \lim_{s \to 0} s\,F(s)$$

**7. Convolutional Integral**

The convolution of functions $f_1(t)$ and $f_2(t)$ results in a function $f(t)$. The convolution integral method is applied to determine the inverse Laplace transform of the product of two functions

$F_1(s)$ and $F_2(s)$ which are Laplace transform of $f_1(t)$ and $f_2(t)$ respectively.

Thus, $$f(t) = £^{-1}[F_1(s)\, F_2(s)] = \int_0^t f_1(\tau)\, f_2(t-\tau)\, d\tau.$$

$$= \int_0^t f_1(t-\tau)\, f_2(\tau)\, d\tau.$$

where, $\tau$ is a dummy variable and integrals are called convolution integrals. The notation $f(t) = f_1(t) * f_2(t)$ stands for the convolution of two functions $f_1(t)$ and $f_2(t)$.

## 8.4 EXAMPLES

Examples given below determine the inverse Laplace transform.

**Example : 8.4.1** *Find The inverse Laplace transform of the following functions*

(i) $F(s) = \dfrac{s+6}{s(s^2+4s+3)}$ (ii) $F(s) = \dfrac{1}{s^2+4s+8}$

(iii) $F(s) = \dfrac{s+2}{s^2+4s+6}$ (iv) $F(s) = \dfrac{5}{s(s^2+4s+5)}$

**Solution :** (i) $$F(s) = \frac{s+6}{s(s^2+4s+3)}$$

The term $(s^2 + 4s + 3)$ can be factored as $(s + 1)(s + 3)$

$$\therefore \quad F(s) = \frac{s+6}{s(s+1)(s+3)}$$

Using partial fraction expansion.

$$\frac{s+6}{s(s+1)(s+3)} = \frac{k_1}{s} + \frac{k_2}{s+1} + \frac{k_3}{s+3}$$

To determine $k_1$, multiply by $s$ on both sides,

$$\therefore \quad \frac{s+6}{(s+1)(s+3)} = k_1 + \frac{k_2\, s}{s+1} + \frac{k_3\, s}{s+3}$$

Put $s = 0$, $k_1 = 2$

To determine $k_2$, multiply by $(s + 1)$ on both sides,

$$\therefore \quad \frac{s+6}{s(s+3)} = \frac{k_1(s+1)}{s} + k_2 + k_3\frac{(s+1)}{s+3}$$

Put $s = -1$, $k_2 = -2.5$

To determine $k_3$, multiply by $(s + 3)$ on both sides.

$$\therefore \quad \frac{s+6}{s(s+1)} = \frac{k_1(s+3)}{s} + k_2\frac{(s+3)}{s+1} + k_3$$

Put $s = -3$ $k_3 = 0.5$

Therefore, $$F(s) = \frac{2}{s} - \frac{2.5}{s+1} + \frac{0.5}{s+3}$$

Taking inverse Laplace on both sides,

$$£^{-1}F(s) = £^{-1}\left[\frac{2}{s} - \frac{2.5}{s+1} + \frac{0.5}{s+3}\right]$$

$$\therefore \quad f(t) = 2 - 2.5e^{-t} + 0.5e^{-3t}, \quad \text{...Ans.}$$

(*ii*) $$F(s) = \frac{1}{s^2 + 4s + 8}$$

On completing the square the term $(s^2 + 4s + 8)$ can be written as $[(s+2)^2 + (2)^2]$

$$\therefore \quad F(s) = \frac{1}{(s+2)^2 + (2)^2}$$

or $$F(s) = \frac{1}{2} \cdot \frac{2}{(s+2)^2 + (2)^2}$$

Taking inverse Laplace transform on both sides

$$£^{-1}F(s) = £^{-1}\frac{1}{2} \cdot \frac{2}{(s+2)^2 + (2)^2}$$

$$\therefore \quad f(t) = \frac{1}{2} \cdot e^{-2t} \sin 2t. \quad \textbf{Ans.}$$

(*iii*) $$F(s) = \frac{5}{s(s^2 + 4s + 5)}$$

The term $(s^2 + 4s + 5)$ can be factored as $(s + 2 - j1)(s + 2 + j1)$

$$\therefore \quad F(s) = \frac{5}{s(s+2-j1)(s+2+j1)}$$

Using partial fraction expansion

$$\frac{5}{s(s+2-j1)(s+2+j1)} = \frac{k_1}{s} + \frac{k_2}{(s+2-j1)} + \frac{k_2^*}{(s+2+j1)}$$

To determine $k_1$ multiply both sides by $s$

$$\frac{5}{(s+2-j1)(s+2+j1)} = k_1 + \frac{k_2\, s}{s+2-j1} + \frac{k_2^* s}{s+2+j1}$$

Put s = 0 , $k_1 = 1$

To determine $k_2$ multiply both sides by $(s + 2 - j1)$

$$\frac{5}{s(s+2+j1)} = \frac{k_1(s+2-j1)}{s} + k_2 + \frac{k_3(s+2-j1)}{s+2+j1}$$

Put $s = -2 + j1$

$$\therefore \quad \frac{5}{(-2+j1)(-2+j1+2+j1)} = k_2$$

or $$\frac{5}{(-2+j1)(j2)} = k_2$$

$$\therefore \quad k_2 = \frac{-5}{2+j4}$$

and $$k_2^* = \frac{-5}{2-j4}$$

$$\therefore \quad F(s) = \frac{1}{s} - \frac{5}{2+j4} \cdot \frac{1}{(s+2-j1)} - \frac{5}{2-j4} \cdot \frac{1}{(s+2+j1)}$$

Taking inverse Laplace transform on both sides,

$$£^{-1} F(s) = £^{-1}\left[\frac{1}{s} - \frac{5}{2+j4} \cdot \frac{1}{(s+2-j1)} - \frac{5}{2-j4} \cdot \frac{1}{(s+2+j1)}\right]$$

$$\therefore \quad f(t) = 1 - \frac{5}{2+j4} e^{-(2-j1)t} - \frac{5}{2-j4} e^{-(2+j1)t}$$

$$= 1 - \frac{5}{2+j4} e^{-2t}(\cos + j \sin t)$$

$$- \frac{5}{2-j4} e^{-2t}(\cos t - j \sin t)$$

$$= 1 - 5e^{-2t}\left[\left(\frac{1}{2+j4} + \frac{1}{2-j4}\right)\cos t + j\left(\frac{1}{2+j4} - \frac{1}{2-j4}\right)\sin t\right]$$

$$= 1 - 5e^{-2t}\left[\frac{4}{20}\cos t + \frac{8}{20}\sin t\right]$$

or $$f(t) = 1 - e^{-2t}\cos t - 2e^{-2t}\sin t \quad \textbf{... Ans.}$$

**Example : 8.4.2** *obtain the inverse Laplace transform given that*

$$F(s) = \frac{1}{s(s+2)(s+1)^2}$$

Using partial fraction expansion

$$\frac{1}{s(s+2)(s+1)^2} = \frac{k_1}{s} + \frac{k_2}{s+2} + \frac{k_{11}}{s+1} + \frac{k_{12}}{(s+1)^2}$$

1. To determine $k_1$, multiply both sides by $s$

$$\therefore \quad \frac{1}{(s+2)(s+1)^2} = k_1 + \frac{k_2\, s}{s+2} + \frac{k_{11}\, s}{s+1} + \frac{k_{12}\, s}{(s+1)^2}$$

Put $s = 0$

$$\therefore \quad k_1 = \frac{1}{(0+2)(0+1)^2} = \frac{1}{2}$$

2. To determine $k_2$, multiply both sides by $(s + 2)$

$$\therefore \quad \frac{1}{s(s+1)^2} = \frac{k_1 (s+2)}{s} + k_2 + \frac{k_{11} (s+2)}{s+1} + \frac{k_{12} (s+2)}{(s+1)^2}$$

Put $s = -2$

$$\therefore \quad k_2 = \frac{1}{(-2)(-2+1)^2} = -\frac{1}{2}$$

3. To determine $k_{12}$, multiply both sides by $(s + 1)^2$

$$\therefore \quad \frac{1}{s(s+2)} = \frac{k_1 (s+1)^2}{s} + \frac{k_2 (s+1)^2}{s+2} + \frac{k_{11} (s+1)^2}{(s+1)} + k_{12}$$

or

$$\frac{1}{s(s+2)} = \frac{k_1 (s+1)^2}{s} + \frac{k_2 (s+1)^2}{s+2} + k_{11} (s+1) + k_{12}$$

Put $s = -1$

$$\therefore \quad k_{12} = \frac{1}{(-1)(-1+2)} = -1$$

4. To determine $k_{11}$ multiply both sides by $(s + 1)^2$

$$\therefore \quad \frac{1}{s(s+2)} = \frac{k_1 (s+1)^2}{s} + \frac{k_2 (s+1)^2}{(s+2)} + k_{11} (s+1) + k_2$$

On differentiating both sides *w.r.t.* $s$ and at $s = -1$ the terms containing $k_1$, $k_2$, $k_{12}$ will be zero.

$$\therefore \quad \frac{d}{ds}\left[\frac{1}{s(s \quad 2)}\right] = k_{11} \frac{d}{ds}(s+1) \Bigg|_{s=-1}$$

$$\therefore \quad k_{11} = -\frac{2s+2}{(s^2+2s)} \Bigg|_{s=-1} = 0$$

Thus, $$F(s) = \frac{1}{2} \cdot \frac{1}{s} - \frac{1}{2} \cdot \frac{1}{(s+2)} - \frac{1}{(s+1)^2}$$

Taking inverse Laplace transform on both sides.

$$£^{-1} F(s) = £^{-1}\left[\frac{1}{2} \cdot \frac{1}{s} - \frac{1}{2} \cdot \frac{1}{(s+2)} - \frac{1}{(s+1)^2}\right]$$

$$\therefore \quad f(t) = \frac{1}{2} - \frac{1}{2} e^{-2t} - t\, e^{-t}. \quad \textbf{...Ans.}$$

**Example : 8.4.3** *Solve The differential equation given below*

$$\frac{d^2 i}{dt^2} + 10 \frac{di}{dt} + 25\, i = 0$$

The initial conditions are $i(0^-) = 2$ and $\frac{di\,(0^-)}{dt} = 0$

**Solution :** Taking Laplace transform on both sides

$$[s^2 I(s) - s\, i(0^-) - i'(0^-)] + 10[I(s) - i(0^-)] + 25I(s) = 0$$

Put $i(0^-) = 2$ and $i'(0^-) = 0$

$\therefore$ $[s^2 I(s) - 2s - 0] + 10[I(s) - 2] + 25I(s) = 0$

On simplification

$$I(s) = \frac{2(s+10)}{s^2 + 10s + 25}$$

or $$I(s) = \frac{2(s+10)}{(s+5)^2}$$

Using partial fraction expansion

$$\frac{2(s+10)}{(s+5)^2} = \frac{k_{11}}{s+5} + \frac{k_{12}}{(s+5)^2}$$

1. To determine $k_{12}$ multiply both sides by $(s+5)^2$

$\therefore$ $2(s+10) = k_{11}(s+5) + k_{12}$ ...(1)

Put $s = -5$

$\therefore$ $k_{12} = 2(-5 + 10) = 10$

2. To determine $k_{11}$ differentiate *Eq.* (1) *w.r.t. s*

$\therefore$ $2(1+0) = k_{11}(1+0)$

or $k_{11} = 2$

Thus, $$I(s) = \frac{2}{s+5} + \frac{10}{(s+5)^2}$$

Taking inverse Laplace transform both sides.

$$£^{-1} I(s) = £^{-1}\left[\frac{2}{s+5} + \frac{10}{(s+5)^2}\right]$$

$\therefore$ $i = 2e^{-t} + 10t\, e^{-5t}$ ... **Ans.**

**Example : 8.4.4** *Determine The inverse Laplace transfore. Apply convolution integral method.*

$$F(s) = \frac{1}{s\,(s+1)}$$

Let $\quad F_1(s) = \frac{1}{s}\ , \quad F_2(s) = \frac{1}{s+1}$

$\therefore \quad f_1(t) = 1\ , \quad f_2(t) = e^{-t}$

and $\quad f_1(\tau) = 1\ , \quad f_2(t-\tau) = e^{-(t-\tau)}$

Applying convolutional integrel,

$$f(t) = \int_0^t f_1(\tau)\, f_2(t-\tau)\, d\tau.$$

$$= \int_0^t 1\, e^{-(t-\tau)}\, d\tau. = e^{-t} \int_0^t e^{\tau}\, d\tau$$

$$= e^{-t}\, [e^{\tau}]_0^t = e^{-t}\, [e^t - e^0]$$

$$= e^{-t}.\, e^t - e^{-t} \times 1$$

$\therefore \quad f(t) = 1 - e^{-t} \quad$ **Ans.**

**Example : 8.4.5** *Use convolution integral to evaluate f(t).*

$$F(s) = \frac{1}{s^2\,(s+2)}$$

**Solution :** Let $\quad F_1(s) = \frac{1}{s^2}\ , \ F_2(s) = \frac{1}{s+2}$

$\therefore \quad f_1(t) = t \ , \quad f_2(t) = e^{-2t}$

$\quad f_1(\tau) = \tau \ , \quad f_2(t-\tau) = e^{-2(t-\tau)}$

As per convolution integral

$$f(t) = \int_0^t f_2(\tau)\, f_2(t-\tau)\, d\tau$$

$\therefore$
$$f(t) = \int_0^t \tau\, e^{-2(t-\tau)}\, d\tau$$

On integrating by parts

$$\int v\, du = u\, v - \int u\, dv$$

Let $\quad v = \tau$

$\therefore \quad d\,v = 1$

and $\quad du = e^{-2(t-\tau)}$

$$\therefore \qquad u = \frac{e^{-2(t-\tau)}}{2}$$

$$\therefore \qquad f(t) = \int_0^t \tau e^{-2(t-\tau)} d\tau$$

$$= \left[ \frac{e^{-2(t-\tau)}}{2} \cdot \tau - \int \frac{e^{-2(t-\tau)}}{2} .1\, d\tau \right]_0^t$$

$$= \left[ \tau \frac{e^{-2(t-\tau)}}{2} - \frac{e^{-2(t-\tau)}}{2 \times 2} \right]_0^t$$

$$= \left( \frac{t}{2} - 0 \right) - \left( \frac{1}{4} - \frac{e^{-2t}}{4} \right)$$

or $$f(t) = \left( \frac{e^{-2t}}{4} + \frac{t}{2} - \frac{1}{4} \right) \qquad \text{... Ans.}$$

## 8.5 IMPEDANCE TRANSFORM

The voltage-current relations formulate network equations in time domain. Further, these relationships can also be transformed in frequency domain ($s$-domain) using Laplace transform

### RESISTOR

The time-domain voltage-current relation for a resistor is given below.

$$v = R\, i(t)$$

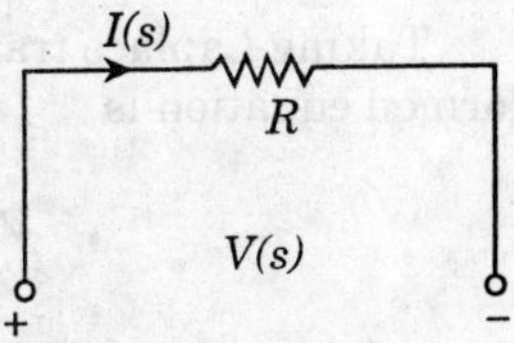

Fig. 8.5.1 Transform of R

Taking Laplace transform on both sides

$$V(s) = R\, I(s)$$

Thus, $$\frac{V(s)}{I(s)} = R$$

The transformed impedance $R$ is indepentent of the frequency "$s$".

### INDUCTOR

The time-domain voltage-current relation for an inductor is given below.

$$v(t) = L \frac{di(t)}{dt}$$

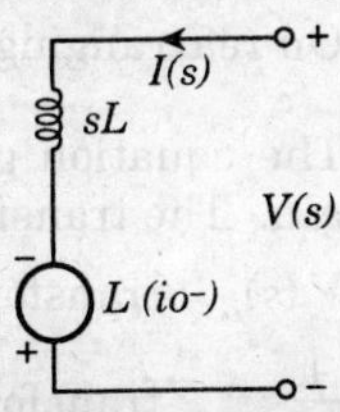

Fig. 8.5.2 Transform of L carrying initial current $i(0^-)$

where, $v(t)$ is the applied voltage across the inductor $L$

Taking Laplace transform on both sides, the transformed eqution is

$$V(s) = L[sI(s) - i(0^-)]$$

$i(0^-)$ is the initial current through the inductor.

On rearranging,

$$sLI(s) - Li(0^-) - V(s) = 0$$

The equation given above satisfies Kirchhoff's voltage law in s - domain. The tranformed network is shown in Fig. 8.5.2

$V(s)$ : tranform of the applied voltage

$sL$ : transform of inductor

$Li(0^-)$ : transform of voltage due to initial current flowing in the inductor.

If the initial current $i(0^-) = 0$, the transform impedance of the inductor is

$$\frac{V(s)}{I(s)} = sL$$

## CAPACITOR

The time-domain voltage-current relation a capacitor is given below,

$$v(t) = \frac{1}{C} \int i(t)\, dt$$

where, $v(t)$ is the applied voltage across the capacitor $C$

Taking Laplace transform on both sides, the transformed equation is

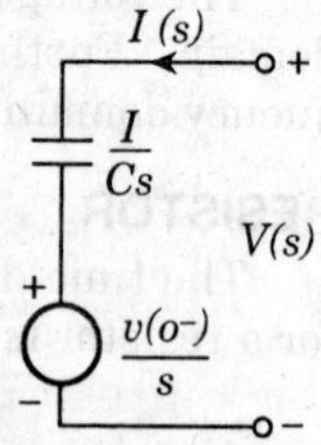


Fig. 8.5.3 Transform of $C$ with initial voltage $v(0^-)$.

$$V(s) = \frac{1}{Cs} . I(s) + \frac{q(0^-)}{Cs}$$

or $$V(s) = \frac{1}{Cs} . I(s) + \frac{v(0^-)}{s}$$

$$\frac{q(0^-)}{C} = v(0^-)$$

is the initial voltage across the capacitor.

On rearranging. $\frac{1}{Cs} . I(s) + \frac{v(0^-)}{s} - V(s) = 0$

The equation given above satisfies Kirchhoff's voltage law is s-domain. The transformed network is shown in Fig. 8.5.3

$V(s)$ : transform of applied voltage

$\frac{1}{Cs}$ : transform of capacitor

$\frac{v(0^-)}{s}$ : transform of initial voltage due to initial charge on The capacitor

If the initial charge on the capacitor is zero, $v(0^-) = 0$ and the transform impedance of the capacitor is

$$\frac{V(s)}{I(s)} = \frac{1}{Cs}$$

## 8.6 SOLVED EXAMPLES (I)

**Example : 8.6.1** *Initially the capacitor is charged to a voltage $V_0$. The switch is closed at t = 0. Determine expression for i (t)*

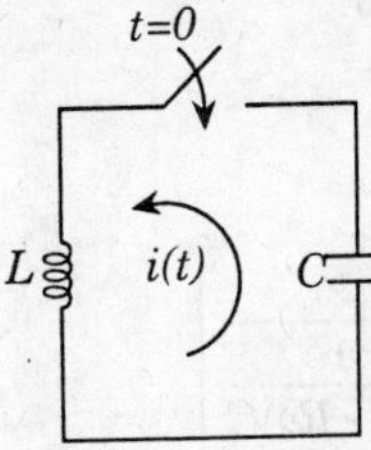


Fig. 8.6.1 Circuit for example 8.6.1

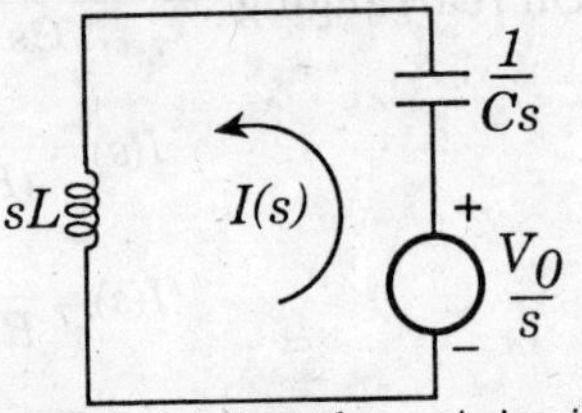


Fig. 8.6.1 (*a*) Transformed circuit of Fig. 8.6.1.

**Solution :** Applying *KVL*

$$\frac{1}{Cs} \cdot I(s) + sLI(s) - \frac{V_0}{s} = 0$$

On simplifying $\quad I(s) = \frac{V_0 C}{s^2 LC + 1}$

or
$$I(s) = \frac{V_0}{L} \cdot \frac{1}{s^2 + \frac{1}{LC}} = \frac{V_0}{L/(1/\sqrt{LC})} \cdot \frac{1/\sqrt{LC}}{s + (1/\sqrt{LC})^2}$$

$$= V_0 \sqrt{\frac{C}{L}} \cdot \frac{1/\sqrt{LC}}{s + (1/\sqrt{LC})^2}$$

Taking inverse Laplace transform on both sides

$$i(t) = V_0 \sqrt{\frac{C}{L}} \cdot \sin \frac{t}{\sqrt{LC}} \quad \textbf{...Ans.}$$

**Example : 8.6.2** *Determine expression for i(t). The switch (Fig. 8.6.2) is closed at t = 0*

**Solution :** $v_c(0^-) = v_c(0^+) = V_0$

The transformed circuit is shown in Fig. 8.6.2 (a). *KVL* equation is written below

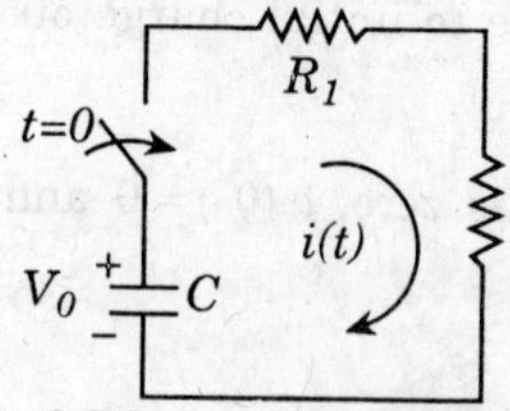

Fig. 8.6.2 circuit for example 8.6.2

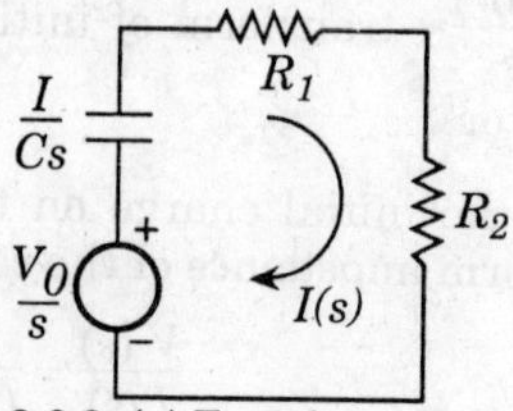

Fig. 8.6.2 (*a*) Transformed circuit of Fig. 8.6.2

$$(R_1 + R_2)\, I(s) - \frac{V_0}{s} + \frac{1}{Cs} I(s) = 0$$

On rearranging $\frac{[(R_1 + R_2)Cs + 1]}{Cs} \,.\, I(s) = \frac{V_0}{s}$

$$\therefore \qquad I(s) = \frac{V_0\, C}{(R_1 + R_2)\, Cs + 1}$$

or
$$I(s) = \frac{V_0}{R_1 + R_2} \cdot \left[\frac{1}{s + \frac{1}{(R_1 + R_2)C}}\right]$$

Taking inverse Laplace transform on both sides

$$i\,(t) = \frac{V_0}{R_1 + R_2}\, e^{\frac{-t}{(R_1 + R_2)\, C}} \qquad \text{...Ans.}$$

**Example : 8.6.3** *In the RC network shown in Fig. 8.6.3 determine expression for voltage across the capacitor. The switch is closed at t = 0 and the capacitor is initially charged to a voltage $V_0$ as shown.*

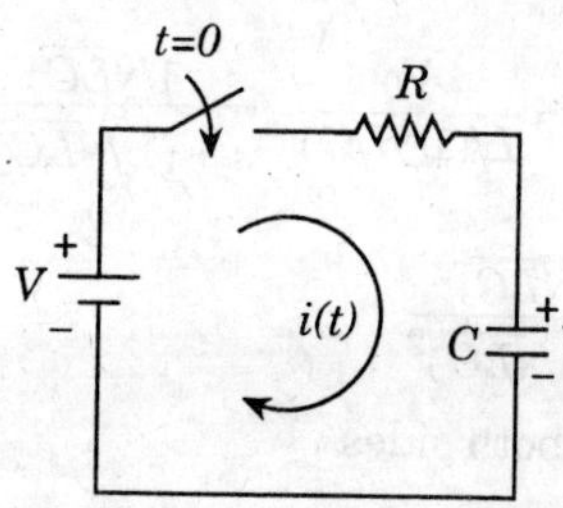

Fig. 8.6.3 Network for example 8.6.3.

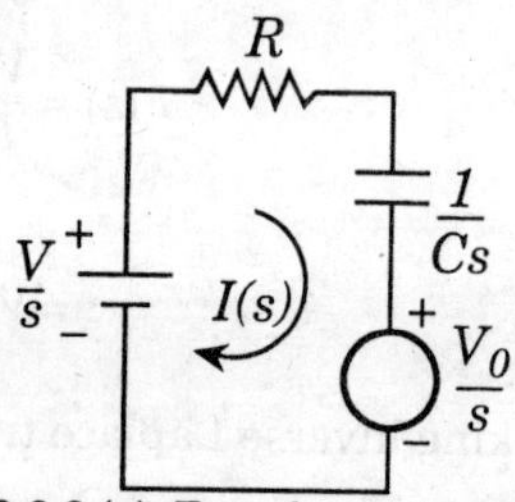

Fig. 8.6.3 (*a*) Transformed network of Fig. 8.6.3

**Solution :** The transformed network is drawn in Fig. 8.6.3 (*a*)

*KVL* equation is written below

$$RI(s) + \frac{1}{Cs} \,.\, I(s) + \frac{V_0}{s} - \frac{V}{s} = 0$$

On rearranging

$$\left(R + \frac{1}{Cs}\right) I(s) = \frac{(V - V_0)}{s}$$

$$\therefore \qquad I(s) = \frac{(V - V_0)\,C}{RCs + 1}$$

$$V_c(s) = \frac{1}{Cs}\,I(s) + \frac{V_0}{s} = \frac{1}{Cs}\cdot\frac{(V - V_0)C}{RCs + 1} + \frac{V_0}{s}$$

$$= \frac{(V - V_0)}{sRC\left(s + \frac{1}{RC}\right)} + \frac{V_0}{s}$$

$$= \frac{V - V_0}{RC}\left(\frac{k_1}{s} + \frac{k_2}{s + \frac{1}{RC}}\right) + \frac{V_0}{s}$$

The coeffs. can be determined as $k_1 = RC$ , $k_2 = -RC$

$$\therefore \qquad V_c(s) = (V - V_0)\left(\frac{1}{s} - \frac{1}{s + \frac{1}{RC}}\right) + \frac{V_0}{s}$$

Taking inverse Laplace transform on both sides

$$v_c(t) = (V - V_0)\,(1 - e^{-t/RC}) + V_0$$

or $$v_c(t) = V - (V - V_0)\,e^{-t/Rc} \qquad \ldots\textbf{Ans.}$$

**Example : 8.6.4** *Determine current i(t) and $v_2(t)$ in the network given in Fig. 8.6.4.*

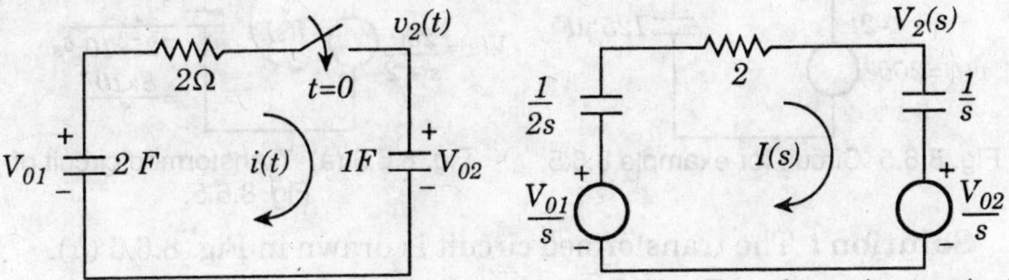


Fig. 8.6.4 Network for example 8.6.4. Fig. 8.6.4 (*a*) Transformed network of Fig. 8.6.4

**Solution :** The capacitors are charged to $V_{01}$ and $V_{02}$ respectively. The transformed network is shown in Fig. 8.6.4 (*a*)

*KVL* equation is written below,

$$\frac{1}{2\,s}\,.\,I(s) + 2I(s) + \frac{1}{s}\,.\,I(s) + \frac{V_{02}}{s} - \frac{V_{01}}{s} = 0$$

On rearranging $$\left(\frac{1}{2s} + \frac{1}{s} + 2\right) I(s) = \frac{(V_{01} - V_{02})}{s}$$

or $$\left(\frac{1.5}{s} + 2\right) I(s) = \frac{(V_{01} - V_{02})}{s}$$

$$\therefore \qquad I(s) = \frac{(V_{01} - V_{02})}{2\,(s + 0.75)}$$

Taking inverse Laplace transform on both sides

$$i\,(t) = \frac{(V_{01} - V_{02})}{2}\, e^{-0.75\,t} \qquad \text{...Ans.}$$

$$V_2\,(s) = \frac{V_{02}}{s} + \frac{1}{s} I\,(s) = \frac{V_{02}}{s} + \frac{1}{s}\frac{(V_{01} - V_{02})}{2\,(s + 0.75)}$$

$$= \frac{V_{02}}{s} + \frac{V_{01} - V_{02}}{2}\left(\frac{k_1}{s} + \frac{k_2}{s + 0.75}\right)$$

The coeffs. can be determined as $k_1 = \frac{1}{0.75}$, $k_2 = -\frac{1}{0.75}$

$$\therefore \qquad V_2\,(s) = \frac{V_{02}}{s} + \frac{V_{01} - V_{02}}{2}\left[\frac{1}{0.75s} - \frac{1}{0.75\,(s + 0.75)}\right]$$

$$= \frac{V_{02}}{s} + \frac{V_{01} - V_{02}}{1.5}\left(\frac{1}{s} - \frac{1}{s + 0.75}\right)$$

Taking inverse Laplace transform on both sides

$$v_2\,(t) = V_{02} + \frac{V_{01} - V_{02}}{1.5}(1 - e^{-0.75t}) \qquad \text{...Ans.}$$

**Example : 8.6.5** *Use convolution integral to determine $v_c\,(t)$*

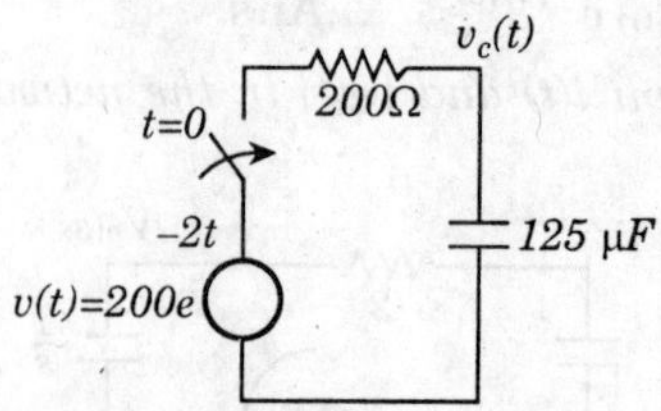


Fig. 8.6.5 Circuit for example 8.6.5.

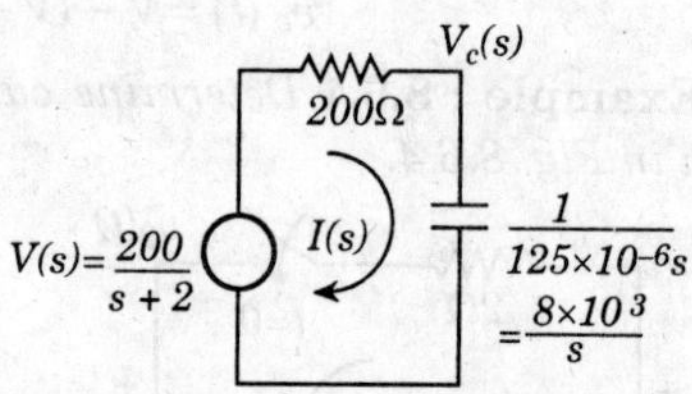


Fig. 8.6.5 (a) Transformed circuit of Fig. 8.6.5.

**Solution :** The transformed circuit is drawn in Fig. 8.6.5 (*a*).

$$I\,(s) = \frac{V\,(s)}{200 + \dfrac{8 \times 10^3}{s}} = \frac{200}{(s + 2)} \cdot \frac{s}{(200s + 8 \times 10^3)}$$

$$= \frac{200\,s}{(s + 2) \times 200\left(s + \dfrac{8 \times 10^3}{200}\right)} = \frac{s}{(s + 2)\,(s + 40)}$$

$$V_c\,(s) = \frac{8 \times 10^3}{s} \times I\,(s)$$

or $$V_c\,(s) = \frac{8 \times 10^3}{s} \times \frac{s}{(s + 2)\,(s + 40)} = \frac{320}{(s + 2)} \cdot \frac{250}{(s + 40)}$$

Let $$F_1\,(s) = \frac{320}{s + 2}$$

$$\therefore \qquad f_1(t) = 320\, e^{-2t}$$

and $$F_2(s) = \frac{250}{s+40}, \quad \therefore \quad \text{and } f_2(t) = 250^{-40t}$$

Using convolution integral

$$v_c(t) = \int_0^t f_1(t-\tau)\, f_2(\tau)\, d\tau$$

$$= \int_0^t 320\, e^{-2(t-\tau)} \,.\, 250 e^{-40\tau}\, d\tau$$

$$= 8000\, e^{-2t} \int_0^t e^{2\tau}\, e^{-40\tau} d\tau$$

$$= 8000\, e^{-2t} \int_0^t e^{-38\tau} d\tau$$

$$= 8000\, e^{-2t} \left[ -\frac{e^{-38\tau}}{38} \right]_0^t$$

$$= 8000\, e^{-2t} \left( -\frac{e^{-38t}}{38} + \frac{1}{38} \right)$$

or $$v_c(t) = \frac{8000}{38} \left( e^{-2t} - e^{-40t} \right) \qquad \text{... Ans.}$$

**Example : 8.6.6** *Find expression for the current through inductor L. The switch is opened at t = 0 in Fig. 8.6.6.*

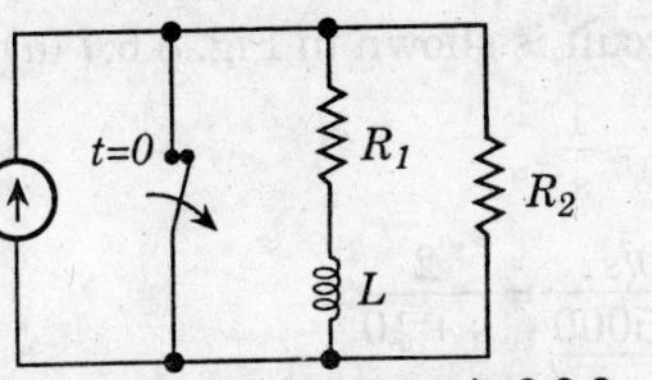


Fig. 8.6.6 Network for example 8.6.6

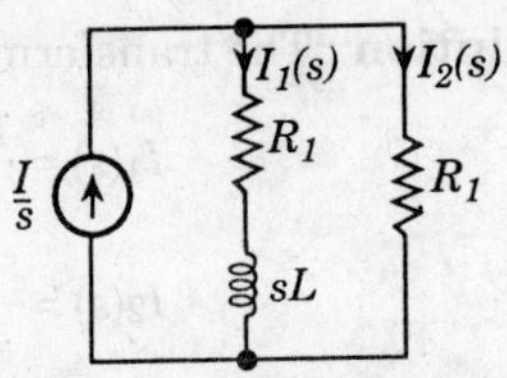


Fig. 8.6.6 (a) Transformed network of Fig. 8.6.6

**Solution :** The transformed circuit is shown in Fig. 8.6.6($a$).

By current division, $$I_1(s) = \frac{I}{s} \cdot \frac{R_2}{(R_1 + sL) + R_2}$$

$$= \frac{IR_2}{s\,(R_1 + R_2 + s\,L)} = \frac{IR_2}{L} \cdot \frac{1}{s\left(s + \dfrac{R_1 + R_2}{L}\right)}$$

$$= \frac{I\,R_2}{L} \left( \frac{k_1}{s} + \frac{k_2}{s + \dfrac{R_1 + R_2}{L}} \right)$$

The coeffs. can be determined as

$$k_1 = \frac{L}{k_1 + k_2} \quad \text{and} \quad k_2 = \frac{-L}{R_1 + R_2}$$

$$\therefore \quad I_1(s) = \frac{I R_2}{L}\left(\frac{L}{R_1+R_2}\cdot\frac{1}{s} - \frac{L}{R_1+R_2}\cdot\frac{1}{s+\dfrac{R_1+R_2}{L}}\right)$$

$$= \frac{IR_2}{R_1+R_2}\left(\frac{1}{s} - \frac{1}{s+\dfrac{R_1+R_2}{L}}\right)$$

Taking inverse Laplace transform on both sides

$$i_1(t) = \frac{IR_2}{R_1+R_2}\left[/1 - e^{-\frac{(R_1+R_2)\,t}{L}}\right] \quad \text{... Ans.}$$

**Example 8.6.7** *obtain expression for the current supplied by the battery and determine time required for the current to reach a value 1.6 A.*

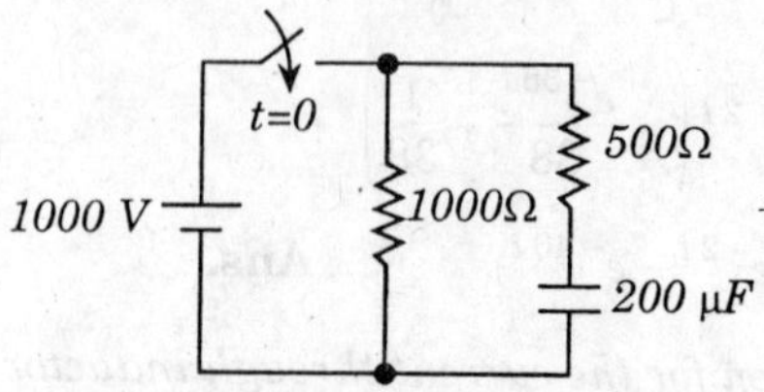


Fig. 8.6.7 Network for example 8.6.7

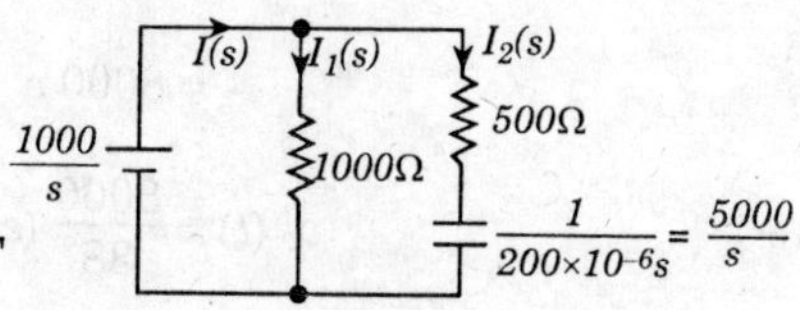


Fig. 8.6.7 (*a*) Transformed network of Fig. 8.6.7.

**Solution :** The transformed circuit is shown in Fig. 8.6.7 (*a*).

$$I_1(s) = \frac{1000/s}{1000} = \frac{1}{s}$$

$$I_2(s) = \frac{1000/s}{500 + \dfrac{5000}{s}} = \frac{2}{s+10}$$

$$I(s) = I_1(s) + I_2(s) = \frac{1}{s} + \frac{2}{s+10}$$

Taking inverse Laplace transform on both sides

$$i(t) = 1 + 2\,e^{-10\,t} \quad \text{... Ans.}$$

$$1.6 = 1 + 2\,e^{-10\,t}$$

$$\therefore \quad e^{-10\,t} = 0.3$$

$$\therefore \quad +10\,t = 1.2$$

$$t = 0.12 \text{ sec.} \quad \text{...Ans.}$$

**Example : 8.6.8** *The RL series circuit shown in Fig. 8.6.8 is connected to a 12V battery through a switch. Determine expression for the current when the switch is moved to 6 V battery after a lapse of 5 ms.*

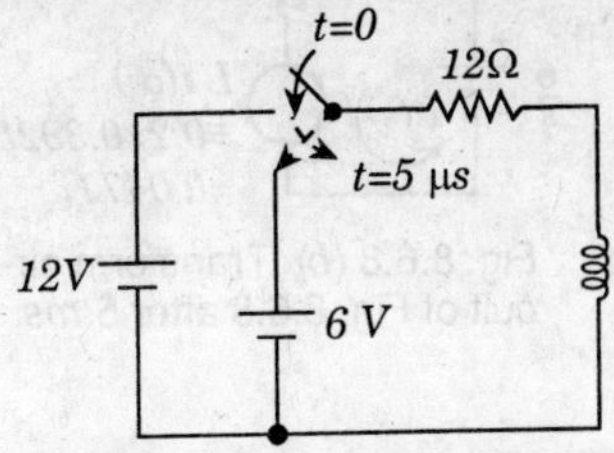

Fig. 8.6.8 circuit for example 8.6.8

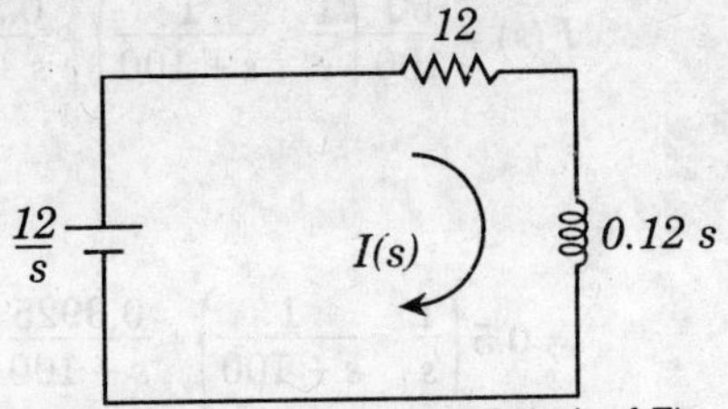

Fig. 8.6.8 (*a*) Transformed ciruit of Fig. 8.6.8

**Solution :** (1) 12*V* battery connection, the transformed circuit is shown in Fig. 8.6.8 (*a*).

$$12\, I(s) + 0.12sI(s) - \frac{12}{s} = 0$$

$$\therefore \qquad I(s) = \frac{12}{s} \cdot \frac{1}{12 + 0.12s} = \frac{12}{0.12} \cdot \frac{1}{s(s+100)}$$

$$= \frac{100}{s(s+100)} = 100\left(\frac{k_1}{s} + \frac{k_{12}}{s+100}\right)$$

The coeffs. can bedetermined as

$$k_1 = \frac{1}{100} \text{ and } k_2 = -\frac{1}{100}$$

$$\therefore \qquad I(s) = \frac{1}{s} - \frac{1}{s+100}$$

Taking inverse Laplace transform on both sides

$$i(t) = (1 - e^{-100\, t})$$

$$i(5ms) = (1 - e^{-100 \times 5 \times 10^{-3}}) = 1 - e^{-0.5} = 0.3935 \text{ A}$$

(2) 6*V* battery connection (switch connected after 5 ms), the transformed circuit is shown in Fig. 8.6.8 (*b*).

$$12I(s) + 0.12I(s) - \frac{6}{s} - 0.0471 = 0$$

or

$$I(s) = \frac{6}{0.12s\,(s+100)} + \frac{0.0471}{0.12\,(s+100)}$$

$$= \frac{50}{s\,(s+100)} + \frac{0.3925}{(s+100)}$$

$$= 50\left(\frac{k_1}{s} + \frac{k_2}{s+100}\right) + \frac{0.3925}{(s+100)}$$

The coeffs. can be determined as

$$k_1 = \frac{1}{100} \text{ and } k_2 = -\frac{1}{100}$$

$$\therefore\ I(s) = \frac{50}{100}\left(\frac{1}{s} - \frac{1}{s+100}\right) + \frac{0.3925}{s+100}$$

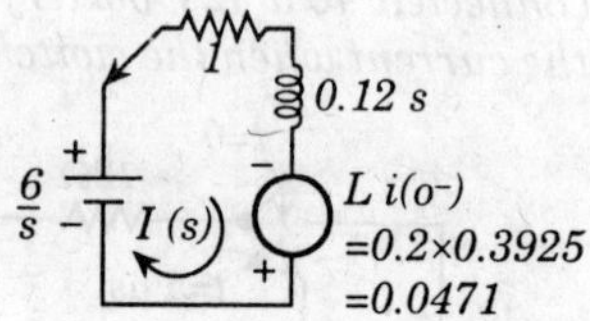


Fig. 8.6.8 (*b*) Transform circuit of Fig. 8.6.8 after 5 *ms*.

$$= 0.5\left(\frac{1}{s} - \frac{1}{s+100}\right) + \frac{0.3925}{s+100}$$

Taking inverse Laplace transform on both sides

$$i(t) = 0.5 - 0.5\, e^{-100\,t} + 0.3925\, e^{-100\,t}$$
$$= 0.5 - 0.1075\, e^{-100\,t}$$

As the time delay $= 5 \times 10^{-3}$ sec

$$i\,(t - 0.5 \times 10^{-3}) = 0.5 - 0.1075\, e^{-100\,(t - 5 \times 10^{-3})} \quad \text{...Ans.}$$

## 8.7 LAPLACE TRANSFORM OF SIGNAL WAVE FORMS

The time functions described below are basic signals useful in construction of signal wave forms.

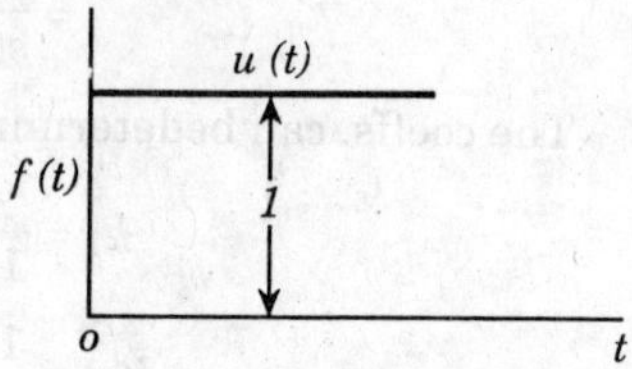


Fig. 8.7.1 Unit step function

### 1. Unit Step Function

As shown in Fig. 8.7.1 the unit step function has zero value for $t < 0$ and $f(t) = 1$ for $t \geq 0$.

The unit step function is represent as

$$f(t) = 0\ ,\ t < 0$$
$$= 1\ ,\ t \geq 0$$

The unit step function is denoted as

$$u(t) = 1$$

and $$\pounds\, u(t) = \frac{1}{s}$$

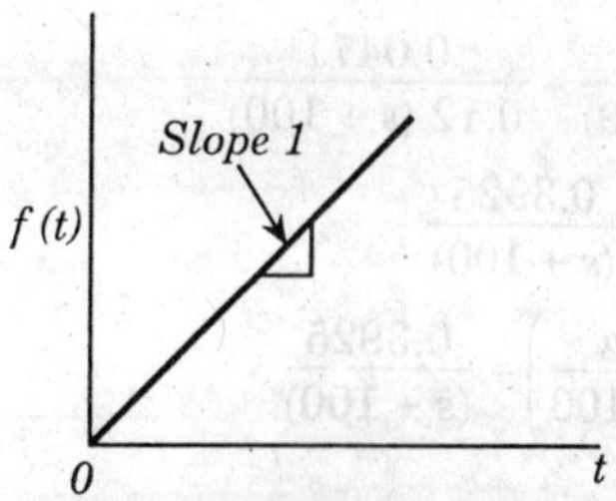


Fig. 8.7.2 Unit ramp function.

### 2. Unit Ramp Function

As shown in Fig. 8.7.2 the unit ramp function has a zero value for $t < 0$ and $f(t) = t$ for $t \geq 0$. The slope of unit ramp function is 1. The unit ramp function is represented as

$$f(t) = 0\ ,\ t < 0$$
$$= t\ ,\ t \geq 0$$

The unit ramp function is denoted as

$$r(t) = t$$

and $$£\, r(t) = \frac{1}{s^2}$$

Any function multiplied by $u(t)$ clearly indicates that the function does not exist for $t < 0$

The function $r(t) = t$ does not exist for $t < 0$, therefore The same can be expressed as

$$r\,(t) = t\,.\,u\,(t)$$

### 3. Impulse Function

The impulse function denoted as $\delta\,(t)$ exists only at $t = 0$ and zero for all other values of time. The area under a unit impulse function is one. The numeral 1 near the arrow head (Fig. 8.7.3) gives strength of the impulse as unity. A pulse having width approaching zero and infinite magnitude with unit area under the pulse is known as unit impulse function.

The Laplace transform of unit impulse function is derived below,

It is a well known fact that step function is a first time derivative of ramp function and in turn impulse function is a first time derivative of step function. Therefore,

$$\text{Unit impulse function } = \frac{d}{dt} \text{ (unit step function)}$$

Hence, the Laplace transform of unit impulse function is derived from the Laplace transform of unit step function as follows

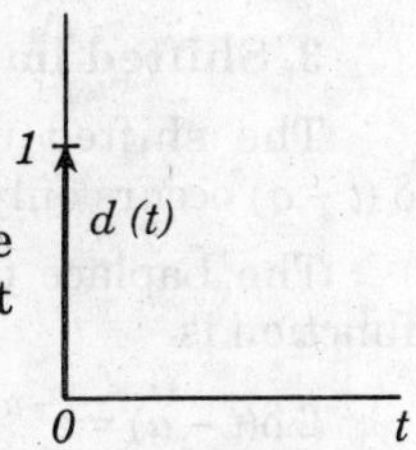

Fig. 8.7.3 Impulse function

$$£ \text{ (unit impulse function)} = £\frac{d}{dt} \text{ (unit step function)}$$

or £ (unit impulse function) = $s$ £ (unit step function)

$$\therefore\ £ \text{ (unit impulse function)} = s\,.\,\frac{1}{s} = 1. \quad i.e.\ £\,\delta\,(t) = 1$$

## 8.7.1 Shifted Functions

In the case of a step function the step occurs at $t = 0$. However, in a shifted step function the step is delayed by a time say $t = a$, $a > 0$ (Fig. 8.7.4)

### 1. Shifted Unit Step Function

The shifted unit step function denoted as $u\,(t - a)$ can be described as

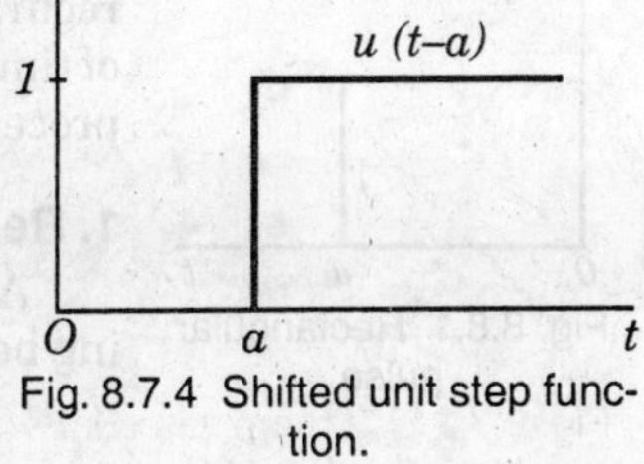

Fig. 8.7.4 Shifted unit step function.

$$u(t-a) = 0\,,\ t < a$$
$$= 1\,,\ t \geq a$$

The Laplace transform of shifted unit step function is

$$£\, u(t-a) = e^{-as}\, £\, u(t)$$

$$\therefore \quad £\, u(t-a) = \frac{e^{-as}}{s}$$

Any function multiplied by $u(t-a)$ indicate that the function exists for $t \geq a$ , at all other times the function is zero.

**2. Shifted Ramp Function**

The shifted unit ramp denoted as $r(t-a)$ can by described as

$$r(t-a) = 0\,,\ t < a$$
$$= t\,,\ t \geq a$$

The Laplace transform of shifted unit ramp function is

$$£\, r(t-a) = e^{-as}\, £\, r(t)$$

$$\therefore \quad £\, r(t-a) = \frac{e^{-as}}{s^2}$$

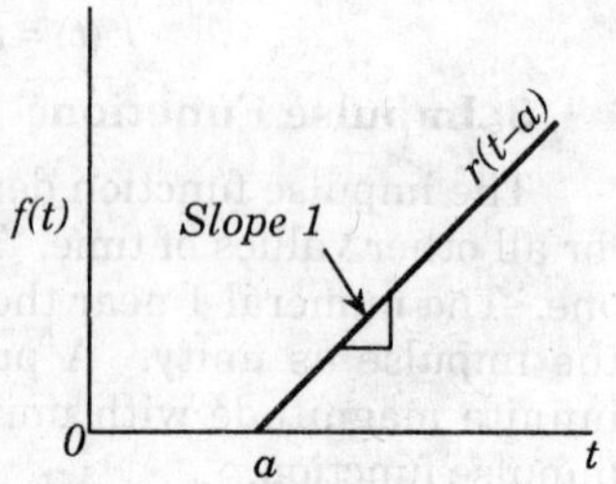

Fig. 8.7.5 Shifted unit ramp function.

**3. Shifted Impulse Function**

The shifted unit impulse function denoted as $\delta(t-a)$ occurs only at $t = a$.

The Laplace transform of a shifted unit impulse function is

$$£\, \delta(t-a) = e^{-as}\, £\, \delta(t)$$

$$\therefore \quad £\, \delta(t-a) = e^{-as} \times 1 . = e^{-as} .$$

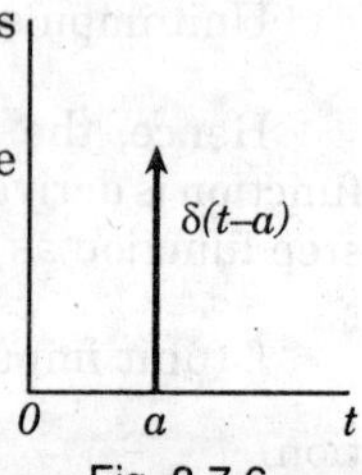

Fig. 8.7.6

## 8.8 LAPLACE TRANSFORM OF WAVE FORMS

The step function and ramp function are useful for the generation of waveforms. The waveforms to be generated are, rectangular pulse, saw-tooth pulse, triangular pulse and like. These pulse waveforms are non-recurring while periodic waveforms are recurring *i.e.* repeating after a regular interval of time. The examples given below describe the procedure of constructing waveforms.

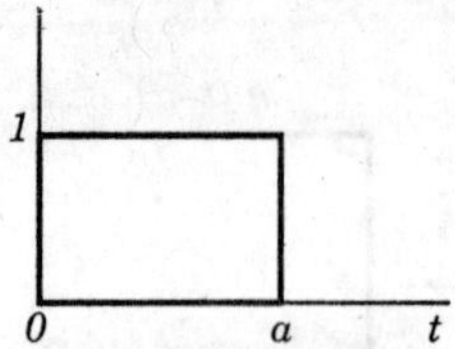

Fig. 8.8.1 Rectangular pulse

**1. Rectangular Pulse**

A rectangular pulse of magnitude 1 occurring between $t = 0$ to $t = a$ is shown in Fig. 8.8.1

wherein a unit step function $u(t)$ exists upto $t = a, a > 0$. Beyond $t = a$ the function does not exist. Thus, at $t = a$ the function $u(t - a)$ is substracted from $u(t)$. Therefore, the expression

$$f(t) = u(t) - u(t - a)$$

represents equation for the rectangular pulse (Fig. 8.8.1)

$$\therefore \quad F(s) = \frac{1}{s} - \frac{e^{-as}}{s} = \frac{1}{s}(1 - e^{-as})$$

**2. Alternate Rectangular Waveform for One Period**

An alternate rectangular waveform for one time period $2a$ is shown in Fig. 8.8.2.

The mathematical expression for the alternate rectangular waveform (Fig. 8.8.2) is written below

$$f(t) = u(t) - u(t - a).$$
$$- u(t - a) + u(t - 2a)$$

or $f(t) = u(t) - 2u(t - a) + u(t - 2a)$

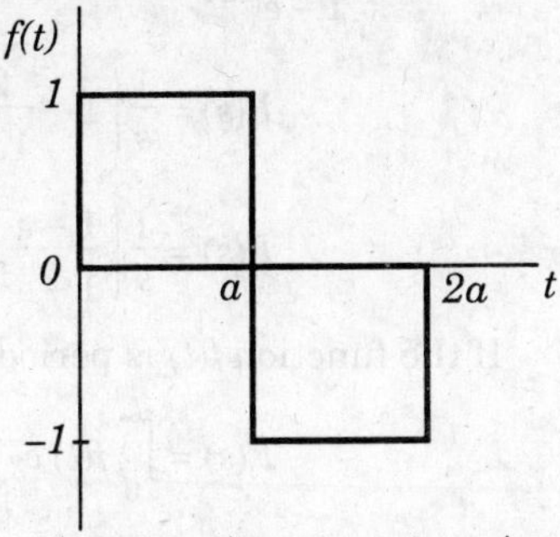

Fig. 8.8.2 Alternate rectangular waveform (one time period)

Taking Laplace transform on both sides

$$F(s) = \frac{1}{s} - \frac{2e^{-as}}{s} + \frac{e^{-2as}}{s}$$

$$= \frac{1}{s}(1 - 2e^{-as} + e^{-2as})$$

or $$F(s) = \frac{(1 - e^{-as})^2}{s}$$

**3. Rectangular Periodic Waveform Having Time Period 2a**

A rectangular periodic waveform having time period $2a$ is shown in Fig. 8.8.3.

The mathematical expression for rectangular periodic waveform is written below

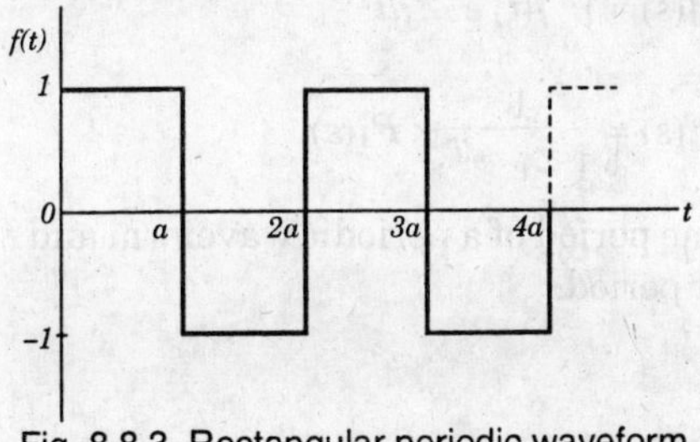

Fig. 8.8.3 Rectangular periodic waveform.

$$f(t) = u(t) - 2u(t-a) + 2u(t-2a) - 2u(t-3a) + 2u(t-4a) + ----$$

Taking Laplace transform both sides

$$F(s) = \frac{1}{s} - \frac{2e^{-as}}{s} + \frac{2e^{-2as}}{s} - \frac{2e^{-3as}}{s} + \frac{2e^{-4as}}{s} + --$$

$$= \frac{1}{s}\,[1 - 2e^{-as}\,(1 - e^{-as} + e^{-2as} - e^{-3as} + --)]$$

$$\therefore \quad \frac{1}{1-e^{-as}} = (1 - e^{-as} + e^{-2as} - e^{-3as} + ------)$$

$$\therefore \quad F(s) = \frac{1}{s}\left(1 - \frac{2e^{-as}}{1+e^{-as}}\right)$$

or

$$F(s) = \frac{1}{s}\left(\frac{1-e^{-as}}{1+e^{-as}}\right)$$

If the function $f(t)$ is periodic, then

$$F(s) = \int_0^\infty f(t)\, e^{-st} dt$$

$$= \int_0^T f(t)\, e^{-st} dt + \int_T^{2T} f(t)\, e^{-st} dt + \int_{2T}^{3T} f(t)\, e^{-st} dt + \ldots$$

where $T$ is the time period.

The term $\int_T^{2T} f(t)\, e^{-st} dt$ ------ is the Laplace transform of a shifted function from time $T$ to $2T$ -------

Therefore, $F(s) = \int_0^T f(t)\, e^{-st}\, dt + e^{-sT} \int_0^T f(t)\, e^{-st} dt$

$$+ e^{-2sT} \int_0^T f(t)\, e^{-st} dt + ------$$

$$\therefore \quad F(s) = (1 + e^{-st} + e^{-2sT} + -----) \int_0^T f(t)\, e^{-st} dt$$

$$\because \quad F_1(s) = \int_0^T f(t)\, e^{-st} dt$$

$$\therefore \quad F(s) = \frac{1}{1-e^{-sT}} \times F_1(s)$$

where $T$ is the time period of a periodic waveform and $F_1(s)$ the Laplace transform of first period.

**4. Saw Tooth Pulse Waveform**

(*i*) A ramp function is shown in Fig. 8.8.4 (solid line). The slope of the ramp function is $\frac{V}{T}$

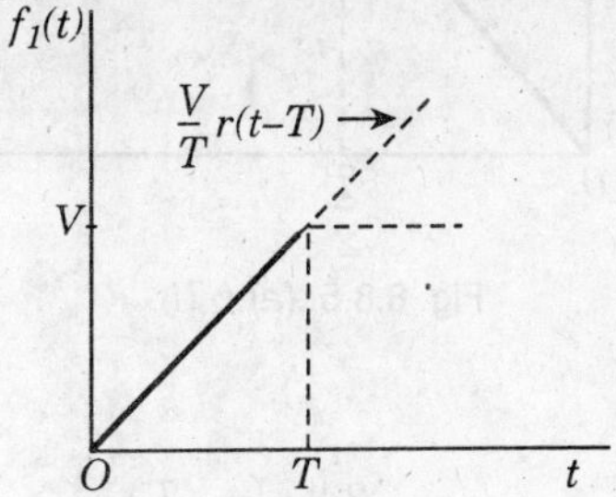


Fig. 8.8.4 $f_1$ (*t*)

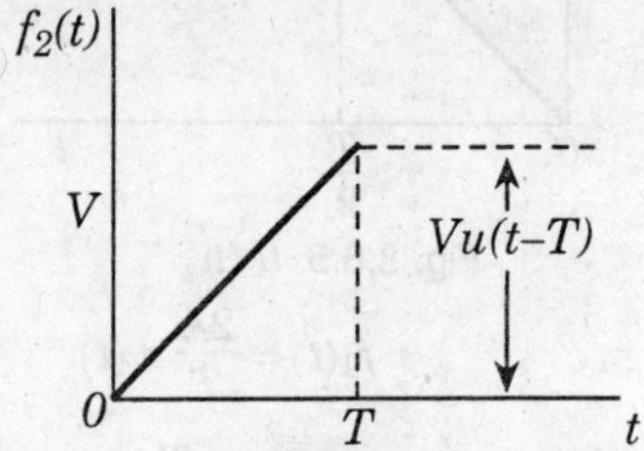


Fig. 8.8.4 (*a*) $f_2$ (*t*)

$$\therefore \quad f_1(t) = \frac{V}{T} t$$

(*ii*) At the instant *T* onwards the function $\frac{V}{T} r(t - T)$ is subtracted from $f_1(t)$ to get $f_2(t)$ shown in Fig. 8.8.4 (*a*).

$$f_2(t) = \frac{V}{T} r(t) - \frac{V}{T} r(t - T)$$

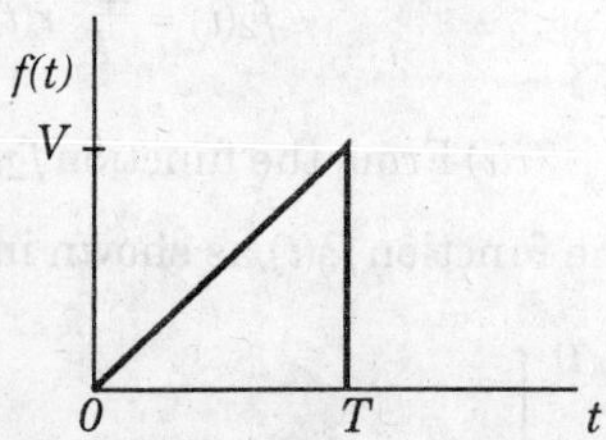


Fig. 8.8.4 (*b*) Saw tooth pulse waveform.

(*iii*) At time *T*, The function $Vu(t - T)$ is subtracted from $f_2(t)$ to get saw tooth pulse waveform shown in Fig. 8.8.4 (*b*)

$$\therefore \quad f(t) = \frac{V}{T} r(t) - \frac{V}{T} r(t - T) - Vu(t - T)$$

Taking Laplace transform on both sides

$$£ f(t) = £\left[\frac{V}{T} r(t) - \frac{V}{T} r(t - T) - V u(t - T)\right]$$

$$\therefore \quad F(s) = \frac{V}{Ts^2} - \frac{V}{Ts^2} \cdot e^{-sT} - \frac{V}{s} \cdot e^{-sT}$$

or

$$F(s) = \frac{V}{Ts^2}\left[1 - e^{-sT}(1 + Ts)\right]$$

**5. Triangular Pulse Waveform**

The expression for the triangular pulse waveform of duration *T* and height *A* is obtained through following steps.

(*i*) The slope of ramp function $f_1(t)$ shown in Fig. 8.8.5 is $\frac{2A}{T}$

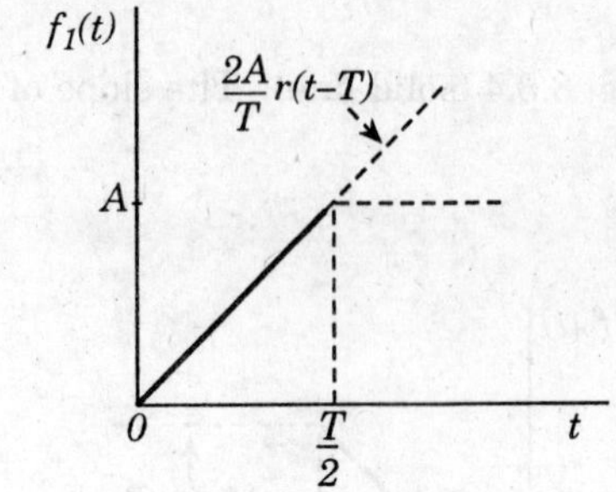


Fig. 8.8.5 $f_1$ (t)

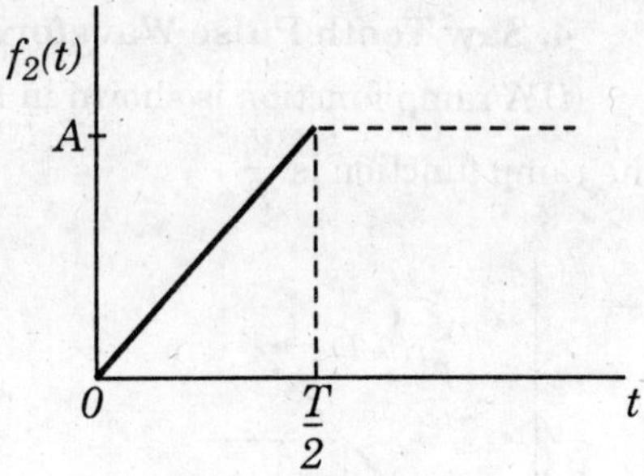


Fig. 8.8.5 (*a*) $f_2$ (*t*)

$$\therefore \qquad f_1(t) = \frac{2A}{T} r(t)$$

(*ii*) At The instant $\frac{T}{2}$ onwards, the function $\frac{2A}{T} r\left(t - \frac{T}{2}\right)$ is subtracted from $f_1(t)$ to obtain $f_2(t)$ as shown in Fig. 8.8.5 (*a*).

$$\therefore \qquad f_2(t) = \frac{2A}{T} r(t) - \frac{2A}{T} r\left(t - \frac{T}{2}\right)$$

(*iii*) From the function $f_2(t)$ subtract the function $\frac{2A}{T} r\left(t - \frac{T}{2}\right)$ to get the function $f_3(t)$ as shown in Fig. 8.8.5 (*b*)

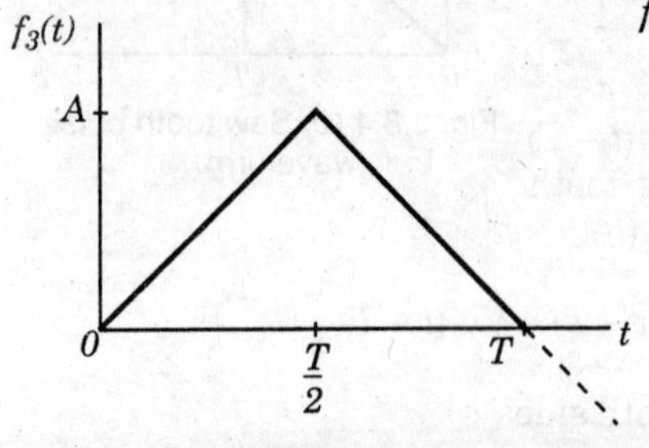


Fig. 8.8.5 (*b*)

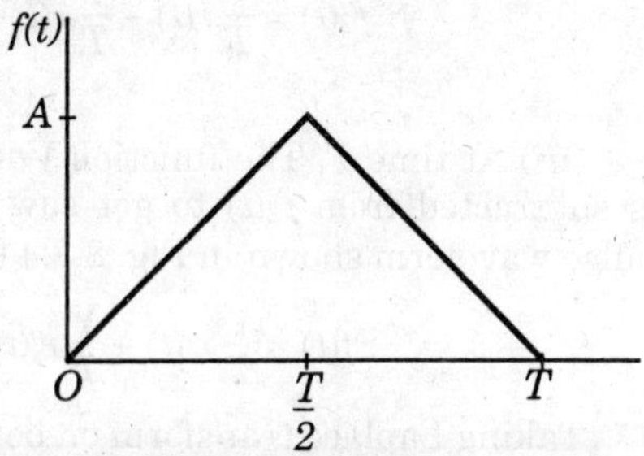


Fig. 8.8.5 (*c*) *f* (*t*)

$$f_3(t) = \frac{2A}{T} r(t) - \frac{2A}{T} r\left(t - \frac{T}{2}\right) - \frac{2A}{T} r\left(t - \frac{T}{2}\right)$$

(*iv*) The expression for triangular pulse is obtained by adding the function $\frac{2A}{T} r(t - T)$ to $f_3(t)$

$$\therefore \qquad f(t) = \frac{2A}{T} r(t) - \frac{2A}{T} r\left(t - \frac{T}{2}\right) - \frac{2A}{T} r\left(t - \frac{T}{2}\right) + \frac{2A}{T} r(t - T)$$

or

$$f(t) = \frac{2A}{T} r(t) - \frac{4A}{T} r\left(t - \frac{T}{2}\right) + \frac{2A}{T} r(t - T)$$

or $$f(t) = \frac{2A}{T}t \cdot u(t) - \frac{4A}{T}t \cdot u\left(t - \frac{T}{2}\right) + \frac{2A}{T}t \cdot u(t - T)$$

Taking inverse Laplace transform

$$F(s) = \frac{2A}{Ts^2} - \frac{4A}{Ts^2} \cdot e^{\frac{-sT}{2}} + \frac{2A}{Ts^2} e^{-sT}.$$

**6. Sinusodial Pulse**

(*i*) A sinusoidal waveform $f_1(t) = \sin \omega t, \quad t \geq 0$ is shown in Fig. 8.8.6.

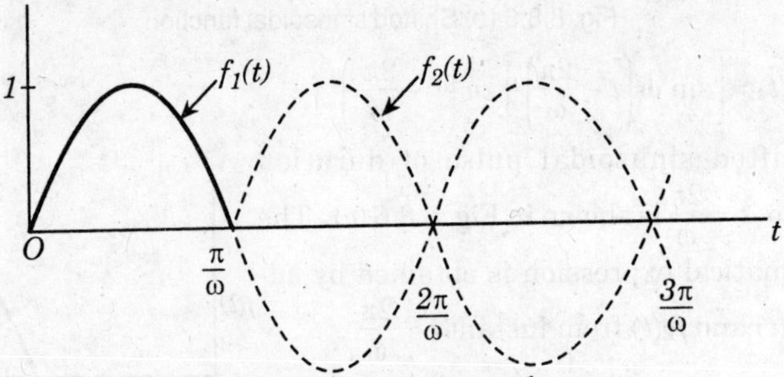


Fig. 8.8.6 Sinusoidal waveforms

In order to obtain sinusoidal pulse of half-cycle duration from $t = 0$ to $t = \frac{\pi}{\omega}$, The function $f_1(t) = \sin \omega t$ is to be cancelled beyond $t = \frac{\pi}{\omega}$. Therefore, add function $f_2(t) = \sin \omega\left(t - \frac{\pi}{\omega}\right)$ at instant $t = \frac{\pi}{\omega}$ to $f_1(t)$. Hence, mathematical expression for the sinusoidal pulse [Fig. 8.8.6 (*a*)] from $t = 0$ to $t = \pi/\omega$ is

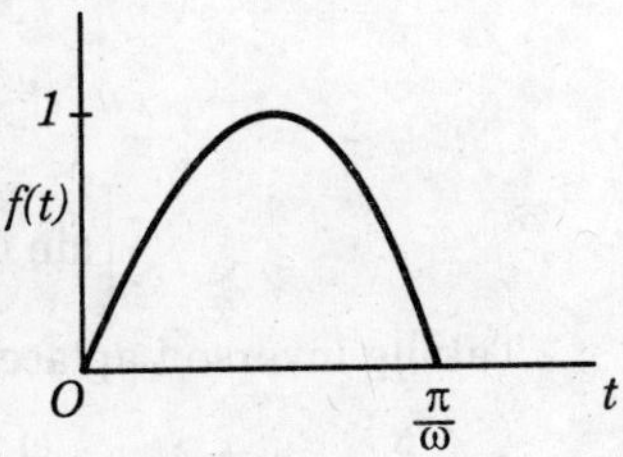


Fig. 8.8.6 (*a*) Sinusoidal pulse

$$f(t) = [\sin \omega t] \cdot u(t) + \left[\sin \omega\left(t - \frac{\pi}{\omega}\right)\right] \cdot u\left(t - \frac{\pi}{\omega}\right)$$

Taking Laplace transform on both sides

$$F(s) = \frac{\omega}{s^2 + \omega^2} + \frac{\omega}{s^2 + \omega^2} \cdot e^{-\frac{s\pi}{\omega}}$$

or $$F(s) = \frac{\omega}{s^2 + \omega^2}(1 - e^{-\frac{s\pi}{\omega}})$$

**(*ii*) Shifted Sinusoidal Pulse**

$$f_1(t) = \left[\sin \omega\left(t - \frac{\pi}{\omega}\right)\right] \cdot u\left(t - \frac{\pi}{\omega}\right)$$

*Fig. 8.8.6(a)*

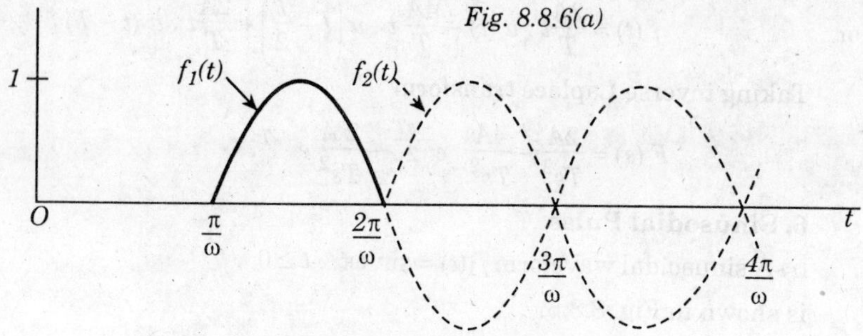

Fig. 8.8.6 (*b*) Shifted sinusoidal function

$$f_2(t) = \left[\sin \omega \left(t - \frac{2\pi}{\omega}\right)\right] . u\left(t - \frac{2\pi}{\omega}\right)$$

Shifted sinusoidal pulse of duration $t = \frac{\pi}{\omega}$ to $t = \frac{2\pi}{\omega}$ is shown in Fig. 8.8.6 (*c*). The mathematical expression is obtained by adding $f_1(t)$ and $f_2(t)$ from instant $t = \frac{2\pi}{\omega}$

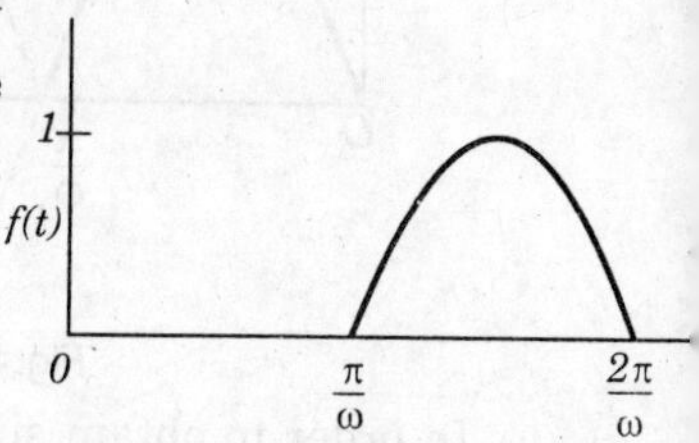

Fig. 8.8.6 (c) Shifted sinusoidal pul

$$\therefore\ f(t) = \left[\sin \omega \left(t - \frac{\pi}{\omega}\right)\right] . u\left(t - \frac{\pi}{\omega}\right) + \left[\sin \omega \left(t - \frac{2\pi}{\omega}\right)\right] . u\left(t - \frac{2\pi}{\omega}\right)$$

Taking inverse Laplace transform on both sides

$$F(s) = \frac{\omega}{s^2 + \omega^2} . e^{-\frac{s\pi}{\omega}} + \frac{\omega}{s^2 + \omega^2} . e^{-\frac{s2\pi}{\omega}}$$

## 8.9 SOLVED EXAMPLES II

**Example . 8.9.1** *Write mathematical expression for the periodic waveform shown in Fig. 8.9.1 and obtain its Laplace transform.*

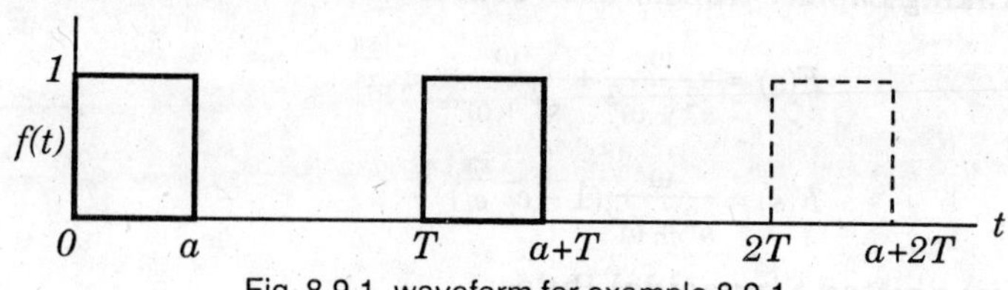

Fig. 8.9.1 waveform for example 8.9.1

**Solution :** $f(t) = u(t) - u(t-a) + u(t-T) - u(t - \overline{a+T})$
$+ u(t-2T) - u(t - \overline{a+2T}) + - - - - - -$

$$f_1(t) = u(t) - u(t-a)$$

$$\therefore \quad F_1(s) = \frac{1}{s} - \frac{1}{s} \cdot e^{-as} = \frac{1}{s}(1 - e^{-as})$$

Time period = $T$

$$F(s) = \frac{1}{1 - e^{-sT}} \times F_1(s)$$

$$\therefore \quad F(s) = \frac{1}{s} \cdot \frac{(1 - e^{-as})}{(1 - e^{-sT})} \quad \text{...Ans.}$$

**Example . 8.9.2** *Determine the Laplace transform of triangular periodic waveform given in Fig. 8.9.2*

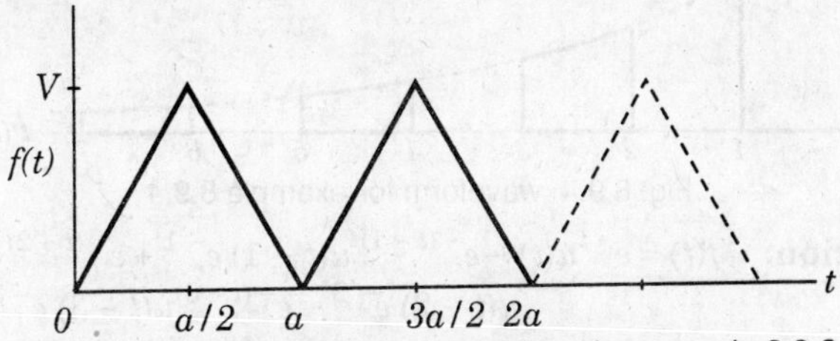


Fig. 8.9.2 Periodic triangular wave form for example 8.9.2

**Solution :** $f_1(t) = \frac{2V}{a} r(t) - \frac{4V}{a} r\left(t - \frac{a}{2}\right) + \frac{2V}{a} r(t-a)$

Taking Laplace transform on both sides

$$F_1(s) = \left(\frac{2V}{as^2} - \frac{4V}{as^2} \cdot e^{-\frac{as}{2}} + \frac{2V}{as^2} \cdot e^{-as}\right)$$

Time period = $a$

$$F(s) = \frac{1}{1 - e^{-as}} \times F_1(s)$$

$$\therefore \quad F(s) = \frac{1}{1 - e^{-as}} \left(\frac{2V}{as^2} - \frac{4V}{as^2} \cdot e^{\frac{-as}{2}} + \frac{2V}{as^2} \cdot e^{-as}\right) \text{...Ans.}$$

**Example . 8.9.3** *Write mathematical equation for the pulse waveform shown in Fig. 8.9.3 and determine Laplace transform.*

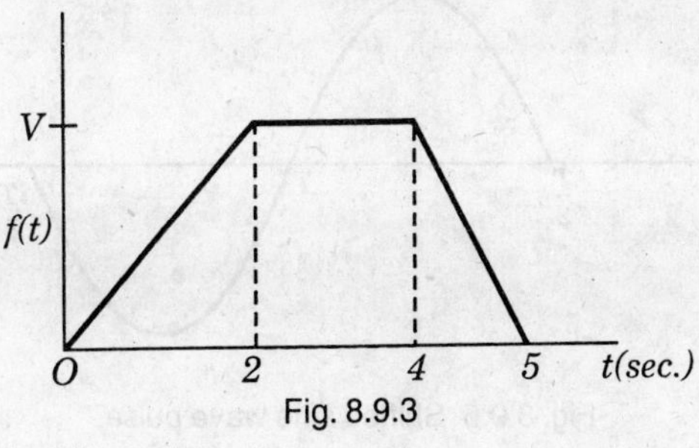


Fig. 8.9.3

**Solution :** $f(t) = \frac{V}{2} r(t) - \frac{V}{2} r(t-2) - V\, r(t-4) + V\, r(t-5)$ ...**Ans.**

Taking Laplace transform on both sides

$$F(s) = \frac{V}{2\,s^2} - \frac{V}{2\,s^2} \cdot e^{-2s} - \frac{V}{s^2} \cdot e^{-4s} + \frac{V}{s^2} \cdot e^{-5s} \quad \text{...Ans.}$$

**Example . 8.9.4** *Determine Laplace transform for decaying exponential waveform shown in Fig. 8.9.4.*

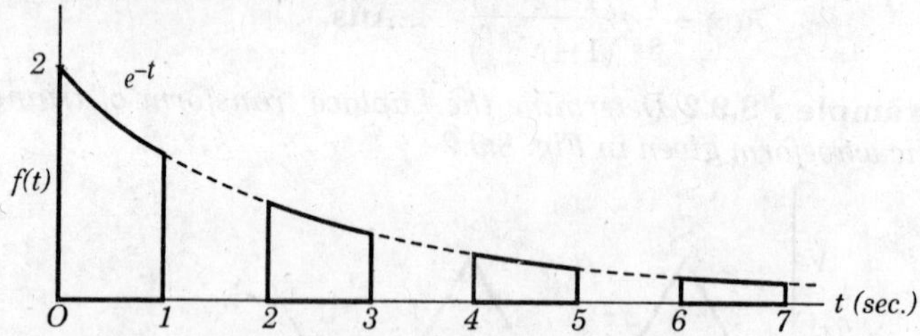


Fig. 8.9.4 waveform for example 8.9.4

**Solution:** $f(t) = e^{-t}u(t) - e^{-(t-1)}\, u(t-1)\, e^{-1} + e^{-(t-2)}$
$u(t-2)\, e^{-2} - e^{-(t-3)} u(t-3)\, e^{-3}$

Taking Laplace transform on both sides

$$F(s) = \frac{1}{s+1} - \frac{1}{s+1} e^{-s} \cdot e^{-1} + \frac{1}{s+1} e^{-2s} e^{-2}$$

$$- \frac{1}{s+1} e^{-3s} \cdot e^{-3} + - - -$$

$$= \frac{1}{(s+1)} \left[ 1 - e^{-(s+1)} + e^{-2(s+1)} - e^{-3(s+1)} + \;--\right]$$

$\because$ $$1 - e^{-(s+1)} + e^{-2(s+1)} - e^{-3(s+1)} + - - - = \frac{1}{1 - e^{-(s+1)}}$$

$\therefore$ $$F(s) = \frac{1}{s+1} \cdot \frac{1}{[1 - e^{-(s+1)}]} \quad \text{... Ans.}$$

**Example . 8.9.5** *Determine Laplace transform of the sine wave pulse shown in Fig. 8.9.5.*

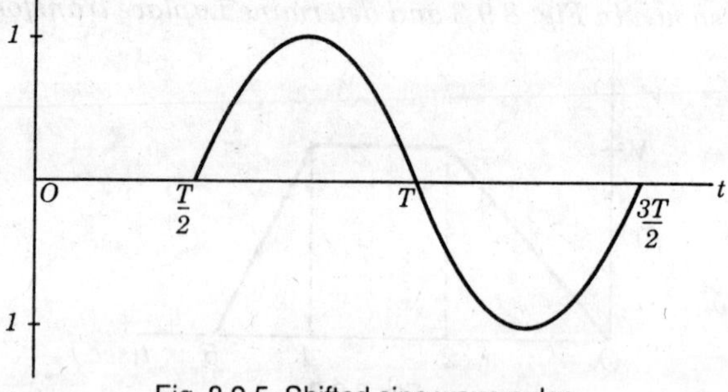


Fig. 8.9.5 Shifted sine wave pulse.

Let the frequency of the wave form ( Fig. 8.9.5 ) be ω. The one cycle sine wave shown is shifted by $t = \frac{T}{2}$. The function $\sin \omega \left(t - \frac{3T}{2}\right)$ is subtracted at $t = 3\,T/2$.

$$\therefore \quad f(t) = \left[\sin \omega \left(t - \frac{T}{2}\right)\right] . u\left(t - \frac{T}{2}\right) - \left[\sin \omega \left(t - \frac{3T}{2}\right)\right] . u\left(t - \frac{3T}{2}\right)$$

Taking inverse Laplace transform on both sides

$$F(s) = \frac{\omega}{s^2 + \omega^2} . e^{-\frac{sT}{2}} - \frac{\omega}{s^2 + \omega^2} . e^{-s\frac{3T}{2}} \qquad \text{...Ans.}$$

where $\omega = \frac{2\pi}{T}$

**Example . 8.9.6** *Determine the Laplace transform of the half - wave sinusoidal rectified periodic wave (Fig. 8.9.6).*

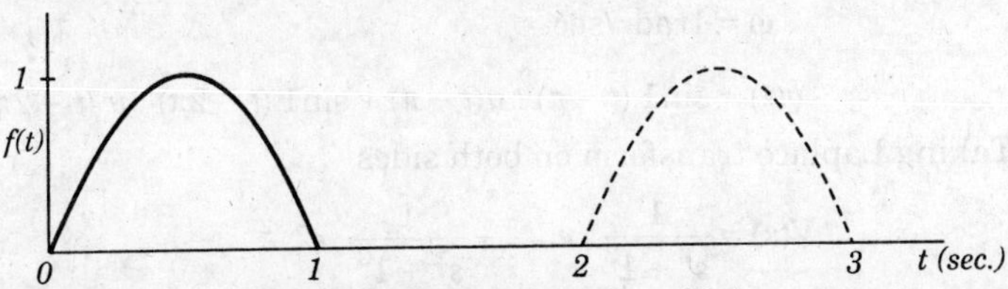


Fig. 8.9.6 Sine wave, half rectified.

**Solution :** The half rectified sine wave (Fig. 8.9.6) is written by a mathematical expression as below

$$f(t) = [\sin \pi t] . u(t) + [\sin \pi(t-1)] . u(t-1) + [\sin \pi(t-2)] . u(t-2) + [\sin \pi (t-3)] . u(t-3) + ....$$

$$\therefore \quad f_1(t) = [\sin \pi t] . u(t) + [\sin \pi (t-1)] . u(t-1)$$

Taking Laplace transform on both sides

$$F_1(s) = \frac{\pi}{s^2 + \pi^2} + \frac{\pi}{s^2 + \pi^2} . e^{-s.1}$$

The time period (repeating time) = 2 sec.

$$\therefore \quad F(s) = \frac{1}{1 - e^{-2s}} \times F_1(s)$$

or

$$F(s) = \frac{1}{1 - e^{-2s}} \left(\frac{\pi}{s^2 + \pi^2} + \frac{\pi}{s^2 + \pi^2} . e^{-s}\right)$$

or

$$F(s) = \frac{\pi}{s^2 + \pi^2} \left(\frac{1 + e^{-s}}{1 - e^{-2s}}\right)$$

$$= \frac{\pi}{s^2+\pi^2}\left[\frac{1+e^{-s}}{(1-e^{-s})\,(1+e^{-s})}\right]$$

$$\therefore \qquad F(s) = \frac{\pi}{s^2+\pi^2}\left(\frac{1}{1-e^{-s}}\right) \qquad \text{...Ans.}$$

**Example . 8.9.7** *A sinusoidal pulse v(t) shown in Fig. 8.9.7 (a) is connected to a series circuit Fig. 8.9.7 (b). Determine the current i(t).*

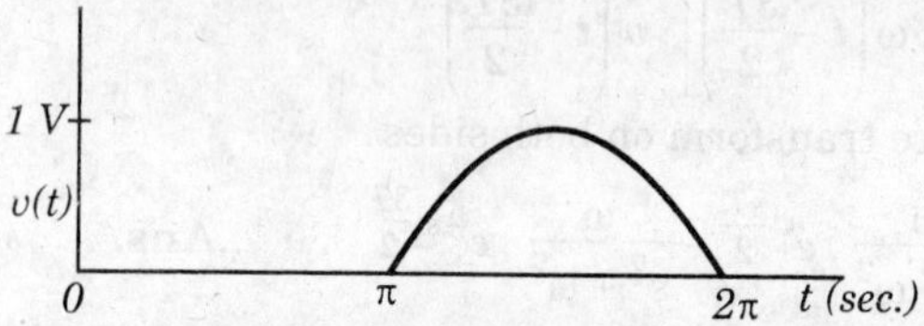


Fig. 8.9.7 (*a*) Sinusoidal pulse.

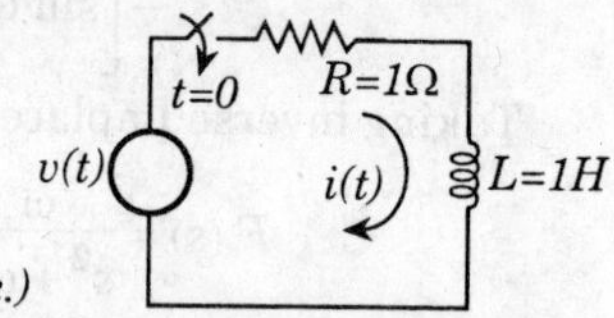


Fig. 8.9.7 (*b*) series circuit

**Solution :** $T = 2\pi$ [Fig.8.9.7.(a)]

$$\therefore \qquad \omega \times 2\pi = 2\pi$$

$$\therefore \qquad \omega = 1 \text{rad. /sec.}$$

$$\therefore \qquad v(t) = \sin 1\,(t-\pi)\,.\,u(t-\pi) + \sin 1\,(t-2\pi)\,.\,u\,(t-2\pi)$$

Taking Laplace transform on both sides

$$V(s) = \frac{1}{s^2+1^2}\,.\,e^{-s\pi} + \frac{1}{s^2+1^2}\,.\,e^{-s2\pi}$$

$$= \frac{1}{s^2+1}(e^{-s\pi} + e^{-s2\pi}).$$

Applying *KVL*

$$v\,(t) = Ri(t) + L\frac{di\,(t)}{dt}$$

Taking Laplace transform on both sides

$$V(s) = RI(s) + sL\,[\,I\,(s) - i\,(0)\,]$$

$$\because \qquad i\,(0) = 0$$

$$\therefore \qquad V(s) = (R + sL)\,I(s)$$

or

$$I(s) = \frac{V(s)}{R + s\,L} = \frac{1}{(s^2+1)\,(s+1)}\,(e^{-s\pi} + e^{-s2\pi})$$

$$\frac{1}{(s^2+1)\,(s+1)} = \frac{1}{(s+j\,1)\,(s-j\,1)\,(s+1)}$$

Let

$$\frac{1}{(s+j\,1)\,(s-j\,1)\,(s+1)} = \frac{k_1}{s+j\,1} + \frac{k_1^*}{s-j\,1} + \frac{k_2}{s+1}$$

or $$1 = k_1 (s - j1)(s+1) + k_1^* (s+j1)(s+1) + k_2 (s+j1)(s-j1)$$

put $s = -1$

$\therefore \quad k_2 = \frac{1}{2}$

put $s = -j\,1$

$\therefore \quad k_1 = -\frac{1}{2\,(1+j\,1)}$

$k_1^* = -\frac{1}{2\,(1-j\,1)}$

$$\therefore I(s) = \left[-\frac{1}{2(1+j\,1)}\cdot\frac{1}{(s+j\,1)} - \frac{1}{2(1-j\,1)}\cdot\frac{1}{(s-j\,1)} + \frac{1}{2}\cdot\frac{1}{(s+1)}\right](e^{-s\pi}+e^{-s2\pi})$$

$$= \left\{-\frac{1}{2\,[(s-1)+j\,(s+1)]} - \frac{1}{2\,[(s-1)-j\,(s+1)]} + \frac{1}{2\,(s+1)}\right\}(e^{-s\pi}+e^{-s2\pi})$$

$$= \left\{-\frac{(s-1)-j\,(s+1)+(s-1)-j\,(s+1)}{2[\,(s-1)+j\,(s+1)]\,[\,(s-1)-j\,(s+1)\,]} + \frac{1}{2(s+1)}\right\}(e^{-s\pi}+e^{-s2\pi})$$

$$= \left[-\frac{(s-1)}{2\,(s^2+1)} + \frac{1}{2\,(s+1)}\right]\left(e^{-\pi s}+e^{-s2\pi}\right)$$

$$= \left[-\frac{s}{2\,(s^2+1)} + \frac{1}{2\,(s^2+1)} + \frac{1}{2\,(s+1)}\right]\left(e^{-\pi s}+e^{-s2\pi}\right)$$

$$= \left[-\frac{s}{2\,(s^2+1)}\,.\,e^{-\pi s} + \frac{1}{2\,(s^2+1)}\,.\,e^{-\pi s} + \frac{1}{2\,(s+1)}\,.\,e^{-\pi s}\right.$$

$$\left. - \frac{s}{2\,(s^2+1)}\,.\,e^{-s2\pi} + \frac{1}{2(s^2+1)}\,.\,e^{-s2\pi} + \frac{1}{2\,(s+1)}\,.\,e^{-s\,2\pi}\right]$$

Taking inverse Laplace transform on both sides

$$i\,(t) = -\frac{1}{2}\cos\,(t-\pi) + \frac{1}{2}\sin\,(t-\pi) + \frac{1}{2}e^{-(t-\pi)} - \frac{1}{2}\cos\,(t-2\pi)$$

$$+\frac{1}{2}\sin\,(t-2\pi) + \frac{1}{2}e^{-(t-2\pi)} \quad \textbf{...Ans.}$$

## PROBLEMS

**8.1** In Fig. 8P-1 the switch is closed at $t = 0$. Determine expression for $i$.

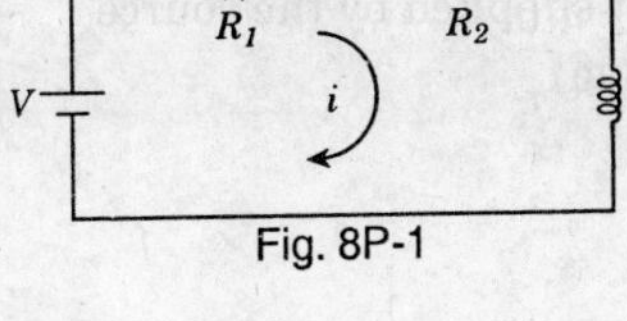


Fig. 8P-1

**Ans.** $i = \frac{V}{R_2}\left(1 - \frac{R_1}{R_1 + R_2} e^{-\frac{R_2 t}{L}}\right)$

**8.2** Determine $v_a(t)$ in the network (Fig. 8 *P* - 2) on closing the switch at $t = 0$

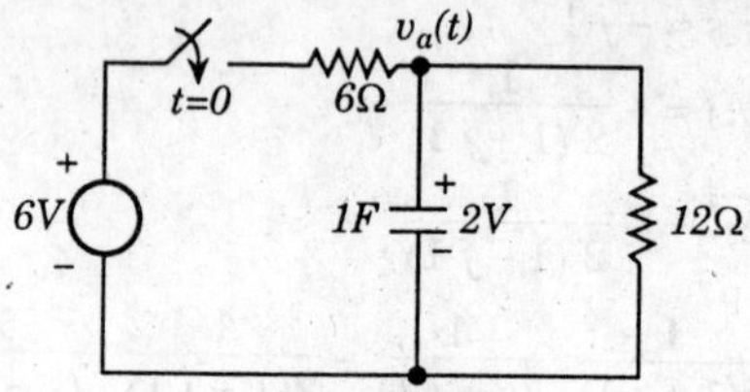


Fig. 8 *P* - 2

**Ans.** $v_a(t) = 4 - 2e^{-\frac{t}{4}}$

**8.3** The circuit in Fig. 8 *P* - 3 is relaxed with the switch at position (*a*). At $t = 0$ , the switch is moved to position (*b*). Determine current flowing through the inductor *L*.

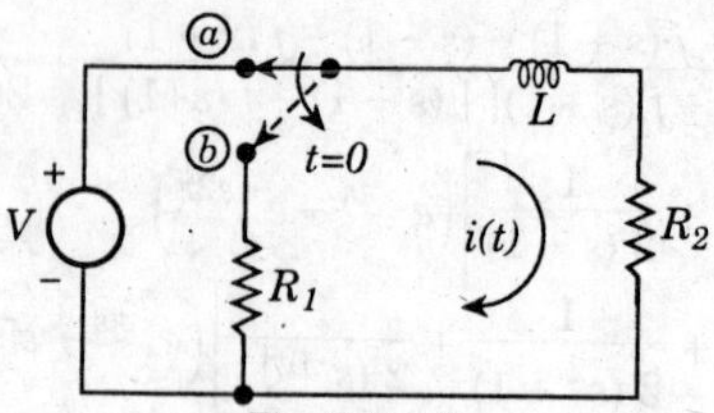


Fig. 8 P - 3

**Ans.** $i(t) = \frac{V}{R_2} e^{-\frac{(R_1 + R_2)t}{L}}$

**8.4** The switch remains at position 1 for a long time, then at $t = 0$ moved to position 2. (Fig. 8P- 4) Determine expression for $i(t)$.

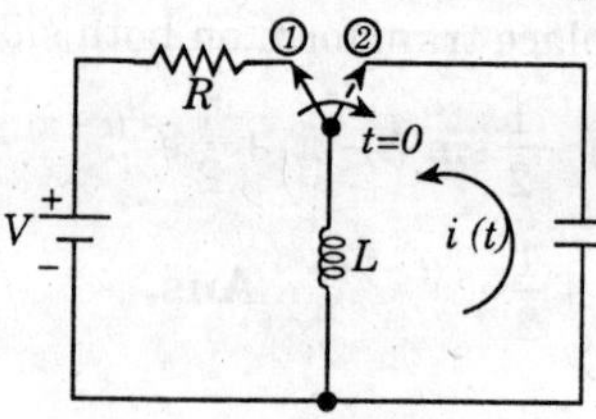


Fig. 8 P - 4

**Ans.** $i(t) = \frac{V}{R} \cos \frac{t}{\sqrt{LC}}$.

**8.5** A network is shown in Fig. 8P - 5 , the switch is closed at $t = 0$. Determine the current supplied by the source

**Ans.** $i = (1 - 0.5e^{-10t})$.

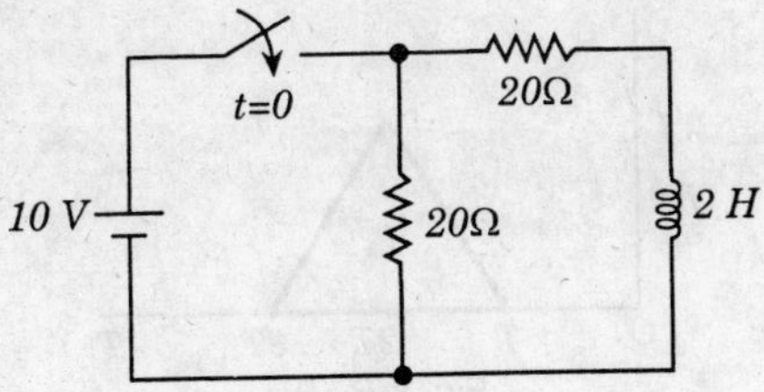


Fig. 8 *P* - 5

**8.6** Obtain expression for the current $i_2$ $(t)$ in the network given in Fig. 8P-6. Determine, time to reach $i_2(t)$ to reach 90% of its final value.

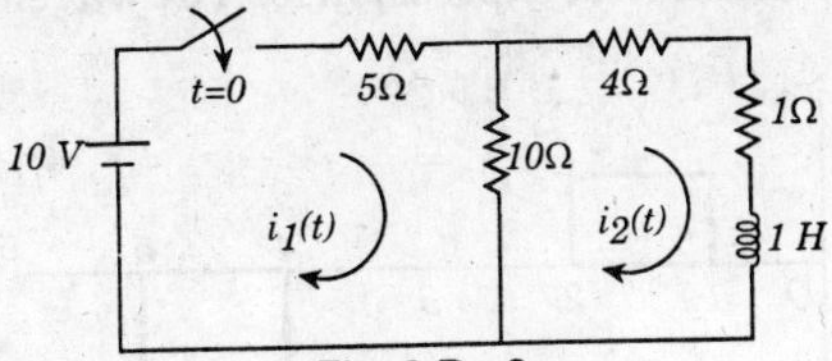


Fig. 8 P - 6

**Ans.** $i_2\,(t) = (0.8 - 0.8\,e^{-\frac{25t}{3}})$, 0.276 sec..

**8.7** Determine Laplace transform of the pulse waveform (Fig. 8P- 7)

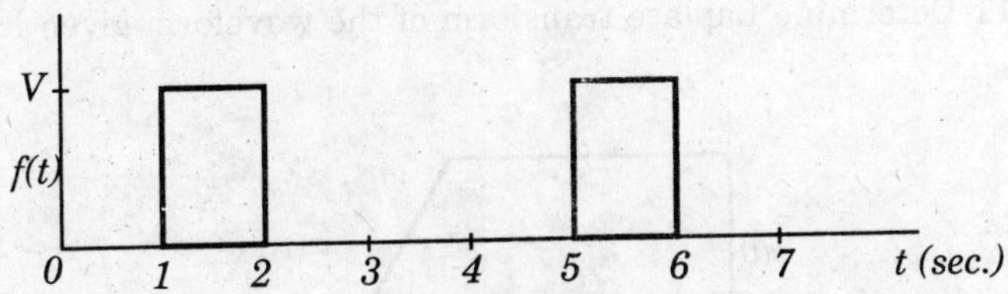


Fig. 8 P - 7

**Ans.** $F(s) = \dfrac{V}{s}\,(e^{-s} - e^{-2s} + e^{-5s} - e^{-6s})$.

**8.8** Determine Laplace transform of the full wave sinusoidal voltage $v\ (t) = V \sin \pi\, t$.

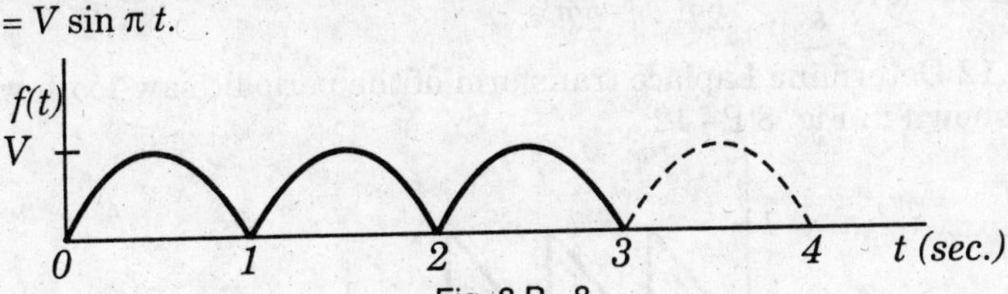


Fig. 8 P - 8

**Ans.** $V(s) = \dfrac{V\pi}{s^2 + \pi^2}\left(\dfrac{1 + e^{-s}}{1 - e^{-s}}\right)$

**8.9** Write mathematical expression and determine Laplace transform of shifted triangular pulse ( Fig. 8P-9 )

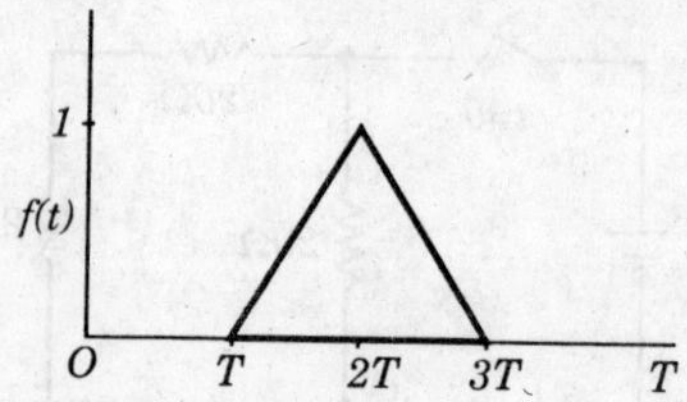


Fig. 8 P - 9

**Ans.** $f(t) = \frac{1}{T} r(t - T) - \frac{2}{T} r(t - 2T) + \frac{1}{T} r(t - 3T)$.

**8.10** Write mathematical expression for The waveform of Fig. 8P-10

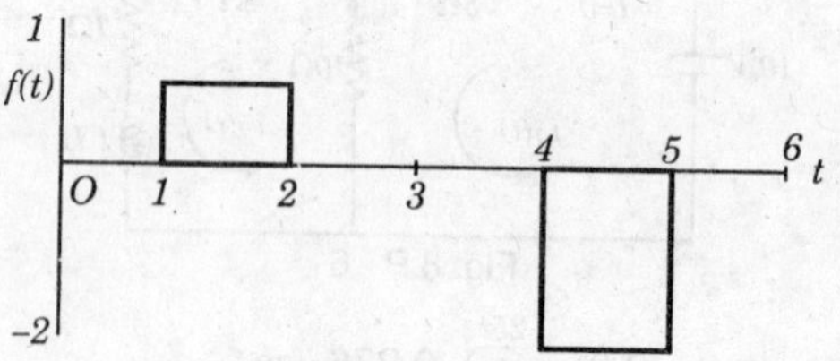


Fig. 8 P - 10

**Ans.** $f(t) = u(t - 1) - u(t - 2) - 2u(t - 4) + 2u(t - 5)$.

**8.11** Determine Laplace transform of the waveform given in Fig. 8P-11

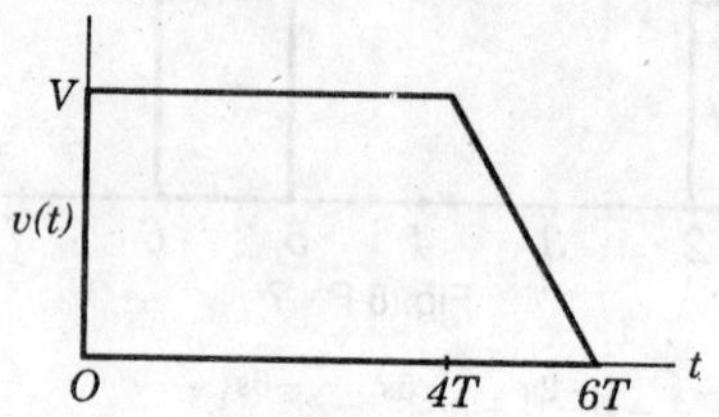


Fig. 8 P - 11

**Ans.** $V(s) = \frac{V}{s} - \frac{Ve^{-4sT}}{2T} + \frac{V}{2T} e^{-6sT}$.

**8.12** Determine Laplace transform of the periodic saw-tooth wave form shown in Fig. 8 P - 12.

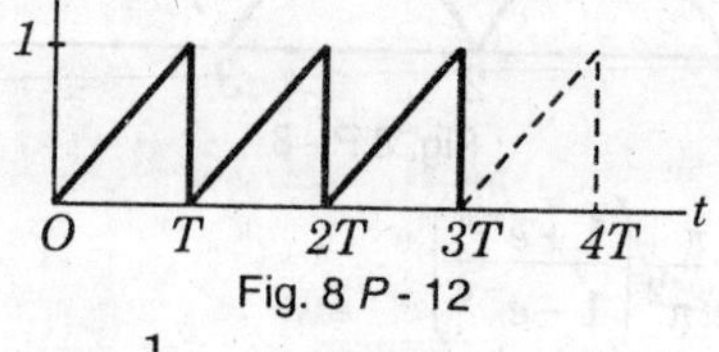


Fig. 8 P - 12

**Ans.** $f_1(t) = \frac{1}{T} r(t) - \frac{1}{T} r(t - T) \cdot u(t - T)$

**8.13** Write expression $f(t)$ for the waveform ( Fig. 8 P - 13 ).

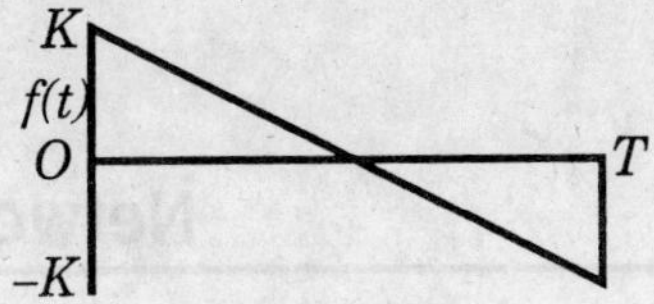


Fig. 8 *P* - 13

**Ans.** $f(t) = \left[ Ku(t) - \dfrac{2K}{T} r(t) \right] + \left[ \dfrac{2K}{T} r(t-T) + Ku(t-T) \right]$

**8.14** A pulse wave form shown in Fig. 8 P - 14 is applied at $t = 0$ to a series circuit consisting $R = 2\ \Omega$ and $L = 1\ H$. Determine current $i(t)$ flowing in the circuit.

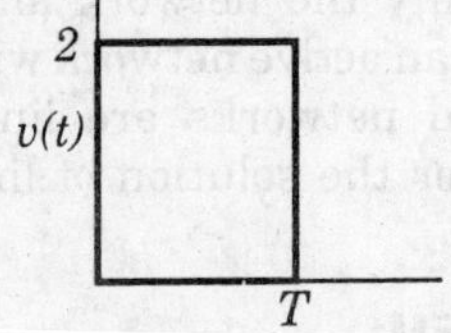


Fig. 8 *P* - 14

**Ans.** $i(t) = (1 - e^{-2t})\, u(t) - (1 - e^{-2(t-T)})\,.\, u(t-T)$

**8.15** Find convolution to determine $f(t)$ given that

$f_1(t) = e^{-at}$ and $f_2(t) = t,\ t \geq 0$

**Ans.** $f(t) = \dfrac{1}{a^2}(at + e^{-at} - 1).$

# 9

# Network Theorems

## 9.1 INTRODUCTION

The network equations based on mesh/node analysis are formulated to solve a given network. The network theorems described below make it possible to simplify the network analysis in relation to a terminal pair connected to an active network with passive elements. In general, passive electrical networks are linear systems. Network theorems are applicable for the solution of linear, bilateral, passive electrical networks.

## 9.2 THEVENIN'S THEOREM

Thevenin's theorem states that any linear active network with output terminals *a*-*b* as shown in Fig. 9.2.1 can be replaced by a singal equivalent voltage source in series with an equivalent resistance as shown in Fig. 9.2.2

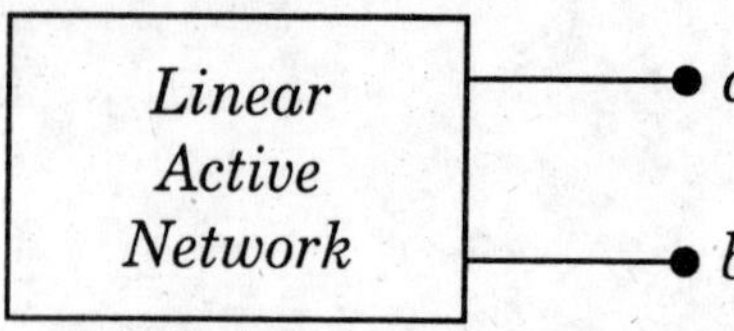

Fig. 9.2.1 Linear active network

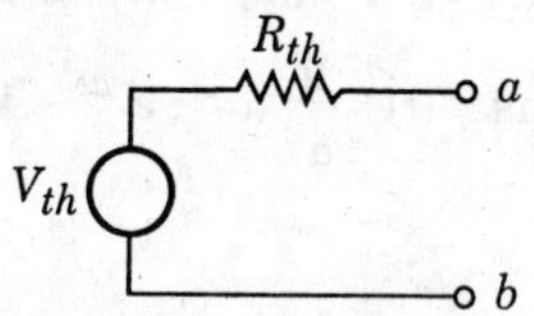

Fig. 9.2.2 Thevenin's equivalent

The Thevenin's equivalent voltage source $V_{th}$ is the open circuit voltage between terminals *a*-*b* of the network.

The series equivalent resistance $R_{th}$ ($\mathbf{Z}_{th}$ for a.c network) is the resistance (impedance) of the network at terminals *a*-*b* Fig. 9.2.1 when all the internal sources (except dependent sources) set to zero, *i.e* independent voltage source replaced by a short circuit and current source open circuited.

### Application of Thevenin's Theorem

Fig. 9.2.3 shows a network wherein the current in branch *a* - *b* ($R_l = 2\ \Omega$) is to be determined. The Thevenin's theorem is applied through following steps.

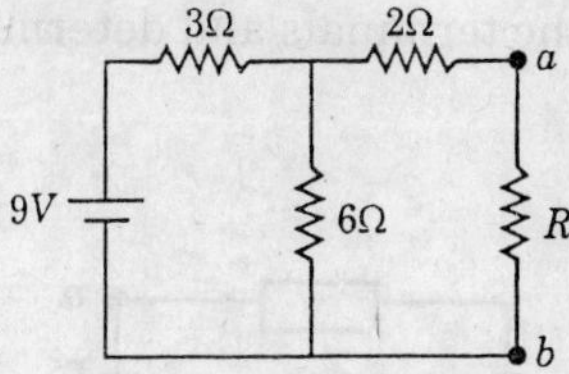


Fig. 9.2.3 Thevenin's theorem application.

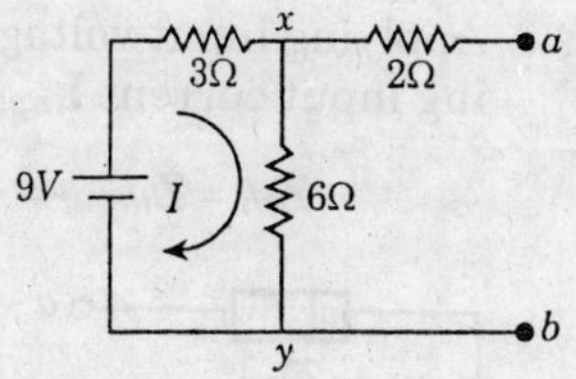


Fig.9.2.4 Terminals a - b o/c

1. Remove the load resistance $R_l$ from the network to open-circuit terminals $a$-$b$ (Fig. 9.2.4).

2. As in Fig. 9.2.4

$$V_{th} = V_{ab} = V_{xy} = I \times 6 = \frac{9}{3+6} \times 6 = 6V$$

3. To determine Thevenin's equivalent resistance $R_{th}$ set $9V$ source to zero (Fig.9.2.5)

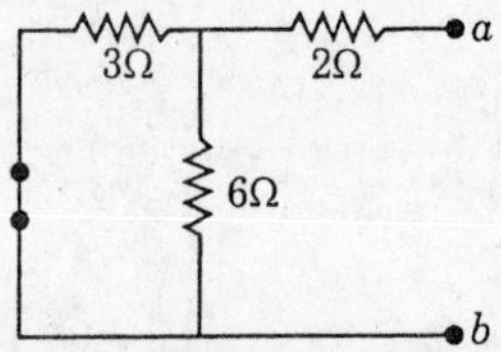


Fig. 9.2.5 Voltage source set to zero.

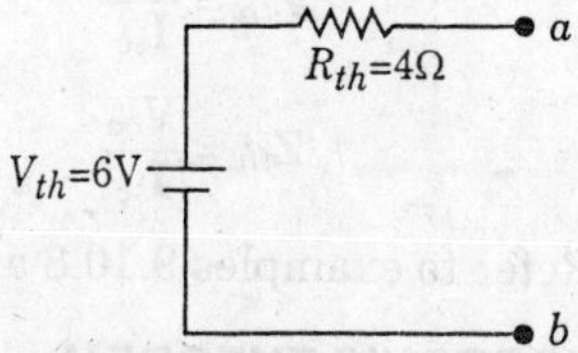


Fig. 9.2.6 Thevenin's equivalence

$$R_{th} = R_{ab} = 2 + \frac{3 \times 6}{3+6} = 4\ \Omega$$

4. The Thevenin's equivalent circuit is shown in Fig. 9.2.6.

5. Insert the load resistance $R_l = 2\ \Omega$ between terminals $a$-$b$ (Fig. 9.2.7).

$$I_{ab} = \frac{V_{th}}{R_{th} + R_L} = \frac{6}{4+2} = 1\ \text{A}$$

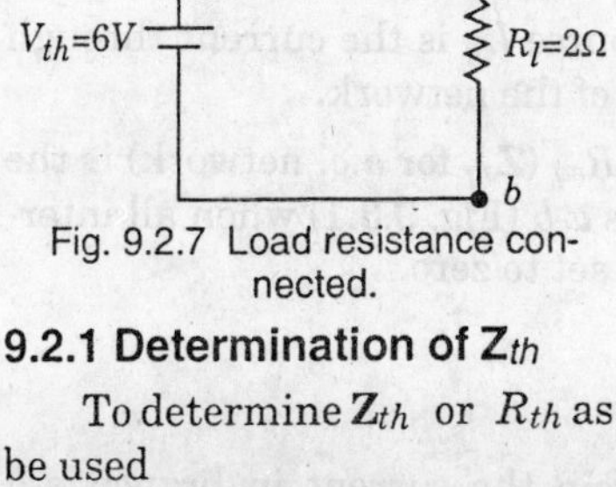


Fig. 9.2.7 Load resistance connected.

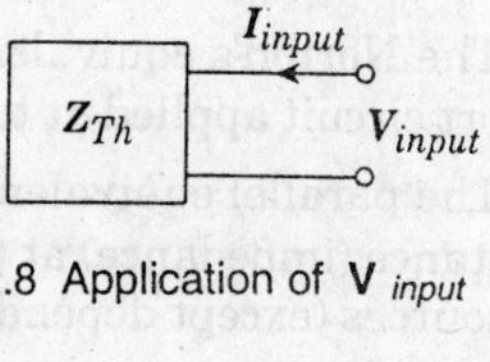


Fig. 9.2.8 Application of **V** $_{input}$

### 9.2.1 Determination of $Z_{th}$

To determine $Z_{th}$ or $R_{th}$ as the case may be, following methods can be used

1. Series- parallel combination of passive elements of the network.

2. Applying input voltage $\mathbf{V}_{input}$ at the terminals and determining input current $\mathbf{I}_{input}$.

$$\mathbf{Z}_{th} = \mathbf{Z}_{input} = \frac{\mathbf{V}_{input}}{\mathbf{I}_{input}}$$

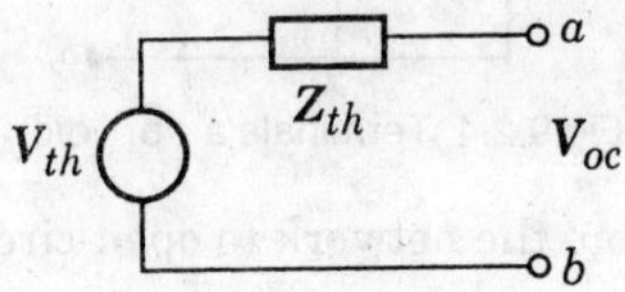

Fig. 9.2.9 *a-b* o/c.

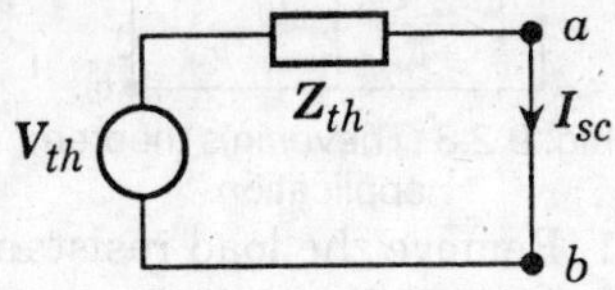

Fig. 9.2.10 *a-b* s/c.

Refer to examples 9.10.5, 9.10.6 & 9.10.7.

3. As per Thevenin's equivalent circuit

(*i*) on open-circuit $\mathbf{V}_{th} = \mathbf{V}_{ab} = \mathbf{V}_{oc}$ (Fig. 9.2.9)

(*ii*) on short-circuit (Fig. 9.2.10)

$$\mathbf{Z}_{th} = \frac{\mathbf{V}_{th}}{\mathbf{I}_{sc}}$$

or

$$\mathbf{Z}_{th} = \frac{\mathbf{V}_{oc}}{\mathbf{I}_{sc}}$$

Refer to examples 9.10.8 and 9.10.13.

## 9.3 NORTON'S THEOREM

Norton's theorem states that any active network with output terminals *a-b* as shown in Fig. 9.3.1 can be replaced by a single equivalent

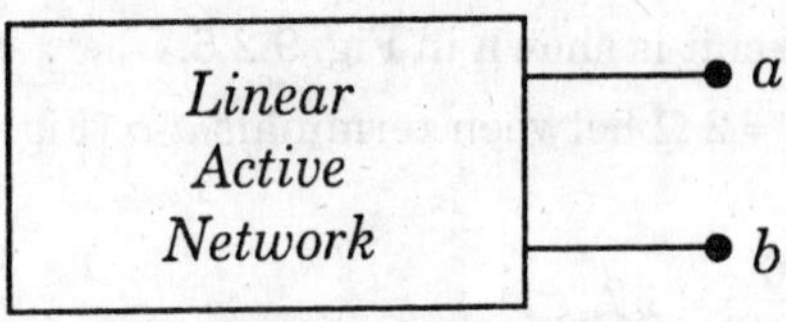

Fig. 9.3.1 Linear active network

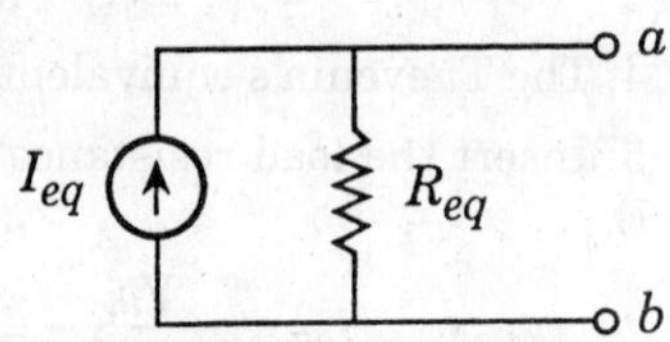

Fig. 9.3.2 Norton's equivalence.

current source in parallel with an equivalent resistance as shown in Fig. 9.3.2

The Norton's equivalent current source $I_{eq}$ is the current through a short circuit applied at terminals *a-b* of the network.

The parallel equivalent resistance $R_{eq}$ ($\mathbf{Z}_{eq}$ for *a.c.* network) is the resistance (impedance) at the terminals *a-b* (Fig. 9.3.1) when all internal sources (except dependent sources) set to zero.

It is noted that $R_{th} = R_{eq}$.

### Application of Norton's Theorem

Fig. 9.3.3 Shows a network wherein the current in branch *a-b* $R_l = 2\Omega$ is to be determined. The Norton's theorem is applied through following steps.

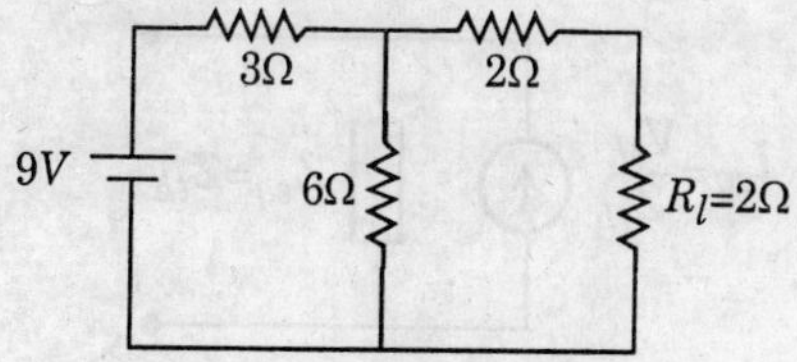


Fig. 9.3.3 Norton's theorem application.

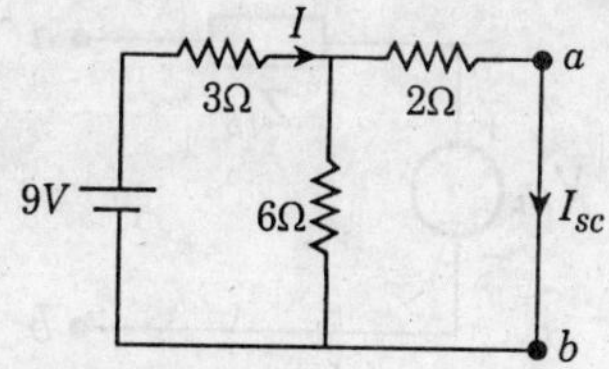


Fig. 9.3.4 Terminals *a-b* s/c

1. Remove the resistance $R_l$ from the network and apply short circuit at terminals *a-b* (Fig. 9.3.4).

$$I = \frac{9}{3 + \dfrac{2 \times 6}{2 + 6}} = 2 \text{ A}$$

$$I_{eq} = I_{sc} = I \times \frac{6}{6 + 2} = 2 \times \frac{6}{8} = \frac{3}{2} \text{ A}$$

2. With terminals *a-b* open, set source to zero (Fig. 9.3.5).

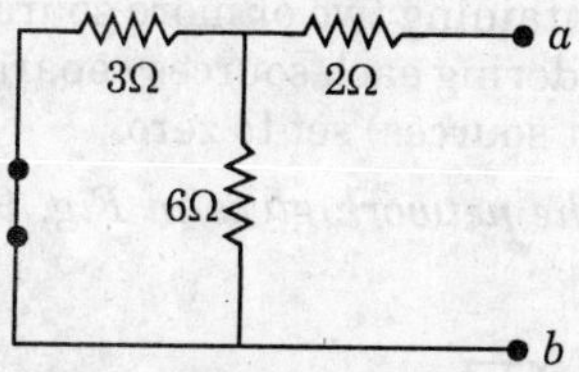


Fig. 9.3.5 Voltage source set to zero

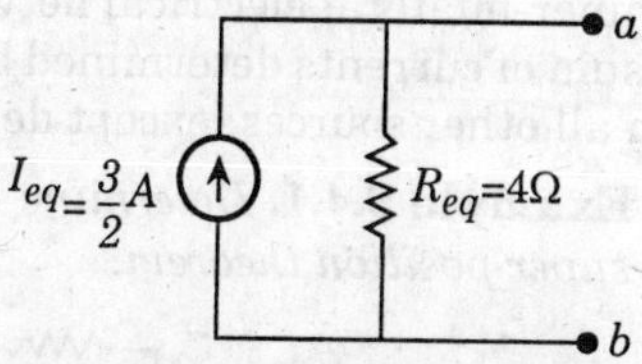


Fig. 9.3.6 Norton's equivalence.

$$R_{eq} = R_{ab} = 2 + \frac{3 \times 6}{3 + 6} = 4 \ \Omega$$

3. The Norton's equivalent network is shown in Fig. 9.3.6.

4. Insert $R_l = 2 \ \Omega$ across terminals a *a-b* (Fig. 9.3.7).

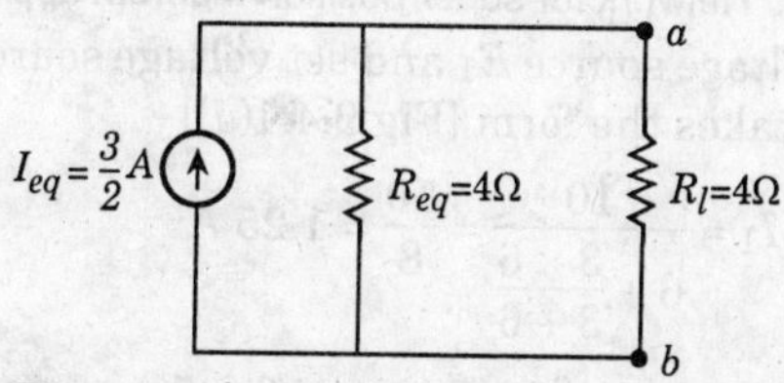


Fig. 9.3.7 Load resistance $R_l$ connected

$$I_{ab} = I_{eq} \times \frac{R_l}{R_{eq} + R_l} = \frac{3}{2} \times \frac{4}{4 + 2} = 1 \text{ A}$$

As per source transformation technique,

1. Thevenin's network can be transformed into equivalent Norton's network.

2. Norton's network can be transformed into equivalent Thevenin's network.

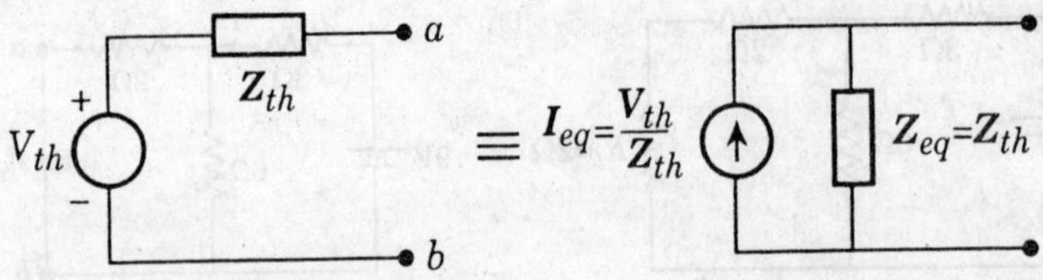

Fig. 9.3.8 Thevenin's network transformed into equivalent Norton's network

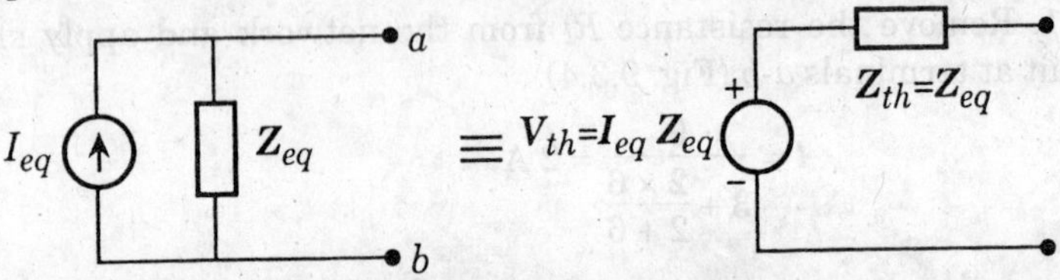

Fig. 9.3.9 Norton's network transformed into equivalent Thevenin's Network.

## 9.4 SUPER POSITION THEOREM

The super position theorem states that the current in any branch of a liner-bilateral electrical network containing two or more sources is the sum of currents determined by considering each sources separately with all other sources (except dependent sources) set to zero.

**Example 9.4.1.** *Determine $I_{ab}$ in the network gives in Fig. 9.4.1. Use super position theorem.*

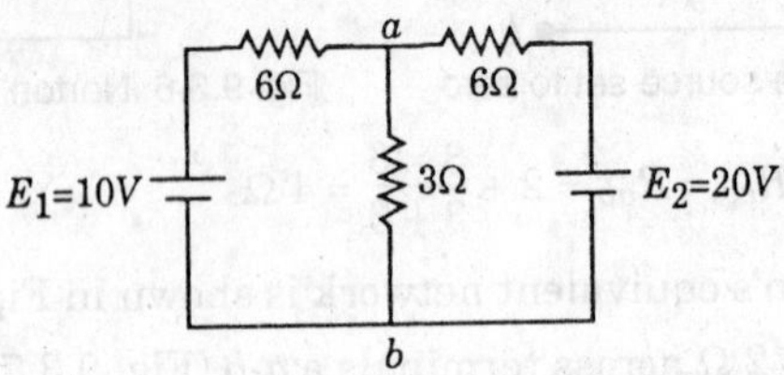

Fig. 9.4.1. Network for super position theorem application.

1. Consider voltage source $E_1$ and set voltage source $E_2 = 0$. Therefore, the network takes the form [Fig.9.4.1(*a*)]

$$I_1 = \frac{10}{6 + \dfrac{3 \times 6}{3 + 6}} = \frac{10}{8} = 1.25 \text{ A}$$

$$\therefore \qquad {}^1I_{ab} = I_1 \times \frac{6}{6+3} = 1.25 \times \frac{6}{9} = \frac{5}{6} = 0.833 \text{ A}$$

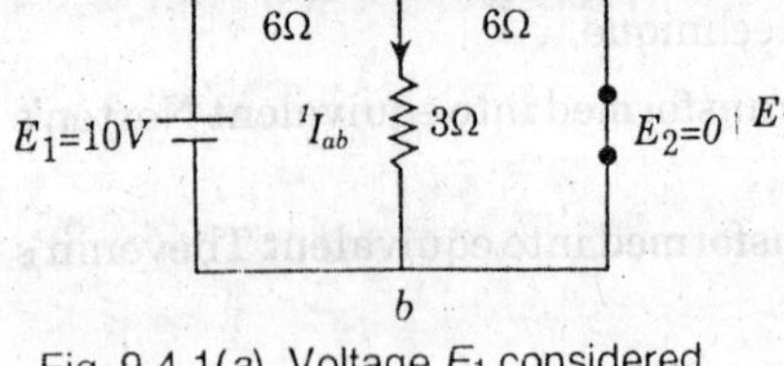

Fig. 9.4.1(*a*) Voltage $E_1$ considered

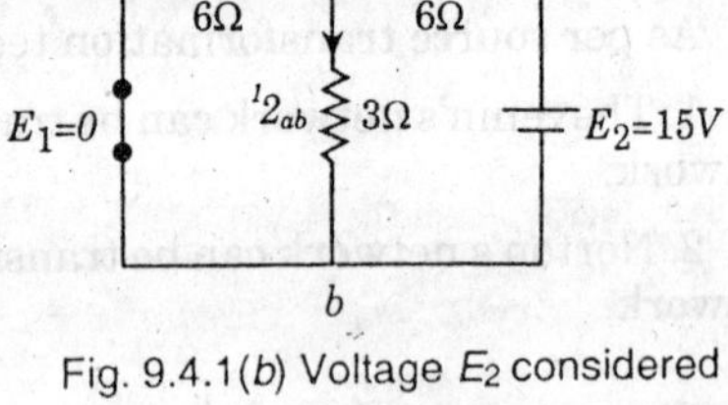

Fig. 9.4.1(*b*) Voltage $E_2$ considered

2. Consider voltage source $E_2$ and set voltage source $E_1 = 0$. therefore, The network takes the form [Fig.9.4.1(*b*)]

$$I_2 = \frac{15}{6 + \frac{3 \times 6}{3 + 6}} = \frac{15}{8} = 1.875 \text{ A}$$

$$\therefore \qquad {}^2I_{ab} = 1.875 \times \frac{6}{6+3} = 1.25 \text{ A}$$

$$I_{ab} = {}^1I_{ab} + {}^2I_{ab}$$

$$= 0.833 + 1.25 = 2.083 \text{ A} \qquad \text{...Ans.}$$

## 9.5 MAXIMUM POWER TRANSFER THEOREM

### 9.5.1 Maximum Power Transfer in a *d.c* Circuit.

A d.c voltage source and its series internal resistance determined for a two port network to the left of terminal pair *a-b* is shown in Fig. 9.5.1. The load resistance $R_l$ can be varied. It is required to determine the value of $R_l$ such that the maximum power transferd from the source to load.

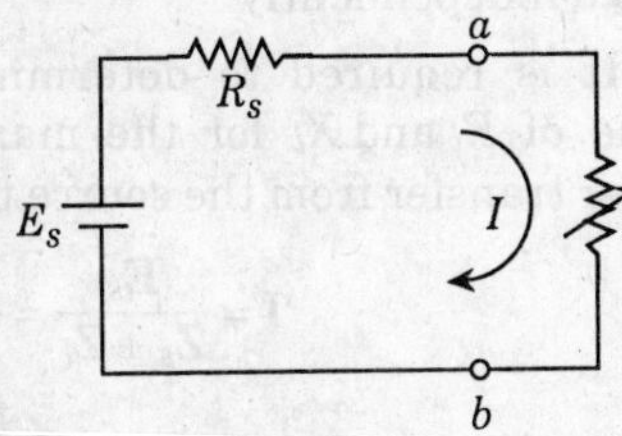

Fig. 9.5.1 Variable load resistance $R_l$

$$I = \frac{E_s}{R_s + R_l}$$

The power consumed in $R_l$ is

$$P = I^2 R_l = \frac{E_s^2}{(R_s + R_l)^2} \,.\, R_l$$

For maximum power,

$$\frac{dP}{dR_l} = 0$$

$$\therefore \qquad \frac{d}{dR_L}\left[\frac{E_s^2\, R_l}{(R_s + R_l)^2}\right] = 0$$

$$\text{or} \qquad E_s 2\left[\frac{(R_s + R_l)^2 \,.\, 1 - R_l\,(2)\,(R_s + R_l) \,.\, 1}{(R_s + R_l)^4}\right] = 0$$

$$\therefore \qquad (R_s + R_l)^2 - 2\,R_l\,(R_s + R_l) = 0$$

$$\text{or} \qquad R_s^2 = R_l^2$$

Therefore, the condition for maximum power flow in $R_l$ is

$$R_s = R_l$$

$$\therefore \qquad P_{\max} = \frac{E_s^2}{(R_l + R_l)^2} \cdot R_l = \frac{E_s^2}{4R_l}$$

The efficiency during maximum power transfer to load is 50%.

### 9.5.2 Maximum Power Transfer in a.c. Circuit

An a.c. voltage source and its equivalent internal impedance determined for a two port network to the left of terminal pair $a$-$b$ is shown in Fig. 9.5.2. The load impedance $\mathbf{Z}_l$ is such that the components $R_l$ and $X_l$ can be varied independently.

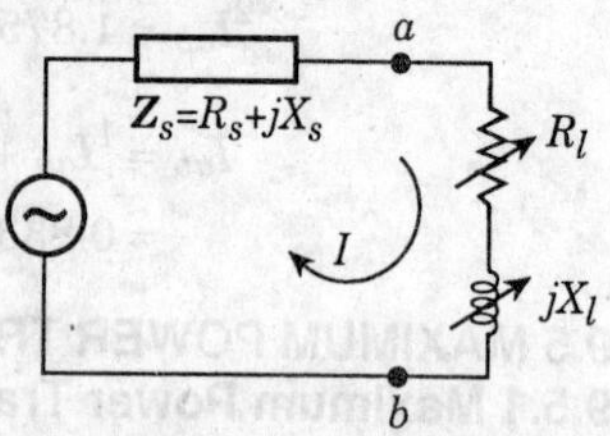


Fig. 9.5.2 Load impedance $\mathbf{Z}_l$ variable

It is required to determine the value of $R_l$ and $X_l$ for the maximum power transfer from the source to load.

$$\mathbf{I} = \frac{\mathbf{E}_s}{\mathbf{Z}_s + \mathbf{Z}_l} = \frac{\mathbf{E}_s}{R_s + j\,X_s + R_l + j\,X_l}$$

$$= \frac{\mathbf{E_s}}{(R_s + R_l) + j\,(X_s + X_l)}$$

The power delivered to the load is given by

$$P = I^2 R_l = \frac{E_s^2 R_l}{(\sqrt{(R_s + R_l)^2 + (X_s + X_l)^2}\,)^2}$$

$$= \frac{E_s^2 R_l}{(R_s + R_l)^2 + (X_s + X_l)^2}$$

The load impedance $\mathbf{Z}_l$ consists of two parts $R_L$ and $X_L$ , both are independently varied to get the maxi minm power. Let $R_l$ be fixed and $X_l$ varied to set the maximum load power. Therefore,

1. The condition for maximum power in relation to variation of $X_l$ and fixed $R_l$ is given below:

$$\frac{\partial P}{\partial X_l} = 0$$

$$\therefore \qquad \frac{\partial}{\partial X_l}\left[\frac{E_s^2 R_l}{(R_s + R_l^2) + (X_s + X_l)^2}\right] = 0$$

or

$$\frac{-\,2\,E_s^2 R_l\,(X_s + X_l)}{[(R_s + R_l^2) + (X_s + X_l)^2]^2} = 0$$

Therefore, for maximum power flow in load

$$X_s = -\,X_l\,, \quad j\,X_l = -\,j\,X_s$$

2. In relation to variation of $R_l$ and fixed $X_l$, the maximum power transfer to load under the condition given below,

$$\frac{\partial}{\partial R_l}\left[\frac{E_s^2 R_l}{(R_s + R_l^2) + (X_s + X_l)^2}\right] = 0$$

For maximum power transfer to load $X_s = -X_l$ as derived above. Therefore,

$$\frac{\partial}{\partial R_l}\left[\frac{E_s^2 R_l}{(R_s + R_l)^2}\right] = 0$$

or $$E_s^2 \left\{\frac{(R_s + R_l)^2 - R_l \times 2\,(R_s + R_l)\,.\,1}{[(R_s + R_l)^2]^2}\right\} = 0$$

$$\therefore \quad (R_s + R_l)\;(R_s - R_l) = 0$$

$$\because \quad R_s + R_l \neq 0$$

$$\therefore \quad R_s = R_l$$

Thus, for maximum power transfer to load

$$\mathbf{Z}_l = R_s - j\,X_s$$

or $$\mathbf{Z}_l = \mathbf{Z}_s^*$$

3. The load consists of $R_l$ only , and $X_l = 0$

$$P = \frac{E_s^2 R_l}{(R_s + R_l) + j\,(X_s + X_l)}$$

$$\because \quad X_l = 0$$

$$P = \frac{E_s^2 R_l}{\left[\sqrt{(R_s + R_l)^2 + X_s^2}\right]^2} = \frac{E_s^2}{(R_s + R_l)^2 + X_s^2}$$

For maximum power flow in the load

$$\therefore \quad \frac{dP}{dR_l} = 0$$

$$\therefore \quad \frac{d}{dR_l}\left[\frac{E_s^2 R_l}{(R_s + R_l)^2 + X_s^2}\right] = 0$$

or $$\left\{\frac{[(R_s + R_l)^2 + X_s^2]\,.\,1 - R_l \times 2\,(R_s + R_l)\,.\,1}{[(R_s + R_l)^2 + X_s^2]^2}\right\} = 0$$

$$\therefore \quad (R_s + R_l)^2 + X_s^2 - 2\,R_l\,(R_s + R_l) = 0$$

or $$R_s + 2\,R_s R_l + R_l^2 + X_s^2 - 2\,R_s R_l - 2\,R_l^2 = 0$$

$$\therefore \quad R_l^2 = R_s^2 + X_s^2$$

Therefore, for maximum power flow is the load,

$$R_l = \sqrt{(R_s^2 + X_s^2)} = |\mathbf{Z}_s|$$

4. The load consists such that $X_l$ is fixed and $R_l$ variable

$$P = \frac{E_s^2 R_l}{[(R_s + R_l) + j(X_s + X_l)]^2}$$

$$= \frac{E_s^2 R_l}{\left[\sqrt{(R_s + R_l)^2 + (X_s + X_l)^2}\right]^2}$$

$$= \frac{E_s^2 R_l}{(R_s + R_l)^2 + (X_s + X_l)^2}$$

For maximum power flow in the load,

$$\frac{dP}{dR_l} = 0$$

$$\therefore \quad \frac{d}{dR_L}\left\{\frac{E_s^2 R_l}{\left[\sqrt{(R_s + R_l)^2 + (X_s + X_l)^2}\right]^2}\right\} = 0$$

$$\therefore \quad E_s^2 \left\{\frac{(R_s + R_l)^2 + (X_s + X_l)^2 \,.\, 1 - R_l \times 2\,(R_s + R_l)\,.\,1}{\left[(R_s + R_l)^2 + (X_s + X_l)^2\right]^2}\right\}$$

or

$$E_s^2 \frac{[R_s^2 - R_l^2 + (X_s + X_l)^2]}{[(R_s + R_l)^2 + (X_s + X_l)^2]^2} = 0$$

$$\therefore \quad R_s^2 - R_l^2 + (X_s + X_l)^2 = 0$$

$$\therefore \quad R_l^2 = R_s^2 + (X_s + X_l)$$

or

$$R_l = |R_s + jX_s + jX_l|$$

$$R_l = |\mathbf{Z}_s + jX_l|$$

Where $\mathbf{Z}_s = R_s + jX_s$

The maximum power transfer theorem is widely applicable in electronics and communication networks.

## 9.6 MILLMAN'S THEOREM

Millman's theorem is applicable to represent parallel connected voltage sources into a single equivalent voltage source.

Millman's theorem states that in any network parallel connected voltage sources $\mathbf{V}_1, \mathbf{V}_2, ----\mathbf{V}_n$ having respective internal impledances $\mathbf{Z}_1, \mathbf{Z}_2, -----\mathbf{Z}_n$ may be replaced by a single equivalent voltage sources $\mathbf{V}'$ having an internal equivalent impedance $\mathbf{Z}'$.

"$n$" voltage sources in parallel are connected in parallel across terminals $a$-$b$ as shown in Fig. 9.6.1. Let $\mathbf{V}_{ab} = \mathbf{V}'$. Applying Kirchhoff's current law,

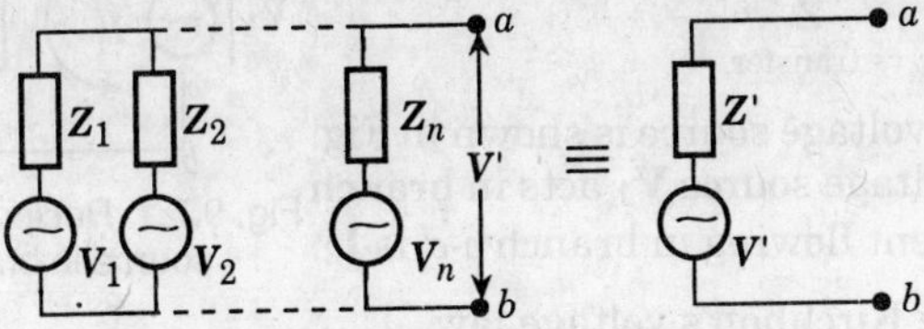

Fig. 9.6.1 Network for Millman's theorem

$$\frac{\mathbf{V}' - \mathbf{V}_1}{\mathbf{Z}_1} + \frac{\mathbf{V}' - \mathbf{V}_2}{\mathbf{Z}_2} + \text{-------} + \frac{\mathbf{V}' - \mathbf{V}_n}{\mathbf{Z}_n} = 0$$

$$\therefore \quad \mathbf{V}'\left(\frac{1}{\mathbf{Z}_1} + \frac{1}{\mathbf{Z}_2} + \text{-------} + \frac{1}{\mathbf{Z}_n}\right) = \left(\frac{\mathbf{V}_1}{\mathbf{Z}_1} + \frac{\mathbf{V}_2}{\mathbf{Z}_2} + \text{-------} + \frac{\mathbf{V}_n}{\mathbf{Z}_n}\right)$$

or

$$\mathbf{V}'(\mathbf{Y}_1 + \mathbf{Y}_2 + \text{--------} + \mathbf{Y}_n) = (\mathbf{V}_1 Y_1 + \mathbf{V}_2 \mathbf{Y}_2 + \text{--------} + \mathbf{V}_n \mathbf{Y}_n)$$

$$\therefore \quad \mathbf{V}' = \frac{\mathbf{V}_1 \mathbf{Y}_1 + \mathbf{V}_2 \mathbf{Y}_2 + \text{--------} + \mathbf{V}_n \mathbf{Y}_n}{\mathbf{Y}_1 + \mathbf{Y}_2 + \text{--------} + \mathbf{Y}_n}$$

To determine equivalent impedance set voltage sources $\mathbf{V}_1, \mathbf{V}_2$, ----- $\mathbf{V}_n$ to zero as shown in Fig. 9.6.2.

$$\frac{1}{\mathbf{Z}'} = \frac{1}{\mathbf{Z}_1} + \frac{1}{\mathbf{Z}_2} + \text{--------} + \frac{1}{\mathbf{Z}_n}$$

$$\therefore \quad \mathbf{Z}' = \frac{1}{\frac{1}{\mathbf{Z}_1} + \frac{1}{\mathbf{Z}_2} + \text{-----} + \frac{1}{\mathbf{Z}_n}}$$

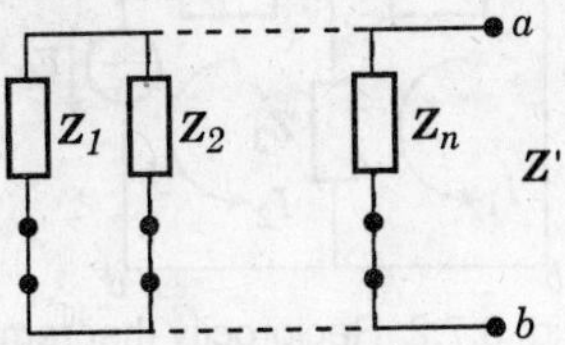

Fig. 9.6.2 Equivalent impedance $\mathbf{Z}'$.

Therefore,

$$\mathbf{Z}' = \frac{1}{\mathbf{Y}_1 + \mathbf{Y}_2 + \text{------} + \mathbf{Y}_n}$$

## 9.7 RECIPROCITY THEOREM

Reciprocity theorem states that in any bilateral, linear single source network, if a source voltage **V** in one branch produces current **I** in any other branch, then the source voltage **V** acting in second branch produces the same current **I** in the first branch.

Thus, as per reciprocity principle the ratio of excitation to response is same when the position of excitation is interchanged to response.

Thus, the transfer impedance

$$\underset{\text{transfer}}{Z} = \frac{V_s}{I_r}$$

or

$$\underset{\text{transfer}}{Z} = \frac{V_r}{I_s}$$

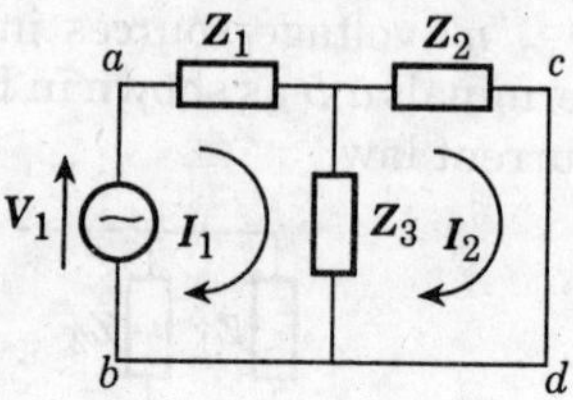


Fig. 9.7.1 Reciprocity theorem, source in branch *a-b*.

A single voltage source is shown in Fig. 9.7.1. The voltage source $V_1$ acts in branch *a-b*, the current flowing in branch *c-d* is $I_2$.

Applying Kirchhoff's voltage law.

$$(Z_1 + Z_3)\, I_1 - Z_3\, I_2 = V_1$$

$$-Z_3\, I_1 + (Z_2 + Z_3)\, I_2 = 0$$

$$\therefore \quad \begin{vmatrix} Z_1 + Z_3 & -Z_3 \\ -Z_3 & Z_2 + Z_3 \end{vmatrix} \begin{vmatrix} I_1 \\ I_2 \end{vmatrix} = \begin{vmatrix} V_1 \\ 0 \end{vmatrix}$$

$$\therefore \quad I_2 = \frac{\begin{vmatrix} Z_1 + Z_3 & V_1 \\ -Z_3 & 0 \end{vmatrix}}{\begin{vmatrix} Z_1 + Z_3 & -Z_3 \\ -Z_3 & Z_2 + Z_3 \end{vmatrix}} = \frac{V_1 Z_3}{Z_1 Z_2 + Z_2 Z_3 + Z_3 Z_1}$$

The ratio of excitation to response is

$$\frac{V_1}{I_2} = \frac{Z_1 Z_2 + Z_2 Z_3 + Z_3 Z_1}{Z_3} \qquad \text{...(1)}$$

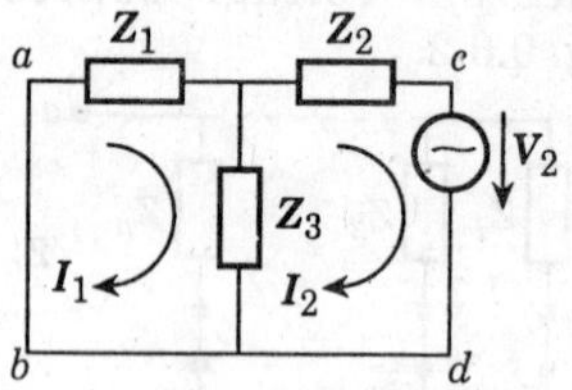


Fig. 9.7.2 Reciprocity theorem, source in branch *c-d*.

On interchanging the position of excitation to response, *i.e.* placing, the source as $V_2$ branch *c-d*. The network takes the form shown in Fig. 9.7.2.

Applying Kirchhoff's voltage law

$$(Z_1 + Z_3) I_1 - Z_3\, I_2 = 0$$

$$-Z_3\, Z_1 + (Z_2 + Z_3) I_2 = V_2$$

$$\therefore \quad \begin{vmatrix} Z_1 + Z_3 & -Z_3 \\ -Z_3 & Z_2 + Z_3 \end{vmatrix} \begin{vmatrix} I_1 \\ I_2 \end{vmatrix} = \begin{vmatrix} 0 \\ V_2 \end{vmatrix}$$

$$I_1 = \frac{\begin{vmatrix} 0 & -Z_3 \\ V_2 & Z_2 + Z_3 \end{vmatrix}}{\begin{vmatrix} Z_1 + Z_3 & -Z_3 \\ -Z_3 & Z_2 + Z_3 \end{vmatrix}} = \frac{V_2 Z_3}{Z_1 Z_2 + Z_2 Z_3 + Z_3 Z_1}$$

$$\therefore \quad \frac{V_2}{I_1} = \frac{Z_1 Z_2 + Z_2 Z_3 + Z_3 Z_1}{Z_3} \qquad \text{...(2)}$$

On comparing relations (1) and (2) $\dfrac{V_1}{I_2} = \dfrac{V_2}{I_1}$

which confirms the statement of reciprocity theorem.

## 9.8 COMPENSATION THEOREM

The compensation theorem states that any element in a network may be replaced by a voltage source of magnitude equal to the current passing through the element multiplied by the value of the element, provided that the current and voltages in other parts of the network remain unaltered.

An active network shown in Fig. 9.8.1 supplies a current **I** in the impedance **Z** connected across terminals *a*-*b*. The element **Z** can be replaced by a compensation voltage $\mathbf{V_c} = \mathbf{I\,Z}$ as shown in Fig. 9.8.2.

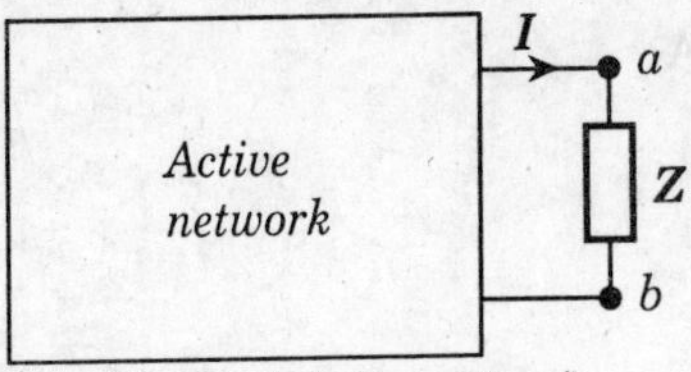


Fig. 9.8.1 Active network.

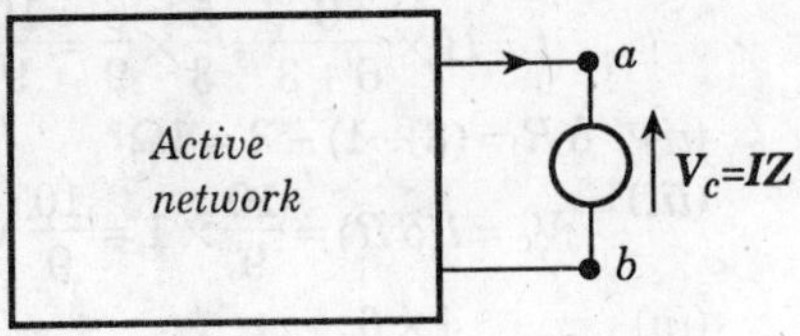


Fig. 9.8.2 Compensation voltage.

The compensation theorem can be extended to determine the change in the current (δ **I**) through an element when the impedance (or resistance) value changes (Fig. 9.8.3)

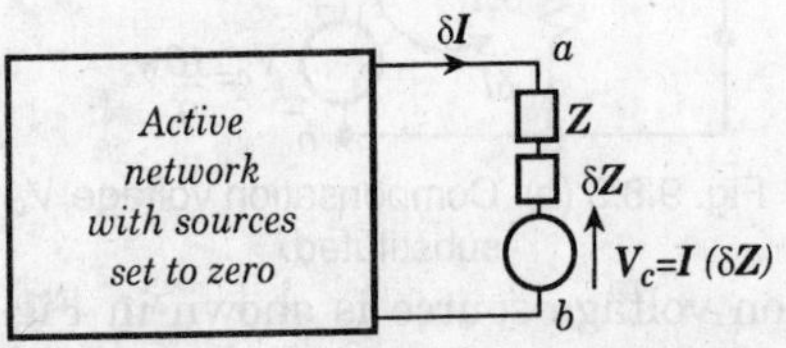


Fig. 9.8.3 Compensation voltage substitution

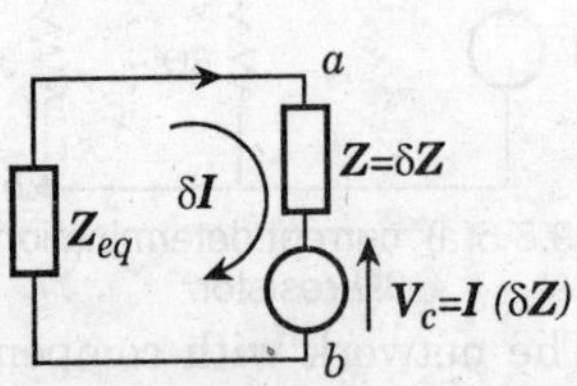


Fig. 9.8.4 Determination of δ **I**

On changing the value of the impedance **Z** to **Z** + δ **Z**, the compensation voltage $\mathbf{V_c} = \mathbf{I}\,\delta\,\mathbf{Z}$ is introduced. The change in current δ **I** is determined setting all sources equal to zero to the left of terminals *a*-*b*.

Let $\mathbf{Z_{eq}}$ be equivalent impedance to the left of terminals *a*-*b* with sources set to zero.

The network takes the form as shown in Fig. 9.8.4.

Applying Kirchhoff's voltage law (Fig. 9.8.4)

$$(\mathbf{Z} + \delta\,\mathbf{Z})\,\delta\,\mathbf{I} + \mathbf{I}\,(\delta\,\mathbf{Z}) + \mathbf{Z_{eq}}\,\delta\,\mathbf{I} = 0$$

$$\therefore \qquad \delta\,\mathbf{I} = \frac{-\,\mathbf{I}\,(\delta\,\mathbf{Z})}{\mathbf{Z_{eq}} + (\mathbf{Z} + \delta\,\mathbf{Z})}$$

**Example 9.8.1** *Determine the current flowing in the ammeter having 1Ω internal resistance connected in 3 Ω resistance in the network Fig. 9.8.5. Apply compensation theorem.*

**Solution :** Determine the current through 3Ω resistor.

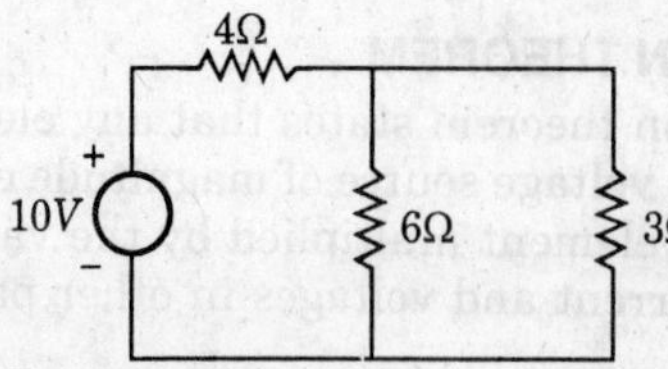


Fig. 9.8.5 Network for example 9.8.1

(*i*) $$I_1 = \frac{10}{4 + \frac{6 \times 3}{6+3}} = \frac{5}{3}\text{ A}$$

$$I = I_1 \times \frac{6}{6+3} = \frac{5}{3} \times \frac{6}{9} = \frac{10}{9}\text{ A}$$

(*ii*) $\delta R = (3 + 1) - 3 = 1\Omega$

(*iii*) $$V_c = I(\delta R) = \frac{10}{9} \times 1 = \frac{10}{9}\text{ V}$$

(*iv*) $$R_{eq} = \frac{4 \times 6}{4 + 6} = 2.4\ \Omega$$

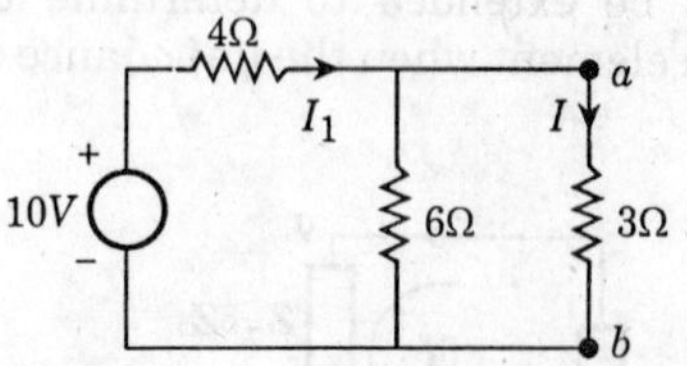


Fig. 9.8.5(*a*) current determination in 3Ω resistor

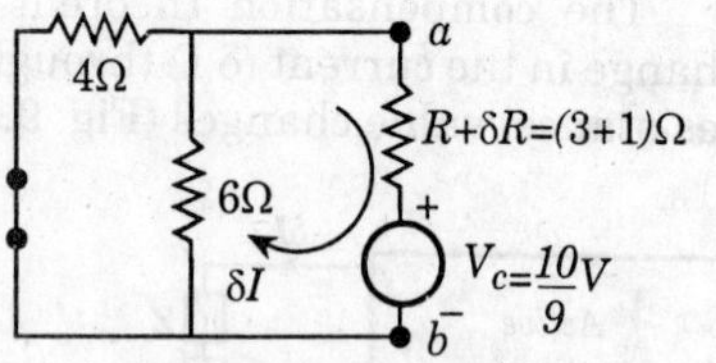


Fig. 9.8.5 (*b*) Compensation voltage $V_c$ substituted.

The network with compensation voltage source is shown in Fig. 9.8.5(*b*)

$$\delta I = \frac{-V_c}{R_{eq} + (R + \delta R)} = \frac{-10/9}{2.4 + 3 + 1} = -0.1736\text{ A}$$

$$I' = I + \delta I$$

$$= \frac{10}{9} + (-0.1736) = 0.9375\text{ A} \quad \textbf{Ans.}$$

**Example 9.8.2** *Use compensation theorem to determine the current flowing in branch a-b of the network given below, when the value of* $R_l$ *is changed from* 5Ω to 4Ω.

(*i*) $R_l = 5\Omega$

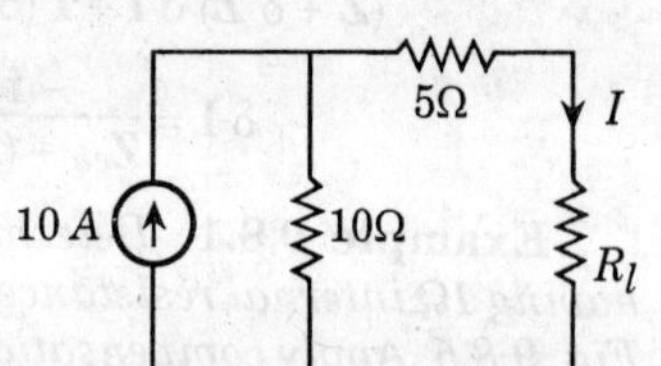


Fig. 9.8.6

$$I = 10 \times \frac{10}{10 + (5 + R_l)}$$

$$= \frac{100}{10 + (5 + 5)} = 5\text{A}$$

(*ii*) $\delta R_L = 4 - 5 = -1\Omega$

(*iii*) $V_c = I(\delta R_L) = 5 \times (-1) = -5$ V

The network with compensation voltage source is shown in Fig. 9.8.6(*a*)

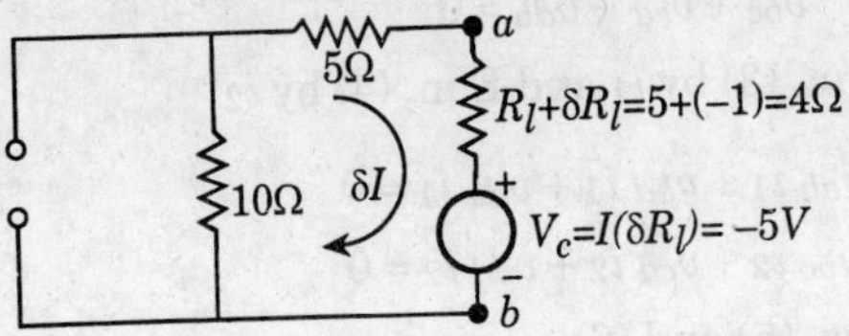


Fig. 9.8.6(*a*) compensation voltage $V_c$ substituted.

$$\delta I = \frac{-V_c}{R_{eq} + (R_t + \delta R_t)}$$

$$= \frac{-(-5)}{10+5+(4)} = \frac{5}{19} \text{ A}$$

$$I' = I + \delta I = 5 + \frac{5}{19} = 5.263 \text{ A} \quad \textbf{Ans.}$$

## 9.9 TELLEGEN'S THEOREM

Tellegen's theorem states that in any electrical network the algebraic sum of products of instantaneous branch voltage and branch currents in zero.

Mathematically Tellegen's theorem can be expressed as

$$\sum_{k=1}^{b} v_k i_k = 0$$

where "*b*" is the number of branches in the network.

Tellegen's theorem is valid for any lumped network which may be linear or non-linear, active or passive, time - variant or time - invariant. All the branch currents and branch voltages in that network must satisfy Kirchhoff's laws.

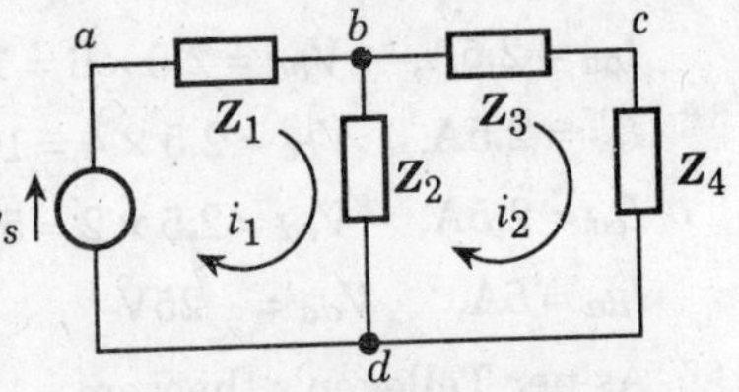


Fig. 9.9.1 Network for Tellegen's theorem

Consider a network given below,

Applying Kirchhoff's voltage law,

$$i_1 Z_1 + (i_1 - i_2) Z_2 - v_s = 0 \quad \text{...(1)}$$

$$i_2 Z_3 + i_2 Z_4 + (i_2 - i_1) Z_2 = 0 \quad \text{...(2)}$$

It is noted that,

$$v_{ab} = i_1 Z_1, \quad v_{bd} = (i_1 - i_2) Z_2, \quad v_{bc} = i_2 Z_3,$$

$$v_{cd} = i_2 Z_4 \text{ and } v_{da} = -v_s$$

Substituting in Eqns. (1) and (2)

$$v_{ab} + v_{bd} + v_{da} = 0 \quad ...(3)$$

and

$$v_{bc} + v_{cd} + v_{db} = 0 \quad ...(4)$$

Multiply Eqn. (3) by $i_1$ and Eqn. (4) by $i_2$

$$\therefore \quad v_{ab}\, i_1 + v_{bd}\, i_1 + v_{da}\, i_1 = 0 \quad ...(5)$$

and

$$v_{bc}\, i_2 + v_{cd}\, i_2 + v_{bd}\, i_2 = 0 \quad ...(6)$$

Adding Eqns. (5) and (6)

$$v_{ab}\, i_1 + v_{bd}\,(i_1 - i_2) + v_{bc}\, i_2 + v_{cd}\, i_2 + v_{da}\, i_1 = 0 \quad ...(7)$$

$$\therefore \quad i_1 = i_{ab} = i_{da}, \quad (i_1 - i_2) = i_{bd}$$

and

$$i_2 = i_{bc} = i_{cd}$$

Substituting in Eqn. (7) and rearranging,

$$v_{da}\, i_{da} + v_{ab}\, i_{ab} + v_{bc}\, i_{bc} + v_{cd}\, i_{cd} + v_{bd}\, i_{bd} = 0$$

**Thus, the statement of Tellegen's theorem is verified.**

**Example 9.9.1** *A network is shown in Fig. 9.9.2. Verify Tellegen's theorem.*

The branch currents and branch voltages can be determined as below,

$I_{ab} = 5\text{A}, \quad V_{ab} = 5 \times 2 = 10\text{V}$

$I_{bd} = 2.5\text{A}, \quad V_{bd} = 2.5 \times 6 = 15\text{V}$

$I_{bc} = 2.5\text{A}, \quad V_{bc} = 2.5 \times 4 = 10\text{V}$

$I_{cd} = 2.5\text{A}, \quad V_{cd} = 2.5 \times 2 = 5\text{V}$

$I_{da} = 5\text{A}, \quad V_{da} = -25\text{V}$

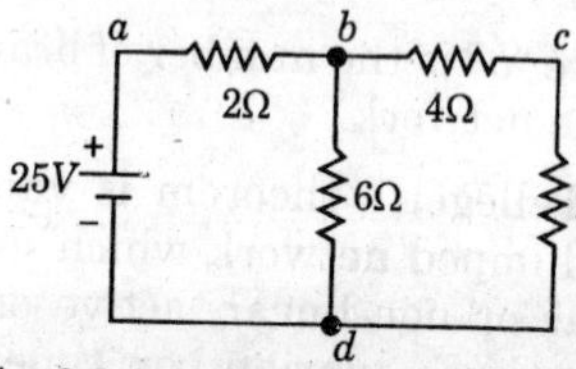

Fig. 9.9.2 Network for verification of Tellegen's theorem.

As per Tellegen's theorem,

$$V_{ab} I_{ab} + V_{bd} I_{bd} + V_{bc} I_{bc} + V_{cd} I_{cd} + V_{da} I_{da} = 0$$

Substituting the values

$$10 \times 5 + 15 \times 2.5 + 10 \times 2.5 + 5 \times 2.5 - 25 \times 5 = 0$$

Tellegen's theorem is verified

## 9.10 SOLVED EXAMPLES

**Example: 9.10.1** *Determine the current flowing in* 10Ω *resistor in the network given (Fig. 9.10.1)*

Use Thevenin's theorem.

**Solution :** The network (Fig. 9.10.1) is redrawn as shown in Fig.9.10.1(a) to include internal resistance of the sources.

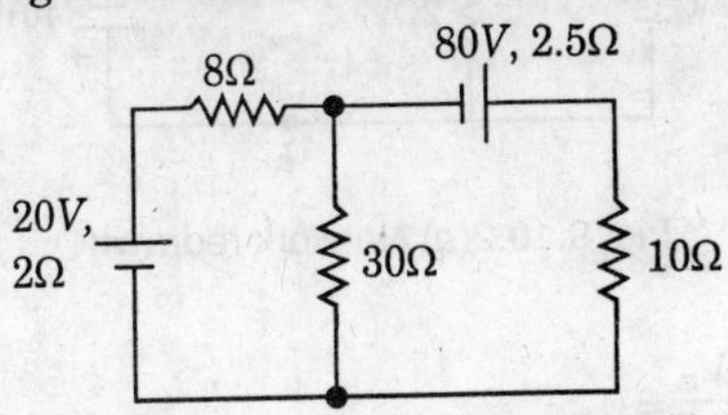


Fig. 9.10.1 Network for example 9.10.1

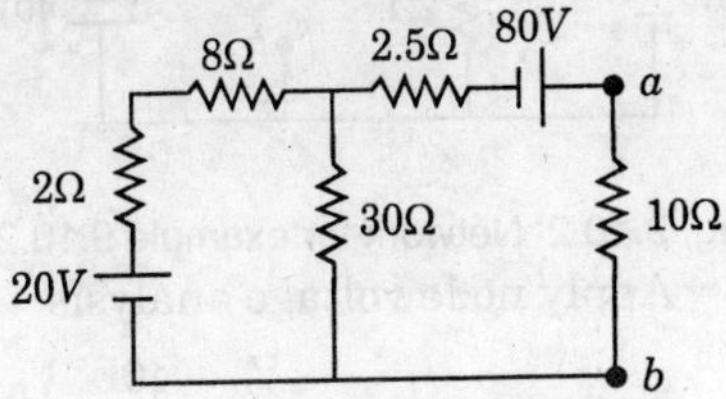


Fig.9.10.1(*a*) Network redrawn

Remove 10 Ω resistor across terminal *a-b* to get Fig. 9.10.1(*b*)

$$V_{th} = V_{ab} = V_{xy} + 80$$

(voltage drop across 2.5 Ω resistor is zero, because no current flows through it)

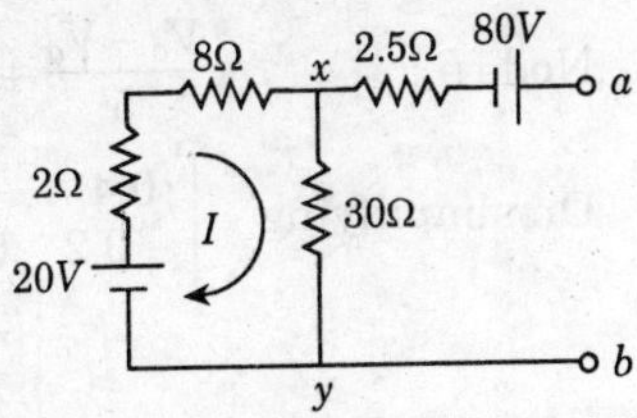


Fig. 9.10.1(*b*) Determination of $V_{th}$

$$= I \times 30 + 80$$

$$= \frac{20}{2+8+30} \times 30 + 80 = 95 \text{ V}$$

To determine $R_{th}$ set voltage sources to zero and draw the circuit as below (Fig. 9.10.1(*c*))

$$R_{th} = R_{ab} = 2.5 + \frac{(2+8) \times 30}{(2+8)+30} = 10\ \Omega$$

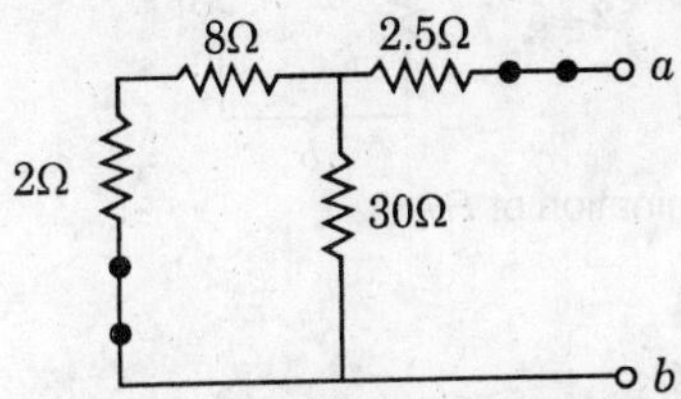


Fig. 9.10.1(*c*) Determination of $R_{th}$

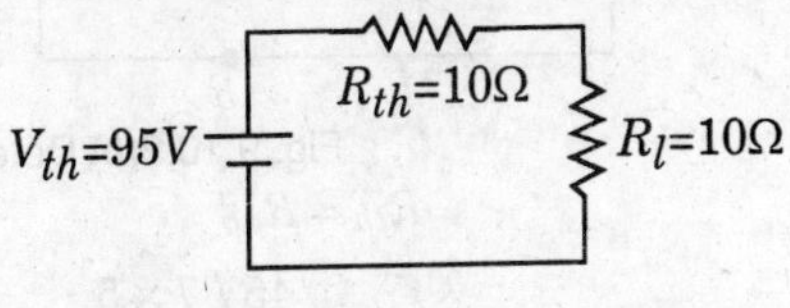


Fig. 9.10.1(*d*) Thevenin's equivalent circuit.

Thevenin's equivalent circuit is shown in Fig. 9.10.1(*d*)

$$I_{ab} = \frac{V_{th}}{R_{th} + R_l}$$

$$= \frac{95}{10+10} = 4.75 \text{ A} \qquad \text{...Ans.}$$

**Example : 9.10.2** *Obtain Thevenin's equivalent at terminals a-b of the network shown in Fig. 9.10.2*

**Solution :** The network is redrawn in Fig. 9.10.2(*a*)

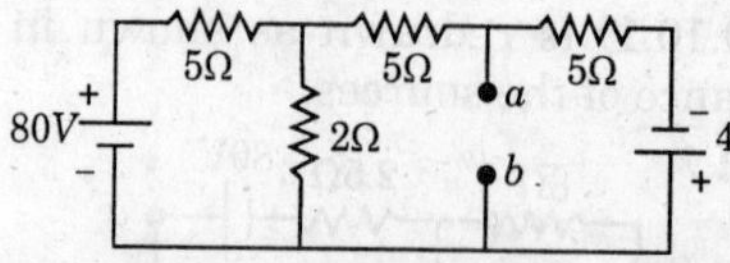


Fig. 9.10.2 Network for example 9.10.2

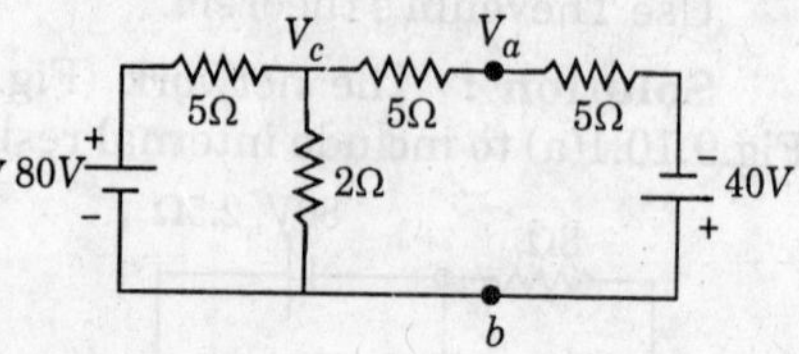


Fig. 9.10.2(*a*) Network redrawn

Apply node voltage analysis

Node *a* : $$\frac{V_a + 40}{5} + \frac{V_a - V_c}{5} = 0$$

Node *b* : $$\frac{V_c - V_a}{5} + \frac{V_c}{2} + \frac{V_c - 80}{5} = 0$$

On simplifying $$\begin{vmatrix} 0.4 & -0.2 \\ -0.2 & 0.9 \end{vmatrix} \begin{vmatrix} V_a \\ V_c \end{vmatrix} = \begin{vmatrix} -8 \\ 16 \end{vmatrix}$$

$$V_{th} = V_a = \frac{\begin{vmatrix} -8 & -0.2 \\ 16 & 0.9 \end{vmatrix}}{\begin{vmatrix} 0.4 & -0.2 \\ -0.2 & 0.9 \end{vmatrix}} = \frac{-4}{0.32} = -12.5 \text{ V}$$

To determine $R_{th}$ set voltage sources to zero as shown in Fig. 9.10.2(*b*).

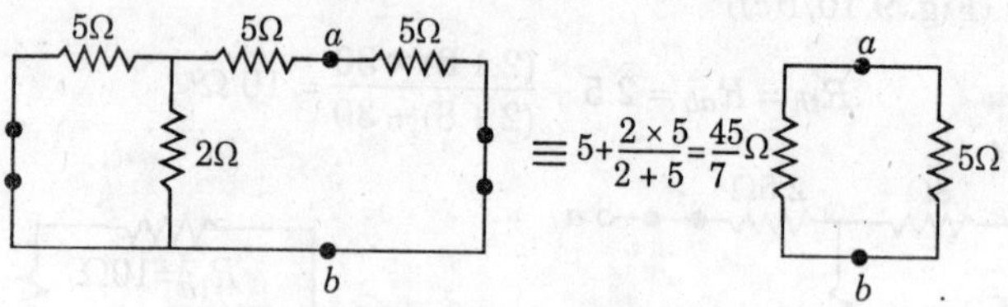


Fig. 9.10.2(*b*) Determination of $R_{th}$

$$R_{th} = R_{ab}$$

$$= \frac{45/7 \times 5}{45/7 + 5} = 2.8\ \Omega$$

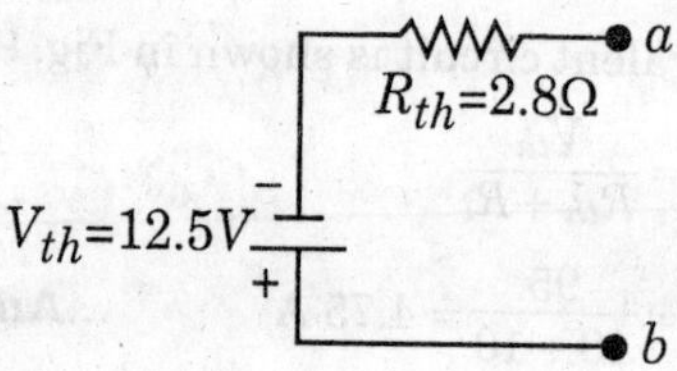


Fig. 9.10.2(*c*) Thevenin's equivalent network

Thevenin's equivalent network is shown in Fig. 9.10.2(*c*).

**...Ans.**

**Example : 9.10.3** *Use Thevenin's theorem to determine the current through 4Ω resistor connected across terminals a-b.*

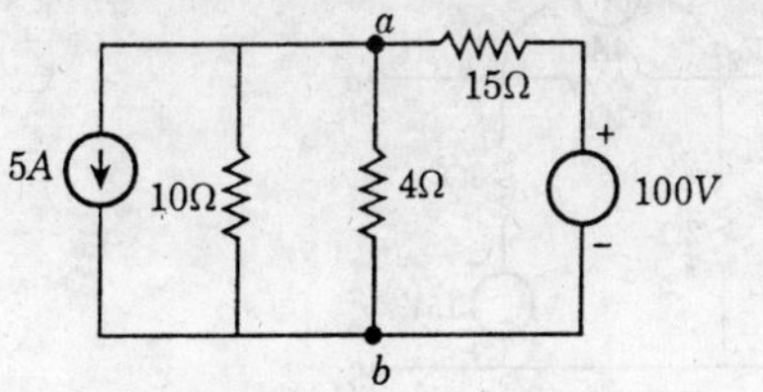


Fig. 9.10.3 Network for example 9.10.3

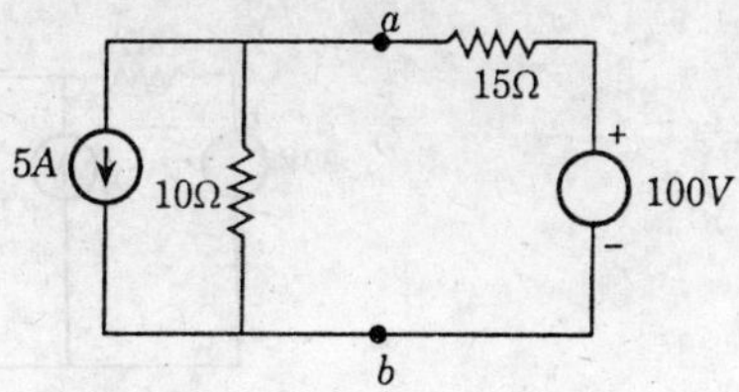


Fig. 9.10.3(*a*) 4Ω resistor removed.

**Solution.** Remove 4Ω resistance to obtain Fig. 9.10.3(*a*).

Apply Kirchhoff's current law at node "*a*""

$$\therefore \qquad \frac{V_a - 100}{15} + \frac{V_a}{10} + 5 = 0$$

Solving, $\quad V_a = 10 \text{ V}$

$$V_{th} = V_a = 10 \text{ V}$$

To determine $R_{th}$ set sources to zero [(Fig. 9.10.3(*b*)]

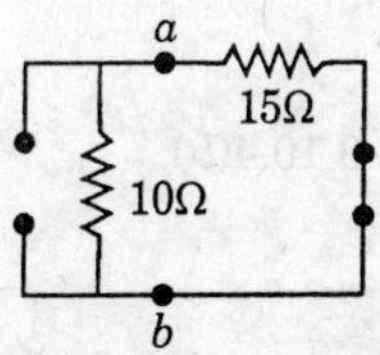


Fig. 9.10.3(*b*) Determination of $R_{th}$

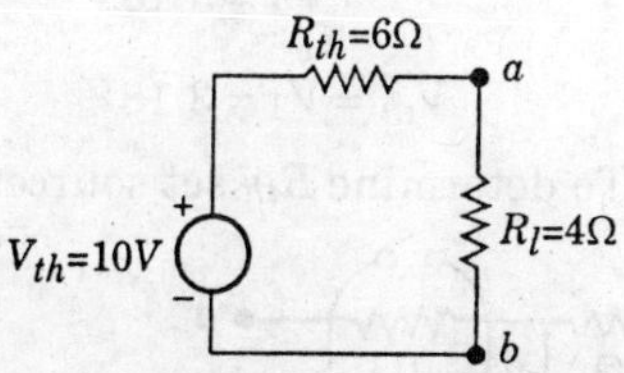


Fig. 9.10.3(*c*) Thevenin's equivalent network

$$R_{th} = R_{ab} = \frac{10 \times 15}{10 + 15} = 6\ \Omega$$

Thevenin's equivalent circuit connected to load $R_l$ is shown in Fig. 9.10.3(*c*).

$$I_{ab} = \frac{V_{th}}{R_{th} + R_l}$$

$$= \frac{10}{6 + 4} = 10 \text{ A} \qquad \text{...Ans.}$$

**Example : 9.10.4** *Find Thevenin's and Norton's equivalent circuits across terminals a-b for the Fig. 9.10.4 given below.*

Apply node voltage analysis,

at node 1 : $\quad \dfrac{V_1 + 15}{3} + \dfrac{V_1 - V_2}{1} - 4 = 0$

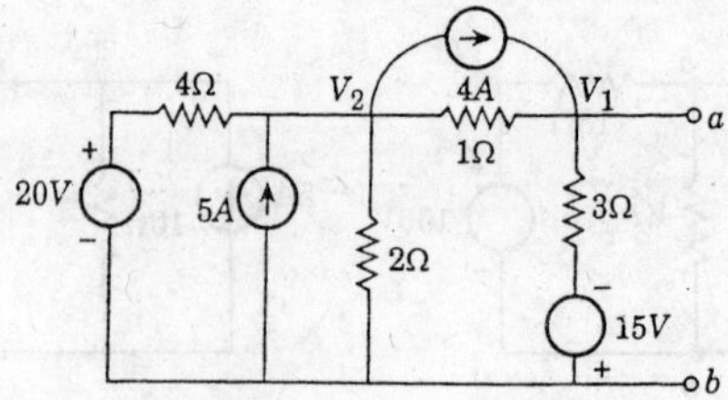


Fig. 9.10.4.(*a*) Network for example 9.10.4.

at node 2 : $\frac{V_2 - 20}{4} + \frac{V_2 - V_1}{1} + \frac{V_2}{2} + 4 - 5 = 0$

Simplifying, $\frac{4}{3} V_1 - V_2 = -1$

$$-V_1 + \frac{7}{4} V_2 = 6$$

Solving above equations,

$$V_1 = 3.18\text{V}$$

$\therefore \quad V_{th} = V_1 = 3.18V$

To determine $R_{th}$ set sources to zero Fig. 9.10.4(*b*).

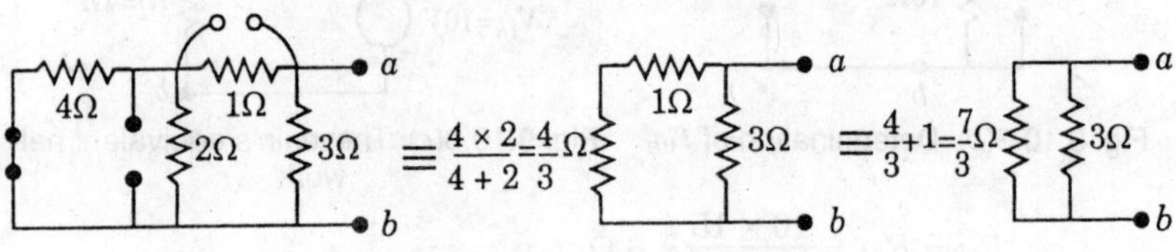


Fig. 9.10.4(*b*) Determination or $R_{th}$.

$$R_{th} = R_{ab} = \frac{7/3 \times 3}{7/3 + 3} = 1.31\Omega$$

Thevenin's equivalent is shown in Fig. 9.10.4(*c*)

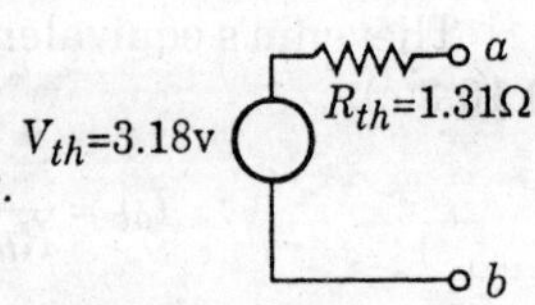


Fig. 9.10.4(*c*) Thevenin's equivalent network

for Norton's equivalent

$$I_{eq} = \underset{\substack{\text{at terminals} \\ a\text{-}b}}{I_{sc}} = \frac{V_{th}}{R_{th}} = \frac{3.18}{1.31} = 2.42 \text{ A}$$

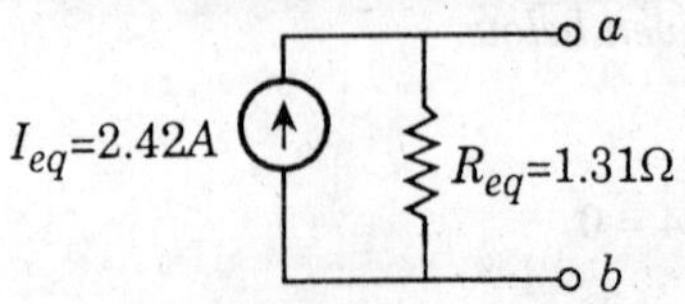


and $R_{eq} = R_{th} = 1.31\ \Omega$

Norton's equivalent is shown in Fig. 9.10.4(*d*)

...**Ans.**

Fig. 9.10.4(*d*) Norton's equivalent network.

**Example 9.10.5.** *Obtain Thevenin's across terminals a-b for the network given in Fig. 9.10.5.*

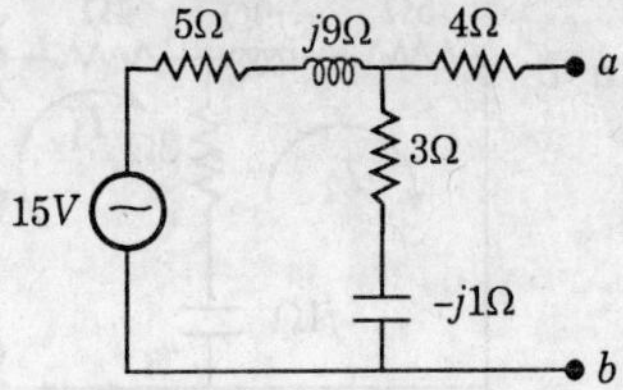


Fig. 9.10.5 Network for example 9.10.5

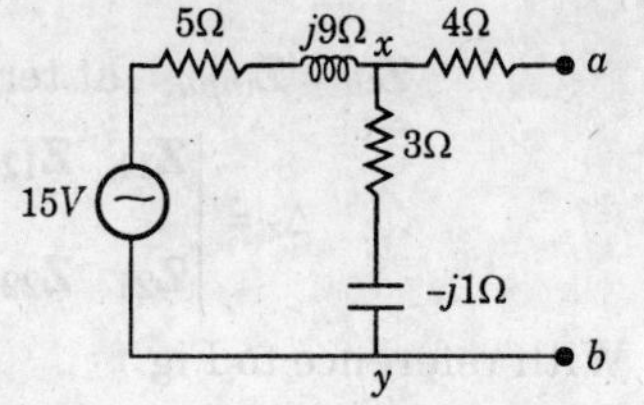


Fig. 9.10.5(*a*) Determination of $\mathbf{V}_{th}$

**Solution .** No current is flowing through the 4Ω resistor, Hence, the voltage drop across it is zero. Therefore.

$$\mathbf{V}_{th} = \mathbf{V}_{ab} = \mathbf{V}_{xy}$$

By voltage division,

$$\mathbf{V}_{th} = \mathbf{V}_{xy} = \frac{15(3 - j\,1)}{(5 + j\,9) + (3 - j\,1)}$$

$$= \frac{15(3 - j\,1)}{8 + j\,8} = \frac{15\sqrt{3^2 + 1^2}\,\angle - \tan^{-1}(1/3)}{\sqrt{8^2 + 8^2}\,\angle \tan^{-1}(8/8)}$$

$$= \frac{15\sqrt{10}\,\angle - 18.43°}{8\sqrt{2}\,\angle 45°} = 4.19\,\angle - 63.43°\text{ V}$$

To determine $\mathbf{Z}_{th}$ set voltage source to zero as in Fig. 9.10.5(*b*)

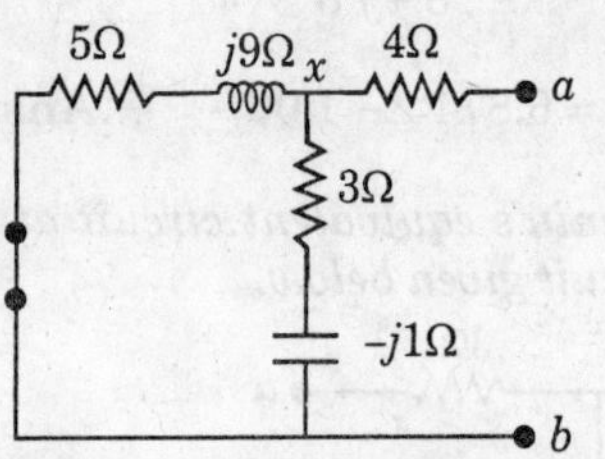


Fig. 9.10.5(*b*) Determination of $\mathbf{Z}_{th}$

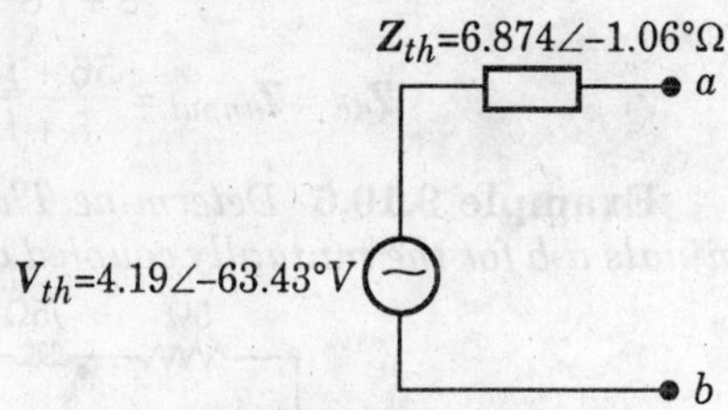


Fig. 9.10.5(*c*)

$$\mathbf{Z}_{th} = \mathbf{Z}_{ab} = 4 + \frac{(5 + j\,9)\,(3 - j\,1)}{(5 + j\,9) + (3 - j\,1)}$$

$$= 4 + \frac{24 + j\,22}{8 + j\,8} = \frac{56 + j\,54}{8 + j\,8} = \frac{56(1 + j0.964)}{8\,(1 + j1)}$$

$$= \frac{56\sqrt{1^2 + 0.964^2}\,\angle\tan^{-1}(0.964/1)}{8\,\sqrt{1^2 + 1^2}\,\angle\tan^{-1}(1/1)}$$

$$= \frac{56\sqrt{1.929}\,\angle 43.94°}{8\sqrt{2}\,\angle 45°} = 6.874\,\angle - 1.06°\ \Omega$$

Thevenin's equivalence is shown in Fig. 9.10.5(*c*)

### Alternative Method to Determine $\mathbf{Z}_{th}$

Apply input voltage $\mathbf{V}_1$ at terminals $a$-$b$ allowing input current flow as $\mathbf{I}_1$

$$\mathbf{Z}_{th} = \mathbf{Z}_{input} \quad \text{at terminals } a\text{–}b$$

$$\Delta_z = \begin{vmatrix} \mathbf{Z}_{11} & \mathbf{Z}_{12} \\ \mathbf{Z}_{21} & \mathbf{Z}_{22} \end{vmatrix}$$

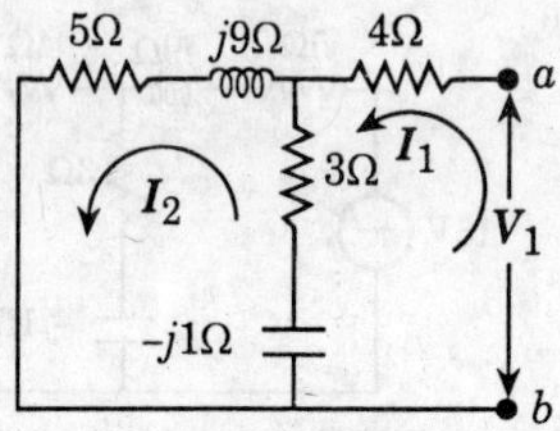

Fig. 9.10.5(*d*) Alternative method for determination of $\mathbf{Z}_{th}$

With reference to Fig.

$$\Delta_z = \begin{vmatrix} (4+3-j\,1) & -(3-j\,1) \\ -(3-j\,1) & (5+j\,9+3-j\,1) \end{vmatrix}$$

or

$$\Delta_z = \begin{vmatrix} (7-j\,1) & -(3-j\,1) \\ -(3-j\,1) & (8+j\,8) \end{vmatrix}$$

$$\mathbf{Z}_{input} = \frac{\mathbf{V}_1}{\mathbf{I}_1} = \frac{\Delta_z}{\Delta_{11}} = \frac{\begin{vmatrix} (7-j\,1) & -(3-j\,1) \\ -(3-j\,1) & (8+j\,8) \end{vmatrix}}{(8+j\,8)}$$

$$= \frac{(7-j\,1)(8+j\,8) - [-(3-j\,1) \times -(3-j\,1)]}{(8+j\,8)}$$

$$= \frac{(64+j\,48)-(8-j\,6)}{8+j\,8} = \frac{56+j\,54}{8+j\,8}$$

$$\therefore \qquad \mathbf{Z}_{th} = \mathbf{Z}_{input} = \frac{56+j\,54}{8+j\,8} = 6.874\angle -1.06° \qquad \text{...Ans.}$$

**Example 9.10.6** *Determine Thevenin's equivalent circuit at terminals a-b for the mutually coupled circuit given below.*

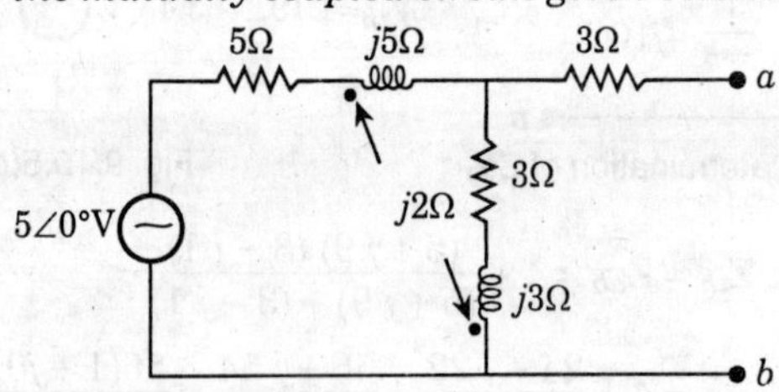

Fig. 9.10.6 Mutually coupled circuit for example 9.10.6

**Solution .** To determine $\mathbf{V}_{th}$

Apply Kirchhoff's voltage law.

$$5\mathbf{I} + j\,5\mathbf{I} - (j\,2\mathbf{I}) + 3\mathbf{I} + j\,3\mathbf{I} - (j\,2\mathbf{I}) - 5\angle 0° = 0$$

In the above equation, the term $-(j\,2\,\mathbf{I})$ gives the mutual inductance effect between $L_1$ and $L_2$.

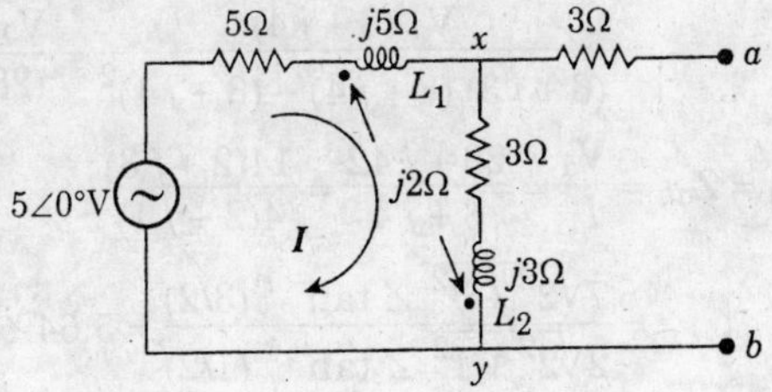

Fig. 9.10.6(*a*) Determination of $\mathbf{V}_{th}$

Solving above equation. $\mathbf{I} = \dfrac{5}{8 + j\,4}$

$$\mathbf{V}_{th} = \mathbf{V}_{xy} = (3 + j\,3)\mathbf{I} - j\,2\,\mathbf{I}$$

↓ mutually induced e.m.f. in $L_2$

$$= (3 + j\,1)\mathbf{I} = (3 + j\,1) \times \frac{5}{8 + j\,4}$$

$$= \frac{5\,(3 + j\,1)}{4\,(2 + j\,1)} = \frac{5\sqrt{3^2 + 1^2}\,\angle \tan^{-1}(1/3)}{4\sqrt{2^2 + 1^2}\,\angle \tan^{-1}(1/2)}$$

or $$\mathbf{V}_{th} = \frac{5\sqrt{10}\,\angle 18.43°}{4\sqrt{5}\,\angle 26.56°} = 1.76\angle -8.13°\text{ V}$$

To determine $\mathbf{Z}_{th}$ set voltage source to zero as in Fig. 9.10.6(*b*)

Apply input voltage $\mathbf{V}_1$ at terminals *a*-*b*. Write mesh eqns.

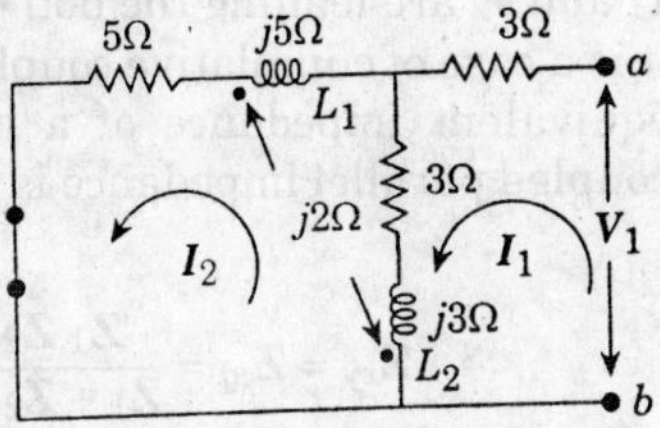

Fig. 9.10.6(*b*) Determination of $\mathbf{Z}_{th}$

Mesh 1 : $3\mathbf{I}_1 + (3 + j\,3)(\mathbf{I}_1 - \mathbf{I}_2) + j\,2\,\mathbf{I}_2 = \mathbf{V}_1$

↓ effect of $L_1$ on $L_2$

Mesh 2 : $(3 + j\,3)(\mathbf{I}_2 - \mathbf{I}_1) + (5 + j\,5)\mathbf{I}_2 - j\,2\,\mathbf{I}_2 - j\,2\,(\mathbf{I}_2 - \mathbf{I}_1) = 0$

↓ effect of $L_1$ on $L_2$ ↓ effect of $L_2$ on $L_1$

On rearranging above equations,

$$\begin{vmatrix} (6 + j\,3) & -(3 + j\,1) \\ -(3 + j\,1) & (8 + j\,4) \end{vmatrix} \begin{vmatrix} \mathbf{I}_1 \\ \mathbf{I}_2 \end{vmatrix} = \begin{vmatrix} \mathbf{V}_1 \\ 0 \end{vmatrix}$$

$$\mathbf{I}_1 = \frac{\begin{vmatrix} \mathbf{V}_1 & -(3 + j\,1) \\ 0 & (8 + j\,4) \end{vmatrix}}{\begin{vmatrix} (6 + j\,3) & -(3 + j\,1) \\ -(3 + j\,1) & (8 + j\,4) \end{vmatrix}}$$

$$= \frac{\mathbf{V}_1 (8 + j\,4)}{(6 + j\,3)(8 + j\,4) - (3 + j\,1)^2} = \frac{\mathbf{V}_1(8 + j\,4)}{(28 + j\,42)}$$

$$\mathbf{Z}_{th} = \mathbf{Z}_{ab} = \frac{\mathbf{V}_1}{I_1} = \frac{28 + j\,42}{8 + j\,4} = \frac{14(2 + j\,3)}{4(2 + j\,1)}$$

$$= \frac{7\sqrt{2^2 + 3^2}\ \angle \tan^{-1}(3/2)}{2\sqrt{2^2 + 1^2}\ \angle \tan^{-1}(1/2)} = 5.64\angle\, 29.74°\ \Omega$$

Thevenin's equivalent circuit is shown in Fig 9.10.6(*c*).

...**Ans.**

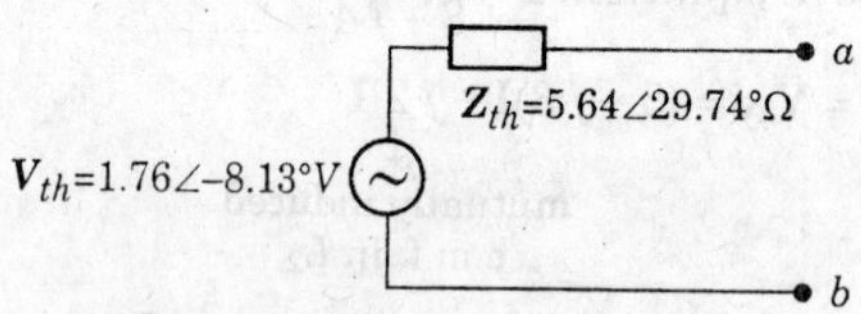


Fig. 9.10.6(*c*) Thevenin's equivalent circuit.

## Alternative Method to Determine $Z_{th}$

The circuit shown in Fig. 9.10.6(*b*) can be redrawn as shown in Fig. 9.10.6(*d*)

As shown in Fig. 9.10.6(*b*), current $\mathbf{I}_1$ and $\mathbf{I}_2$ are leaning the dot(•). Thus, it is a case of cumulative coupling. The equivalent impedance of a mutually coupled parallel impedance is given by

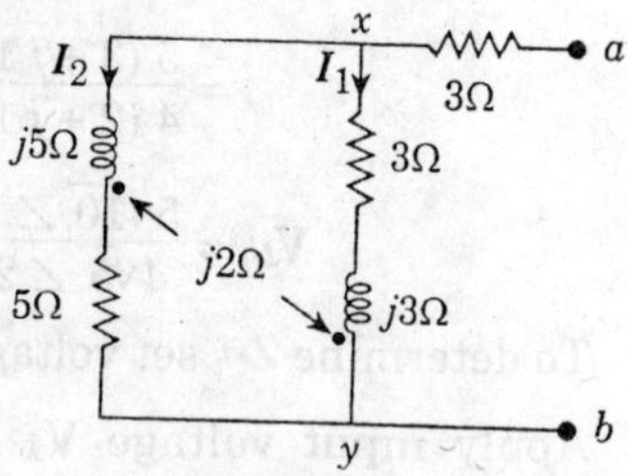


Fig. 9.10.6(*d*) circuit in Fig. 9.10.6(*b*) redrawn

$$\mathbf{Z}_{xy} = \mathbf{Z}_{eq} = \frac{\mathbf{Z}_1\,\mathbf{Z}_2 - \mathbf{Z}_m^2}{\mathbf{Z}_1 + \mathbf{Z}_2 - 2\,\mathbf{Z}_m} \quad \text{for cumulative coupling}$$

(Refer chapter Five)

put
$$\mathbf{Z}_1 = 3 + j\,3$$
$$\mathbf{Z}_2 = 5 + j\,5$$
$$\mathbf{Z}_m = j\,2$$

$$\therefore \quad \mathbf{Z}_{eq} = \frac{(3 + j\,3)(5 + j\,5) - (j\,2)^2}{(3 + j\,3) + (5 + j\,5) - 2(j\,2)}$$

$$= \frac{4 + j\,30}{8 + j\,4}$$

$$\mathbf{Z}_{th} = \mathbf{Z}_{eq} + 3$$

$$= \frac{4 + j\,30}{8 + j\,4} + 3 = \frac{4 + j\,30 + 24 + j\,12}{8 + j\,4}$$

$$= \frac{28 + j\,42}{8 + j\,4} = 5.64 \angle 29.74° \ \Omega$$

**Example 9.10.7** *Determine the voltage across the capacitor using Thevenin's theorem.*

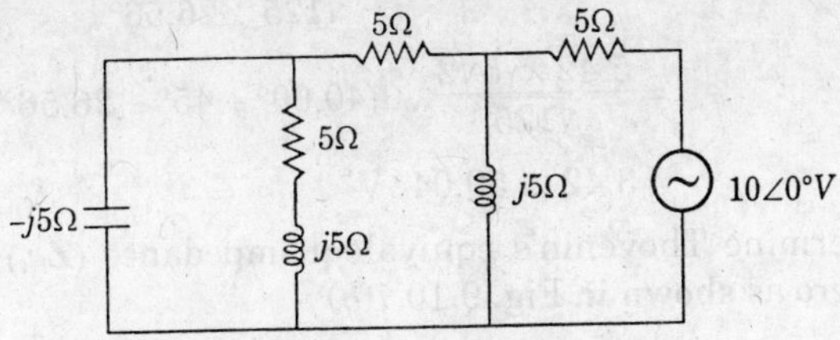

Fig. 9.10.7 Network for example 9.10.7

**Solution .** To determine $\mathbf{V}_{th}$, remove $-j\,5\Omega$ capacitor to get the network (Fig. 9.10.7(*a*)). Apply node voltage analysis to determine $v_x$.

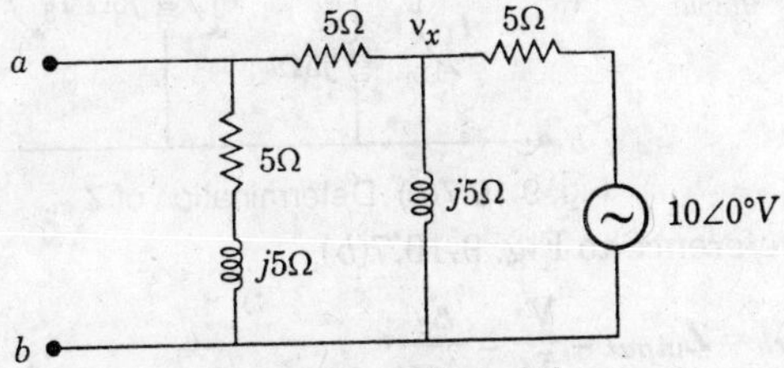

Fig. 9.10.7(*a*) Determination of **V** *th*.

Thus,

$$\frac{v_x - 10}{5} + \frac{v_x}{j\,5} + \frac{v_x}{5 + (5 + j\,5)} = 0$$

$\therefore$
$$v_x \left( \frac{1}{5} + \frac{1}{j\,5} + \frac{1}{10 + j\,5} \right) = 2$$

or
$$\left( 0.2 - j\,0.2 + \frac{10 - j\,5}{10^2 + 5^2} \right) = 2$$

or
$$v_x\,(0.2 + j\,0.2 + 0.08 - j\,0.04) = 2$$

or
$$v_x\,(0.28 - j\,0.24) = 2$$

$\therefore$
$$v_x = \frac{2}{0.28 - j\,0.24} = \frac{2}{\sqrt{0.28^2 + 0.24^2} \angle - \tan^{-1}\left(\frac{0.24}{0.28}\right)}$$

$$= 5.42 \angle 40.60 \text{ V}$$

By voltage division,

$$\mathbf{V}_{th} = \mathbf{V}_{ab} = v_x \times \frac{(5 + j\,5)}{5 + (5 + j\,5)}$$

$$= 5.42 \angle 40.60° \times \frac{\sqrt{5^2 + 5^2} \angle \tan^{-1}(5/5)}{\sqrt{10^2 + 5^2} \angle \tan^{-1}(5/10)}$$

$$= 5.42 \angle 40.60° \times \frac{5\sqrt{2} \angle 45°}{\sqrt{125} \angle 26.56°}$$

$$= \frac{5.42 \times 5\sqrt{2}}{\sqrt{125}} \angle (40.60° + 45° - 26.56°)$$

$$= 3.42 \angle 59.04° \text{ V}$$

To determine Thevenin's equivalent impedance ($\mathbf{Z}_{th}$) set voltage source to zero as shown in Fig. 9.10.7(*b*)

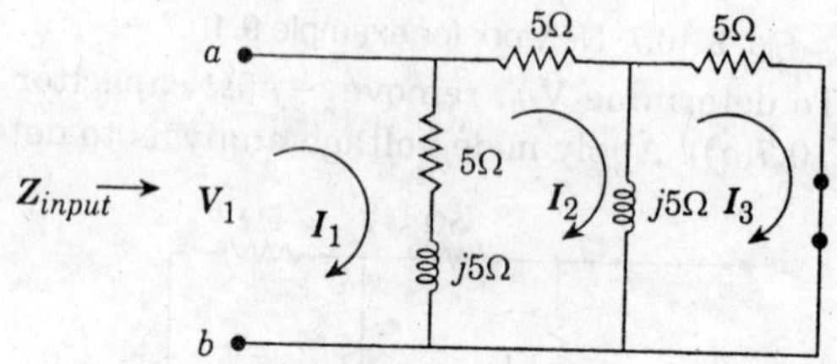


Fig. 9.10.7(*b*) Determination of $\mathbf{Z}_{th}$.

With reference to Fig. 9.10.7(*b*),

$$\mathbf{Z}_{th} = \mathbf{Z}_{input} = \frac{\mathbf{V}_I}{\mathbf{I}_1} = \frac{\Delta_z}{\Delta_{11}}$$

where,
$$\Delta_z = \begin{vmatrix} \mathbf{Z}_{11} & \mathbf{Z}_{12} & \mathbf{Z}_{13} \\ \mathbf{Z}_{21} & \mathbf{Z}_{22} & \mathbf{Z}_{23} \\ \mathbf{Z}_{31} & \mathbf{Z}_{32} & \mathbf{Z}_{33} \end{vmatrix}$$

$$\Delta_z = \begin{vmatrix} (5+j5) & -(5+j5) & 0 \\ -(5+j5) & (10+j10) & -j5 \\ 0 & -j5 & (5+j5) \end{vmatrix}$$

$$= (5+j5)\begin{vmatrix} (10+j10) & -j5) \\ (-j5) & (5+j5) \end{vmatrix}$$

$$+ (5+j5)\begin{vmatrix} -(5+j5) & -j5 \\ 0 & (5+j5) \end{vmatrix} + 0$$

$$= (5+j5)(j100+25) + (5+j5)[-(5+j5)(5+j5) - 0]$$

$$= 5 \times 25(1+j1)(1+j4) - (5+j5)^3$$

$$= 5 \times 25(-3+j5) - 125 \times 2(-1+j1)$$

$$= 125[(-3+j5) - 2(-1+j1)] = 125(-1+j3)$$

$$\Delta_{11} = \begin{vmatrix} (10 + j\,10) & -j\,5 \\ -j\,5 & (5 + j\,5) \end{vmatrix}$$

$$= (10 + j\,10)\,(5 + j\,10) - (-j\,5)\,(-j\,5) = 25(1 + j\,4)$$

$$\therefore \quad \mathbf{Z}_{th} = \mathbf{Z}_{input} = \frac{125\,(-1 + j\,3)}{25\,(1 + j\,4)}$$

$$= \frac{125\sqrt{1^2 + 3^2}\ \angle\,180° - \tan^{-1}(3/1)}{5\sqrt{1^2 + 4^2}\ \tan^{-1}(4/1)}$$

$$= \frac{125\sqrt{10}\ \angle\,(180° - 71.56°)}{5\sqrt{17}\ \angle\,75.96°}$$

$$= 3.83\,\angle\,(180° - 71.56° - 75.96°)$$

$$= 3.83\,\angle\,32.48°\Omega$$

Thevenin's equivalent circuit is shown in Fig. 9.10.7(*c*).

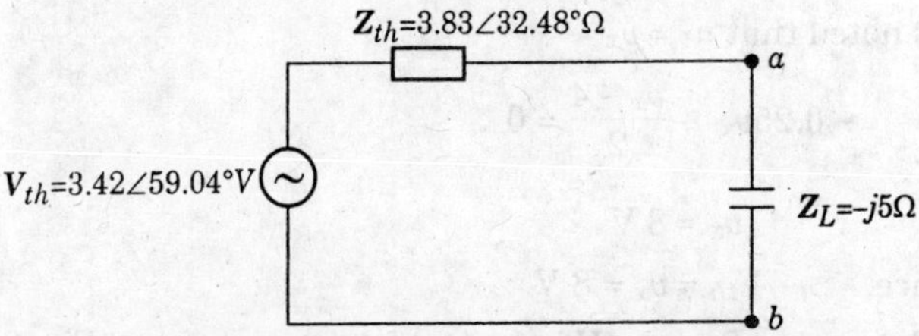


Fig. 9.10.7(*c*) Thevenin's equivalent network

The voltage across the capacitor,

$$\mathbf{V}_{ab} = \mathbf{V}_{th} \times \frac{\mathbf{Z}_L}{\mathbf{Z}_{th} + \mathbf{Z}_L} \qquad \text{By voltage division}$$

$$= 3.42\,\angle\,59.04° \times \frac{-j5}{3.83\,\angle\,32.48° - j\,5}$$

$$= 3.42\,\angle\,59.04° \times \frac{5\,\angle -90°}{3.83\,(\cos 32.48 + j \sin 32.48) - j\,5}$$

$$= 3.42\,\angle\,59.04° \times \frac{5\,\angle -90°}{3.23 + j\,2.056 - j\,5}$$

$$= 3.42\,\angle\,59.04° \times \frac{5\,\angle -90°}{3.23 - j\,2.94}$$

$$= 3.42\,\angle\,59.04° \times \frac{5\,\angle -90°}{\sqrt{3.23^2 + 2.94^2}\ \angle -\tan^{-1}\left(\frac{2.94}{3.23}\right)}$$

$$= \frac{3.42\,\angle\,59.04° \times 5\,\angle -90°}{4.367\,\angle -42.30}$$

or $\quad \mathbf{V}_{ab} = 3.91\,\angle\,11.34° \qquad$ **...Ans.**

**Example 9.10.8** *Obtain Thevenin's equivalent at terminals a-b.*

**Solution :** To determine $V_{th}$, The network is shown in Fig. 9.10.8(*a*)

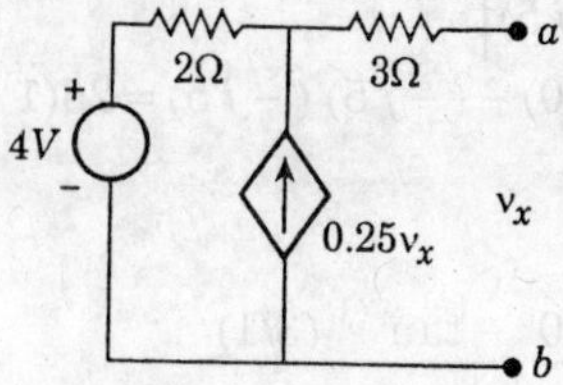


Fig. 9.10.8 Network for example 9.10.8

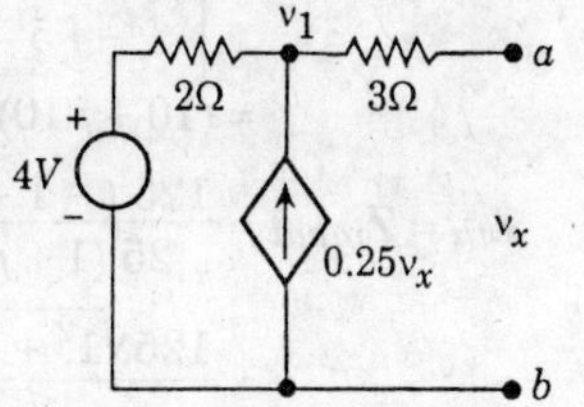


Fig. 9.10.8(*a*) Determination of $V_{th}$

Terminals *a-b* are open circuit, Hence, no current flows through 3Ω resistor.

Apply Kirchhoff's current law at node "1"

$$\therefore \quad -0.25v_x + \frac{v_1 - 4}{2} + 0 = 0$$

It is noted that $v_1 = v_x$

$$\therefore \quad -0.25v_x + \frac{v_x - 4}{2} = 0$$

$$\therefore \quad v_x = 8 \text{ V}$$

Hence, $\quad V_{th} = v_x = 8$ V

To determine $R_{th}$ set 4V independent source to zero (Fig. 9.10.8(*b*))

Let a voltage $v_x$ be applied at terminals *a-b* and resulting a current $i_x$

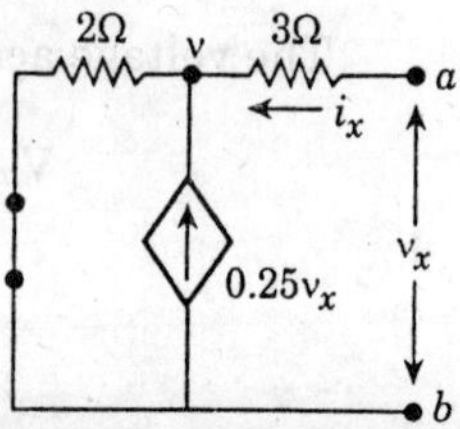


Fig. 9.10.8(*b*) Determination of $R_{th}$

Applying Kirchhoff's current law,

$$\frac{v}{2} - 0.25\, v_x - \frac{v_x - v}{3} = 0$$

Solving above equation

$$v = 0.7v_x$$

$$i_x = \frac{v_x - v}{3} = \frac{v_x - 0.7v_x}{3} = \frac{0.3v_x}{3}$$

$$R_{th} = R_{ab} = \frac{v_x}{i_x} = \frac{v_x}{(0.3\,/\,3)v_x} = 10\ \Omega$$

## Alternative Method to Determine $R_{th}$

To determine $I_{sc}$ apply short circuit at terminals *a-b* [Fig. 9.10.8(*c*)]

On short circuiting terminals *a-b*, $v_x = 0$. Therefore, the dependent current source $0.25v_x$ sets to zero Fig. 9.10.8(*c*)

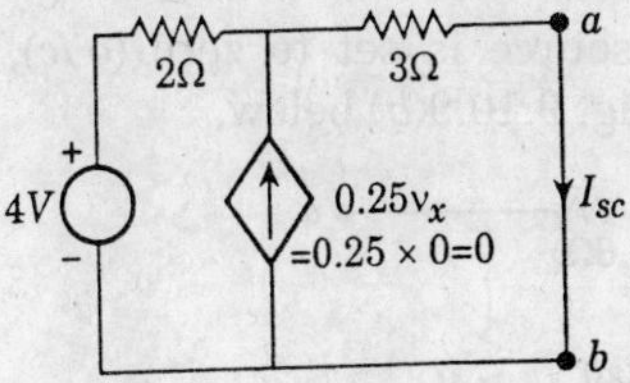

Fig. 9.10.8 (c) Determination of $R_{th}$ (alternative method)

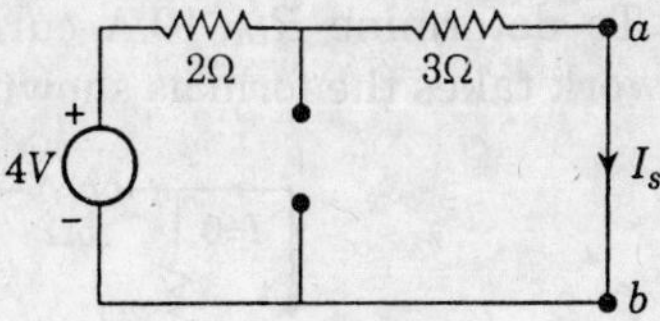

Fig. 9.10.8 (d) Network of Fig. 9.10.8 (c) redrawn

$$I_{sc} = \frac{4}{2+3} = 0.8 \text{ A}$$

$$R_{th} = \frac{V_{th}}{I_{sc}} = \frac{8}{0.8} = 10\ \Omega$$

Thevenin's equivalent is shown in Fig.9.10.8(*e*)

...**Ans.**

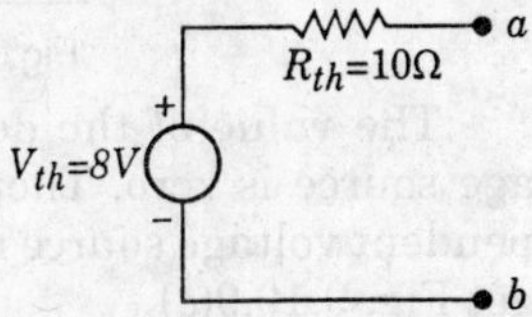

Fig. 9.10.8(*e*) Thevenin's equivalent network

**Example 9.10.9.** *Apply Thevenin's theorem to determine the current through* 5.6Ω *resistor connected across terminals a-b.*

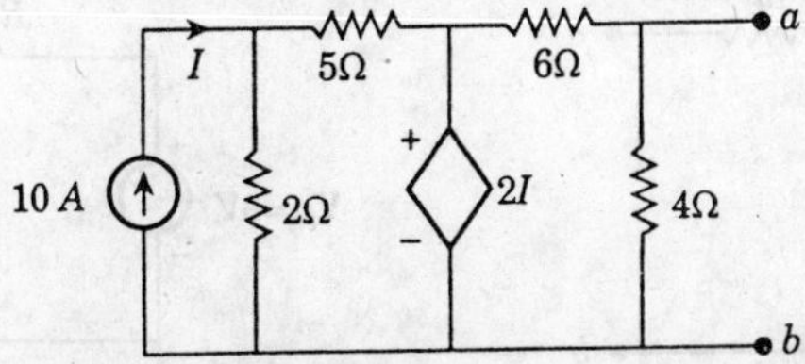

Fig. 9.10.9 Network for example 9.10.9.

**Solution :** By inspection , (*i*) the voltage drop across 2 Ω resistor is $2 \times 10 = 20$ V

(*ii*) the voltage of dependent voltage of source is $2 \times I = 2 \times 10 = 20$ V

Thus, no current flows through the 5 Ω resistor. The network takes the form as shown in Fig. 9.10.9 (*a*).

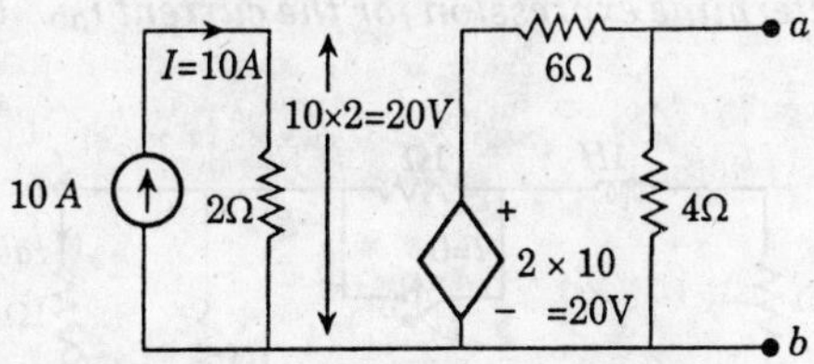

Fig. 9.10.9(*a*) Determination of $V_{th}$

$$V_{th} = V_{ab} = 20 \times \frac{4}{4+6} \qquad \text{By voltage division}$$

$$= 8 \text{ V}$$

To determine $R_{th}$, 10 A current source is set to zero (o /c), the network takes the form as shown in Fig. 9.10.9(b) below,

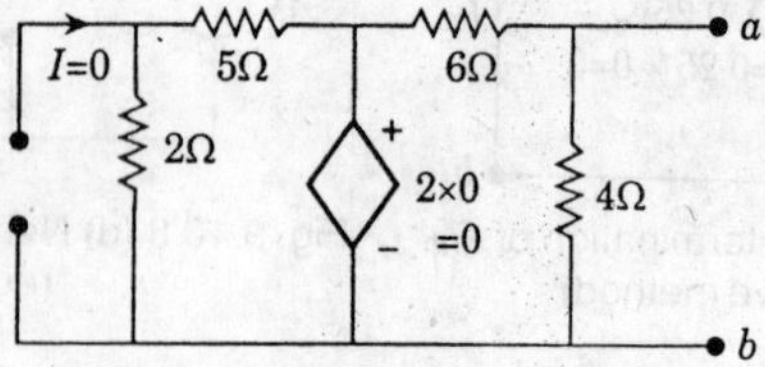


Fig. 9.10.9(b) Determination of $R_{th}$

The value of the dependent voltage source is zero. Therefore, the dependent voltage source is set to zero to get Fig. 9.10.9(c)

$$R_{th} = R_{ab} = \frac{6 \times 4}{6+4} = 2.4\ \Omega$$

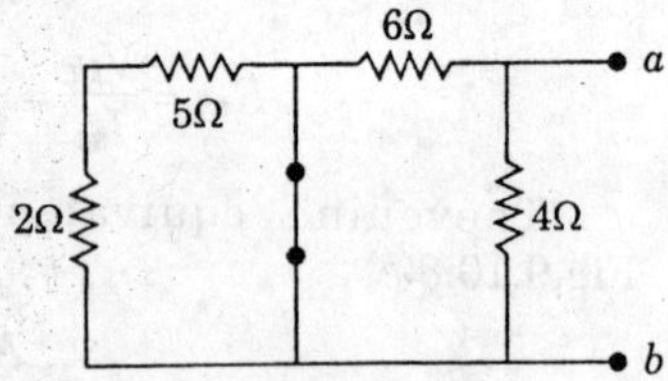


Fig. 9.10.9(c) Dependent source set to zero

Thevenin's equivalent network is shown in Fig. 9.10.9(d).

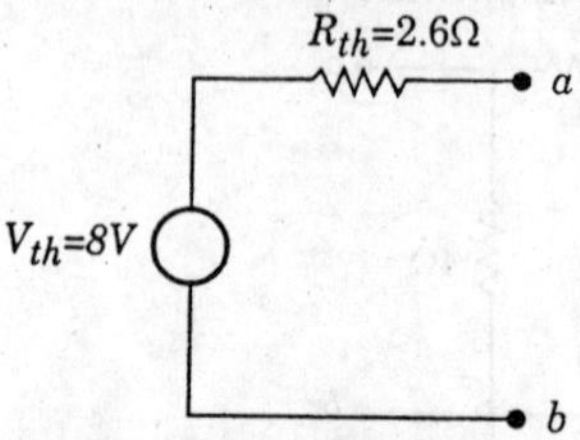


Fig. 9.10.9(d) Thevenin's equivalent network

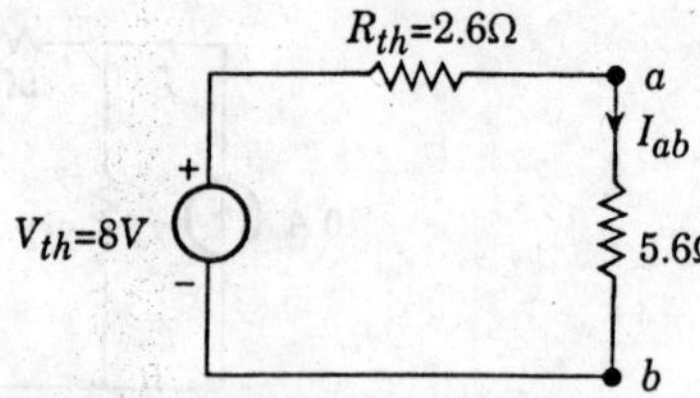


Fig. 9.10.9(e) 5.6 Ω resistor inserted between terminals a-b

$$I_{ab} = \frac{V_{th}}{R_{th} + 5.6}$$

$$= \frac{8}{2.4 + 5.6} = 1.0\text{ A} \qquad \text{...Ans.}$$

**Example . 9.10.10** *In the network shown below, The switch k is closed at t = 0. Determine expression for the current $i_{ab}$. Use Thevenin's theorem.*

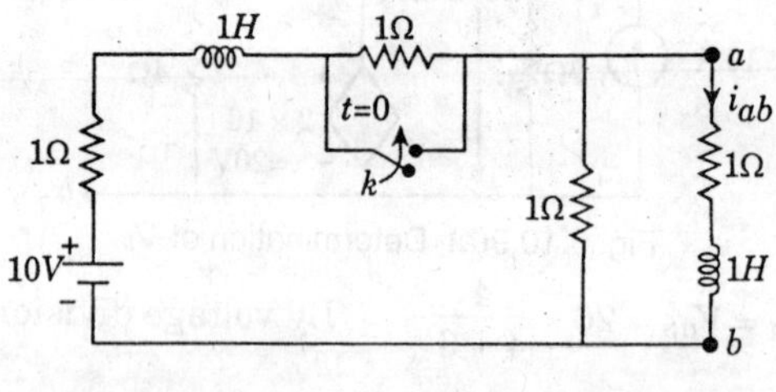


Fig. 9.10.10 Network for example 9.10.10

**Solution :** With switch $k$ open, under steady state condition the network is drawn as shown in Fig.9.10.10($a$)

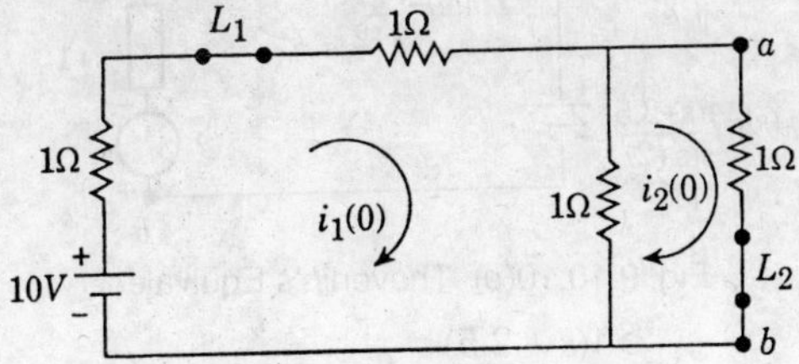


Fig. 9.10.10 ($a$) switch "$k$" closed.

$$i_1(0) = \frac{10}{1+1+\frac{1\times 1}{1+1}} = 4 \text{ A} \qquad i_1(0) = 4\times\frac{1}{1+1} = 2 \text{ A}$$

The transformed network for $t \geq 0$ is shown in Fig.9.10.10($b$)

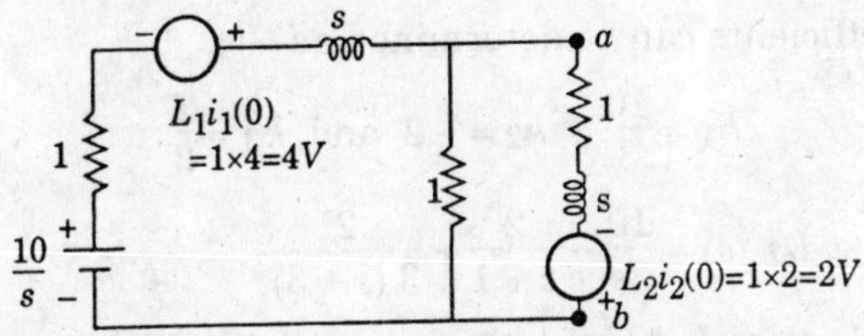


Fig. 9.10.10($b$) Transformed network.

Open circuit at terminals $a$-$b$ to get Fig. 9.10.10($c$)

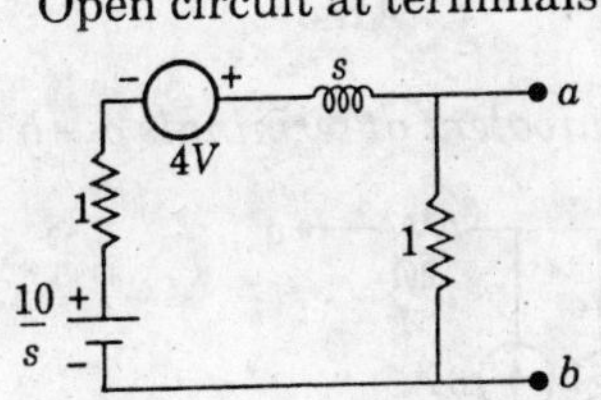


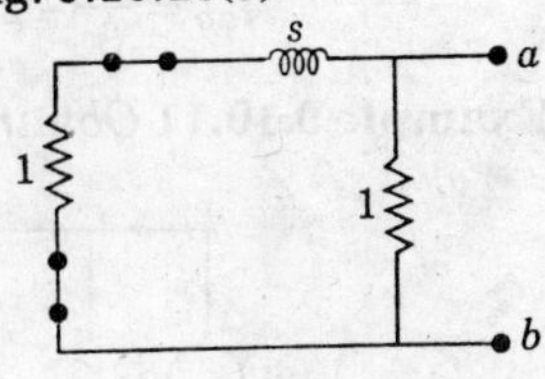


Fig. 9.10.10($c$) Determination of $V_{th}$ ($s$) Fig. 9.10.10($d$) Determination of $Z_{th}$ ($s$).

$$V_{th}(s) = V_{ab}(s) = \left(\frac{10}{s}+4\right)\times\frac{1}{s+1+1} \qquad \text{By voltage division}$$

$$= \frac{4(s+2.5)}{s\,(s+2)}$$

To determine $Z_{th}$ ($s$), set voltages to zero as shown in Fig. 9.10.10($d$)

$$Z_{th}\,(s) = \frac{1\times(s+1)}{1+(s+1)} = \frac{s+1}{s+2}$$

Thevenin's equivalent network with branch $a$-$b$ inserted is shown in Fig. 9.10.10($e$)

$$I_{ab}\,(s) = \frac{V_{th}\,(s)+2}{Z_{th}\,(s)+(s+1)}$$

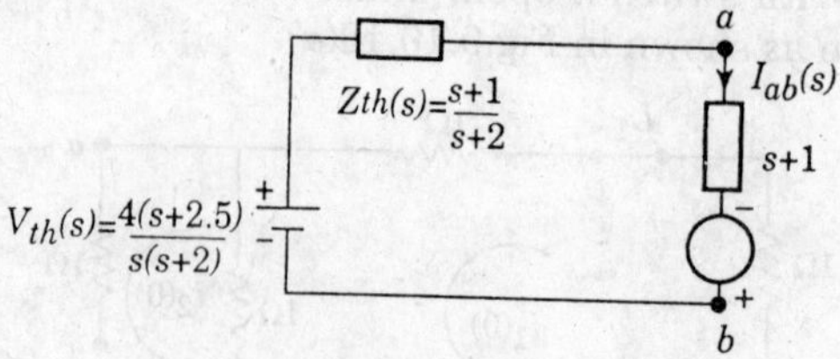


Fig. 9.10.10(*e*) Thevenin's Equivalent

$$= \frac{\frac{4(s+2.5)}{s(s+2)}+2}{\frac{(s+1)}{(s+2)}+(s+1)} = \frac{2s^2+8s+10}{s(s^2+4s+3)}$$

$$= \frac{k_1}{s} + \frac{k_2}{s+1} + \frac{k_3}{s+3}$$

The coefficients can be determined as

$$k_1 = \frac{10}{3}, \quad k_2 = -2 \text{ and } k_3 = \frac{2}{3}$$

$$\therefore \qquad I_{ab}(s) = \frac{10}{3s} - \frac{2}{s+1} + \frac{2}{3(s+3)}$$

Taking inverse Laplace transform on both sides,

$$i_{ab} = \frac{10}{3} - 2e^{-t} + \frac{2}{3}e^{-3t} \qquad \textbf{...Ans.}$$

**Example 9.10.11** *Obtain Norton's equivalent at terminals a – b.*

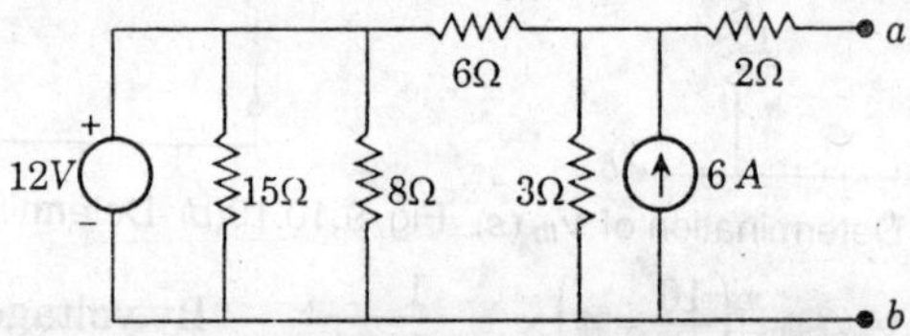


Fig. 9.10.11 Network for example 9.10.11.

**Solution :** As the 100V source is ideal (independent), the 15 Ω and 8Ω resistors will not affect the short circuit current through terminals *a* – *b*. Hence, the network in Fig. 9.10.11 is redrawn below [Fig. 9.10.11(*a*) ].

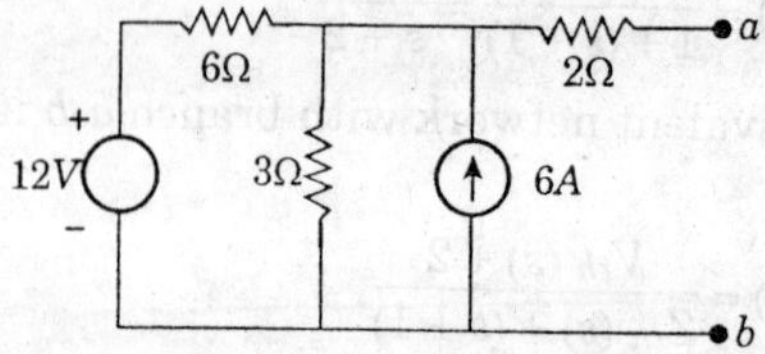


Fig. 9.10.11 (*a*) Network redrawn.

To determine Norton's $I_{eq}$, apply short circuit at terminals $a - b$ [Fig. 9.10.11 ($c$)]

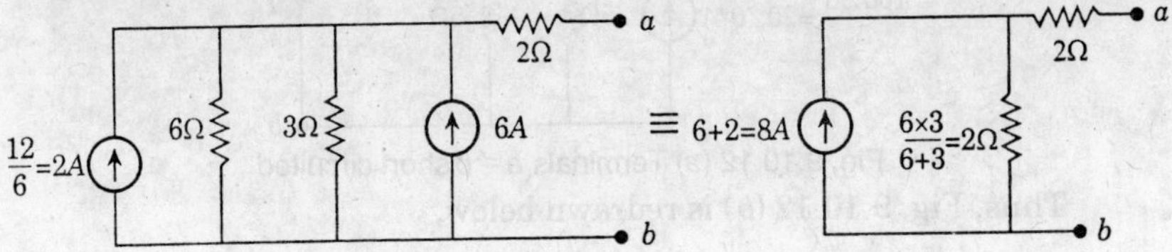


Fig. 9.10.11 ($b$) Determination of $I_{eq}$.

To determine $I_{eq}$ short circuit terminals $a - b$.

$$I_{eq} = I_{sc} = 8 \times \frac{2}{2+2}$$

$= 4A$ By current division

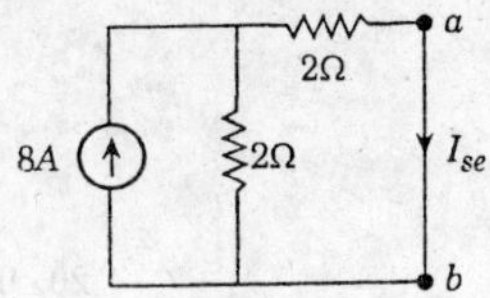


Fig. 9.10.11 ($c$) Determination of $I_{eq}$. (s/c a-b)

To determine $R_{eq}$ set 8A current source to zero as shown below [ Fig. 9.10.11 ($c$) ]

$$R_{eq} = R_{ab} = 2 + 2 = 4\ \Omega$$

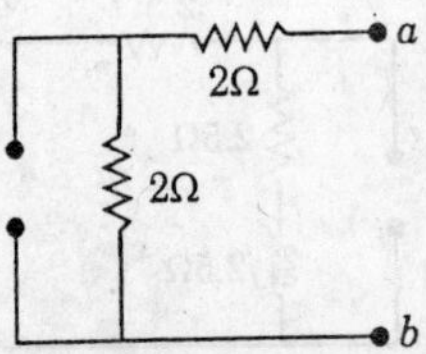


Fig. 9.10.11 ($d$) Determination of $R_{eq}$.

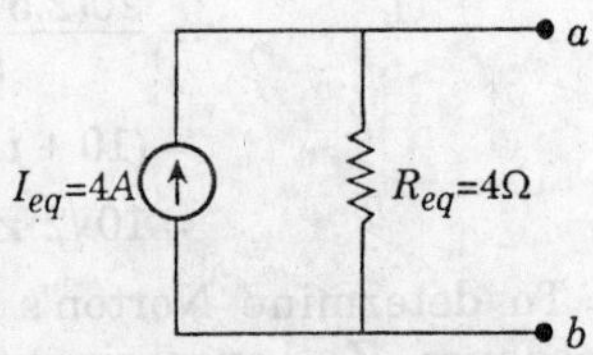


Fig. 9.10.11 ($e$) Norton's equivalent.

Norton's equivalent is shown in Fig. 9.10.11 ($e$)

**Example 9.10.12** *Obtain Norton's equivalent for the network shown below and determine the load current if the load impedance* $\mathbf{Z}_L = j\,5\ \Omega$

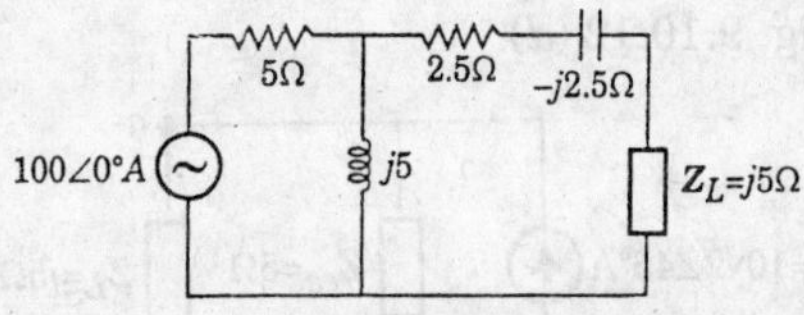


Fig. 9.10.12 Network for example 9.10.12

**Solution.** Remove load impedance $\mathbf{Z}_L$ and apply short circuit at terminals $a - b$ convert $100 \angle 0°\ V$ to equivalent current source as shown in Fig. 9.10.12 ($a$)

Combine 5 Ω and $j$ 5 in parallel

$$\mathbf{Z}' = \frac{j\,5 \times 5}{5 + j\,5} = \frac{25 \angle 90°}{5\sqrt{2} \angle 45°} = \frac{5}{\sqrt{2}} \angle 45° = (2.5 + j\,2.5)\ \Omega$$

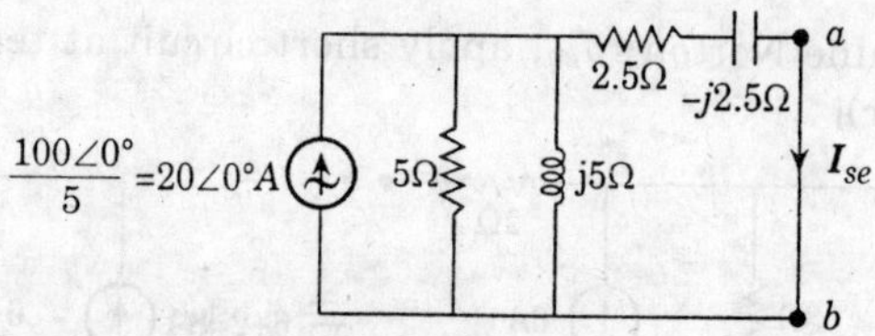


Fig. 9.10.12 (*a*) Terminals *a* – *b* short circuited

Thus, Fig. 9.10.12 (*b*) is redrawn below,

$$\mathbf{I}_{eq} = \mathbf{I}_{sc} = 20 \times \frac{2.5 + j\,2.5}{(2.5 + j\,2.5) + (2.5 - j\,2.5)}$$

By current division

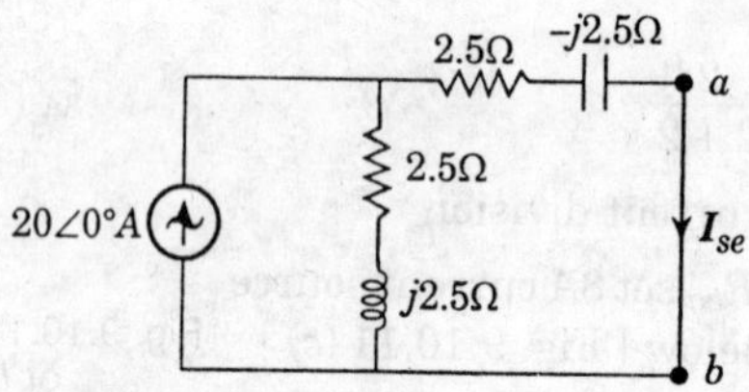


Fig. 9.10.12 (*b*) Determination of $I_{eq}$.

$$= \frac{20(2.5 + j\,2.5)}{5}$$

$$= (10 + j\,10)$$

$$= 10\sqrt{2} \angle 45° \text{ A}$$

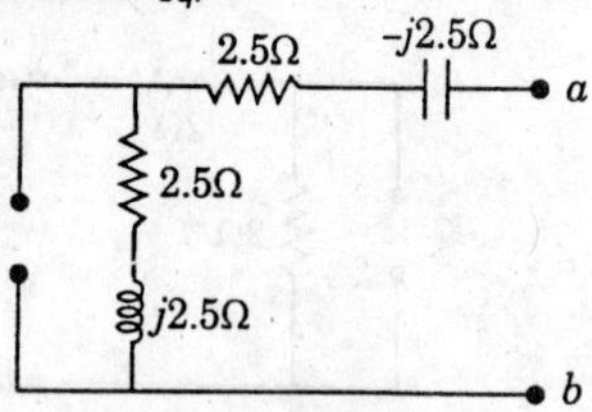


Fig. 9.10.12 (*c*) Determination of $\mathbf{Z}_{eq}$

To determine Norton's equivalent impedance, $\mathbf{Z}_{eq}$, open circuit terminals $a - b$ and set current source to zero (Fig. 9.10.11(*c*))

$$\mathbf{Z}_{eq} = \mathbf{Z}_{ab} = (2.5 - j\,2.5) + (2.5 + j\,2.5) = 5\Omega$$

Norton's equivalent with load impedance $\mathbf{Z}_L$ inserted at terminals $a - b$ is shown in Fig. 9.10.12 (*d*).

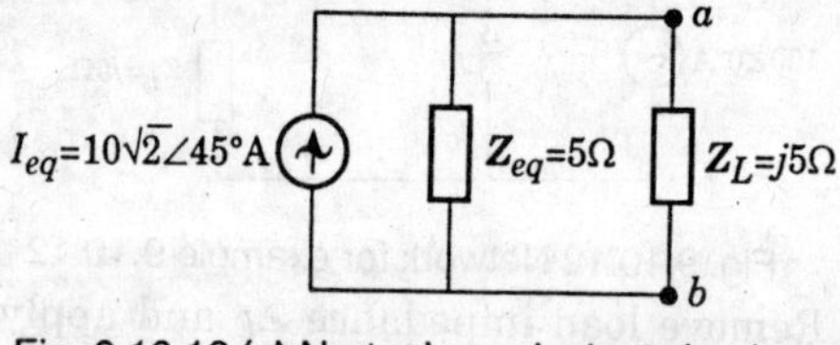


Fig. 9.10.12 (*d*) Norton's equivalent circuit.

$$\mathbf{I}ab = \mathbf{I}_{eq} \times \frac{\mathbf{Z}_{eq}}{\mathbf{Z}_{eq} + \mathbf{Z}_L} = 10\sqrt{2} \angle 45° \times \frac{5}{5 + j\,5}$$

$$= 10\sqrt{2} \angle 45° \times \frac{5}{5\sqrt{2}\angle 45°} = 10 \text{ A} \ldots \textbf{Ans.}$$

**Example . 9.10.13.** *Determine Thevenin's equivalent between terminals a – b for the network shown in Fig. 9.12.13.*

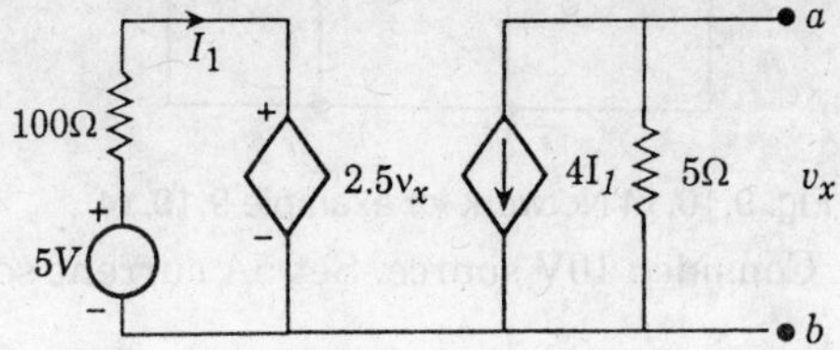


Fig. 9.10.13 Network for example 9.10.13.

**Solution :** Terminals $a - b$ being open circuit $V_{th} = V_x$

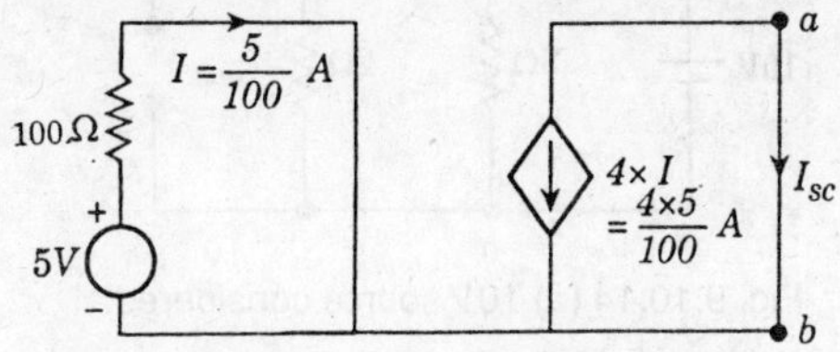


Fig. 9.10.13 (*a*) Determination of $R_{th}$.

Apply Kirchhoffs voltage law,

Loop 1 : $100\, I_1 + 2.5 V_x = 5$

Loop 2 : $V_x = 5(-4\, I)$

Put $V_x = V_{th}$ in above equtions,

$$100\, I_1 + 2.5\, V_{th} = 5 \quad ...(1)$$

$$V_{th} = -\, 20 I \quad ...(2)$$

Solving above equations,

$$V_{th} = -\, 2\ V$$

To determine $R_{th}$ short circuit terminals $a - b$. [Fig. 9.10.13 (a)]

The short circuit results in $V_x = 0$. Therefore, the value of 2.5 $V_x$ is zero. The network takes the form as below,

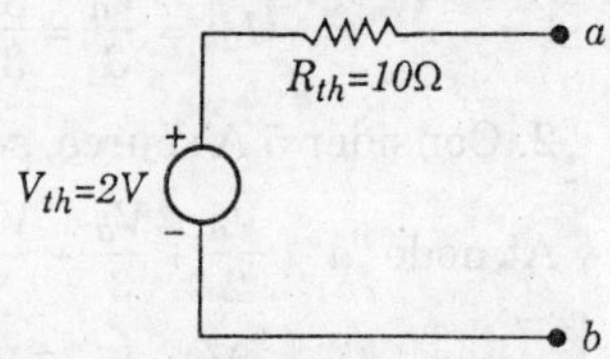


Fig. 9.10.13 (*b*) Thevenin's equivalent network.

$$I_{sc} = -\frac{4 \times 5}{100} = -\frac{1}{5} A \text{ flowing from } b \text{ to } a$$

$$R_{th} = \frac{V_{th}}{I_{sc}} = \frac{-\,2}{(-\,1/5)} = 10\ \Omega$$

Thevenin's equivalent is shown in Fig. 9.10.13 (*b*)

**...Ans.**

**Example 9.10.14.** *Use superposition theorem to determine the current $I_{ab}$ in the network given below.*

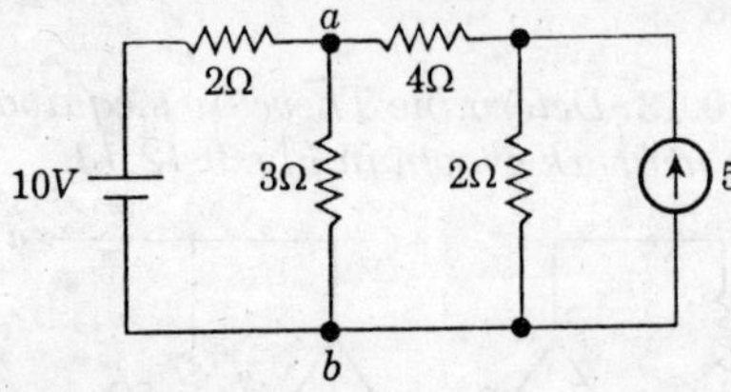


Fig. 9.10.14 Network for example 9.10.14

**Solution :** 1. Consider 10V source. Set 5$A$ current source to zero, *i.e.* open circuit

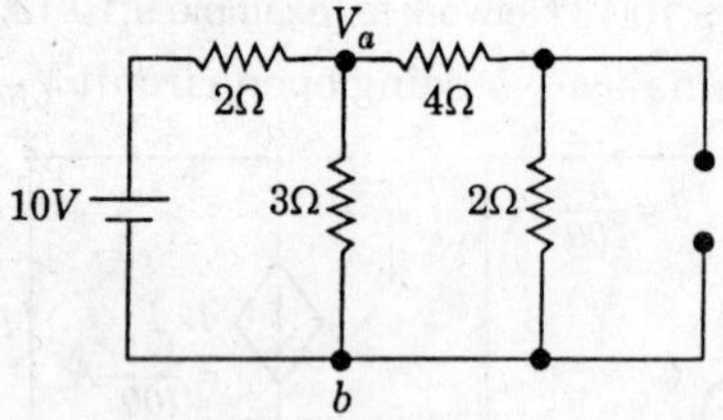


Fig. 9.10.14 (*a*) 10*V* source considered.

Apply node voltage aualysis

$$\frac{V_a - 10}{2} + \frac{V_a}{3} + \frac{V_a}{(4+2)} = 0$$

Rearranging.

$$\left(\frac{1}{2} + \frac{1}{3} + \frac{1}{6}\right)V_a = 5$$

$$\therefore \qquad V_a = 5$$

$${}^1I_{ab} = \frac{V_a}{3} = \frac{5}{3} \text{ A}$$

2. Consider 5 A source, set 10 V source to zero

At node "$a$" $\quad \dfrac{V_a}{2} + \dfrac{V_a}{3} + \dfrac{V_a - V_c}{4} = 0$

At node "$c$" $\quad \dfrac{V_c - V_a}{4} + \dfrac{V_c}{2} - 5 = 0$

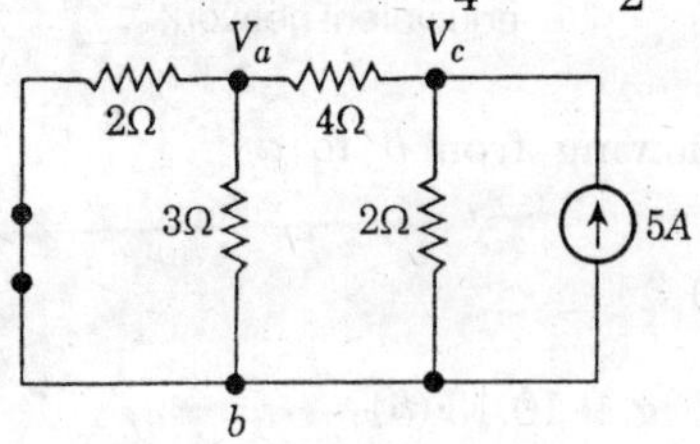


Fig. 9.10.14 (*b*) 5 *A* source considered.

Rearranging above equations,

$$\begin{vmatrix} \frac{13}{12} & -\frac{1}{4} \\ -\frac{1}{4} & \frac{3}{4} \end{vmatrix} \begin{vmatrix} V_a \\ V_c \end{vmatrix} = \begin{vmatrix} 0 \\ 5 \end{vmatrix}$$

$$V_a = \frac{\begin{vmatrix} 0 & -\frac{1}{4} \\ 5 & \frac{3}{4} \end{vmatrix}}{\begin{vmatrix} \frac{13}{12} & -\frac{1}{4} \\ -\frac{1}{4} & \frac{3}{4} \end{vmatrix}} = \frac{0 - 5\left(-\frac{1}{4}\right)}{\frac{13}{12} \times \frac{3}{4} - \left(-\frac{1}{4}\right)\left(-\frac{1}{4}\right)} = \frac{5}{3}\text{ V}$$

$$^2I_{ab} = \frac{V_a}{3} = \frac{5/3}{3} = \frac{5}{9}\text{ A}$$

$$\therefore \qquad I_{ab} = {}^1I_{ab} + {}^2I_{ab} = \frac{5}{3} + \frac{5}{9} = \frac{20}{9}\text{ A} \quad \ldots \textbf{ Ans.}$$

**Example . 9.10.15.** *Determine the current through j 10Ω inductor in the circuit given below. Apply superposition theorem.*

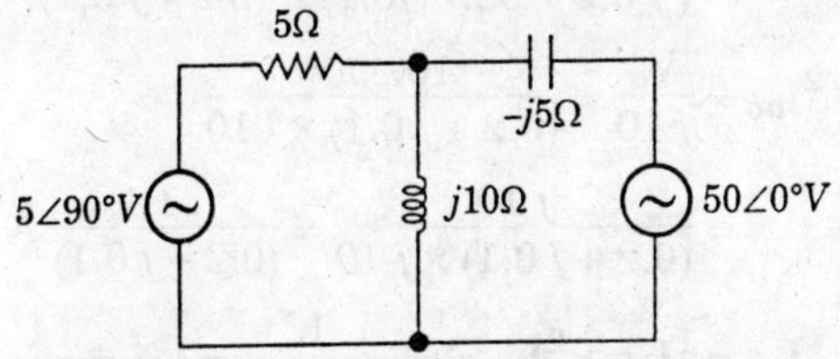


Fig. 9.10.15 Network for example 9.10.15.

1. Consider 50∠90*V* source. Set 50∠0°*V* to zero [ Fig. 9.10.15 (*a*) ]

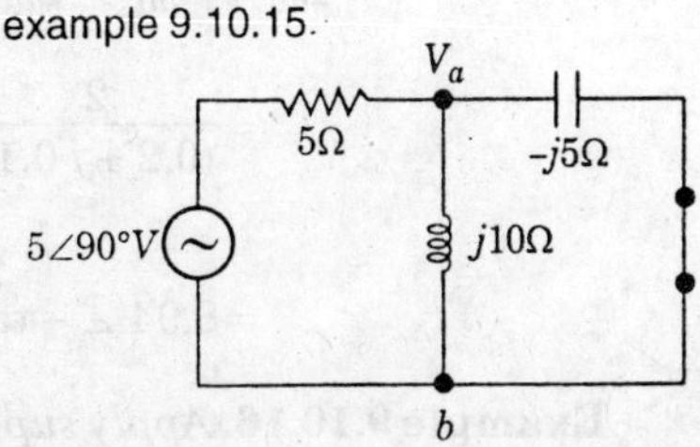


Fig. 9.10.15 (*a*) 5∠90° *V* source considered

Apply Kirchhoff's current law at node "*a*"

$$\frac{\mathbf{V}_a - 50\angle 90^\circ}{5} + \frac{\mathbf{V}_a}{j\,10} + \frac{\mathbf{V}_a}{-j\,5} = 0$$

Rearranging,

$$\mathbf{V}_a \left(\frac{1}{5} + \frac{1}{j}\,10 + \frac{1}{-j\,5}\right) = 10\angle 90^\circ$$

or $\quad \mathbf{V}_a\,(0.2 - j\,0.1 + j\,0.2) = 10\angle 90^\circ$

$$\therefore \qquad \mathbf{V}_a = \frac{10\angle 90^\circ}{(0.2 - j\,0.1 + j\,0.2)} = \frac{10\angle 90^\circ}{(0.2 + j\,0.1)}$$

$$^1\mathbf{I}_{ab} = \frac{\mathbf{V}_a}{j10} = \frac{10\angle 90^\circ}{(0.2 + j\,0.1) \times j\,10}$$

$$= \frac{j\,10}{(0.2 + j\,0.1) \times j\,10} = \frac{1}{(0.2 + j\,0.1)}\text{ A}$$

2. Consider 50∠0°*V* source. Set 50∠90°*V* source to zero. Fig. 9.10.15 (*b*)

Apply Kirchhoffi current law at node "$a$"

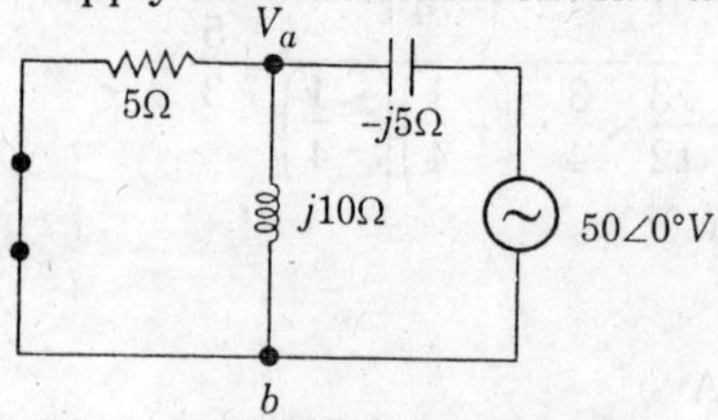


Fig. 9.10.15 (*b*) 50∠0° *V* source considered

$$\frac{\mathbf{V}_a - 50\angle 0^\circ}{-j\,5} + \frac{\mathbf{V}_a}{5} + \frac{\mathbf{V}_a}{j\,10} = 0$$

Rearranging,

$$\mathbf{V}_a\left(\frac{1}{-j\,5} + \frac{1}{5} + \frac{1}{j\,10}\right) = \frac{50\angle 0^\circ}{-j\,5} = j\,10$$

or

$$\mathbf{V}_a\,(j\,0.2 + 0.2 - j\,0.1) = 10\angle 90^\circ$$

$$\mathbf{V}_a = \frac{10\angle 90^\circ}{(j\,0.2 + 0.2 - j0.1)} = \frac{10\angle 90^\circ}{(0.2 + j\,0.1)}$$

$$^2\mathbf{I}_{ab} = \frac{\mathbf{V}_a}{j\,10} = \frac{10\angle 90^\circ}{(0.2 + j\,0.1) \times j\,10}$$

$$= \frac{j\,10}{(0.2 + j\,0.1) \times j\,10} = \frac{1}{(0.2 + j\,0.1)}\text{ A}$$

$$\mathbf{I}_{ab} = {}^1\mathbf{I}_{ab} + {}^2\mathbf{I}_{ab} = \frac{1}{(0.2 + j\,0.1)} + \frac{1}{(0.2 + j\,0.1)}$$

$$= \frac{2}{(0.2 + j\,0.1)} = \frac{2}{\sqrt{0.2^2 + 0.1^2}\ \angle \tan^{-1}\left(\frac{0.1}{0.2}\right)}$$

$$= 8.94\ \angle -\tan^{-1}\left(\frac{0.1}{0.2}\right) = 8.94\ \angle -26.56^\circ\text{ A} \ldots \textbf{Ans.}$$

**Example 9.10.16.** *Apply superposition theorem to determine $V_{xy}$ in the circuit shown in Fig. 9.10.16.*

**Solution.** The presence of 3V Voltage source in series with current source does not affect the value of 5 A current source. The circuit takes the form as shown in Fig. 9.10.16(*a*).

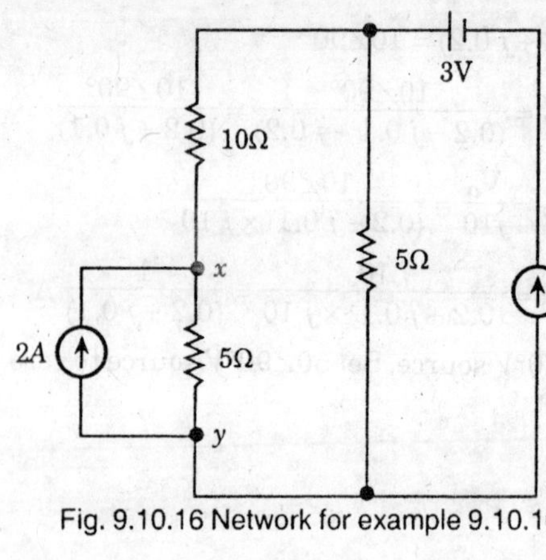


Fig. 9.10.16 Network for example 9.10.16.

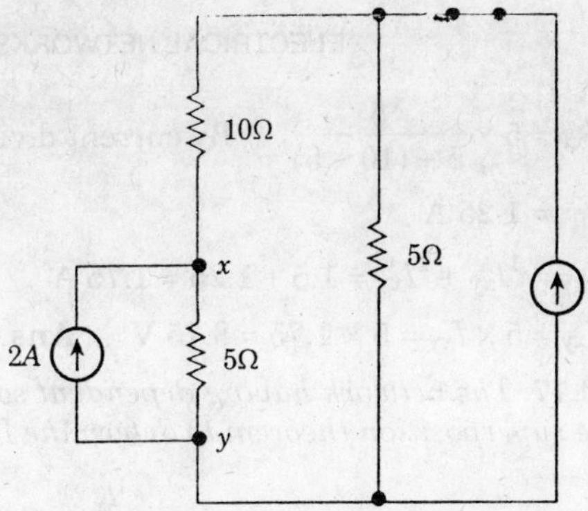


Fig. 9.10.16 (*a*) Network redrawn

1. Consider 2A current source. Set 5 A current source to zero *i.e.* open circuit [Fig. 9.10.16 (*b*)]

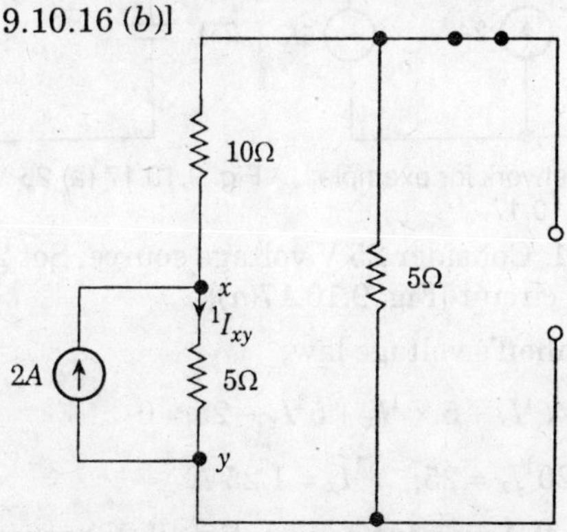


Fig. 9.10.16 (*b*) 2 *A* source considered.

$$^1I_{xy} = 2 \times \frac{(10+5)}{(10+5)+5} \qquad \text{By current division.} = 1.5 \text{ A}$$

2. Consider 5 A current source. Set 2 A current source to zero *i.e.* open circuit [Fig. 9.10.16 (*c*)]

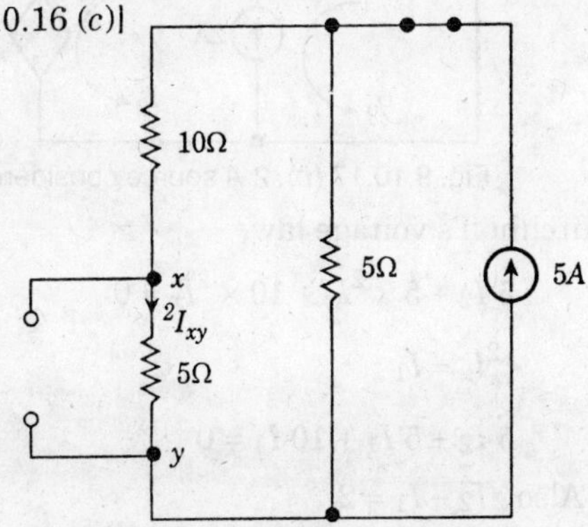


Fig. 9.10.16(c). 5*A* source considered.

$$^2I_{xy} = 5 \times \frac{5}{5 + (10 + 5)} \quad \text{By current division.}$$

$$= 1.25 \text{ A}$$

$$I_{xy} = {}^1I_{xy} + {}^2I_{xy} = 1.5 + 1.25 = 1.75 \text{ A}$$

$$V_{xy} = 5 \times I_{xy} = 5 \times 1.75 = 8.75 \text{ V} \quad \textbf{... Ans.}$$

**Example 9.10.17.** *The network having dependent source is shown in Fig. 9.10.17. Use superposition theorem to determine $I_x$.*

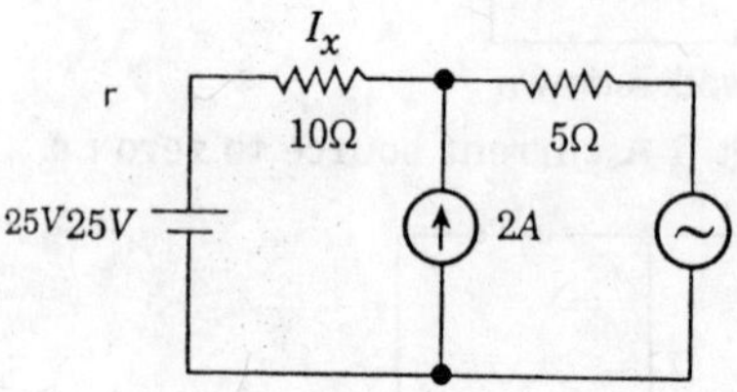


Fig. 9.10.17 Network for example 9.10.17.

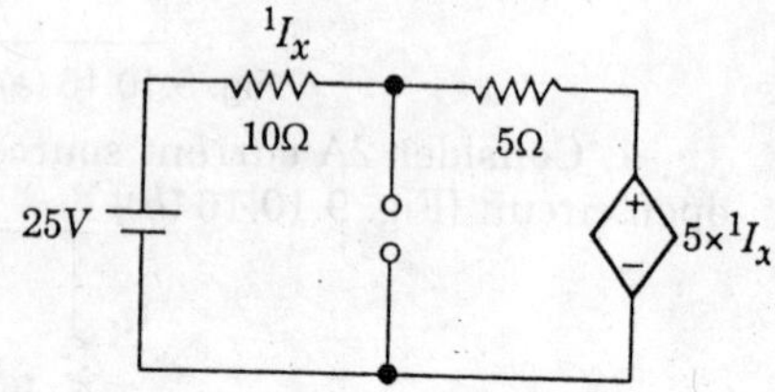


Fig. 9.10.17 (*a*) 25 *V* source considered.

**Solution :** 1. Consider 25 V voltage source. Set 2 A current source to zero *i.e.* open circuit [Fig. 9.10.17(*a*)]

Apply Kirchhoff's voltage law,

$$10 \times {}^1I_x + 5 \times {}^1I_x + 5\,{}^1I_x - 25 = 0$$

or $\quad 20\,{}^1I_x = 25, \quad {}^1I_x = 1.25 \text{ A}$

2. Consider 2 A current source. Set 25 V source to zero *i.e.* short circuit [Fig. 9.10.17(*b*)]

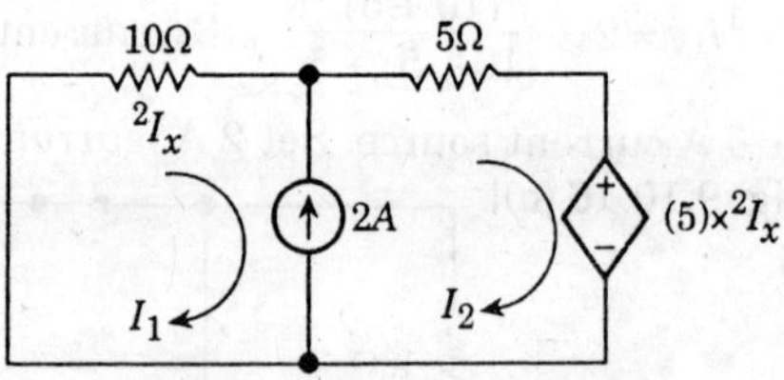


Fig. 9.10.17 (*b*). 2 *A* source considered.

Apply Kirchhoff's voltage law,

$$5\,I_2 + 5 \times {}^2I_x + 10 \times {}^2I_x = 0$$

$\because \quad {}^2I_x = I_1$

$\therefore \quad 5\,I_2 + 5\,I_1 + 10\,I_1 = 0 \quad \text{...(1)}$

Also $\quad I_2 - I_1 = 2 \quad \text{...(2)}$

Solving Eqns. (1) and (2)

$$I_1 = -\,0.5\,, \quad \therefore \quad {}^2I_x = -\,0.5$$

$$I_x = {}^1I_x + {}^2I_x = 1.25 + (-0.5) = 0.75\ A \ \dots \textbf{Ans.}$$

**Example 9.10.18.** *Determine the maximum power transfer to $R_L$ in the network shown below.*

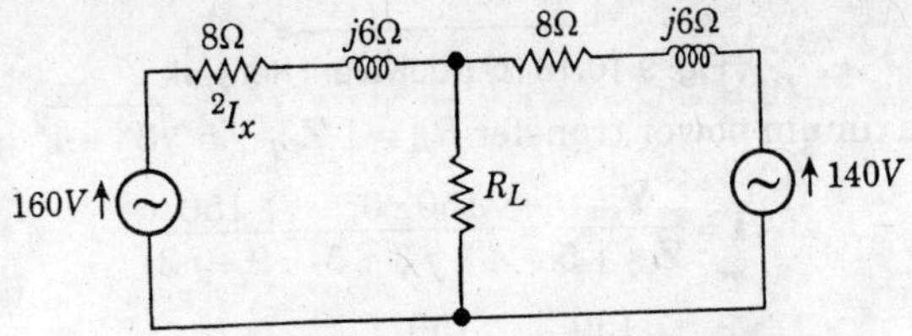


Fig. 9.10.18 Network for example 9.10.18.

**Solution :** Remove $R_L$ to obtain the network drawn below.

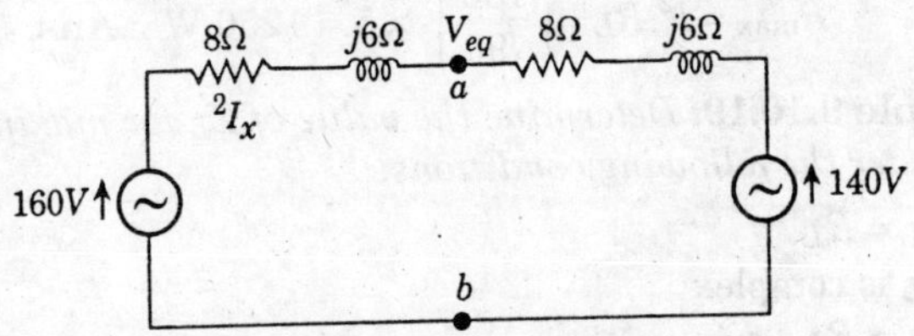


Fig. 9.10.18 (*a*) Network redrawn.

Apply node voltage analysis to determine

$\mathbf{V}_{eq}$ (*o/c* voltage between terminals $a-b$).

$$\frac{\mathbf{V}_{eq} - 160}{8 + j\,6} + \frac{\mathbf{V}eq - 140}{8 + j\,6} = 0$$

$$\therefore \quad \mathbf{V}_{eq}\left(\frac{1}{8 + j\,6} + \frac{1}{8 + j\,6}\right) = \frac{300}{8 + j\,6}$$

$$\therefore \quad \mathbf{V}_{eq} = 150 \angle 0°\ V$$

To determine $\mathbf{Z}_{eq}$ set voltage sources to zero in Fig. 9.10.18 (*b*) Thus,

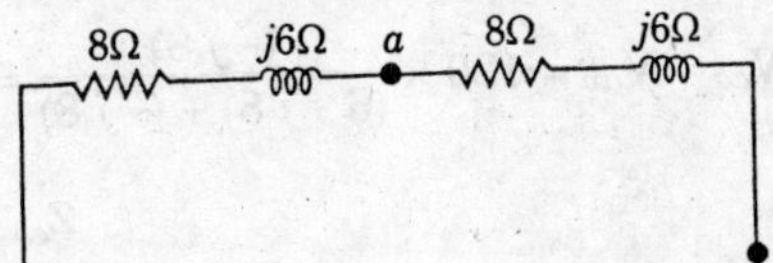


Fig. 9.10.18.(*b*) Determination of **Z** *eq*.

$$\mathbf{Z}_{eq} = \mathbf{Z}_{ab} = \frac{(8 + j\,6)\,(8 + j\,6)}{(8 + j\,6) + (8 + j\,6)}$$

$$= \frac{(8 + j\,6)\,(8 + j\,6)}{2\,(8 + j\,6)} = 4 + j\,3$$

The equivalent network across terminals $a - b$ is drawn below,

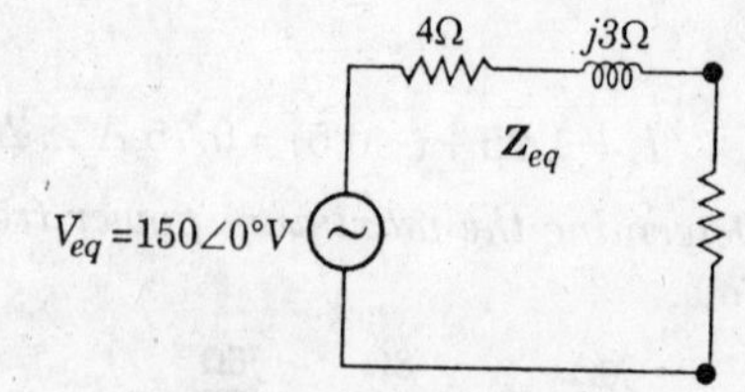


Fig. 9.10.18 (*c*) Equivalent network

For maximum power transfer $R_L = |\ \mathbf{Z}_{eq}\ | = \sqrt{3^2 + 4^2} = 5\ \Omega$

$$\mathbf{I} = \frac{\mathbf{V}_{eq}}{\mathbf{Z}_{eq} + 5} = \frac{150\angle 0°}{4 + j\,3 + 5} = \frac{150}{9 + j\,3}$$

$$\therefore \qquad I = \frac{150}{\sqrt{9^2 + 3^2}} = \frac{150}{\sqrt{90}}\ \text{A}$$

$$P_{\max} = I^2 R_L = \left(\frac{150}{\sqrt{90}}\right)^2 \times 5 = 1250\ \text{W} \ \textbf{...Ans.}$$

**Example 9.10.19.** *Determine the value of* $\mathbf{Z}_L$ *for maximum power transfer under the following conditions.*

(*a*) $\mathbf{Z}_L = R_L$

(*b*) $\mathbf{Z}_L$ is complex

(*c*) $\mathbf{Z}_L = R_L + j\,4$

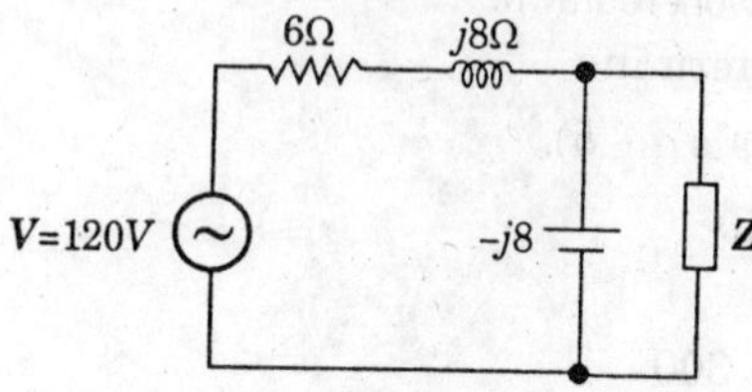


Fig. 9.10.19 Network for example 9.10.19

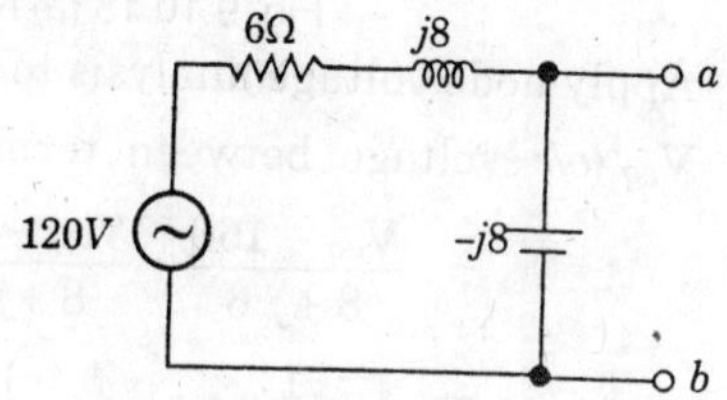


Fig. 9.10.19 (*a*) Impedance $\mathbf{Z}_L$ removed.

Determine the value of maximum power in each case.

Remove $\mathbf{Z}_L$ to obtain Fig. 9.10.19 (*a*)

$$\mathbf{V}_{eq} = \mathbf{V}_{ab} = 120 \times \frac{(-j\,8)}{(6 + j\,8) + (-j\,8)} = -j\,160\ \text{V}$$

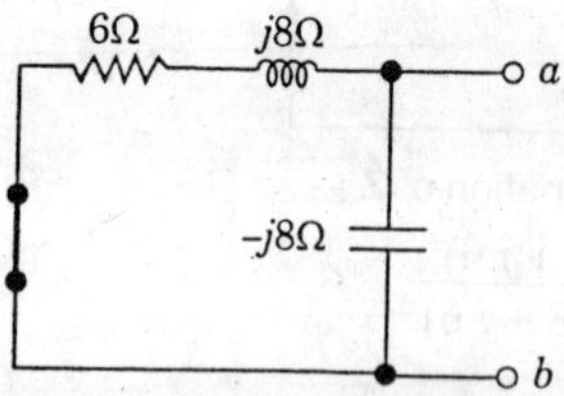


Fig. 9.10.19 (*b*) Determination of $\mathbf{Z}_{eq}$.

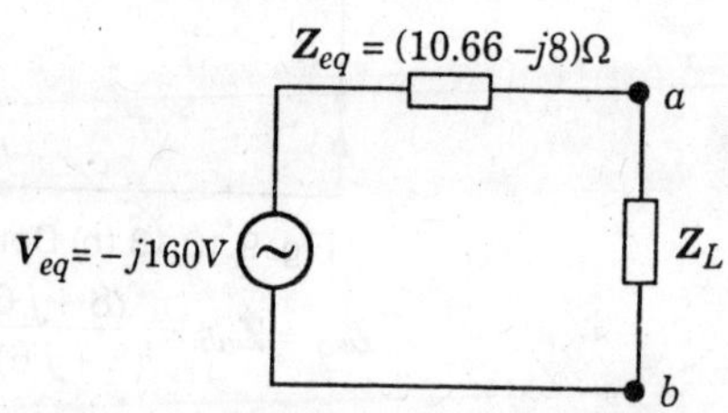


Fig. 9.10.19 (*c*) Equivalent network

To determine $\mathbf{Z}_{eq} = \mathbf{Z}_{ab}$ set voltage source to zero, as shown in Fig. 9.10.19 (*b*).

$$\mathbf{Z}_{eq} = \frac{(6 + j\,8)\,(-j\,8)}{(6 + j\,8) + (-j\,8)} = (10.66 - j\,8)\ \Omega$$

The equivalent network with $\mathbf{Z}_L$ connected across terminals $a - b$ is shown in Fig. 9.10.19 (*c*).

(*a*) $\mathbf{Z}_L = R_L$

For maximum power transfer

$$R_L = |\,\mathbf{Z}_{eq}\,|$$

$$= \sqrt{10.66^2 + 8^2} = 13.32\ \Omega \text{ ...}\textbf{Ans.}$$

$$I = \left|\frac{-j\,160}{(10.66 - j\,8) + 13.32}\right| = \left|\frac{-j\,160}{23.98 - j\,8}\right|$$

$$= \frac{160}{\sqrt{23.98^2 + 8^2}} = 6.33\text{ A}$$

$$P_{\max} = I^2 R_L$$

$$= (6.33)^2 \times 13.32 = 533.7\text{ W} \quad \text{...}\textbf{Ans.}$$

(*b*) For max. power $\mathbf{Z}_L = \mathbf{Z}_{eq}^* = (10.66 + j\,8)\Omega$ ...**Ans.**

$$I = \left|\frac{j\,160}{(10.66 - j\,8) + 10.66 - j\,8}\right|$$

$$= \frac{160}{2 \times 10.66} = \frac{80}{10.66}\text{ A}$$

$$P_{\max} = I^2\,R_L$$

$$= \left(\frac{80}{10.66}\right)^2 \times 10.66 = 600.3\text{W} \text{ ...}\textbf{Ans.}$$

or $$P_{\max} = \frac{V^2}{4\,R_L} = \frac{160^2}{4 \times 10.66} = 600.3\text{ W}$$

(*c*) For max. power $R_L = |\,\mathbf{Z}_{eq} + j\,4\,|$

$$\therefore \quad R_L = |\,10.66 - j\,8 + j\,4\,| = |\,10.66 - j\,4\,|$$

$$= \sqrt{10.66^2 + 4^2} = 11.38\ \Omega \text{ ... }\textbf{Ans.}$$

$$\therefore \quad Z_L = 13.38 + j\,4$$

$$I = \left|\frac{-j\,160}{10.66 - j8 + 13.38 + j\,4}\right| = \left|\frac{-j\,160}{24.04 - j4}\right|$$

$$= \frac{160}{\sqrt{24.04^2 + 4^2}} = \frac{160}{24.37}\text{ A}$$

$$P_{max} = I^2 R_L = \left(\frac{160}{24.37}\right)^2 \times 11.38 = 490.5 \text{ W ... \textbf{Ans.}}$$

**Example . 9.10.20.** *Determine the value of $R_L$ for maximum power flow with reference to network (Fig. 9.10.20)*

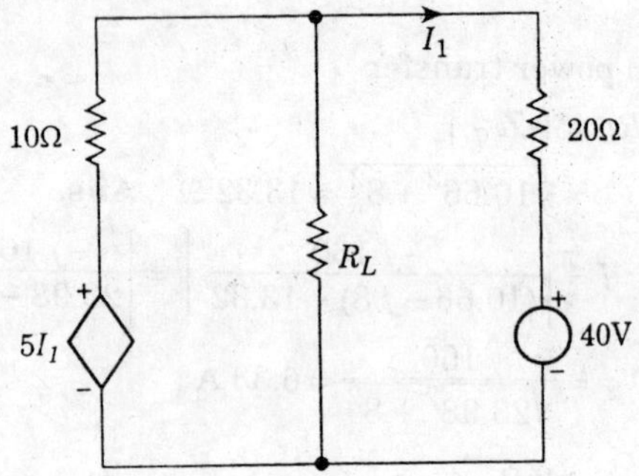


Fig. 9.10.20 Network for example 9.10.20.

**Solution :** Remove $R_L$ to obtain Fig. 9.10.20(*a*)

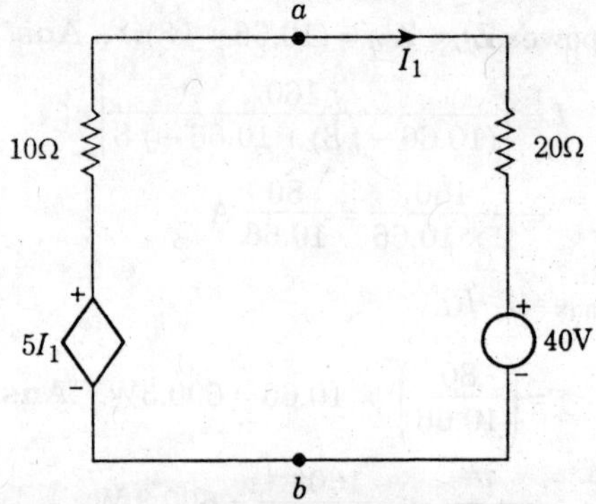


Fig. 9.10.20 (*a*). $R_L$ removed.

Apply Kirchhoff's voltage law

$$-5 I_1 + 10 I_1 + 20 I_1 + 40 = 0$$

or $$25 I_1 = -40$$

$\therefore$ $$I_1 = -1.6 \text{ A}$$

$$V_{eq} = V_{ab} = 5 I_1 - 10 I_1$$

$$= 5(-1.6) - 10(-1.6) = 8 \text{ V}$$

Apply short circuit at terminals $a - b$ ( Fig. 9.10.20 (*b*)

Apply Kirchhoff's voltage law,

Loop 1 : $20 I_1 + 40 = 0$

Loop 2 : $10 I_2 - 5 I_1 = 0$

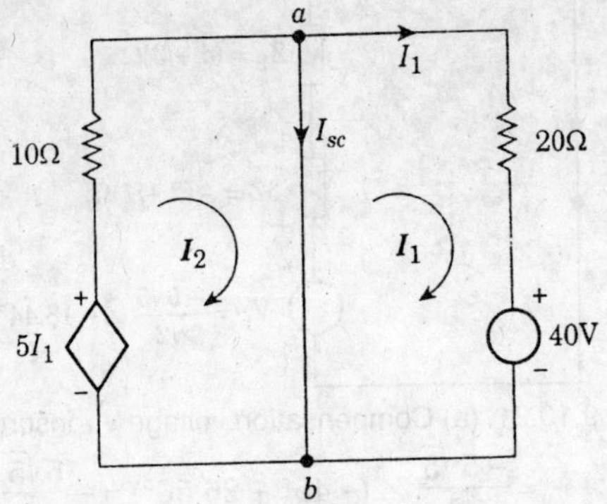


Fig. 9.10.20 (*b*) Short-circuit applied at terminals *a* – *b*.

Solving, $I_1 = -2\text{A}$

$I_2 = -1\text{ A} \quad , \quad I_{sc} = I_2 - I_1 = -1 - (-2) = 1\text{ A}$

$$\therefore \quad R_{eq} = \frac{V_{eq}}{I_{sc}} = \frac{8}{1} = 8\ \Omega$$

For maximum power transfer to $R_L$

$$R_L = R_{eq} = 8\ \Omega$$

**Example . 9.10.21.** *Use compensation theorem to determine the change in current when the impedance* $\mathbf{Z}_2$ *is changed to* $(2 + j\,2)\ \Omega$.

**Solution:** 1. $\mathbf{I} = \dfrac{25 \angle 0°}{(1 + j\,2) + (4 + j\,3)} = \dfrac{25}{5 + j\,5}$

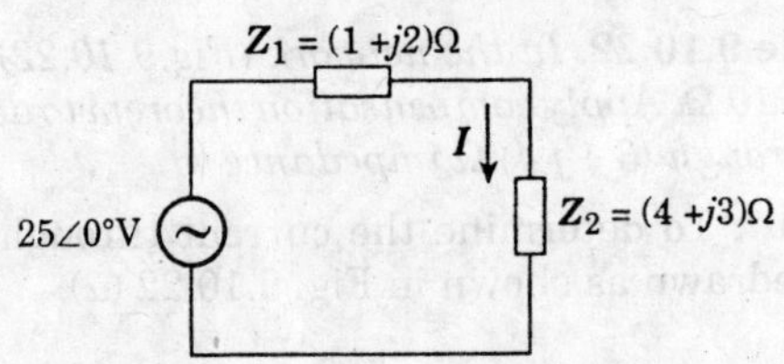


Fig. 9.10.21 Network for example 9.10.21.

$$= \frac{25}{\sqrt{5^2 + 5^2} \angle \tan^{-1}(5/5)}$$

$$= \frac{25}{5\sqrt{2}} \angle -45° = \frac{5}{\sqrt{2}} \angle -45°\text{ A}$$

2. $\delta\,\mathbf{Z} = (2 + j\,2) - (4 + j\,3) = -(2 + j\,1)\ \Omega$

3. $\mathbf{V}_c = \mathbf{I}\,\delta\,\mathbf{Z} = \dfrac{5\angle -45°}{\sqrt{2}} \times -(2 + j\,1)$

$$= -\frac{5\angle -45°}{\sqrt{2}} \times \sqrt{2^2 + 1^2} \angle \tan^{-1}(1/2)$$

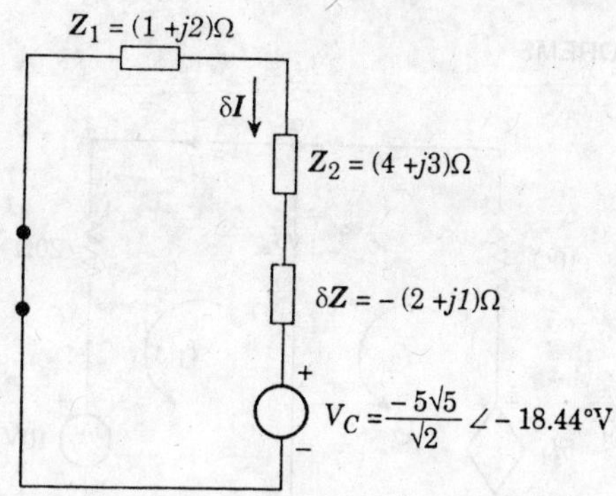


Fig. 9.10.21. (a) Compensation voltage $V_C$ inserted

$$= \frac{-5\sqrt{5}}{\sqrt{2}} \angle (-45° + 26.56°) = -\frac{5\sqrt{5}}{\sqrt{2}} \angle -18.44° \text{ V}$$

4. Set $25 \angle 0°$ *V* source to zero and insert $\mathbf{V}_c$ as shown in Fig. 9.10.21

Apply Kirchhoff's voltage law,

$$(1 + j\,2)\,\delta\,\mathbf{I} + (4 + j\,3)\,\delta\,\mathbf{I} - (2 + j\,1)\,\delta\,\mathbf{I} + \left(-\frac{5\sqrt{5}}{\sqrt{2}} \angle -18.44°\right) = 0$$

$$\therefore \qquad \delta\,\mathbf{I} = \frac{5\sqrt{5}}{\sqrt{2}} \angle -18.44° \times \frac{1}{3 + j\,4}$$

$$= 7.94 \angle -18.44° \times \frac{1}{\sqrt{3^2 + 4^2} \angle \tan^{-1}(4/3)}$$

$$= 7.94 \angle -18.44° \times \frac{1}{5 \angle 53.13°}$$

$$= 1.58 \angle -71.57° \text{ A}$$ **Ans.**

**Example 9.10.22.** *In the network (Fig.9.10.22), the resistance 5 Ω is changed to 10 Ω. Apply compensation theorem to determine the change in current through (3 + j 4) Ω impedance*

**Solution :** To determine the current through 5Ω resistance the network is redrawn as shown in Fig. 9.10.22 (*a*).

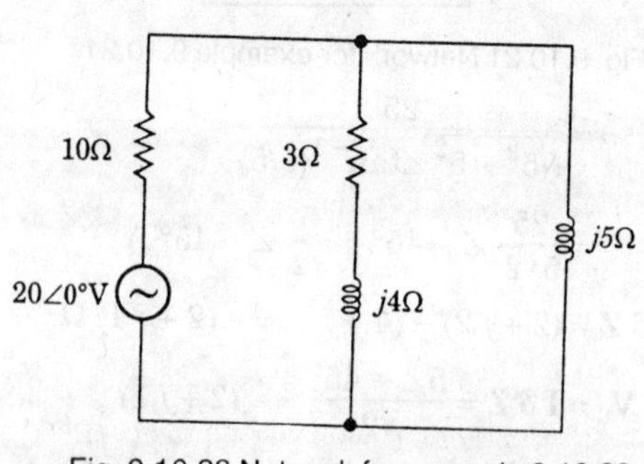


Fig. 9.10.22 Network for example 9.10.22.

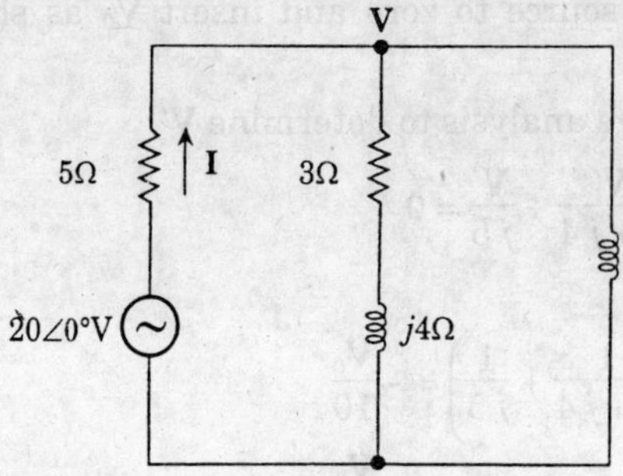


Fig. 9.10.22 (*a*) Network redrawn

Apply node voltage analysis to determine **V**

$$\frac{\mathbf{V} - 20\angle 0°}{5} + \frac{\mathbf{V}}{3 + j\,4} + \frac{\mathbf{V}}{j\,5} = 0$$

$$\therefore \quad \mathbf{V}\left(\frac{1}{5} + \frac{1}{3 + j\,4} + \frac{1}{j\,5}\right) = \frac{20}{5}$$

or $$\mathbf{V}\,(0.2 + 0.12 - j\,0.16 - j\,0.2) = 4$$

or $$\mathbf{V} = \frac{4}{0.32 - j0.36} = \frac{4}{\sqrt{0.32^2 + 0.36^2}\ \angle -\tan^{-1}(0.36/0.32)}$$

$$= \frac{4}{0.481\angle -48.36°} = 8.316\angle 48.36°\ V$$

1. $$\mathbf{I} = \frac{10 - \mathbf{V}}{5}$$

$$= \frac{10 - 8.316\angle 48.36°}{5} = 2 - 1.663\angle 48.36°$$

$$= 2 - 1.663\,(\cos 48.36° + j\sin 48.36°)$$

$$= 2 - 1.663\,(0.664 + j\,0.747)$$

$$= (2.896 - j\,1.242) = 3.15\angle -23.21°\ \text{A}$$

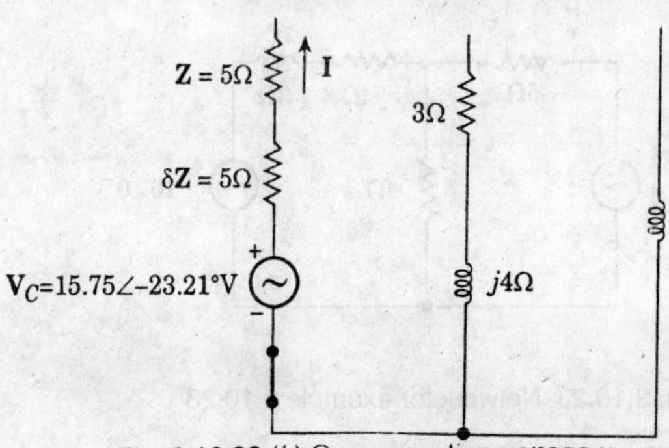


Fig. 9.10.22 (*b*) Compensation voltage **v** *c* inserted.

2. $\delta \mathbf{Z} = (10 - 5) = 5\ \Omega$

3. $\mathbf{V}_c = \mathbf{I}\,\delta \mathbf{Z} = 3.15 \angle -23.21° \times 5 = 15.75 \angle -23.21°$ V

4. Set $20 \angle 0°$ V source to zero and insert $\mathbf{V}_c$ as shown in Fig. 9.10.22(b)

Apply node voltage analysis to determine $\mathbf{V}'$

$$\frac{\mathbf{V}' + \mathbf{V}_c}{5 + 5} + \frac{\mathbf{V}'}{3 + j4} + \frac{\mathbf{V}'}{j5} = 0$$

Rearranging,

$$\mathbf{V}'\left(\frac{1}{10} + \frac{1}{3 + j4} + \frac{1}{j5}\right) = -\frac{\mathbf{V}_c}{10}$$

or $\mathbf{V}'(0.1 + 0.12 - j\,0.16 - j\,0.2) = -\dfrac{\mathbf{V}_c}{10}$

or $$\mathbf{V}'(0.22 - j\,0.36) = -\frac{\mathbf{V}_c}{10}$$

$\therefore$ $$\mathbf{V}' = -\frac{\mathbf{V}_c}{10\,(0.22 - j\,0.36)}$$

$$= -\frac{15.75 \angle -23.21°}{10 \times \sqrt{0.22^2 + 0.36^2} \angle -\tan^{-1}(0.36/0.22)}$$

$$= -\frac{1.575 \angle -23.21°}{0.421 \angle -58.5°} = -3.73 \angle 35.29° \text{ V}$$

$$\delta \mathbf{I} = \frac{\mathbf{V}'}{(3 + j4)} = -\frac{3.73 \angle 35.29°}{\sqrt{3^2 + 4^2} \angle \tan^{-1}(4/3)}$$

$$= -\frac{3.73 \angle 35.29°}{5 \angle 53.13°} = -0.746 \angle -17.84° \text{ A} \ldots \textbf{Ans.}$$

**Example 9.10.23.** *Use Millman's theorem to determine the current through 4Ω resistance.*

**Solution:** On removing 4 Ω resistance, the circuit is redrawn as shown in Fig. 9.10.23 (*a*)

As per Millman's theorem

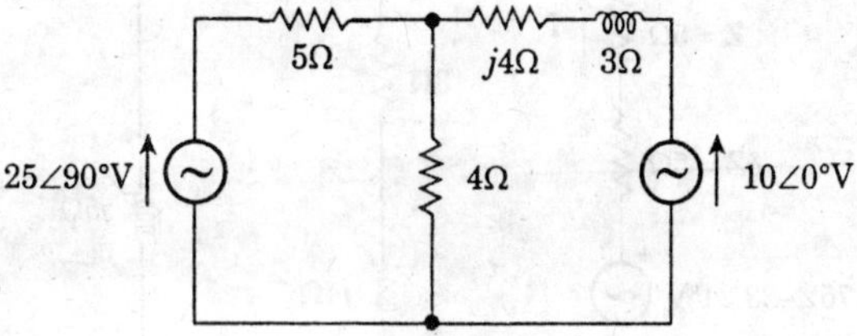


Fig. 9.10.23. Network for example 9.10.23

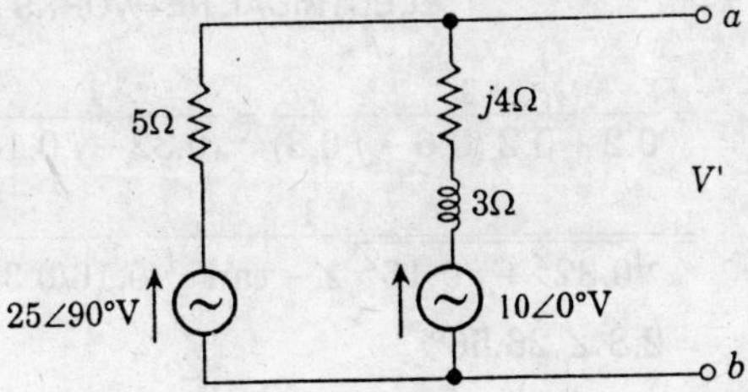


Fig. 9.10.23 (*a*). 4 Ω resistor removed.

$$\mathbf{V}' = \frac{\mathbf{V}_1\,\mathbf{Y}_1 + \mathbf{V}_2\,\mathbf{Y}_2}{\mathbf{Y}_1 + \mathbf{Y}_2}$$

$$\mathbf{V}_1 = 25 \angle 90° V, \quad \mathbf{Y}_1 = \frac{1}{5} = 0.2\angle 0° \;℧$$

$$\mathbf{V}_2 = 10 \angle 0° \;V, \quad \mathbf{Y}_2 = \frac{1}{3 + j\,4} = 0.2 \angle -53.13° \;℧$$

$$\therefore \quad \mathbf{V}' = \frac{25 \angle 90° \times 0.2 \angle 0° + 10 \angle 0° \times 0.2 \angle -53.13°}{0.2 \angle 0° + 0.2 \angle -53.13°}$$

$$= \frac{5 \angle 90° + 2 \angle -53.13°}{0.2 + 0.2\,(\cos 53.13° - j \sin 53.13°}$$

$$= \frac{j\,5 + 2\,(\cos 53.13° - j \sin 53.13°)}{0.2 + 0.2\,(0.6 - j\,0.8)}$$

$$= \frac{j\,5 + 2\,(0.6 - j\,0.8)}{(0.32 - j\,0.16)} = \frac{1.2 + j\,3.4}{0.32 - j\,0.16}$$

$$= \frac{\sqrt{1.2^2 + 3.4^2} \angle \tan^{-1}(3.4/1.2)}{\sqrt{0.32^2 + 0.16^2} \angle -\tan^{-1}(0.16/0.32)}$$

$$= \frac{3.6 \angle 70.56°}{0.357 \angle -26.56°} = 10.08 \angle 97.12° \text{ V}$$

$$\mathbf{Z}' = \frac{1}{\mathbf{Y}_1 + \mathbf{Y}_2} = \frac{1}{0.2 + 0.2 \angle -51.13°}$$

$$= \frac{1}{0.2 + 0.2\,(\cos 53.13° - j \sin 53.13°)}$$

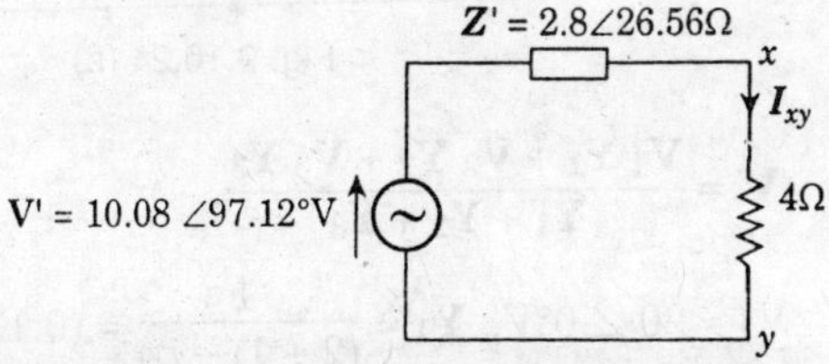


Fig. 9.10.23 (*b*) Millman's equivalent network.

$$= \frac{1}{0.2 + 0.2\,(0.6 - j\,0.8)} = \frac{1}{(0.32 - j\,0.16)}$$

$$= \frac{1}{\sqrt{0.32^2 + j\,0.16^2}\ \angle -\tan^{-1}(0.16/0.32)}$$

$$= 2.8 \angle 26.56°$$

The equivalent circuit with inclusion of 4Ω resistance is shown in Fig. 9.10.23 (*b*)

$$\mathbf{I}_{xy} = \frac{\mathbf{V}'}{\mathbf{Z}' + 4} = \frac{10.08 \angle 97.12°}{2.8 \angle 26.56° + 4}$$

$$= \frac{10.08 \angle 97.12°}{2.8\,(\cos 97.12° + j \sin 97.12°) + 4}$$

$$= \frac{10.08 \angle 97.12°}{2.8\,(0.894 + j\,0.491) + 4} = \frac{10.08 \angle 97.12°}{6.6 \angle 10.45}$$

$$= 1.527 \angle 86.67° \text{ A ...Ans.}$$

**Example 9.10.24.** *Determine the current through*

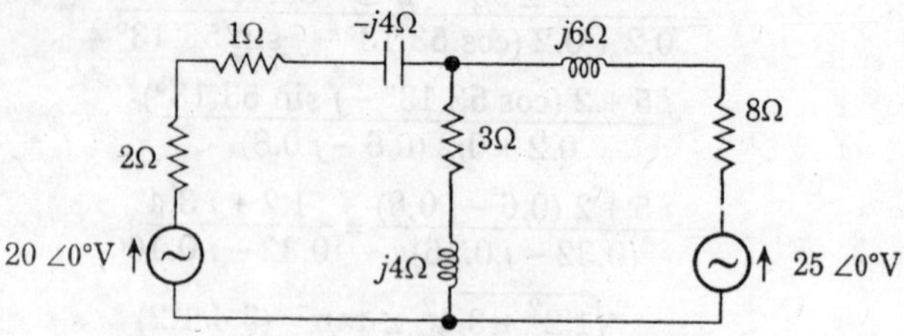


Fig. 9.10.24 Network for example 9.10.24.

(*i*) 2 Ω resistor.

(*ii*) (3 + *j* 4) Ω impedance.

Apply Millman's theorem.

**Solution :** As per Millman's theorem

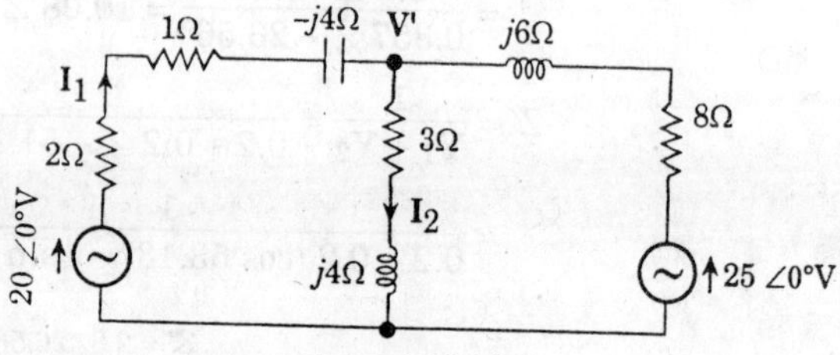


Fig. 9.10.24 (a)

$$\mathbf{V}' = \frac{\mathbf{V_1\,Y_1} + \mathbf{V_2\,Y_2} + \mathbf{V_3\,Y_3}}{\mathbf{Y_1} + \mathbf{Y_2} + \mathbf{Y_3}}$$

$$\mathbf{V_1} = 20 \angle 0°V,\ \ \mathbf{Y_1} = \frac{1}{(2+1) - j\,4} = (0.12 + j\,0.16)\ \mho$$

$$\mathbf{V_2} = 0,\ \ \mathbf{Y_2} = \frac{1}{3 + j\,4} = (0.12 - j\,0.16)\ \mho$$

$$\mathbf{V_3} = 25 \angle 0°V, \quad \mathbf{Y_3} = \frac{1}{8 + j\,6} = (0.08 - j\,0.06)\ ℧$$

Substituting the values.

$$\mathbf{V'} = \frac{20 \angle 0° \times (0.12 + j\,0.16) + 0 \times (0.12 - j\,0.16) + 25(0.08 - j\,0.06)}{(0.12 + j\,0.16) + (0.12 - j\,0.16) + (0.08 - j\,0.06)}$$

$$= \frac{4.4 + j1.7}{0.32 - j0.06} = \frac{\sqrt{4.4^2 + 1.7^2}\ \angle \tan^{-1}(1.7/4.4)}{\sqrt{0.32^2 + 0.06^2}\ \angle{-\tan^{-1}}(0.06/0.2)}$$

$$= \frac{4.716 \angle 21.12°}{0.25 \angle -10.61°} = 14.51 \angle 31.73°\ \text{V}$$

$$\mathbf{I_1} = \frac{20 \angle 0° - \mathbf{V'}}{(2 + 1) - j\,4} = \frac{20 \angle 0° - 14.51 \angle 31.73°}{(3 - j\,4)}$$

$$= \frac{20 - 14.51\,(\cos 31.73° + j\,31.73°)}{(3 - j\,4)}$$

$$= \frac{20 - 14.51\,(0.85 + j\,0.525)}{(3 - j\,4)} = \frac{7.66 - j\,7.63}{(3 - j\,4)}$$

$$= \frac{\sqrt{7.66^2 + 7.63^2}\ \angle -\tan^{-1}(7.63/7.66)}{\sqrt{3^2 + 4^2}\ \angle -\tan^{-1}(4/3)}$$

$$= \frac{10.81 \angle -48.88°}{5 \angle -53.13} = 2.16 \angle 4.25°\ \text{A} \ \ldots \textbf{Ans.}$$

$$\mathbf{I_2} = \frac{\mathbf{V'}}{3 + j\,4} = \frac{14.51 \angle 31.73°}{\sqrt{3^2 + 4^2}\ \angle \tan^{-1}(4/3)}$$

$$= \frac{14.51 \angle 31.73°}{5 \angle 53.13°} = 2.9 \angle -21.4°\ \text{A} \ \ldots \textbf{Ans.}$$

**Example. 9.10.25.** *Verify reciprocity theorem by interchanging voltage drop a cross terminals c – d and current source across a – b as shown in Fig. 9.10.25.*

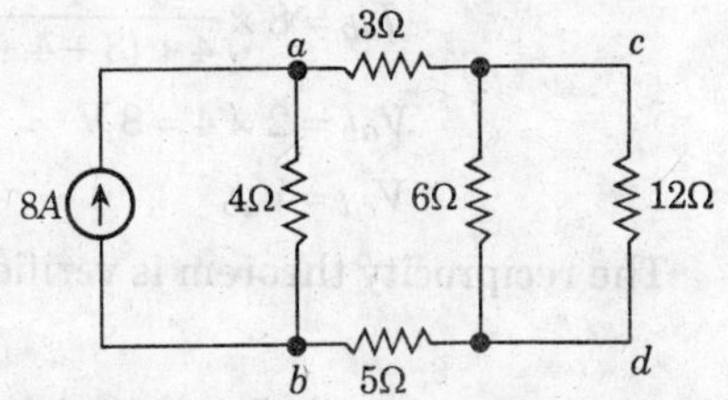

Fig. 9.10.25 Network for example 9.10.25.

**Solution :** The resistances 6Ω and 12Ω are in parallel. The circuit is reduced as shown in Fig. 9.10.25 (*a*)

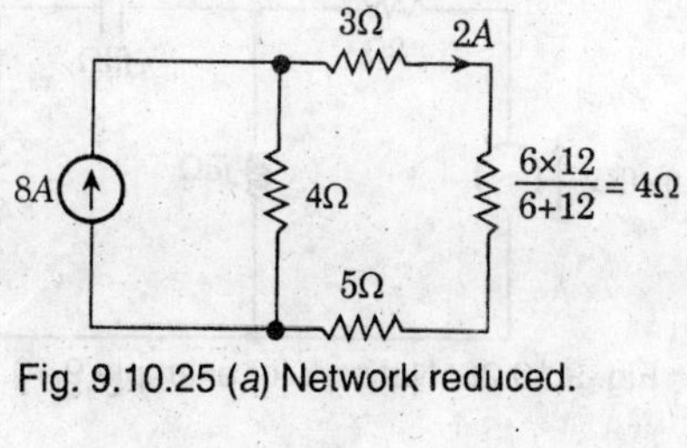

Fig. 9.10.25 (*a*) Network reduced.

The current through 3Ω resistor $= 8 \times \frac{4}{4 + (3 + 4 + 5)} = 2$ A

The current through 12Ω resistor $= 2 \times \frac{6}{6 + 12} = \frac{2}{3}$ A

The voltage drop $V_{cd} = \frac{2}{3} \times 12 = 8$ V

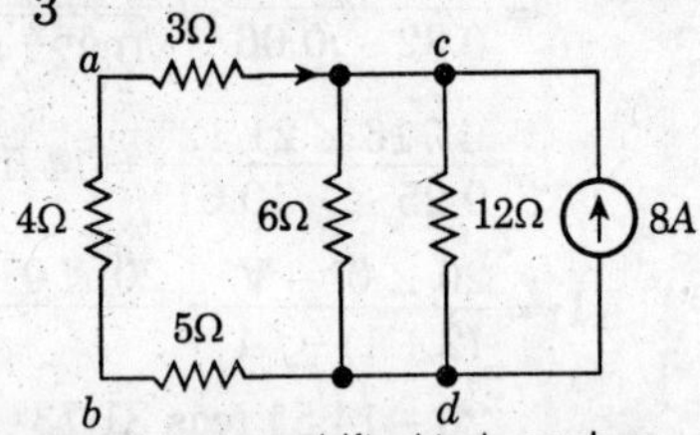


Fig. 9.10.25 (*b*). current source shifted to branch *c* – *d*

On connecting current source across the terminals *c* – *d*, the circuit takes the form as shown in Fig. 9.10.25(*b*)

The resistances 6Ω and 12Ω are in parallel, the circuit takes the form as shown in Fig. 9.10.25 (*c*)

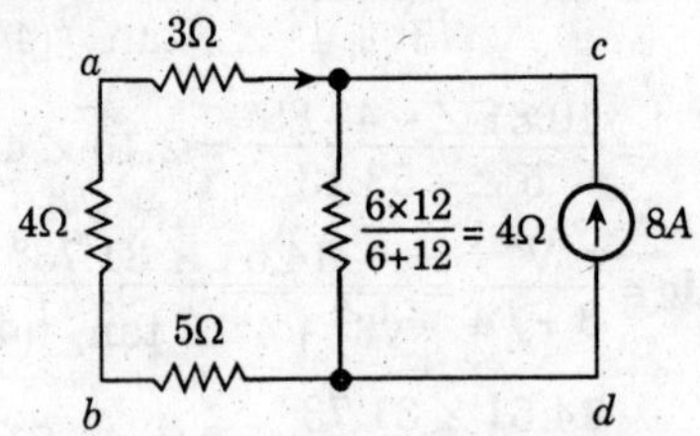


Fig. 9.10.25 (*c*). Network to determine $I_{ab}$

$$I_{ab} = 8 \times \frac{4}{4 + (3 + 4 + 5)} = 2 \text{ A}$$

$$V_{ab} = 2 \times 4 = 8 \text{ V}$$

$$V_{cd} = V_{ab}$$

The reciprocity theorem is verified.

**Example 9.10.26.** *Determine the current in 4Ω resistor and verify reciprocity theorem for the network shown in Fig. 9.10.26.*

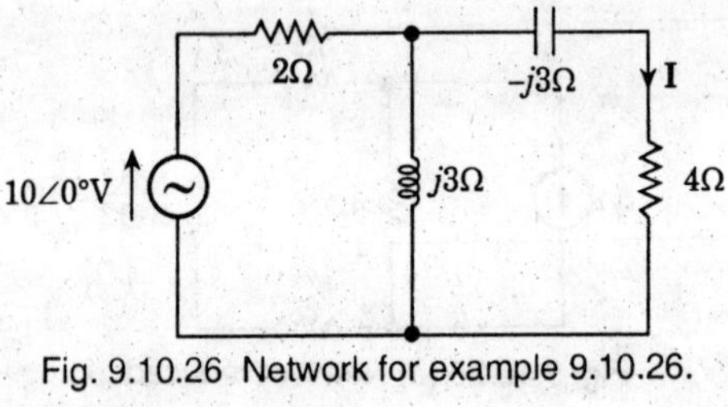


Fig. 9.10.26 Network for example 9.10.26.

**Solution :** Determine the current **I** as below

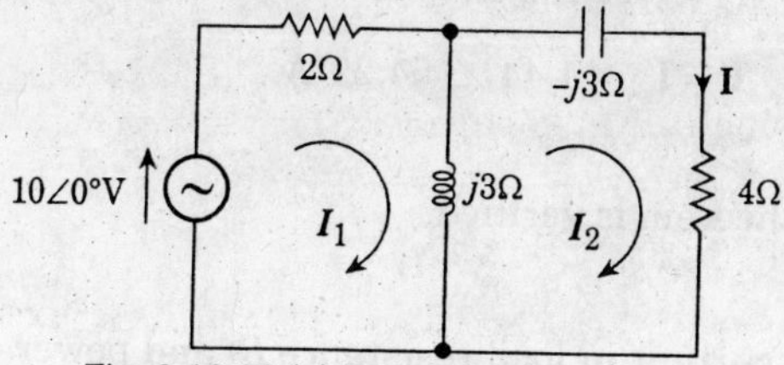


Fig. 9.10.26 (*a*) Determination of current I

Applying Kirchhoff's voltage law,

$$(2 + j\,3)\,\mathbf{I}_1 - j\,3\,\mathbf{I}_2 = 10 \angle 0°$$

$$-j\,3\,\mathbf{I}_1 + [4 + (j\,3 - j\,3)]\,\mathbf{I}_2 = 0$$

$$\therefore \quad \begin{vmatrix} 2 + j\,3 & -j\,3 \\ -j\,3 & 4 \end{vmatrix} \begin{vmatrix} \mathbf{I}_1 \\ \mathbf{I}_2 \end{vmatrix} = \begin{vmatrix} 10 \angle° \\ 0 \end{vmatrix}$$

$$\therefore \quad \mathbf{I}_2 = \frac{\begin{vmatrix} 2 + j\,3 & 10\angle 0° \\ -j\,3 & 0 \end{vmatrix}}{\begin{vmatrix} 2 + j\,3 & -j\,3 \\ -j\,3 & 4 \end{vmatrix}} = \frac{j\,30}{17 + j\,12}$$

$$= \frac{30 \angle 90°}{20.8\angle 35.21°} = 1.44 \angle 54.79° \text{ A}$$

$$\therefore \quad \mathbf{I} = \mathbf{I}_2 = 1.44 \angle 54.79° \text{ A}$$

Insert source in the 4 Ω branch as shown in Fig. 9.10.26 (*b*)

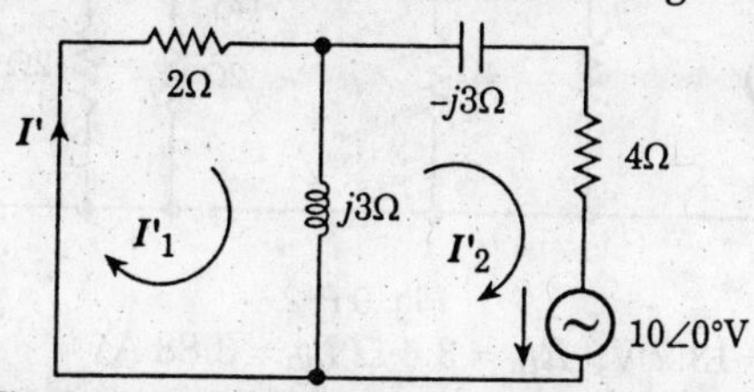


Fig. 9.10.26 (*b*) Determination of current I ′

Applying Kirchhoff's voltage law,

$$(2 + j\,3)\,\mathbf{I'}_1 - j\,3\,\mathbf{I'}_2 = 0$$

$$-j\,3\,\mathbf{I'}_1\,[4 + (j\,3 - j\,3)]\,\mathbf{I'}_2 = 10\angle 0°$$

$$\therefore \quad \begin{vmatrix} 2 + j\,3 & -j\,3 \\ -j\,3 & 4 \end{vmatrix} \begin{vmatrix} \mathbf{I'}_1 \\ \mathbf{I'}_2 \end{vmatrix} = \begin{vmatrix} 0 \\ 10 \angle 0° \end{vmatrix}$$

$$\therefore \quad \mathbf{I'}_1 = \frac{\begin{vmatrix} 0 & -j\,3 \\ 10 \angle 0° & 4 \end{vmatrix}}{\begin{vmatrix} 2 + j\,3 & -j\,3 \\ -j\,3 & 4 \end{vmatrix}} = \frac{j\,30}{17 + j\,12} = \frac{30 \angle 90°}{20.8\angle 35.21°}$$

$$= 1.44 \angle 54.79° \text{ A}$$

$$\therefore \quad \mathbf{I'} = \mathbf{I'}_1 = 1.44 \angle 54.29° \text{A}$$

Reciprocity theorem is verified.

## PROBLEMS

**9.1** Find the current in load resistance $R_l$ and power consumed in it. Use Thevenin's theorem.

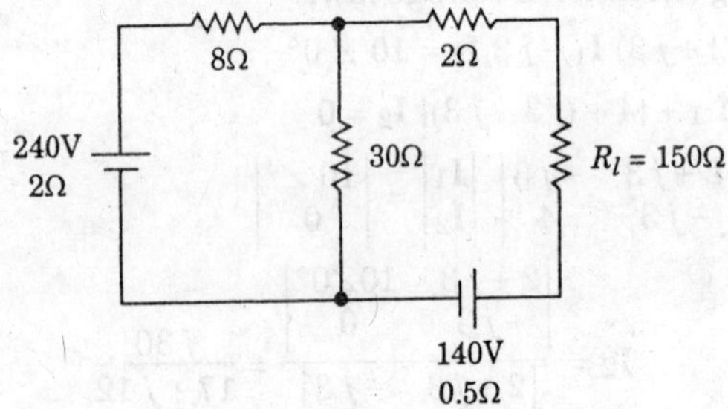


Fig. 9 P-1

(**Ans:** $I_l = 0.25$ A, $P = 9.375$ W)

**9.2** Apply Thevenin's theorem to determine $I_{ab}$.

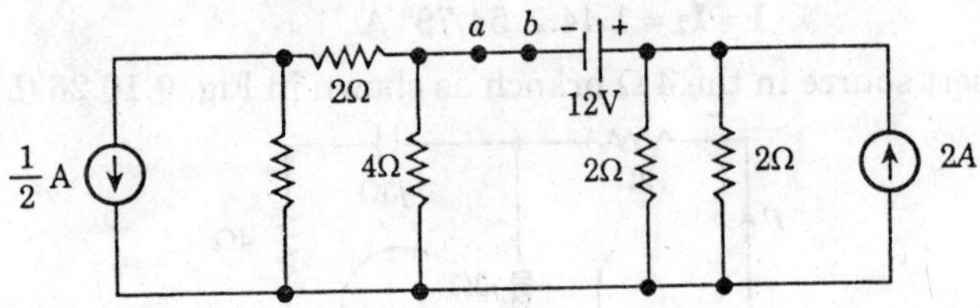


Fig. 9 P-2

(**Ans:** $V_{th} = 13.2$ V, $R_{th} = 3.4\ \Omega$ $I_{ab} = 3.88$ A)

**9.3** Determine the current through branch $a - b$ of The network shown on next page. Apply Thevenin's theorem. Verify the answer using Norton's theorem.

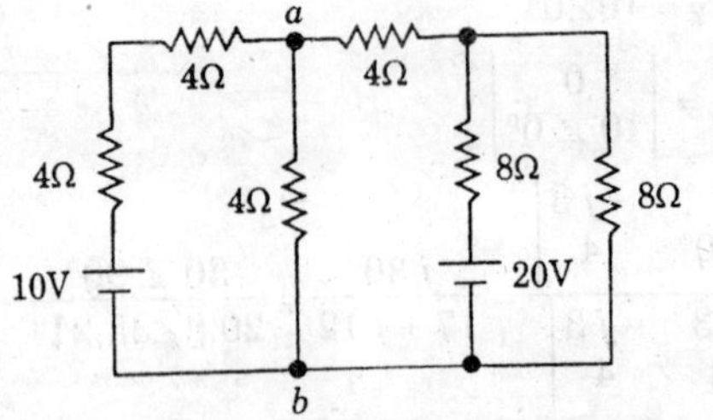


Fig. 9 P-3

(**Ans:** $I_{ab} = 1.25$A)

**9.4.** Use source transformation technique to obtain Thevenin's equivalent at terminals $a - b$.

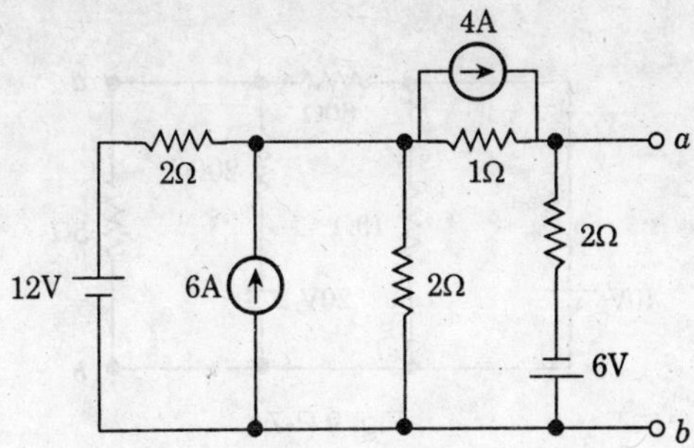


Fig. 9 P-4

(**Ans**: $V_{th} = 5$ V, $R_{th} = 1\ \Omega$)

**9.5.** The switch is closed at $t = 0$. Determine the expression for $i(t)$ through terminals $x - y$. Use Thevenin's theorem. Verify the answer using Norton's theorem

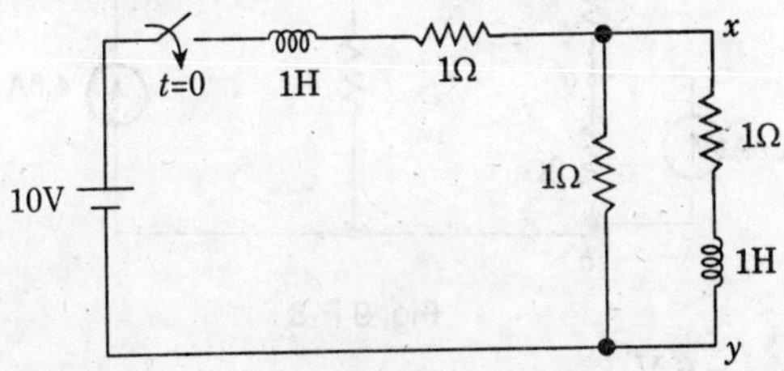


Fig. 9 P-5

[**Ans**: $i(t) = \frac{10}{3} - 5\,e^{-t} + \frac{5}{3}\,e^{-3t}$]

**9.6.** Apply Thevenin's theorem to determine the current through inductor.

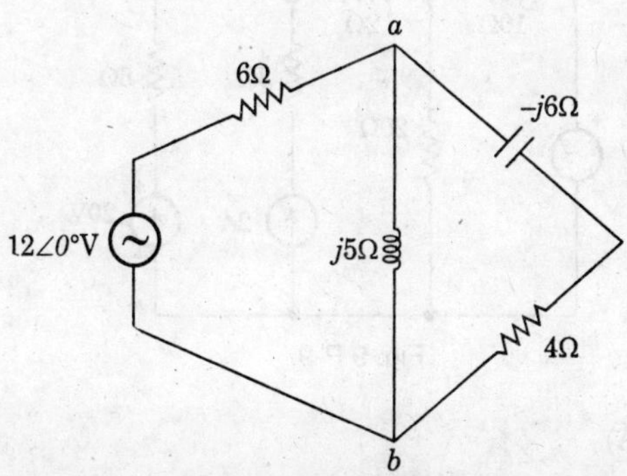


Fig. 9 P-6

(**Ans**: $\mathbf{I}_{ab} = 1.55\ \angle -70.93°$ A)

**9.7** Apply Norton's theorem to determine $I_{ab}$ in the network given below.

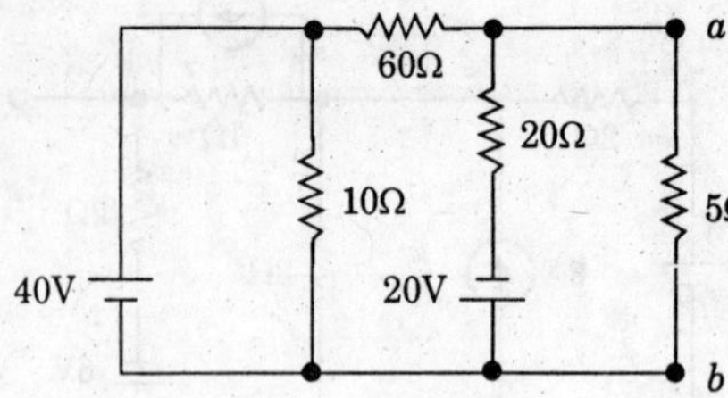


Fig. 9 P-7

(**Ans**: $I_{ab} = -0.25$ A)

**9.8.** Find $V_{ab}$ using superposition theorem.

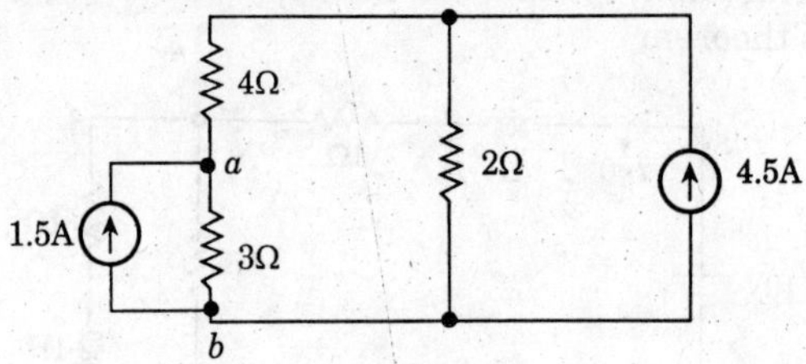


Fig. 9 P-8

(**Ans**: $V_{ab} = 6$ V

**9.9** Determine the current through 2 Ω resistor. Apply superposition theorem.

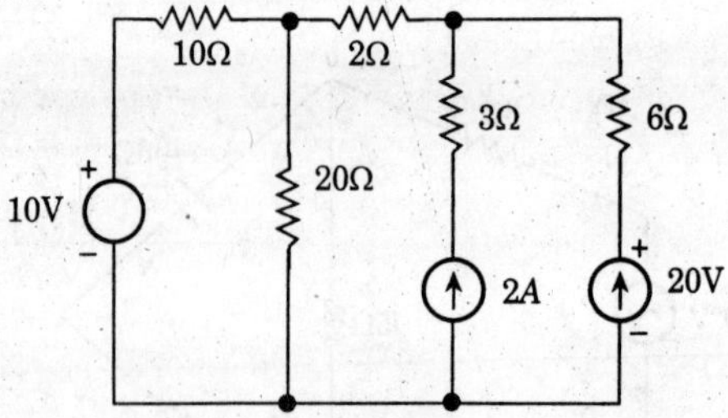


Fig. 9 P-9

(**Ans**: $I = \frac{16}{11}$ A)

**9.10.** Use superposition theorem to determine the current $I_{xy}$

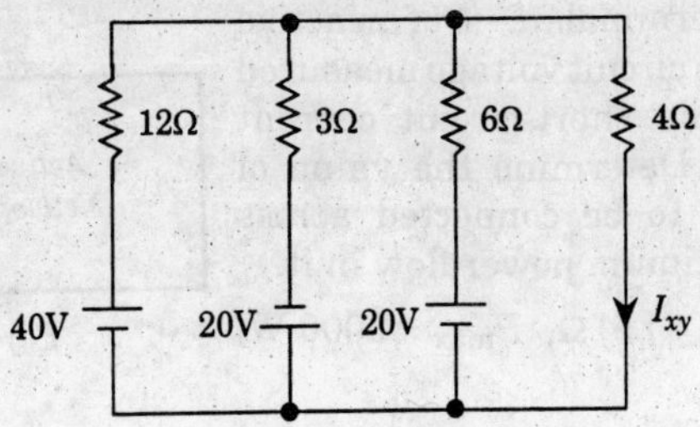


Fig. 9 P-10

(**Ans**: $I_{xy} = 0$)

**9.11** Apply superposition theorem to determine the current flowing through $(3 - j\,4)\ \Omega$ impedance.

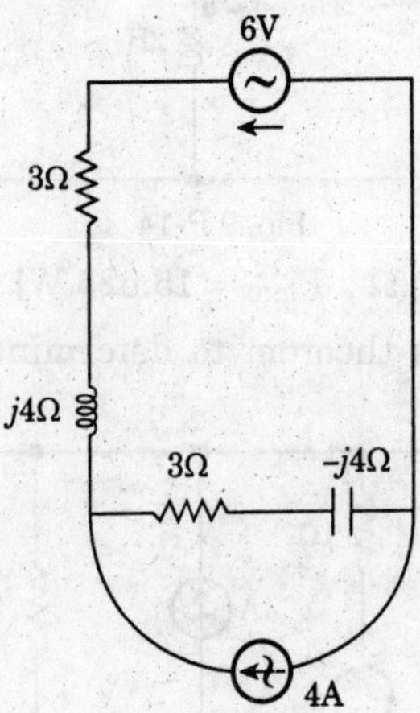


Fig. 9 P-11

(**Ans**: $I = 4.01 \angle 41.63°$ A)

**9.12** In The network given below determine the value of $\mathbf{Z}_l$ for maximum power transfer.

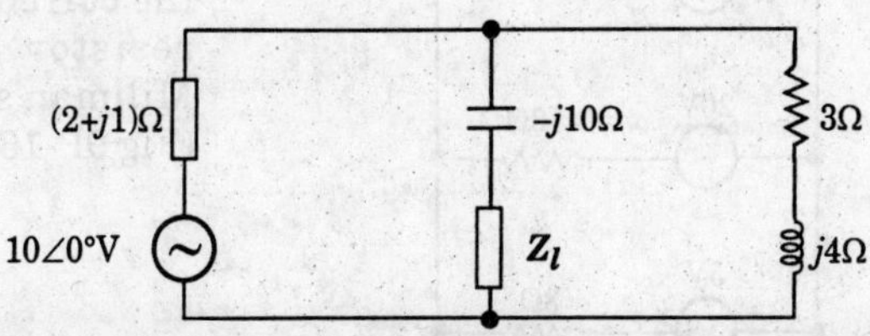


Fig. 9 P-12

(**Ans**: $\mathbf{Z}_l = 9.19 \angle 81.86°\ \Omega$)

**9.13** At the terminals $a-b$ of an active network the open circuit voltage measured is 200 V and the short-circuit current $(40/\sqrt{2}) \angle 45°$ A. Determine the value of load impedance to be connected across $a-b$ for the maximum power flow in it.

[**Ans**: $\mathbf{Z}_l = (5 + j\,5)\ \Omega$, $P_{max} = 2000$ W]

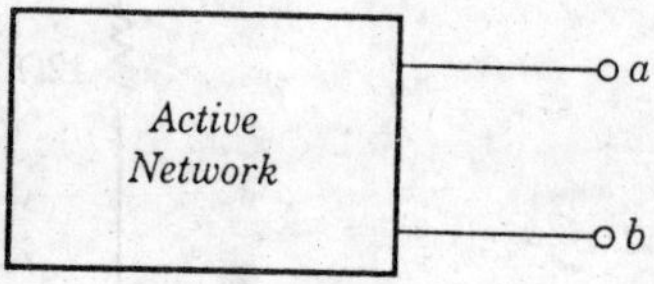


Fig. 9 P-13

**9.14** A mutually coupled network is shown below. Determine the value of load impedance to be connected across terminals $a-b$ to absorb maximum power. Calculate the maximum power flow in the load.

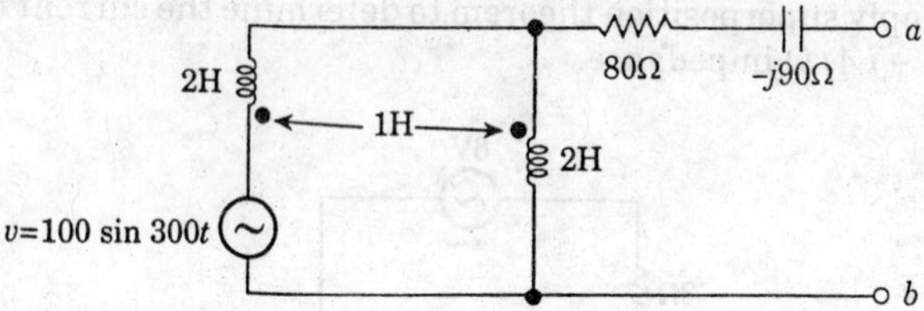


Fig. 9 P-14

[**Ans**: $\mathbf{Z}_l = (80 - j\,60)\ \Omega$ , $P_{max} = 15.625$ W]

**9.15** Use Millman's theorem to determine the current $I$ in the network given below.

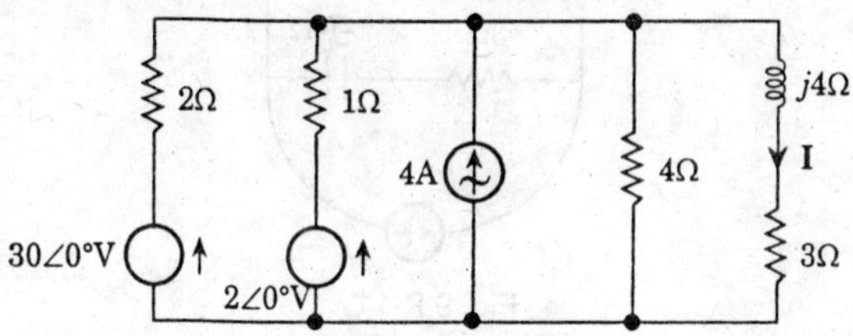


Fig. 9 P-15

(**Ans**: $I = 0.798$ A)

**9.16.** Determine the current in 7.42 Ω resistor using Millman's theorem. (Fig 9P-16)

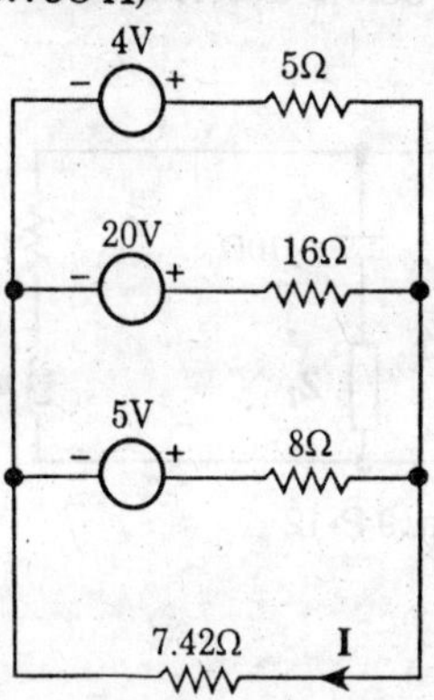


Fig. 9 P-16

(**Ans**: $I = 0.69$ A)

**9.17** Determine the current through $j\,10\ \Omega$ reactane. Apply Millman's theorem. (Fig 9P-17)

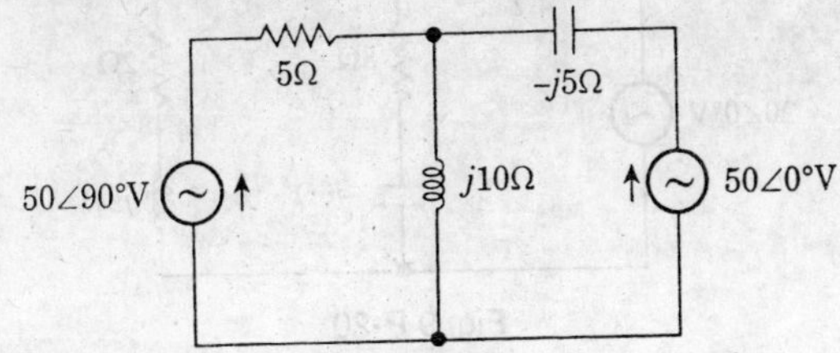


Fig. 9 P-17

(**Ans:** $I = 8.94$ A)

**9.18** A network is shown below. Determine the current $\mathbf{I_2}$ flowing in 3Ω resistor. Verify reciprocity theorem with respect to terminal pair *a-b* and *c-d*.

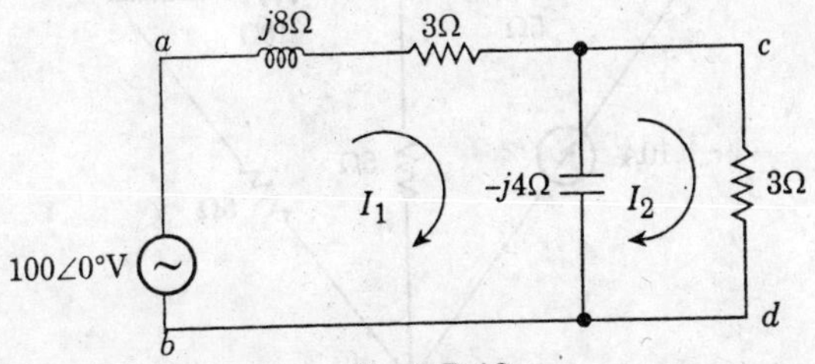


Fig. 9 P-18

(**Ans:** $I_2 = \dfrac{400}{41} \angle -90°$)

**9.19** Determine the change of current in 5 Ω resistor. when it is changed to 2Ω. Use compensation theorem. The network is given in Fig. 9P-19

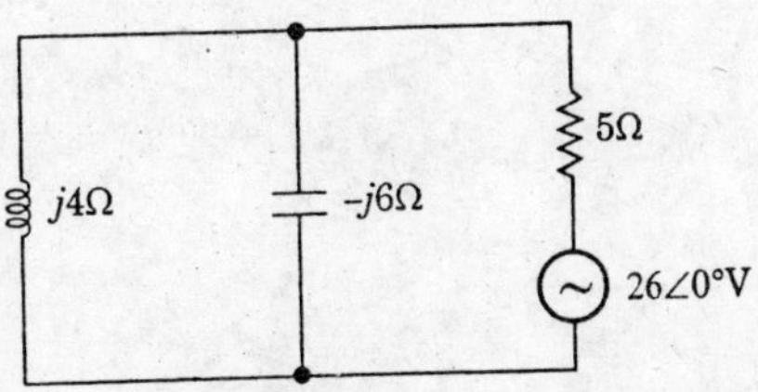


Fig. 9 P-19

(**Ans:** $\delta\,\mathbf{I} = 0.495 \angle -147.9°$ A)

**9.20** In the network shown below, the impedance $(2 + j\,2)\ \Omega$ is changed to $(3 + j4\ \Omega)$. Use compensation theorem to determine change of current in it.

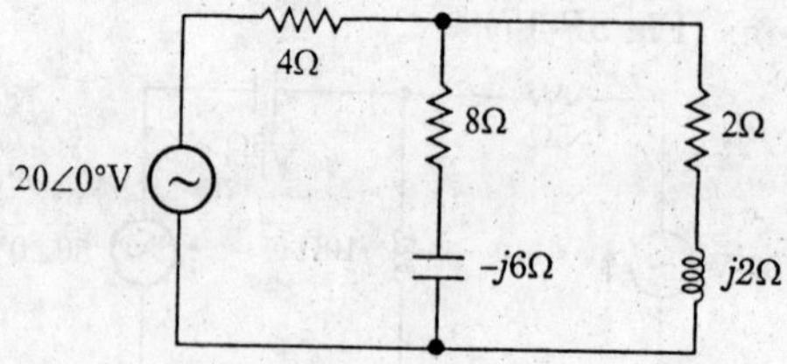


Fig. 9 P-20

**(Ans:** $\delta \mathbf{I} = -0.421 \angle -57.14°A$)

**9.21** Verify Tellegen's theorem for the network given below.

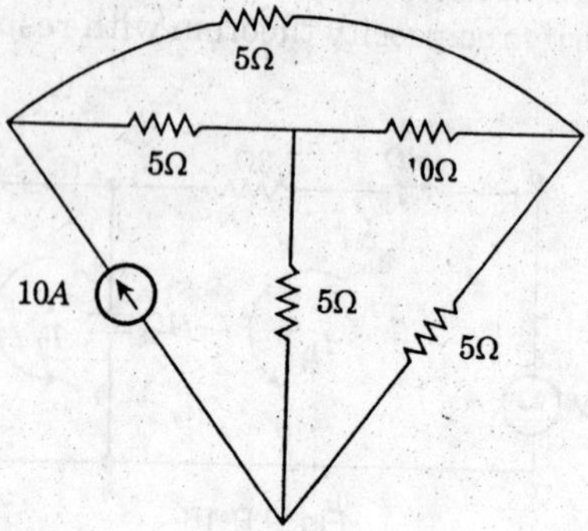


Fig. 9 P-21

# 10

# Network Functions

## 10.1 INTRODUCTION

An electrical network consists of inter-connection of passive elements such as resistors, inductors and capacitors. The excitation (input) applied to two terminals of the network. The application of excitation results in the response (output). The excitation may be a voltage and the response being a flow of current. Also, the current may produce responsive voltage drop across some other elements.

In a network having one-part, a pair of terminals is available as shown in Fig. 10.1.1

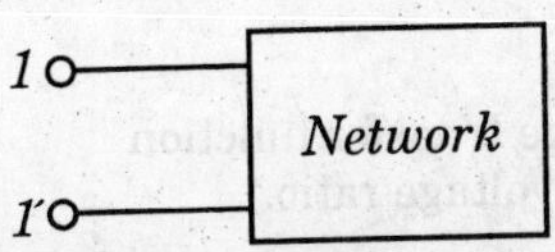


Fig. 10.1.1. One-port network

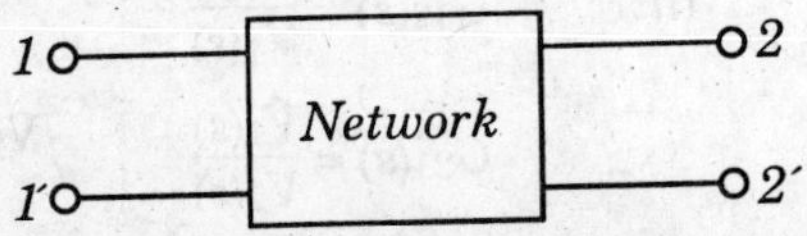


Fig. 10.1.2. Two-port network

A two-port network has two pairs of terminals as shown in Fig. 10.1.2

The network function is given by the ratio of Laplace transform of one quantity to Laplace transform of another quantity with initial conditions set to zero.

## 10.2 NETWORK FUNCTIONS FOR ONE-PORT NETWORK

The network functions in relation to one-port network are described below :

(*i*) *Impedance Function* : The impedance function $Z(s)$ is given by the ratio of Laplace transform of the input voltage $V(s)$ to Laplace transform of the input current $I(s)$ with the network in relaxed state.

$$Z(s) = \frac{V(s)}{I(s)}$$

(*ii*) *Admittance Function* : The admittance function $Y(s)$ is given the ratio of Laplace transform of the input current $I(s)$ to Laplace transform of the input voltage $V(s)$ with the network in relaxed state.

$$Y(s) = \frac{I(s)}{V(s)}$$

The names impedance and admittance functions can be combined to be written as immitance function.

The impedance and admittance functions are driving point functions.

(Network in relaxed state indicates that the initial conditions are set to zero and dependent sources if any are kept as it is.)

## 10.3 NETWORK FUNCTIONS OF TWO-PORT NETWORK

In general for a relaxed two-port the ratio of Laplace transform of one quantity to Laplace transform of another quantity gives the network function.

In relation to two-port network following network functions are possible :

(*i*) $Z_{11}(s) = \dfrac{V_1(s)}{I_1(s)}$ Driving point impedance (Input impedance)

(*ii*) $Y_{11}(s) = \dfrac{I_1(s)}{V_1(s)}$ Driving point admittance (Input admittance)

(*iii*) $G_{12}(s) = \dfrac{V_2(s)}{V_1(s)}$

$G_{21}(s) = \dfrac{V_1(s)}{V_2(s)}$ Voltage transfer function (voltage ratio.)

(*iv*) $\alpha_{12}(s) = \dfrac{I_2(s)}{I_1(s)}$

$\alpha_{21}(s) = \dfrac{I_1(s)}{I_2(s)}$ Current transfer ratio.

(*v*) $Z_{12}(s) = \dfrac{V_2(s)}{I_1(s)}$

$Z_{21}(s) = \dfrac{V_1(s)}{I_2(s)}$ Transfer impedance function

(*vi*) $Y_{12}(s) = \dfrac{I_2(s)}{V_1(s)}$

$Y_{21}(s) = \dfrac{I_1(s)}{V_2(s)}$ Transfer admittance function

The network functions mentioned above are determined by writing network equations using loop/mesh current or node voltage analysis, taking Laplace transform of equations considering initial conditions as zero and solving for the ratio of the specified output and input.

The network function (*iii*) and (*iv*) are called transfer functions. The symbol for transfer function has the order of subscript* as 1, 2, *e.g.*

$Z_{12}(s) = \dfrac{V_2(s)}{I_1(s)}$ ... etc.

## 10.4 DETERMINATION OF NETWORK FUNCTIONS

### 1. Driving Point (input) Impedance for Ladder Network

A ladder network is shown in Fig. 10.4.1. The branch impedances are considered as series elements, while admittances as parallel elements

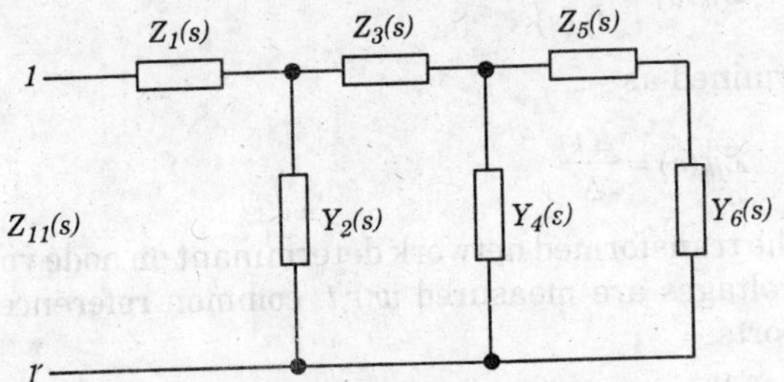


Fig. 10.4.1 Ladder network

Starting from R.H.S., $\left[Z_5(s) + \dfrac{1}{Y_6(s)}\right]$ in parallel with $Y_4(s)$ and this process continues towards left. The driving point impedance function $Z_{11}(s)$ at terminals 1 – 1′ is given by

$$Z_{11}(s) = Z_1(s) + \cfrac{1}{Y_2(s) + \cfrac{1}{Z_3(s) + \cfrac{1}{Y_4(s) + \cfrac{1}{Z_5(s) + \cfrac{1}{Y_6(s)}}}}}$$

The equation given above is a continued fraction formed to determine the driving point impedance function of a ladder network.

### 2. Network Functions for Multi Mesh/Loop Networks

In the multiloop network other then ladder type, simultaneous equations based on loop/mesh current or mode voltage basis are formed and the ratio of Laplace transform of respective quantities is to be obtained for the required network function. Thus, the network function is expressed as a quotient of determinants based on loop/mesh current or node voltage analysis.

(*i*) Admittance network function.

---

* See, Network Analysis, M.E. Van Valken burg, 3rd. Ed. *P&H* (India), *p.* 281.

$$Y_{jk}(s) = \frac{I_k(s)}{V_j(s)}$$

can be determined as

$$Y_{jk}(s) = \frac{\Delta_{kj}}{\Delta}$$

where $\Delta$ is the transformed network determination loop/mesh current basis.

(*ii*) Impedance network function.

$$Z_{jk}(s) = \frac{V_k(s)}{I_j(s)}$$

can be determined as

$$Z_{jk}(s) = \frac{\Delta'_{kj}}{\Delta'}$$

where $\Delta'$ is the transformed network determinant on node voltage basis. The node voltages are measured *w.r.t.* common reference node between two ports.

(*iii*) The following two-port transfer functions can also be determined as below :

$$G_{12}(s) = \frac{V_2(s)}{V_1(s)} = \frac{\Delta'_{12}}{\Delta'_{11}}$$

$$\alpha_{12}(s) = \frac{I_2(s)}{I_1(s)} = \frac{\Delta_{12}}{\Delta_{11}}$$

## 10.5 POLES AND ZEROS OF A NETWORK FUNCTION

The network function is a quotient of polynomials in s expressed as,

$$F(s) = \frac{p(s)}{q(s)} = \frac{a_0 s^n + a_1 s^{n-1} + \ldots + a_n}{b_0 s^m + b_1 s^{m-1} + \ldots + b_m}$$

The network function is a rational function of $s$ with real constant coefficients and $n$ and $m$ are integers. The degree of $p(s)$ is $n$ and that of $q(s)$ $m$.

The driving point functions $Z_{11}(s)$ and $Y_{11}(s)$ are called immitance functions. The network function $Z_{12}(s)$, $Z_{21}(s)$, $Y_{12}(s)$, $Y_{21}(s)$, $G_{12}(s)$ and $\alpha_{12}(s)$ are transfer functions being the ratio Laplace transform of one parameter to another assuming initial conditions zero. In general the transfer function is denoted as $H(s)$.

The network function

$$\frac{p(s)}{q(s)} = \frac{a_0 s^n + a_1 s^{n-1} + \ldots + a_n}{b_0 s^m + b_1 s^{m-1} + \ldots + b_m}$$

can be factored for $p(s)$ and $q(s)$ as below :

$$\frac{p(s)}{q(s)} = \frac{K\,(s - z_1)\,(s - z_2)...(s - z_n)}{(s - p_1)\,(s - p_2)\,...(s - p_m)}$$

where, $K = \frac{a_0}{b_0}$ known as gain factor or scale factor.

The variable $s$ is a complex number. Thus,

$$s = \sigma + j\,\omega$$

is known as complex frequency. The imaginary part $\omega$ is radian frequency (rad./sec.). The real part termed as neper frequency is the decrement factor.

(i) On equating the numerator $p(s) = 0$, the roots are $s = z_1, z_2 ... z_n$ know as zeros of the network function. Substituting $s = z_1, z_2, ... z_n$, The network function attains a zero value. The zeros $z_1, z_2, ..., z_n$ are the complex frequencies due to the zeros of a network function. At these complex frequencies the network function behaves like a short-circuit.

(ii) On equating the denominator $q(s) = 0$, the roots are $s = p_1, p_2, ... p_m$ known as poles of the network function. Substituting $s = p_1, p_2, ... p_m$, The network function attains an infinite value. The poles $p_1, p_2, ..., p_m$ are the complex frequencies due to the poles of a transfer function. At these complex frequencies the network function behaves like an open-circuit.

The poles and zeros are the critical frequencies of a network function.

At complex frequencies other than critical frequencies the network function has finite non-zero value.

The poles and zero along with the gain factor completely specify a network function.

The poles and zeros are plotted by symbol × (small cross) and O (small circle) respectively in a complex s-plane.

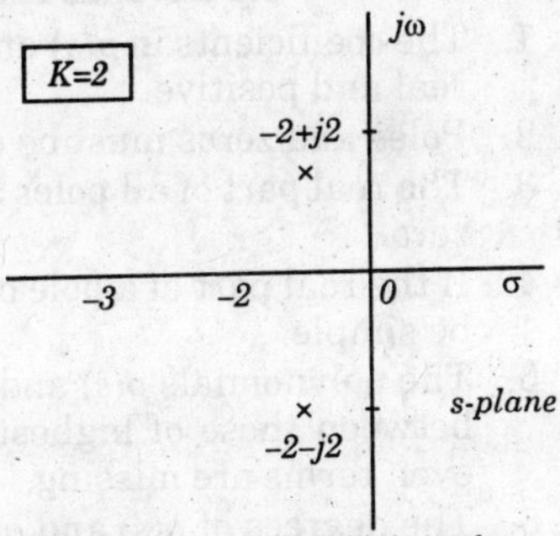


Fig.10.5.1. Pole-zero plot for $F(s) = \frac{2\,(s+2)}{s\,(s+3)\,(s+2+j2)\,(s+2-j2)}$

Let (i) $F(s) = \frac{2\,(s + 2)}{s\,(s + 3)\,(s + 2 + j\,2)\,(s + 2 - j\,2)}$

The zero is located at $s = -2$ (simple zero)

The poles are located at

$s = 0$ (simple pole)

$s = -3$ (simple pole)

$s = -2 \pm j\,2$ (complex poles)

Gain factor : $K = 2$

The pole-zero plot is shown in Fig. 10.5.1.

$$(ii)\ F(s) = \frac{K\,(s+1)}{s^2\,(s+2)^2\,(s+1+j\,1)\,(s+1-j\,1)}$$

The zero is located at

$s = -1$ (simple zero)

The poles are located at

$s = 0, 0$

(multiple pole of order 2)

$s = -2, -2$

(multiple pole of order 2)

$s = (-1 \pm j\,1)$ (complex poles)

Gain factor : $K$

The pole - zero plot is shown in Fig. 10.5.2.

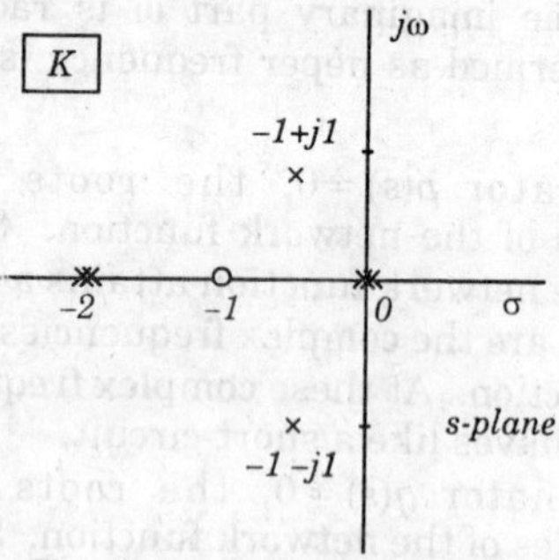


Fig. 10.5.2. Pole-zero plot for $F(s) = \dfrac{K\,(s+1)}{s^2\,(s+2)^2\,(s+1+j\,1)\,(s+1-j\,1)}$

## Restrictions on Pole Zero Locations for Driving Point Functions

1. The coefficients in $p(s)$ and $q(s)$ of a network function must be real and positive.
2. Poles and zeros must be conjugate if complex or imaginary.
3. The real part of all poles and zeros must be either negative or zero.
4. If the real part of a pole or zero is zero, that pole or zero must be simple.
5. The polynomials $p(s)$ and $q(s)$ should not have missing terms between those of highest or lowest degree unless all odd or even terms are missing.
6. The degrees of $p(s)$ and $q(s)$ *i.e.*, $n$ and $m$ may differ by 1 or 0 only.
7. The terms of lowest degree in $p(s)$ and $q(s)$ may differ in degree by one at the most.

## Restrictions on Pole Zero Locations for Transfer Functions

1. The coefficients of different terms in $p(s)$ and $q(s)$ must be real and those for $q(s)$ must be positive.
2. If poles and zeros are complex or imaginary they must be conjugate.

3. The real part of a pole must be negative or zero. If the real part is zero then that pole must be simple.
4. The polynomial $q(s)$ should not have any missing term between those of the highest and lowest degree unless all the even or odd terms are missing.
5. The polynomial $p(s)$ may have missing terms between those of the highest and lowest degree.
6. The degree of $p(s)$ may be as small as zero, independent of the degree of $q(s)$.
7. For $G_{12}(s)$ and $\alpha_{12}(s)$, the maximum degree of $p(s)$ is the degree of $q(s)$. For $Z_{12}(s)$ and $Y_{12}(s)$, the maximum degree of $p(s)$ is the degree of $q(s)$ plus one.

## 10.6 TIME RESPONSE FROM THE POLE-ZERO PLOT

The time response for a system can be assessed from the location of poles and zeros plotted in the $s$ - plane. The poles explain the time response and the zeros are useful in determining the coefficients of partial fraction expansion of a network function

Let, $$F(s) = \frac{K(s - z_1)(s - z_2) \dots (s - z_n)}{(s - p_1)(s - p_2) \dots (s - p_m)}$$

Expanding into partial fractions

$$F(s) = \frac{k_1}{s - p_1} + \frac{k_2}{s - p_2} + \frac{k_3}{s - p_3} \dots + \frac{k_m}{s - p_m}$$

The residue $k_m$ at pole $p_m$ is determined by taking the ratio of product of vectors from zeros to the pole $p_m$ to the product of vectors from other poles to the pole $p_m$. The residues at complex conjugate poles are also conjugate.

**Example 10.6.1.** *A network function is given below,*

$F(s) = \dfrac{2\,s}{(s+2)(s^2+2\,s+2)}$. Determine residue at the poles and $f(t)$.

**Solution :**

$$F(s) = \frac{2\,s}{(s+2)(s^2+2\,s+2)}$$

$$= \frac{2\,s}{(s+2)(s+1+j\,1)(s+1-j\,1)}$$

Expanding into partial fractions

$$F(s) = \frac{k_1}{(s+2)} + \frac{k_2}{(s+1+j\,1)} + \frac{k_2^*}{(s+1-j\,1)}$$

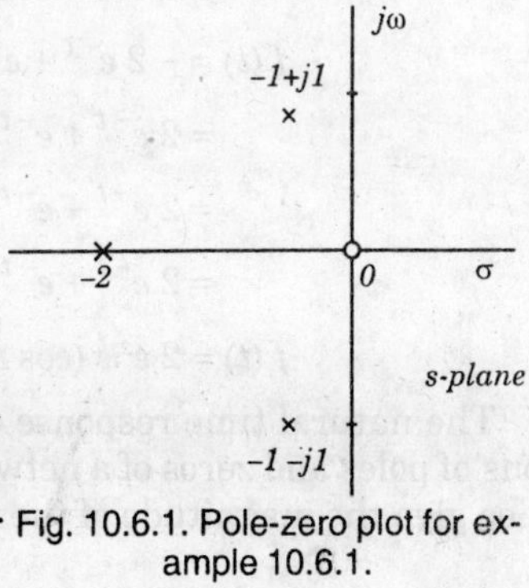


Fig. 10.6.1. Pole-zero plot for example 10.6.1.

The pole-zero plot is shown in Fig. 10.6.1

(*i*) To determine $k_1$ (residue at the pole $s = -2$).

Draw vectors from zero $s = 0$ and poles $s = -1 \pm j1$ towards the pole $s = -2$ as shown in Fig. 10.6.1 (*a*).

$$k_1 = \frac{2 \times 2 \angle 180°}{\sqrt{2} \angle -135° \times \sqrt{2} \angle 135°}$$

$$= 2 \angle 180° = -2 \quad \text{... Ans.}$$

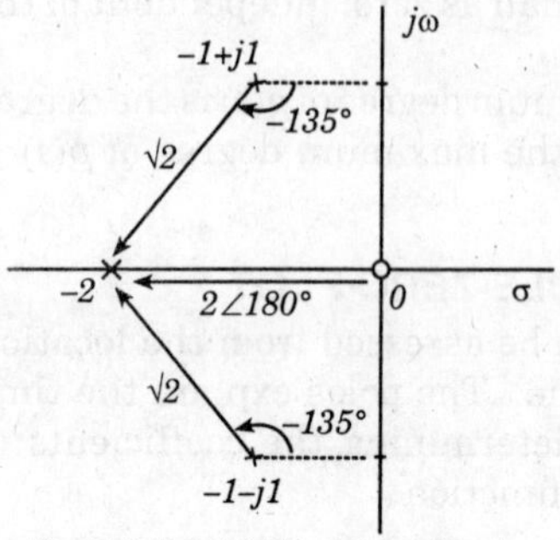


Fig. 10.6.1 (*a*) To determine $k_1$

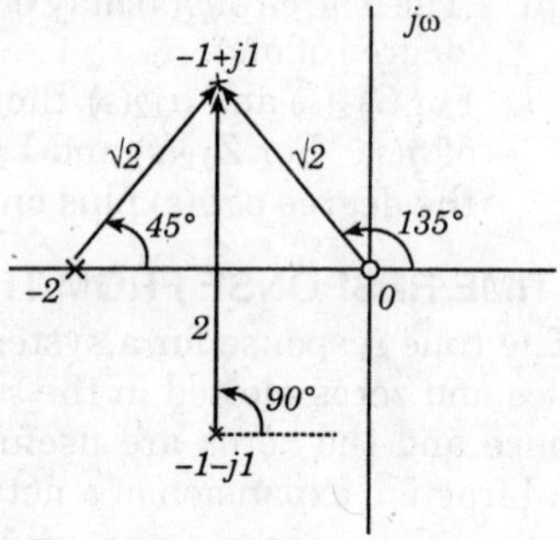


Fig. 10.6.1 (*b*) To determine $k_2$

(*ii*) To determine $k_2$ (residue at pole $s = -1 + j1$)

Draw vectors from zero $s = 0$ and poles $s = -2$, $s = -1 - j1$ towards the pole $s = -1 + j1$ as shown in Fig. 10.6.1 (*b*).

$$k_2 = \frac{2 \times \sqrt{2} \angle 135°}{\sqrt{2} \angle 45° \times 2 \angle 90°} = 1 \angle 0° = 1 + j0 \quad \text{... Ans.}$$

(*iii*) $\quad k_2^* = 1 - j0. \quad$ **... Ans.**

$$F(s) = \frac{k_1}{s+2} + \frac{k_2}{s+1+j1} + \frac{k_2^*}{s+1-j1}$$

$\because \quad k_1 = -2, \quad k_2 = 1 + j0 \quad \text{and } k_2^* = 1 - j0$

$$\therefore \quad F(s) = \frac{-2}{s+2} + \frac{1}{s+1+j1} + \frac{1}{s+1-j1}$$

Taking inverse Laplace transform on both sides

$$f(t) = -2e^{-t} + e^{-(1+j1)t} + e^{-(1-j1)t}$$

$$= 2e^{-t} + e^{-t}(e^{-jt} + e^{jt})$$

$$= 2e^{-t} + e^{-t}(\cos t - j\sin t + \cos t + j\sin t)$$

$$= 2e^{-t} + e^{-t}\, 2\cos t$$

or $\quad f(t) = 2e^{-t}(\cos t - 1) \quad$ **... Ans.**

The natural time response can be obtained from the *s*-plane locations of poles and zeros of a network fucntion. The zeros along with the poles give the magnitude of the time response.

Consider a second order system network function given below,

$$F(s) = \frac{\omega_n^2}{s^2 + 2\,\xi\,\omega_n\,s + \omega_n^2}$$

where, $\xi$ = damping ratio

and $\omega_n$ = natural (undamped) freqency of oscillations.

On factoring the denominator,

$$F(s) = \frac{\omega_n^2}{(s + \xi\,\omega_n + j\,\omega_n\sqrt{1-\xi^2})\,(s + \xi\,\omega_n - j\,\omega_n\sqrt{1-\xi^2})}$$

Expanding into partial fractions,

$$F(s) = \frac{k_1}{(s + \xi\,\omega_n + j\,\omega_n\sqrt{1-\xi^2})} + \frac{k_2}{(s + \xi\,\omega_n - j\,\omega_n\sqrt{1-\xi^2})}$$

The coefficients can be determined as

$$k_1 = \frac{j\,\omega_n}{2\sqrt{1-\xi^2}} \quad \text{and}$$

$$k_2 = \frac{-j\,\omega_n}{2\sqrt{1-\xi^2}}$$

$$\therefore \quad F(s) = \frac{j\,\omega_n}{2\sqrt{1-\xi^2}\;(s + \xi\,\omega_n + j\,\omega_n\sqrt{1-\xi^2})} - \frac{j\,\omega_n}{2\sqrt{1-\xi^2}\;(s + \xi\,\omega_n - j\,\omega_n\sqrt{1-\xi^2})}$$

Taking inverse Laplace transform on both sides,

$$\pounds^{-1} F(s) = \pounds^{-1}\left[\frac{j\,\omega_n}{2\sqrt{1-\xi^2}\;(s + \xi\,\omega_n + j\,\omega_n\sqrt{1-\xi^2})} - \frac{j\,\omega_n}{2\sqrt{1-\xi^2}\;(s + \xi\,\omega_n - j\,\omega_n\sqrt{1-\xi^2})}\right]$$

$$\therefore \quad f(t) = \frac{j\,\omega_n}{2\sqrt{1-\xi^2}}\,e^{-\xi\,\omega_n\,t}\,(e^{-j\,\omega_n\sqrt{1-\xi^2}\,t} - e^{+j\,\omega_n\sqrt{1-\xi^2}\,t})$$

$$= \frac{j\,\omega_n}{2\sqrt{1-\xi^2}}\,e^{-\xi\,\omega_n\,t}\,(\cos\omega_n\sqrt{1-\xi^2}\,t - j\sin\omega_n\sqrt{1-\xi^2}\,t - \cos\omega_n\sqrt{1-\xi^2}\,t - j\sin\omega_n\sqrt{1-\xi^2}\,t)$$

$$= \frac{j\,\omega_n}{2\sqrt{1-\xi^2}}\,e^{-\xi\,\omega_n\,t}\,(-j\,2\sin\omega_n\sqrt{1-\xi^2}\,t)$$

or

$$f(t) = \frac{\omega_n}{\sqrt{1-\xi^2}}\,e^{-\xi\,\omega_n\,t}\,\sin\omega_n\sqrt{1-\xi^2}\,t.$$

***(i)* For $\xi < 1$.** The poles $s_1, s_2 = (-\xi\,\omega_n \pm j\,\omega_n\sqrt{1-\xi^2})$ are complex located in *s*-plane as shown in Fig. 10.6.2 (*a*). The corrosponding time response having damped oscillation is shown in Fig. 10.6.2 (*b*)

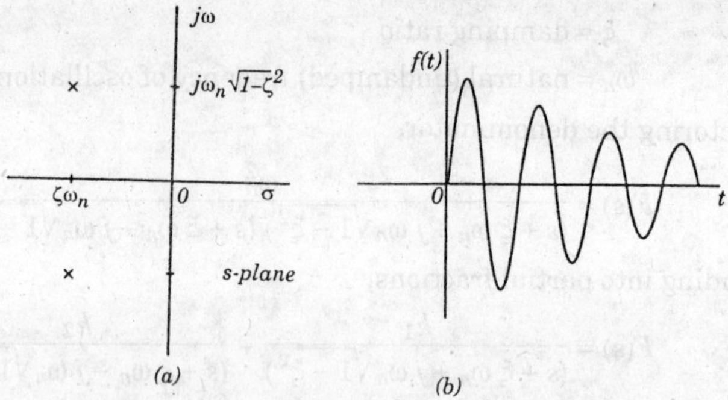


Fig. 10.6.2. pole locations in s-plane (damped oscillations)

***(ii)* For $\xi = 0$.** The poles $s_1, s_2 = \pm j\,\omega_n$ are imaginary located in *s*-plane as shown in Fig. 10.6.3 (*a*). The corresponding time response in given by

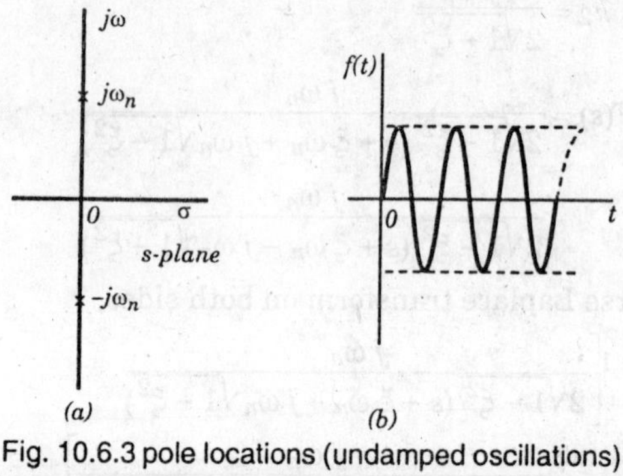


Fig. 10.6.3 pole locations (undamped oscillations)

$$f(t) = \omega_n \sin \omega_n t$$

The time response is undamped (sustained oscillations) as shown in Fig. 10.6.3 (*b*).

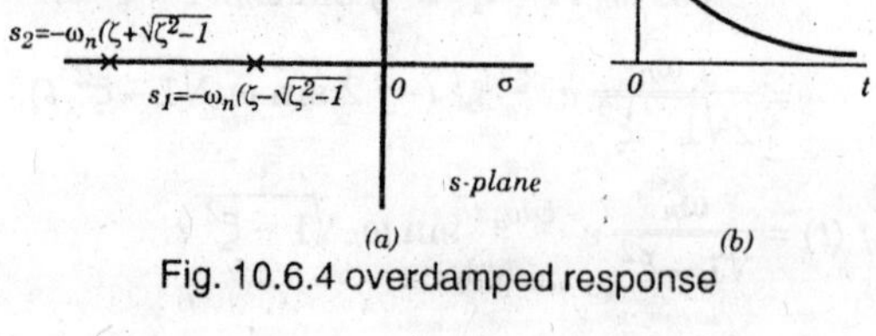


Fig. 10.6.4 overdamped response

*(iii)* $\xi > 1$ The poles $s_1$, $s_2 = -\xi\,\omega_n \pm \omega_n\sqrt{\xi^2 - 1}$ $= -\omega_n\,(\xi \pm \sqrt{\xi^2 - 1})$ are negative real located in $s$-plane as shown in Fig. 10.6.4(*a*)

The corresponding time response is given below,

$$f(t) = \frac{\omega_n}{j\sqrt{\xi^2 - 1}}\, e^{-\xi\,\omega_n t} \sin j\,\omega_n \sqrt{\xi^2 - 1}\, t$$

$$= \frac{\omega_n}{j\sqrt{\xi^2 - 1}}\, e^{-\xi\,\omega_n t}\, j \sinh \omega_n \sqrt{\xi^2 - 1}\, t$$

$$= \frac{\omega_n}{\sqrt{\xi^2 - 1}}\, e^{-\xi\,\omega_n t}\, \frac{(e^{\omega_n \sqrt{\xi^2 - 1}\, t} - e^{-\omega_n \sqrt{\xi^2 - 1}\, t})}{2}$$

or
$$f(t) = \frac{\omega_n}{\sqrt{\xi^2 - 1}}\, [e^{-\omega_n(\xi - \sqrt{\xi^2 - 1})\, t} - e^{-\omega_n(\xi + \sqrt{\xi^2 - 1})\, t}]$$

The pole $s_2 = -\omega_n(\xi + \sqrt{\xi^2 - 1})$ is located away towards left of pole $s_1 = -\omega_n\,(\xi - \sqrt{\xi^2 - 1})$ as such the effect of pole $s_2$ with regard to time response vanishes faster as compared to that of $s_1$. (In other words the time constant due to pole $s_2$ acts faster as compared to that due to pole $s_1$ ). Hence, to a fair approximation the effect of pole $s_2$ on the time response can be neglected. Thus, the time response can be written as

$$f(t) = \frac{\omega_n}{2\sqrt{\xi^2 - 1}}\, e^{-\omega_n\,(\xi - \sqrt{\xi^2 - 1})\, t}$$

The time response is overdamped as shown in Fig. 10.6.4 (*b*)

(*iv*) Consider a network function given below,

$$F(s) = \frac{K}{s + a}$$

The single pole is located at $s = -a$ [ Fig. 10.6.5 (*a*) ]

Taking inverse Laplace transform for $F(s)$ on both sides

$$\pounds^{-1} F(s) = \pounds^{-1} \frac{K}{s - a}$$

$$\therefore \qquad f(t) = K\, e^{-at}$$

The pole $s = -a$ is negative real. The time response is shown in Fig. 10.6.5 (*b*)

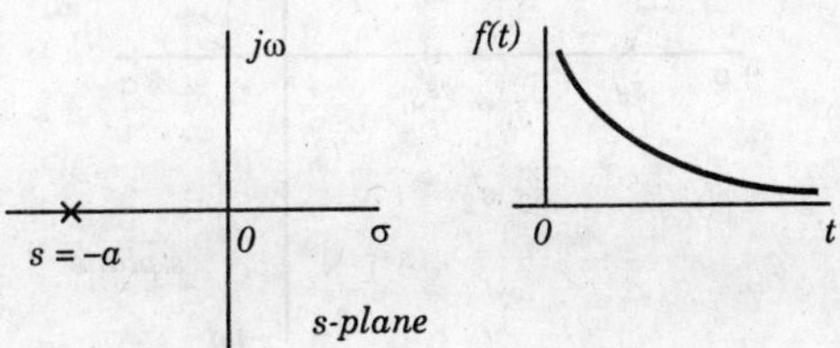


Fig. 10.6.5 Negative real pole: time response.

(*v*) Consider a network function given below,

$$F(s) = \frac{\omega_n^2}{s^2 - 2\,\xi\,\omega_n\,s + \omega_n^2}$$

(Note that the coefficient of *s* term in the denominator has negative sign.)

The poles are $s_1, s_2 = \xi\,\omega_n \pm j\,\omega_n\sqrt{1-\xi^2}$.

**For $\xi < 1$,** The time response can be determined as

$$f(t) = \frac{\omega_n}{\sqrt{1-\xi^2}}\,e^{\xi\,\omega_n\,t}\,\sin\omega_n\sqrt{1-\xi^2}\;t$$

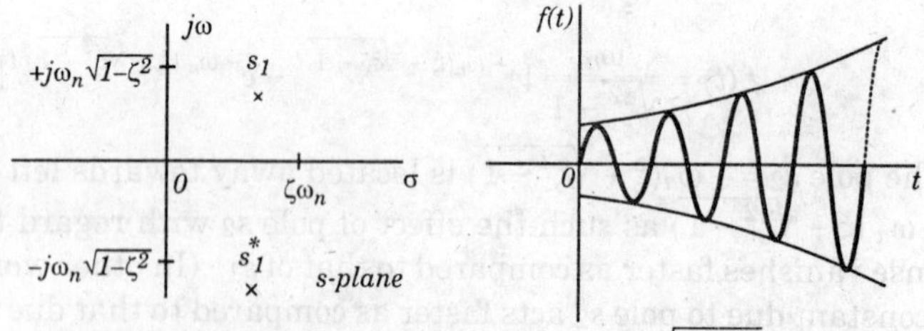


Fig. 10.6.6 Pole location $s_1, s_2 = \xi\,\omega_n \pm j\,\omega_n\sqrt{1-\xi^2}$, $\xi < 1$. Time response (growing oscillations).

The poles $s_1, s_2 = \xi\,\omega_n \pm j\,\omega_n\sqrt{1-\xi^2}$ are complex having +ive real part located in s - plane as shown in Fig. 10.6.6(*a*). The corresponding time response where the oscillations grow with time is shown in Fig. 10.6.6(*b*). This type of response is unstable and not desirable.

Simple poles and complex poles of multiplicity 1 should have a negative real part for stable response. However, complex poles of multiplicity 1 located on the imaginary axis lead to sustained oscillations in the response.

The poles whether simple or complex having positive real part are not permitted because they make the response unstable (growing response).

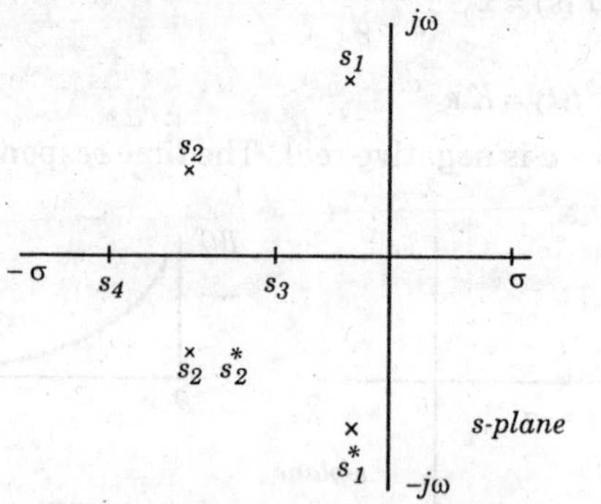


Fig. 11.6.7 pole locations in s-place.

Fig. 11.6.7 shows the pole locations in s-place. The complex poles $s_1, s_1^*$ give damped oscillatory response. The complex poles $s_2, s_2^*$ also give damped oscillatory response with more damping as compared to $s_1, s_1^*$.

The simple poles $s_3$ and $s_4$ lead to over damped response but the response due to $s_4$ provides more damping as compared to $s_3$.

It is noted that as the poles move away towards *L.H.S.* from the imaginary axis in the s - plane their effect on the response decreases because of relative decrease in the time constant.

The response is dominated by the *L.H.S.* poles nearer to the imaginary axis of s - plane. Hence, these poles are called dominant poles.

## 10.7 SOLVED EXAMPLES.

**Example 10.7.1** *Determine the driving point impedance at terminals* 1 – 1′ *for the network shown in Fig. 10.7.1.*

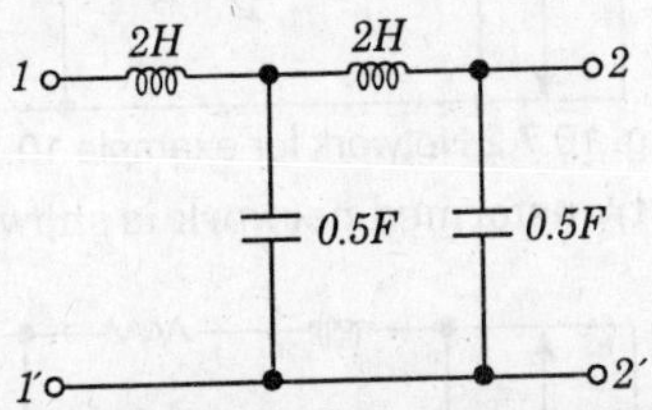


Fig. 10.7.1 Network for example 10.7.1

**Solution :** The transformed network is shown in Fig. 10.7.1 (*a*).

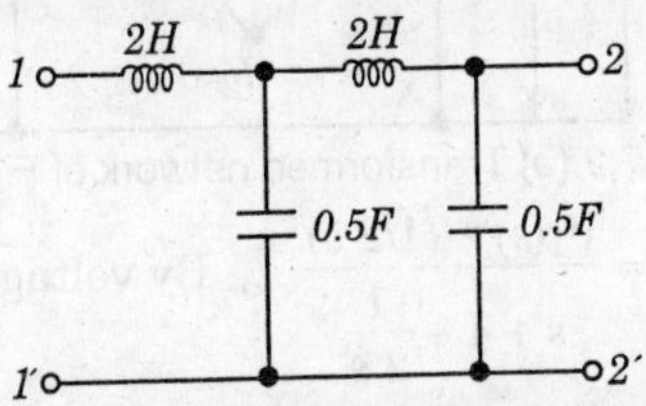


Fig. 10.7.1 (*a*). Transformed network

$$Z_{11}(s) = Z_1(s) + \cfrac{1}{Y_2(s) + \cfrac{1}{Z_3(s) + \cfrac{1}{Y_4(s)}}}$$

Substituting the values,

$$Z_{11}(s) = 2\,s + \cfrac{1}{\cfrac{s}{2} + \cfrac{1}{2\,s + \cfrac{1}{s/2}}}$$

$$= 2\,s + \cfrac{1}{\cfrac{s}{2} + \cfrac{1}{2\,s + \cfrac{2}{s}}} = 2\,s + \cfrac{1}{\cfrac{s}{2} + \cfrac{s}{2\,s^2 + 2}}$$

$$= 2\,s + \frac{2\,(2\,s^2 + 2)}{2\,s^3 + 2\,s + 2\,s} = \frac{4\,s^4 + 8\,s^2 + 4\,s^2 + 4}{2\,s^3 + 4\,s}$$

or $$Z_{11}(s) = \frac{2\,s^4 + 6\,s^2 + 2}{s^3 + 2\,s} \text{ ... Ans.}$$

**Example . 10.7.2** *Determine* $V_2(s)/V_1(s)$, $I_2(s)/I_1(s)$ and $Z_{12}(s)$. *The network is shown in Fig. 10.7.2*

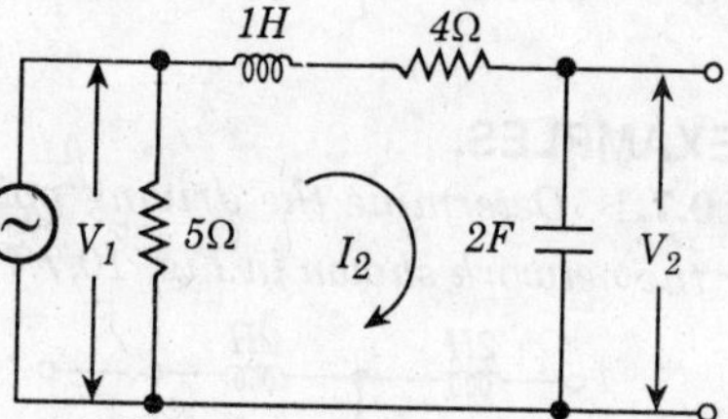


Fig. 10.7.2 Network for example 10.7.2.

**Solution :** The transformed network is shown in Fig. 10.7.2 (*a*).

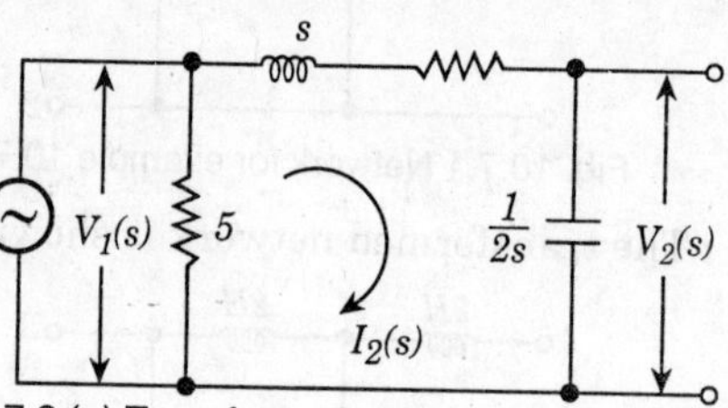


Fig. 10.7.2 (*a*) Transformed network of Fig. 10.7.2

(*i*) $$V_2(s) = \frac{V_1(s) \times (1/2\,s)}{s + 4 + \dfrac{1}{2\,s}} \text{ ... By voltage division}$$

$$\therefore \quad \frac{V_2(s)}{V_1(s)} = \frac{1}{2\,s^2 + 8\,s + 1} \text{ ... Ans.}$$

(*ii*) $$I_2(s) = I_1(s) \times \frac{5}{5 + s + 4 + \dfrac{1}{2s}}$$

$$\therefore \quad \frac{I_2(s)}{I_1(s)} = \frac{10\,s}{2\,s^2 + 18\,s + 1} \text{ ... Ans.}$$

(*iii*) $$V_2(s) = I_2(s) \times \frac{1}{2\,s} = I_1(s) \times \frac{5}{5 + s + 4 + \dfrac{1}{2s}} \times \frac{1}{2\,s}$$

$$\therefore \quad Z_{12}(s) = \frac{V_2(s)}{I_1(s)} = \frac{5}{2\,s^2 + 18\,s + 1} \quad \text{... Ans.}$$

**Example . 10.7.3** *Determine* $G_{12}$, $Z_{12}$, $\alpha_{12}$ and $Y_{12}$ *for the network shown in Fig. 10.7.3.*

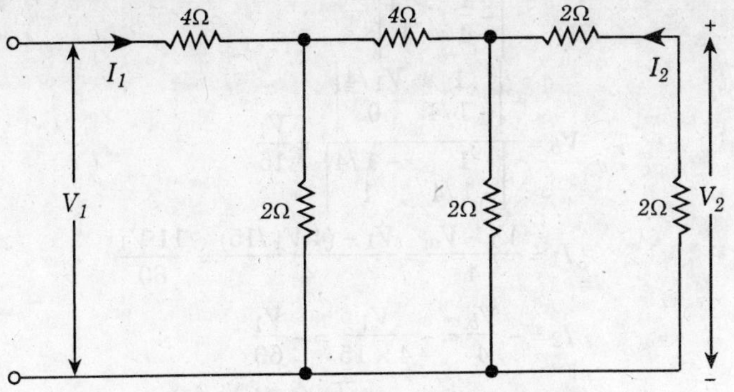

Fig. 10.7.3 Network for example 10.7.3.

**Solution :** The network of Fig. 10.7.3 is redrawn as shown in Fig. 10.7.3 (*a*).

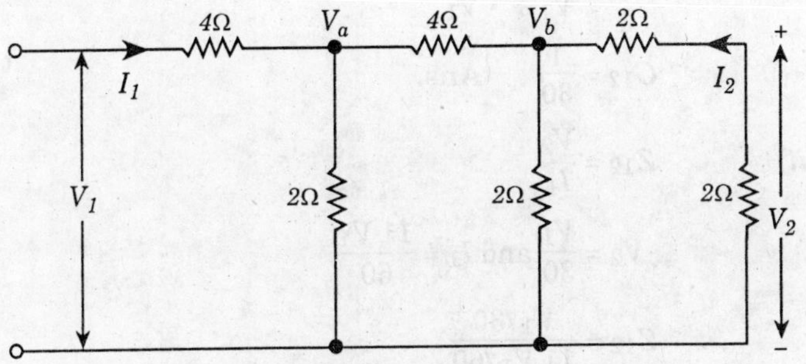

Fig. 10.7.3 (*a*). Network of Fig. 10.7.3 redrawn.

The node voltage equations are written below,

$$\text{At node } a \;:\; -\frac{(V_1 - V_a)}{4} + \frac{V_a - V_b}{4} + \frac{V_a}{2} = 0$$

$$\text{At node } b \;:\; \frac{V_b - V_a}{4} + \frac{V_b}{2} + \frac{V_b}{2+2} = 0$$

The equations given above are simplified and determinant form written below,

$$\begin{vmatrix} 1 & -\frac{1}{4} \\ -\frac{1}{4} & 1 \end{vmatrix} \begin{vmatrix} V_a \\ V_b \end{vmatrix} = \begin{vmatrix} V_1/4 \\ 0 \end{vmatrix}$$

$$V_a = \frac{\begin{vmatrix} \frac{V_1}{4} & -\frac{1}{4} \\ 0 & 1 \end{vmatrix}}{\begin{vmatrix} 1 & -\frac{1}{4} \\ -\frac{1}{4} & 1 \end{vmatrix}} = \frac{4\,V_1}{15}$$

$$V_b = \frac{\begin{vmatrix} 1 & V_1/4 \\ -1/4 & 0 \end{vmatrix}}{\begin{vmatrix} 1 & -1/4 \\ -1/4 & 1 \end{vmatrix}} = \frac{V_1}{15}$$

$$I_1 = \frac{V_1 - V_a}{4} = \frac{V_1 - (4\,V_1/15)}{4} = \frac{11\,V_1}{60}$$

$$I_2 = -\frac{V_b}{4} = -\frac{V_1}{4 \times 15} = -\frac{V_1}{60}$$

$$V_2 = 2 \times (-I_2) = 2 \times \left[-\left(-\frac{V_1}{60}\right)\right] = \frac{V_1}{30}$$

(*i*) $$G_{12} = \frac{V_2}{V_1} = \frac{V_1/30}{V_1}$$

or $$G_{12} = \frac{1}{30} \quad \textbf{Ans.}$$

(*ii*) $$Z_{12} = \frac{V_2}{I_1}$$

$\because$ $$V_2 = \frac{V_1}{30} \text{ and } I_1 = \frac{11\,V_1}{60}$$

$\therefore$ $$Z_{12} = \frac{V_1/30}{11\,V_1/60}$$

or $$Z_{12} = \frac{2}{11}\,\Omega \quad \textbf{Ans.}$$

(*iii*) $$\alpha_{12} = \frac{I_2}{I_1}$$

$\because$ $$I_2 = -\frac{V_1}{60} \text{ and } I_1 = \frac{11\,V_1}{60}$$

$\therefore$ $$\alpha_{12} = \frac{-V_1/60}{11\,V_1/60} = -\frac{1}{11} \quad \textbf{Ans.}$$

(*iv*) $$Y_{12} = \frac{I_2}{V_1}$$

$\because$ $$I_2 = -\frac{V_1}{60}$$

$$\therefore \qquad Y_{12} = \frac{-V_1/60}{V_1} = -\frac{1}{60} \ \mho \ \textbf{Ans.}$$

**Example 10.7.4** *Determined driving point and admittance $Y_{11}(s)$ and transfer admittance $Y_{12}(s)$. The network is shown in Fig. 10.7.4*

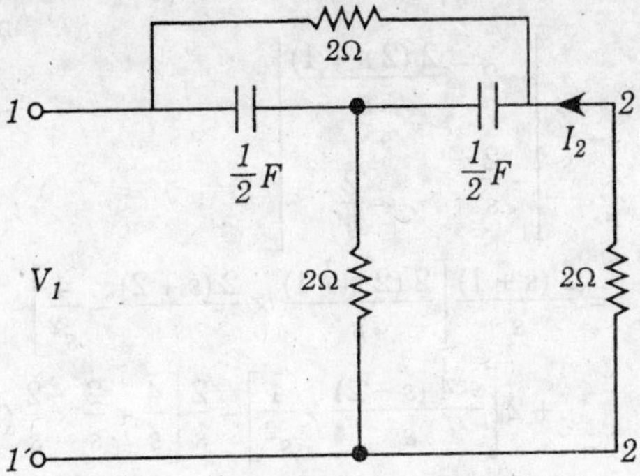


Fig. 10.7.4 Network for example 10.7.4

**Solution :** The transformed network is shown in Fig. 10.7.4 (*a*)

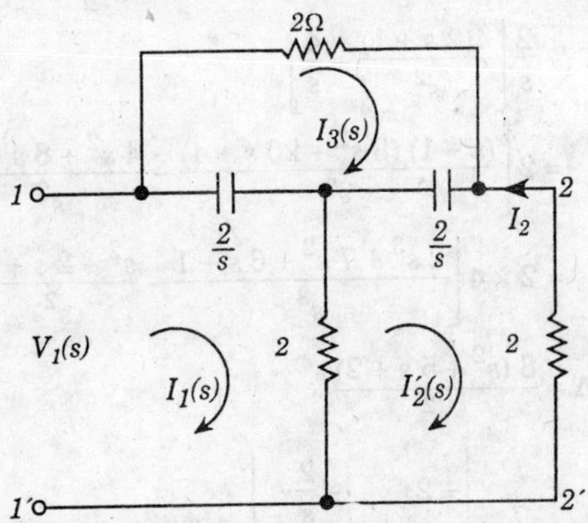


Fig. 10.7.4 (a) Transformed network of Fig. 10.7.4

As per Fig. 10.7.4 (*a*), the determinant on loop analysis basis is written below.

$$\Delta = \begin{vmatrix} \dfrac{2(s+1)}{s} & -2 & -\dfrac{2}{s} \\ -2 & \dfrac{2(2s+1)}{s} & -\dfrac{2}{s} \\ -\dfrac{2}{s} & -\dfrac{2}{s} & \dfrac{2(s+2)}{s} \end{vmatrix}$$

The value of the determinant is determined below,

$$\Delta = \frac{2(s+1)}{s}\begin{vmatrix} \frac{2(s+1)}{s} & -\frac{2}{s} \\ -\frac{2}{s} & \frac{2(s+2)}{s} \end{vmatrix} - (-2)\begin{vmatrix} -2 & -\frac{2}{s} \\ -\frac{2}{s} & \frac{2(s+2)}{s} \end{vmatrix}$$

$$-\frac{2}{s}\begin{vmatrix} -2 & \frac{2(2s+1)}{s} \\ -\frac{2}{s} & -\frac{2}{s} \end{vmatrix}$$

$$= \frac{2(s+1)}{s}\left[\frac{2(2s+1)}{s} \times \frac{2(s+2)}{s} - \frac{4}{s^2}\right]$$

$$+ 2\left[\frac{-4(s+2)}{s} - \frac{4}{s^2}\right] - \frac{2}{s}\left[\frac{4}{s} + \frac{2}{s} \times \frac{2}{s}(2s+1)\right]$$

$$= \frac{2(s+1)}{s}\left[\frac{4(2s^2+5s+2)}{s^2} - \frac{4}{s^2}\right] + 2\left[\frac{-4s-8}{s} - \frac{4}{s^2}\right]$$

$$-\frac{2}{s}\left[\frac{4(2s+1)}{s^2} + \frac{4}{s}\right]$$

$$= 2\left[\frac{(s+1)(8s^2+20s+4)}{s^3} - \frac{4s^2+8s+4}{s^2} - \frac{12s+4}{s^3}\right]$$

$$= 2 \times 4\left[\frac{2s^3+7s^2+6s+1}{s^3} - \frac{s^2+2s+1}{s^2} - \frac{3s+1}{s^3}\right]$$

or
$$\Delta = \frac{8(s^2+5s+2)}{s^2}$$

$$\Delta_{21} = (-1)\begin{vmatrix} -2 & -\frac{2}{s} \\ -\frac{2}{s} & \frac{2(s+2)}{s} \end{vmatrix} = \frac{4(s^2+2s+1)}{s^2}$$

$$\Delta_{11} = (+1)\begin{vmatrix} \frac{2(2s+1)}{s} & -\frac{2}{s} \\ -\frac{2}{s} & \frac{2(2s+1)}{s} \end{vmatrix} = \frac{4(2s^2+5s+1)}{s^2}$$

$$Y_{11}(s) = \frac{\Delta_{11}}{\Delta} = \frac{4(2s^2+5s+1)/s^2}{8(s^2+5s+2)/s^2} = \frac{2s^2+5s+1}{2(s^2+5s+2)} \quad \textbf{Ans.}$$

$$\frac{I'_2(s)}{V_1(s)} = \frac{\Delta_{21}}{\Delta}$$

$\because \quad I_2(s) = -I'_2(s)$

$$\therefore \quad Y_{12}(s) = -\frac{\Delta_{21}}{\Delta}$$

$$\text{or} \quad Y_{12}(s) = -\frac{4\,(s^2 + 2\,s + 1)/s^2}{8\,(s^2 + 5\,s + 2)/s^2}$$

$$= -\frac{(s^2 + 2\,s + 1)}{2\,(s^2 + 5\,s + 2)} \quad \textbf{Ans.}$$

**Example 10.7.5** *The network shown in Fig. 10.7.5 consists of resistors and controlled sources. Determine voltage transfer function* $G_{12} = \dfrac{V_2}{V_1}$ *and transfer impedance* $Z_{12} = \dfrac{V_2}{I_1}$

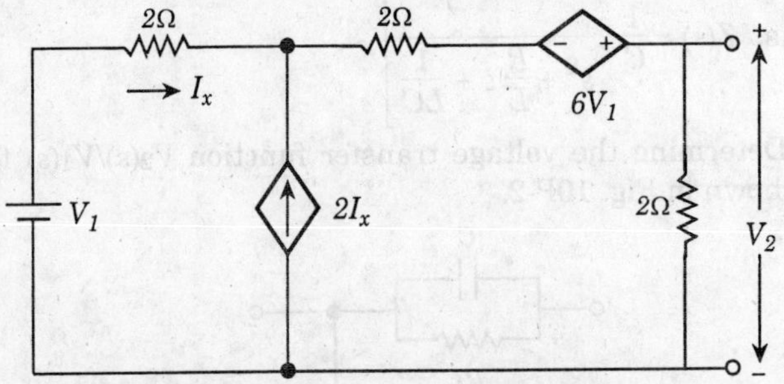


Fig. 10.7.5 Network for example 10.7.5.

**Solution :** Applying Kirchhoff's voltage law

$$2\,I_x + 2\,(I_x + 2\,I_x) - 6\,V_1 + 2\,(I_x + 2\,I_x) - V_1 = 0$$

$$\text{or} \quad 7\,V_1 = 14\,I_x$$

$$\therefore \quad V_1 = 2\,I_x$$

$$V_2 = 2 \times (I_x + 2\,I_x) = 6\,I_x$$

$$(i) \quad G_{12} = \frac{V_2}{V_1}$$

$$= \frac{6\,I_x}{2\,I_x} = 3 \quad \textbf{Ans.}$$

$$(ii) \quad Z_{12} = \frac{V_2}{V_1}$$

$$\because \quad V_2 = 6\,I_x \text{ and } I_1 = I_x$$

$$\therefore \quad Z_{12} = \frac{6\,I_x}{I_x}$$

$$= 6\ \Omega \quad \textbf{Ans.}$$

## PROBLEMS

**10.1** Determine the input impedance. The network is shown in Fig. 10P-1.

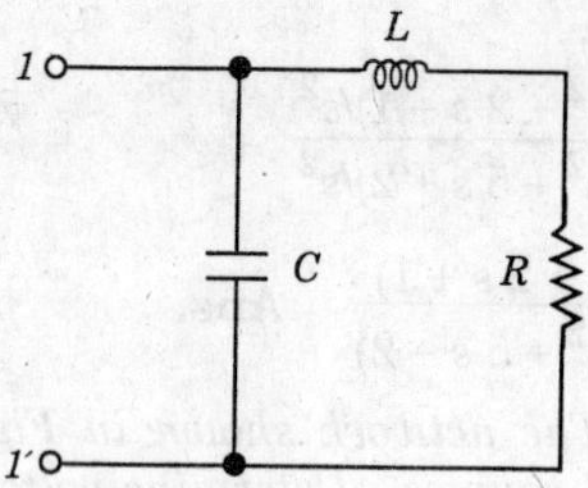


Fig. 10 P-1

$$\left[\textbf{Ans. } Z(s) = \frac{1}{C}\cdot\frac{\left(s+\dfrac{R}{L}\right)}{s^2+\dfrac{R}{L}s+\dfrac{1}{LC}}\right]$$

**10.2** Determine the voltage transfer function $V_2(s)/V_1(s)$ for the network shown in Fig. 10P-2.

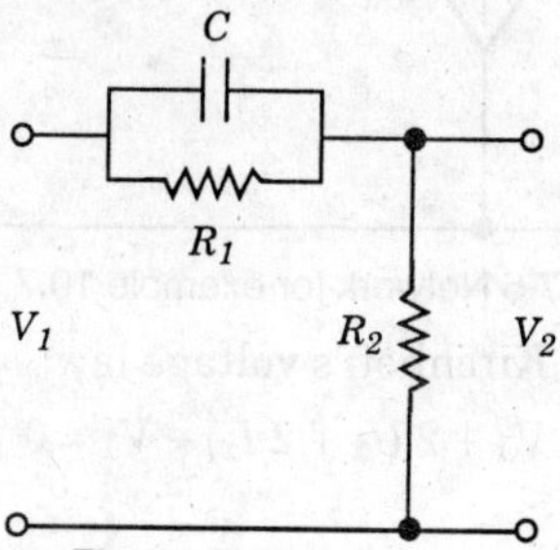


Fig. 10 P-2

$$\left[\textbf{Ans. } \frac{V_2(s)}{V_1(s)} = \frac{s+\dfrac{1}{R_1C}}{s+\left(\dfrac{R_1+R_2}{R_1R_2C)}\right)}\right]$$

**10.3** Obtain voltage ratio transfer function. The network is shown in Fig. 10P-3.

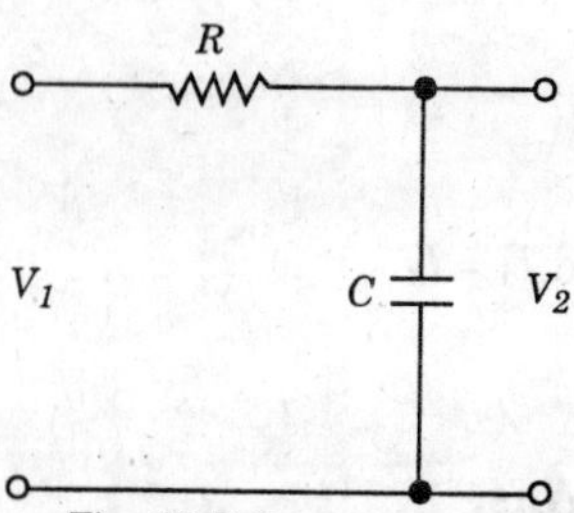


Fig. 10 P-3

**Ans.** $\dfrac{V_2(s)}{V_1(s)} = \dfrac{1}{RC\,(s + \frac{1}{RC})}$

**10.4** Determine the driving point impedance for the network is shown in Fig. 10P-4.

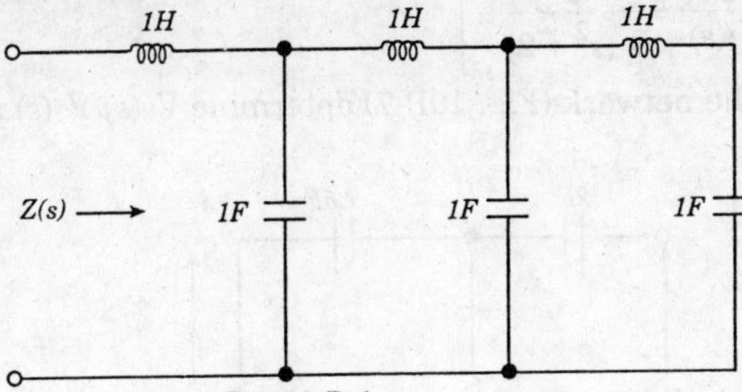


Fig. 10 P-4

$$\left[\textbf{Ans. } Z(s) = \frac{s^6 + 5\,s^4 + 6\,s^2 + 1}{s\,(s^4 + 4\,s^2 + 3}\right]$$

**10.5** Determine $G_{12}(s) = \dfrac{V_2(s)}{V_1(s)}$ and $Z_{12}(s) = \dfrac{V_2(s)}{I_1(s)}$. The network is shown in Fig. 10P-5.

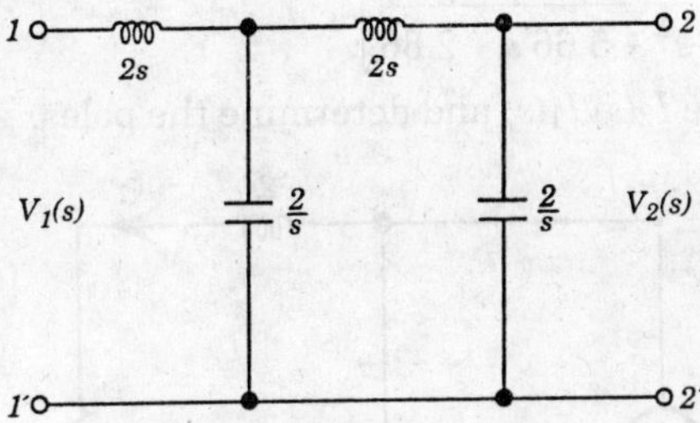


Fig. 10 P-5

$$\left[\textbf{Ans. } G_{12}(s) = \frac{1}{s^4 + 3\,s^2 + 1},\ Z_{12}(s) = \frac{2}{s\,(s^2 + 2)}\right]$$

**10.6** Determine $\dfrac{V_1(s)}{I_1(s)}$, $\dfrac{V_2(s)}{V_1(s)}$ and $\dfrac{V_2(s)}{I_1(s)}$ for the network is given below.

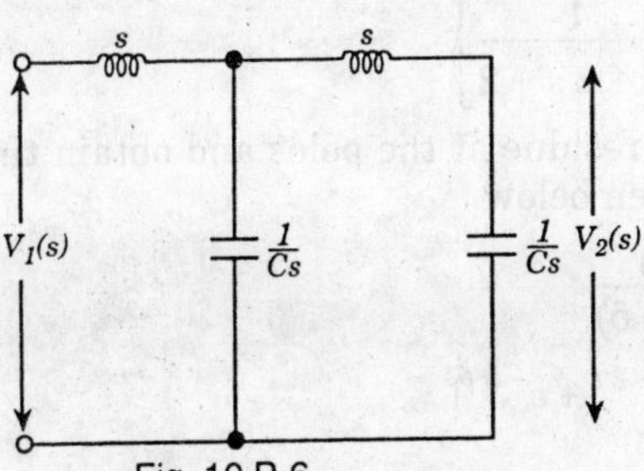


Fig. 10 P-6

$$\left[\textbf{Ans.}\ \frac{V_1(s)}{I_1(s)} = \frac{s^4 + 3s^2 + 1}{s(s^2+2)},\quad \frac{V_2(s)}{V_1(s)} = \frac{1}{s^4 + 3s^2 + 1},\quad \frac{V_2(s)}{I_1(s)} = \frac{1}{s(s^2+2)}\right]$$

**10.7** For the network (Fig. 10P-7) determine $V_2(s)/V_1(s)$ and draw pole-zero plot.

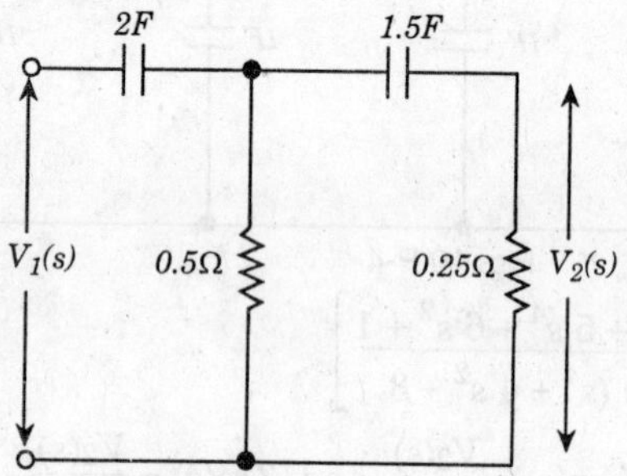


Fig. 10 P-7

$$\left[\textbf{Ans.}\ \frac{V_2(s)}{V_1(s)} = \frac{s^2}{s^2 + 5.66\,s + 2.66}\right]$$

**10.8** Determine $I_2(s)/I_1(s)$ and determine the poles.

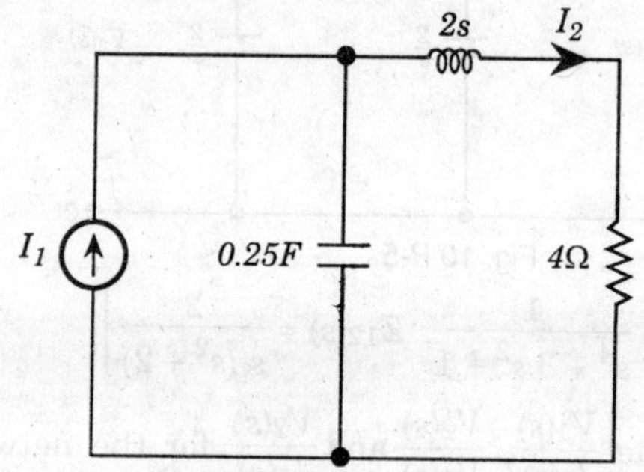


Fig. 10 P-8

$$\left[\textbf{Ans.}\ \frac{I_2(s)}{I_1(s)} = \frac{1}{s^2 + 2s + 2}\right]$$

**10.9** Determine residue at the poles and obtain time response for the $V(s)$ function given below.

$$V(s) = \frac{3(s+4)}{(s+2)(s+5)}$$

[**Ans.** $v(t) = 2e^{-2t} + e^{-5t}$]

**10.10** Determine the expression on for $i(t)$ having given

$$I(s) = \frac{4\,s}{(s+1)\,(s^2 + 2\,s + 5)}$$

[**Ans.** $i(t) = e^{-t}\,(\cos 2\,t + 2\,\sin 2\,t - 1)$]

# 11

# TWO-PORT PARAMETERS

## 11.1 INTRODUCTION

A two-port network is shown in Fig. 11.1.1 wherein terminals at the two ports are 1 – 1′ (*input*) and 2 – 2′ (*output*). The internal network

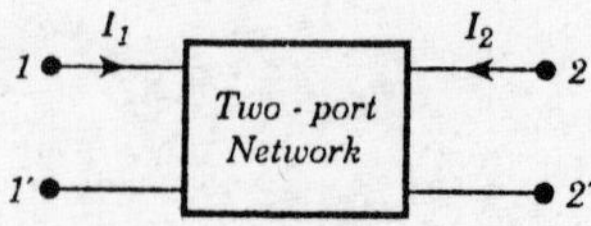


Fig. 11.1.1 Two-port network

contains passive, bilateral, linear, time-invariant elements. The internal network may or may not have active elements. The internal variables in a two-port network are not measurable. However, the variables, $V_1$, $I_1$ and $V_2$, $I_2$ at the respective ports are available for measurement. Thus, there are four $V_1$, $I_1$, $V_2$ and $I_2$ to be considered. Out of these four variables any two are independent variables while the remaining dependent variables. The variables can be selected in six combination as below :

1. Open-circuit impedance parameters relating $V_1, V_2$ with $I_1, I_2$ are as below :

$$V_1 = z_{11} I_1 + z_{12} I_2$$

$$V_2 = z_{21} I_1 + z_{22} I_2$$

2. Short-circuit admittance parameters relating, $I_1, I_2$ with $V_1, V_2$ are as below :

$$I_1 = y_{11} V_1 + y_{12} V_2$$

$$I_2 = y_{21} V_1 + y_{22} V_2$$

3. Transmission (chain) parameters relating $V_1, I_1$ with $V_2, I_2$ are as below :

$$V_1 = AV_2 - BI_2$$

$$I_1 = CV_2 - DI_2$$

4. Inverse transmission parameters relating $V_2, I_2$ with $V_1, I_1$ are as below :

$$V_2 = A' V_1 - B' I_1$$

$$I_2 = C' V_1 - D' I_1$$

5. Hybrid parameters relating $V_1$, $I_2$ with $I_1$, $V_2$ are as below :

$$V_1 = h_{11} I_1 + h_{12} V_2$$

$$I_2 = h_{21} I_1 + h_{22} V_2$$

6. Inverse hybrid parameters relating $I_1$, $V_2$ with $V_1$, $I_2$ are as below

$$I_1 = g_{11} V_1 + g_{12} I_2$$

$$V_2 = g_{21} V_1 + g_{22} I_2$$

## 11.2 DETERMINATION OF TWO-PORT PARAMETERS

(1) Open-circuit impedance parameters : $z_{11}, z_{12}, z_{21}, z_{22}$

$$V_1 = z_{11} I_1 + z_{12} I_2$$

$$V_2 = z_{21} I_1 + z_{22} I_2$$

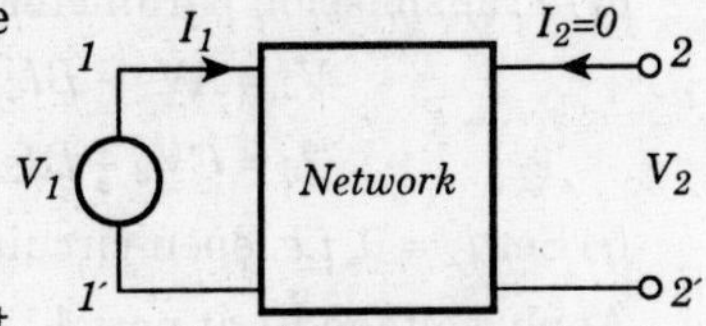


Fig. 11.2.1(a) Determination of $z_{11}$, $z_{21}$

(i) Set $I_2 = 0$, *i.e.* open-circuit at port 2.

Apply voltage $V_1$ at port 1

$$\therefore \quad z_{11} = \frac{V_1}{I_1}\bigg|_{I_2 = 0}$$

and $$z_{21} = \frac{V_2}{I_1}\bigg|_{I_2 = 0}$$

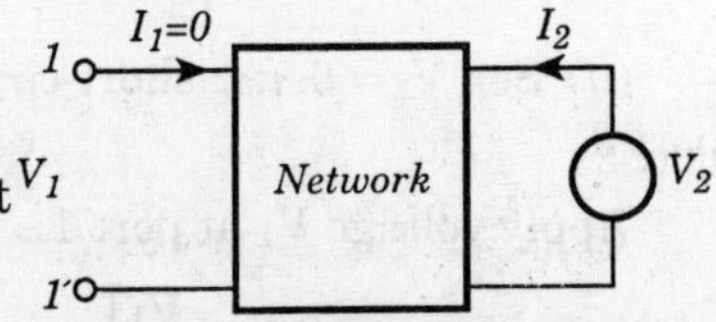


Fig. 11.2.1(b) Determination of $z_{12}$, $z_{22}$

(ii) Set $I_1 = 0$, open-circuit at port

Apply voltage $V_2$ at port 2.

$$\therefore \quad z_{12} = \frac{V_1}{I_2}\bigg|_{I_1 = 0}$$

and $$z_{22} = \frac{V_2}{I_2}\bigg|_{I_1 = 0}$$

(2) Short-circuit admittance parameters : $y_{11}, y_{12}, y_{21}, y_{22}$ .

$$I_1 = y_{11} V_1 + y_{12} V_2$$

$$I_2 = y_{21} V_1 + y_{22} V_2$$

(i) Set $V_2 = 0$, *i.e.*., short-circuit port 2.

Apply voltage $V_1$ at port 1.

$$\therefore \quad y_{11} = \frac{I_1}{V_1}\bigg|_{V_2 = 0}$$

and $$y_{21} = \frac{I_2}{V_1}\bigg|_{V_2 = 0}$$

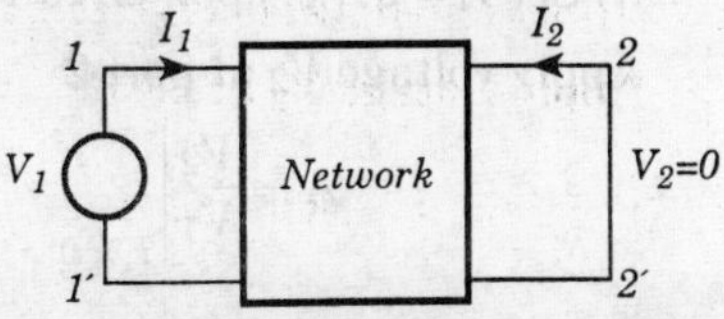


Fig. 11.2.2 (a) Determination of $y_{11}$, $y_{21}$

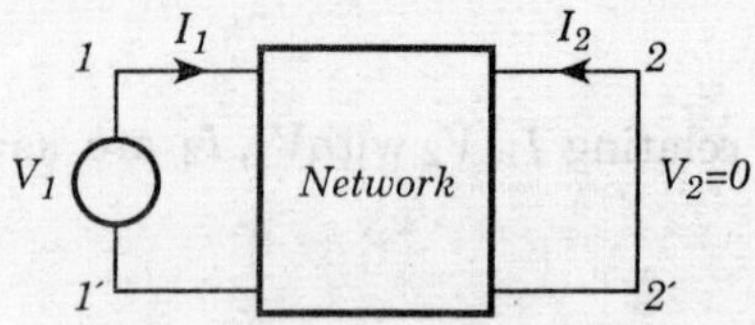


Fig. 11.2.2 (*a*) Determination of $y_{12}$, $y_{22}$

(*ii*) Set $V_1 = 0$, *i.e.* short-circuit port 1.

Apply voltage $V_2$ at port 2 .

$$\therefore \; y_{12} = \frac{I_1}{V_1} \Big| V_1 = 0$$

and $$y_{22} = \frac{I_2}{V_2} \Big| V_1 = 0$$

(3) Transmission parameters : $A, B, C, D$ .

$$V_1 = AV_2 - BI_2$$

$$I_1 = CV_2 - DI_2$$

(*i*) Set $I_2 = 0$, *i.e.* open-circuit at port 2.

Apply voltage $V_1$ at port 1

$$\therefore \quad A = \frac{V_1}{V_2}\Big|_{I_2 = 0}$$

and $$C = \frac{I_1}{V_2} \Big| I_2 = 0$$

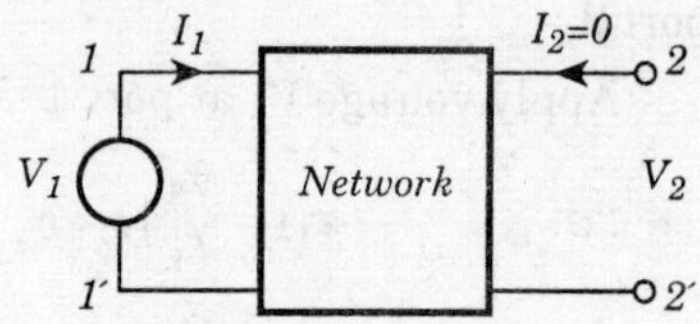


Fig. 11.2.3(*a*) Determination of $A$, $C$ .

(*ii*) Set $V_2 = 0$, *i.e.* short-circuit at port 2.

Apply voltage $V_1$ at port 1

$$\therefore \quad B = -\frac{V_1}{I_2}\Big|_{V_2 = 0}$$

and $$D = -\frac{I_1}{I_2}\Big|_{V_2 = 0}$$

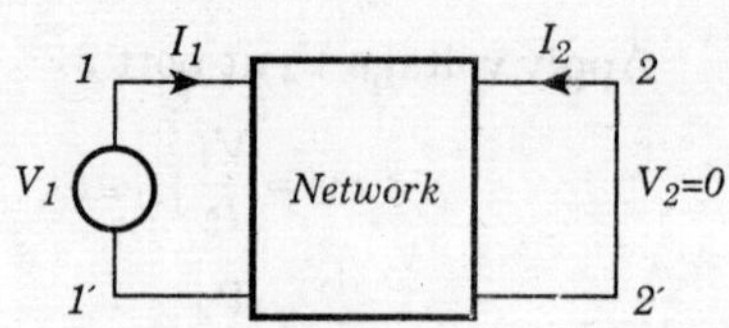


Fig. 11.2.3(*b*) Determination of $B$, $D$ .

(4) Inverse transmission parameters : $A', B', C' D'$

$$V_2 = A' V_1 - B' I_1$$

$$I_2 = C' V_1 - D' I_1$$

(*i*) Set $I_1 = 0$, *i.e.* open-circuit at port 1.

Apply voltage $V_2$ at port 2

$$\therefore \quad A' = \frac{V_2}{V_1}\Big|_{I_1 = 0}$$

and $$C' = \frac{I_2}{V_1}\Big|_{I_2 = 0}$$

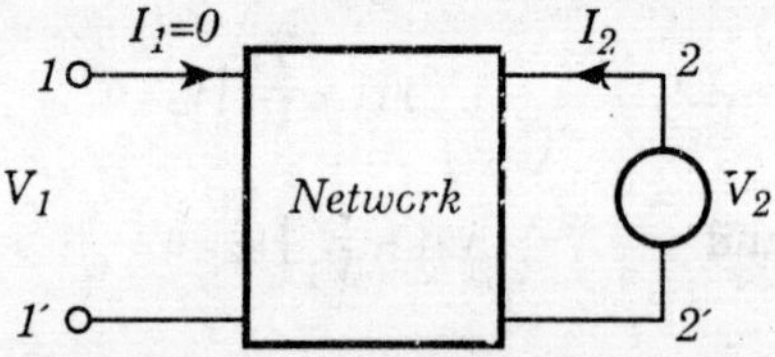


Fig. 11.2.4(*a*) Determination of $A'$, $C'$.

(*ii*) Set $V_1 = 0$, *i.e.* short-circuit at port 1.

Apply voltage $V_2$ at port 2

$$\therefore \quad B' = -\left.\frac{V_2}{I_1}\right|_{V_1 = 0}$$

and

$$D' = -\left.\frac{I_2}{I_1}\right|_{V_1 = 0}$$

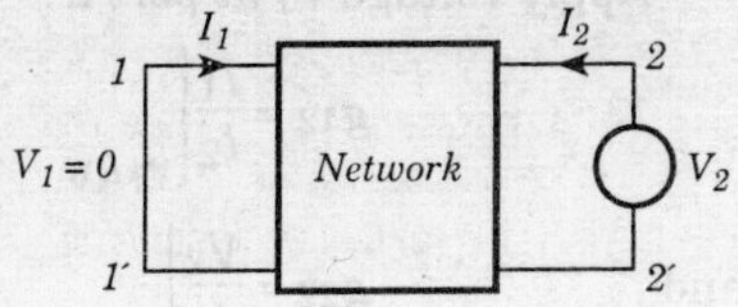


Fig. 11.2.4(*b*) Determination of *B*′, *D*′

(5) Hybrid (*h*) parameters :

$$V_1 = h_{11} I_1 + h_{12} V_2$$

$$I_2 = h_{21} I_1 + h_{22} V_2$$

(*i*) Set $V_2 = 0$, *i.e* .short-circuit port 2.

Apply voltage $V_1$ at port 1.

$$\therefore \quad h_{11} = \left.\frac{V_1}{I_1}\right|_{V_2 = 0}$$

and

$$h_{21} = \left.\frac{I_2}{I_1}\right|_{V_2 = 0}$$

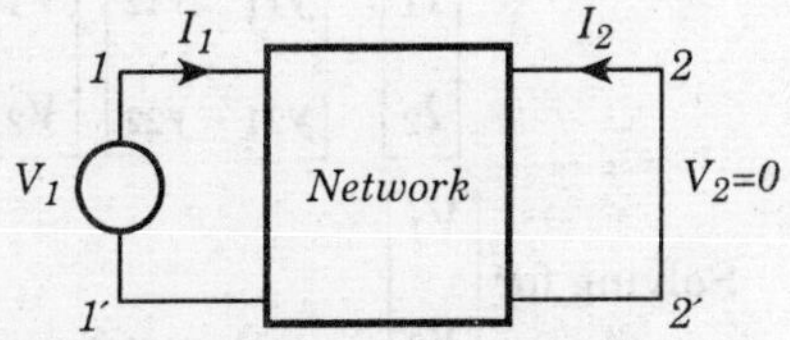


Fig. 11.2.5(*a*) Determination of $h_{11}$, $h_{21}$.

(*ii*) Set $I_1 = 0$, *i.e.* open-circuit port 1.

Apply voltage $V_2$ at port 2

$$\therefore \quad h_{12} = \left.\frac{V_1}{V_2}\right|_{I_1 = 0}$$

and

$$h_{22} = \left.\frac{I_2}{V_2}\right|_{I_1 = 0}$$

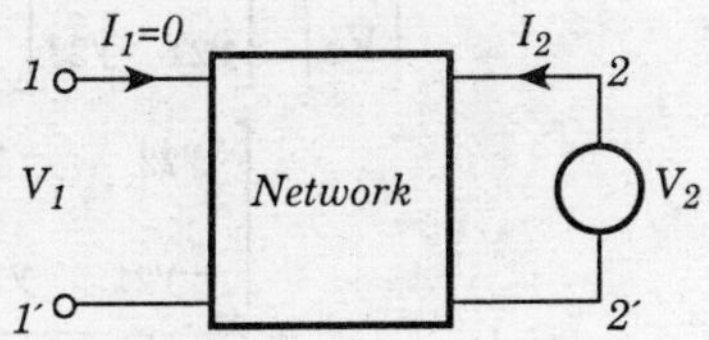


Fig. 11.2.5(*b*) Determination of $h_{12}$, $h_{22}$

(6) Inverse hybrid (*g*) parameters:

$$I_1 = g_{11} V_1 + g_{12} I_2$$

$$V_2 = g_{21} V_1 + g_{22} I_2$$

(*i*) Set $I_2 = 0$, *i.e* .open-circuit port 2.

Apply voltage $V_1$ at port 1.

$$\therefore \quad g_{11} = \left.\frac{I_1}{V_1}\right|_{I_2 = 0}$$

and

$$g_{21} = \left.\frac{V_2}{V_1}\right|_{I_2 = 0}$$

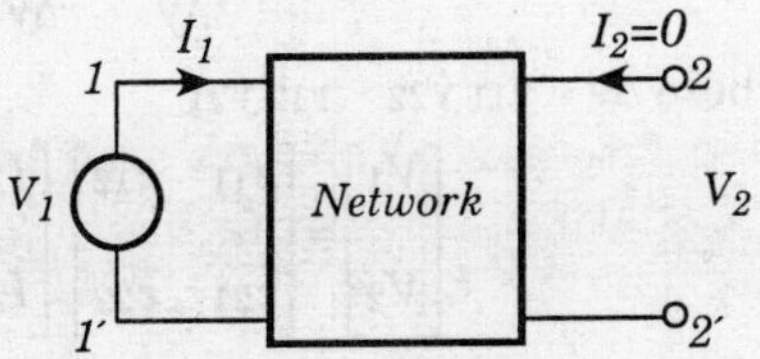


Fig. 11.2.6(*a*) Determination of $g_{11}$, $g_{21}$.

(*ii*) Set $V_1 = 0$, *i.e.* short-circuit port 1.

Apply voltage $V_1$ at port 2

$$\therefore \quad g_{12} = \left.\frac{I_1}{I_2}\right|_{V_1=0}$$

and

$$g_{22} = \left.\frac{V_2}{I_2}\right|_{V_1=0}$$

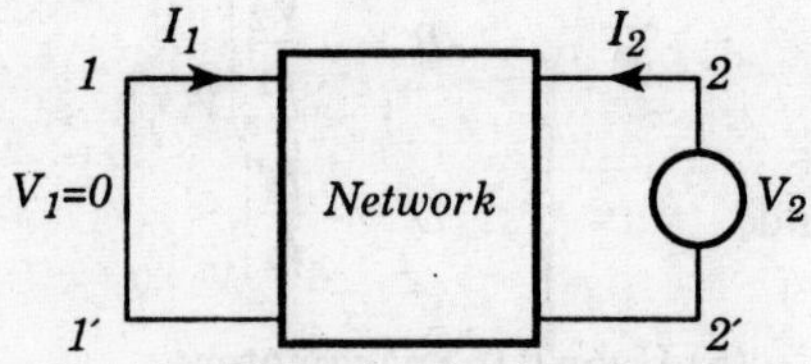


Fig. 11.2.6(*b*) Determination of $g_{12}$, $g_{22}$

## 11.3 RELATIONSHIPS BETWEEN TWO-PORT PARAMETERS.

### (1) *z*-parameters in Terms of *y*-parameters.

In matrix form the relation for *y*-parameters are

$$\begin{bmatrix} I_1 \\ I_2 \end{bmatrix} = \begin{bmatrix} y_{11} & y_{12} \\ y_{21} & y_{22} \end{bmatrix} \begin{bmatrix} V_1 \\ V_2 \end{bmatrix}$$

Solving for $\begin{bmatrix} V_1 \\ V_2 \end{bmatrix}$

$$\begin{bmatrix} V_1 \\ V_2 \end{bmatrix} = \begin{bmatrix} y_{11} & y_{12} \\ y_{21} & y_{22} \end{bmatrix}^{-1} \begin{bmatrix} I_1 \\ I_2 \end{bmatrix}$$

$$= \frac{\begin{bmatrix} y_{22} & -y_{12} \\ -y_{21} & y_{11} \end{bmatrix}\begin{bmatrix} I_1 \\ I_2 \end{bmatrix}}{\begin{vmatrix} y_{11} & y_{12} \\ y_{21} & y_{22} \end{vmatrix}} = \frac{\begin{bmatrix} y_{22} & -y_{12} \\ -y_{21} & y_{11} \end{bmatrix}\begin{bmatrix} I_1 \\ I_2 \end{bmatrix}}{y_{11}y_{22} - y_{12}y_{21}}$$

or

$$\begin{bmatrix} V_1 \\ V_2 \end{bmatrix} = \begin{bmatrix} \dfrac{y_{22}}{\Delta y} & -\dfrac{y_{12}}{\Delta y} \\ -\dfrac{y_{21}}{\Delta y} & \dfrac{y_{11}}{\Delta y} \end{bmatrix} \begin{bmatrix} I_1 \\ I_2 \end{bmatrix}$$

where $\Delta y = y_{11}y_{22} - y_{12}y_{21}$

$$\because \quad \begin{bmatrix} V_1 \\ V_2 \end{bmatrix} = \begin{bmatrix} z_{11} & z_{12} \\ z_{21} & z_{22} \end{bmatrix} \begin{bmatrix} I_1 \\ I_2 \end{bmatrix}$$

$$\therefore \quad \begin{bmatrix} z_{11} & z_{12} \\ z_{21} & z_{22} \end{bmatrix} = \begin{bmatrix} \dfrac{y_{22}}{\Delta y} & \dfrac{-y_{12}}{\Delta y} \\ \dfrac{-y_{21}}{\Delta y} & \dfrac{y_{11}}{\Delta y} \end{bmatrix}$$

### (2) *z*-parameters in Terms of (*ABCD*) Parameters

The relationships for *ABCD* (transmission) parameters are given below :

$$V_1 = AV_2 - BI_2 \qquad ...(1)$$

$$I_1 = CV_2 - DI_2 \qquad ...(2)$$

Substitute for $V_2$ in Eqn. (1) from Eqn. (2)

$$\therefore \quad V_1 = \frac{A\,(D\,I_2 + I_1)}{C} - B\,I_2 \qquad ...(3)$$

On rearranging Eqns. (3) and (2) ,

$$V_1 = \frac{A}{C} I_1 + \frac{(A\,D - B\,C)}{C} I_2$$

$$V_2 = \frac{1}{C} I_1 + \frac{D}{C} I_2$$

$$\therefore \quad \begin{bmatrix} V_1 \\ V_2 \end{bmatrix} = \begin{bmatrix} \dfrac{A}{C} & \dfrac{(AD - BC)}{C} \\ \dfrac{1}{C} & \dfrac{D}{C} \end{bmatrix} \begin{bmatrix} I_1 \\ I_2 \end{bmatrix}$$

or

$$\begin{bmatrix} V_1 \\ V_2 \end{bmatrix} = \begin{bmatrix} \dfrac{A}{C} & \dfrac{\Delta_T}{C} \\ \dfrac{1}{C} & \dfrac{D}{C} \end{bmatrix} \begin{bmatrix} I_1 \\ I_2 \end{bmatrix}$$

where $\Delta_T = AD - BC$

$$\because \quad \begin{bmatrix} V_1 \\ V_2 \end{bmatrix} = \begin{bmatrix} z_{11} & z_{12} \\ z_{21} & z_{22} \end{bmatrix} \begin{bmatrix} I_1 \\ I_2 \end{bmatrix}$$

$$\therefore \quad \begin{bmatrix} z_{11} & z_{12} \\ z_{21} & z_{22} \end{bmatrix} = \begin{bmatrix} \dfrac{A}{C} & \dfrac{\Delta_T}{C} \\ \dfrac{1}{C} & \dfrac{D}{C} \end{bmatrix}$$

### (3) z-parameters in Terms of *A′*, *B′*, *C′*, *D′* Parameters

The relationships for $A', B', C', D'$ (inverse transmission) parameters are given below :

$$V_2 = A'\,V_1 - B'\,I_1 \qquad ...(1)$$

$$I_2 = C' V_1 - D' I_1 \quad ...(2)$$

Substitute for $V_1$ in Eqn. (1) from Eqn. (2)

$$\therefore \quad V_2 = A' \frac{(D' I_1 + I_2)}{C'} - B' I_1 \quad ...(3)$$

Rearranging Eqns. (2) and (3),

$$V_1 = \frac{D'}{C'} I_1 + \frac{1}{C'} I_2$$

$$V_2 = \frac{(A' D' - B' C')}{C'} I_1 + \frac{A'}{C'} I_2$$

$$\therefore \quad \begin{bmatrix} V_1 \\ V_2 \end{bmatrix} = \begin{bmatrix} \dfrac{D'}{C'} & \dfrac{1}{C'} \\ \dfrac{A' D' - B' C'}{C'} & \dfrac{A'}{C'} \end{bmatrix} \begin{bmatrix} I_1 \\ I_2 \end{bmatrix}$$

or

$$\begin{bmatrix} V_1 \\ V_2 \end{bmatrix} = \begin{bmatrix} \dfrac{D'}{C'} & \dfrac{1}{C'} \\ \dfrac{\Delta_{T'}}{C'} & \dfrac{A'}{C'} \end{bmatrix} \begin{bmatrix} I_1 \\ I_2 \end{bmatrix}$$

where $\Delta_{T'} = A' D' - B' C'$

$$\because \quad \begin{bmatrix} V_1 \\ V_2 \end{bmatrix} = \begin{bmatrix} z_{11} & z_{12} \\ z_{21} & z_{22} \end{bmatrix} \begin{bmatrix} I_1 \\ I_2 \end{bmatrix}$$

$$\therefore \quad \begin{bmatrix} z_{11} & z_{12} \\ z_{21} & z_{22} \end{bmatrix} = \begin{bmatrix} \dfrac{D'}{C'} & \dfrac{1}{C'} \\ \dfrac{\Delta_{T'}}{C'} & \dfrac{A'}{C'} \end{bmatrix}$$

### (4) z-parameters in Terms of *h*-parameters

The relationship for $h$ (hybrid) parameters are given below :

$$V_1 = h_{11} I_1 + h_{12} V_2 \quad ...(1)$$

$$I_1 = h_{21} I_1 + h_{22} V_2 \quad ...(2)$$

Substitute for $V_2$ in Eqn. (1) from Eqn. (2)

$$\therefore \quad V_1 = h_{11} I_1 + h_{12} \frac{(I_2 - h_{22} I_1)}{h_{22}} \quad ...(3)$$

On rearranging Eqns. (3) and (1)

$$V_1 = \frac{(h_{11} h_{22} - h_{12} h_{21})}{h_{22}} I_1 + \frac{I_{12}}{h_{22}} I_2$$

$$V_2 = -\frac{h_{21}}{h_{22}} I_1 + \frac{1}{h_{22}} I_2$$

$$\therefore \quad \begin{bmatrix} V_1 \\ V_2 \end{bmatrix} = \begin{bmatrix} \dfrac{(h_{11}\,h_{22} - h_{12}\,h_{21}}{h_{22}} I_1 & \dfrac{h_{12}}{h_{22}} \\ -\dfrac{h_{21}}{h_{22}} I_1 & \dfrac{1}{h_{22}} \end{bmatrix} \begin{bmatrix} I_1 \\ I_2 \end{bmatrix}$$

or
$$\begin{bmatrix} V_1 \\ V_2 \end{bmatrix} = \begin{bmatrix} \dfrac{\Delta_h}{h_{22}} & \dfrac{h_{12}}{h_{22}} \\ -\dfrac{h_{21}}{h_{22}} & \dfrac{1}{h_{22}} \end{bmatrix} \begin{bmatrix} I_1 \\ I_2 \end{bmatrix}$$

where $\Delta_h = h_{11}\,h_{22} - h_{12}\,h_{21}$

$$\because \quad \begin{bmatrix} V_1 \\ V_2 \end{bmatrix} = \begin{bmatrix} z_{11} & z_{12} \\ z_{21} & z_{22} \end{bmatrix} \begin{bmatrix} I_1 \\ I_2 \end{bmatrix}$$

$$\therefore \quad \begin{bmatrix} z_{11} & z_{12} \\ z_{21} & z_{22} \end{bmatrix} = \begin{bmatrix} \dfrac{\Delta_h}{h_{22}} & \dfrac{h_{12}}{h_{22}} \\ -\dfrac{h_{21}}{h_{22}} & \dfrac{1}{h_{22}} \end{bmatrix}$$

### (5) *z*-parameters in Terms of *g*-parameters

The relationships for $g$ (inverse hybrid) parameters are given below.

$$I_1 = g_{11}\,V_1 + g_{12}\,I_2 \qquad \text{...(1)}$$

$$V_2 = g_{21}\,V_1 + g_{22}\,I_2 \qquad \text{...(2)}$$

Substitute for $V_1$ in Eqn. (2) from Eqn. (1)

$$\therefore \quad V_2 = \frac{g_{21}}{g_{11}} I_1 + \frac{(g_{11}\,g_{22} - g_{12}\,g_{21})}{g_{11}} I_2 \qquad \text{...(3)}$$

Rearrange Eqns. (1)

$$V_1 = \frac{1}{g_{11}} I_1 \quad - \frac{g_{12}}{g_{11}} I_2$$

$$\therefore \quad \begin{bmatrix} V_1 \\ V_2 \end{bmatrix} = \begin{bmatrix} \dfrac{1}{g_{11}} & -\dfrac{g_{12}}{g_{11}} \\ \dfrac{g_{21}}{g_{11}} & \dfrac{(g_{11}\,g_{22} - g_{12}\,g_{21})}{g_{11}} \end{bmatrix} \begin{bmatrix} I_1 \\ I_2 \end{bmatrix}$$

or
$$\begin{bmatrix} V_1 \\ V_2 \end{bmatrix} = \begin{bmatrix} \dfrac{1}{g_{11}} & -\dfrac{g_{12}}{g_{11}} \\ \dfrac{g_{21}}{g_{11}} & \dfrac{\Delta_g}{g_{11}} \end{bmatrix} \begin{bmatrix} I_1 \\ I_2 \end{bmatrix}$$

where $\Delta_g = g_{11}\,g_{22} - g_{12}\,g_{21}$

$$\because \quad \begin{bmatrix} V_1 \\ V_2 \end{bmatrix} = \begin{bmatrix} z_{11} & z_{12} \\ z_{21} & z_{22} \end{bmatrix} \begin{bmatrix} I_1 \\ I_2 \end{bmatrix}$$

$$\therefore \quad \begin{bmatrix} z_{11} & z_{12} \\ z_{21} & z_{22} \end{bmatrix} = \begin{bmatrix} \dfrac{1}{g_{11}} & -\dfrac{g_{12}}{g_{11}} \\ \dfrac{g_{21}}{g_{11}} & \dfrac{\Delta_g}{g_{11}} \end{bmatrix}$$

## Condition for Reciprocal Two-port Networks

$$z_{12} = z_{21}$$

$$y_{12} = y_{21}$$

$$\Delta_T = 1$$

$$\Delta_{T'} = 1$$

$$h_{12} = -h_{21}$$

$$g_{12} = -g_{21}$$

## Conditions for Symmetrical Two-port Networks

$$z_{11} = z_{12}$$

$$y_{11} = y_{22}$$

$$A = D$$

$$A' = D'$$

$$\Delta_h = 1$$

$$\Delta_g = 1$$

Relationship between different two-port networks is given in Table 11.1.

$\Delta_z = z_{11}\, z_{22} - z_{12}\, z_{21}$ , $\Delta_y = y_{11}\, y_{22} - y_{12}\, y_{21}$

$\Delta_T = AD - BC$ , $\Delta_{T'} = A'\, D' - B'\, C'$

$\Delta_h = h_{11}\, h_{22} - h_{12}\, h_{21}$ , $\Delta_g = g_{11}\, g_{22} - g_{12}\, g_{21}$

## 11.4 INTERCONNECTION OF TWO-PORT NETWORKS

### (1) Series Connection

The series combination of two-port networks "$a$" and "$b$" is shown in Fig. 11.4.1

The $z$-parameters of the respective network are

$$[z_a] = \begin{bmatrix} z_{11a} & z_{12a} \\ z_{21a} & z_{22a} \end{bmatrix} \text{ and } [z_b] = \begin{bmatrix} z_{11b} & z_{12b} \\ z_{21b} & z_{22b} \end{bmatrix}$$

**Table 11.1**

| | $z$ | $y$ | $ABCD(T)$ | $A'B'C'D'(T')$ | $h$ | $g$ |
|---|---|---|---|---|---|---|
| $z$ | $\begin{matrix} z_{11} & z_{12} \\ z_{21} & z_{22} \end{matrix}$ | $\begin{matrix} \frac{y_{22}}{\Delta_y} & -\frac{y_{12}}{\Delta_y} \\ -\frac{y_{21}}{\Delta_y} & \frac{y_{11}}{\Delta_y} \end{matrix}$ | $\begin{matrix} \frac{A}{C} & \frac{\Delta_T}{C} \\ \frac{1}{C} & \frac{D}{C} \end{matrix}$ | $\begin{matrix} \frac{D'}{C'} & \frac{1}{C'} \\ \frac{\Delta_{T'}}{C'} & \frac{A'}{C'} \end{matrix}$ | $\begin{matrix} \frac{\Delta h}{h_{22}} & \frac{h_{12}}{h_{22}} \\ \frac{-h_{21}}{h_{22}} & \frac{1}{h_{22}} \end{matrix}$ | $\begin{matrix} \frac{1}{g_{11}} & \frac{-g_{12}}{g_{11}} \\ \frac{g_{21}}{g_{11}} & \frac{\Delta_g}{g_{11}} \end{matrix}$ |
| $y$ | $\begin{matrix} \frac{z_{22}}{\Delta_z} & -\frac{z_{12}}{\Delta_z} \\ -\frac{z_{21}}{\Delta_z} & \frac{z_{11}}{\Delta_z} \end{matrix}$ | $\begin{matrix} y_{11} & y_{12} \\ y_{21} & y_{22} \end{matrix}$ | $\begin{matrix} \frac{D}{B} & \frac{-\Delta_T}{B} \\ \frac{-1}{B} & \frac{A}{B} \end{matrix}$ | $\begin{matrix} \frac{A'}{B'} & \frac{-1}{B'} \\ \frac{-\Delta_{T'}}{B'} & \frac{D'}{B'} \end{matrix}$ | $\begin{matrix} \frac{1}{h_{11}} & \frac{-h_{12}}{h_{11}} \\ \frac{h_{21}}{h_{11}} & \frac{\Delta_h}{h_{11}} \end{matrix}$ | $\begin{matrix} \frac{\Delta_g}{g_{22}} & \frac{g_{12}}{g_{22}} \\ \frac{-g_{21}}{g_{22}} & \frac{1}{g_{22}} \end{matrix}$ |
| $ABCD(T)$ | $\begin{matrix} \frac{z_{11}}{z_{21}} & \frac{\Delta_z}{z_{21}} \\ \frac{1}{z_{21}} & \frac{z_{22}}{z_{21}} \end{matrix}$ | $\begin{matrix} -\frac{y_{22}}{y_{21}} & -\frac{1}{y_{21}} \\ -\frac{\Delta_y}{y_{21}} & -\frac{y_{11}}{y_{21}} \end{matrix}$ | $\begin{matrix} A & B \\ C & D \end{matrix}$ | $\begin{matrix} \frac{D'}{\Delta_{T'}} & \frac{B'}{\Delta_{T'}} \\ \frac{C'}{\Delta_{T'}} & \frac{A'}{\Delta_{T'}} \end{matrix}$ | $\begin{matrix} \frac{\Delta h}{h_{21}} & \frac{h_{11}}{h_{21}} \\ \frac{-h_{22}}{h_{21}} & \frac{-1}{h_{21}} \end{matrix}$ | $\begin{matrix} \frac{1}{g_{21}} & \frac{g_{22}}{g_{21}} \\ \frac{g_{11}}{g_{12}} & \frac{\Delta_g}{g_{11}} \end{matrix}$ |
| $A'B'C'D'(T')$ | $\begin{matrix} \frac{z_{22}}{z_{12}} & \frac{\Delta_z}{z_{12}} \\ \frac{1}{z_{12}} & \frac{z_{11}}{z_{12}} \end{matrix}$ | $\begin{matrix} -\frac{y_{11}}{y_{12}} & -\frac{1}{y_{12}} \\ -\frac{\Delta_y}{y_{12}} & -\frac{y_{22}}{y_{12}} \end{matrix}$ | $\begin{matrix} \frac{D}{\Delta_T} & \frac{B}{\Delta_T} \\ \frac{C}{\Delta_T} & \frac{A}{\Delta_T} \end{matrix}$ | $\begin{matrix} A' & B' \\ C' & D' \end{matrix}$ | $\begin{matrix} \frac{1}{h_{12}} & \frac{h_{11}}{h_{12}} \\ \frac{h_{22}}{h_{12}} & \frac{\Delta_h}{h_{12}} \end{matrix}$ | $\begin{matrix} \frac{-\Delta_g}{g_{12}} & \frac{-g_{12}}{g_{12}} \\ \frac{-g_{11}}{g_{22}} & -\frac{1}{g_{22}} \end{matrix}$ |
| $h$ | $\begin{matrix} \frac{\Delta_z}{z_{22}} & \frac{z_{12}}{z_{22}} \\ -\frac{z_{21}}{z_{22}} & \frac{1}{z_{22}} \end{matrix}$ | $\begin{matrix} \frac{1}{y_{11}} & -\frac{y_{12}}{y_{11}} \\ \frac{y_{21}}{y_{11}} & \frac{\Delta_y}{y_{11}} \end{matrix}$ | $\begin{matrix} \frac{B}{D} & \frac{\Delta_T}{D} \\ \frac{-1}{D} & \frac{C}{D} \end{matrix}$ | $\begin{matrix} \frac{B'}{A'} & \frac{1}{A'} \\ \frac{\Delta_{T'}}{A'} & \frac{C'}{A'} \end{matrix}$ | $\begin{matrix} h_{11} & h_{12} \\ h_{21} & h_{22} \end{matrix}$ | $\begin{matrix} \frac{g_{22}}{\Delta_g} & \frac{-g_{12}}{\Delta_g} \\ \frac{-g_{21}}{\Delta_g} & \frac{g_{11}}{\Delta_g} \end{matrix}$ |
| $g$ | $\begin{matrix} \frac{1}{z_{11}} & -\frac{z_{12}}{z_{11}} \\ \frac{z_{21}}{z_{11}} & \frac{\Delta_z}{z_{11}} \end{matrix}$ | $\begin{matrix} \frac{\Delta_y}{y_{22}} & \frac{y_{12}}{y_{22}} \\ -\frac{y_{21}}{y_{22}} & \frac{1}{y_{22}} \end{matrix}$ | $\begin{matrix} C_A & \frac{-\Delta_T}{A} \\ \frac{1}{A} & \frac{B}{A} \end{matrix}$ | $\begin{matrix} \frac{C'}{D'} & \frac{-1}{D'} \\ \frac{\Delta_{T'}}{D'} & \frac{B'}{D'} \end{matrix}$ | $\begin{matrix} \frac{h_{22}}{\Delta_h} & \frac{-h_{12}}{\Delta_h} \\ \frac{-h_{21}}{\Delta_h} & \frac{h_{11}}{\Delta_h} \end{matrix}$ | $\begin{matrix} g_{11} & g_{12} \\ g_{21} & g_{22} \end{matrix}$ |

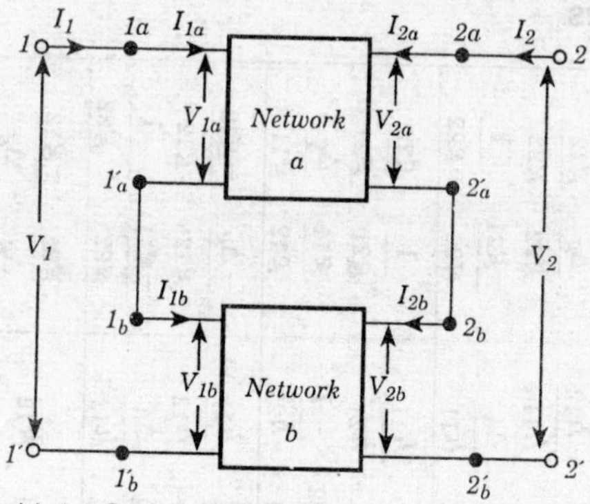


Fig.11.4.1 Series Connection of two-port networks.

Therefore, $$\begin{bmatrix} V_{1a} \\ V_{2a} \end{bmatrix} = \begin{bmatrix} z_{11a} & z_{12a} \\ z_{21a} & z_{22a} \end{bmatrix} \begin{bmatrix} I_{1a} \\ I_{2a} \end{bmatrix} \quad ...(1)$$

and $$\begin{bmatrix} V_{1b} \\ V_{2b} \end{bmatrix} = \begin{bmatrix} z_{11b} & z_{12b} \\ z_{21b} & z_{22b} \end{bmatrix} \begin{bmatrix} I_{1b} \\ I_{2b} \end{bmatrix} \quad ...(2)$$

Adding (1) and (2)

$$\begin{bmatrix} V_{1a} + V_{1b} \\ V_{2a} + V_{2b} \end{bmatrix} = \begin{bmatrix} z_{11a} & z_{12a} \\ z_{21a} & z_{22a} \end{bmatrix} \begin{bmatrix} I_{1a} \\ I_{2a} \end{bmatrix} + \begin{bmatrix} z_{11b} & z_{12b} \\ z_{21b} & z_{22b} \end{bmatrix} \begin{bmatrix} I_{1b} \\ I_{2b} \end{bmatrix}$$

As the two networks are connected in series at the input and output ports. Thus,

$$I_1 = I_{1a} = I_{1b}$$

and $$I_2 = I_{2a} = I_{2b}$$

Also, $$V_1 = V_{1a} + V_{1b}$$

and $$V_2 = V_{2a} + V_{2b}$$

$$\therefore \quad \begin{bmatrix} V_1 \\ V_2 \end{bmatrix} = \begin{bmatrix} z_{11a} & z_{12a} \\ z_{21a} & z_{22a} \end{bmatrix} \begin{bmatrix} I_1 \\ I_2 \end{bmatrix} + \begin{bmatrix} z_{11b} & z_{12b} \\ z_{21b} & z_{22b} \end{bmatrix} \begin{bmatrix} I_1 \\ I_2 \end{bmatrix}$$

or $$\begin{bmatrix} V_1 \\ V_2 \end{bmatrix} = \begin{bmatrix} z_{11a} + z_{11b} & z_{12a} + z_{12b} \\ z_{21a} + z_{21b} & z_{22a} + z_{22b} \end{bmatrix} \begin{bmatrix} I_1 \\ I_2 \end{bmatrix}$$

Thus, for series connected two-port networks,

$$[z_{eq}] = \begin{bmatrix} z_{11a} + z_{11b} & z_{12a} + z_{12b} \\ z_{21a} + z_{21b} & z_{22a} + z_{22b} \end{bmatrix}$$

### (2) Cascade Connection

The cascade combination of two-port networks "$a$" and "$b$" is shown in Fig. 11.4.2

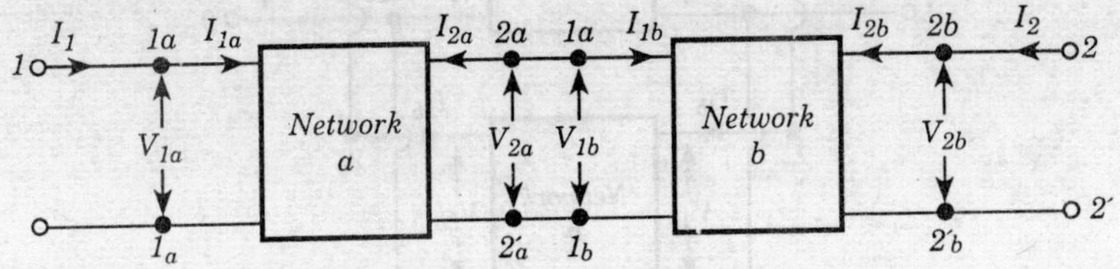


Fig. 11.4.2 Cascade connection of two-port networks.

As per $ABCD$-parameters matrix notation,

$$\begin{bmatrix} V_{1a} \\ I_{1a} \end{bmatrix} = \begin{bmatrix} A_a & B_a \\ C_a & D_a \end{bmatrix} \begin{bmatrix} V_{2a} \\ -I_{2a} \end{bmatrix} \text{ and } \begin{bmatrix} V_{1b} \\ I_{1b} \end{bmatrix} = \begin{bmatrix} A_b & B_b \\ C_b & D_b \end{bmatrix} \begin{bmatrix} V_{2b} \\ -I_{2b} \end{bmatrix}$$

$\because \quad V_{1b} = V_{2a} \quad ; \quad I_{1b} = -I_{2a}$

$$\therefore \quad \begin{bmatrix} V_{2a} \\ I_{1b} \end{bmatrix} = \begin{bmatrix} A_b & B_b \\ C_b & D_b \end{bmatrix} \begin{bmatrix} V_{2b} \\ -I_{2b} \end{bmatrix}$$

$$\text{Thus} \quad \begin{bmatrix} V_{1a} \\ I_{1a} \end{bmatrix} = \begin{bmatrix} A_a & B_a \\ C_a & D_a \end{bmatrix} \begin{bmatrix} A_b & B_b \\ C_b & D_b \end{bmatrix} \begin{bmatrix} V_{2b} \\ -I_{2b} \end{bmatrix}$$

$\because \quad V_1 = V_{1a}, \quad I_1 = I_{1a}$

and $\quad V_2 = V_{2b}, \quad I_2 = I_{2b}$

Thus, for cascade connected two-port network equivalent $A\ B\ C\ D$ parameters are,

$$\begin{bmatrix} A & B \\ C & D \end{bmatrix} = \begin{bmatrix} A_a & B_a \\ C_a & D_a \end{bmatrix} \begin{bmatrix} A_b & B_b \\ C_b & D_b \end{bmatrix}$$

### (3) Parallel Connection

The parallel combination of two-port networks "$a$" and "$b$" is shown in Fig. 11.4.3

As per $y$-parameters matrix notation,

$$\begin{bmatrix} I_{1a} \\ I_{2a} \end{bmatrix} = \begin{bmatrix} y_{11a} & y_{12a} \\ y_{21a} & y_{22a} \end{bmatrix} \begin{bmatrix} V_{1a} \\ V_{2a} \end{bmatrix}$$

$$\begin{bmatrix} I_{1b} \\ I_{2b} \end{bmatrix} = \begin{bmatrix} y_{11b} & y_{12b} \\ y_{21b} & y_{22b} \end{bmatrix} \begin{bmatrix} V_{1b} \\ V_{2b} \end{bmatrix}$$

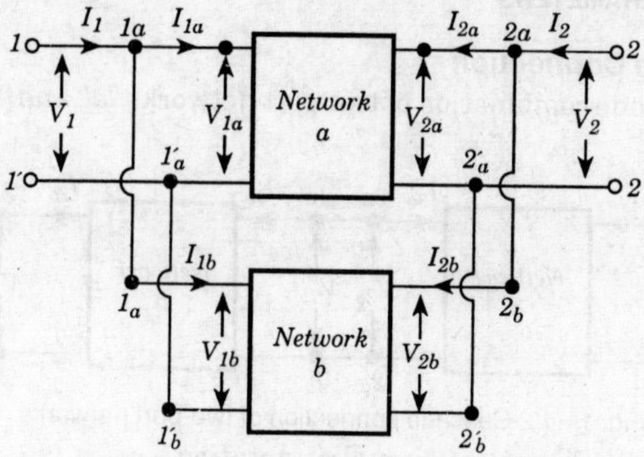


Fig. 11.4.3 Parallel connection of two-port networks.

On adding

$$\begin{bmatrix} I_{1a}+I_{1b} \\ I_{2a}+I_{2b} \end{bmatrix} = \begin{bmatrix} y_{11a} & y_{12a} \\ y_{21a} & y_{22a} \end{bmatrix}\begin{bmatrix} V_{1a} \\ V_{2a} \end{bmatrix} + \begin{bmatrix} y_{11b} & y_{12b} \\ y_{21b} & y_{22b} \end{bmatrix}\begin{bmatrix} V_{1b} \\ V_{2b} \end{bmatrix}$$

$\because$ $$I_1 = I_{1a} + I_{1b}\ ,\ I_2 = I_{2a} + I_{2b}$$

and $$V_1 = V_{1a} = V_{1b}\ ,\ V_2 = V_{2a} = V_{2b}$$

$\therefore$ $$\begin{bmatrix} I_1 \\ I_2 \end{bmatrix} = \begin{bmatrix} y_{11a}+y_{11b} & y_{12a}+y_{12b} \\ y_{21a}+y_{21b} & y_{22a}+y_{22b} \end{bmatrix}\begin{bmatrix} V_1 \\ V_2 \end{bmatrix}$$

Thus, for parallel connected two-port network the equivalent $y$-parameters are

$$\begin{bmatrix} y_{11} & y_{12} \\ y_{21} & y_{22} \end{bmatrix} = \begin{bmatrix} y_{11a}+y_{11b} & y_{12a}+y_{12b} \\ y_{21a}+y_{21b} & y_{22a}+y_{22b} \end{bmatrix}$$

The two-port network $N_a$ and $N_b$ can be connected in parallel with the condition that the nature of the network elements is not altered due to such a connection.

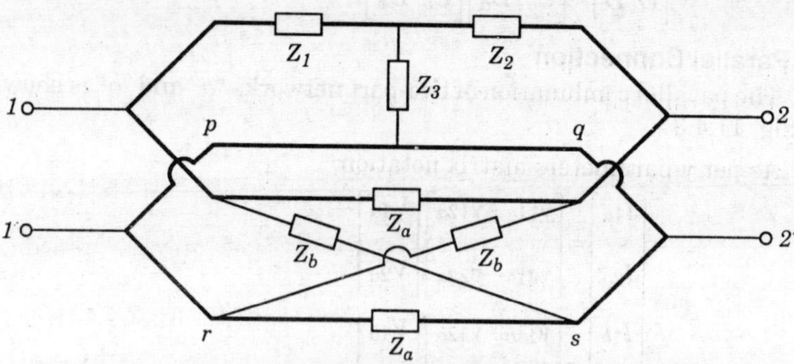

Fig. 11.4.4 $T$-network and lattice network connected in parallel.

For example consider combination $T$-network and lattice network (Fig. 11.4.4). This combination can not be connected in parallel because the terminals $p$-$q$ of the $T$-network short circuit the terminals $r$-$s$ of the lattic network. Thus, the short circuit alters the nature of the lattice network.

In order to ensure that the connecting one two-port network with another does not alter the nature of the other, an isolation transformer is used as shown in Fig. 11.4.5.

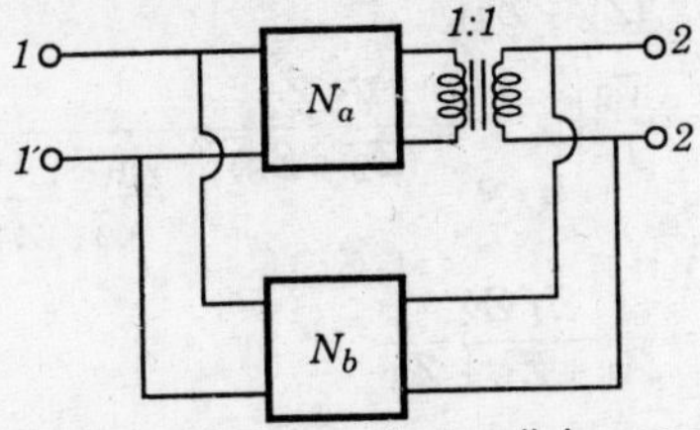


Fig. 11.4.5 Use of isolation transformer in parallel connection of two-port networks.

If the parallel connected two-port networks have a common datum (reference) node, The isolation transformer is not required.

## 11.5 SOLVED EXAMPLES

**Example : 11.5.1** *Determine z-parameters for the π network shown in Fig. 11.5.1.*

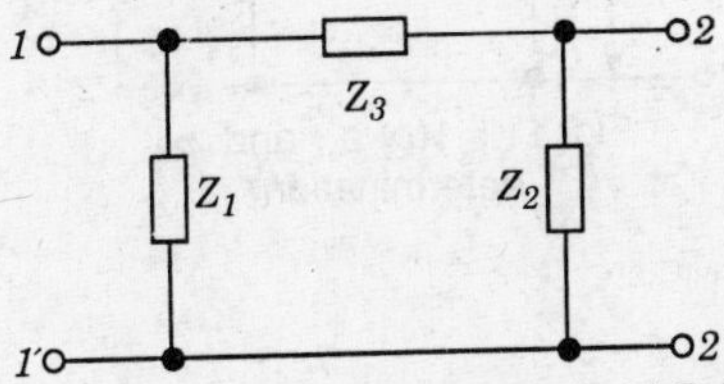


Fig. 11.5.1 Network for example 11.5.1.

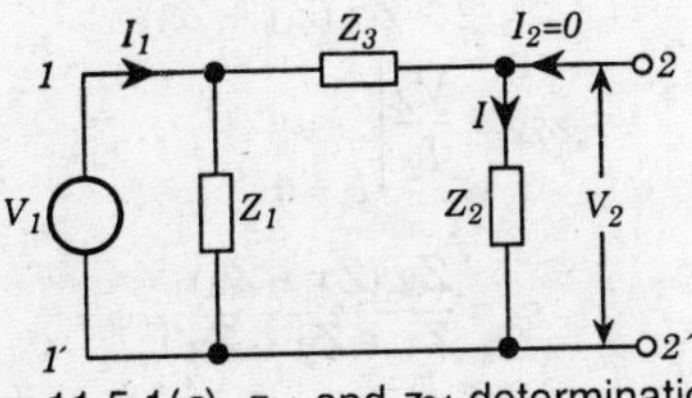


Fig. 11.5.1($a$). $z_{11}$ and $z_{21}$ determination

**Solution :** ($i$) Set $I_2 = 0$ *i.e.* open-circuit port 2 [Fig. 11.5.1($a$)]. Apply voltage $V_1$ at port 1.

$$I_1 = \frac{V_1}{\dfrac{Z_1(Z_2+Z_3)}{Z_1+(Z_2+Z_3)}}$$

or

$$I_1 = \frac{V_1(Z_1+Z_2+Z_3)}{Z_1(Z_2+Z_3)}$$

$$z_{11} = \left.\frac{V_1}{I_1}\right|_{I_2=0} = \frac{Z_1(Z_2+Z_3)}{Z_1+Z_2+Z_3}$$

$$I = I_1 \times \frac{Z_1}{Z_1+(Z_2+Z_3)} \quad \text{By current division}$$

$$= V_1 \frac{(Z_1 + Z_2 + Z_3)}{Z_1(Z_2 + Z_3)} \times \frac{Z_1}{(Z_1 + Z_2 + Z_3)}$$

or $$I = \frac{V_1}{(Z_2 + Z_3)}$$

$$V_2 = I\, Z_2$$

$\therefore$ $$V_2 = \frac{V_1\, Z_2}{(Z_2 + Z_3)}$$

$$z_{21} = \left.\frac{V_2}{I_1}\right|_{I_2 = 0} = \frac{V_1\, Z_2}{(Z_2 + Z_3)} \times \frac{1}{\dfrac{V_1(Z_1 + Z_3 + Z_3)}{Z_1\,(Z_1 + Z_3)}}$$

or $$z_{21} = \frac{Z_1\, Z_2}{Z_1 + Z_2 + Z_3}$$

(*ii*) Set $I_1 = 0$, *i.e.* open-circuit port 1.

Apply voltage $V_1$ at port 2

$$I_2 = \frac{V_2}{\dfrac{Z_2\,(Z_1 + Z_3)}{Z_2 + (Z_1 + Z_3)}}$$

or $$I_2 = \frac{V_2\,(Z_1 + Z_2 + Z_3)}{Z_2\,(Z_1 + Z_3)}$$

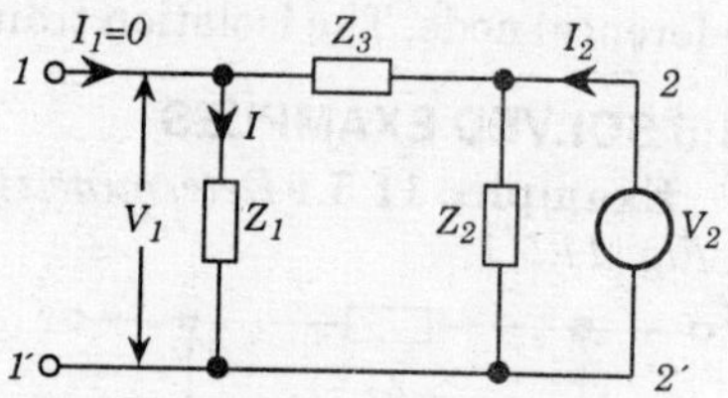

Fig. 11.5.1(*b*) $z_{12}$ and $z_{22}$ determination

$$z_{22} = \left.\frac{V_2}{I_2}\right|_{I_1 = 0}$$

$$= \frac{Z_2\,(Z_1 + Z_3)}{Z_1 + Z_2 + Z_3}$$

$$I = I_2 \times \frac{Z_2}{Z_1 + Z_2 + Z_3}$$

$$= \frac{V_2\,(Z_1 + Z_2 + Z_3)}{Z_2\,(Z_1 + Z_3)} \times \frac{Z_2}{(Z_1 + Z_2 + Z_3)}$$

or $$I = \frac{V_2}{Z_1 + Z_3}$$

$$V_1 = I\, Z_1$$

$\therefore$ $$V_1 = \frac{V_2\, Z_1}{Z_1 + Z_3}$$

$$z_{12} = \left.\frac{V_1}{I_2}\right|_{I_1 = 0} = \frac{V_2\, Z_1}{Z_1 + Z_3} \times \frac{1}{\dfrac{V_2(Z_1 + Z_2 + Z_3)}{Z_2(Z_1 + Z_3)}}$$

$$\therefore \qquad z_{12} = \frac{Z_1 Z_2}{Z_1 + Z_2 + Z_3}$$

$z$-parameters are,

$$[z] = \begin{bmatrix} z_{11} & z_{12} \\ z_{21} & z_{22} \end{bmatrix} = \begin{bmatrix} \dfrac{Z_1 (Z_2 + Z_3)}{Z_1 + Z_2 + Z_3} & \dfrac{Z_1 Z_2}{Z_1 + Z_2 + Z_3} \\ \dfrac{Z_1 Z_2}{Z_1 + Z_2 + Z_3} & \dfrac{Z_2 (Z_1 + Z_3)}{Z_1 + Z_2 + Z_3} \end{bmatrix} \quad \textbf{Ans.}$$

**Example : 11.5.2** *Determine y-parameters for the two-port network shown in Fig. 11.5.2.*

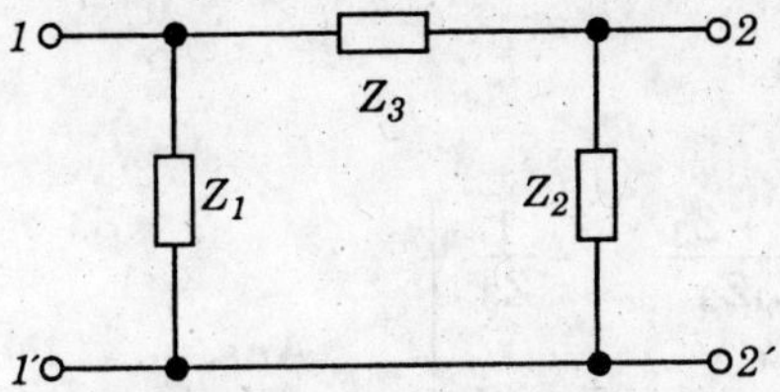


Fig. 11.5.2 Network for example 11.5.2

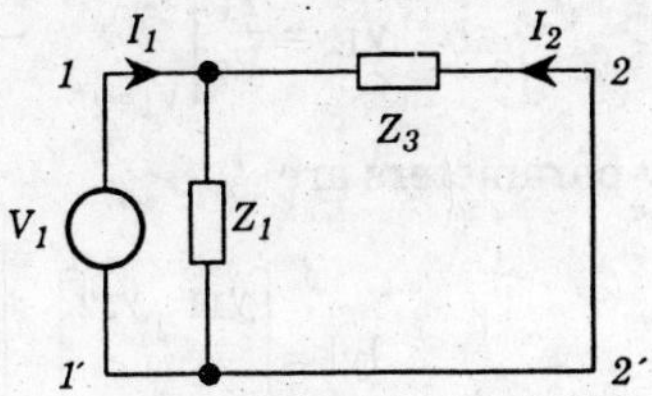


Fig. 11.5. 2 (a) $V_2 = 0$

**Solution :** (*i*) Set $V_2 = 0$ *i.e.* short-circuit port 2 Fig. 11.5.2(*a*).

Apply voltage $V_1$ at port 1.

$$I_1 = \frac{V_1}{\dfrac{Z_1 Z_3}{Z_1 + Z_3}} = \frac{V_1 (z_1 + Z_3)}{Z_1 Z_3}$$

$$y_{11} = \left.\frac{I_1}{V_1}\right|_{V_2 = 0} = \frac{Z_1 + Z_3}{Z_1 Z_3}$$

$$I_2 = -I_1 \times \frac{Z_1}{Z_1 + Z_3} \quad \text{By current division.}$$

$$= -\frac{V_1 (Z_1 + Z_3)}{Z_1 Z_3} \times \frac{Z_1}{Z_1 + Z_3}$$

or

$$I_2 = -\frac{V_1}{Z_3}$$

$$y_{21} = \left.\frac{I_2}{V_1}\right|_{V_2 = 0} = -\frac{V_1}{Z_3} \times \frac{1}{V_1}$$

or

$$y_{21} = -\frac{1}{Z_3}$$

(*ii*) Set $V_1 = 0$, *i.e.* short-circuit port 1 Fig. 11.5.2(*b*). Apply voltage $V_2$ at port 2.

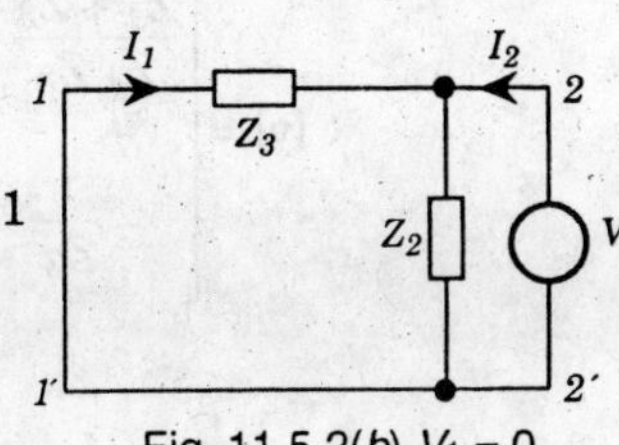


Fig. 11.5.2(*b*) $V_1 = 0$

$$I_2 = \frac{V_2}{\frac{Z_2 Z_3}{Z_2 + Z_3}} = \frac{V_2 (Z_2 + Z_3)}{Z_2 Z_3}$$

$$y_{22} = \left.\frac{I_2}{V_2}\right|_{V_1=0} = \frac{Z_2 + Z_3}{Z_2 Z_3}$$

$$I_1 = -I_2 \times \frac{Z_2}{Z_2 + Z_3} = -\frac{V_2(Z_2 + Z_3)}{Z_2 Z_3} \times \frac{Z_2}{Z_2 + Z_3}$$

or $$I_1 = -\frac{V_2}{Z_3}$$

$$y_{12} = \left.\frac{I_1}{V_2}\right|_{V_1=0} = -\frac{1}{Z_3}$$

$y$-parameters are

$$[y] = \begin{bmatrix} y_{11} & y_{12} \\ y_{21} & y_{22} \end{bmatrix} = \begin{bmatrix} \frac{Z_1 + Z_3}{Z_1 Z_3} & -\frac{1}{Z_3} \\ -\frac{1}{Z_3} & \frac{Z_2 + Z_3}{Z_2 Z_3} \end{bmatrix}$$ **Ans.**

## ALTERNATIVE METHOD

The equation for $y$-parameters are

$$I_1 = y_{11} V_1 + y_{12} V_2$$
$$I_2 = y_{21} V_1 + y_{22} V_2$$

Applying node voltage analysis at node 1 and 2 [Fig. 11.5.2(*c*)]

At node 1 : $$-I_1 + \frac{V_1}{Z_1} + \frac{V_1 - V_2}{Z_3} = 0$$

At node 2 : $$-I_2 + \frac{V_2}{Z_2} + \frac{V_2 - V_1}{Z_3} = 0$$

Simplifying above equations

$$I_1 = \left(\frac{1}{Z_1} + \frac{1}{Z_3}\right) V_1 - \frac{1}{Z_3} V_2$$

$$I_2 = -\frac{1}{Z_3} V_1 + \left(\frac{1}{Z_2} + \frac{1}{Z_3}\right) V_2$$

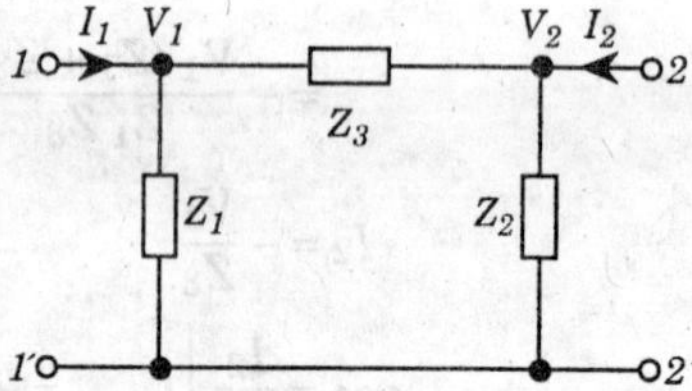

Fig. 11.5.2(c)

$y$-parameters are

$$[y] = \begin{bmatrix} \frac{Z_1 + Z_3}{Z_1 Z_3} & -\frac{1}{Z_3} \\ -\frac{1}{Z_3} & \frac{Z_2 + Z_3}{Z_2 Z_3} \end{bmatrix}$$ **Ans.**

**Example 11.5.3** *Determine z and y parameters for the two port network (Fig. 11.5.3)*

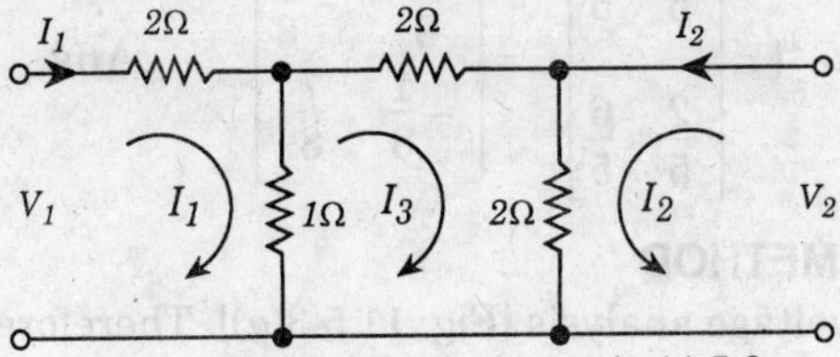


Fig. 11.5.3 Network for example 11.5.3

**Solution :** Apply loop current analysis for the given network

Loop 1 : $2I_1 + 1(I_1 - I_3) - V_1 = 0$ ...(1)

Loop 2 : $2\,(I_2 + I_3) - V_2 = 0$ ...(2)

Loop 3 : $2\,I_3 + 2\,(I_2 + I_3) + 1\,(I_3 - I_1) = 0$ ...(3)

Simplifying Eqn.(3)

$$I_3 = \frac{I_1 - I_2}{5} \quad ...(4)$$

Rearranging Eqns. (1) and (2)

$$V_1 = 3\,I_1 - I_3 \quad ...(5)$$

$$V_2 = 2\,I_2 + 2\,I_3 \quad ...(6)$$

Substitute for $I_3$ in Eqns. (5) and (6) from Eqn. (4) Therefore,

$$V_1 = 3\,I_1 - \frac{(I_1 - 2\,I_2)}{5} \quad ...(7)$$

$$V_2 = 2\,I_2 - \frac{2\,(I_1 - 2I_2)}{5} \quad ...(8)$$

Rearranging Eqns. (7) and (8)

$$V_1 = \frac{14}{5} I_1 + \frac{2}{5} I_2$$

$$V_2 = \frac{2}{5} I_1 + \frac{6}{5} I_2$$

*z*-parameters are given by following equation

$$V_1 = z_{11}\, I_1 + z_{12}\, I_2$$

$$V_2 = z_{21}\, I_1 + z_{22}\, I_2$$

$$\therefore \qquad [z] = \begin{bmatrix} z_{11} & z_{12} \\ z_{21} & z_{22} \end{bmatrix} = \begin{bmatrix} \frac{14}{5} & \frac{2}{5} \\ \frac{2}{5} & \frac{6}{5} \end{bmatrix} \quad \textbf{...Ans.}$$

$$[y] = [z^{-1}] = \begin{bmatrix} \frac{14}{5} & \frac{2}{5} \\ \frac{2}{5} & \frac{6}{5} \end{bmatrix}^{-1} = \begin{bmatrix} \frac{3}{8} & -\frac{1}{8} \\ -\frac{1}{8} & \frac{7}{8} \end{bmatrix} \quad \text{...Ans.}$$

## ALTERNATIVE METHOD

Apply node voltage analysis [Fig. 11.5.3(*a*)]. Therefore,

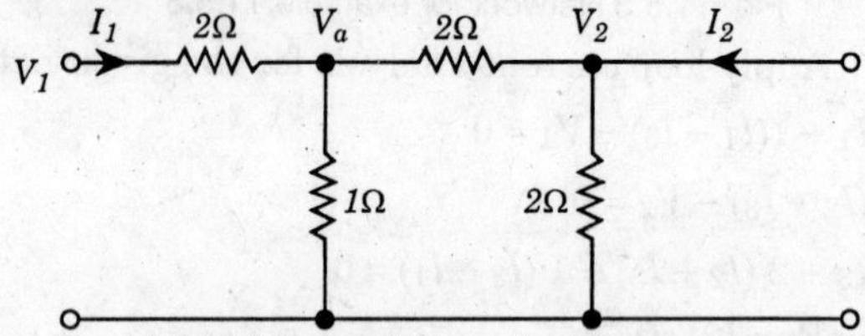


Fig. 11.5.3(*a*) Network for node voltage analysis.

At node *a* : $-I_1 + \dfrac{V_a}{1} + \dfrac{V_a - V_2}{2} = 0$

Simplifying above equation

$$I_1 = \frac{3}{2} V_a - \frac{V_2}{2}$$

$$\because \qquad V_a = V_1 - 2I_1$$

$$\therefore \qquad I_1 = \frac{3}{2} (V_1 - 2 I_1) - \frac{V_2}{2}$$

or
$$I_1 = \frac{3}{8} V_1 - \frac{1}{8} V_2 \qquad \text{...(1)}$$

At node 2 : $-I_2 + \dfrac{V_2}{2} + \dfrac{V_2 - V_a}{2} = 0$

Rearranging above equation,

$$I_2 = \frac{V_2}{2} + \frac{V_2}{2} - \frac{V_a}{2}$$

$$\because \qquad V_a = V - 2I_1$$

$$\therefore \qquad I_2 = V_2 - \frac{1}{2} (V_1 - 2 I_1)$$

or
$$I_2 = V_2 - \frac{V_1}{2} + I_1$$

From Eqn. (1)

$$I_1 = \frac{3}{8} V_1 - \frac{1}{8} V_2$$

$$\therefore \qquad I_2 = V_2 - \frac{V_1}{2} + \left(\frac{3}{8}V_1 - \frac{1}{8}V_2\right)$$

Simplifying above equation

$$I_2 = -\frac{1}{8}V_1 + \frac{7}{8}V_2 \qquad \text{...(2)}$$

As per Eqns. (1) and (2) is

$$\begin{bmatrix} I_1 \\ I_2 \end{bmatrix} = \begin{bmatrix} \frac{3}{8} & -\frac{1}{8} \\ -\frac{1}{8} & \frac{7}{8} \end{bmatrix} \begin{bmatrix} V_1 \\ V_2 \end{bmatrix}$$

The equation for $y$-parameters are

$$\begin{bmatrix} I_1 \\ I_2 \end{bmatrix} = \begin{bmatrix} y_{11} & y_{12} \\ y_{21} & y_{22} \end{bmatrix} \begin{bmatrix} V_1 \\ V_2 \end{bmatrix}$$

$$\therefore \qquad \begin{bmatrix} y_{11} & y_{12} \\ y_{21} & y_{22} \end{bmatrix} = \begin{bmatrix} \frac{3}{8} & -\frac{1}{8} \\ -\frac{1}{8} & \frac{7}{8} \end{bmatrix} \qquad \text{...Ans.}$$

**Example 11.5.4** *A two-port network is given in Fig. 11.5.4. Determine y-parameters.*

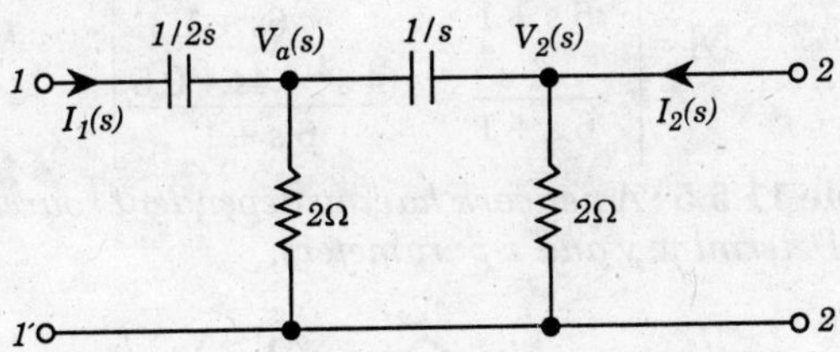


Fig. 11.5.4 Two-port network for example 11.5.4

**Solution :** Apply node voltage analysis,

$$\text{At node 1}: \frac{V_a(s) - V_1(s)}{1/2s} + \frac{V_a(s)}{2} + \frac{V_a(s) - V_2}{1/s} = 0$$

Simplifying

$$(3s + 0.5)\,V_a(s) - 2s\,V_1(s) - s\,V_2(s) = 0 \qquad \text{...(1)}$$

$$\because \qquad I_1(s) = \frac{V_1(s) - V_a(s)}{1/2\,s}$$

$$\text{or} \qquad V_a(s) = V_1(s) - \frac{I_1(s)}{2\,s}$$

$$\therefore \qquad (3s + 0.5)\left[V_1(s) - \frac{I_1(s)}{2\,s}\right] - 2s\,V_1(s) - s\,V_2 = 0$$

or $$I_1(s) = \frac{2s(s+1)}{(6s+1)} V_1 - \frac{2s^2}{3s+0.5} V_2 \quad ...(2)$$

At node 2 : $-I_2(s) + \dfrac{V_2(s)}{2} + \dfrac{V_2(s) - V_a(s)}{1/s} = 0$

Simplifying, $I_2(s) = (s+0.5)\,V_2(s) - s\,V_a(s)$

From Eqn. (1)

$$V_a(s) = \frac{2s\,V_1(s)}{3s+0.5} + \frac{s\,V_2(s)}{3s+0.5}$$

$$\therefore \quad I_2(s) = (s+0.5)\,V_2(s) - s\left[\frac{2s\,V_1(s)}{3s+0.5} + \frac{s\,V_2(s)}{3s+0.5}\right]$$

or $$I_2(s) = -\frac{4s^2}{6s+1} V_1(s) + \frac{(4s^2+4s+0.5)}{6s+1} V_2(s) \quad ...(3)$$

In matrix form Eqns. (2) and (3) are written as

$$\begin{bmatrix} I_1(s) \\ I_2(s) \end{bmatrix} = \begin{bmatrix} \dfrac{2s(s+1)}{6s+1} & -\dfrac{4s^2}{6s+1} \\ \dfrac{-4s^2}{6s+1} & \dfrac{4s^2+4s+0.5}{6s+1} \end{bmatrix} \begin{bmatrix} V_1(s) \\ V_2(s) \end{bmatrix}$$

$$\therefore \quad [y] = \begin{bmatrix} \dfrac{2s(s+1)}{6s+1} & -\dfrac{4s^2}{6s+1} \\ \dfrac{-4s^2}{6s+1} & \dfrac{4s^2+4s+0.5}{6s+1} \end{bmatrix} \quad ...\textbf{Ans.}$$

**Example 11.5.5 :** *A network having dependent sources is shown in Fig. 11.5.5. Determine y and z-parameters.*

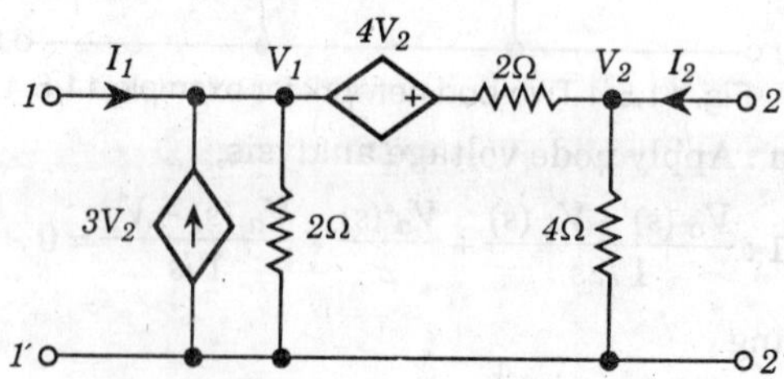


Fig. 11.5.5 Network for example 11.5.5.

**Solution :** Apply Kirchhoff's current law.

At node 1 : $-I_1 - 3V_2 + \dfrac{V_1}{2} + \dfrac{(V_1 + 4V_1) - V_2}{2} = 0 \quad ...(1)$

At node 2 : $-I_2 - \dfrac{V_2}{4} + \dfrac{(V_2 + 4V_1) - V_1}{2} = 0 \quad ...(2)$

Rearranging Eqns. (1) and (2)

$$I_1 = 3V_1 - 3.5V_2 \quad ...(3)$$

$$I_2 = -2.5V_1 + 0.75V_2 \quad \text{...(4)}$$

In matrix form Eqns. (3) and (4) are written as

$$\begin{bmatrix} I_1 \\ I_2 \end{bmatrix} = \begin{bmatrix} 3 & -3.5 \\ -2.5 & 0.75 \end{bmatrix} \begin{bmatrix} V_1 \\ V_2 \end{bmatrix}$$

$$\therefore \quad [y] = \begin{bmatrix} y_{11} & y_{12} \\ y_{21} & y_{22} \end{bmatrix} \begin{bmatrix} 3 & -3.5 \\ -2.5 & 0.75 \end{bmatrix} \quad \textbf{...Ans.}$$

$$[z] = [y]^{-1} = \begin{bmatrix} y_{11} & y_{12} \\ y_{21} & y_{22} \end{bmatrix}^{-1} = \begin{bmatrix} 3 & -3.5 \\ -2.5 & 0.75 \end{bmatrix}^{-1}$$

$$= \begin{bmatrix} -0.115 & -0.538 \\ -0.384 & -0.461 \end{bmatrix} \quad \textbf{...Ans}$$

**Example 11.5.6 :** *Use two-port parameter definitions to obtain z-parameters for the network shown in Fig. 11.5.6.*

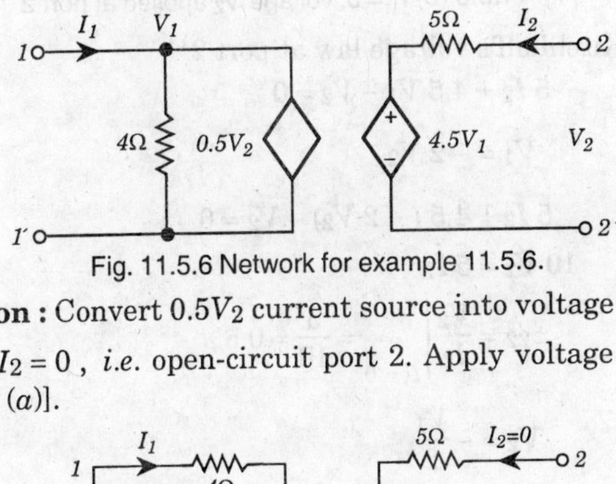


Fig. 11.5.6 Network for example 11.5.6.

**Solution :** Convert $0.5V_2$ current source into voltage source.

(*i*) Set $I_2 = 0$ , *i.e.* open-circuit port 2. Apply voltage $V_1$ at port 1 [Fig. 11.5.6 (*a*)].

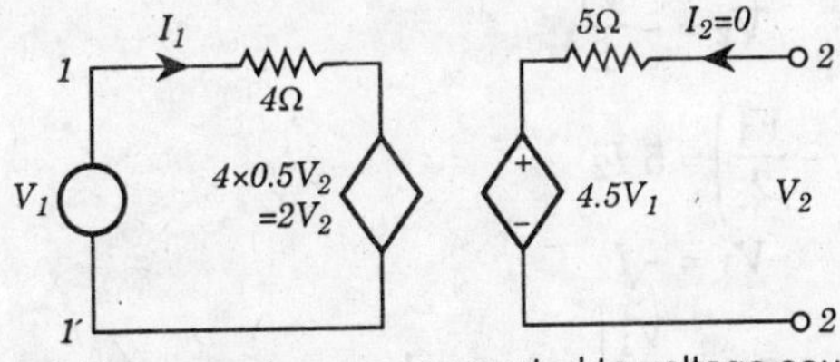


Fig. 11.5.6(*a*) $0.5V_2$ current source converted to voltage source and $I_2 = 0$

Apply Kirchhoff's voltage law,

$$\therefore \quad 4\,I_1 - 2\,V_2 - V_1 = 0$$

$$\because \quad V_2 = 4.5\,V_1$$

$$\therefore \quad 4\,I_1 - 2 \times 4.5V_1 - V_1 = 0$$

or $$10\,V_1 = 4\,I_1$$

$$z_{11} = \left.\frac{V_1}{I_1}\right|_{I_2=0} = \frac{4}{10} = 0.4$$

$$I_1 = \frac{10}{4}\,V_1$$

and $$V_2 = 4.5\,V_1$$

$$z_{21} = \left.\frac{V_2}{I_1}\right|_{I_2=0} = \frac{4.5\,V_1}{(10/4)V_1} = 1.8$$

*(ii)* Set $I_1 = 0$, *i.e.* open-circuit port 1. Apply voltage $V_2$ at port [Fig. 11.5.6(*b*)].

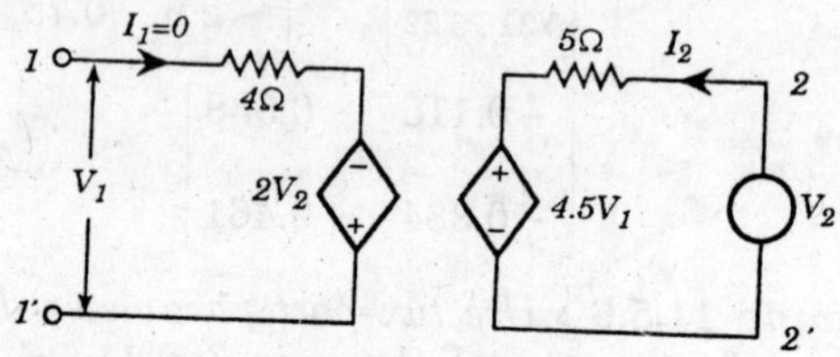


Fig. 11.5.6.(*b*) $I_1 = 0$, voltage $V_2$ applied at port 2

Apply Kirchhoff's voltage law at port 2

$$5\,I_2 + 4.5\,V_1 - V_2 = 0$$

$\because$ $$V_1 = -2\,V_2$$

$\therefore$ $$5\,I_2 + 4.5\,(-2\,V_2) - V_2 = 0$$

or $$10\,V_2 = 5\,I_2$$

$$z_{22} = \left.\frac{V_2}{I_2}\right|_{I_1=0} = \frac{5}{10} = 0.5$$

$\because$ $$V_2 = -\frac{V_1}{2}$$

$\therefore$ $$10\left(-\frac{V_1}{2}\right) = 5\,I_2$$

or $$V_1 = -I_2$$

$$z_{12} = \left.\frac{V_1}{I_2}\right|_{I_1=0} = -1$$

$$[z] = \begin{bmatrix} z_{11} & z_{12} \\ z_{21} & z_{22} \end{bmatrix} = \begin{bmatrix} 0.4 & -1 \\ 1.8 & 0.5 \end{bmatrix} \quad \text{...Ans.}$$

**Example 11.5.7 :** *Find the open-circuit parameters for the network given in Fig. 11.5.7.*

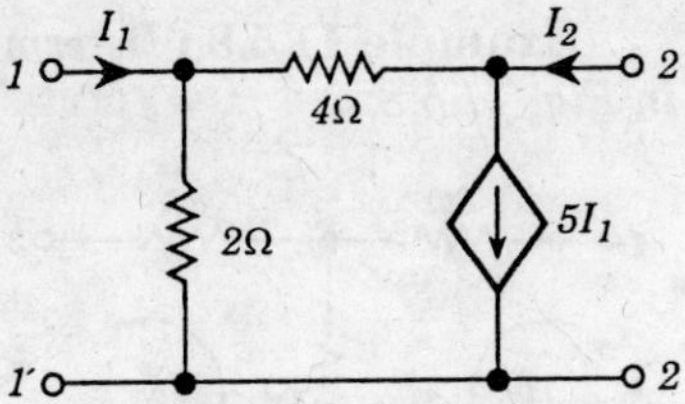


Fig. 11.5.7 Network for example 11.5.7

**Solution :** (*i*) Set $I_2 = 0$ , *i.e.* open-circuit port 2. Apply voltage at port 1 Fig. 11.5.7(*a*)

Apply Kirchhoff's current law at node a

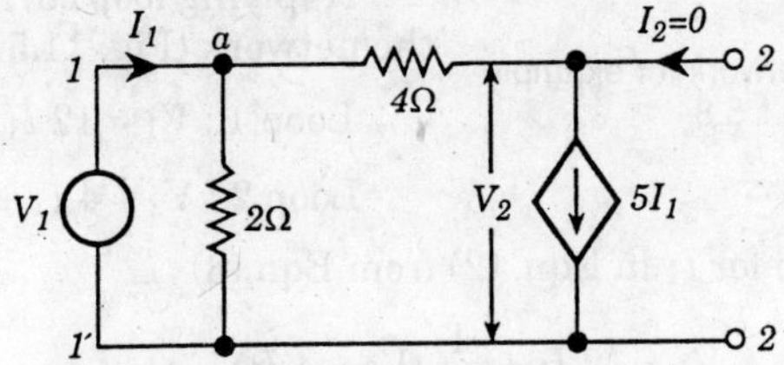


Fig. 11.5.7(*a*) port two open-circuit , $I_2 = 0$

$$I_1 = I + 5\,I_1$$

$\therefore$ $$I = -\,4\,I_1$$

$$V_1 = 2 \times I = 2 \times (-\,4I_1) = -\,8\,I_1$$

$$z_{11} = \left.\frac{V_1}{I_1}\right|_{I_2 = 0} = -\,8$$

$$V_2 = V_1 - 4 \times 5\,I_1$$

or $$V_2 = -\,8\,I_1 - 20\,I_1 = -\,28\,I_1$$

$$z_{21} = \left.\frac{V_1}{I_1}\right|_{I_2 = 0} = -\,28$$

(*ii*) Set $I_1 = 0$ , *i.e.* open-circuit port 1. Since $I_1 = 0$, the current source $5I_1 = 0$. Apply voltage $V_2$ at port 2 [Fig. 11.5.7(*b*)].

$$I_2 = \frac{V_2}{2+4} = \frac{V_2}{6}$$

$$z_{22} = \left.\frac{v_2}{I_2}\right|_{I_1 = 0} = 6$$

$$V_1 = 2\,I_2$$

$$z_{12} = \left.\frac{V_1}{I_2}\right|_{I_1 = 0} = 2$$

$$\begin{bmatrix} z_{11} & z_{12} \\ z_{21} & z_{22} \end{bmatrix} = \begin{bmatrix} -\,8 & 2 \\ -\,28 & 6 \end{bmatrix}$$ **...Ans.**

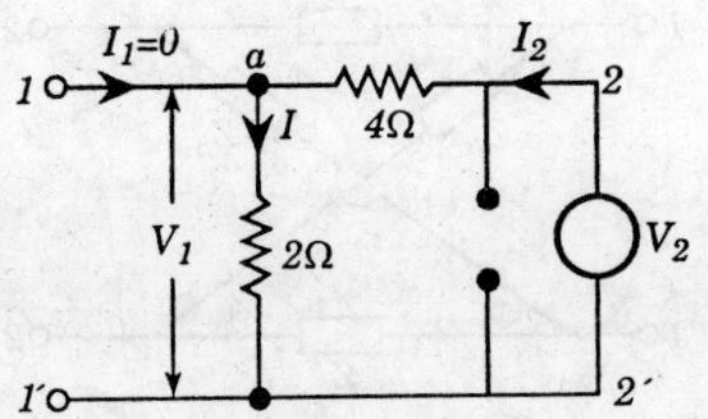


Fig. 11.5.7(*b*) port 1 open-circuit , $I_1 = 0$

**Example 11.5.8 :** *Determine h-parameters for the network shown in Fig. 11.5.8.*

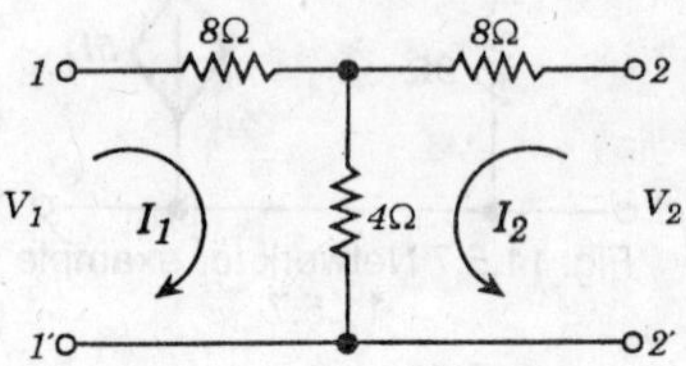


Fig. 11.5.8 Network for example 11.5.8

**Solution :** Relationship for h-parameters is given by

$$\begin{bmatrix} V_1 \\ I_2 \end{bmatrix} = \begin{bmatrix} h_{11} & h_{12} \\ h_{21} & h_{22} \end{bmatrix} \begin{bmatrix} I_1 \\ V_2 \end{bmatrix} \quad ...(1)$$

Applying loop current analysis for the network (Fig. 11.5.8)

$$\text{Loop 1}: V_1 = 12\,I_1 + 4\,I_2 \quad ...(2)$$

$$\text{Loop 2}: V_2 = 4\,I_1 + 12\,I_2 \quad ...(3)$$

Substitute for $I_1$ in Eqn. (2) from Eqn.(3)

$$\therefore \quad V_1 = 12\,I_1 + \frac{4}{12}(V_2 - 4\,I_1) \quad ...(4)$$

Simplifying, $V_1 = \frac{32}{3} I_1 + \frac{1}{3} V_2$

Rearranging Eqn. (2)

$$I_2 = -\frac{1}{3} I_1 + \frac{1}{12} V_2 \quad ...(5)$$

Eqns. (4) and (5) can be arranged in matrix form as

$$\begin{bmatrix} V_1 \\ I_2 \end{bmatrix} = \begin{bmatrix} \frac{32}{3} & \frac{1}{3} \\ -\frac{1}{3} & \frac{1}{12} \end{bmatrix} \begin{bmatrix} I_1 \\ V_2 \end{bmatrix} \quad ...(6)$$

Comparing matrix (1) & (6)

$$[h] = \begin{bmatrix} h_{11} & h_{12} \\ h_{21} & h_{22} \end{bmatrix} = \begin{bmatrix} \frac{32}{3} & \frac{1}{3} \\ -\frac{1}{3} & \frac{1}{12} \end{bmatrix} \quad ...\textbf{Ans.}$$

**Example 11.5.9 :** *Obtain z-parameters for the lattice network shown in Fig. 11.5.9.*

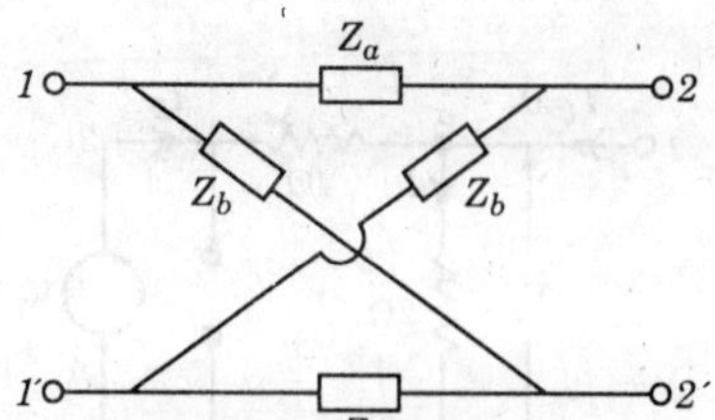


Fig. 11.5.9 Lattice network for example 11.5.9.

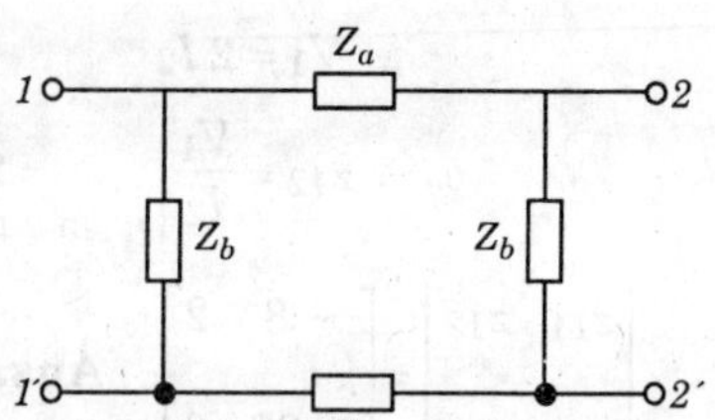


Fig. 11.5.9(*a*) Lattice network redrawn.

**Solution :** The given lattice network can be redrawn as shown in Fig. 11.5.9(*a*).

For the determination of *z*-parameters, the network [Fig. 11.5.9(*a*)] is arranged below as shown in Fig. 11.5.9(*b*) and (*c*).

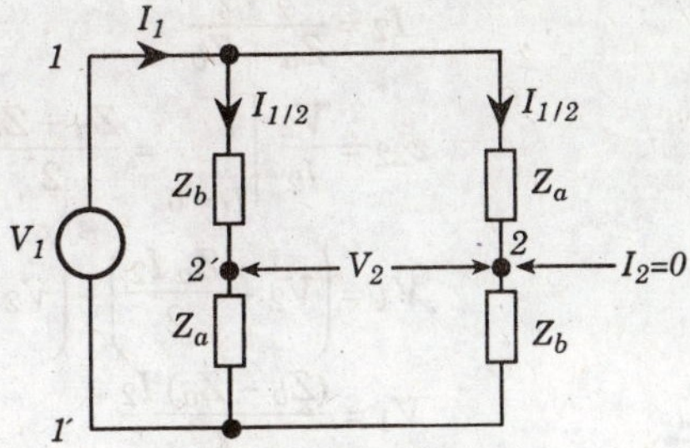


Fig. 11.5.9(*b*) Voltage $V_1$ applied at port 1 , $I_1 = 0$

(*i*) Set $I_2 = 0$. Apply voltage $V_1$ at port 1 [Fig. 11.5.9(*b*)]

$$I_1 = \frac{V_1}{Z_b + Z_a} + \frac{V_1}{Z_a + Z_b}$$

or $$I_1 = \frac{Z\,V_1}{Z_a + Z_b}$$

$\therefore$ $$z_{11} = \frac{V_1}{I_1}\bigg|_{I_2=0} = \frac{Z_a + Z_b}{2}$$

$$V_2 = \left(V_1 - \frac{Z_a I_1}{2}\right) - \left(V_1 - \frac{Z_b I_1}{2}\right)$$

or $$V_2 = \frac{(Z_b - Z_a)\,I_1}{2}$$

$\therefore$ $$z_{21} = \frac{V_2}{I_1}\bigg|_{I_2=0} = \frac{Z_b - Z_a}{2}$$

(*ii*) Set $I_1$ 0. Apply voltage $V_2$ at port 2 [Fig. 11.5.9(*c*)]

$$I_2 = \frac{V_2}{Z_b + Z_a} + \frac{V_2}{Z_a + Z_b}$$

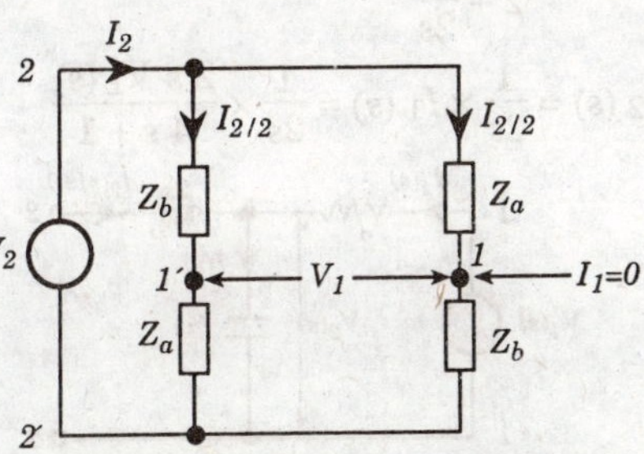


Fig. 11.5.9(*c*) Voltage $V_2$ applied at port 2, $I_1 = 0$

or $$I_2 = \frac{2\,V_2}{Z_a + Z_b}$$

$$\therefore \quad z_{22} = \left.\frac{V_2}{I_2}\right|_{I_1=0} = \frac{Z_a + Z_b}{2}$$

$$V_1 = \left(V_2 - \frac{Z_a\,I_2}{2}\right) - \left(V_2 - \frac{Z_b\,I_2}{2}\right)$$

or $$V_1 = \frac{(Z_b - Z_a)\,I_2}{2}$$

$$\therefore \quad z_{12} = \left.\frac{V_1}{I_2}\right|_{I_1=0} = \frac{Z_b - Z_a}{2}$$

$$[z] = \begin{bmatrix} z_{11} & z_{12} \\ z_{21} & z_{22} \end{bmatrix} = \begin{bmatrix} \dfrac{Z_a + Z_b}{2} & \dfrac{Z_b - Z_a}{2} \\ \dfrac{Z_b - Z_a}{2} & \dfrac{Z_a + Z_b}{2} \end{bmatrix} \qquad \text{...Ans.}$$

**Example 11.5.10 :** *Use two-port parameter definitions to determine transmission (chain) parameters for the network shown in Fig. 11.5.10*

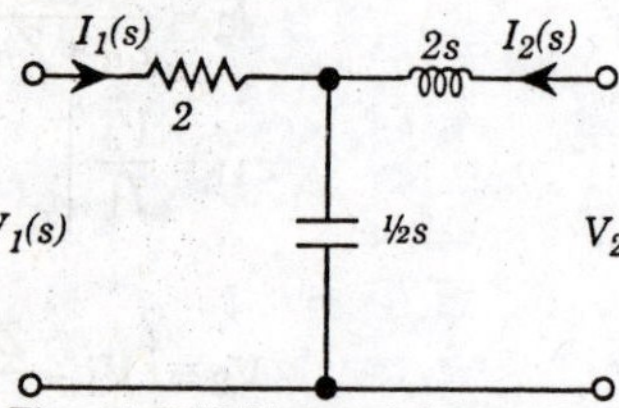


Fig. 11.5.10 Network for example 11.5.10

**Solution :** Transmission parameters are given by the following equations.

$$V_1(s) = AV_2(s) - BI_2(s)$$

$$I_1(s) = DV_2(s) - DI_2(s)$$

or $$\begin{bmatrix} V_1(s) \\ I_1(s) \end{bmatrix} = \begin{bmatrix} A & B \\ C & D \end{bmatrix} \begin{bmatrix} V_2(s) \\ -I_2(s) \end{bmatrix}$$

(*i*) Set $I_2(s) = 0$, *i.e.* open-circuit port 2. Apply $V_1(s)$ at port 1 [Fig. 11.5.10(*a*)]

$$I_1(s) = \frac{V_1(s)}{2 + \dfrac{1}{2s}} = \frac{2s\,V_1(s)}{4\,s + 1}$$

$$V_2(s) = \frac{1}{2s} \times I_1(s) = \frac{1}{2s} \times \frac{2\,s\,V_1(s)}{4\,s + 1}$$

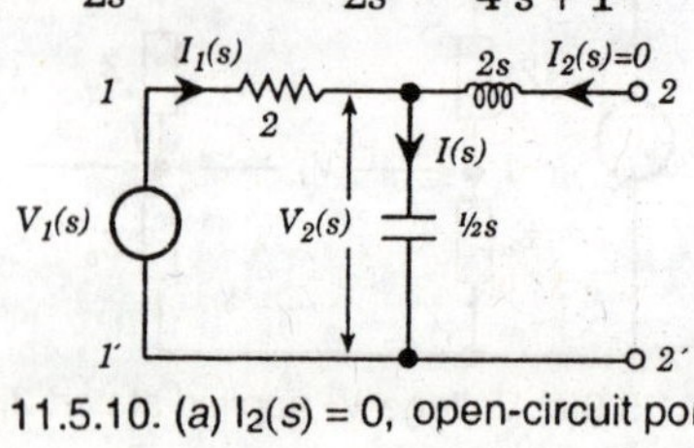


Fig. 11.5.10. (*a*) $I_2(s) = 0$, open-circuit port 2

or $$V_2(s) = \frac{V_1(s)}{4s+1}$$

$$A = \left.\frac{V_1(s)}{V_2(s)}\right|_{I_2(s)=0} = 4s+1$$

$$C = \left.\frac{I_1(s)}{V_2(s)}\right|_{I_2(s)=0} = 2s$$

(*ii*) Set $V_2(s) = 0$, *i.e.* short-circuit port 2. Apply $V_1(s)$ at port 1 [Fig. 11.5.10(*b*)]

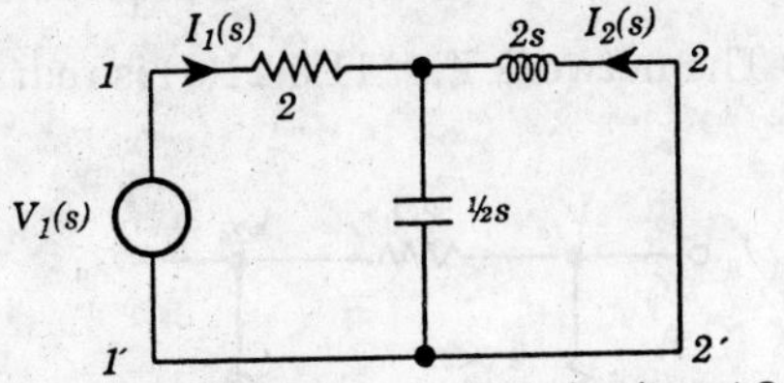


Fig. 11.5.10(*b*) $V_2(s) = 0$ short-circuit port 2

$$I_1(s) = \frac{V_1(s)}{2 + \dfrac{2s \times 1/2s}{2s + \dfrac{1}{2s}}}$$

or $$I_1(s) = \frac{(4s^2+1)V_1(s)}{8s^2+2s+2}$$

$$I_2(s) = -I_1(s) \times \frac{1/2s}{2s + 1/2s}$$

or $$I_2(s) = -\frac{(4s^2+1)V_1(s)}{(8s^2+2s+2)} \times \frac{1}{(4s^2+1)} = -\frac{V_1(s)}{(8s^2+2s+2)}$$

$$B = -\left.\frac{V_1(s)}{I_2(s)}\right|_{V_2(s)=0} = -\frac{V_1(s)}{-V_1(s)/(8s^2+2s+2)}$$

$$= 8s^2+2s+2$$

$$D = -\left.\frac{I_1(s)}{I_2(s)}\right|_{V_2(s)=0} = -\frac{V_1(s)(4s^2+1)}{(8s^2+2s+2)}$$

$$\times \frac{1}{[-V_1(s)/(8s^2+2s+2)]} = 4.\,s^2+1$$

$$[T] = \begin{bmatrix} A & B \\ C & D \end{bmatrix} = \begin{bmatrix} 4s+1 & 8s^2+2s+2 \\ 2s & 4s^2+1 \end{bmatrix} \quad \text{...Ans}$$

**Example 11.5.11 :** *Determine the transmission parameters for the two-port networks shown in Fig. 11.5.11 (a) and (b) and verify that AD – BC = 1. If the networks (a) and (b) are connected in cascade, obtain equivalent ABCD parameters.*

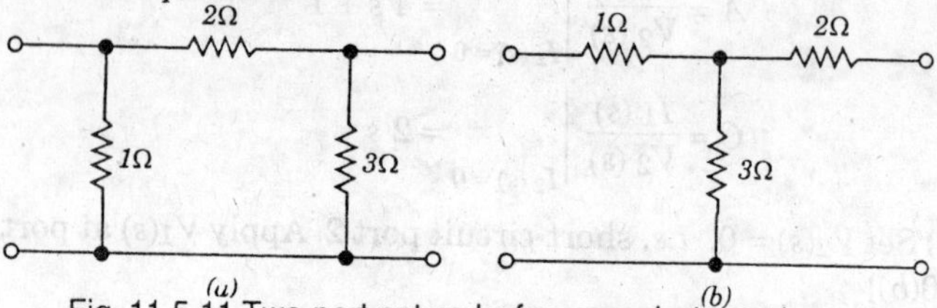


Fig. 11.5.11 Two-port networks for example 11.5.11.

**Solution :** (*a*) The network Fig. 11.5.11(*a*) is redrawn as shown in Fig. 11.5.11(*c*).

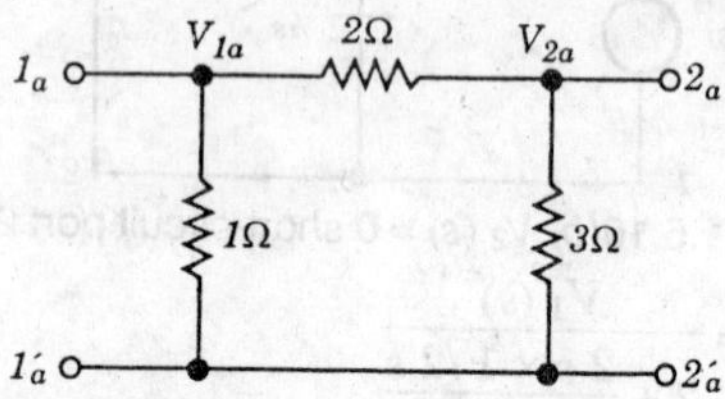


Fig. 11.5.11.(*c*) Transmission parameters network (*a*)

The transmission parameters are given as,

$$\begin{bmatrix} V_{1a} \\ I_{1a} \end{bmatrix} = \begin{bmatrix} A_a & B_a \\ C_a & D_a \end{bmatrix} \begin{bmatrix} V_{2a} \\ -I_{2a} \end{bmatrix}$$

Apply Kirchhoff's current law at nodes 1a and 2a,

At node 1 a : $-I_{1a} + \dfrac{V_{1a}}{1} + \dfrac{(V_{1a} - V_{2a})}{2} = 0$

or $$I_{1a} = 1.5V_a - 0.5V_{2a} \qquad ...(1a)$$

At node 2 a : $-I_{2a} + \dfrac{V_{2a}}{3} + \dfrac{(V_{2a} - V_{1a})}{2} = 0$

or $$I_{2a} = -0.5\,V_{1a} + \frac{5}{6}V_{2a} \qquad ...(2a)$$

Rearrange Eqn. (2*a*) as below,

$$V_{1a} = \frac{5}{3}V_{2a} - 2\,I_{2a} \qquad ...(3a)$$

Substitute for $V_{1a}$ in Eqn. (1*a*) from Eqn. (2*a*)

$\therefore$ $$I_{1a} = 1.5\left(\frac{5}{3}V_{2a} - 2\,I_{2a}\right) - 0.5\,V_{2a}$$

or $$I_{1a} = 2\,V_{2a} - 3\,I_{2a} \qquad ...(4a)$$

In matrix form Eqns. (3$a$) and (4$a$) can be written as

$$\begin{bmatrix} V_{1a} \\ I_{1a} \end{bmatrix} = \begin{bmatrix} 5/3 & 2 \\ 2 & 3 \end{bmatrix} \begin{bmatrix} V_{2a} \\ -I_{2a} \end{bmatrix}$$

$$\therefore \quad \begin{bmatrix} A_a & B_a \\ C_a & D_a \end{bmatrix} = \begin{bmatrix} 5/3 & 2 \\ 2 & 3 \end{bmatrix} \quad \text{...Ans.}$$

$$A_a D_a - B_a C_a = \frac{5}{3} \times 3 - 2 \times 2 = 1$$

($b$) The network Fig. 11.5.11($b$) is redrawn as shown in Fig. 11.5.11($d$).

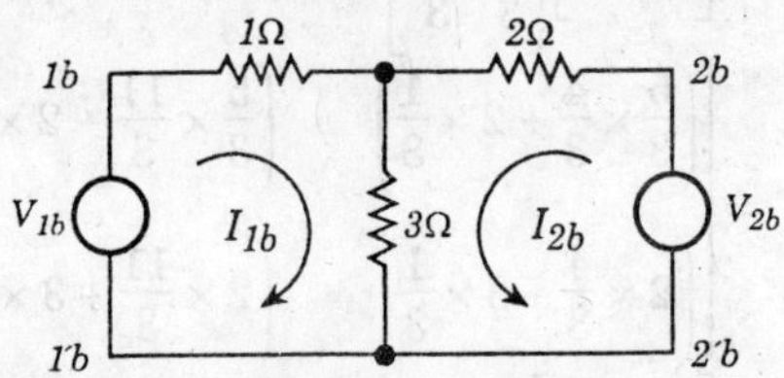


Fig. 11.5.11($d$) Transmission parameters for network ($b$)

Select mesh current as shown in Fig. 11.5.11($d$). As per mesh current analysis,

Mesh no 1 : $1\, I_{1b} + 3\,(I_{1b} + I_{2b}) - V_{1b} = 0$

Mesh no 2 : $2\, I_{2b} + 3\,(I_{1b} + I_{2b}) - V_{2b} = 0$

Rearrange above equations

$$V_{1b} = 4I_{1b} + 3I_{2b} \quad \text{...(1}b\text{)}$$

$$V_{2b} = 3I_{1b} + 5I_{2b} \quad \text{...(2}b\text{)}$$

Substitute for $I_{1b}$ in Eqn. (1$b$) from Eqn. (2$b$)

$$\therefore \quad V_{1b} = \frac{4\,(V_{2b} - 5I_{2b})}{3} + 3I_b$$

Simplifying above equation,

$$V_{1b} = \frac{4}{3} V_{2b} - \frac{11}{3} I_{2b} \quad \text{...(3}b\text{)}$$

Rearrange Eqn. (2$b$)

$$\therefore \quad I_{1b} = \frac{1}{3} V_{2b} - \frac{5}{3} I_{2b} \quad \text{...(4}b\text{)}$$

In matrix form Eqns. (3$a$) and Eqns. (4$b$) can be written as

$$\begin{bmatrix} V_{1b} \\ I_{1b} \end{bmatrix} = \begin{bmatrix} \frac{4}{3} & \frac{11}{3} \\ \frac{1}{3} & \frac{5}{3} \end{bmatrix} \begin{bmatrix} V_{2b} \\ -I_{2b} \end{bmatrix}$$

$$\therefore \quad \begin{bmatrix} A_b & B_b \\ C_b & D_b \end{bmatrix} = \begin{bmatrix} \frac{4}{3} & \frac{11}{3} \\ \frac{1}{3} & \frac{5}{3} \end{bmatrix} \quad \text{...Ans.}$$

$$A_b D_b - B_b C_b = \frac{4}{3} \times \frac{5}{3} - \frac{11}{3} \times \frac{1}{3} = 1$$

The equivalent transmission parameters on connecting networks (*a*) and (*b*) in cascade are determined below :

$$\begin{bmatrix} A & B \\ C & D \end{bmatrix} = \begin{bmatrix} 5/3 & 2 \\ 2 & 3 \end{bmatrix} \begin{bmatrix} \frac{4}{3} & \frac{11}{3} \\ \frac{1}{3} & \frac{5}{3} \end{bmatrix}$$

$$= \begin{bmatrix} \left(\frac{5}{3} \times \frac{4}{3} + 2 \times \frac{1}{3}\right) & \left(\frac{5}{3} \times \frac{11}{3} + 2 \times \frac{5}{3}\right) \\ \left(2 \times \frac{4}{3} + 3 \times \frac{1}{3}\right) & \left(2 \times \frac{11}{3} + 3 \times \frac{5}{3}\right) \end{bmatrix}$$

$$= \begin{bmatrix} \frac{26}{9} & \frac{85}{9} \\ \frac{11}{3} & \frac{37}{3} \end{bmatrix} \quad \text{...Ans.}$$

$$AD - BC = \frac{26}{9} \times \frac{37}{3} - \frac{85}{9} \times \frac{11}{3} = 1$$

**Example 11.5.12 :** *Determine y-parameters for the twin-T network shown in Fig. 11.5.12*

**Solution :** The transformed network is shown in Fig. 11.5.12(*a*)

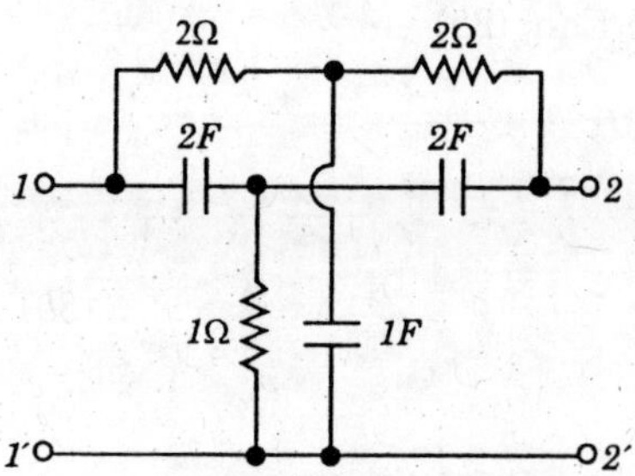

Fig. 11.5.12 Twin-T network for example 11.5.12

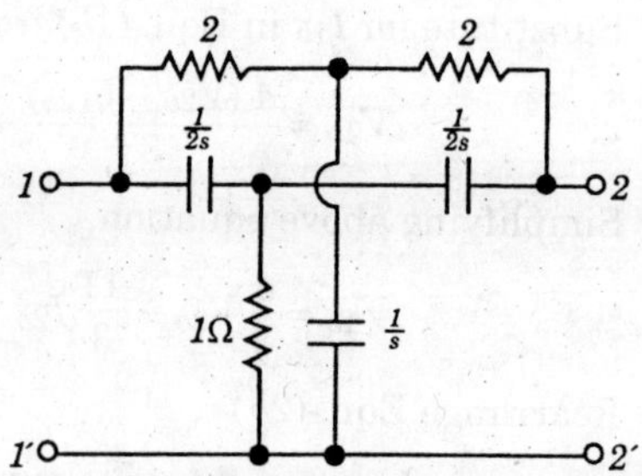

Fig. 11.5.12 (*a*) Transformed network.

The network shown in Fig. 11.5.12(*b*) consists of parallel connection of two *T*-networks as shown in Figs. 11.5.12(*b*) and 11.5.17(*c*).

Apply $V_{1a}(s)$ and $V_{2a}(s)$ at ports 1 and 2 respectively [Fig.11.5.12(b)] As per node voltage analysis,

(a)

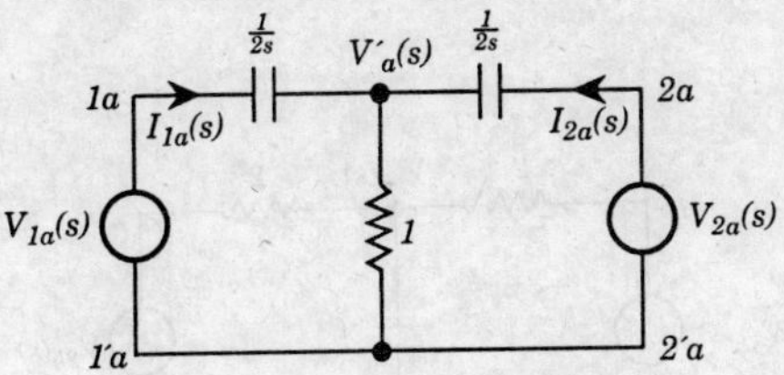


Fig. 11.5.12(*b*) *T*-network "*a*"

At node $a$ : $\dfrac{V'_a(s) - V_{1a}(s)}{1/2s} + \dfrac{V'_a(s) - V_{2a}(s)}{1/2s} + \dfrac{V'_a(s)}{1} = 0$

Simplifying, $(2s + 2s + 1)\, V'_a(s) = 2s\, V_{1a}(s) + 2s\, V_{2a}(s)$

$$\therefore \qquad V'_a(s) = \frac{2s\, V_{1a}(s)}{4s+1} + \frac{2s\, V_{2a}(s)}{4s+1}$$

$$\because \qquad I_{1a}(s) = \frac{V_{1a}(s) - V'_a(s)}{1/2s}$$

$$\therefore \qquad I_{1a}(s) = 2s\, V_{1a}(s) - 2s\left[\frac{2s\, V_{1a}(s)}{4s+1} + \frac{2s\, V_{2a}(s)}{4s+1}\right]$$

Simplifying,

$$I_{1a}(s) = \frac{2s\,(s+1)}{4s+1} V_{1a}(s) - \frac{4s^2}{4s+1} V_{2a}(s) \qquad \text{...(1a)}$$

$$I_{2a}(s) = \frac{V_{2a}(s) - V'_a(s)}{1/2s}$$

$$= 2s\, V_{2a}(s) - 2s\left[\frac{2s\, V_{1a}(s)}{4s+1} + \frac{2s\, V_{2a}(s)}{4s+1}\right]$$

Simplifying,

$$I_{2a}(s) = -\frac{4s^2}{4s+1} V_{1a}(s) + \frac{2s\,(2s+1)}{4s+1} V_{2a}(s) \qquad \text{...(2a)}$$

In matrix form Eqns. (1$a$) and (2$a$) can be written as

$$\begin{bmatrix} I_{1a}(s) \\ I_{2a}(s) \end{bmatrix} = \begin{bmatrix} \dfrac{2s\,(2s+1)}{4s+1} & -\dfrac{4s^2}{4s+1} \\ -\dfrac{4s^2}{4s+1} & \dfrac{2s\,(2s+1)}{4s+1} \end{bmatrix} \begin{bmatrix} V_{1a}(s) \\ V_{2a}(s) \end{bmatrix}$$

$$\therefore \qquad [y_a] = \begin{bmatrix} y_{11a} & y_{12a} \\ y_{21a} & y_{22a} \end{bmatrix} = \begin{bmatrix} \dfrac{2s\,(2s+1)}{4s+1} & -\dfrac{4s^2}{4s+1} \\ -\dfrac{4s^2}{4s+1} & \dfrac{2s\,(2s+1)}{4s+1} \end{bmatrix}$$

Apply $V_{1b}(s)$ and $V_{2b}(s)$ at port 1 and 2 respectively [Fig.11.5.12(c)]. As per node voltage analysis,

At node $b$ :

($b$)

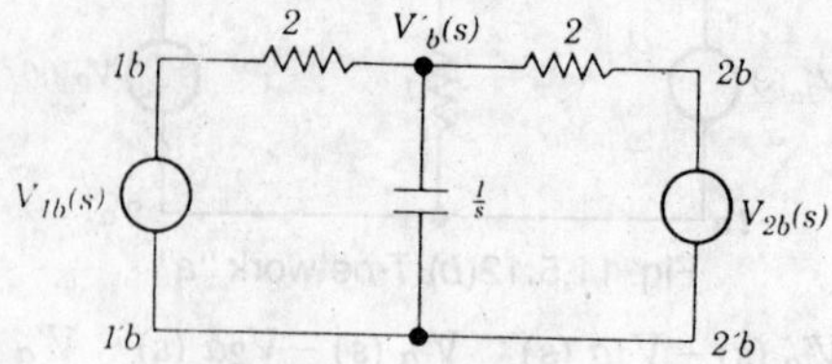


Fig. 11.5.12($c$) $T$-network "b"

$$\frac{V'_b(s) - V_{1b}(s)}{2} + \frac{V'_b(s) - V_{2b}(s)}{2} + \frac{V'_b(s)}{1/s} = 0$$

Simplifying $$\left(\frac{1}{2} + \frac{1}{2} + s\right) V'_b(s) = \frac{V_{1b}(s)}{2} + \frac{V_{2b}(s)}{2}$$

or $$(s+1)\, V'_b(s) = \frac{V_{1b}(s)}{2} + \frac{V_{2b}(s)}{2}$$

$\therefore$ $$V'_b(s) = \frac{V_{1b}(s)}{2(s+1)} + \frac{V_{2b}(s)}{2(s+1)}$$

$$I_{1b}(s) = \frac{V_{1b}(s) - V'_b(s)}{2} = \frac{V_{1b}(s)}{2} - \frac{1}{2}\left[\frac{V_{1b}(s)}{2(s+1)} + \frac{V_{2b}(s)}{2(s+1)}\right]$$

$$= \left[\frac{1}{2} - \frac{1}{4(s+1}\right] V_{1b}(s) - \frac{1}{4(s+1)} V_{2b}(s)$$

or $$I_{1b}(s) = \frac{2s+1}{4(s+1)} V_{1b}(s) - \frac{1}{4(s+1)} V_{2b}(s) \qquad \text{...(1a)}$$

$$I_{2b}(s) = \frac{V_{2b}(s) - V'_b(s)}{2} = \frac{V_{2b}(s)}{2} - \frac{1}{2}\left[\frac{V_{1b}(s)}{2(s+1)} + \frac{V_{2b}(s)}{2(s+1)}\right]$$

Simplifying,

$$I_{2b}(s) = -\frac{1}{4(s+1)} V_{1b}(s) + \frac{2s+1}{4(s+1)} V_{2b}(s) \qquad \text{...(2b)}$$

In matrix form Eqns. (1$a$) and (2$b$) can be written as

$$\begin{bmatrix} I_{1b}(s) \\ I_{2b}(s) \end{bmatrix} = \begin{bmatrix} \frac{2s+1}{4(s+1)} & -\frac{1}{4(s+1)} \\ -\frac{1}{4(s+1)} & \frac{2s+1}{4(s+1)} \end{bmatrix} \begin{bmatrix} V_{1b}(s) \\ V_{2b}(s) \end{bmatrix}$$

$\therefore$ $$[y_b] = \begin{bmatrix} \frac{2s+1}{4(s+1)} & -\frac{1}{4(s+1)} \\ -\frac{1}{4(s+1)} & \frac{2s+1}{4(s+1)} \end{bmatrix}$$

The equivalent $y$-parameters are given by

$$[y] = [y_a] + [y_b]$$

$$= \begin{bmatrix} y_{11a} + y_{11b} & y_{12a} + y_{12b} \\ y_{21a} + y_{21b} & y_{22a} + y_{22b} \end{bmatrix}$$

$$= \begin{bmatrix} \frac{2\,s\,(2\,s+1)}{4\,(s+1)} + \frac{2\,s+1}{4\,(s+1)} & \frac{-4\,s^2}{4\,(s+1)} - \frac{1}{4\,(s+1)} \\ \frac{-4\,s^2}{4\,(s+1)} - \frac{1}{4\,(s+1)} & \frac{2\,s\,(2\,s+1)}{4\,(s+1)} + \frac{2\,s+1}{4\,(s+1)} \end{bmatrix} \quad \text{...Ans.}$$

**Example 11.5.13** *Determine y-parameters for the bridged-T network (Fig. 11.5.13).*

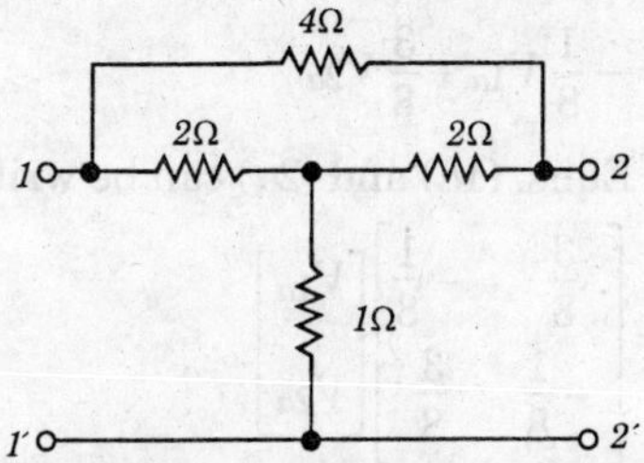


Fig. 11.5.13 Bridged-*T* network for example 11.5.13.

**Solution :** The bridged-*T* network shown in Fig. 11.5.13 consists of parallel connection of network ($a$) and ($b$) shown below,

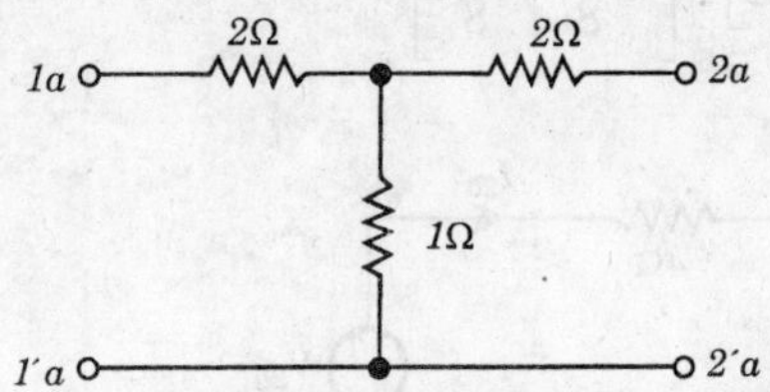


Fig. 11.5.13($a$) Network "($a$)"

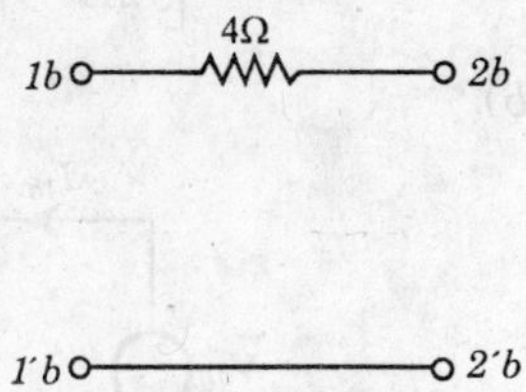


Fig. 11.5.13($b$) Network "($b$)"

($a$)

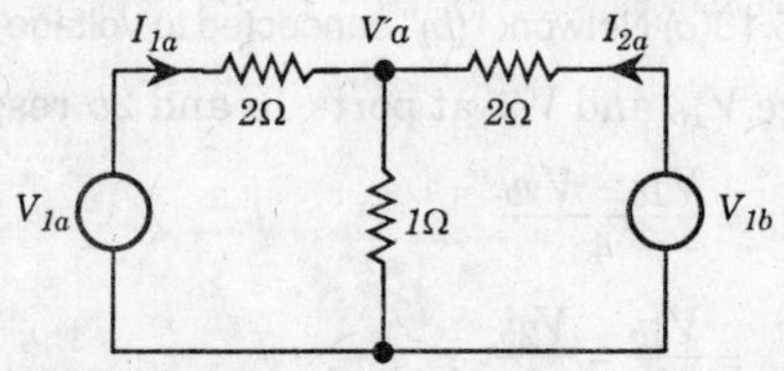


Fig. 11.5.13 ($c$) Network "($a$)" connected to voltage sources.

Apply voltages $V_{1a}$ and $V_{2a}$ at port $1a$ and $2a$ respectively.

As per node voltage analysis,

$$\text{At node } (a): \frac{V'_a - V_{1a}}{2} + \frac{V'_a - V_{2a}}{2} + \frac{V'_a}{1} = 0$$

Simplifying,

$$2V'_a = \frac{V_{1a}}{2} + \frac{V_{2a}}{2}$$

$$\therefore \quad V'_a = \frac{V_{1a}}{4} + \frac{V_{2a}}{4}$$

$$I_{1a} = \frac{V_{1a} - V'_a}{2} = \frac{V_{1a}}{2} - \frac{1}{2}\left(\frac{V_{1a}}{4} + \frac{V_{2a}}{4}\right)$$

or
$$I_{1a} = \frac{3}{8} V_{1a} - \frac{1}{8} V_{2a} \qquad ...(1a)$$

$$I_{2a} = \frac{V_{2a} - V'_a}{2} = \frac{V_{2a}}{2} - \frac{1}{2}\left(\frac{V_{1a}}{4} + \frac{V_{2a}}{4}\right)$$

or
$$I_{2a} = -\frac{1}{8} V_{1a} + \frac{3}{8} V_{2a} \qquad ...(2a)$$

In matrix form Eqns. (1*a*) and (2*a*) can be written as

$$\begin{bmatrix} I_{1a} \\ I_{2a} \end{bmatrix} = \begin{bmatrix} \frac{3}{8} & -\frac{1}{8} \\ -\frac{1}{8} & \frac{3}{8} \end{bmatrix} \begin{bmatrix} V_{1a} \\ V_{2a} \end{bmatrix}$$

$$\therefore \quad [y_a] = \begin{bmatrix} y_{11a} & y_{12a} \\ y_{21a} & y_{22a} \end{bmatrix} = \begin{bmatrix} \frac{3}{8} & -\frac{1}{8} \\ -\frac{1}{8} & \frac{3}{8} \end{bmatrix}$$

(*b*)

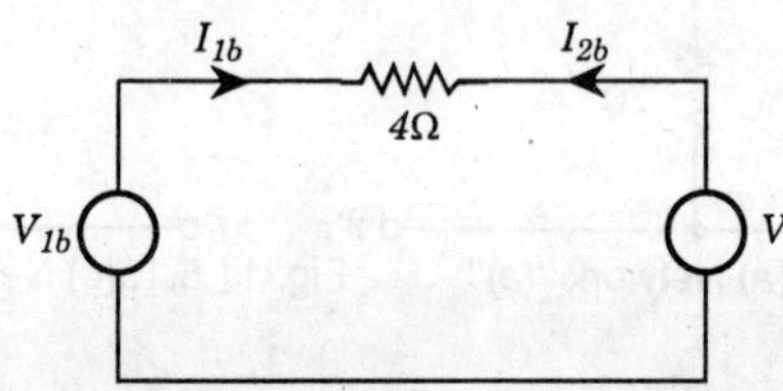


Fig. 11.5.13(*d*) Network "(*b*)" connected to voltage sources.

Apply voltage $V_{1b}$ and $V_{2b}$ at ports 1*b* and 2*b* respectively.

$$I_{1b} = \frac{V_{1b} - V_{2b}}{4}$$

or
$$I_{1b} = \frac{V_{1b}}{4} - \frac{V_{2b}}{4} \qquad ...(1b)$$

$$I_{2b} = \frac{V_{2b} - V_{1b}}{4}$$

or
$$I_{2b} = -\frac{V_{1b}}{4} + \frac{V_{2b}}{4} \qquad ...(2b)$$

In matrix form Eqns. (1*b*) and (2*b*) can be written as

$$\begin{bmatrix} I_{1b} \\ I_{2b} \end{bmatrix} = \begin{bmatrix} \frac{1}{4} & -\frac{1}{4} \\ \frac{1}{4} & -\frac{1}{4} \end{bmatrix} \begin{bmatrix} V_{1b} \\ V_{2b} \end{bmatrix}$$

$$\therefore \qquad [y_b] = \begin{bmatrix} y_{11b} & y_{12b} \\ y_{21b} & y_{22b} \end{bmatrix} = \begin{bmatrix} \frac{1}{4} & -\frac{1}{4} \\ -\frac{1}{4} & \frac{1}{4} \end{bmatrix}$$

The equivalent *y*-parameters are

$$[y] = \begin{bmatrix} y_{11a} + y_{11b} & y_{12a} + y_{12b} \\ y_{21a} + y_{21b} & y_{22a} + y_{22b} \end{bmatrix}$$

$$= \begin{bmatrix} \frac{3}{8} + \frac{1}{4} & -\frac{1}{8} - \frac{1}{4} \\ -\frac{1}{8} - \frac{1}{4} & \frac{3}{8} + \frac{1}{4} \end{bmatrix} = \begin{bmatrix} \frac{5}{8} & -\frac{3}{8} \\ -\frac{3}{8} & \frac{5}{8} \end{bmatrix} \quad \text{...Ans.}$$

## PROBLEMS

**11.1** Use two-port network parameter definitions to obtain open-circuit parameters for the network shown in Fig. 11P-1

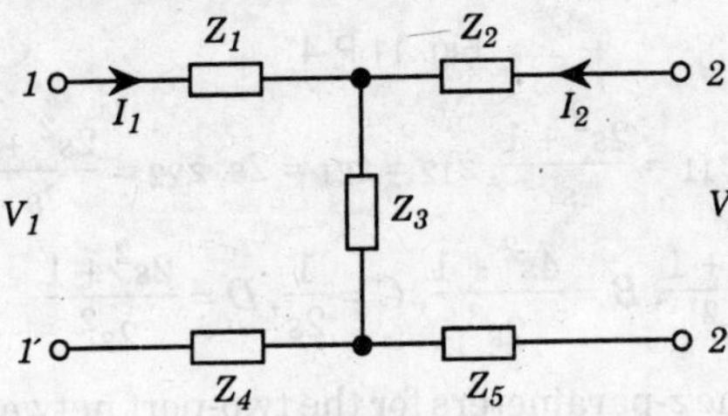

Fig. 11P-1

(**Ans**: $z_{11} = z_1 + z_3 + z_4$, $z_{12} = z_{21} = z_3$, $z_{22} = z_2 + z_3 + z_4$)

**11.2** Find *z*-parameters for the network given in Fig. 11P-2. Check for symmetry and reciprocity

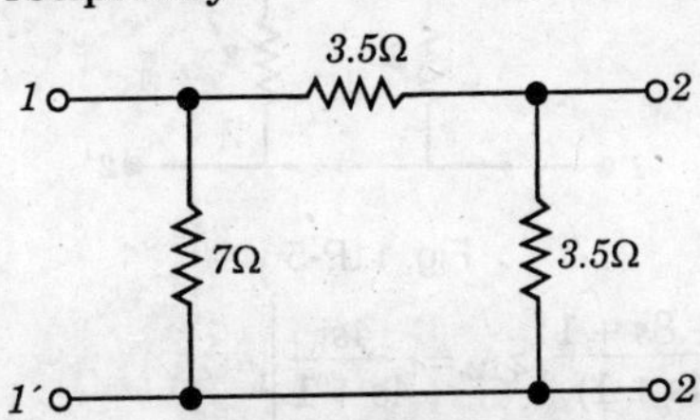

Fig. 11P-2

(**Ans**: $z_{11} = 3.5$, $z_{12} = 1.75$, $z_{21} = 1.75$, $z_{21} = 2.625$)

**11.3** Determine (*i*) *z*-parameters (*ii*) *ABCD* parameters. The two-port network is shown in Fig. 11P-3

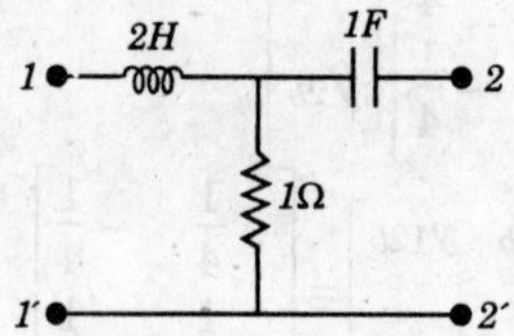


Fig. 11 P-3

**Ans** : (*i*) $z_{11} = (2s + 1), z_{12} = z_{21} = 1, z_{22} = \frac{s+1}{s}$

(*ii*) $A = (2s + 1), B = \frac{2s^2 + 2s + 1}{s}, C = 1, D = \frac{s+1}{s}$

**11.4** For The T-network shown in Fig.11P-4, obtain (*a*) *z*-parameters (*b*) *ABCD* parameters.

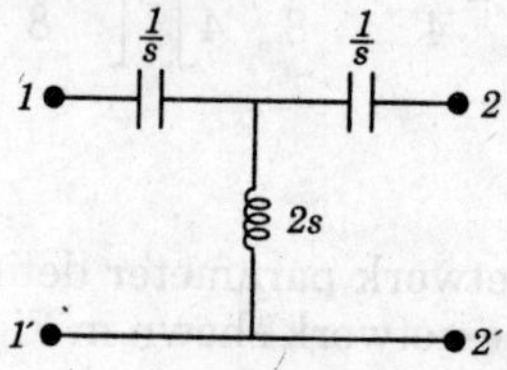


Fig. 11 P-4

**Ans**:(*a*)$z_{11} = \frac{2s^2+1}{s}, z_{12} = z_{21} = 2s, z_{22} = \frac{2s^2+1}{s}$

(*b*)$A = \frac{2s^2+1}{2s^2}, B = \frac{4s^2+1}{2s^3}, C = \frac{1}{2s}, D = \frac{2s^2+1}{2s^2}$

**11.5** Determine *z*-parameters for the two-port network given in Fig. 11P-5

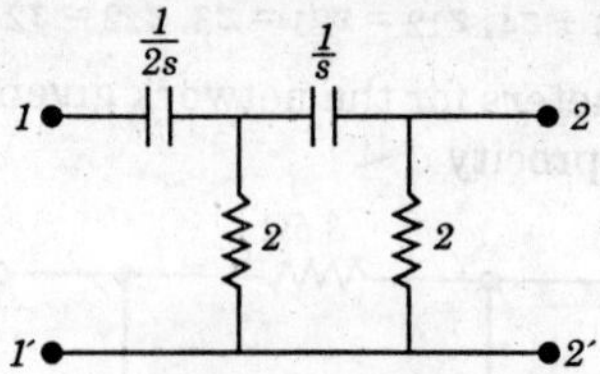


Fig. 11P-5

**Ans**: $z_1 = \frac{8s^2 + 8s + 1}{2s(4s+1)}, z_{12} = \frac{4s}{4s+1}$

$z_{21} = \frac{4s}{s+1}, z_{22} = \frac{2(2s+1)}{4s+1}$

**11.6** Obtain $z$-parameters for the network (Fig. 11P-6)

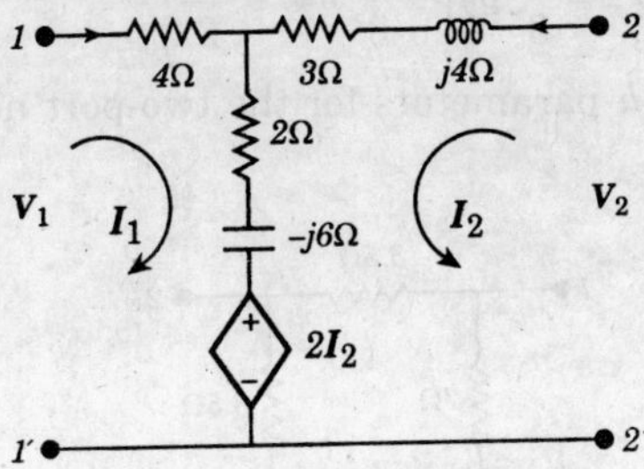


Fig. 11P-6

[**Ans**: $z_{11} = (6 - j6), z_{12} = (4 - j6), z_{21} = (2 - j6), z_{22}(7 - j2)$]

**11.7** Determine $y$-parameters. The network is given in Fig. 11P-7.

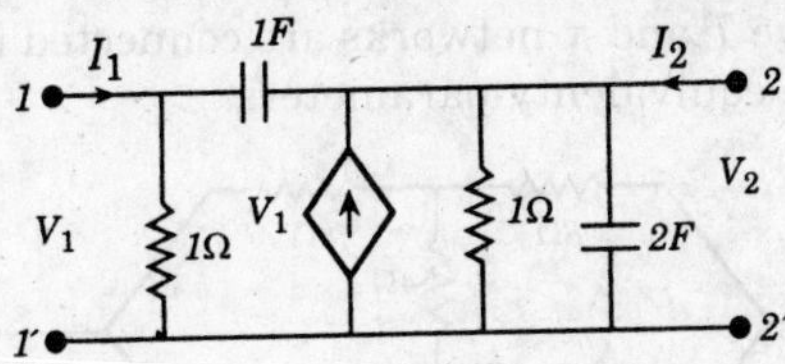


Fig. 11P-7

[**Ans**: $y_{11} = \dfrac{1+4s}{2}, y_{12} = -2s, y_{21} = -(1+2s), y_{22} = (1+3s)$]

**11.8** Use two-port parameter definitions to determine $y$-parameters (Fig. 11P-8).

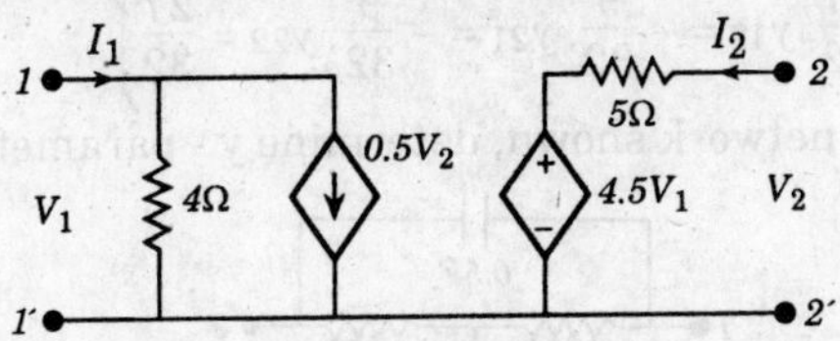


Fig. 11P-8

(**Ans**: $y_{11} = 0.25, y_{12} = 0.5, y_{21} = -0.9, y_{22} = 0.2$)

**11.9** Obtain $g$-parameters for the network shown in Fig. 11P-9.

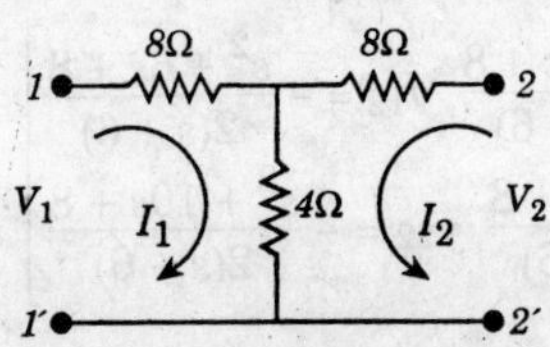


Fig. 11P-9

$\left(\textbf{Ans:} g_{11} = \frac{1}{12}, g_{12} = -\frac{1}{3}, g_{21} = \frac{1}{3}, g_{22} = \frac{32}{3}\right)$

**11.10** Determine $h$-parameters for the two-port network given in Fig. 11P-10

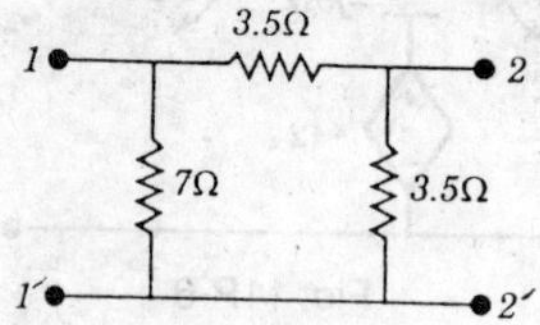


Fig. 11P-10

(**Ans**: $h_{11} = 2.33$, $h_{12} = 0.66$, $h_{21} = -0.66$, $h_{22} = 0.38$)

**11.11** A resistive $T$ and $\pi$ networks are connected in parallel (Fig. 11P-11). Obtain the equivalenty-parameters.

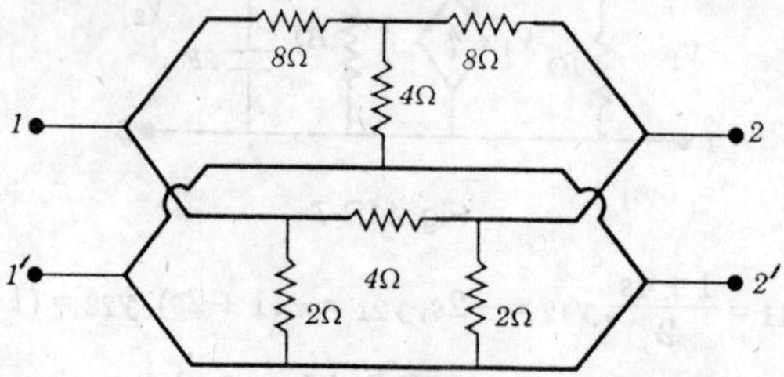


Fig. 11P-11

$\left(\textbf{Ans:}\ y_{11} = \frac{27}{32}, y_{12} = -\frac{9}{32}, y_{21} = -\frac{9}{32}, y_{22} = \frac{27}{32}\right)$

**11.12** For the network shown, determine y - parameters

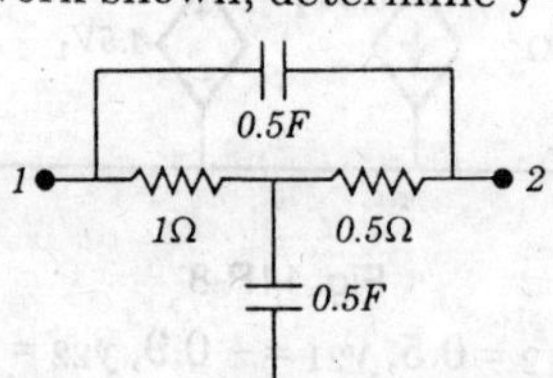


Fig. 11P-12

$$\left[\begin{array}{l}\textbf{Ans:}\ y_{11} = \frac{s^2 + 8s + 8}{2(s+6)}, y_{12} = -\frac{s^2 + 6s + 8}{2(s+6)} \\ y_{21} = -\frac{s^2 + 6s + 8}{2(s+6)}, y_{22} = -\frac{s^2 + 10s + 8}{2(s+6)}\end{array}\right]$$

# 12

# ELECTRICAL NETWROK TOPOLOGY (Graph Theory)

## 12.1 INTRODUCTION

The branch of geometry which concerns with the properties of geometrical figures is known as topology. A general configuration of electric network wherein each element appears in the form of a line and a junction such that the line is placed between junction points is a graph representation of the network.

Following terms are used in electrical network topology.

Node : A point at which two or more elements have a common connection forming a junction.

Branch : A single path containing one element which connects one node to any other node.

Loop : A set of elements that may be traversed through a closed path without passing a node twice.

Mesh : A loop which does not contain any other loop inside it.

Planar Circuit : A circuit which may be drawn on a plane surface such that no branch crosses over or under any other branch.

Non-Planar Circuit : Any circuit which is not planar.

In a network graph each element is represented by a line segment, potential source elements as a short circuit and current source as open circuit.

## 12.2 NETWORK GRAPH

A network graph is defined as a collection of branches and nodes in which each branch (edge) contains two nodes.

Fig. 12.2.1 Shows a network and its corresponding graph

Nodes : $a$, $b$, $c$ and $d$

Branches : 1, 2, 3, 4, 5, 6 and 7

The current source (branch no. 7) being shown as open circuit in network graph, voltage source (in branch no.1) is shown as short circuit.

Loop : $a$–$b$–$c$–$d$–$a$ formed by branch nos. 4, 5, 3, 1

$a$–$c$–$b$–$d$–$a$ formed by branch nos. 2, 5, 6, 1

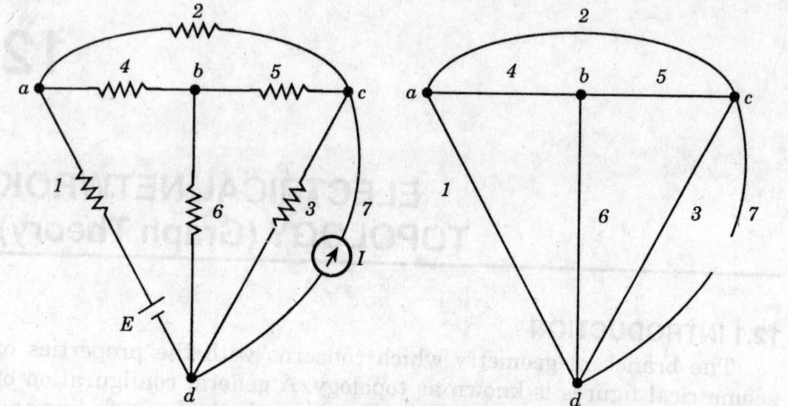


Fig. 12.2.1 Network and its corresponding graph

| | | |
|---|---|---|
| | $a–b–d–c–a$ | formed by branch nos. 4, 6, 3, 2 |
| | $a–c–d–a$ | formed by branch nos. 2, 3, 1 |
| Mesh: | $a–b–d–a$ | formed by branch nos. 1, 4, 6 |
| | $b–c–d–b$ | formed by branch nos. 5, 3, 6 |
| | $a–b–c–a$ | formed by branch nos. 2, 4, 5 |

### 12.2.1 Oriented Graph

The reference in a graph is indicated by the orientation of a branch. This is done by placing an arrow on the branch. The direction of the arrow is arbitrary. A network graph where the branch have orientation (direction) is known as oriented (directed) graph. An oriented graph is shown in Fig. 12.2.2

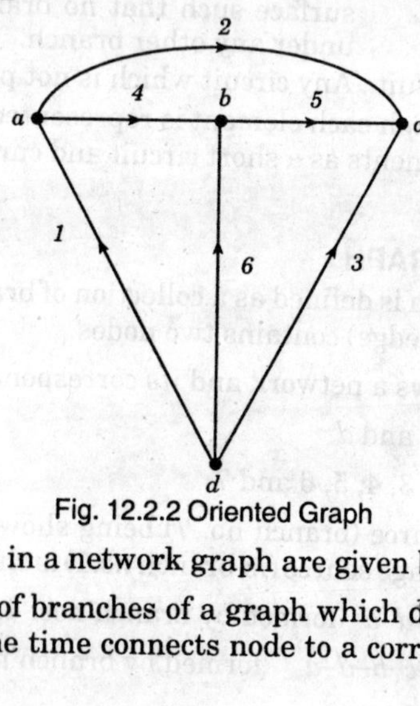


Fig. 12.2.2 Oriented Graph

The terms used in a network graph are given below.

**Tree** : Any set of branches of a graph which does not contain any loop and at the same time connects node to a corresponding node. All the nodes of a graph are present in a tree graph. A number of trees can be drawn for a graph. The branches of a tree graph are called tree branches or twigs or simply branches.

**Co-tree** : Those branches of a graph which are not parts of a tree, form a co-tree. The co-tree is a complement of a tree.

**Link** : The branch of a co-tree is called link.

In a network graph the tree branches are drawn by solid lines, where as links by broken lines.

Fig. 12.2.3(*a*) shows a graph. There can be a number of tree of a graph. One set of tree for the graph Fig. 12.2.3(*a*) is shown in Fig. 12.2.3(*b*) and co-tree in Fig. 12.2.3(*c*)

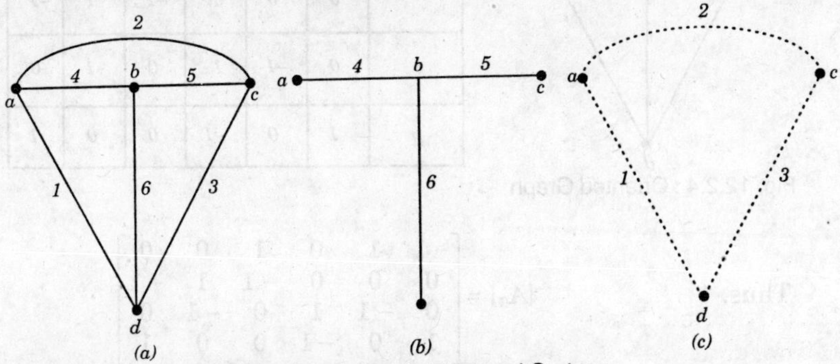


Fig. 12.2.3 Graph, Tree and Co-tree

As shown in Fig. 12.2.3

The number of nodes $n = 4$, $a$, $b$, $c$ and $d$

The total number of graph branches (edges) :

$$b_t = 6, (1, 2, 3, 4, 5 \& 6)$$

The number of tree branches (twigs) : $b = 3$, (4, 5 & 6)

The number of co-tree branches (links) : $l = 3$, (1, 2 & 3)

The relationship between the total number of graph branches $b_t$ number of links $l$, number of tree branches $b$ and number of nodes $n$ is determined below:

If the number of nodes in a graph is $n$, then $(n - 1)$ nodes are needed to form a tree, thus,

$$b = n - 1$$

and $$l = (b_t - b)$$

or $$l = b_t - (n - 1)$$

## 12.2.2 INCIDENCE MATRIX:[$A_a$]

The incidence matrix [$A_a$] relates rectangular array of numbers 1, –1 and 0 to an oriented (directed) graph. The branch converging to a node is assigned a coefficient –1 and that diverging 1. Any other branch not connected to a node under consideration is assigned a coefficient 0.

For the oriented graph shown in Fig. 12.2.4 the incidence matrix $[A_a]$ is formed below:

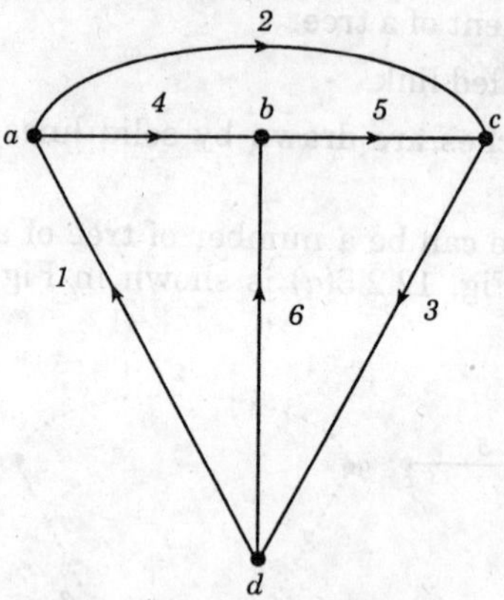


Fig. 12.2.4 : Oriented Graph

| Branch / node | 1 | 2 | 3 | 4 | 5 | 6 |
|---|---|---|---|---|---|---|
| a | -1 | 1 | 0 | 1 | 0 | 0 |
| b | 0 | 0 | 0 | -1 | 1 | -1 |
| c | 0 | -1 | 1 | 0 | -1 | 0 |
| d | 1 | 0 | -1 | 0 | 0 | 1 |

Thus.
$$[A_a] = \begin{bmatrix} -1 & 1 & 0 & 1 & 0 & 0 \\ 0 & 0 & 0 & -1 & 1 & -1 \\ 0 & -1 & 1 & 0 & -1 & 0 \\ 1 & 0 & -1 & 0 & 0 & 1 \end{bmatrix}$$

The columns of incidence matrix has two entries as there are two nodes for each branch and the sum of these entries is zero.

The incidence matrix translates geometrical information into an algebraic information as follows:

The rows of incidence matrix satisfy Kirchhoff's current law (*KCL*) at nodes. For example, if the branch (edge) currents are $I_1, I_2, I_3, I_4, I_5$ and $I_6$ then :

at node $a$ : $-I_1 + I_2 + I_4 = 0$

at node $b$ : $-I_4 + I_5 - I_6 = 0$

at node $c$ : $-I_2 + I_3 - I_5 = 0$

at node $d$ : $I_1 - I_3 + I_6 = 0$

Thus $[A_a]\ [I_b] = 0$

$[I_b]$: branch current matrix is column vector

The transpose of incidence matrix gives relation between branch voltage in terms of node voltages.

$$[A_a]^T = \begin{array}{c} \text{branch} \\ 1 \\ 2 \\ 3 \\ 4 \\ 5 \\ 6 \end{array} \overset{\text{node}}{\overset{\begin{array}{cccc} a & b & c & d \end{array}}{\begin{bmatrix} -1 & 0 & 0 & 1 \\ 1 & 0 & -1 & 0 \\ 0 & 0 & 1 & -1 \\ 1 & -1 & 0 & 0 \\ 0 & 1 & -1 & 0 \\ 0 & -1 & 0 & 1 \end{bmatrix}}}$$

As per the rows of transpose incidence matrix, the relation between branch voltage and node voltages is given below :

$$V_1 = -e_a + e_d$$

$$V_2 = e_a - e_c$$

$$V_3 = e_c - e_d$$

$$V_4 = e_a - e_b$$

$$V_5 = e_b - e_c$$

$$V_6 = -e_b + e_d$$

Thus, $$[V_b] = [A_a]^T [e_n]$$

where $[V_b]$ : branch voltage matrix is column vector.

$[e_n]$ : node voltage matrix is column vector.

### 12.2.3 Reduced Incidence Matrix : [*A*]

Reduced incidence matrix [*A*] is obtained from incidence matrix by removing any row from it. This removal is usually for the row concerning reference node. For the graph shown in Fig. 12.2.4 the node d is considered as reference node and the reduced incidence matrix [A] is given below :

| node \ Branch | 1 | 2 | 3 | 4 | 5 | 6 |
|---|---|---|---|---|---|---|
| a | –1 | 1 | 0 | 1 | 0 | 0 |
| b | 0 | 0 | 0 | –1 | 1 | –1 |
| c | 0 | –1 | 1 | 0 | –1 | 0 |

Thus, $$[A] = \begin{bmatrix} -1 & 1 & 0 & 1 & 0 & 0 \\ 0 & 0 & 0 & -1 & 1 & -1 \\ 0 & -1 & 1 & 0 & -1 & 0 \end{bmatrix}$$

The transpose of reduced incidence matrix gives relation between the branch voltage and node pair voltages. The voltage of reference node is considered to be zero.

$$[A]^T = \begin{array}{c} \text{branch} \\ 1 \\ 2 \\ 3 \\ 4 \\ 5 \\ 6 \end{array} \overset{\text{node}}{\overset{\begin{array}{ccc} a & b & c \end{array}}{\begin{bmatrix} & & \\ -1 & 0 & 0 \\ 1 & 0 & -1 \\ 0 & 0 & 1 \\ 1 & -1 & 0 \\ 0 & 1 & -1 \\ 0 & -1 & 0 \end{bmatrix}}}$$

The relation between branch voltage and node voltages (*w.r.t.* reference node) is given by the rows of $[A]^T$ as given below :

$$V_1 = -e_a$$
$$V_2 = e_a - e_c$$
$$V_3 = e_c$$
$$V_4 = e_a - e_b$$
$$V_5 = e_b - e_c$$
$$V_6 = -e_b$$

Thus $$[V_b] = [A]^T [e_n]$$

The reference node voltage is zero. Out of $n$ nodes of a graph $(n\text{-}1)$ nodes are considered after deleting the reference node.

### 12.2.4 Number of Possible Trees of a Network Graph

The number of possible trees of a graph is given by $|[A][A]^T|$ where $A$ is reduced incidence matrix. This is verified by the example given below :

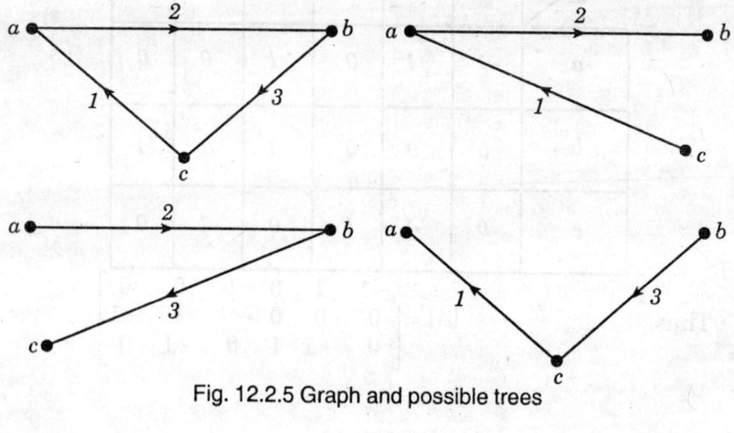


Fig. 12.2.5 Graph and possible trees

It is observed from the graph shown in Fig. 12.2.5 that the number of possible graph tree is 3 as shown.

The incidence matrix for the graph shown in Fig. 12.2.5 is given below :

| Branch / node | 1 | 2 | 3 |
|---|---|---|---|
| a | -1 | 1 | 0 |
| b | 0 | -1 | 1 |
| c | 1 | 0 | 1 |

Considering the node $c$ as reference node, the reduced incidence matrix is :

| Branch / node | 1 | 2 | 3 |
|---|---|---|---|
| a | -1 | 1 | 0 |
| b | 0 | -1 | 1 |

Therefore, $$[A] = \begin{bmatrix} -1 & 1 & 0 \\ 0 & -1 & 1 \end{bmatrix}$$

and $$[A]^T = \begin{bmatrix} -1 & 0 \\ 1 & -1 \\ 0 & 1 \end{bmatrix}$$

$$[A]\,[A]^T = \begin{bmatrix} -1 & 1 & 0 \\ 0 & -1 & 1 \end{bmatrix}\begin{bmatrix} -1 & 0 \\ 1 & -1 \\ 0 & 1 \end{bmatrix} = \begin{bmatrix} 2 & -1 \\ -1 & 2 \end{bmatrix}$$

and $$[A]\,[A]^T = \begin{vmatrix} 2 & -1 \\ -1 & 2 \end{vmatrix} = 2 \times 2 - (-1)(-1) = 3$$

Hence, the number of possible trees for the network graph in Fig. 12.2.5 is 3.

## 12.3 MESH-MATRIX : $[B_m]$

Fig 12.3.1 shows the graph of a network containing 3 meshes and 6 branches, the three mesh current are denoted as $i_1$, $i_2$ and $i_3$ while the branch current as $I_1$, $I_2$, $I_3$, $I_4$, $I_5$ and $I_6$.

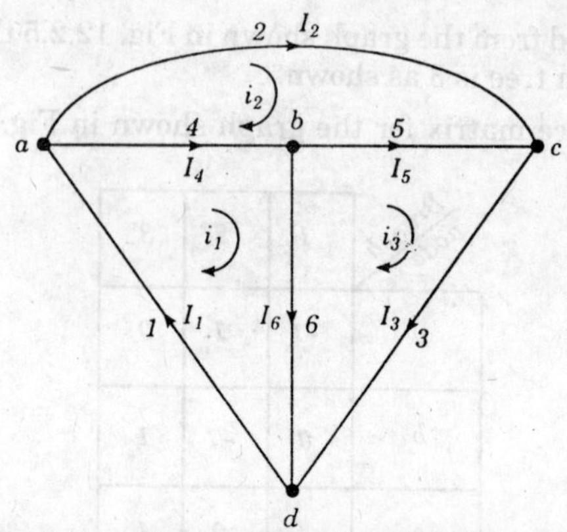


Fig. 12.3.1 Network graph for mesh matrix : $[B_m]$

The mesh matrix $[B_m]$ concerns with the interaction of mesh currents with branch currents. The mesh currents and branch currents having same direction, are assigned a coefficient 1 while the opposite direction are assigned a coefficient –1. For no interaction, the coefficient 0 is assigned. The mesh matrix for network graph (Fig. 12.3) is formed below.

| Branch / mesh | 1 | 2 | 3 | 4 | 5 | 6 |
|---|---|---|---|---|---|---|
| 1 | 1 | 0 | 0 | 1 | 0 | 1 |
| 2 | 0 | 1 | 0 | –1 | –1 | 0 |
| 3 | 0 | 0 | 1 | 0 | 1 | –1 |

Thus $$[B_m] = \begin{bmatrix} 1 & 0 & 0 & 1 & 0 & 1 \\ 0 & 1 & 0 & -1 & -1 & 0 \\ 0 & 0 & 1 & 0 & 1 & -1 \end{bmatrix}$$

The rows of mesh matrix satisfy Kirchhoff's voltage law (*KVL*) for the network as follows:

for mesh 1 : $V_1 + V_4 + V_6 = 0$

for mesh 2 : $V_2 - V_4 - V_5 = 0$

for mesh 3 : $V_3 + V_5 - V_6 = 0$

Thus, $[B_m]\ [V_b] = 0$

The columns of mesh matrix relate branch current and mesh current as given below :

$$I_1 = i_1$$
$$I_2 = i_2$$
$$I_3 = i_3$$
$$I_4 = i_1 - i_2$$
$$I_5 = -i_2 + i_3$$
$$I_6 = i_1 - i_3$$

Thus $\quad [I_b] = [B_m]^T [i_m]$

$[I_b]$ : branch current matrix is column vector.

$[B_m]^T$ : transpose mesh matrix.

$[i_m]$ : mesh current matrix is column vector.

## 12.4 FUNDAMENTAL CIRCUITS AND FUNDAMENTAL CIRCUIT MATRIX : $[B_f]$

In a network tree graph each link of a co-tree is associated with a mesh or loop. A closed circuit consisting of a link and the associated tree branches is called a fundamental circuit. There are as many fundamental circuit as there are links. The example given below illustrate the formation of f-circuit matrix $[B_f]$.

**Example : 1.**

For the graph shown in Fig. 12.4.1

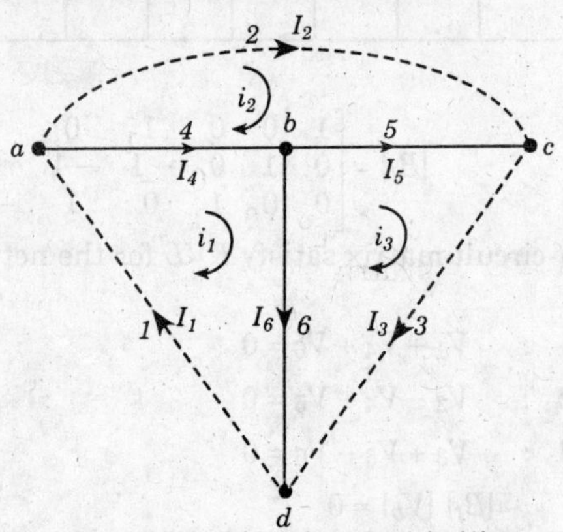


Fig. 12.4.1 Graph for example (1)

Tree branches : 4, 5 & 6

Links : 1, 2 & 3

As there are 3 links, the number of *f*-circuits is 3, *f*-circuits are formed as :

| | link | tree branches |
|---|---|---|
| *f*-circuit no.1 | 1 | 4 , 6 |
| *f*-circuit no.2 | 2 | 4 , 5 |
| *f*-circuit no.3 | 3 | 5 , 6 |

The loop/mesh formed by a *f*-circuit is assigned a loop/mesh current such as $i_1$, $i_2$, $i_3$ etc. and branch current as $I_1$, $I_2$, $I_3$ etc.

While forming *f*-circuit matrix $[B_f]$ link/tree branch current associated with the same direction of mesh/loop current is assigned a coefficient 1, while opposite -1. the link/tree branch not associated with the mesh/loop is assigned a coefficient 0.

As per above reasoning f-circuit matrix $[B_f]$ for the network graph shown in Fig. 12.4.1 is formed below :

*Link / tree branch*

| *f-circuit* | *1* | 2 | 3 | 4 | 5 | 6 |
|---|---|---|---|---|---|---|
| *1* | *1* | *0* | *0* | *1* | *0* | *1* |
| 2 | *0* | *1* | *0* | *–1* | *–1* | *0* |
| 3 | *0* | *0* | *1* | *0* | *1* | *-1* |

Thus, $$[B_f] = \begin{bmatrix} 1 & 0 & 0 & 1 & 0 & 1 \\ 0 & 1 & 0 & -1 & -1 & 0 \\ 0 & 0 & 1 & 0 & 1 & -1 \end{bmatrix}$$

The rows of *f*-circuit matrix satisfy *KVL* for the network branches i.e.

for *f*-circuit 1 : $V_1 + V_4 + V_6 = 0$

for *f*-circuit 2 : $V_2 - V_4 - V_5 = 0$

for *f*-circuit 3 : $V_3 + V_5 - V_6 = 0$

Therefore, $[B_f]\,[V_b] = 0$

The columns of f-circuit matrix relate branch current and mech/loop current i.e.

$$I_1 = i_1$$

$$I_2 = i_2$$

$$I_3 = i_3$$
$$I_4 = i_1 - i_2$$
$$I_5 = - i_2 + i_3$$
$$I_6 = i_1 - i_3$$

**Example : 2.**

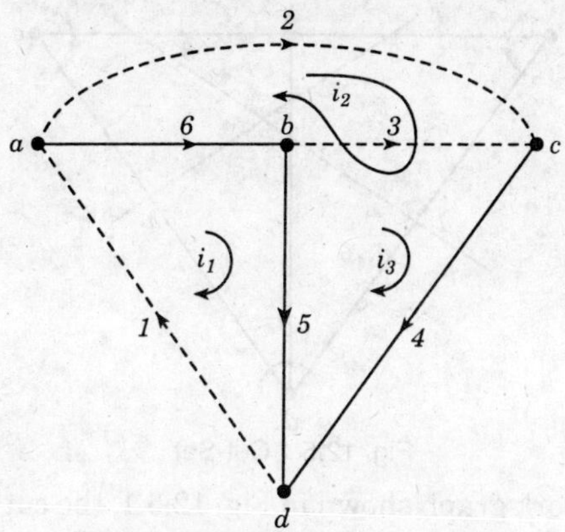


Fig. 12.4.2 Graph for example (2)

For the graph shown in Fig. 12.4.2
Tree branches : 4, 5 & 6
Links : 1, 2 & 3

As there are 3 links the number of *f*-circuits is 3, *f*-circuits are formed as :

| | Link | Tree branches |
|---|---|---|
| *f*-circuit no.1 | 1 | 6, 5 |
| *f*-circuit no.2 | 2 | 4, 5, 6 |
| *f*-circuit no.3 | 3 | 4, 5 |

The loop/mesh formed by a *f*-circuit is assigned a loop/mesh current such as $i_1$, $i_2$, $i_3$ *etc.*

*f*-circuit matrix for the network graph (Fig. 12.4.2) is formed below:

*Link / tree branch*

| *f-circuit* | 1 | 2 | 3 | 4 | 5 | 6 |
|---|---|---|---|---|---|---|
| 1 | 1 | 0 | 0 | 0 | 1 | 1 |
| 2 | 0 | 1 | 0 | 1 | –1 | –1 |
| 3 | 0 | 0 | 1 | 1 | –1 | 0 |

Thus, $$[B_f] = \begin{bmatrix} 1 & 0 & 0 & 0 & 1 & 1 \\ 0 & 1 & 0 & 1 & -1 & -1 \\ 0 & 0 & 1 & 1 & -1 & 0 \end{bmatrix}$$

## 12.5 CUT-SET

Cut-set is a set of branches that separates a network graph into two parts such that replacement of any one element destroys this property.

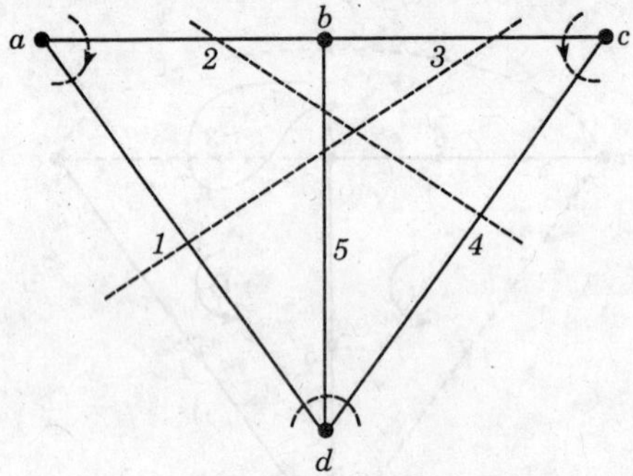


Fig. 12.5.1 Cut-Set

For the network graph shown in Fig. 12.5.1, the cut sets Fig. 12.5.2 formed are given below:

Cut-set no. 1 : 1, 2

Cut-set no. 2 : 3, 4

Cut-set no. 3 : 1, 5, 4

Cut-set no. 4 : 1, 5, 3

Cut-set no. 5 : 2, 3, 5

Cut-set no. 6 : 2, 5, 4

### 12.5.1 Fundamental Cut-sets : *f*-cut-sets

*f*-cut set concerns with a tree graph where in one tree branch and other connected links are cut to separate the graph into two parts. The

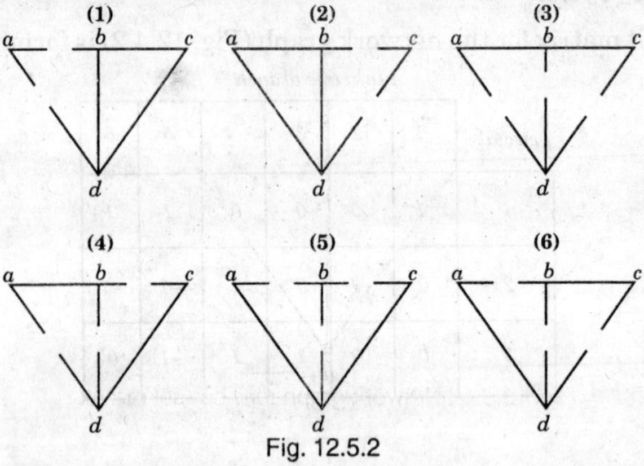


Fig. 12.5.2

tree branch cut specifies *f*-cutset for that branch. There are as many *f*-cutsets as tree branches Fig. 12.5.3

As shown in Fig. 12.5.3 the number of tree branches is 3, hence the number of *f*-cutsets is 3.

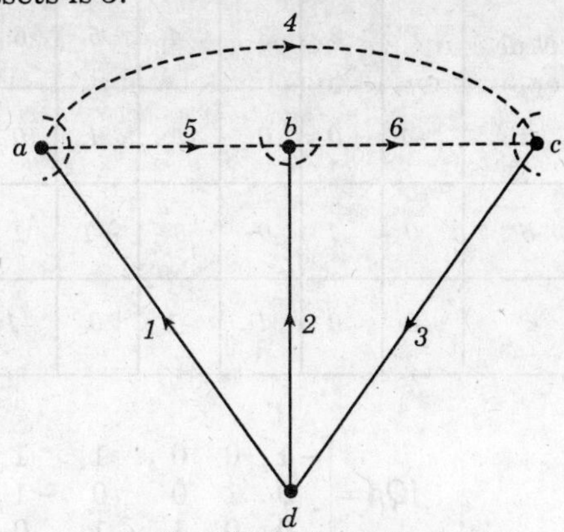


Fig. 12.5.3 : *f*-cutsets.

The *f*-cuts sets are

| | | Branch | Link |
|---|---|---|---|
| *f*-cutset no. 1 | : | 1 | 5, 4 |
| *f*-cutset no. 2 | : | 2 | 5, 6 |
| *f*-cutset no. 3 | : | 3 | 6, 4 |

In a network tree graph each node is associated with a tree branch and links. A cut applied to this combination forms *f*-cut set. The tree branch/link diverging from the node is assigned coefficient 1 and that converging – 1. The tree branch and link which is not connected to the node under consideration are assigned coefficient 0.

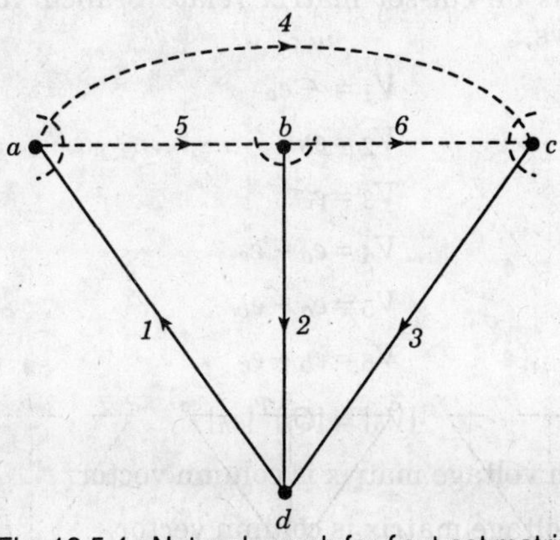


Fig. 12.5.4 : Network graph for *f*-cut-set matrix

With the assigned coefficients as above, the fundamental cut-set matrix $[Q_f]$ is formed below for the network graph shown in Fig. 12.5.4

*Tree branch / Link*

| *Node* | *1* | *2* | *3* | *4* | *5* | *6* |
|---|---|---|---|---|---|---|
| *a* | *–1* | *0* | *0* | *1* | *1* | *0* |
| *b* | *0* | *1* | *0* | *0* | *–1* | *1* |
| *c* | *0* | *0* | *1* | *–1* | *0* | *–1* |

Thus. $$[Q_f] = \begin{bmatrix} -1 & 0 & 0 & 1 & 1 & 0 \\ 0 & 1 & 0 & 0 & -1 & 1 \\ 0 & 0 & 1 & -1 & 0 & -1 \end{bmatrix}$$

The rows of $f$-cut-set matrix $[Q_f]$ satisfy Kirchhof's current law ($KCL$) at nodes as follows :

at node a : $-I_1 + I_4 + I_5 = 0$

at node b : $I_2 - I_5 + I_6 = 0$

at node c : $I_3 - I_4 - I_6 = 0$

Thus, $[Q_f]\,[I_b] = 0$

$[Q_f]$ : $f$-cut set matrix

$[I_b]$ : branch current matrix is column vector.

The columns off-cut-set matrix relate branch voltage and node voltage as follows,

$$V_1 = -e_a$$

$$V_2 = e_b$$

$$V_3 = e_c$$

$$V_4 = e_a - e_c$$

$$V_5 = e_a - e_b$$

$$V_6 = e_b - e_c$$

Thus, $[V_b] = [Q_f]^T [e_n]$

$[V_b]$ : branch voltage matrix is column vector.

$[e_n]$ : node voltage matrix is column vector.

## 12.6 TIE-SET SCHEDULE

Tie set schedule is used to form a set equations for a network in terms of loop currents. In a network tree graph a loop (or mesh) is formed by a link and corresponding tree branches. The loop current $i_l$, is assumed to flow in the direction of link (branch) current $I_b$. Tie-set schedule is formed by relating the loop currents and branch currents.

Tie-set is a set of branches contained in a loop of a network graph such that each loop contains one link and the remainder are tree branches. Fig. 12.6.1 given shows a tree graph.

In Fig. 12.6.1, tree branches, links and loop currents, branch currents and tie sets are identified as given below :

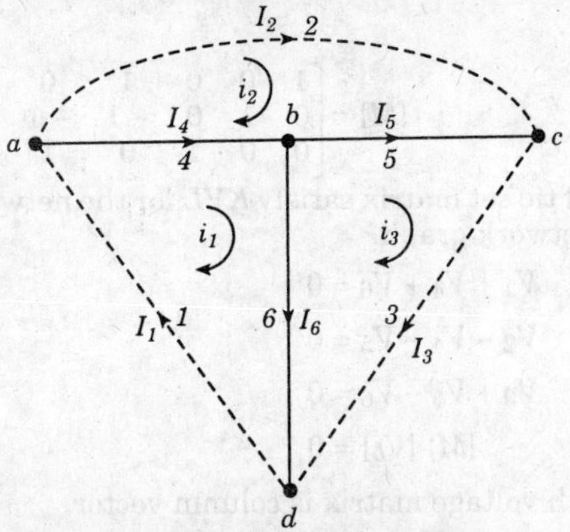


Fig. 12.6.1 tree graph : tie set

| | | |
|---|---|---|
| tree branch nos. | : | 4 , 5 , 6 |
| link nos. | : | 1 , 2, 3 |
| loop currents | : | $i_1, i_2, i_3$ |
| link/branch currents | : | $I_1, I_2, I_3, I_4, I_5, I_6$ |

| | link no | branch nos. |
|---|---|---|
| tie set no. 1 | 1 | 4, 6 |
| tie set no. 2 | 2 | 4, 5 |
| tie set no. 3 | 3 | 6, 5 |

It is convenient to assign the direction of loop currents same as that of link current in the concerned loop and as such the loop current is identified same as the corresponding link current.

While forming a tie-set schedule the branch/link current that are in the same direction of loop current are assigned a coefficient 1 and opposite −1. The branch/link current not appearing in a loop are assigned a coefficient 0. As per this explanation, the tie-set schedule for the network graph shown in Fig. 12.6.1 is formed below :

The matrix formed by the tie set schedule is called tie set matrix and denoted as $[M]$.

| Node | Tree branch / Link 1 | 2 | 3 | 4 | 5 | 6 |
|---|---|---|---|---|---|---|
| 1 | 1 | 0 | 0 | 1 | 0 | 1 |
| 2 | 0 | 1 | 0 | –1 | –1 | 0 |
| 3 | 0 | 0 | 1 | 0 | 1 | –1 |

Thus, $$[M] = \begin{bmatrix} 1 & 0 & 0 & 1 & 0 & 1 \\ 0 & 1 & 0 & -1 & -1 & 0 \\ 0 & 0 & 1 & 0 & 1 & -1 \end{bmatrix}$$

The rows of tie set matrix satisfy *KVL* for the network branches *i.e.* for the given network graph.

$$V_1 + V_4 + V_6 = 0$$

$$V_2 - V_4 - V_5 = 0$$

$$V_3 + V_5 - V_6 = 0$$

Thus, $$[M]\,[V_b] = 0$$

$[V_b]$ : branch voltage matrix is column vector.

The transpose of tie set matrix gives relation between the branch currents and loop currents as follows :

$$[I_b] = [M]^T [i_l]$$

$[I_b]$ : branch current matrix is column vector.

$[I_l]$ : loop current matrix is column vector.

Thus, for the network graph (Fig. 12.6.1)

$$\begin{bmatrix} l_1 \\ l_2 \\ l_3 \\ l_4 \\ l_5 \\ l_6 \end{bmatrix} = \begin{bmatrix} 1 & 0 & 0 \\ 0 & 1 & 0 \\ 0 & 0 & 1 \\ 1 & -1 & 0 \\ 0 & -1 & 1 \\ 1 & 0 & -1 \end{bmatrix} \begin{bmatrix} i_1 \\ i_2 \\ i_3 \end{bmatrix}$$

Verification of above equations from network graph shown in Fig. 12.6.1 is given below :

$$I_1 = i_1$$

$$I_2 = i_2$$
$$I_3 = i_3$$
$$I_4 = i_1 - i_2$$
$$I_5 = -i_2 + i_3$$
$$I_6 = i_1 - i_3$$

## 12.7 NETWORK EQUILIBRIUM EQUATIONS ON MESH/LOOP CURRENT BASIS:

For the network shown in Fig. 12.7.1, the branches are

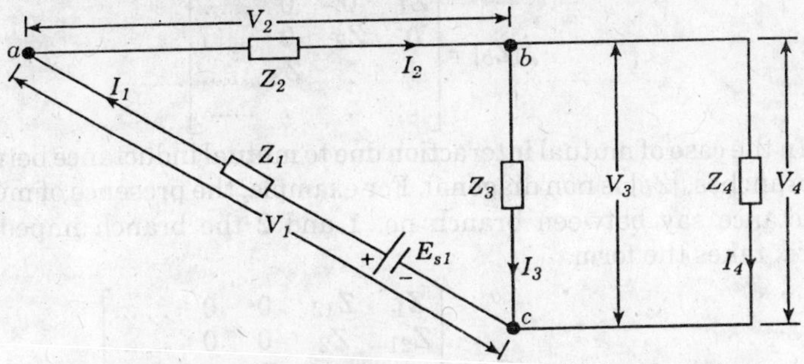


Fig. 12.7.1 : Network : mesh/loop current equilibrium equations

no. 1 : from node $c$ to $a$

no. 2 : from node $a$ to $b$

no. 3 : from node $b$ to $c$ through $Z_3$

no. 4 : from node $b$ to c through $Z_4$

The branch voltages $V_1$, $V_2$, $V_3$, and $V_4$ are related to respective branch currents $I_1$, $I_2$, $I_3$ and $I_4$ as follows :

$$V_1 = I_1 Z_1 - E_{s1}$$
$$V_2 = I_2 Z_2$$
$$V_3 = I_3 Z_3$$
$$V_4 = I_4 Z_4$$

Above set of equations can be written in matrix form as :

$$[V_b] + [E_s] = [Z_b]\,[I_b]$$

If current source $I_s$ is present across a branch, then on converting the same into equivalent voltage source the above equation is modified as :

$$[V_b] + [E_s] = [Z_b]\,[I_b] + [Z_b]\,[I_s]$$

or $$[V_b] + [E_s] = [Z_b]\,\{[I_b] + [I_s]\}$$

$[V_b]$ : Column vector of branch voltage

$[E_s]$ : Column vector of branch source voltage

$[I_b]$ : Column vector of branch current

$[I_s]$ : Column vector of branch source current

$[Z_b]$ : branch impedance matrix

The branch impedance matrix is a diagonal matrix provided no mutual interaction is present between the branches. Hence,

$$[Z_b] = \begin{bmatrix} Z_1 & 0 & 0 & \ldots\ldots \\ 0 & Z_2 & 0 & \ldots\ldots \\ . & . & Z_3 & \ldots\ldots \\ . & . & . & \ldots\ldots \end{bmatrix}$$

In the case of mutual interaction due to mutual inductance between the branches, $[Z_b]$ is non diagonal. For example, the presence of mutual inductance say between branch no. 1 and 2 the branch impedance matrix takes the form.

$$[Z_b] = \begin{bmatrix} Z_1 & Z_{12} & 0 & 0 & \ldots\ldots \\ Z_{21} & Z_2 & 0 & 0 & \ldots\ldots \\ 0 & 0 & Z_3 & 0 & \ldots\ldots \\ . & . & . & . & \ldots\ldots \\ . & . & . & . & \ldots\ldots \end{bmatrix}$$

It is required to form equilibrium equations based on *KVL* to determine mesh/loop currents. The equation derived above forms the basis for this purpose, on premulipling the same on both side by tie set matrix [M],

$$[M]\ [V] + [M]\ [E_s] = [M]\ [Z_b] \{[I_b] + [I_s]\}$$

or
$$[M]\ [V_b] = [M] \{[Z_b]\ [I_b] + [Z_b]\ [I_s] - [E_s]\}$$

It has been already shown that $[M][V_b] = 0$ Therefore,

$$[M] \{[Z_b]\ [I_b] + [Z_b]\ [I_s] - [E_s]\} = 0$$

or
$$[M]\ [Z_b]\ [I_b] = [M] \{[E_s] - [Z_b]\ [I_s]\}$$

It has already been shown that $[I_b] = [M]^T [i_l]$ therefore

$$\{[M]\ [Z_b]\ [M]^T\}[i_l] = [M] \{[E_s] - [Z_b]\ [I_s]\}$$

The equation derived above is known as equation on loop current basis for a given network and loop currents are determined from this equation.

The product $[M]\ [Z_b]\ [M]^T$ is known as triple matrix or mesh/loop impedance matrix denoted as :

$$[Z_l] = [M]\ [Z_b]\ [M]^T$$

or
$$[Z_m] = [M]\,[Z_b]\,[M]^T$$

where $[Z_m]$ = Mesh impedance matrix

## 12.8 CUT-SET SCHEDULE :

Cut set schedule is used to form a set of equations for a network in terms of node pair voltages of a tree branch. In a network tree graph cut-set is formed by a tree branch and other links meeting at a node. Fig. 12.8.1 given below shows a tree graph.

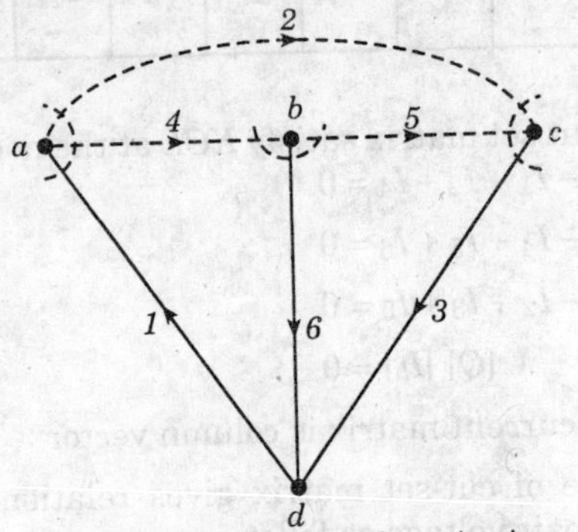


Fig. 12.8.1 Tree graph : cut set

In Fig. 12.8.1 tree branches, link and cut sets are identified as given below :

tree branch now. : 1, 6, 3

link nos. : 2, 4, 5

node pair voltage : $e_a, e_b, e_c$ (*w.r.t.* reference node $d$ at zero potential)

| **Cut-Set** | **Branch no** | **Link nos** |
|---|---|---|
| at node $a(1)$ | 1 | 2, 4 |
| at node $b(2)$ | 6 | 4, 5 |
| at node $c(3)$ | 3 | 5, 2 |

While forming a cut-set schedule the tree branch and link converging at the node is assigned a coefficient –1 and diverging 1. Other tree branches and links not meeting at the node under consideration are assigned a coefficient 0. As per this explanation the cut-set schedule for the network graph shown in Fig. 12.8.1 is formed on next page :

The matrix formed by the cut-set schedule is called cut-set matrix and denoted as $[Q]$, thus

$$[Q] = \begin{bmatrix} -1 & 1 & 0 & 1 & 0 & 0 \\ 0 & 0 & 0 & -1 & 1 & 1 \\ 0 & -1 & 1 & 0 & -1 & 0 \end{bmatrix}$$

| Branch / node | 1 | 2 | 3 | 4 | 5 | 6 |
|---|---|---|---|---|---|---|
| a | –1 | 1 | 0 | 1 | 0 | 0 |
| b | 0 | 0 | 0 | –1 | 1 | 1 |
| c | 0 | –1 | 1 | 0 | –1 | 0 |

The rows of cut set matrix satisfy *KCL* at the nodes of the network

*i.e.*

$$-I_1 + I_2 + I_4 = 0$$

$$-I_4 + I_5 + I_6 = 0$$

$$-I_2 + I_3 + I_5 = 0$$

Thus,

$$[Q]\,[I_b] = 0$$

$[I_b]$ : branch current matrix is column vector

The transpose of cut-set matrix gives relation between branch voltage and node pair voltage as follows:

$$[V_b] = [Q]^T [e_n]$$

$[V_b]$ : branch voltage matrix is column vector.

$[e_n]$ : node voltage matrix is column vector.

Verification of the above equation from the network graph Fig. 12.8.1 is given below.

$$\begin{bmatrix} V_1 \\ V_2 \\ V_3 \\ V_4 \\ V_5 \\ V_6 \end{bmatrix} = \begin{bmatrix} -1 & 0 & 0 \\ 1 & 0 & -1 \\ 0 & 0 & 1 \\ 1 & -1 & 0 \\ 0 & 1 & -1 \\ 0 & 1 & 0 \end{bmatrix} \begin{bmatrix} e_a \\ e_b \\ e_c \end{bmatrix}$$

Hence,

$$V_1 = -e_a$$

$$V_2 = e_a - e_c$$

$$V_3 = e_c$$

$$V_4 = e_a - e_b$$

$$V_5 = e_b - e_c$$

$$V_6 = e_b$$

## 12.9 NETWORK EQUILIBRIUM EQUATIONS ON NODE VOLTAGE BASIS:

For then network shown in Fig. 12.9.1 the nodes are

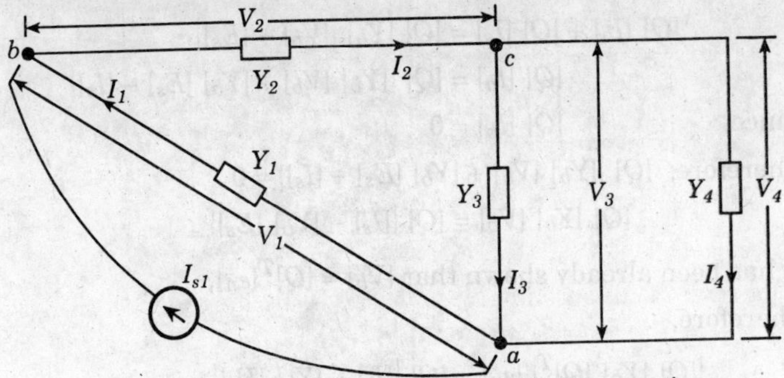


Fig 12.9.1 : Network: Node voltage equilibrium equation

no. 1 : $b$

no. 2 : $c$

no. 3 : $a$ (reference node)

The branch current $I_1$, $I_2$, $I_3$ and $I_4$ are related to branch voltages $V_1$, $V_2$, $V_3$ and $V_4$ as follows :

$$I_1 = Y_1V_1 - I_{s1}$$

$$I_2 = Y_2V_2$$

$$I_3 = Y_3V_3$$

$$I_4 = Y_4V_4$$

Above set of equations can be written in matrix form as :

$$[I_b] + [I_s] = [Y_b]\,[V_b]$$

If the voltage source $E_s$ is present in a branch, then on converting the same into equivalent current source above equation is modified as:

$$[I_b] + [I_s] = [Y_b]\,[V_b] + [Y_b]\,[E_s]$$

or

$$[I_b] + [I_s] = [Y_b]\,\{[V_b] + [E_s]\}$$

$[I_b]$ : Column vector of branch current.

$[I_s]$ : Column vector of source current.

$[V_b]$ : Column vector of branch voltage.

$[E_s]$ : Column vector of source voltage.

$[Y_b]$ : Branch admittance matrix.

The branch admittance matrix is a diagonal one provided no mutual interaction is present between branches.

It is required to form equilibrium equations based on $KCL$ to determine node voltages (tree branch voltages). The equation derived above forms the basis for this purpose, on premultiplying the same on both side by cut-set matrix $[Q]$.

$$[Q]\,[I_b] + [Q]\,[I_s] = [Q]\,[Y_b]\,\{[V_b] + [E_s]\}$$

or
$$[Q]\,[I_b] = [Q]\,\{[Y_b]\,[V_b] + [Y_b]\,[E_s] - [I_s]\}$$

Since,
$$[Q]\,[I_b] = 0$$

Therefore, $[Q]\,\{[Y_b]\,[V_b] + [Y_b]\,[E_s] - [I_s]\} = 0$

$$[Q]\,[Y_b]\,[V_b] = [Q]\,\{[I_s] - [Y_b]\,[E_s]\}$$

It has been already shown that $[V_b] = [Q]^T [e_n]$,

Therefore,

$$\{[Q]\,[Y_b]\,[Q]^T\}\,[e_n] = [Q]\,\{[I_s] - [Y_b]\,[E_s]\}$$

The equation derived above is known as equilibrium equation on node voltage basis for a given network and node voltages w.r.t. ref. node are determined from this equation.

The product $[Q][Y_b][Q]^T$ is known as triple product matrix or node admittance matrix denoted as:

$$[Y_n] = [Q]\,[Y_b]\,[Q]^T$$

## 12.10 SOLVED EXAMPLES

**Example 12.10.1 :** *Write tie set schedule and formulate equlibrium equation on loop current basis for the network given below:*

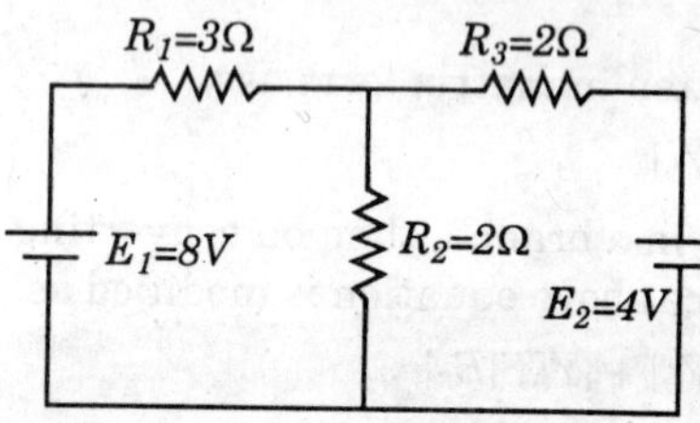


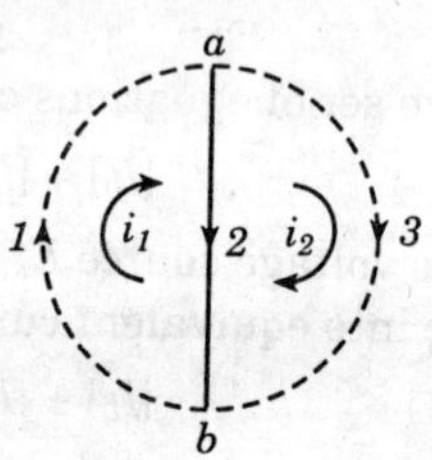


*Tie-set schedule*

| Loop \ Branch | 1 | 2 | 3 |
|---|---|---|---|
| 1 | 1 | 1 | 0 |
| 2 | 0 | −1 | 1 |

Fig. 12.10.1 (*a*)

Fig. 12.10.1 (*b*)

**Solution:**

$$[M] = \begin{bmatrix} 1 & 1 & 0 \\ 0 & -1 & 1 \end{bmatrix}, \quad [Z_b] = \begin{bmatrix} R_1 & 0 & 0 \\ 0 & R_2 & 0 \\ 0 & 0 & R_3 \end{bmatrix}$$

$$[E_s] = \begin{bmatrix} E_1 \\ 0 \\ -E_2 \end{bmatrix} \quad [I_s] = \begin{bmatrix} 0 \\ 0 \\ 0 \end{bmatrix}, \quad [M]^T = \begin{bmatrix} 1 & 0 \\ 1 & -1 \\ 0 & 1 \end{bmatrix}$$

Equilibrium equation on loop current basis is given by :

$$\{[M]\ [Z_b]\ [M]^T\}\ [i_l] = [M]\ \{[E_s] - [Z_b]\ [I_s]\}$$

Since, $[I_s] = 0$ above equation is written as

$$\{[M]\ [Z_b]\ [M]^T\}\ [i_l] = [M]\ \{[E_s]\}$$

$$\therefore \quad [M]\ [Z_b]\ [M]^T = \begin{bmatrix} 1 & 1 & 0 \\ 0 & -1 & 1 \end{bmatrix} \begin{bmatrix} R_1 & 0 & 0 \\ 0 & R_2 & 0 \\ 0 & 0 & R_3 \end{bmatrix} \begin{bmatrix} 1 & 0 \\ 1 & -1 \\ 0 & 1 \end{bmatrix}$$

$$= \begin{bmatrix} R_1 + R_2 & -R_2 \\ -R_2 & R_2 + R_3 \end{bmatrix}$$

$$\therefore \quad \begin{bmatrix} R_1 + R_2 & -R_2 \\ -R_2 & R_2 + R_3 \end{bmatrix} \begin{bmatrix} i_1 \\ i_2 \end{bmatrix} = \begin{bmatrix} 1 & 1 & 0 \\ 0 & -1 & 1 \end{bmatrix} \begin{bmatrix} E_1 \\ 0 \\ -E_2 \end{bmatrix}$$

or

$$\begin{bmatrix} R_1 + R_2 & -R_2 \\ -R_2 & R_2 + R_3 \end{bmatrix} \begin{bmatrix} i_1 \\ i_2 \end{bmatrix} = \begin{bmatrix} E_1 \\ -E_2 \end{bmatrix}$$

substituting given values,

$$\begin{bmatrix} 3+2 & -2 \\ -2 & 2+2 \end{bmatrix} \begin{bmatrix} i_1 \\ i_2 \end{bmatrix} = \begin{bmatrix} 8 \\ -4 \end{bmatrix}$$

or

$$\begin{bmatrix} 5 & -2 \\ -2 & 4 \end{bmatrix} \begin{bmatrix} i_1 \\ i_2 \end{bmatrix} = \begin{bmatrix} 8 \\ -4 \end{bmatrix} \quad \text{....Ans.}$$

**Example 12.10.2.** *Write cut-set schedule and formulate equilibrium equation on node voltage basis for the network given below and determine node voltage $e_a$ & $e_b$ w.r.t. to reference node c.*

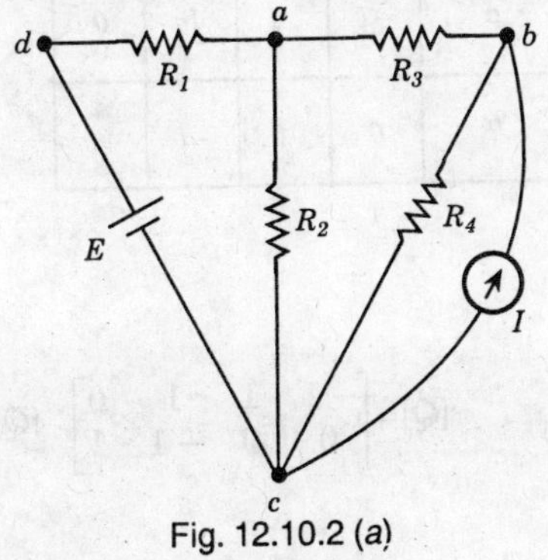


Fig. 12.10.2 (a)

**Solution:**

The network graph is shown below, the orientation of the graph is selected arbitrarily. Tree branches are selected as 2 & 4. Tree graph is given below.

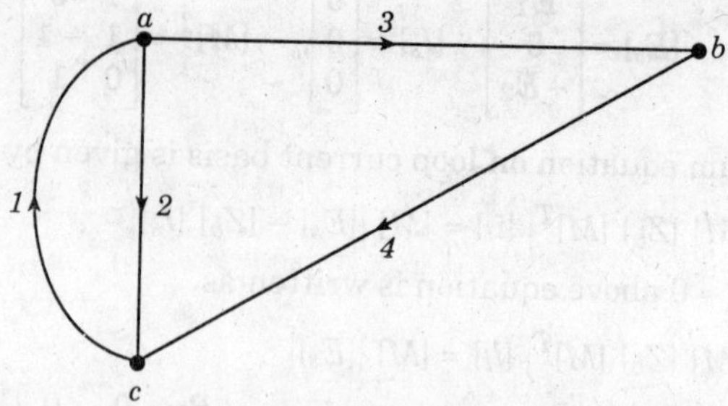

Fig. 12.10.2 (*b*)

Cut-set for branch no. 2 : 1, 2, 3

Cut-set for tree branch no. 4 : 4, 3

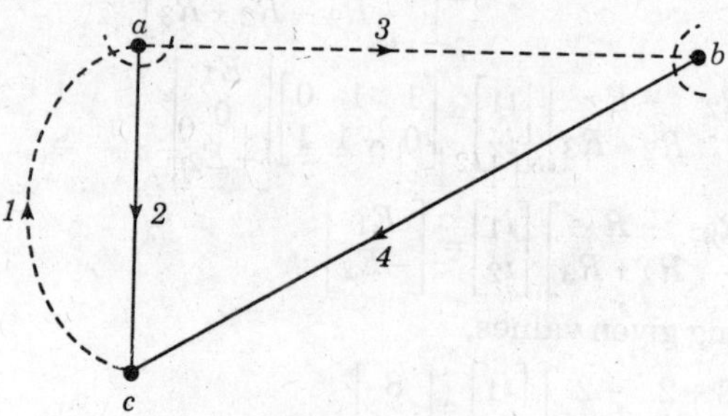

Fig. 12.10.2 (*c*)

Cut-set schedule

| Node \ Branch | 1 | 2 | 3 | 4 |
|---|---|---|---|---|
| *a* | –1 | 1 | 1 | 0 |
| *b* | 0 | 0 | –1 | 1 |

Cut-set matrix

$$[Q]=\begin{bmatrix} -1 & 1 & 1 & 0 \\ 0 & 0 & -1 & 1 \end{bmatrix}, \quad [Q]^T\begin{bmatrix} -1 & 0 \\ 1 & 0 \\ 1 & -1 \\ 0 & 1 \end{bmatrix}$$

$$[Y_b] = \begin{bmatrix} 1/R_1 & 0 & 0 & 0 \\ 0 & 1/R_2 & 0 & 0 \\ 0 & 0 & 1/R_3 & 0 \\ 0 & 0 & 0 & 1/R_4 \end{bmatrix},$$

$$[E_s] = \begin{bmatrix} E \\ 0 \\ 0 \\ 0 \end{bmatrix}$$

$$[I_s] = \begin{bmatrix} 0 \\ 0 \\ 0 \\ 1 \end{bmatrix}$$

Equilibrium equation on node voltage basis is given by

$$\{[Q]\ [Y_b]\ [Q]^T[e_n] = [Q]\ \{[I_s] - [Y_b]\ [E_s]\}$$

$$\left\{ \begin{bmatrix} -1 & 1 & 1 & 0 \\ 0 & 0 & -1 & 1 \end{bmatrix} \begin{bmatrix} 1/R_1 & o & 0 & 0 \\ 0 & 1/R_2 & 0 & 0 \\ 0 & 0 & 1/R_3 & 0 \\ 0 & 0 & 0 & 1/R_4 \end{bmatrix} \begin{bmatrix} -1 & 0 \\ 1 & 0 \\ 1 & -1 \\ 0 & 1 \end{bmatrix} \right\} \begin{bmatrix} e_a \\ e_b \end{bmatrix}$$

$$= \begin{bmatrix} -1 & 1 & 1 & 0 \\ 0 & 0 & -1 & 1 \end{bmatrix} \left\{ \begin{bmatrix} 0 \\ 0 \\ 0 \\ 1 \end{bmatrix} - \begin{bmatrix} 1/R_1 & 0 & 0 & 0 \\ 0 & 1/R_2 & 0 & 0 \\ 0 & 0 & 1/R_3 & 0 \\ 0 & 0 & 0 & 1/R_4 \end{bmatrix} \begin{bmatrix} E \\ 0 \\ 0 \\ 0 \\ 0 \end{bmatrix} \right\}$$

or

$$\begin{bmatrix} \frac{1}{R_1} + \frac{1}{R_2} + \frac{1}{R_3} & -\frac{1}{R_3} \\ -\frac{1}{R_3} & \frac{1}{R_3} + \frac{1}{R_4} \end{bmatrix} \begin{bmatrix} e_a \\ e_b \end{bmatrix} = \begin{bmatrix} \frac{E}{R_1} \\ I \end{bmatrix} \quad \textbf{Ans.}$$

**Example 12.10.3.** *Write tie-set schedule and formulate equlibrium equation on loop current basis for the network given belows :*

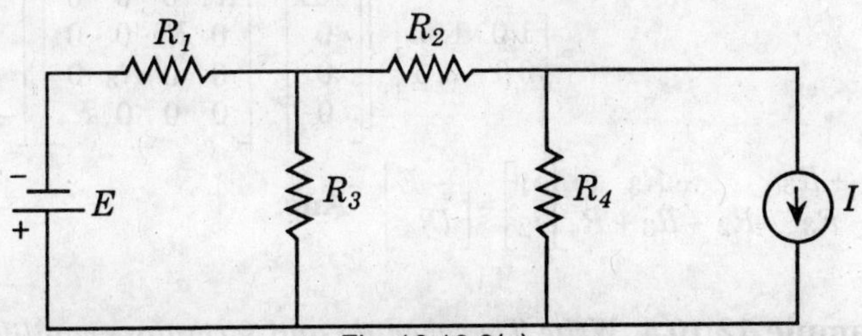


Fig. 12.10.3(*a*)

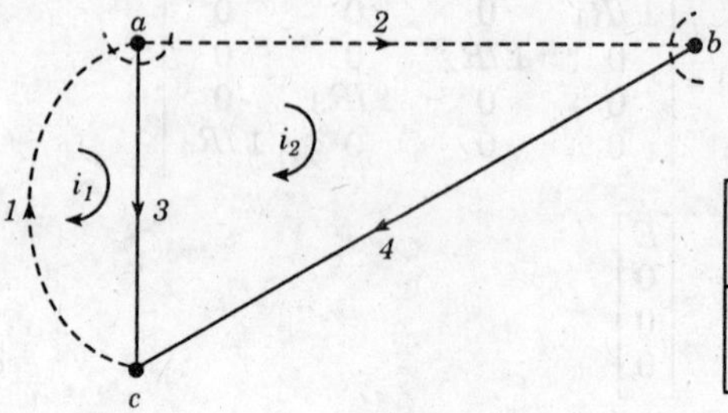


Tie-set schedule

| Loop \ Branch | 1 | 2 | 3 | 4 |
|---|---|---|---|---|
| 1 | 1 | 0 | 1 | 0 |
| 2 | 0 | 1 | -1 | 1 |

Fig. 12.10.3(*b*)

**Tie-set matrix**

$$[M] = \begin{bmatrix} 1 & 0 & 1 & 0 \\ 0 & 1 & -1 & 1 \end{bmatrix}, \; [M]^T = \begin{bmatrix} 1 & 0 \\ 0 & 1 \\ 1 & -1 \\ 0 & 1 \end{bmatrix}$$

$$[Z_b] = \begin{bmatrix} R_1 & 0 & 0 & 0 \\ 0 & R_2 & 0 & 0 \\ 0 & 0 & R_3 & 0 \\ 0 & 0 & 0 & R_4 \end{bmatrix}, \; [E_s] = \begin{bmatrix} -E \\ 0 \\ 0 \\ 0 \end{bmatrix}$$

$$[I_s] = \begin{bmatrix} 0 \\ 0 \\ 0 \\ -1 \end{bmatrix}$$

Equilibrium equations on loop current basis is given by

$$\{[M]\ [Z_b]\ [M]^T\}\ [i_l] = [M]\ \{[E_s] - [Z_b]\ [I_s]\}$$

$$\left\{ \begin{bmatrix} 1 & 0 & 1 & 0 \\ 0 & 1 & -1 & 1 \end{bmatrix} \begin{bmatrix} R_1 & 0 & 0 & 0 \\ 0 & R_2 & 0 & 0 \\ 0 & 0 & R_3 & 0 \\ 0 & 0 & 0 & R_4 \end{bmatrix} \begin{bmatrix} 1 & 0 \\ 0 & 1 \\ 1 & -1 \\ 0 & 1 \end{bmatrix} \right\} \begin{bmatrix} i_1 \\ i_2 \end{bmatrix}$$

$$= \begin{bmatrix} 1 & 0 & 1 & 0 \\ 0 & 1 & -1 & 1 \end{bmatrix} \left\{ \begin{bmatrix} -E \\ 0 \\ 0 \\ 0 \end{bmatrix} - \begin{bmatrix} R_1 & 0 & 0 & 0 \\ 0 & R_2 & 0 & 0 \\ 0 & 0 & R_3 & 0 \\ 0 & 0 & 0 & R_4 \end{bmatrix} \begin{bmatrix} 0 \\ 0 \\ 0 \\ -1 \end{bmatrix} \right\}$$

or $$\begin{bmatrix} R_1 + R_3 & -R_3 \\ -R_3 & R_2 + R_3 + R_4 \end{bmatrix} \begin{bmatrix} i_1 \\ i_2 \end{bmatrix} = \begin{bmatrix} -E \\ IR_4 \end{bmatrix}$$ **Ans.**

**Example 12.10.4.** *Write Tie schedule and formulate equilibrium equation on loop current basis for the network given in Fig. 12.10.4 (a).*

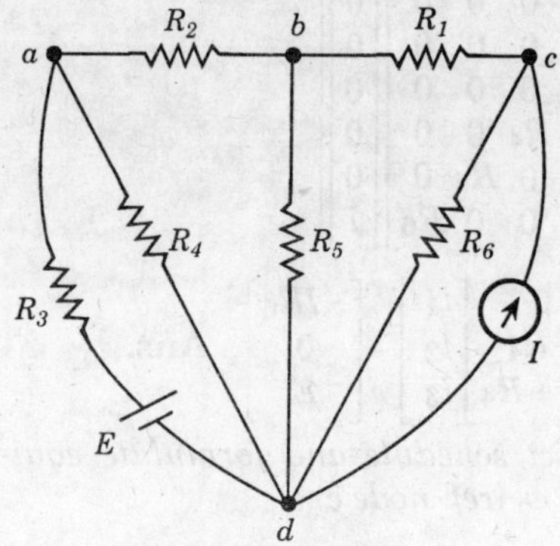


Fig. 12.10.4(*a*)

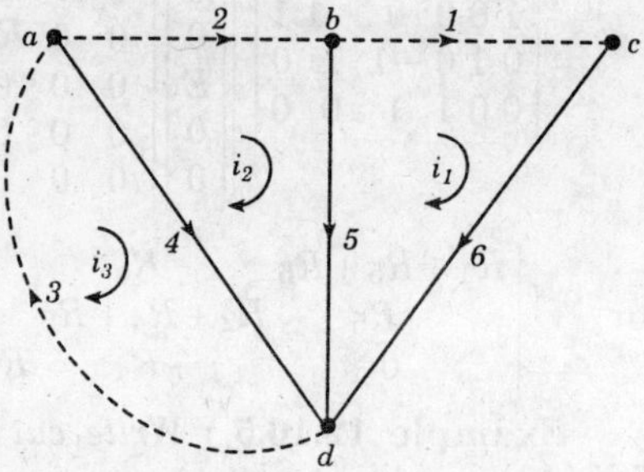


Fig. 12.10.4(*b*)

**Solution:**

*Tie-set Schedule*

| Link \ Branch | 1 | 2 | 3 | 4 | 5 | 6 |
|---|---|---|---|---|---|---|
| 1 | 1 | 0 | 0 | 0 | –1 | 1 |
| 2 | 0 | 1 | 0 | –1 | –1 | 0 |
| 3 | 0 | 0 | 1 | 1 | 0 | 0 |

**Tie-set matrix**

$$[M] = \begin{bmatrix} 1 & 0 & 0 & 0 & -1 & 1 \\ 0 & 1 & 0 & -1 & 1 & 0 \\ 0 & 0 & 1 & 1 & 0 & 0 \end{bmatrix}, \quad [M]^T = \begin{bmatrix} 1 & 0 & 0 \\ 0 & 1 & 0 \\ 0 & 0 & 1 \\ 0 & -1 & 1 \\ -1 & 1 & 0 \\ 1 & 0 & 0 \end{bmatrix}, \quad [E_s] = \begin{bmatrix} 0 \\ 0 \\ 0 \\ E \\ 0 \\ 0 \end{bmatrix}$$

$$[I_s] = \begin{bmatrix} 0 \\ 0 \\ 0 \\ 0 \\ 0 \\ I \end{bmatrix}, \quad [Z_b] = \begin{bmatrix} R_1 & 0 & 0 & 0 & 0 & 0 \\ 0 & R_2 & 0 & 0 & 0 & 0 \\ 0 & 0 & R_3 & 0 & 0 & 0 \\ 0 & 0 & 0 & R_4 & 0 & 0 \\ 0 & 0 & 0 & 0 & R_5 & 0 \\ 0 & 0 & 0 & 0 & 0 & R_6 \end{bmatrix}$$

Equilibrium equation on loop current basis is given below

$$\{[M]\ [Z_b]\ [M]^T\}\ [i_l] = [M]\ \{[E_s] - [Z_b]\ [I_s]\}$$

$$\left\{ \begin{bmatrix} 1 & 0 & 0 & 0 & -1 & 1 \\ 0 & 1 & 0 & -1 & 1 & 0 \\ 0 & 0 & 1 & 1 & 0 & 0 \end{bmatrix} \begin{bmatrix} R_1 & 0 & 0 & 0 & 0 & 0 \\ 0 & R_2 & 0 & 0 & 0 & 0 \\ 0 & 0 & R_3 & 0 & 0 & 0 \\ 0 & 0 & 0 & R_4 & 0 & 0 \\ 0 & 0 & 0 & 0 & R_5 & 0 \\ 0 & 0 & 0 & 0 & 0 & R_6 \end{bmatrix} \begin{bmatrix} 1 & 0 & 0 \\ 0 & 1 & 0 \\ 0 & 0 & 1 \\ 0 & -1 & 1 \\ -1 & 1 & 0 \\ 1 & 0 & 0 \end{bmatrix} \right\} \begin{bmatrix} i_1 \\ i_2 \\ i_3 \end{bmatrix}$$

$$= \begin{bmatrix} 1 & 0 & 0 & 0 & -1 & 1 \\ 0 & 1 & 0 & -1 & 1 & 0 \\ 0 & 0 & 1 & 1 & 0 & 0 \end{bmatrix} \left\{ \begin{bmatrix} 0 \\ 0 \\ 0 \\ E \\ 0 \\ 0 \end{bmatrix} \begin{bmatrix} R_1 & 0 & 0 & 0 & 0 & 0 \\ 0 & R_2 & 0 & 0 & 0 & 0 \\ 0 & 0 & R_3 & 0 & 0 & 0 \\ 0 & 0 & 0 & R_4 & 0 & 0 \\ 0 & 0 & 0 & 0 & R_5 & 0 \\ 0 & 0 & 0 & 0 & 0 & R_6 \end{bmatrix} \begin{bmatrix} 0 \\ 0 \\ 0 \\ 0 \\ 0 \\ I \end{bmatrix} \right\}$$

or $$\begin{bmatrix} R_1+R_5+R_6 & -R_5 & 0 \\ -R_5 & R_2+R_4+R_6 & -R_4 \\ 0 & -R_4 & R_3+R_4 \end{bmatrix} \begin{bmatrix} i_1 \\ i_2 \\ i_3 \end{bmatrix} = \begin{bmatrix} -IR_6 \\ 0 \\ E \end{bmatrix}$$ **Ans.**

**Example 12.10.5 :** *Write cut set schedule and formulate equilibrium equation to determine* $e_a$ and $e_b$ *(ref. node c) :*

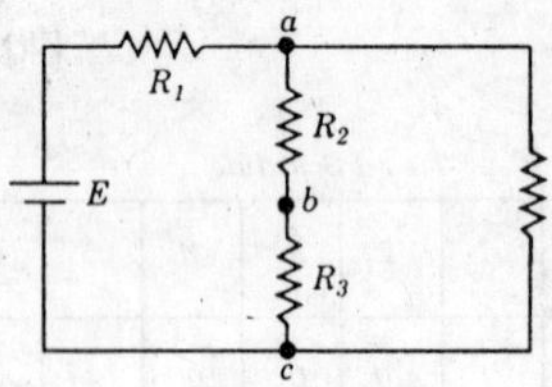


Fig. 12.10.5

**Solution:**

Cut-set schedule

*Cut-set schedule*

| Node \ Branch | 1 | 2 | 3 | 4 |
|---|---|---|---|---|
| a | −1 | 1 | 0 | 1 |
| b | 0 | −1 | 1 | 0 |

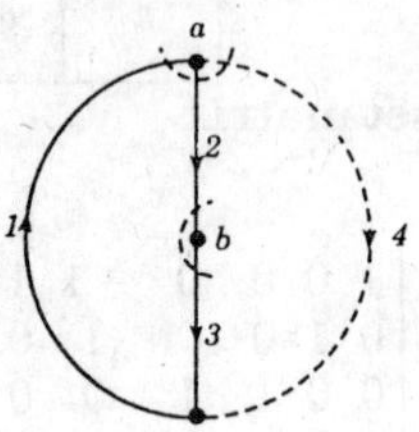


Fig.12.10.5(a)Tree-Graph

Cut-set matrix

$$[Q] = \begin{bmatrix} -1 & 1 & 0 & 1 \\ 0 & -1 & 1 & 0 \end{bmatrix}, [Q]^T = \begin{bmatrix} -1 & 0 \\ 1 & -1 \\ 0 & 1 \\ 1 & 0 \end{bmatrix}, [E_s] = \begin{bmatrix} E \\ 0 \\ 0 \\ 0 \end{bmatrix}$$

$$[I_s] = \begin{bmatrix} 0 \\ 0 \\ 0 \\ 0 \end{bmatrix}, [Y_b] = \begin{bmatrix} \frac{1}{R_1} & 0 & 0 & 0 \\ 0 & \frac{1}{R_2} & 0 & 0 \\ 0 & 0 & \frac{1}{R_3} & 0 \\ 0 & 0 & 0 & \frac{1}{R_4} \end{bmatrix}$$

Equilibrium equation on node voltage basis is

$$\{[Q]\,[Y_b]\,[Q]^T\}[e_n] = [Q]\{[I_s] - [Y_b]\,[E_s]\}$$

$$\therefore \left\{\begin{bmatrix} -1 & 1 & 0 & 1 \\ 0 & -1 & 1 & 0 \end{bmatrix}\begin{bmatrix} \frac{1}{R_1} & 0 & 0 & 0 \\ 0 & \frac{1}{R_2} & 0 & 0 \\ 0 & 0 & \frac{1}{R_3} & 0 \\ 0 & 0 & 0 & \frac{1}{R_4} \end{bmatrix}\begin{bmatrix} -1 & 0 \\ 1 & -1 \\ 0 & 1 \\ 1 & 0 \end{bmatrix}\right\}\begin{bmatrix} e_a \\ e_b \end{bmatrix}$$

$$= \begin{bmatrix} -1 & 1 & 0 & 1 \\ 0 & -1 & 1 & 0 \end{bmatrix}\left\{\begin{bmatrix} 0 \\ 0 \\ 0 \\ 0 \end{bmatrix} - \begin{bmatrix} \frac{1}{R_1} & 0 & 0 & 0 \\ 0 & \frac{1}{R_2} & 0 & 0 \\ 0 & 0 & \frac{1}{R_3} & 0 \\ 0 & 0 & 0 & \frac{1}{R_4} \end{bmatrix}\begin{bmatrix} E \\ 0 \\ 0 \\ 0 \end{bmatrix}\right\}$$

or

$$\begin{bmatrix} \frac{1}{R_1} + \frac{1}{R_2} + \frac{1}{R_4} & -\frac{1}{R_2} \\ -\frac{1}{R_2} & \frac{1}{R_2} + \frac{1}{R_3} \end{bmatrix}\begin{bmatrix} e_a \\ e_b \end{bmatrix} = \begin{bmatrix} \frac{E}{R_1} \\ 0 \end{bmatrix} \quad \text{...Ans.}$$

**Example : 12.10.6** *Draw the oriented network graph. Select tree write (i) Tie set schedule (ii) Cut-set schedule for the network shown in Fig. 12.10.6(a)*

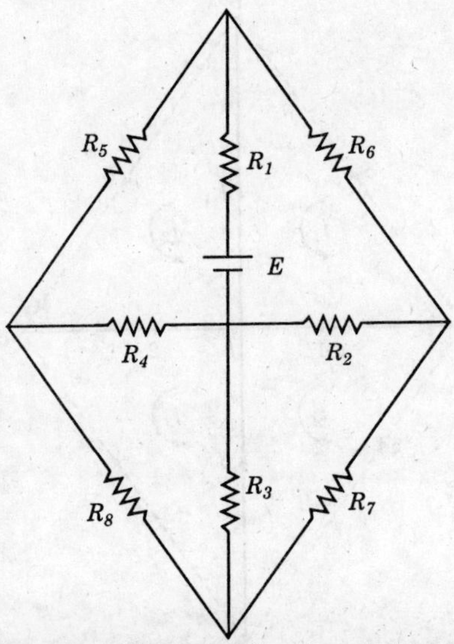


Fig. 12.10.6(*a*) Network for example 12.10.6

**Solution :** The oriented (directed) network graph is shown is Fig. 12.10.6($b$)

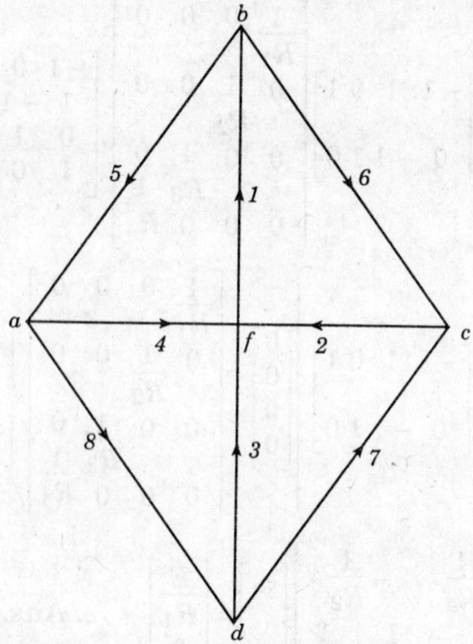


Fig. 12.10.6(*b*) oriented network graph of Fig. 12.10.6(*a*)

($i$) The branches 1, 2, 3, 4 are selected as tree branches, branches 5, 6, 7, 8 as links. As per Fig. 12.10.6($c$), the tie set schedule is formed below

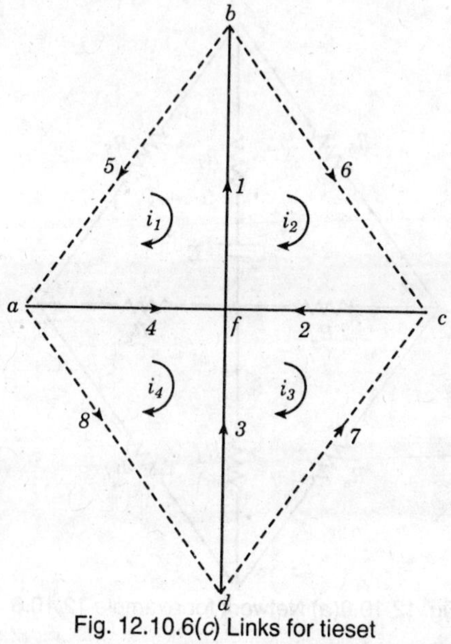


Fig. 12.10.6(*c*) Links for tieset

*Tie-set schedule*

| Mesh \ Branch | 1 | 2 | 3 | 4 | 5 | 6 | 7 | 8 |
|---|---|---|---|---|---|---|---|---|
| 1 | –1 | 0 | 0 | –1 | –1 | 0 | 0 | 0 |
| 2 | 1 | 1 | 0 | 0 | 0 | 1 | 0 | 0 |
| 3 | 0 | –1 | 1 | 0 | 0 | 0 | –1 | 0 |
| 4 | 0 | 0 | –1 | 1 | 0 | 0 | 0 | –1 |

**Ans.**

(*ii*) For cutset, tree branches are 1, 2, 3, 4 with corresponding links [Fig. 12.10.6(*d*)].

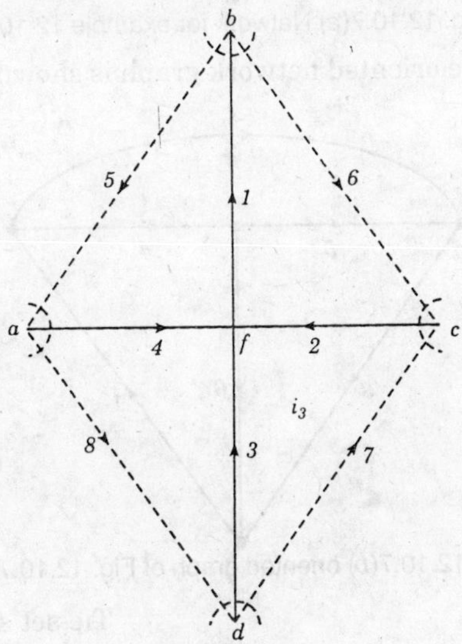


Fig. 12.10.6(*d*)

The cut set schedule is formed below.

*Cut-set schedule Brands*

| Node | 1 | 2 | 3 | 4 | 5 | 6 | 7 | 8 |
|---|---|---|---|---|---|---|---|---|
| a | 0 | 0 | 0 | 1 | –1 | 0 | 0 | 0 |
| b | –1 | 0 | 0 | 0 | 1 | 1 | 0 | 0 |
| c | 0 | 1 | 0 | 0 | 0 | –1 | –1 | 0 |
| d | 0 | 0 | 1 | 0 | 0 | 0 | 1 | –1 |

**Ans.**

**Example 12.10.7.** *For the network shown in Fig. 12.10.7 select tree graph. Write tie-set and determine KVL equations in matrix form.*

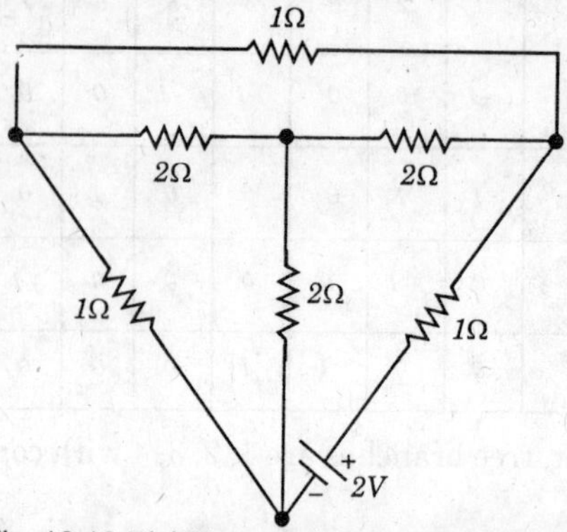


Fig. 12.10.7(*a*) Network for example 12.10.7

**Solution :** The oriented network graph is shown in Fig. 12.10.7(*b*)

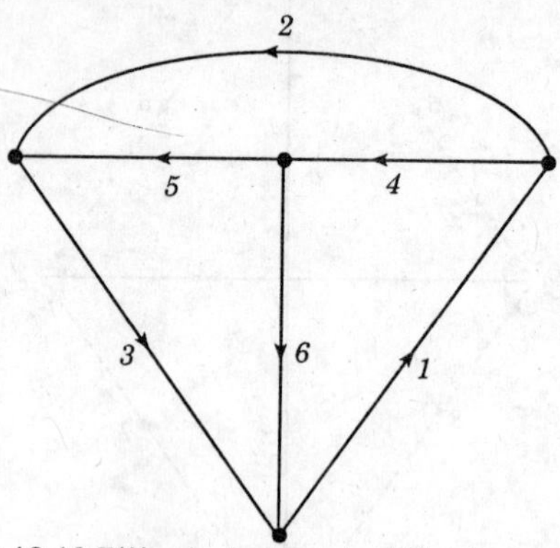


Fig. 12.10.7(*b*) oriented graph of Fig. 12.10.7(*a*)

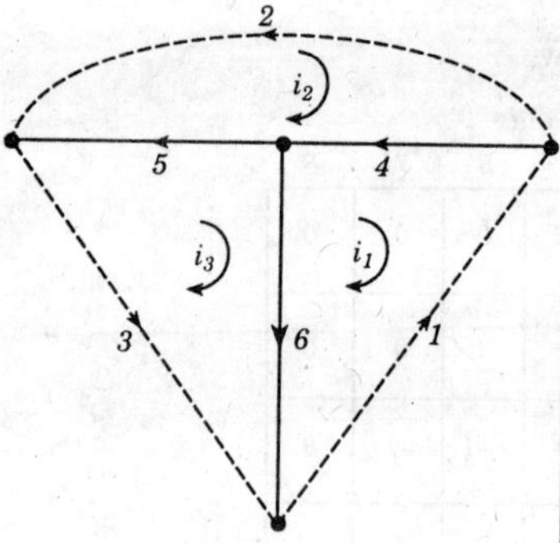


Fig. 12.10.7(*c*) Tree and link of Fig. 12.10.7(*b*)

Tie-set schedule

| Mesh \ Branch/Link | 1 | 2 | 3 | 4 | 5 | 6 |
|---|---|---|---|---|---|---|
| 1 | −1 | 0 | 0 | −1 | 0 | −1 |
| 2 | 0 | −1 | 0 | 1 | 1 | 0 |
| 3 | 0 | 0 | −1 | 0 | −1 | 1 |

The tie-set matrix is

$$M = \begin{bmatrix} -1 & 0 & 0 & -1 & 0 & -1 \\ 0 & -1 & 0 & 1 & 1 & 0 \\ 0 & 0 & -1 & 0 & -1 & 1 \end{bmatrix}, \quad \therefore [M]^T = \begin{bmatrix} -1 & 0 & 0 \\ 0 & -1 & 0 \\ 0 & 0 & -1 \\ -1 & 1 & 0 \\ 0 & 1 & -1 \\ -1 & 0 & 1 \end{bmatrix}$$

$$[Z_b] = \begin{bmatrix} 1 & 0 & 0 & 0 & 0 & 0 \\ 0 & 1 & 0 & 0 & 0 & 0 \\ 0 & 0 & 1 & 0 & 0 & 0 \\ 0 & 0 & 0 & 2 & 0 & 0 \\ 0 & 0 & 0 & 0 & 2 & 0 \\ 0 & 0 & 0 & 0 & 0 & 2 \end{bmatrix}$$

$$[E_s] = \begin{bmatrix} 2 \\ 0 \\ 0 \\ 0 \\ 0 \\ 0 \end{bmatrix}$$

The $KVL$ equation matrix is given by

$$\{[M]\ [Z_b]\ [M]^T\}\ [i_m] = [M]\{[E_s] - [Z_b]\ [I_s]\}$$

$$\because \qquad [I_s] = 0$$

$$\therefore \qquad \{[M]\ [Z_b]\ [M]^T\}\ [i_m] = [M]\ \{[E_s]\}$$

$$\therefore \left\{ \begin{bmatrix} -1 & 0 & 0 & -1 & 0 & -1 \\ 0 & -1 & 0 & 1 & 1 & 0 \\ 0 & 0 & -1 & 0 & -1 & 1 \end{bmatrix} \begin{bmatrix} 1 & 0 & 0 & 0 & 0 & 0 \\ 0 & 1 & 0 & 0 & 0 & 0 \\ 0 & 0 & 1 & 0 & 0 & 0 \\ 0 & 0 & 0 & 2 & 0 & 0 \\ 0 & 0 & 0 & 0 & 2 & 0 \\ 0 & 0 & 0 & 0 & 0 & 2 \end{bmatrix} \begin{bmatrix} -1 & 0 & 0 \\ 0 & -1 & 0 \\ 0 & 0 & -1 \\ -1 & 1 & 0 \\ 0 & 1 & -1 \\ -1 & 0 & 1 \end{bmatrix} \right\} \begin{bmatrix} i_1 \\ i_2 \\ i_3 \end{bmatrix}$$

$$= \begin{bmatrix} -1 & 0 & 0 & -1 & 0 & -1 \\ 0 & -1 & 0 & 1 & 1 & 0 \\ 0 & 0 & -1 & 0 & -1 & 1 \end{bmatrix} \left\{ \begin{bmatrix} 2 \\ 0 \\ 0 \\ 0 \\ 0 \\ 0 \end{bmatrix} \right\}$$

or

$$\begin{bmatrix} 11 & -2 & -6 \\ -2 & 11 & -5 \\ -6 & -5 & 14 \end{bmatrix} \begin{bmatrix} i_1 \\ i_2 \\ i_3 \end{bmatrix} = \begin{bmatrix} -2 \\ 0 \\ 0 \end{bmatrix} \qquad \textbf{...Ans.}$$

**Example 12.10.8.** *Obtain the cut set matrix. Obtain node voltage equations in matrix form at nodes a and b in the network shown in Fig. 12.10.8(a)*

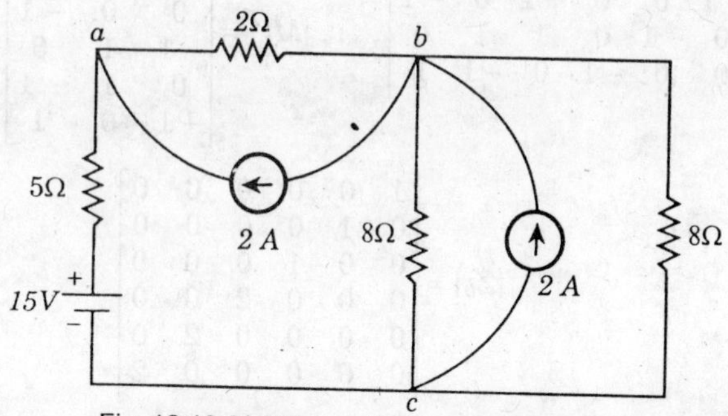


Fig. 12.10.8(*a*) Network for example 12.10.8

**Solution :** The network graph is shown in Fig. 12.10.8(*b*)

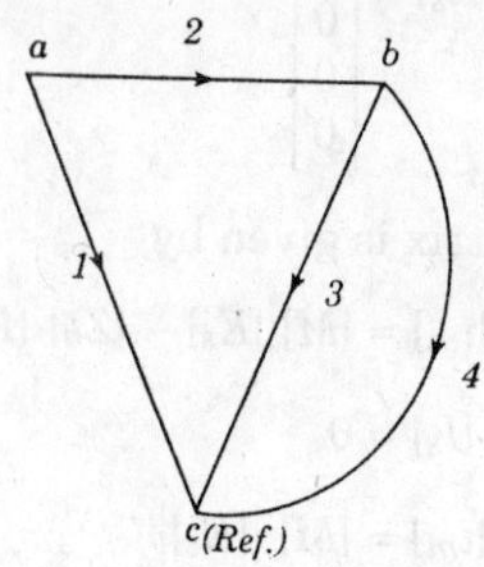


Fig. 12.10.8(*b*) Network graph of Fig. 12.10.8(*a*)

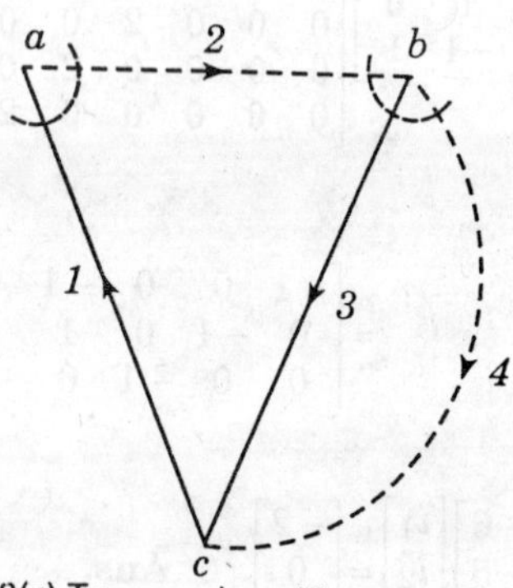


Fig. 12.10.8(*c*) Tree graph and links for Fig. 12.10.8(*b*)

Cut-set schedule for Fig.12.10.8(c) is written below,

**Cut-set Schedule**

| Node \ Branch/Link | 1 | 2 | 3 | 4 |
|---|---|---|---|---|
| a | –1 | 1 | 0 | 0 |
| b | 0 | –1 | 1 | 1 |

$$[Q]=\begin{bmatrix}-1 & 1 & 0 & 0\\ 0 & -1 & 1 & 1\end{bmatrix},\ [Q]^T=\begin{bmatrix}-1 & 0\\ 1 & -1\\ 0 & 1\\ 0 & 1\end{bmatrix},\ [I_s]=\begin{bmatrix}0\\2\\2\\0\end{bmatrix},\ [E_s]=\begin{bmatrix}15\\0\\0\\0\end{bmatrix}$$

Branch admittance matrix

$$[Y_b]=\begin{bmatrix}1/5 & 0 & 0 & 0\\ 0 & 1/2 & 0 & 0\\ 0 & 0 & 1/8 & 0\\ 0 & 0 & 0 & 1/8\end{bmatrix}=\begin{bmatrix}0.2 & 0 & 0 & 0\\ 0 & 0.5 & 0 & 0\\ 0 & 0 & 0.125 & 0\\ 0 & 0 & 0 & 0.125\end{bmatrix}$$

$$[Q][Y_b][Q]^T=\begin{bmatrix}-1 & 1 & 0 & 0\\ 0 & -1 & 1 & 1\end{bmatrix}\begin{bmatrix}0.2 & 0 & 0 & 0\\ 0 & 0.5 & 0 & 0\\ 0 & 0 & 0.125 & 0\\ 0 & 0 & 0 & 0.125\end{bmatrix}\begin{bmatrix}-1 & 0\\ 1 & -1\\ 0 & 1\\ 0 & 1\end{bmatrix}$$

$$=\begin{bmatrix}0.7 & -0.5\\ -0.5 & 0.75\end{bmatrix}$$

$$Q\left\{[I_s]-[Y_b]\,[E_s]\right\}=\begin{bmatrix}-1 & 1 & 0 & 0\\ 0 & -1 & 1 & 1\end{bmatrix}\left\{\begin{bmatrix}0\\2\\2\\0\end{bmatrix}-\begin{bmatrix}0.2 & 0 & 0 & 0\\ 0 & 0.5 & 0 & 0\\ 0 & 0 & 0.125 & 0\\ 0 & 0 & 0 & 0.125\end{bmatrix}\begin{bmatrix}15\\0\\0\\0\end{bmatrix}\right\}$$

$$=\begin{bmatrix}5\\ \\0\end{bmatrix}$$

The node voltage equation in matrix form is given by

$$\left\{[Q]\,[Y_b]\,[Q]^T\right\}[e_n]=[Q]\left\{[I_s]-[Y_b]\,[E_s]\right\}$$

$$\therefore\quad \begin{bmatrix}0.7 & -0.5\\ -0.5 & 0.75\end{bmatrix}\begin{bmatrix}e_a\\ e_b\end{bmatrix}=\begin{bmatrix}5\\0\end{bmatrix}\quad \textbf{...Ans.}$$

**Example 12.10.9.** *Draw the network graph. Write cut-set schedule and determine transform of the node admittance matrix. The network is given is Fig. 12.10.9(a)*

$L_1 = L_2 = 1H$, $R_3 = R_4 = 1\Omega$ and $C = 1F$

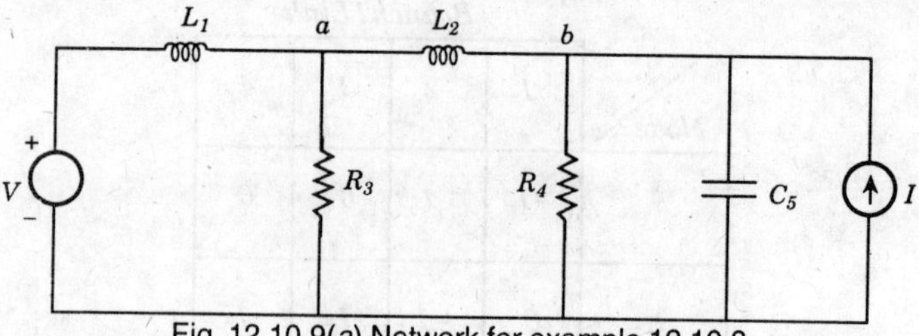


Fig. 12.10.9(*a*) Network for example 12.10.8

**Solution :** The oriented network graph is shown in Fig. 12.10.9(*b*)

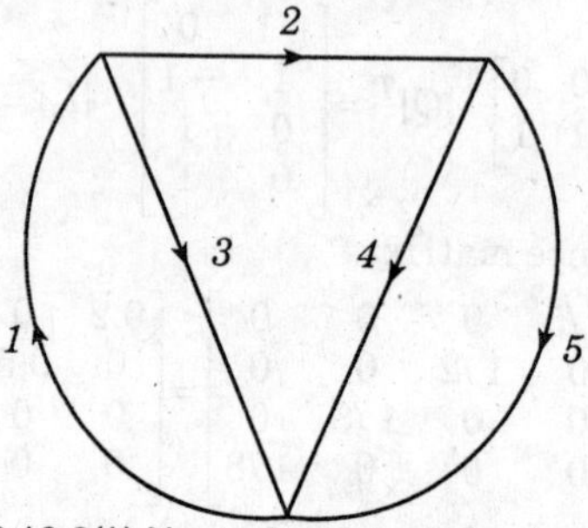


Fig. 12.10.9(*b*) Network graph of Fig. 12.10.9(*a*)

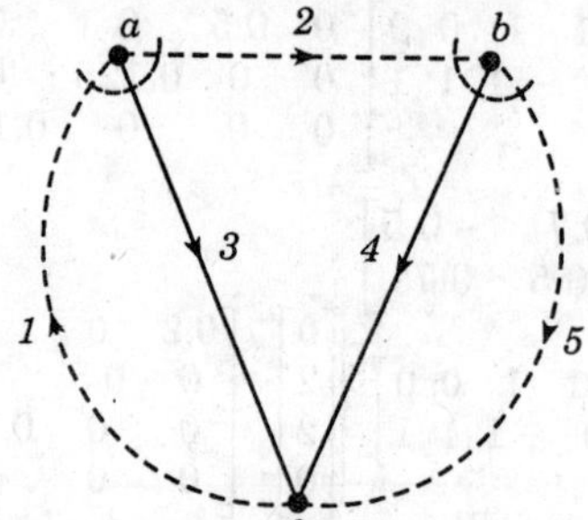


Fig. 12.10.9(*c*) Tree graph and links for Fig. 12.10.9(*b*)

The cut-set schedule is written below.

**Cut-set Schedule**

| Node \ Branch/Link | 1 | 2 | 3 | 4 | 5 |
|---|---|---|---|---|---|
| *a* | –1 | 1 | 1 | 0 | 0 |
| *b* | 0 | –1 | 0 | 1 | 1 |

The cut-set matrix

$$[Q] = \begin{bmatrix} -1 & 1 & 1 & 0 & 0 \\ 0 & -1 & 0 & 1 & 1 \end{bmatrix}, \quad [Q]^T = \begin{bmatrix} -1 & 0 \\ 1 & -1 \\ 1 & 0 \\ 0 & 1 \\ 0 & 1 \end{bmatrix}$$

Transform of branch admittance matrix

$$[Y_b(s)] = \begin{bmatrix} 1/sL_1 & 0 & 0 & 0 & 0 \\ 0 & 1/sL_2 & 0 & 0 & 0 \\ 0 & 0 & 1/R_3 & 0 & 0 \\ 0 & 0 & 0 & 1/R_4 & 0 \\ 0 & 0 & 0 & 0 & sC \end{bmatrix} = \begin{bmatrix} 1/s & 0 & 0 & 0 & 0 \\ 0 & 1/s & 0 & 0 & 0 \\ 0 & 0 & 1 & 0 & 0 \\ 0 & 0 & 0 & 1 & 0 \\ 0 & 0 & 0 & 0 & s \end{bmatrix}$$

$$[Y_n(s)] = [Q]\,[Y_b(s)]\,[Q]^T$$

$$= \begin{bmatrix} -1 & 1 & 1 & 0 & 0 \\ 0 & -1 & 0 & 0 & 1 \end{bmatrix} \begin{bmatrix} 1/s & 0 & 0 & 0 & 0 \\ 0 & 1/s & 0 & 0 & 0 \\ 0 & 0 & 1 & 0 & 0 \\ 0 & 0 & 0 & 1 & 0 \\ 0 & 0 & 0 & 0 & s \end{bmatrix} \begin{bmatrix} -1 & 0 \\ 1 & -1 \\ 1 & 0 \\ 0 & 1 \\ 0 & 1 \end{bmatrix}$$

$$\therefore \; [Y_n(s)] = \begin{bmatrix} \dfrac{s+2}{2} & -\dfrac{1}{s} \\ -\dfrac{1}{s} & \dfrac{s^2+s+1}{s} \end{bmatrix} \quad \textbf{...Ans.}$$

**Example 12.9.10.** *Determine the branch admittance matrix for the network given below.*

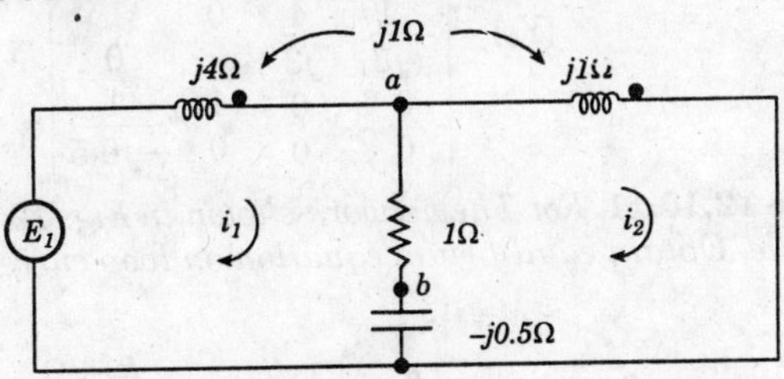


Fig. 12.10.10(*a*)

**Solution:**

The network for graph is shown in Fig. 12.10.10(*b*)

As the inductance given in the network are mutually coupled, the branch adittancces matrix $[Y_b]$, is not diagonal. For this case the branch impedance matrix $[Z_b]$ is formed and branch admittance matrix is determined using the relation $[Y_b] = [Z_b]^{-1}$

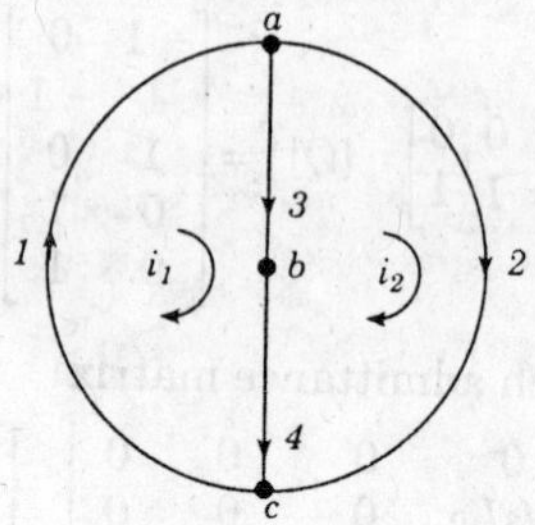


Fig. 12.10.10(*b*)

$$[Z_b] = \begin{bmatrix} Z_1 & Z_{12} & Z_{13} & Z_{14} \\ Z_{21} & Z_2 & Z_{23} & Z_{24} \\ Z_{31} & Z_{32} & Z_3 & Z_{34} \\ Z_{41} & Z_{42} & Z_{43} & Z_4 \end{bmatrix} = \begin{bmatrix} j4 & j1 & 0 & 0 \\ j1 & j1 & 0 & 0 \\ 0 & 0 & 1 & 0 \\ 0 & 0 & 0 & -j0.5 \end{bmatrix}$$

$$[Y_b] = [Z_b]^{-1} = \begin{bmatrix} j4 & j1 & 0 & 0 \\ j1 & j1 & 0 & 0 \\ 0 & 0 & 1 & 0 \\ 0 & 0 & 0 & -j0.5 \end{bmatrix}^{-1}$$

$$= \begin{bmatrix} \begin{bmatrix} j\,4 & j\,1 \\ j\,1 & j\,1 \end{bmatrix}^{-1} & \begin{matrix} 0 \\ 0 \end{matrix} & \begin{matrix} 0 \\ 0 \end{matrix} \\ \begin{matrix} 0 & 0 \\ 0 & 0 \end{matrix} & \begin{matrix} 1 \\ 0 \end{matrix} & \begin{matrix} 0 \\ \dfrac{1}{-1j\,0.5} \end{matrix} \end{bmatrix}$$

or

$$[Y_b] = \begin{bmatrix} \dfrac{1}{j3} & \dfrac{1}{j3} & 0 & 0 \\ -\dfrac{1}{j3} & \dfrac{4}{j3} & 0 & 0 \\ 0 & 0 & 1 & 0 \\ 0 & 0 & 0 & \dfrac{1}{-j0.5} \end{bmatrix} \quad \text{...Ans.}$$

**Example 12.10.11.** *For The network shown in Fig. 12.10.11. Write tie-set schedule. Obtain equilibrium equation on loop current basis.*

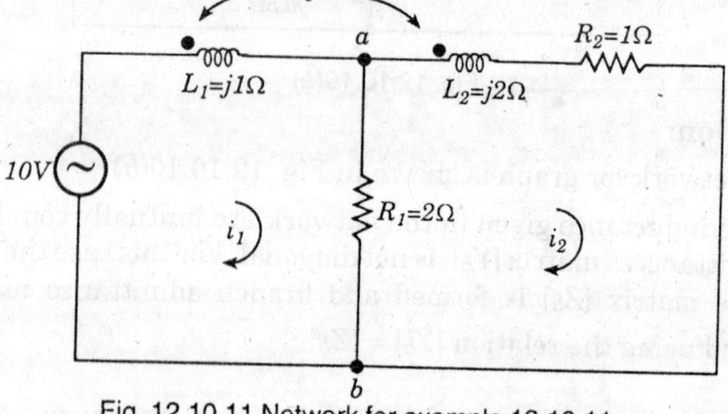


Fig. 12.10.11 Network for example 12.10.11

**Solution :** The tree graph with links is drawn in Fig 12.10.11($a$)

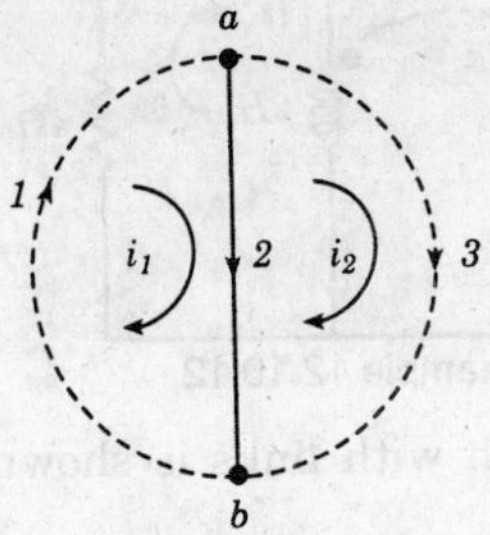


*Tie-set Schedule*
*Branch / Link*

| Loop \ Branch/Link | 1 | 2 | 3 |
|---|---|---|---|
| 1 | 1 | 1 | 0 |
| 2 | 0 | –1 | 1 |

Fig. 12.10.11($a$) Tree graph with links for the network shown is Fig. 12.10.11

The tie-set schedule is written above.

Tie-set matrix

$$[M] = \begin{bmatrix} 1 & 1 & 0 \\ 0 & -1 & 1 \end{bmatrix}, \ [M]^T = \begin{bmatrix} 1 & 0 \\ 1 & -1 \\ 0 & 1 \end{bmatrix}, \ [E_s] = \begin{bmatrix} 10 \\ 0 \\ 0 \end{bmatrix}$$

Branch impedance matrix (mutual inductance between branch 1 and 2) is written below

$$[Z_b] = \begin{bmatrix} Z_1 & Z_{12} & 0 \\ Z_{21} & Z_2 & 0 \\ 0 & 0 & Z_3 \end{bmatrix} = \begin{bmatrix} j1 & j1 & 0 \\ j1 & 2 & 0 \\ 0 & 0 & 1+j2 \end{bmatrix}$$

Since, currents $i_1$ and $i_2$ are entering dots

$$\therefore \qquad Z_{12} = Z_{21} = +jM = +j1\Omega$$

Equilibrium equation based on loop current basis is

$$\{[M]\ [Z_b]\ [M]^T\}\ [i_l] = [M]\ \{[E_s] - [Z_b]\ [I_s]\}$$

$$\because \qquad [I_s] = 0$$

$$\therefore \qquad \{[M]\ [Z_b]\ [M]^T\}\ [i_l] = [M]\ [E_s]$$

or
$$\left\{\begin{bmatrix} 1 & 1 & 0 \\ 0 & -1 & 1 \end{bmatrix} \begin{bmatrix} j1 & j1 & 0 \\ j1 & 2 & 0 \\ 0 & 0 & 1+j2 \end{bmatrix} \begin{bmatrix} 1 & 0 \\ 1 & -1 \\ 0 & 1 \end{bmatrix}\right\} \begin{bmatrix} i_1 \\ i_2 \end{bmatrix} = \begin{bmatrix} 1 & 1 & 0 \\ 0 & -1 & 1 \end{bmatrix} \begin{bmatrix} 10 \\ 0 \\ 0 \end{bmatrix}$$

$$\therefore \qquad \begin{bmatrix} 2+j1 & -2+j1 \\ -2+j1 & 3+j2 \end{bmatrix} \begin{bmatrix} i_1 \\ i_2 \end{bmatrix} = \begin{bmatrix} 10 \\ 0 \end{bmatrix} \qquad \text{...Ans.}$$

**Example 12.10.12.** *Draw the network graph for the Fig. 12.10.12. Using tie-set matrix obtain equilibrium equation in s-domain on loop current basis*

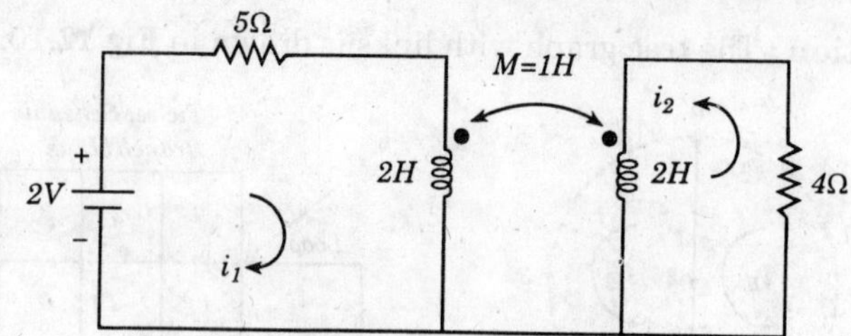


Fig. 12.10.12 Network for example 12.10.12

**Solution :** The network tree graph with links is shown in Fig. 12.10.12($a$)

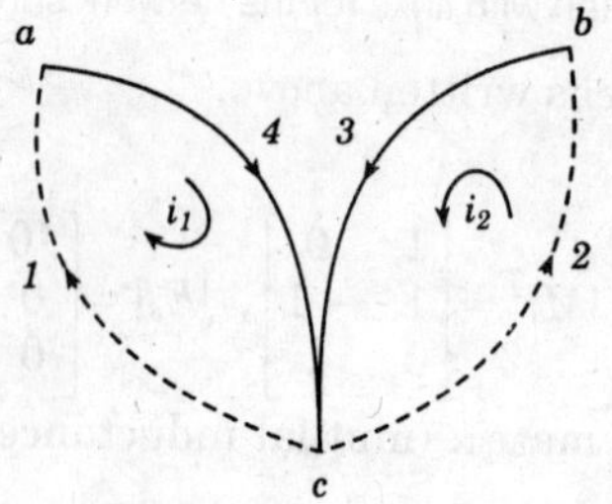


Fig. 12.10.12($a$) Tree graph with links of Fig. 12.10.12

Tie-set schedule

| Loop \ Branch/Link | 1 | 2 | 3 | 4 |
|---|---|---|---|---|
| 1 | 1 | 0 | 0 | 1 |
| 2 | 0 | 1 | 1 | 0 |

$$\therefore \quad [M] = \begin{bmatrix} 1 & 0 & 0 & 1 \\ 0 & 1 & 1 & 0 \end{bmatrix}, \quad [M]^T = \begin{bmatrix} 1 & 0 \\ 0 & 1 \\ 0 & 1 \\ 1 & 0 \end{bmatrix}, \quad [E_s(s)] = \begin{bmatrix} 2/s \\ 0 \\ 0 \\ 0 \end{bmatrix}$$

$$Z_b\,(s) = \begin{bmatrix} Z_1(s) & 0 & 0 & 0 \\ 0 & Z_2(s) & 0 & 0 \\ 0 & 0 & Z_3(s) & Z_{34}(s) \\ 0 & 0 & Z_{43}(s) & Z_4(s) \end{bmatrix} = \begin{bmatrix} 5 & 0 & 0 & 0 \\ 0 & 4 & 0 & 0 \\ 0 & 0 & 2s & s \\ 0 & 0 & s & 2s \end{bmatrix}$$

$Z_{34}(s) = Z_{43}(s)$ is the transformed mutual inductance between branch no. 3 and 4.

$$\{[M]\ [Z_b(s)]\ [M]^T\} = \begin{bmatrix} 1 & 0 & 0 & 1 \\ 0 & 1 & 1 & 0 \end{bmatrix} \begin{bmatrix} 5 & 0 & 0 & 0 \\ 0 & 4 & 0 & 0 \\ 0 & 0 & 2s & s \\ 0 & 0 & s & 2s \end{bmatrix} \begin{bmatrix} 1 & 0 \\ 0 & 1 \\ 0 & 1 \\ 1 & 0 \end{bmatrix}$$

$$= \begin{bmatrix} 2s+5 & s \\ s & 2s+4 \end{bmatrix}$$

$$[M]\ [E_s(s)] = \begin{bmatrix} 2/s \\ 0 \\ 0 \\ 0 \end{bmatrix}$$

Equilibrium equation on loop current basis is given by

$$\{[M]\ [Z_b(s)]\ [M]^T\}\ [I_l(s)] = [M]\{[E_s(s) - [Z_b(s)]\ [I_s(s)]\}$$

$$\because \qquad [I_s(s)] = 0$$

$$\therefore\ \{[M]\ [Z_b(s)]\ [M]^T\}\ [I_l(s)] = [M]\ [E_s(s)]$$

$$\therefore \begin{bmatrix} 2s+5 & s \\ s & 2s+4 \end{bmatrix} \begin{bmatrix} I_1(s) \\ I_2(s) \end{bmatrix} = \begin{bmatrix} 2/s \\ 0 \end{bmatrix} \qquad \text{...Ans.}$$

**Example : 12.10.13** *Use network topological approach to obtain mesh current equilibrium equations for the network shown in Fig. 12.10.13*

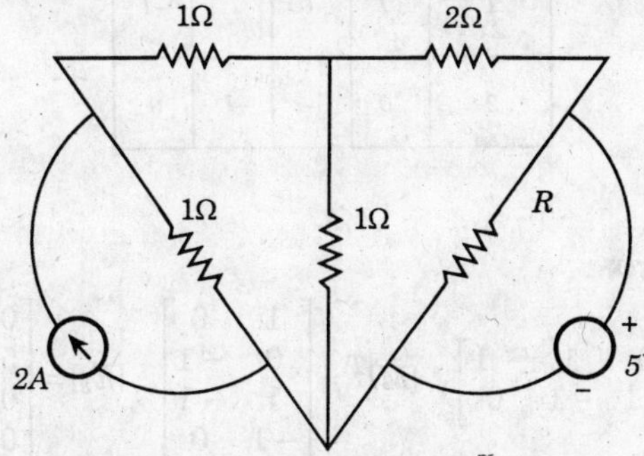


Fig. 12.10.13 Network for example 12.10.13

**Solution:** Since the voltage source is shunted by resistor R, The same is omitted from the network. The network takes the form as shown in Fig. 12.10.13(*a*)

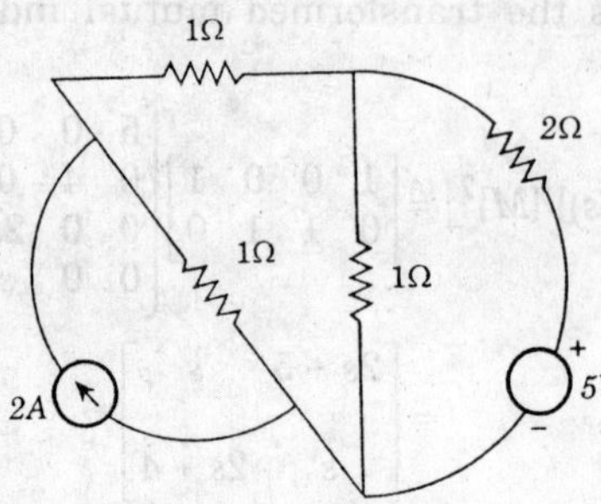


Fig. 12.10.13(*a*) Network of Fig. 12.10.13 redrawn.

The tree graph with links for Fig. 12.10.13(*a*) is drawn in Fig. 12.10.13(*b*)

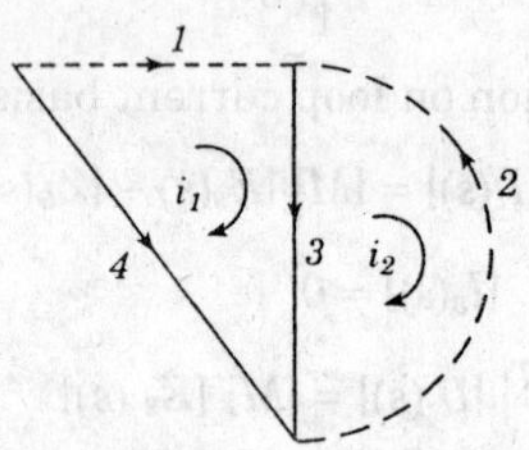


Fig. 12.10.13(*b*) Tree branch graph of Fig. 12.10.13(*a*)

Tie-set schedule

| Mesh \ Branch / Link | 1 | 2 | 3 | 4 |
|---|---|---|---|---|
| 1 | 1 | 0 | 1 | −1 |
| 2 | 0 | −1 | −1 | 0 |

Tie-set matrix

$$[M] = \begin{bmatrix} 1 & 0 & 1 & -1 \\ 0 & -1 & -1 & 0 \end{bmatrix}, \ [M]^T = \begin{bmatrix} 1 & 0 \\ 0 & -1 \\ 1 & -1 \\ -1 & 0 \end{bmatrix}, \ [E_s] = \begin{bmatrix} 0 \\ 5 \\ 0 \\ 0 \end{bmatrix}, \ I_s = \begin{bmatrix} 0 \\ 0 \\ 0 \\ 2 \end{bmatrix}$$

$$[Z_b] = \begin{bmatrix} 1 & 0 & 0 & 0 \\ 0 & 2 & 0 & 0 \\ 0 & 0 & 1 & 0 \\ 0 & 0 & 0 & 1 \end{bmatrix}$$

$$[M][Z_b][M]^T = \begin{bmatrix} 1 & 0 & 1 & -1 \\ 0 & -1 & -1 & 0 \end{bmatrix} \begin{bmatrix} 1 & 0 & 0 & 0 \\ 0 & 2 & 0 & 0 \\ 0 & 0 & 1 & 0 \\ 0 & 0 & 0 & 1 \end{bmatrix} \begin{bmatrix} 1 & 0 \\ 0 & -1 \\ 1 & -1 \\ -1 & 0 \end{bmatrix}$$

$$= \begin{bmatrix} 3 & -1 \\ -1 & 3 \end{bmatrix}$$

$$[M]\{[E_s] - [Z_b][I_s]\} = \begin{bmatrix} 1 & 0 & 1 & -1 \\ 0 & -1 & -1 & 0 \end{bmatrix} \left\{ \begin{bmatrix} 0 \\ 5 \\ 0 \\ 0 \end{bmatrix} - \begin{bmatrix} 1 & 0 & 0 & 0 \\ 0 & 2 & 0 & 0 \\ 0 & 0 & 1 & 0 \\ 0 & 0 & 0 & 1 \end{bmatrix} \begin{bmatrix} 0 \\ 0 \\ 0 \\ 2 \end{bmatrix} \right\}$$

$$= \begin{bmatrix} 2 \\ -5 \end{bmatrix}$$

The mesh current equilibrium equation is given by

$$\{[M]\ [Z_b]\ [M]^T\}\ [i_m] = [M]\ \{[E_s] - [Z_b]\ [I_s]\}$$

$$\therefore \qquad \begin{bmatrix} 3 & -1 \\ -1 & 3 \end{bmatrix} \begin{bmatrix} i_1 \\ i_2 \end{bmatrix} = \begin{bmatrix} 2 \\ -5 \end{bmatrix} \qquad \text{...Ans.}$$

## PROBLEMS

**12.1** The incidence matrix of a network is given below. Draw the oriental graph.

| Node | Branch 1 | 2 | 3 | 4 | 5 | 6 |
|---|---|---|---|---|---|---|
| *a* | -1 | 0 | 0 | 1 | 0 | 1 |
| *b* | 0 | 1 | 0 | -1 | 1 | 0 |
| *c* | 0 | 0 | 1 | 0 | -1 | -1 |
| *d* | 1 | -1 | -1 | 0 | 0 | 0 |

**12.2** A network graph is shown in Fig 12P-1. Select tree and determine (*i*) incidence matrix (*ii*) fundamental circuit matrix

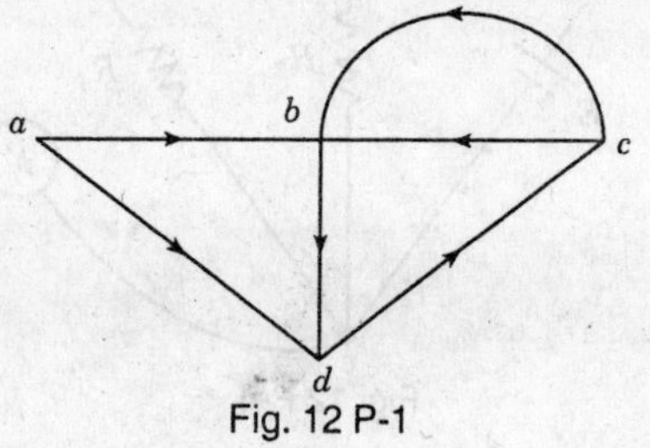


Fig. 12 P-1

**12.3** Obtain fundamental loop matrix for the oriented network graph shown in Fig. 12 P-2

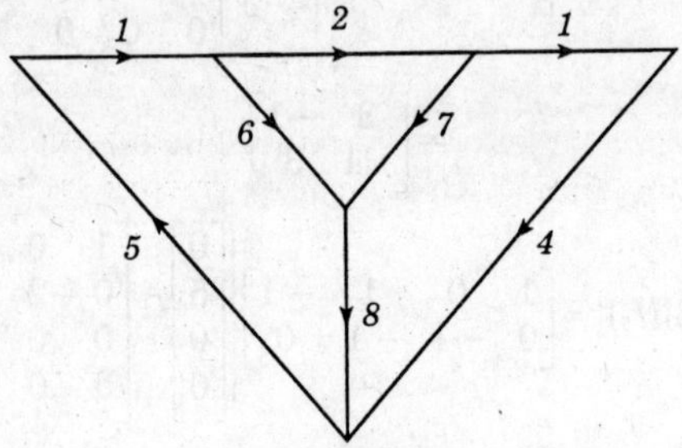


Fig. 12 P-2

**12.4** Write tie set schedule and formulate equilibrium equation on loop current basis for the network given below:

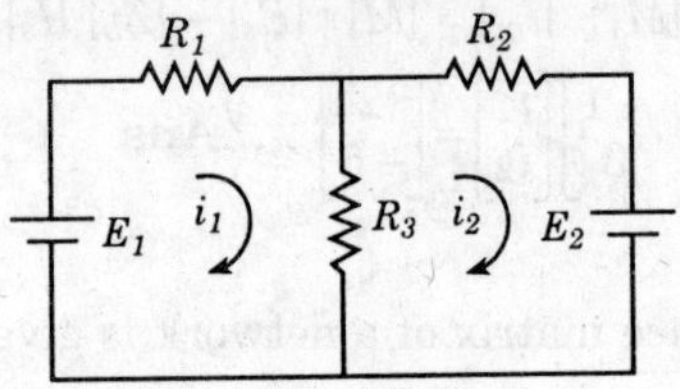


Fig. 12 P-3

**Ans:** $$\begin{bmatrix} R_1 + R_3 & -R_3 \\ -R_3 & R_2 + R_3 \end{bmatrix} \begin{bmatrix} i_1 \\ i_2 \end{bmatrix} = \begin{bmatrix} E_1 \\ E_2 \end{bmatrix}$$

**12.5** Write equilibrium equation based on node voltage basis for the network given below and determine node voltages *a* & *b* with respect to reference node *c*.

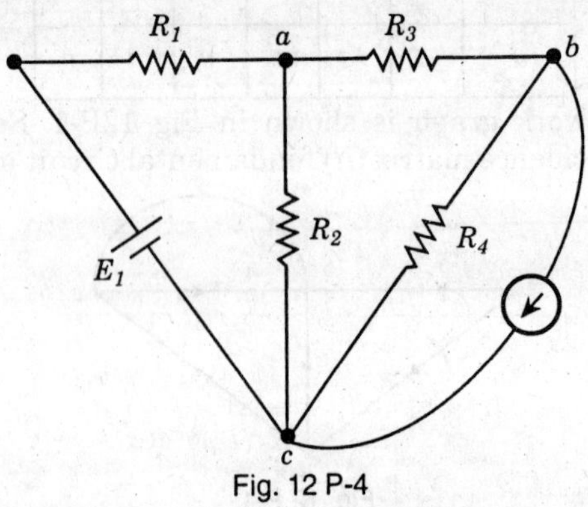


Fig. 12 P-4

$$\textbf{Ans :} \begin{bmatrix} \frac{1}{R_1}+\frac{1}{R_2}+\frac{1}{R_3} & -\frac{1}{R_3} \\ -\frac{1}{R_3} & \frac{1}{R_3}+\frac{1}{R_4} \end{bmatrix} \begin{bmatrix} e_a \\ e_b \end{bmatrix} = \begin{bmatrix} \frac{E}{R_1} \\ -I \end{bmatrix}$$

**12.6** Select tree and write cur-set schedule to form equlibrium equations on mode voltage basis for the network given below :

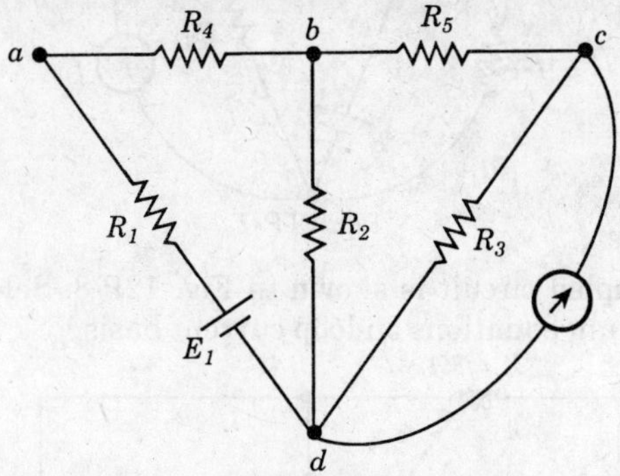


Fig. 12 P-5

$$\textbf{Ans:} \begin{bmatrix} \frac{1}{R_1}+\frac{1}{R_4} & -\frac{1}{R_4} & 0 \\ -\frac{1}{R_4} & \frac{1}{R_2}+\frac{1}{R_4}+\frac{1}{R_5} & -\frac{1}{R_5} \\ 0 & -\frac{1}{R_5} & \frac{1}{R_3}+\frac{1}{R_5} \end{bmatrix} \begin{bmatrix} e_a \\ e_b \\ e_b \end{bmatrix} = \begin{bmatrix} E/R_1 \\ 0 \\ 0 \end{bmatrix}$$

**12.7** Draw the oriented graph and determine equilibrium equations on mode voltage basis to determine voltage $V_a$ and $V_b$ in the network of Fig. 12P-6

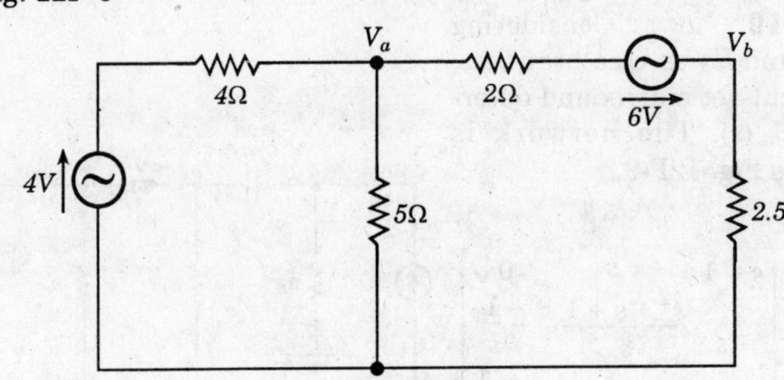


Fig. 12 P-6

$$\textbf{Ans:} \begin{bmatrix} 0.95 & -0.5 \\ -0.5 & 0.9 \end{bmatrix} \begin{bmatrix} V_a \\ V_b \end{bmatrix} = \begin{bmatrix} 4 \\ -3 \end{bmatrix}$$

**12.8** For The network shown in Fig. 12P-7, draw the network graph. Select tree and write equilibrium equation on node voltage basis.

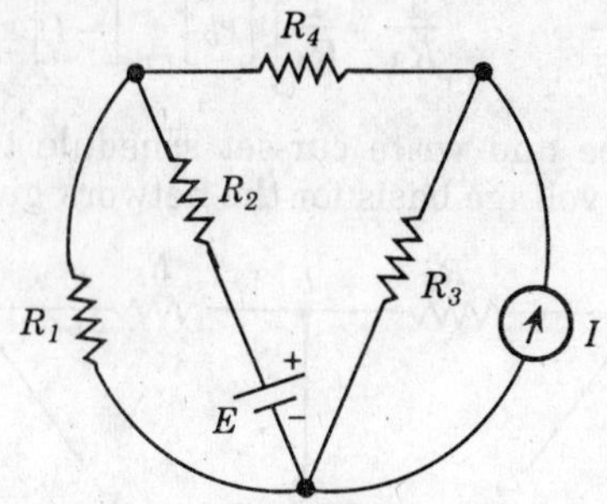


Fig. 12 P-7

**12.9** A coupled circuit is shown in Fig. 12P-8. Select tree graph. Write equilibrium equations on loop current basis.

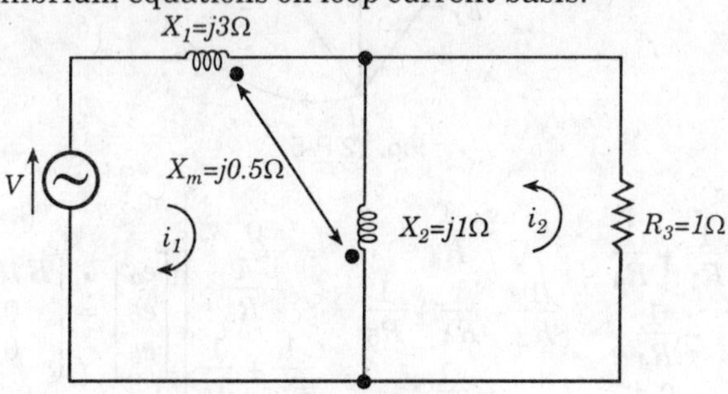


Fig. 12 P-8

**Ans:** $\begin{bmatrix} j\,5 & j\,1.5 \\ j\,1.5 & 1+j\,1 \end{bmatrix} \begin{bmatrix} i_1 \\ i_2 \end{bmatrix} = \begin{bmatrix} V \\ 0 \end{bmatrix}$

**12.10** Considering $R_1$, $R_2$ and $R_3$ as tree branches, obtain cut-set matrix and determine $Y_n(s)$. The network is shown is Fig. 12P-9.

$$Y_m(s) = \begin{bmatrix} s+1 & -s & 0 \\ -s & \dfrac{s^2+s+1}{s} & -\dfrac{1}{s} \\ 0 & -\dfrac{1}{s} & \dfrac{s+1}{s} \end{bmatrix}$$

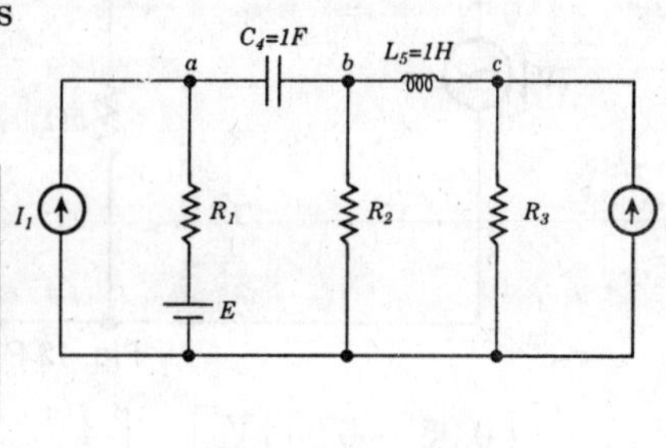


Fig. 12 P-9

# 13

# Fourier Analysis

## 13.1. Introduction

The response of an electrical network to sinusoidal excitation (input) can be easily determined. Sometimes, the excitation is non-sinusoidal. The non-sinusoidal periodic signal waveforms can be represented as a series of simple harmonic function having frequencies which are integral multiples of fundamental frequency, and such a series is known as Fourier series. For linear circuit elements, the principal of superposition holds good therefore, the response due to sinusoidal signals of different frequencies can be determined independently. The total response is obtained by adding individual responses.

The periodic function $f(t)$ repeats after a time period $T$. Thus,

$$f(t) = f(t \pm T)$$

For periodic function to have a Fourier series following conditions known as "Dirichlet conditions" must be satisfied.

The periodic function

1. has finite number of discontinuties in a time period $T$.
2. has finite number of maxima and minima.
3. has a finite average value over a time period *i.e.* $\int_{-T/2}^{T/2} f(t)\, dt$ is finite.

## 13.2 TRIGONOMETRIC FORM OF FOURIER SERIES FOR A PERIODIC FUNCTION *f(t)*

$$f(t) = a_0 + a_1 \cos\omega t + a_2 \cos 2\omega t + \dots + a_n \cos n\omega t + b_1 \sin\omega t$$
$$+ b_2 \sin 2\omega t + \dots + b_n \sin n\omega t.$$

$\omega$ is fundamental frequency, $2\omega$, $3\omega$, ... *2nd*, *3rd*, ... harmonic frequency $a_0, a_n$ and $b_n$ are Fourier coefficients. The evaluation of Fourier coefficients is as follows :

### (1) $a_0$

Multiply $f(t)$ by 1 and integrate over the time period $T$.

Therefore,

$$\int_0^T f(t).\ 1.\ dt = \int_0^T a_0 \,.\, 1 \,.\, dt + \int_0^T (a_1 \cos \omega\, t \,.\, 1 \,.\, dt + ...$$

$$+ a_n \cos n\, \omega\, t \,.\, 1\, dt) + \int_0^T (b_1 \sin \omega t \,.\, 1 \,.\, dt + ...$$

$$+ b_n \sin n\, \omega\, t \,.\, 1 \,.\, dt)$$

The definite integrals $\int_0^T (a_1 \cos\omega \,.\, 1dt + ...a_n \cos n\omega t \,.\, 1 \,.\, dt)$

and $\int_0^T (b_1 \sin\omega t + ... + b_n \sin n\, \omega t \,.\, 1 \,.\, dt)$ equal zero

Hence,

$$\int_0^T f(t) \,.\, dt = \int_0^T a_0\, dt$$

$$\therefore \qquad a_0 = \frac{1}{T}\int_0^T f(t)\, dt$$

$$\text{Graphically, } a_0 = \frac{\text{Area under } f(t) \text{ for one time period}}{\text{Time period } (T)}$$

**(2) $a_n$**

Multiply $f(t)$ by $\cos n\omega t$ and integrate over the time period $T$. Therefore,

$$\int_0^T f(t) \cos n\omega t\, dt = \int_0^T a_0 \cos n\omega t + \int_0^T a_1 \cos \omega t \cos n\omega t + ...$$

$$+ \int_0^T a_n \cos^2 n\, \omega t\, dt + \int_0^T b_1 \sin \omega t \cos n\omega t dt + ...$$

$$+ \int_0^T b_n \sin \omega t \cos n\, \omega t\, dt.$$

The definite integrals on the *R.H.S.* of above equation equal zero except $\int_0^T a_n \cos^2 n\, \omega t\, dt$.

$$\text{Hence, } \int_0^T f(t) \cos n\omega t\, dt = \int_0^T a_n \cos^2 \omega t\, dt \,. = \frac{aT}{2}$$

$$\therefore \qquad a_n = \frac{2}{T}\int_0^2 f(t) \cos n\omega t\, dt.$$

**(3) $b_n$**

Multiply $f(t)$ by $\sin n\omega t$ and integrate over the time period $T$. Therefore,

$$\int_0^T f(t)\sin n\omega t\, dt \;. = \int_0^T a_0 \sin n\omega t + \int_0^T a_1 \cos \omega t \sin n\omega t\, dt + \ldots$$

$$+ \int_0^T a_n \cos n\omega t \sin n\omega t\, dt + \int_0^T b_1 \sin\omega t \sin n\omega t\, dt + \ldots$$

$$+ \int_0^T b_n \sin^2 n\omega t dt \;.$$

The definite integrals on The *R.H.S.* of above equation equal zero except $\int_0^T b_n \sin^2 n\omega t dt$.

Hence,

$$\int_0^T f(t) \sin n\, \omega t dt = \int_0^T b_n \sin^2 n\, \omega t\, dt = \frac{b_n T}{2}$$

$$\therefore \qquad b_n = \frac{2}{T}\int_0^T f(t) \sin n\, \omega t\, dt$$

## 13.3 COMPACT FORM OF FOURIER SERIES

The trigonometric form of Fourier series can be expressed in compact form as below :

$$f(t) = a_0 + \sum_{n=1}^{\infty} (a_n \cos n\, \omega t + b_n \sin n\, \omega t)$$

The second term of the above expression can be written as

$$(a_n \cos n\omega t + b_n \sin n\omega t)$$

$$= \sqrt{a_n^2 + b_n^2}\left(\frac{a_n}{\sqrt{a_n^2 + b_n^2}} \cos n\omega t + \frac{b_n}{\sqrt{a_n^2 + b_n^2}} \sin n\omega t\right)$$

Let $\dfrac{a_n}{\sqrt{a_n^2 + b_n^2}} = \cos \theta_n$ and $\dfrac{b_n}{\sqrt{a_n^2 + b_n^2}} = \sin \theta_n$

$$\therefore \quad (a_n \cos n\, \omega t + b_n \sin n\, \omega t)$$

$$= \sqrt{a_n^2 + b_n^2}(\cos \theta_n \cos n\, \omega t + \sin \theta_n \sin n\, \omega t)$$

or $$(a_n \cos n\, \omega t + b_n \sin n\, \omega t) = \sqrt{a_n^2 + b_n^2} \cos(n\, \omega t - \theta_n)$$

Put $$C_n = \sqrt{a_n^2 + b_n^2}$$

$$\therefore \quad f(t) = a_0 + C_n \cos (n\, \omega t + \theta_n) \;\ldots\; \text{cosine form } n = 1, 2, 3, \ldots$$

where, $$\theta_n = -\tan^{-1}\left(\frac{b_n}{a_n}\right)$$

Let $\dfrac{a_n}{\sqrt{a_n^2 + b_n^2}} = \sin \phi_n$ and $\dfrac{b_n}{\sqrt{a_n^2 + b_n^2}} = \cos \phi_n$

$$\therefore (a_n \cos n\omega t + b_n \sin n\omega t) = \sqrt{a_n^2 + b_n^2}$$

$$(\sin \phi_n \cos n\omega t + \cos \phi_n \sin n\omega t)$$

$$\therefore \quad f(t) = a_0 + C_n \sin (n\omega t + \phi_n) \text{ ... sine form } n = 1, 2, 3, \ldots$$

where, $\phi_n = \tan^{-1}\left(\dfrac{a_n}{b_n}\right)$

$a_0$, $C_n = \sqrt{a_n^2 + b_n^2}$ and $\theta_n = -\tan^{-1}\left(\dfrac{b_n}{a_n}\right)$ or $\theta_n = \tan^{-1}\left(\dfrac{a_n}{b_n}\right)$

contain all needed information with regards to Fourier series of a periodic function $f(t)$.

$C_n$ is the $n^{th}$ harmonic amplitude and $\theta_n$ or $\phi_n$ $n^{th}$ harmonic phase angle

## 13.4 LINE SPECTRA

The plot of amplitude and phase angle of a periodic function $f(t)$ at the integer value of $n$ is known as line spectrum of a Fourier series.

**(1) Amplitude spectrum**

The amplitude spectrum is obtained by determining the value of

$$C_n = \sqrt{a_n^2 + b_n^2} \quad \text{at} \quad n = 1, 2, 3, \ldots$$

where $C_n$ is the amplitude of $n^{th}$ component of a Fourier series.

**(2) Phase spectrum**

The phase angle of $n^{th}$ harmonic component of a Fourier series is given by

$$\theta_n = \tan^{-1}\left(\frac{b_n}{a_n}\right) \quad \text{for cosine expression.}$$

$$\phi_n = \tan^{-1}\left(\frac{a_n}{b_n}\right) \quad \text{for sine expression.}$$

The phase spectrum is obtained by determining the value of $\theta_n$ or $\phi_n$ at $n = 1, 2, 3, \ldots$

## 13.5 WAVEFORM SYMMETRY

The determination of Fourier coefficients $a_0$, $a_n$ and $b_n$ depends on the waveform of a given periodic function $f(t)$. However, in some cases either one or two of these coefficients need not be determined. This is decided by the waveform symmetry described below.

**(1) Even function**

The periodic function $f(t)$ is said to be an even function if, it satisfies the following condition

$$f(t) = f(-t)$$

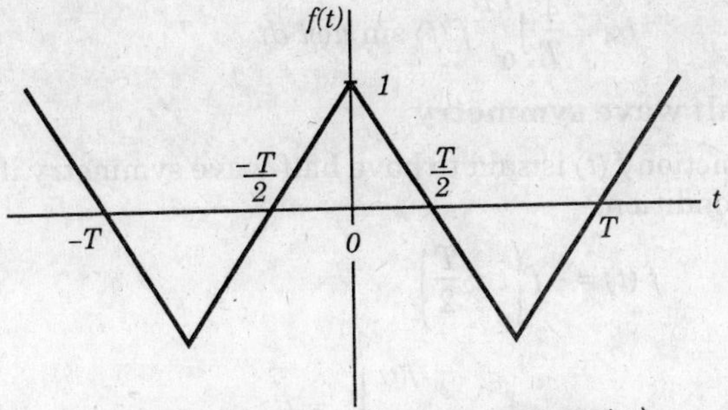


Fig. 13.5.1 Even function (mirror symmetry)

The even function is shown in Fig. 13.5.1. The Fourier series of an even function contains cosine terms only. Thus, the coefficient $a_n$ is to be determined only. The coefficient $b_n = 0$. Also, if the even function is symmetrical about the time axis its average value over a time period $T$ is zero. Hence, $a_0 = 0$, otherwise the coefficient $a_0$ is to be determined.

For the even function, the coefficient $a_n$ can also be determined as

$$a_n = \frac{4}{T}\int_0^{T/2} f(t) \cos n\,\omega t\, dt$$

**(2) Odd function**

The periodic function $f(t)$ is said to be an odd function if, it satisfies the following condition

$$f(t) = -f(-t)$$

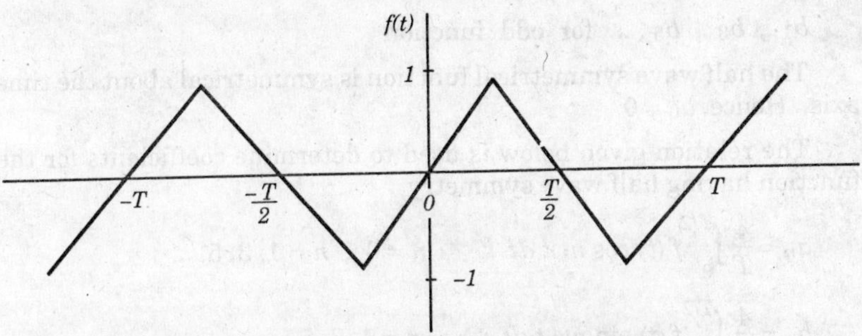


Fig. 13.5.2 Odd function (skew symmetry)

The odd function is shown in Fig. 13.5.2. The Fourier series of an odd function contains sine terms. Thus the coefficient $b_n$ is to be determined only. The coefficient $a_n = 0$. Also, if the odd function is symmetrical about the time axis its average value over a time period $T$ is zero. Hence, $a_0 = 0$ , otherwise the coefficient $a_0$ is to be determined.

For the odd function, the coefficient $b_n$ can also be determined as

$$b_n = \frac{4}{T}\int_0^{T/2} f(t) \sin n\omega t \, dt$$

**(3) Half wave symmetry**

The function $f(t)$ is said to have half-wave symmetry if, it satisfies following condition.

$$f(t) = -f\left(t \pm \frac{T}{2}\right)$$

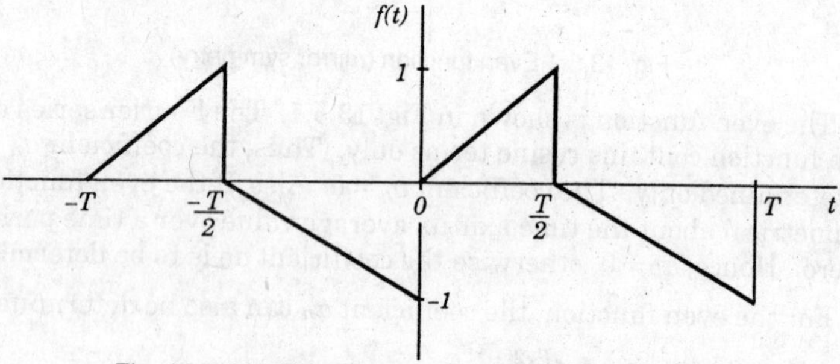


Fig. 13.5.3 Half wave symmetry (alternate symmetry)

The function having half wave symmetry is shown in Fig. 13.5.3. For a halfwave symmetrical function in addition to fundamental, only odd harmonies are present in its Fourier series.

Thus, following Fourier coefficients are to be determined

$a_1$ , $a_3$ , $a_5$ , ... for even function

$b_1$ , $b_3$ , $b_5$ , ... for odd function

The half wave symmetrical function is symmetrical about the time axis. Hence, $a_0 = 0$

The relation given below is used to determine coefficients for the function having half wave symmetry

$$a_n = \frac{4}{T}\int_0^{T/2} f(t) \cos n\omega t \, dt \qquad n \neq 0 \ , \ n = 1, 3, 5, ...$$

$$b_n = \frac{4}{T}\int_0^{T/2} f(t) \sin n\omega \, t \, dt \qquad n = 1, 3, 5, ...$$

The coefficients $a_n$ or $b_n$ are to be evaluated as the given function is even or odd.

## 13.6 EXPONENTIAL FOURIER SERIES

The exponential form of Fourier series is obtained by substituting equivalent of sine and cosine terms in the trigonometric form. The trigonometric form of Fourier series is given below.

$$f(t) = a_0 + \sum_{n=1}^{\infty} (a_n \cos n\omega t + b_n \sin n\omega t)$$

$$\because \quad \cos n\omega t = \frac{e^{jn\omega t} + e^{-jn\omega t}}{2}$$

and $$\sin n\omega t = \frac{e^{jn\omega t} - e^{-jn\omega t}}{j2}$$

$$\therefore \quad f(t) = a_0 + \sum_{n=1}^{\infty} \left( a_n \frac{e^{jn\omega t} + e^{-jn\omega t}}{2} + b_n \frac{e^{jn\omega t} - e^{-jn\omega t}}{j2} \right)$$

$$= a_0 + \sum_{n=1}^{\infty} \left( a_n \frac{e^{jn\omega t} + e^{-jn\omega t}}{2} - j\, b_n \frac{e^{jn\omega t} - e^{-jn\omega t}}{2} \right)$$

$$= a_0 + \sum_{n=1}^{\infty} \left( \frac{a_n - j\, b_n}{2} e^{jn\omega t} + \frac{a_n + j\, b_n}{2} e^{-jn\omega t} \right)$$

put $$\overline{C}_n = \frac{a_n - j\, b_n}{2}, \quad \overline{C}_{-n} = \frac{a_n + j\, b_n}{2} \quad \text{and} \quad C_0 = a_0$$

$$\therefore \quad f(t) = C_0 + \sum_{n=1}^{\infty} (\overline{C}_n e^{jn\omega t} + \overline{C}_{-n} e^{-jn\omega t})$$

On expanding *R.H.S.* of the above expression complete spectrum for $n = -\infty$ to $n = \infty$ is obtained below :

$$f(t) = \overline{C}_{-n} e^{-jn\omega t} + \ldots + \overline{C}_{-2} e^{-j2\omega t} + \overline{C}_{-1} e^{-j\omega t} + \overline{C}_0 + \ldots$$
$$\ldots + \overline{C}_1 e^{j\omega t} + \overline{C}_2 e^{j2\omega t} + \ldots + \overline{C}_n e^{jn\omega t}$$

Multiply on both sides by $e^{-jn\omega t}$ and integrate with limits 0 to $T$. Therefore,

$$\int_0^T f(t)\, e^{-jn\omega t}\, dt = \ldots + \int_0^T \overline{C}_{-2} e^{-j2\omega t} \cdot e^{-jn\omega t}\, dt + \int_0^T \overline{C}_{-1} e^{-j\omega t} \cdot e^{-jn\omega t}\, dt$$
$$+ \int_0^T \overline{C}_0 e^{-jn\omega t} dt + \int_0^T \overline{C}_1 e^{j\omega t} \cdot e^{-jn\omega t}\, dt + \ldots$$
$$+ \int_0^T \overline{C}_n\, dt$$

On *R.H.S.* of the above expression all the definite integrals are zero except $\int_0^T \overline{C}_n dt$

$$\therefore \quad \int_0^T f(t)\, e^{-jn\omega t} = \int_0^T \overline{C}_n\, dt$$

$\because \quad \int_0^T \overline{C}_n \, dt = \overline{C}_n \, T$

$$\therefore \quad \overline{C}_n = \frac{1}{T}\int_0^T f(t)\, e^{-jn\omega t} dt$$

$\overline{C}_n$ and $\overline{C}_{-n}$ are complex conjugate

$$\therefore \quad \overline{C}_{-n} = \frac{1}{T}\int_0^T f(t)\, e^{jn\omega t} dt$$

The trigonometric Fourier coefficients $a_n$ and $b_n$ are determinated in terms of exponential Fourier coefficients as below

$$\overline{C}_n = \frac{a_n - j\, b_n}{2}$$

$$\overline{C}_{-n} = \frac{a_n + j\, b_n}{2}$$

$$\therefore \quad a_n = \overline{C}_n + \overline{C}_{-n}$$

and $\quad b_n = j(\overline{C}_n - \overline{C}_{-n})$

$$a_0 = \overline{C}_0$$

## 13.7 SOLVED EXAMPLES

**Example 13.7.1** *Determine the Fourier series for the waveform shown in Fig. 13.7.1.*

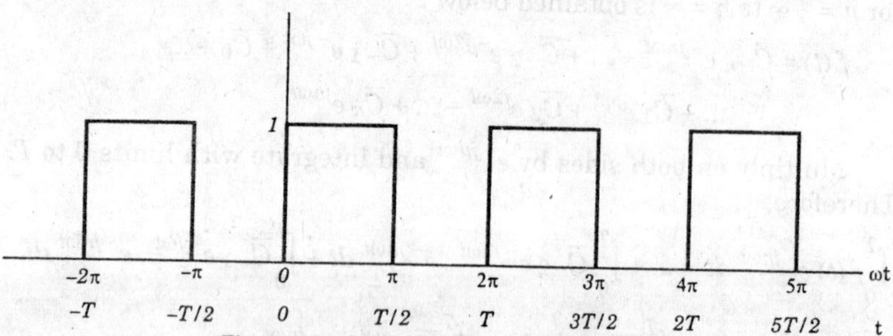


Fig. 13.7.1 Waveform for example 13.7.1.

1. $a_0$ = Average value of $f(t)$ for one period

$$= \frac{\text{Area of the waveform for one period}}{T}$$

$$= \frac{1 \times (T/2)}{T}, \quad \therefore a_0 = \frac{1}{2}$$

2. $f(t) = 1 \quad$ from $t = 0$ to $t = T/2$

$\quad = 0 \quad$ from $t = T/2$ to $T$

$$a_n = \frac{2}{T}\int_0^T f(t) \cos n\omega t \, dt.$$

$$= \frac{2}{T}\left[\int_0^{T/2} 1 \,.\, \cos n\omega t \, dt + \int_{T/2}^{T} 0 \,.\, \cos n\omega t \, dt\right]$$

$$= \frac{2}{T}\left[\frac{\sin n\omega t}{n\omega}\right]_0^{T/2}$$

$$= \frac{2}{n\omega T}\left[\sin\left(\frac{n\omega T}{2}\right) - \sin n\omega \times 0\right]$$

$$\because \quad \omega = \frac{2\pi}{T}$$

$$\therefore \quad a_n = \frac{1}{n\pi} \sin n\pi$$

$$\therefore \quad a_n = 0 \qquad \text{for } n = 1, 2, 3, \ldots$$

3. $$b_n = \frac{2}{T}\int_0^T f(t) \sin n\omega t \, dt.$$

$$= \frac{2}{T}\left[\int_0^{T/2} 1 \,.\, \sin n\omega t \, dt + \int_{T/2}^{T} 0 \sin n\omega t \, dt\right]$$

$$= \frac{2}{T}\left[-\frac{\cos n\,\omega\, t}{n\,\omega}\right]_0^{T/2}$$

$$= \frac{2}{n\omega T}\left[\left(-\frac{\cos n\omega T}{2}\right) - (-\cos n\omega \times 0)\right]$$

$$= \frac{2}{n\omega t}\left[1 - \omega s n \frac{\omega}{2} T\right]$$

put $$\omega T = 2\pi$$

$$\therefore \quad b_n = \frac{1}{n\pi}(1 - \cos n\,\pi)$$

$$n = 2, 4, 6, \ldots, \cos n\pi = 1$$

$$n = 1, 3, 5, \ldots, \cos n\pi = -1$$

$$\therefore \quad b_n = 0 \qquad \text{for } n = 2, 4, 6, \ldots$$

$$b_n = \frac{2}{n\pi} \qquad \text{for } n = 1, 3, 5, \ldots$$

$$f(t) = a_0 + b_1 \sin \omega t + b_3 \sin 3\,\omega t + b_5 \sin 5\omega t$$

or $$f(t) = \frac{1}{2} + \frac{2}{\pi} \sin \omega t + \frac{2}{3\pi} \sin 3\,\omega t + \frac{2}{5\pi} + \ldots$$ **Ans.**

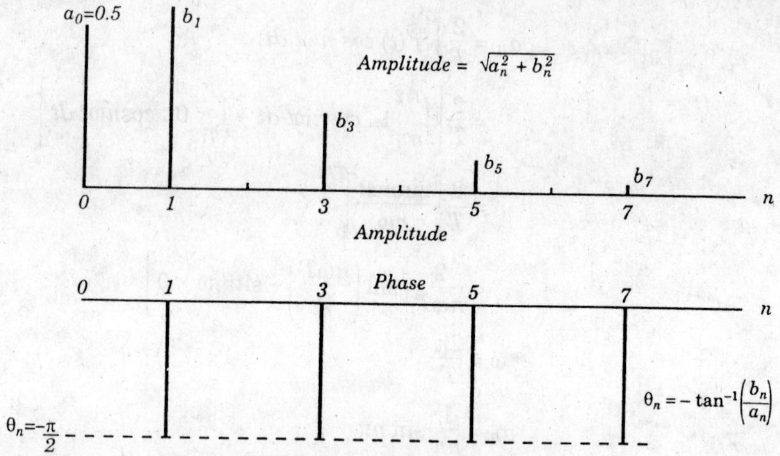


Fig. 13.7.1 (*a*) Line spectra for example 13.7.1

**Example 13.7.2** *Determine the Fourier coefficients and Fourier series for the wave form given in Fig. 13.7.2*

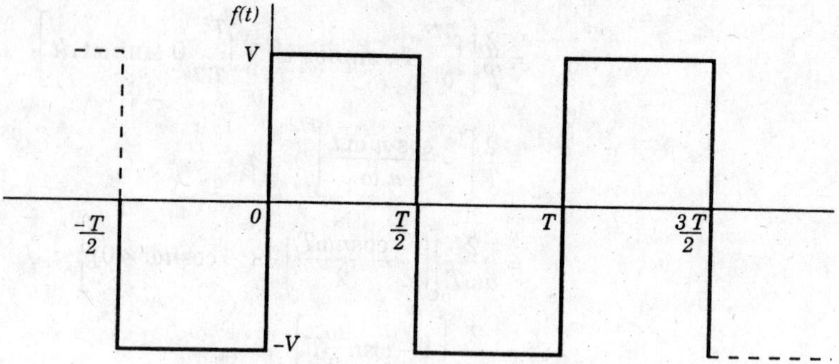


Fig. 13.7.2 periodic wave form for example 13.7.2

**Solution:** $f(t) = V$ from 0 to $T/2$

$= -V$ from $T/2$ to $T$

$f(t)$ is symmetrical about time axis, $a_0 = 0$

$f(t)$ is an odd function with half-wave symmetry.

The coefficient $b_n$ is to be determined for odd harmonics.

For odd function $a_n = 0$

$$b_n = \frac{4}{T}\int_0^{T/2} f(t) \sin n\omega t \, dt$$

$$= \frac{4}{T}\int_0^{T/2} V \sin n\omega t \, dt$$

$$= \frac{4V}{T}\int_0^{T/2} \sin n\omega t \, dt$$

$$= -\frac{4V}{n\omega T}[\cos n\omega t]_0^{T/2}$$

$$= -\frac{4V}{n\omega T}\left(\cos n\frac{\omega}{2}T - 1\right)$$

put $\omega T = 2\pi$

$$\therefore \quad b_n = \frac{2V}{n\pi}(\cos n\pi - 1)$$

or
$$b_n = \frac{2V}{n\pi}(1 - \cos n\pi)$$

$$n = 2, 4, 6, \ldots \qquad \cos n\pi = 1$$

$$n = 1, 3, 5, \ldots \qquad \cos n\pi = -1$$

$$\therefore \quad b_n = 0 \quad \text{for } n = 2, 4, 6, \ldots$$

and
$$b_n = \frac{4V}{n\pi} \quad \text{for } n = 1, 3, 5, \ldots$$

$$f(t) = b_1 \sin\omega t + b_3 \sin 3\omega t + b_5 \sin 5\omega t + \ldots$$

$$= \frac{4V}{\pi}\left(\sin\omega t + \frac{1}{3}\sin 3\omega t + \frac{1}{5}\sin 5\omega t + \ldots\right)$$

...**Ans.**

**Example 13.7.3** *Determine the trigonometric form of Fourier series for the periodic pulse wave-form shown in Fig. 13.7.3.*

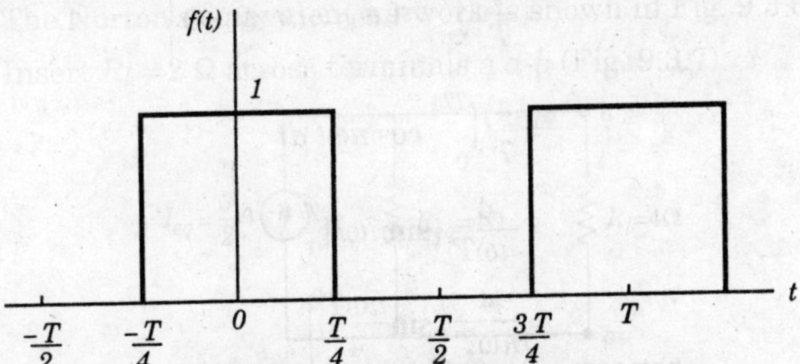


Fig. 13.7.3 Pulse waveform for example 13.7.3

**Solution:**
$$f(t) = 0 \qquad -\frac{T}{2} < t < -\frac{T}{4}$$

$$= 1 \qquad -\frac{T}{4} < t < \frac{T}{4}$$

$$= 0 \qquad \frac{T}{4} < t < \frac{T}{2}$$

$f(t)$ is not symmetrical about time axis.

$$\therefore \quad a_0 = \frac{1}{T}\int_{-T/2}^{T/2} f(t)\,dt$$

$$= \frac{1}{T}\left[\int_{1\,T/2}^{-T/4} o\,dt + \int_{-T/4}^{T/4} 1\,dt + \int_{T/4}^{T/2} 0\,dt\right]$$

$$= \frac{1}{T}\int_{-T/4}^{T/4} 1\,dt$$

$$= \frac{1}{T}[\,t\,]_{-T/4}^{T/4}$$

$$= \frac{1}{T}\left[\frac{T}{4} - \left(-\frac{T}{4}\right)\right]$$

$$= 0.5$$

$f(t)$ is an even function, $b_n = 0$. The coefficient $a_n$ is determined below,

$$a_n = \frac{2}{T}\int_0^T f(t)\cos n\omega t\,dt \qquad n \neq 0$$

For even function

$$a_n = \frac{4}{T}\int_0^{T/2} f(t)\cos n\omega t\,dt$$

$$= \frac{4}{T}\left[\int_0^{T/4} f(t)\cos n\omega t\,dt + \int_{T/4}^{T/2} f(t)\cos n\omega t\,dt\right]$$

$$= \frac{4}{T}\left[\int_0^{T/4} 1\cos n\omega t\,dt + 0\right]$$

$$= \frac{4}{T}\int_0^{T/4} \cos n\omega t\,dt$$

$$= \frac{4}{n\omega T}[\sin n\omega t]_0^{T/4}$$

$$= \frac{4}{n\omega T}\left(\sin\frac{n\omega T}{4}\right)$$

put $\omega T = 2\pi$

$$\therefore \quad a_n = \frac{2}{n\pi}\sin\frac{n\pi}{2}$$

$$a_n = 0 \qquad \text{for } n = 2, 4, 6, \ldots$$

$$a_n = \frac{2}{n\pi} \qquad \text{for } n = 1, 5, 9, \ldots$$

$$a_n = -\frac{2}{n\pi} \quad \text{for } n = 3, 7, 11, \ldots$$

$$\therefore f(t) = \frac{1}{2} + \frac{2}{\pi}\left(\cos \omega t - \frac{1}{3}\cos 3\omega t + \frac{1}{5}\cos 5\omega t - \frac{1}{7}\cos 7\omega t + \ldots\right) \ldots\textbf{Ans.}$$

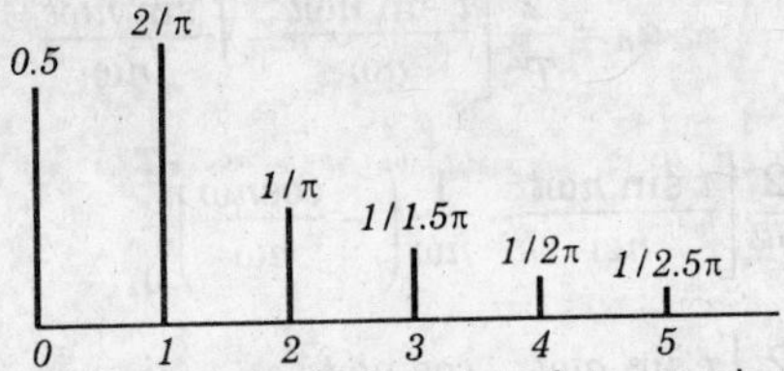

Fig. 13.7.3(a) Amplitude Spectrum for example 13.7.3

**Example. 13.7.4** *Obtain the Fourier series expansion. The saw-tooth waver form is shown in Fig. 13.7.4. Plot amplitude and phase spectra.*

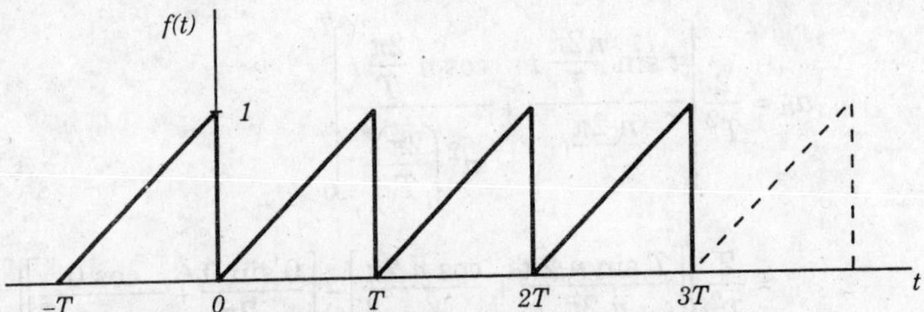

Fig. 13.7.4 Saw-tooth waveform for example 13.7.4

1. $$a_0 = \frac{1}{T}\int_0^T f(t)\,dt$$

$$= \frac{1}{T}\int_0^T \frac{1}{T}\,.\,t\,dt$$

$$= \frac{1}{T}\left[\frac{1}{T}\cdot\frac{t^2}{2}\right]_0^T$$

$$= 0.5$$

2. $$a_n = \frac{2}{T}\int_0^T f(t)\cos n\omega t\,dt.$$

$$= \frac{2}{T}\int_0^T \frac{1}{T}\,.\,t\cos n\omega t\,dt.$$

$$= \frac{2}{T^2}\int_0^T t\,.\cos n\omega t\,dt.$$

Let $u = t$ and $dv = \cos n\omega t\,dt$

$$\therefore \quad du = 1 \text{ and } v = \int \cos n\,\omega t\, dt = \frac{\sin n\omega t}{n\omega}$$

$$\int u dv = uv - \int v du$$

$$\therefore \quad a_n = \frac{2}{T^2}\left[\frac{t \sin n\omega t}{n\omega} - \int \frac{\sin n\omega t}{n\omega} \cdot 1\, dt\right]_0^T$$

$$= \frac{2}{T^2}\left[\frac{t \sin n\omega t}{n\omega} - \frac{1}{n\omega}\left(-\frac{\cos n\omega}{n\omega}\right)\right]_0^T$$

$$= \frac{2}{T^2}\left[\frac{t \sin n\omega t}{n\omega} + \frac{\cos n\omega t}{n^2\omega^2}\right]_0^T$$

put $\omega = \frac{2\pi}{T}$

$$\therefore \quad a_n = \frac{2}{T^2}\left[\frac{t \sin \frac{n2\pi}{T} t}{\frac{n\,2\pi}{T}} + \frac{\cos n\,\frac{2\pi}{T} t}{n^2\left(\frac{2\pi}{T}\right)^2}\right]_0^T$$

$$= \frac{2}{T^2}\left\{\left[\frac{T \sin n\,2\pi}{\frac{n\,2\pi}{T}} + \frac{\cos n\,2\pi}{n^2\left(\frac{2\pi}{T}\right)^2}\right] - \left[\frac{0 \sin 0}{n\frac{2\pi}{T}} + \frac{\cos 0}{n^2\left(\frac{2\pi}{T}\right)^2}\right]\right\}$$

$$= \frac{2}{T^2}\left\{\left[0 + \frac{+1}{n^2\left(\frac{2\pi}{T}\right)^2}\right] - \left[0 + \frac{1}{n^2\left(\frac{2\pi}{T}\right)^2}\right]\right\}$$

or $\quad a_n = 0$

3. $$b_n = \frac{2}{T}\int_0^T f(t) \sin n\omega t\, dt$$

$$= \frac{2}{T}\int_0^T \frac{1}{T} \cdot t \sin n\omega t\, dt$$

$$= \frac{2}{T^2}\int_0^T t \sin n\omega t\, dt$$

Let $\quad u = t \text{ and } dv = \sin n\omega t$

$$\therefore \quad du = 1 \text{ and } v = \int \sin n\omega t = -\frac{\cos n\omega t}{n\omega}$$

$$\int u dv = uv - \int v du$$

$$\therefore \quad b_n = \frac{2}{T^2}\left[-\frac{t\cos n\omega t}{n\omega} - \int -\frac{\cos n\omega t}{n\omega} \cdot 1 \cdot dt\right]_0^T$$

$$= \frac{2}{T^2}\left[-\frac{t\cos n\omega t}{n\omega} + \frac{\sin n\omega t}{n^2\omega^2}\right]_0^T$$

put $\omega = \dfrac{2\pi}{T}$

$$\therefore \quad b_n = \frac{2}{T^2}\left[\left(\frac{-T\cos n\frac{2\pi}{T}.T}{n\cdot\frac{2\pi}{T}} + \frac{\sin n\frac{2\pi}{T}.T}{n^2\left(\frac{2\pi}{T}\right)^2}\right) - \left(\frac{-0\ \omega s\ 0}{n\omega} + \frac{\sin 0}{n^2(2\pi/T)^2}\right)\right]$$

$$= \frac{2}{T^2}\left[\left(-\frac{T\cos 2\pi n}{n\frac{2\pi}{T}} + 0\right) - (0+0)\right]$$

or $$b_n = -\frac{1}{n\pi}$$

$$\therefore \quad f(t) = a_0 + \sum_{n=1}^{\infty} b_n \sin n\omega t$$

or $$f(t) = 0.5 - \frac{1}{\pi}\sin\omega t - \frac{1}{2\pi}\sin 2\omega t - \frac{1}{3\pi}\sin 3\omega t \ \dots \textbf{Ans.}$$

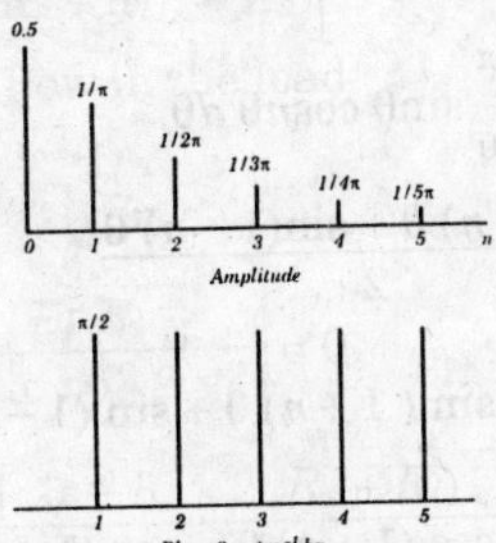


Fig. 13.7.4 (*a*) Line spectra for example 13.7.4

**Example 13.7.5.** *Obtain Fourier series for the full-wave rectified sinusoidal voltage shown in Fig. 13.7.5*

**Solution:** $f(\theta) = E_m \sin\theta, \quad 0 \le \theta \le \pi,$

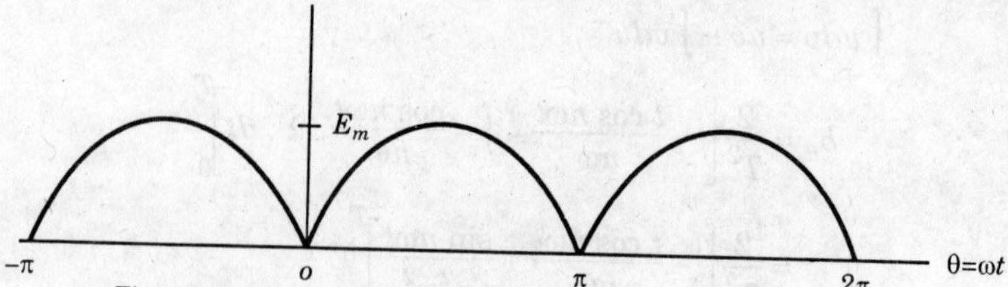


Fig. 13.7.5 Full-wave rectified sine wave for example 13.7.5.

$f(\theta)$ is an even function. Therefore, $b_n = 0$

**1. The Fourier coefficient $a_0$**

$$a_0 = \frac{1}{\pi}\int_0^{\pi} f(\theta)\, d\theta$$

$$= \frac{1}{\pi}\int_0^{\pi} E_m \sin\theta\, d\theta$$

$$= \frac{E_m}{\pi}[-\cos\theta]_0^{\pi}$$

$$= \frac{E_m}{\pi}[-(-1-1)]$$

$$= \frac{2E_m}{\pi}$$

**2. The Fourier coefficient $a_n$**

$$a_n = \frac{2}{\pi}\int_0^{\pi} f(\theta)\cos n\theta\, d\theta$$

$$= \frac{2}{\pi}\int_0^{\pi} E_m \sin\theta \cos n\theta\, d\theta$$

$$= \frac{2E_m}{\pi}\int_0^{\pi} \sin\theta \cos n\theta\, d\theta$$

$$\because \sin\theta\cos n\theta = \frac{\sin(1+n)\theta + \sin(1-n)\theta}{2}$$

$$\therefore \quad a_n = \frac{E_m}{\pi}\int_0^{\pi} [\sin(1+n)\theta + \sin(1-n)\theta]\, d\theta$$

$$= \frac{E_m}{\pi}\left[-\frac{\cos(1+n)\theta}{1+n} - \frac{\cos(1-n)\theta}{1-n}\right]_0^{\pi}$$

$$= -\frac{E_m}{\pi}\left[\frac{\cos(1+n)\theta}{1+n} + \frac{\cos(1-n)\theta}{1-n}\right]_0^{\pi}$$

$$= -\frac{E_m}{\pi}\left[\frac{\cos(1+n)\pi}{1+n} - \frac{\cos(1+n)\,0}{1+n} + \frac{\cos(1-n)\pi}{1-n} - \frac{\cos(1-n)0}{1-n}\right]$$

$$= -\frac{E_m}{\pi}\left[\frac{\cos(1+n)\pi}{1+n} + \frac{\cos(1-n)\,\pi}{1-n} - \frac{1}{1+n)} - \frac{1}{1-n}\right]$$

For odd values of $n$ except $n = 1$ $\quad a_n = 0$

The coefficient $a_1$ is determined below :

$$a_1 = \frac{1}{\pi}\int_0^{\pi} f(\theta)\cos\theta\, d\theta$$

$$= \frac{1}{\pi}\int_0^{\pi} E_m \sin\theta\cos\theta\, d\theta$$

$$\because \sin\theta\cos\theta = \frac{\sin 2\theta}{2}$$

$$\therefore \quad a_1 = \frac{E_m}{2\pi}\int_0^{\pi}\frac{\sin 2\theta}{2}\, d\theta$$

$$= \frac{E_m}{2\pi}\left[-\frac{\cos 2\theta}{2}\right]_0^{\pi}$$

$$= -\frac{E_m}{2\pi}[1-1], \quad \therefore \; a_1 = 0$$

For even values $n = 2, 4, 6, \ldots$

$$a_{2,4,6,\ldots} = -\frac{E_m}{\pi}\left[-\frac{1}{1+n} - \frac{1}{1-n} - \frac{1}{1+n} - \frac{1}{1-n}\right]$$

$$= \frac{4\,E_m}{\pi(1-n^2)}$$

$$f(\theta) = a_0 + a_2\cos 2\theta + a_4\cos 4\theta + a_6\cos 6\theta + \ldots$$

$$= \frac{2\,E_m}{\pi} - \frac{4\,E_m}{3\pi}\cos 2\theta - \frac{4\,E_m}{15\pi}\cos 4\theta - \frac{4E_m}{35\pi}\cos 6\theta \ldots$$

$$\because \quad \theta = \omega t$$

or $$f(t) = \frac{2\,E_m}{\pi} - \frac{4\,E_m}{3\pi}\cos 2\omega t - \frac{4\,E_m}{15\pi}\cos 4\omega t - \frac{4E_m}{35\pi}\cos 6\omega t \ldots$$ **Ans.**

**Example 13.7.6.** *The half-rectified sinusoidal voltage waveform is shown in Fig. 13.7.6. Determine the trigonometric form of Fourier series.*

*Fig. 13.7.5*

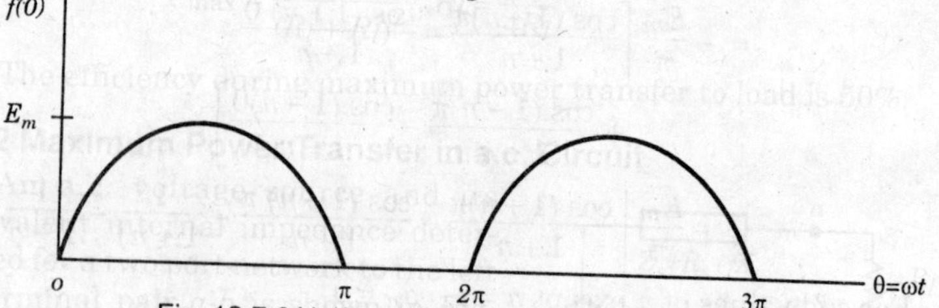


Fig. 13.7.6 Half-rectified wave for example 13.7.6

**Solution:** The function $f(\theta)$ does not possess any wave symmetry.

$$f(\theta) = E_m \sin\theta \ , \quad 0 \le \theta \le \pi$$
$$= 0 \qquad , \quad \pi \le \theta \le 2\pi$$

**1. The coefficient $a_0$**

$$a_0 = \frac{1}{2\pi}\int_0^{2\pi} f(\theta)\, d\theta = \frac{1}{2\pi}\left[\int_0^{2\pi} E_m \sin\theta\, d\theta + \int_\pi^{2\pi} 0 d\theta\right]$$

$$= \frac{E_m}{2\pi}\int_0^{\pi} \sin\theta\, d\theta$$

$$= \frac{E_m}{2\pi}(-\cos\theta)_0^{\pi} = \frac{E}{2\pi}[-(\cos\pi - \cos 0)]$$

$$= \frac{E_m}{2\pi}[-(-1-1)] = \frac{E_m}{\pi}$$

**2. The coefficient $a_n$**

$$a_n = \frac{2}{2\pi}\left[\int_0^{\pi} E_m \sin\theta \cos n\theta\, d\theta + \int_\pi^{2\pi} 0\, d\theta\right]$$

$$= \frac{E_m}{\pi}\int_0^{\pi} \sin\theta \cos n\theta\, d\theta$$

$$\because \sin\theta \cos n\theta = \frac{\sin(1+n)\theta + \sin(1-n)\theta}{2}$$

$$\therefore \quad a_n = \frac{E_m}{2\pi}\int_0^{\pi} [\sin(1+n)\theta + \sin(1-n)\theta]\, d\theta$$

$$= \frac{E_m}{2\pi}\left[-\frac{\cos(1+n)\theta}{1+n} - \frac{\cos(1-n)\theta}{1-n}\right]_0^{\pi}$$

$$= \frac{E_m}{2\pi}\left\{-\left[\frac{\cos(1+n)\pi}{1+n} - \frac{\cos(1+n)0}{1+n}\right] - \left[\frac{\cos(1-n)\pi}{1-n} - \frac{\cos(1-n)0}{1-n}\right]\right\}$$

$$= \frac{E_m}{2\pi}\left[-\frac{\cos(1+n)\pi}{1+n} + \frac{1}{1+n} - \frac{\cos(1-n)\pi}{1-n} + \frac{1}{1-n}\right]$$

For odd values of $n = 3, 5, 7, \ldots$ except $n = 1$

$$a_{3,5,7\ldots} = \frac{E_m}{2\pi}\left[-\frac{1}{1+n} + \frac{1}{1+n} - \frac{1}{1-n} + \frac{1}{1-n}\right] = 0$$

For even values of $n = 2, 4, 6, \ldots$

$$a_{2,4,6,\ldots} = \frac{E_m}{2\pi}\left[\frac{1}{1+n} + \frac{1}{1+n} + \frac{1}{1-n} + \frac{1}{1-n}\right] = \frac{2E_m}{\pi(1-n^2)}$$

For $n = 1$

$$a_1 = \frac{2}{2\pi}\left[\int_0^{\pi} E_m \sin\theta\cos\theta\, d\theta + \int_{\pi}^{2\pi} 0\, d\theta\right]$$

$$= \frac{E_m}{\pi}\int_0^{\pi} \sin\theta\cos\theta\, d\theta$$

$$\because \sin\theta\cos\theta = \frac{\sin 2\theta}{2}$$

$$\therefore \quad a_1 = \frac{E_m}{2\pi}\int_0^{\pi} \sin 2\theta\, d\theta$$

$$= \frac{E_m}{2\pi}\left[-\frac{\cos 2\theta}{2}\right]_0^{\pi}$$

$$= \frac{E_m}{2\pi}\left[-\left(\frac{\cos 2\pi}{2} - \frac{\cos 2\times 0}{2}\right)\right]$$

$$= \frac{E_m}{2\pi}\left[-\left(\frac{1}{2} - \frac{1}{2}\right)\right]$$

$$= 0$$

**3. The coefficient $b_n$**

$$b_n = \frac{2}{2\pi}\left[\int_0^{\pi} E_m \sin\theta \sin n\theta\, d\theta + \int_{\pi}^{2\pi} 0\, d\theta\right]$$

$$= \frac{E_m}{\pi}\int_0^{\pi} \sin\theta \sin n\theta\, d\theta$$

$$\because \sin\theta\sin n\theta = \frac{\cos(1-n)\theta - \cos(1+n)\theta}{2}$$

$$\therefore \quad b_n = \frac{E_m}{2\pi}\int_0^{\pi} [\cos(1-n)\theta - \cos(1+n)\theta]\, d\theta$$

$$= \frac{E_m}{2\pi}\left[\frac{\sin(1-n)\theta}{1-n} - \frac{\sin(1+n)\theta}{1+n}\right]_0^{\pi}$$

$$= \frac{E_m}{2\pi}\left[\frac{\sin(1-n)\pi}{1-n} - \frac{\sin(1-n)\,0}{1-n} - \frac{\sin(1+n)\pi}{1+n} + \frac{\sin(1+n)0}{1+n}\right]$$

$\therefore \quad b_n = 0 \quad$ for $\; n = 2, 3, 4, \ldots$

For $n = 1$

$$b_1 = \frac{2}{2\pi}\left[\int_0^{\pi} E_m \sin\theta \sin\theta \, d\theta + \int_{\pi}^{2\pi} 0 \, d\theta\right]$$

$$= \frac{E_m}{\pi}\int_0^{\pi} \sin^2\theta \, d\theta = \frac{E_m}{\pi}\int_0^{\pi}\left(\frac{1-\cos 2\theta}{2}\right)d\theta$$

$$= \frac{E_m}{2\pi}\left[\theta - \frac{\sin 2\theta}{2}\right]_0^{\pi} = \frac{E_m}{2\pi}\left[(\pi - 0) - \frac{(\sin 2\pi - \sin 2\times 0)}{2}\right]$$

$$= \frac{E_m}{2\pi}\left[(\pi - 0) - \frac{(0-0)}{2}\right]$$

$$\therefore \quad b_1 = \frac{E_m}{2}$$

$$f(\theta) = a_0 + (a_2 \cos 2\theta + a_4 \cos 4\theta + a_6 \cos 6\theta + \ldots) + b_1 \sin\theta$$

$$= \frac{E_m}{\pi} + \left(\frac{2}{3\pi}E_m \cos 2\theta + \frac{2E_m}{15\pi}\cos 4\theta + \frac{2E_m}{35\pi}\cos 6\theta + \ldots\right) + \frac{E_m}{2}\sin\theta$$

$\because \quad \theta = \omega t$

or $$f(t) = \frac{E_m}{\pi}\left[\left(1 - \frac{2}{3}\cos 2\omega t + \frac{2}{15}\cos 4\omega t + \frac{2}{35}\cos 6\omega t + \ldots\right) + \frac{\pi}{2}\sin\omega t\right]$$

... **Ans.**

**Example 13.7.7** *Determine the Fourier coefficients for the waveform shown in Fig. 13.7.7 and write the Fourier series expression.*

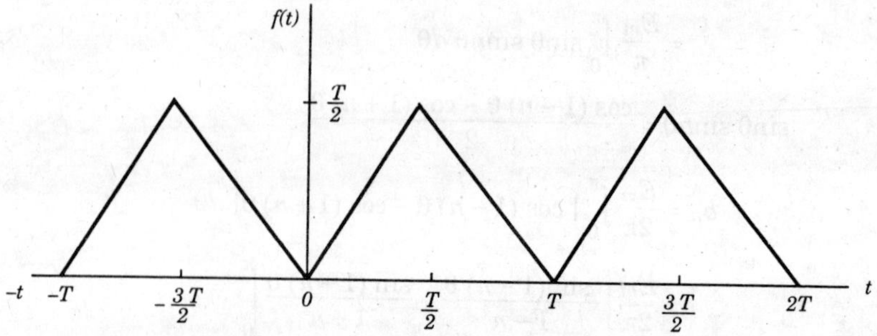


Fig. 13.7.7 Triangular waveform for example 13.7.7

**Solution.** The waveform $f(t)$ is not symmetrical about the time axise

(1) The coeffcient $a_0$

$$a_0 = \frac{Area}{Base} = \frac{1}{2} \cdot \frac{T \times T/2}{T}$$

$$\therefore \quad = \frac{T}{4}$$

The function $f(t)$ is an even function $[f(t) = f(-t)]$, therefore, the Fourier coefficient $a_n$ is to be determined.

(2) The coefficient $a_n$

$$a_n = \frac{4}{T}\int_0^{T/2} f(t) \cos n\omega t \, dt \text{ --- (for even function)}$$

$$f(t) = t \;, \; 0 \le t \le \frac{T}{2}$$

$$\therefore \quad a_n = \frac{4}{T}\int_0^{T/2} f(t) \cos n\omega t \, dt .$$

$$\int u dv = uv - \int v du$$

Let, $u = t$, $du = 1$

and $dv = \cos n\omega t$,

$$v = \int \cos n\omega t$$

$$= \frac{\sin n\omega t}{n\omega}$$

$$\therefore \quad a_n = \frac{4}{T}\left[\frac{t \sin n\omega t}{n\omega} - \int \frac{\sin n\omega t}{n\omega} . 1\, dt\right]_0^{\frac{T}{2}}$$

$$= \frac{4}{T}\left[\frac{t \sin n\omega t}{n\omega} + \frac{\cos n\omega t}{n^2\omega^2}\right]_0^{\frac{T}{2}}$$

$$= \frac{4}{T}\left[\frac{T/2 \sin n\frac{\omega T}{2} t}{n\omega} + \frac{\cos n\frac{\omega T}{2} t}{n^2\omega^2} - \frac{0 \sin n\omega \times 0}{n\omega} - \frac{\cos n\omega \times 0}{n^2\omega^2}\right]$$

$$\because \quad \omega T = 2\pi$$

$$a_n = \frac{4}{T}\left[\frac{T/2 \sin n\pi}{n\, 2\pi/T} + \frac{\cos n\pi}{n^2(2\pi/T)^2} - 0 - \frac{1}{n^2(2\pi/T)^2}\right]$$

$$= \frac{4}{T}\left[0 + \frac{\cos n\pi}{n\left(\frac{2\pi}{T}\right)^2} - 0 - \frac{1}{n^2\left(\frac{2\pi}{T}\right)^2}\right]$$

or $$a_n = \frac{T}{n^2\pi^2}\ (\cos n\pi - 1)$$

$\cos n\pi = 1 \quad$ for $\; n = 2, 4, 6, -----$

$\therefore\; a_{2,4,6,------} = 0$

$\cos n\pi = -1 \quad$ for $\; n = 1, 3, 5, -----$

$\therefore\; a_{1,3,5,-----} = -\dfrac{2T}{n^2\pi^2}$

$$f(t) = a_0 + a_2 \cos \omega t + a_3 \cos 3\omega t + a_5 \omega s\, 5\omega t + -----$$

or $$f(t) = \frac{T}{4} - \frac{2T}{\pi^2}\cos\omega t - \frac{2T}{9\pi^2}\cos 3\omega t$$

$$- \frac{2T}{25\pi^2}\cos 5\omega t ------ \textbf{ Ans.}$$

**Example 13.7.8** *Determine Fourier Series for the waveform shown in Fig. 13.7.8*

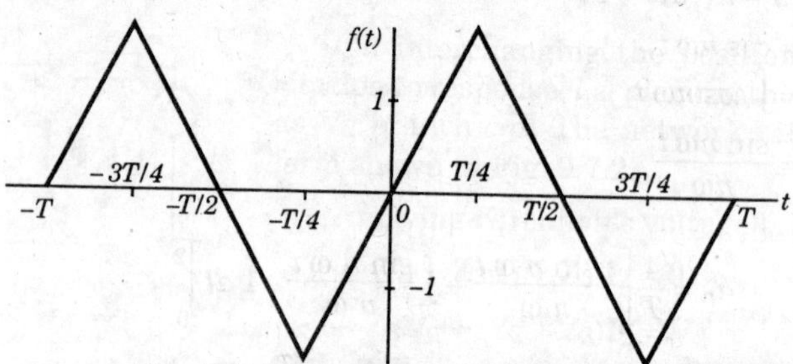


Fig. 13.7.8 Waveform for example 13.7.8

**Solution.** The function $f(t)$ is symmetrical about the time axis. Thus,

$$a_0 = 0$$

The function possesses half wave symmetry, contains odd harmonic terms.

The function is odd $[f(t)] = [-f(-t)]$, only the Fourier coefficient $b_n$ is to be determineal

$$b_n = \frac{4}{T}\int_{-\frac{T}{4}}^{\frac{T}{4}} f(t)\sin n\omega t\, dt \qquad \text{(for odd function)}$$

$$f(t) = \frac{4}{T} \cdot t \quad \text{from } t = -\frac{T}{4} \text{ to } t = \frac{T}{4}$$

$$\therefore \quad b_n = \frac{4}{T}\int_{-\frac{T}{4}}^{\frac{T}{4}} \frac{4}{T} \cdot t \ \sin n\,\omega\, t\, dt = \frac{16}{T^2}\int_{-\frac{T}{4}}^{\frac{T}{4}} t \sin n\,\omega\, t\, dt$$

Let, $\quad u = t \ , \ du = 1$

and $\quad dv = \sin n\,\omega\, t \ , \quad v = \int \sin n\,\omega\, t = -\dfrac{\cos n\,\omega t}{n\,\omega}$

$$\int u\, d\,v = u\,v - \int v\, du$$

$$\therefore \quad b_n = \frac{16}{T^2}\left[-\frac{t \cos n\omega\, t}{n\omega} - \int -\frac{\cos n\,\omega\, t}{n\omega} \cdot 1\, dt\right]_{-\frac{T}{4}}^{\frac{T}{4}}$$

$$= \frac{16}{T^2}\left[-\frac{t\cos n\omega\, t}{n\omega} + \frac{\sin n\,\omega\, t}{n^2\omega^2}\right]_{-\frac{T}{4}}^{\frac{T}{4}}$$

$$= \frac{16}{T^2}\left\{-\left[\frac{\frac{T}{4}\cos n\omega\frac{T}{4}}{n\omega} - \frac{\frac{T}{4}\cos(-n\,\omega\, T/4)}{n\omega}\right] + \left[\frac{\sin n\frac{\omega}{4}T}{n^2\omega^2} - \frac{\sin\left(-n\,\frac{\omega}{4}T\right)}{n^2\omega^2}\right]\right\}$$

$$= \frac{16}{T^2}\left\{-\frac{T}{4n\omega}\left[\cos n\,\frac{\omega}{4}\,T - \cos\left(-\frac{n\omega T}{4}\right)\right] + \frac{1}{n^2\omega^2}\left[\left(\sin n\,\frac{\omega}{4}\,T\right) - \sin\left(-\frac{n\,\omega\,T}{4}\right)\right]\right\}$$

$$\because \quad \omega T = 2\pi$$

$$= \frac{16}{T^2}\left\{-\frac{T^2}{4\,n \times 2\pi}\left[\cos\frac{n}{2}\pi - \cos\left(-\frac{n}{2}\pi\right)\right] + \frac{T^2}{n^2 4\pi^2}\left[\sin\frac{n\pi}{2} - \sin\left(-\frac{n\pi}{2}\right)\right]\right\}$$

$$= \frac{16}{T^2}\left\{-\frac{T^2}{8\,n\pi}\left[\cos\frac{n}{2}\pi - \cos\frac{n}{2}\pi\right] + \frac{T^2}{4n^2\pi^2}\left[\sin\frac{n\pi}{2} + \sin\frac{n\pi}{2}\right]\right\}$$

$$= \frac{16}{T^2}\left[-\frac{T^2}{8\,n\pi}(0) + \frac{2T^2}{4n^2\pi^2}\left(\sin\frac{n\pi}{2}\right)\right]$$

Or $\quad b_n = \frac{8}{n^2\pi^2}\sin\frac{n\pi}{2}$, for $n = 2, 4, 6$, $\sin\frac{n\pi}{2} = 0$

$\therefore\ b_{2,4,6,------} = 0$

for $\quad n = 1, 5, 9, ------,\ \sin\frac{n\pi}{2} = 1$

and $\quad n = 3, 7, 11, ------, \sin\frac{n\pi}{2} = -1$

$\therefore\ b_{1,5,9,---} = \frac{8}{n^2\pi^2}$ and $b_{3,7,11---}, = -\frac{8}{n^2\pi^2}$

$$f(t) = b_1 \sin\omega t + b_3 \sin 3\omega t + b_5 \sin 5\omega t + b_7 \sin 7\omega t + ------$$

$$= \frac{8}{\pi^2}\sin\omega t - \frac{8}{3^2\pi^2}\sin 3\omega t + \frac{8}{5^2\pi^2}\sin 5\omega t - \frac{8}{7^2\pi^2}\sin 7\omega t + ----$$ **Ans.**

**Example 13.7.9.** *Determine exponential form of Fourier series for the waveform shown in Fig. 13.7.9.*

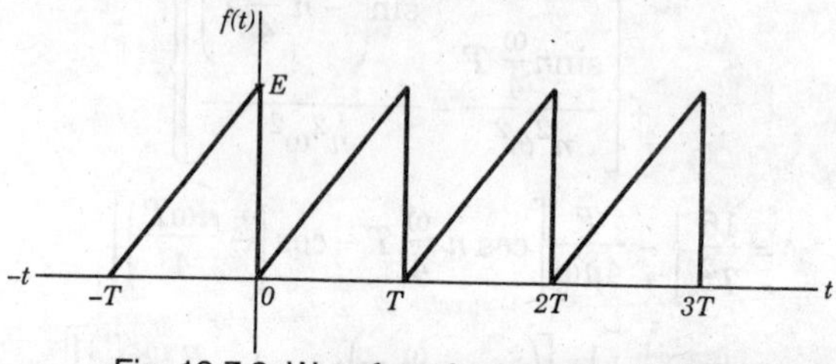


Fig. 13.7.9 Waveform for example 13.7.9.

**Solution:** $f(t) = \frac{V}{T}\cdot t$

(1) $\quad C_0 = \frac{1}{T}\int_0^T f(t)\,dt = \frac{1}{T}\int_0^T \frac{E}{T}\cdot t\,dt = \frac{E}{T_2}\left[\frac{t^2}{2}\right]_0^T$

$$= \frac{E}{2}$$

(2) $\quad \overline{C}_n = \frac{1}{T}\int_0^T f(t)\,e^{-j\,n\omega t}\,dt = \frac{1}{T}\int_0^T \frac{E}{T}\cdot t\,e^{-j\,n\omega t}\,dt$

$$= \frac{E}{T^2}\int_0^T t\, e^{-jn\omega t}\, dt$$

$$\int u\, dv = u\, v - \int v\, du$$

put $u = t$ , $du = 1$

and $\quad dv = e^{-jn\omega t}$ , $v = \dfrac{e^{-jn\omega t}}{-jn\omega t}$

$$= \frac{E}{T^2}\left[\frac{t\, e^{-jn\omega t}}{-jn\omega} - \int \frac{e^{-jn\omega t}}{-jn\omega}.\, 1\, dt\right]_0^T$$

$$= \frac{E}{T^2}\left[\frac{jt\, e^{-jn\omega t}}{n\,\omega} - \frac{e^{-jn\omega t}}{(-jn\omega)\,(-jn\omega)}\right]_0^T$$

$$= \frac{E}{T^2}\left[\frac{jt\, e^{-jn\omega t}}{n\,\omega} + \frac{e^{-jn\omega t}}{n^2\omega^2}\right]_0^T = \frac{E}{T^2}\left[\frac{e^{-jn\omega t}}{n^2\omega^2}\,(j\, n\omega\, t + 1)\right]_0^T$$

$$= \frac{E}{T^2\, n^2\, \omega^2}\left[e^{-jn\omega T}(jn\omega\, T + 1) - e^{-jn\omega \times 0}\,(jn\omega \times 0 + 1)\right]$$

$$= \frac{E}{T^2\, n^2\, \omega^2}\left[j\, n\, \omega\, T\, e^{-jn\omega T} + e^{-jn\omega T} - 1\right]$$

$\because \quad \omega T = 2\pi$

$$\therefore \quad \overline{C}_n = \frac{E}{n^2(2\,\pi)^2}\left[j\, n 2\pi\, e^{-jn2\pi} + e^{-jn2\pi} - 1\right]$$

$$= \frac{E}{n^2(2\pi)^2}\,[\,j\, 2\pi\, n(\cos 2\pi\, n - j\sin 2\pi\, n)$$

$$+ (\cos 2\pi\, n - j\sin 2\pi\, n) - 1]$$

$\because \ \cos 2\pi\, n = 1$

and $\quad \sin 2\pi\, n = 0$

$$\therefore \quad \overline{C}_n = \frac{E}{n^2(2\pi)^2}\,[\,j\, 2\pi\, n(1 - 0) + (1 - 0) - 1]$$

$$= \frac{jE}{2\pi\, n} \quad \text{for } n \neq 0 \quad \text{and } \overline{C}_{-n} = \frac{-jE}{2\pi\, n} \quad \text{for } n \neq 0$$

The exponential form of Fourier series given below

$$f(t) = - - - \frac{-jE}{2 \times 5\pi}\, e^{-j5\omega t}\, \frac{-jE}{2 \times 4\pi}\, e^{-j4\omega t} - - - \frac{jE^{-j\omega t}}{2\pi} - - -$$

$$+ \frac{V}{2} + \frac{jE\, e^{j\omega t}}{2 \times \pi} + - - - - + \frac{jE\, e^{-jn\omega t}}{2 \times n\pi}$$

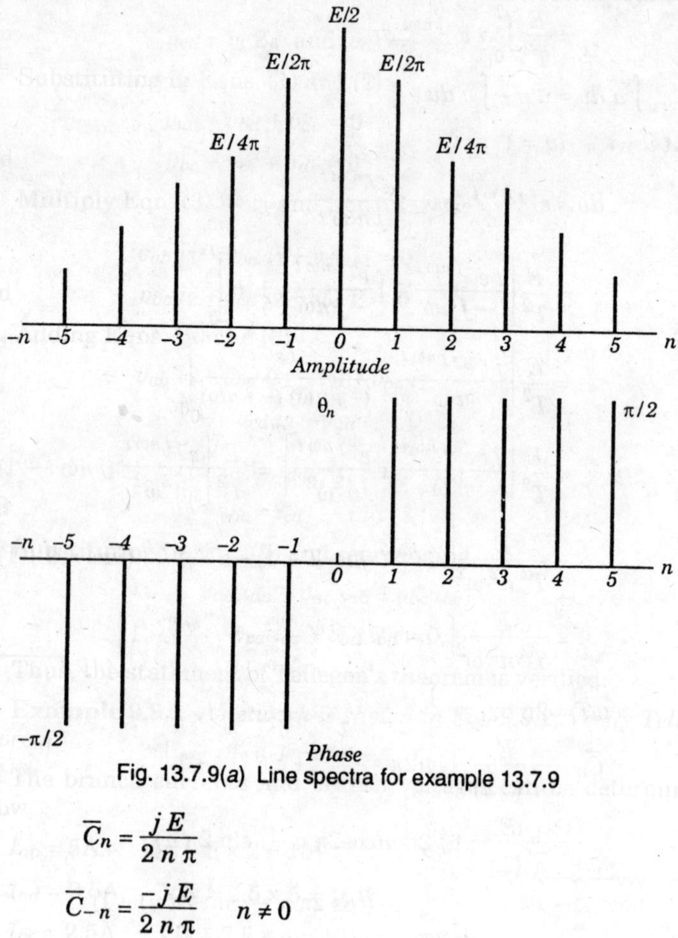


Fig. 13.7.9(a) Line spectra for example 13.7.9

$$\overline{C}_n = \frac{jE}{2n\pi}$$

$$\overline{C}_{-n} = \frac{-jE}{2n\pi} \qquad n \neq 0$$

$$\therefore \quad a_n = \overline{C}_n + \overline{C}_{-n} = 0$$

$$b_n = j(\overline{C}_n - \overline{C}_{-n}) = -\frac{E}{n\pi}$$

$$a_0 = E/2$$

$$\theta_n = -\tan^{-1}\frac{b_n}{a_n} = \frac{\pi}{2} \quad n = 1, 2, 3, ------$$

$$= -\frac{\pi}{2} \quad n = -1, -2, -3, ------$$

## PROBLEMS

**13.1** For the full wave rectified wave form shown in Fig. 13P-1 determine Fourier coefficients and plot amplitude spectrum.

$$\left[\textbf{Hint}: f(t) = E_m \cos\left(\frac{\omega t}{2}\right)\right]$$

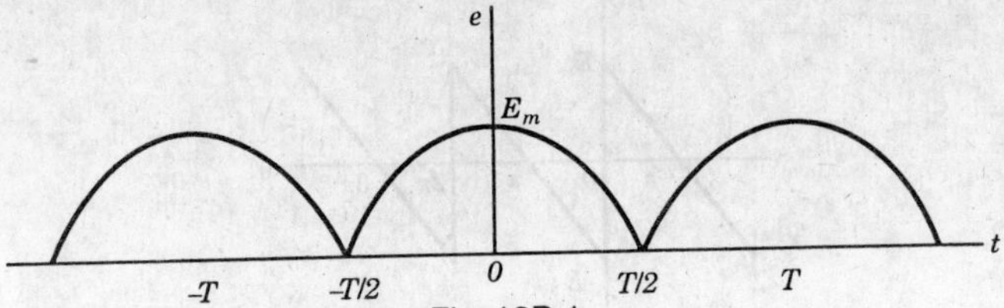


Fig. 13P-1

**Ans**. $a_0 = \frac{2\, E_m}{\pi}$ , $a_n = \frac{4\, E_m \cos n\pi}{\pi\,(1 - 4\, n^2)}$ , $n = 1 , 3 ,5 , -----$

$a_n = -\frac{4\, E_m \cos(n\pi)}{\pi\,(1 - 4\, n^2)}$ , $n = 2 , 4 ,6 ,----$

**13.2** Determine the Fourier series in trigonometric form for the waveform shown in Fig. 13P-2.

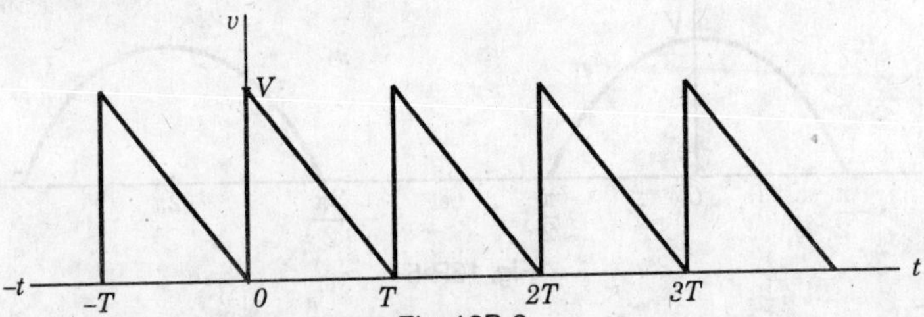


Fig. 13P-2

$\left(\textbf{Ans}: a_0 = \frac{V}{2} , b_n = \frac{V}{n\,\pi} , n = 1 , 2 ,3 , -----\right)$

**13.3** Expand the square wave voltage into trigonometric Fourier series form

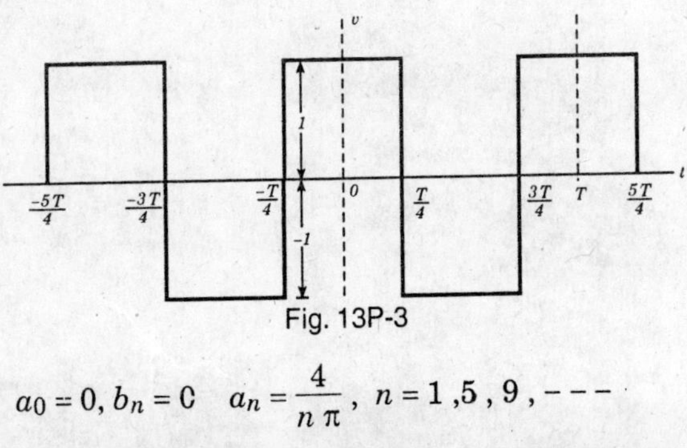


Fig. 13P-3

**Ans** : $a_0 = 0, b_n = 0 \quad a_n = \frac{4}{n\,\pi}$ , $n = 1 ,5 , 9 , ---$

$= -\frac{4}{n\,\pi}$ , $n = 3 , 7 , 11 ----$

**13.4** Determine the Fourier coefficients. The periodic waveform is shown in Fig. 13P-4.

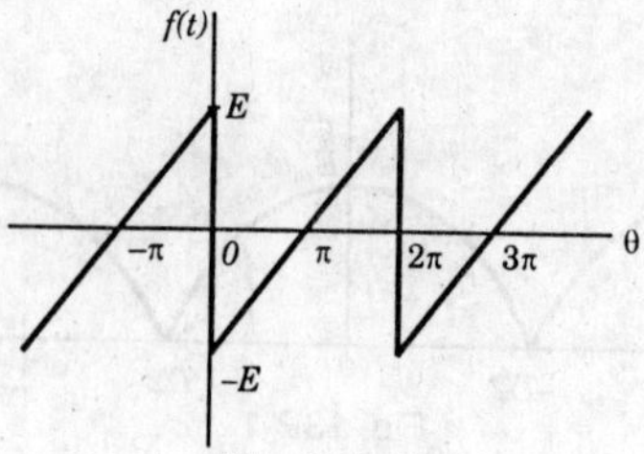


Fig. 13P-4

$$\left[ \textbf{Ans:} a_o = 0\ ,\ a_n = 0 \quad b_n = -\frac{2\pi}{n\pi} \quad n = 1, 2, 3, --- \right]$$

**13.5** Evaluate Fourier series expansion for the rectified wave form shown in Fig. 13P-5

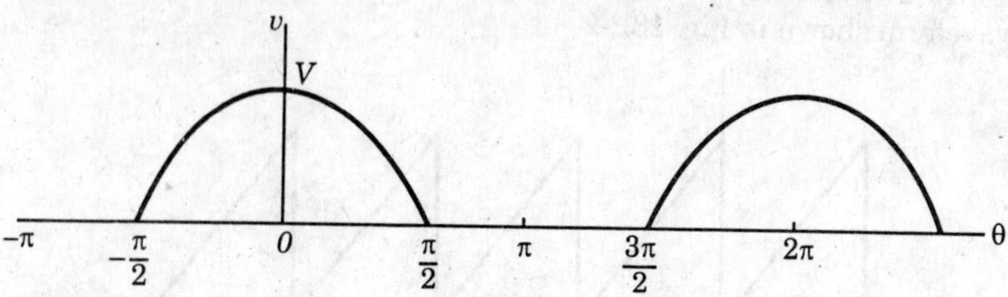


Fig. 13P-5

$$\left[ \textbf{Ans} : a_0 = \frac{V}{\pi}\ ,\ a_1 = \frac{V}{2} \quad a_n = \frac{2V\cos(n\pi/2)}{\pi(1-n^2)} \quad n = 2, 4, 6, -- \right]$$

# APPENDIX

## Objective Type Questions

(✓) Tick mark the correct answer.

**1.** The value of $R$ in the circuit given below is

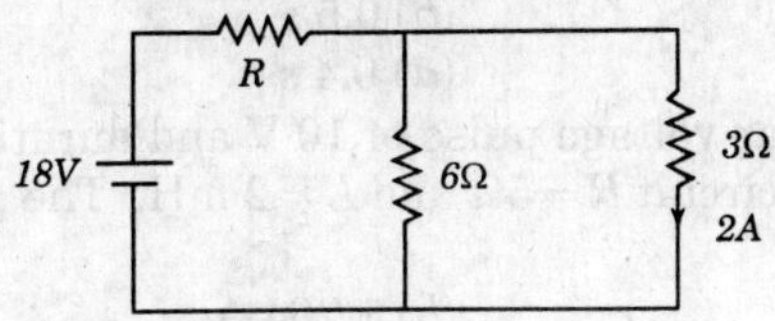


(a) 2 Ω (b) 9 Ω
(c) 4 Ω (d) 3 Ω

**2.** For the circuit given below to be in resonance at $f_0$ = 1000 Hz.

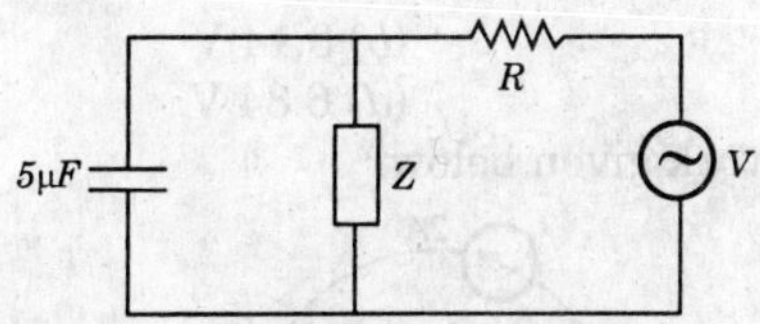


(a) $Z = j\dfrac{100}{\pi}\ \Omega$ (b) $Z = -j\dfrac{100}{\pi}\ \Omega$

(c) $Z = j\dfrac{200}{\pi}\ \Omega$ (d) $Z = -j\dfrac{50}{\pi}\ \Omega$

**3.** For the circuit shown the current **I** is.

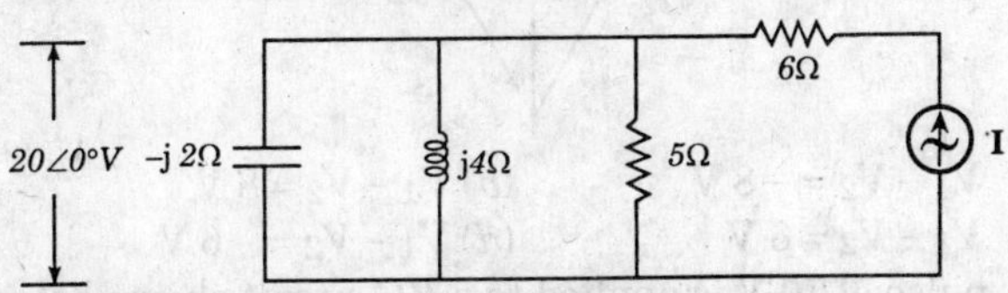


(a) (5 + j 4) A (b) (4 + j 5) A
(c) (3 + j 4) A (d) (4 + j 3) A

**4.** The time constant of the circuit given is

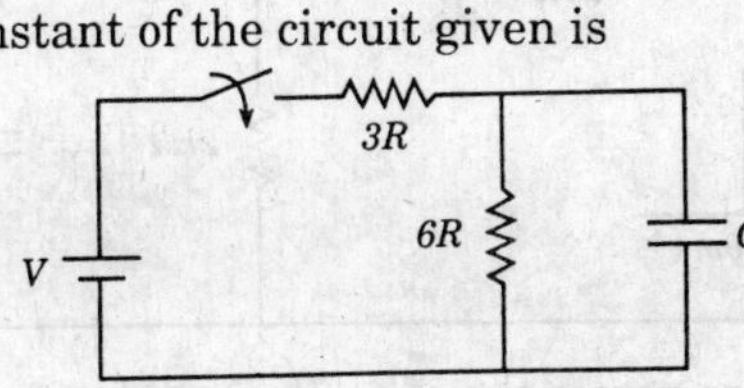

(*a*) 2 *RC* (*b*) *RC*/2
(*c*) 3 *RC* (*d*) 4 *RC*

**5.** The time constant for The given network is

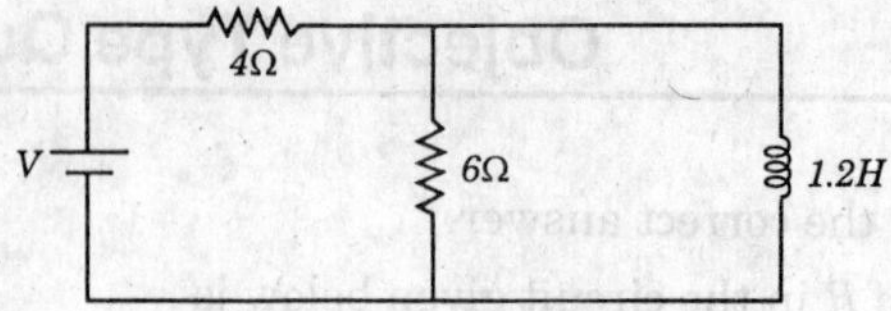


(*a*) 0.25 *s* (*b*) 0.5 *s*
(*c*) 0.025 *s* (*d*) 0.4 *s*

**6.** A rectangular voltage pulse of 10 V and duration 0 to 0.4 ms is applied to a series circuit $R = 5\Omega$ and $L = 2$ mH. The peak value of the current reached is

(*a*) 1.562 A (*b*) 1.264 A
(*c*) 1.414 A (*d*) 1.732 A

**7.** A rectangular voltage pulse of 10 V and duration 0 to 2ms is applied to a series circuit $R = 1$ kΩ and $c = 2$ μF. The peak value of the voltage across the capacitor is

(*a*) 6.28 V (*b*) 3.14 V
(*c*) 12.64 V (*d*) 6.84 V

**8.** In the network given below.

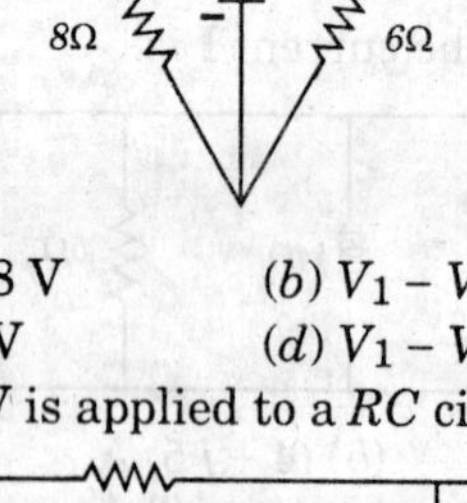


(*a*) $V_1 - V_2 = -8$ V (*b*) $V_1 - V_2 = 8$ V
(*c*) $V_1 - V_2 = 6$ V (*d*) $V_1 - V_2 = -6$ V

**9.** A pulse of 10 V is applied to a *RC* circuit shown below.

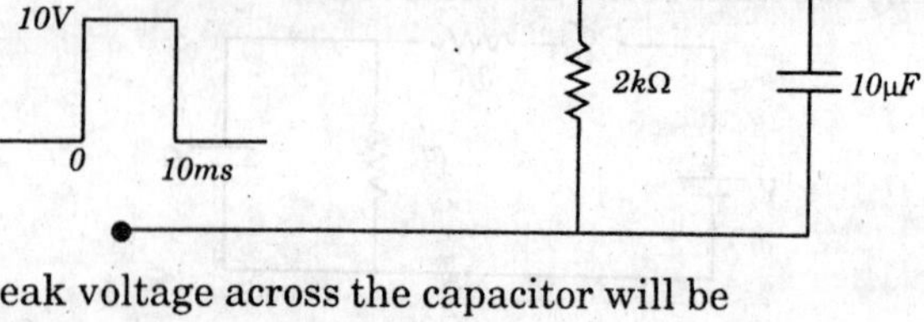


The peak voltage across the capacitor will be

(a) $\frac{10}{3}$ V (b) 5 V

(c) 3.16 V (d) 10 V

**10.** A rectangular pulse of magnitude $V$ and duration $T$ is applied to a series combination of resistor R and inductor L. The maximum current flowing in the circuit is

(a) $i_m = \frac{V}{R}(1 - e^{-RT/L})$ (b) $i_m = V\,T\,e^{-LT/R}$

(c) $i_m = \frac{V}{R}(1 - e^{-LT/R})$ (d) $i_m = \frac{V}{R}e^{-RT/L}$

**11.** The time constant for the network given below is

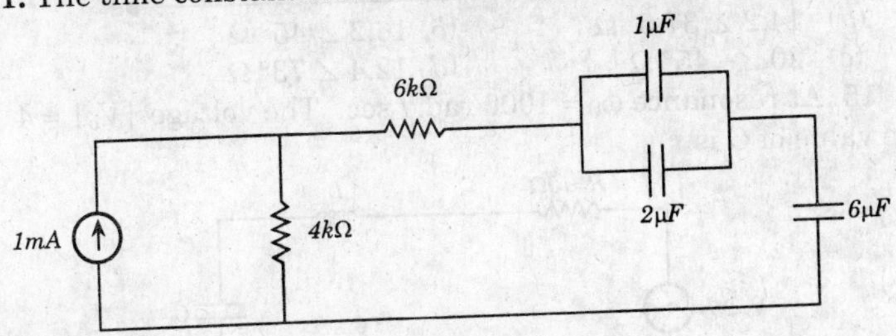


(a) 10 ms. (b) 12 ms.

(c) 20 ms. (d) 3 ms.

**12.** A set of two mutually coupled coils and $R = 8\ \Omega$, $X_c = -j\,6$ are connected in series as shown in figure given below. It is desired to have u.p.f. at the terminals. The value of $k$ is

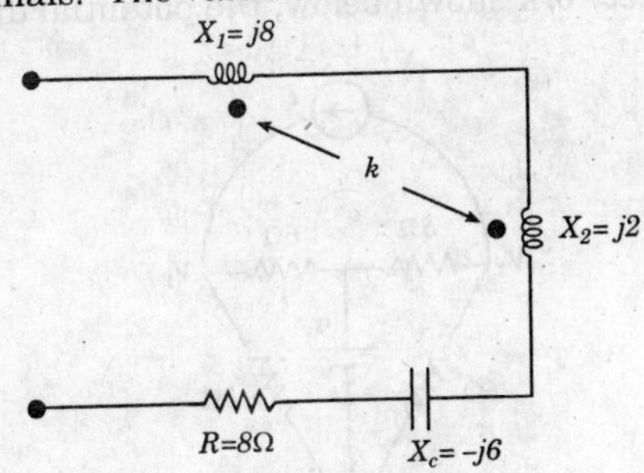


(a) $k = 0.125$ (b) $k = 0.5$

(c) $k = 0.2$ (d) $k = 0.4$

**13.** The most appropriate value of $\mathbf{Z}_{th}$ is

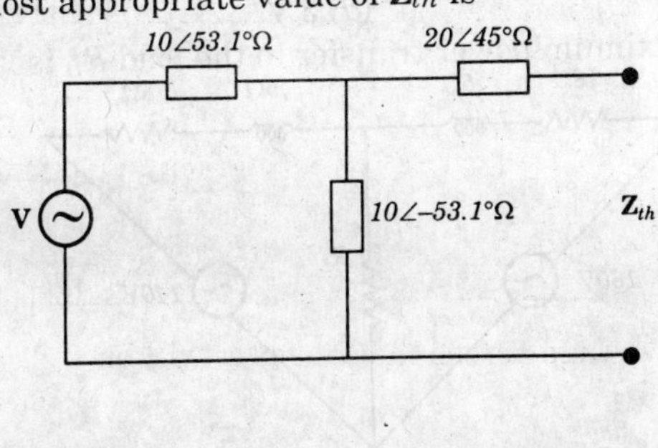

(a) 30 ∠ 45° Ω (b) 25 ∠ 40° Ω
(c) 26 ∠ 32° Ω (d) 20 ∠ 22.5° Ω

**14.** The value of $\mathbf{Z}_{eq}$ is

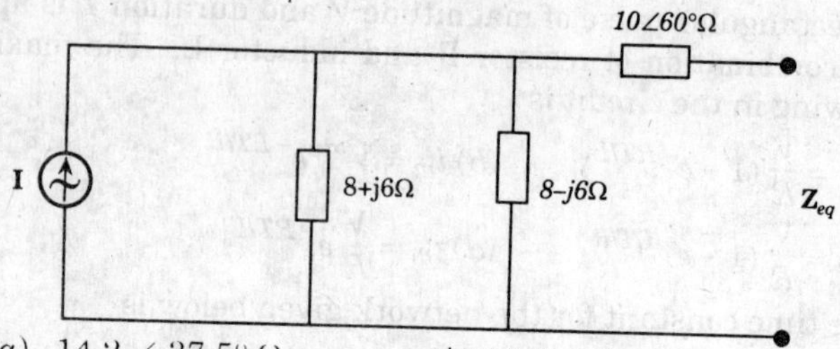


(a) 14.2 ∠ 37.5° Ω (b) 16.2 ∠ 45° Ω
(c) 20 ∠– 45° Ω (d) 12.4 ∠ 73° Ω

**15.** At resonance $\omega_0 = 1000$ rad. / sec. The voltage $|V_c| = 4\,|V_R|$. The value of $C$ is

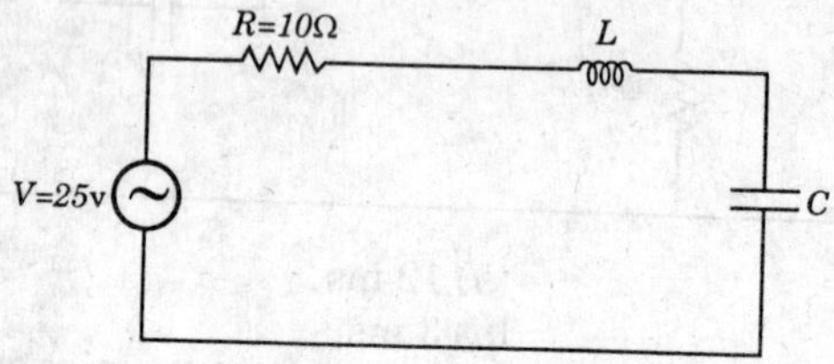


(a) 40 μ F (b) 25 μ F
(c) 35 μ F (d) 20 μ F

**16.** In the network shown below, the potential difference $(V_1 - V_2)$ is

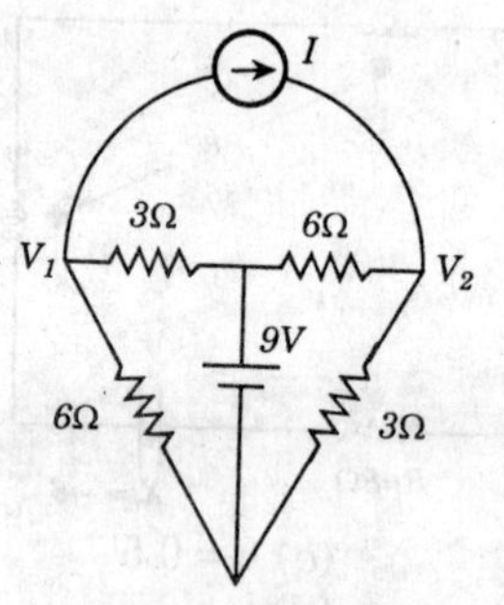


(a) 6 V (b) 4 V
(c) 4.5 V (d) 3 V

**17.** The maximum power transfer to the load $R_L$ is

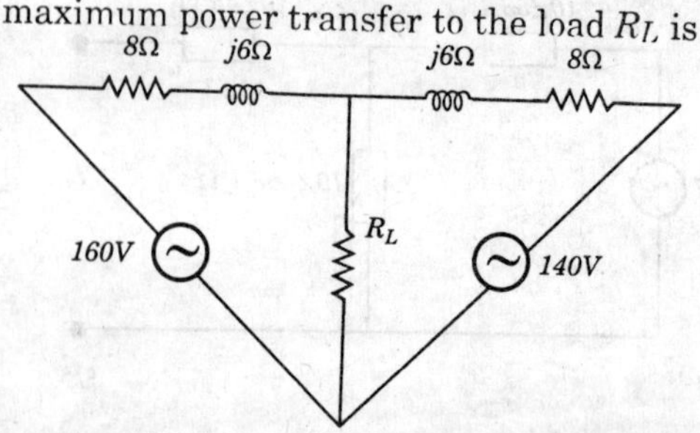

(a) 1250 W (b) 750 W
(c) 1000 W (d) 1500 W

**18.** The initial charge on the capacitor is 1.25 coulomb. The switch is closed at $t = 0$. The current flowing in the circuit at $t = 2.5$sec. will be,

(a) 5 mA (b) 0.1 A
(c) 54 mA (d) 2.5 mA

**19.** The expression for the voltage across the inductor is

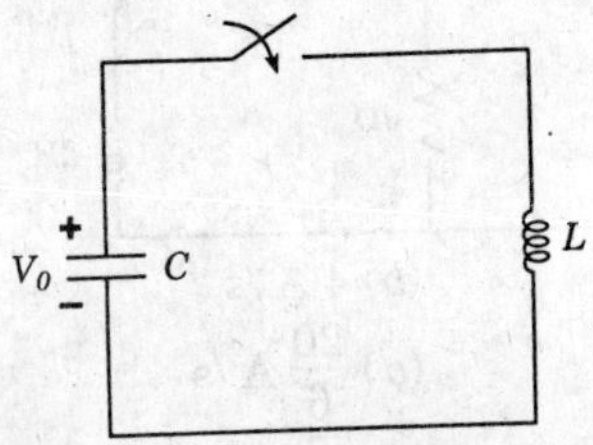


(a) $V_0 \sin \frac{t}{\sqrt{LC}}$ (b) $\frac{V_0}{L} \cos \frac{t}{\sqrt{LC}}$

(c) $\frac{V_0}{C} \cos \frac{t}{\sqrt{LC}}$ (d) $V_0 \cos \frac{t}{\sqrt{LC}}$

**20.** At resonance the phasor diagram for the circuit given below is,

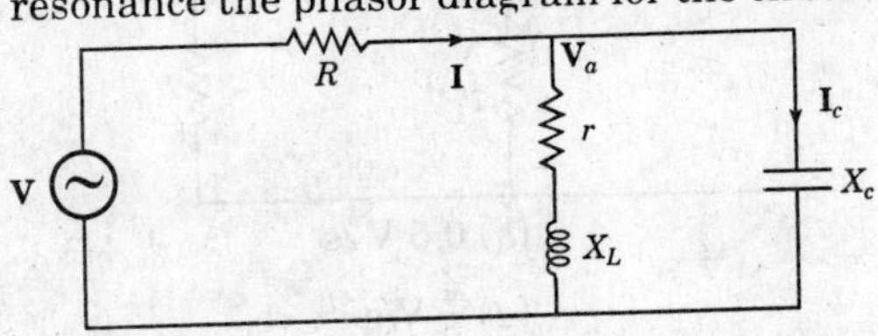


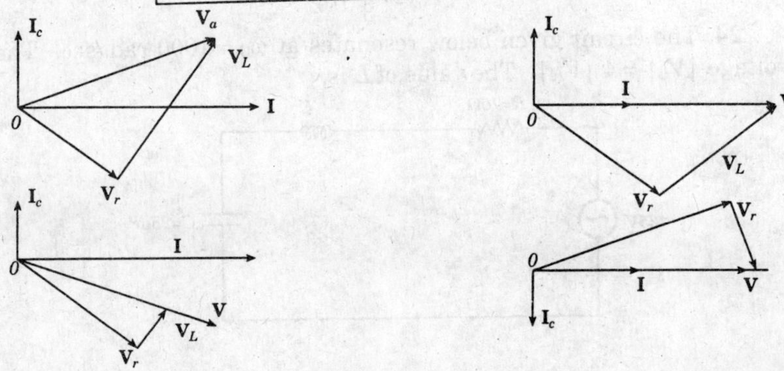

**21.** The network shown below remains in steady state. The current I equals,

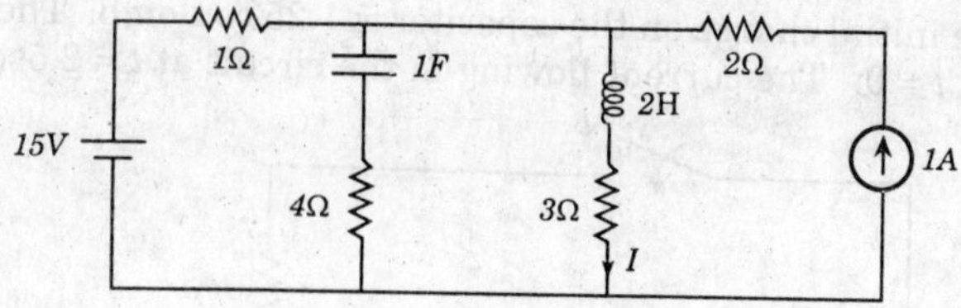


(*a*) 4 A (*b*) 5 A
(*c*) 1 A (*d*) 2 A

**22.** The switch is closed at $t = 0$, The $\dfrac{di\,(0^+)}{dt}$ equals

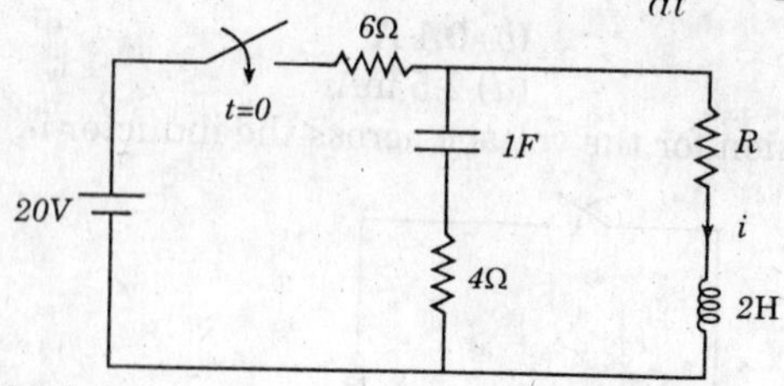


(*a*) 10 A/s (*b*) 4 A/s
(*c*) 5 A/s (*d*) $\dfrac{20}{6}$ A/s

**23.** The switch is closed at $t = 0$. The value of $\dfrac{dv\,(0^+)}{dt}$ is

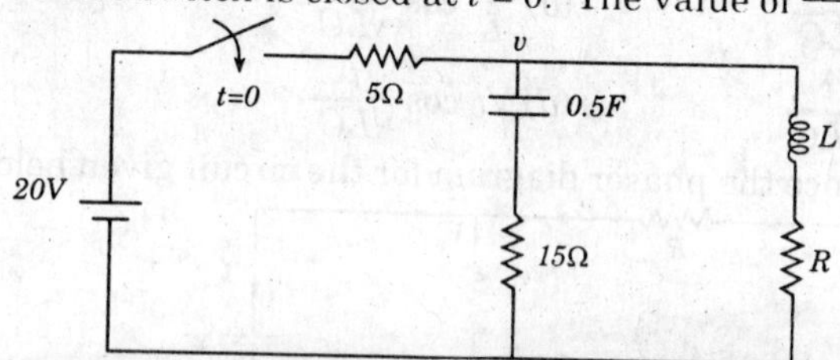


(*a*) 2 V/s (*b*) 0.5 V/s
(*c*) 4 V/s (*d*) $\dfrac{4}{3}$ V/s

**24.** The circuit given below resonates at $\omega_0 = 1000$ rad./sec. The voltage $|V_c| = 4\,|V_R|$. The value of $L$ is,

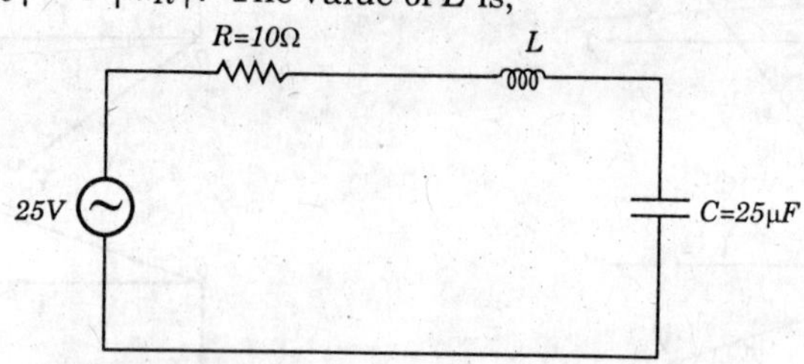

(a) 150 mH (b) 100 π mH

(c) $\frac{100}{\pi}$ mH (d) 100 mH

**25.** In the network shown below, for u.p.f.

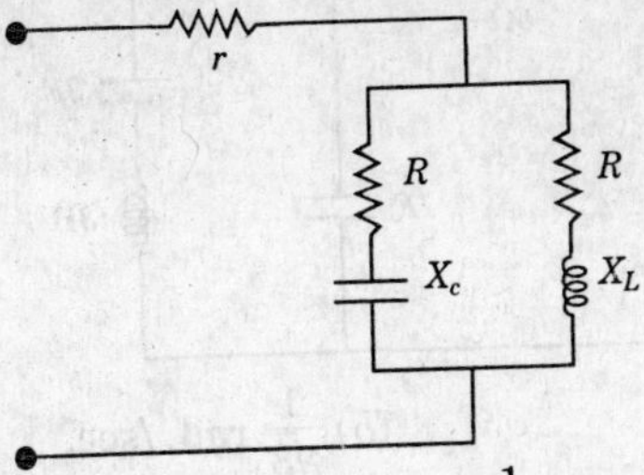


(a) $X_L = X_c$ (b) $X_L = \frac{1}{X_c}$

(c) $X_L < X_c$ (d) $X_L > X_c$

**26.** The time constant of the circuit shown below is,

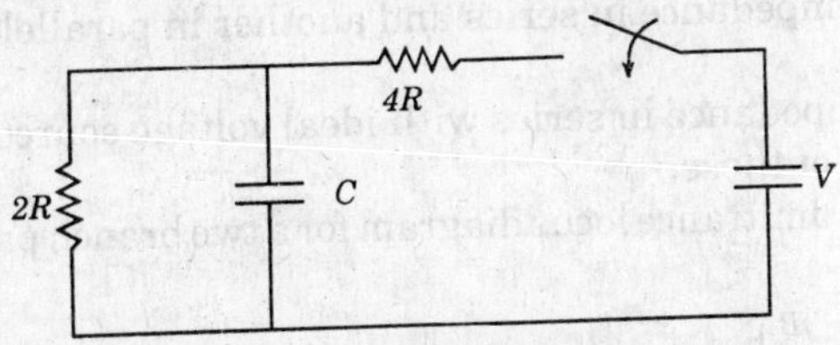


(a) $\frac{4\,RC}{3}$ (b) $\frac{3\,RC}{4}$

(c) $\frac{RC}{2}$ (d) $\frac{RC}{3}$

**27.** $V_{th}$ at terminals $a - b$ is

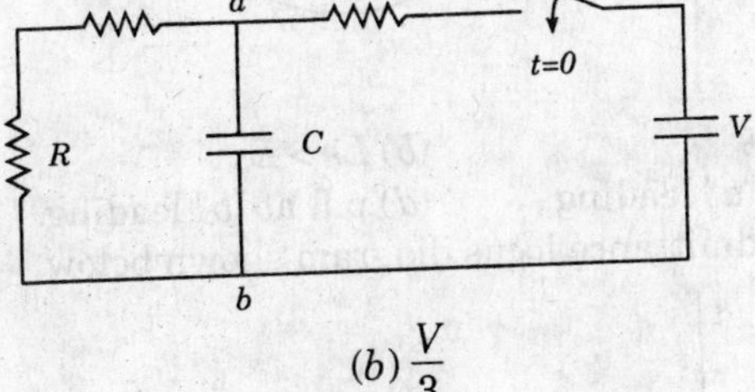


(a) $\frac{V}{4}$ (b) $\frac{V}{3}$

(c) 3 V (d) $\frac{V}{2}$

**28.** A series $RL$ circuit switched on to a d.c. supply voltage $V$. The rate of change of current at $t = 0$ is

(a) $e^{-(R/L)}$ (b) $\frac{V}{R}$

(c) $\frac{V}{L}$ (d) $e^{-\frac{L}{R}}$

**29.** The resonance frequency for the circuit given below is

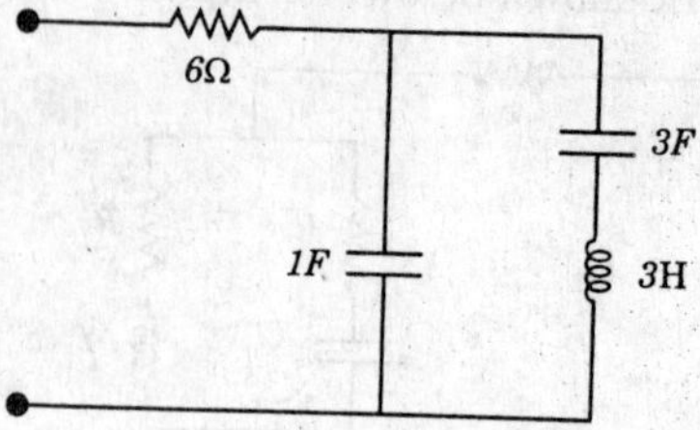


(a) $\sqrt{3}$ rad. /sec. (b) $\frac{1}{\sqrt{3}}$ rad. /sec.

(c) 3 rad. /sec. (d) $\frac{1}{3}$ rad. /sec.

**30.** The representation of a practical voltage source is given by

(a) An impedance in parallel with ideal voltage source.

(b) One impedance in series and another in parallel with ideal voltage source.

(c) An impedance in series with ideal voltage source.

(d) None of these.

**31.** In the admittance locus diagram for a two branch parallel circuit given below,

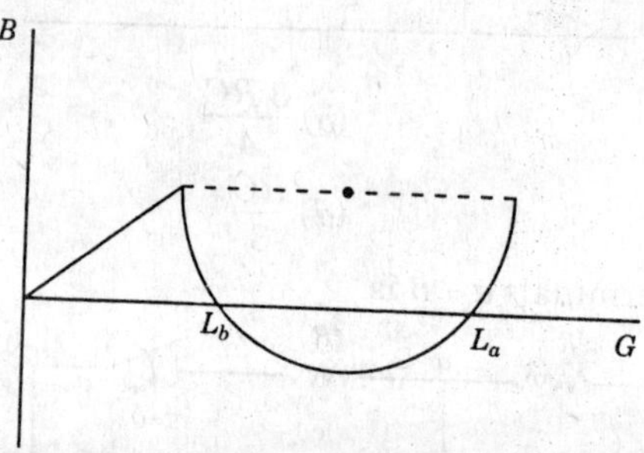


(a) $L_a < L_b$ (b) $L_a > L_b$

(c) p.f. at "a" leading (d) p.f. at "b" leading.

32. In the admittance locus diagram shown below

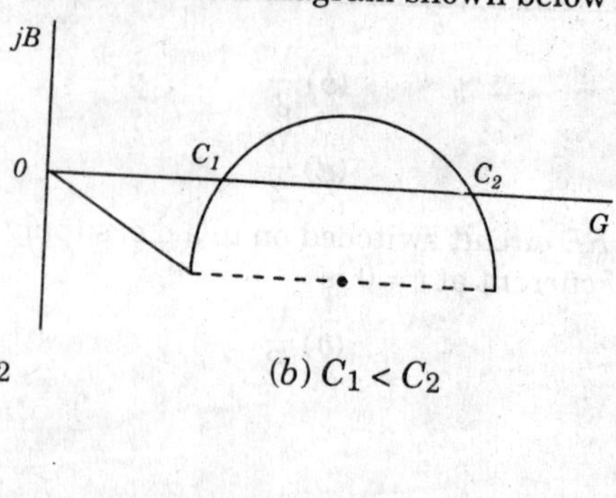


(a) $C_1 > C_2$ (b) $C_1 < C_2$

(c) $\omega_1 < \omega_2$ (d) $\omega_1 > \omega_2$

**33.** The locus diagram given below consists of a parallel combination of

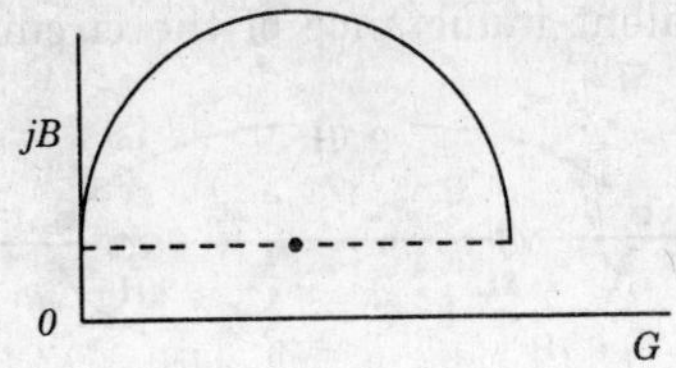


(a) L, $C_2$ (variable) and $C_1$ (b) R, $C_1$ series (variable) and $C_2$
(c) R, $C_2$ (variable) and $C_1$ (d) R (variable), $C_2$ series and $C_1$

**34.** The locus diagram given below consists of a parallel combination of

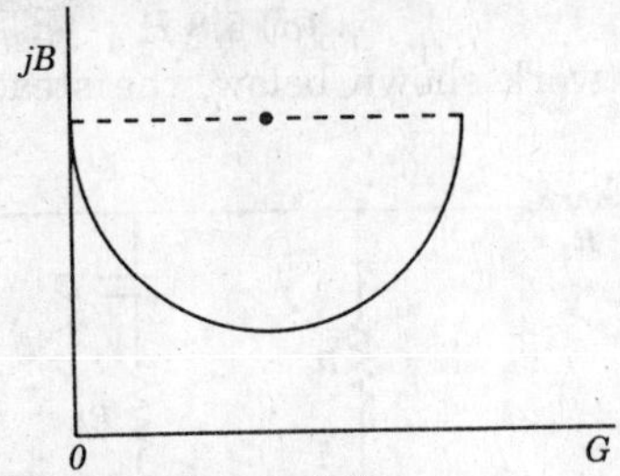


(a) R, C (variable) in series and C.
(b) R, L (variable) in series and C.
(c) R (variable), L in series and C.
(d) R, L in series and C (variable).

**35.** A simusoidal voltage V of fixed frequency is connected to a series circuit consisting fixed R and variable X. The current locus is
(a) a circle having radius V/2 R and center (0, V/2 R).
(b) a straight line having slope X/R.
(c) a semi-circle having radius V/2 R and center (0, V/2 R).
(d) a circle with R/2 as diameter and center (0, R/2).

**36.** A series circuit consisting of a resistor, inductor and capacitor resonates at a frequency of $\omega_0$. If the component values reduced to half. The new resonant frequency will be
(a) $\omega_0 /\sqrt{2}$ (b) $\omega_0 \sqrt{2}$
(c) $\omega_0 /2$ (d) $2\ \omega_0$

**37.** A network is shown below. Its equivalence at the terminals a – b will be

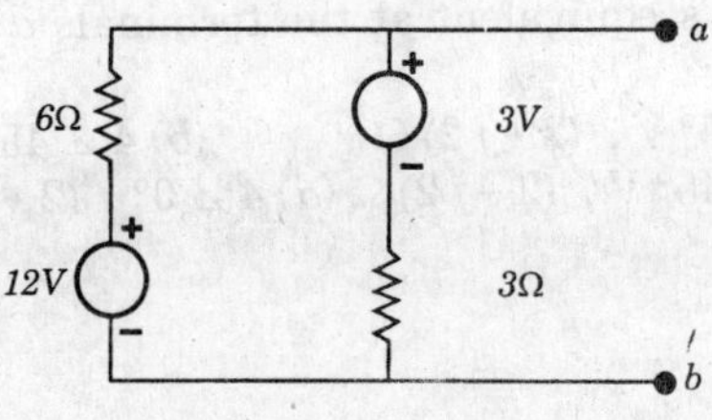

(*a*) a 6V source in series with 3Ω resistor.
(*b*) a 7.5V source in series with 7.5Ω resistor.
(*c*) a 6V source in series with 2Ω resistor.
(*d*) a 9V source in series with 6Ω resistor.

**38.** The equivalent inductance of the circuit between terminals $a - b$ is

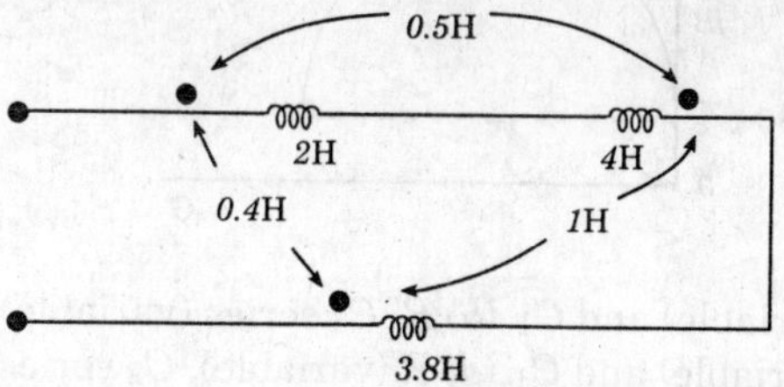


(*a*) 10 H (*b*) 12 H
(*c*) 6 H (*d*) 5.8 H

**39.** In the network shown below, the steady state value of the current is

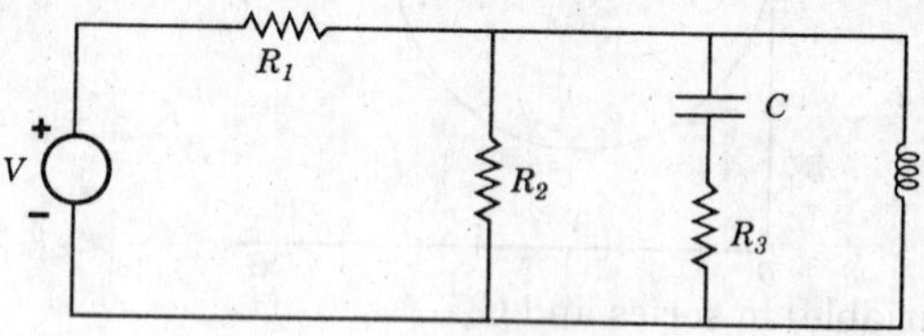


(*a*) $\frac{V}{R_2}$ (*b*) $\frac{V}{R_1}$
(*c*) $\frac{V}{R_1 + R_2}$ (*d*) $\frac{V}{R_3}$

**40.** In a series circuit $\omega_0$ = 400 rad./sec., $\omega_1$ = 200 rad./sec. $\omega_2$ is
(*a*) 1600 rad./sec. (*b*) 1200 rad./sec.
(*c*) 600 rad./sec. (*d*) 800 rad./sec.

**41.** In the circuit shown, the value of $C$ for u.p.f. is

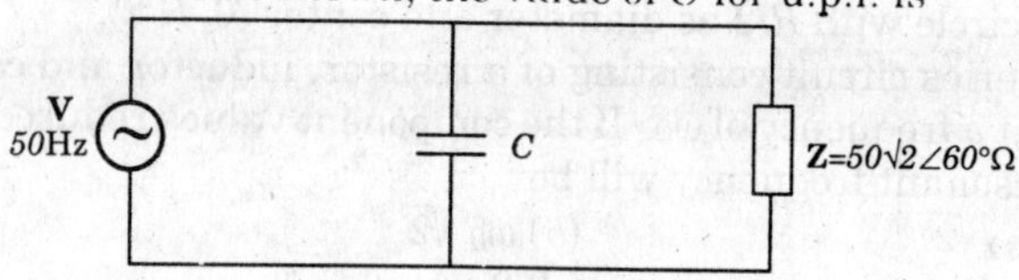


(*a*) 15.9 μF (*b*) 31.8 μF
(*c*) 63.6 μF (*d*) 47.7 μF

**42.** Thevenin's equivalent at the terminals $a - b$ of the network given is
(*a*) $4\sqrt{2} \angle 45° \, V$, $(2 + j\,2)\,\Omega$ (*b*) $4 \angle 45° \, V$, $(2 + j\,4)\,\Omega$
(*c*) $4\sqrt{2} \angle -45° \, V$, $(2 - j\,2)\,\Omega$ (*d*) $4 \angle 0°$, $(2 + j\,6)\,\Omega$

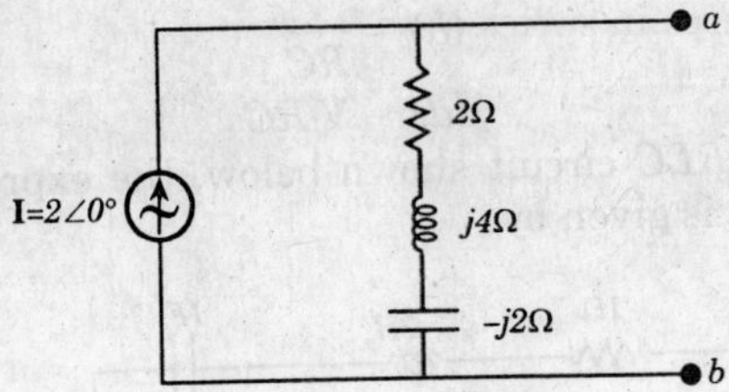


**43.** The switch is closed at $t = 0$. $\dfrac{dv\,(0^+)}{dt}$ is

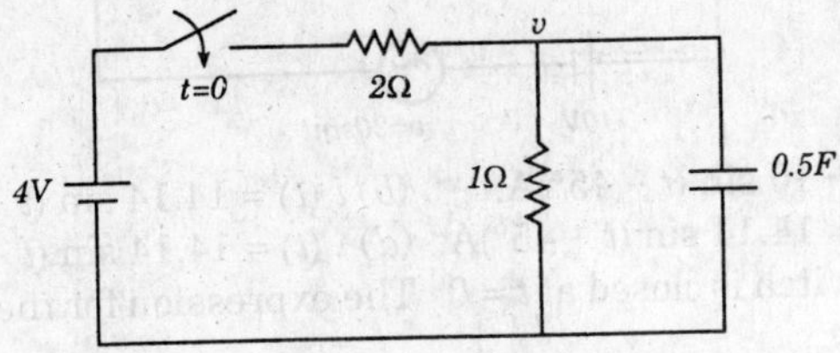


(*a*) 4 V/sec. (*b*) 2 V/sec.
(*c*) 8 V/sec. (*d*) 1 V/sec.

**44.** In the circuit shown below, the switch closed at $t = 0$. The steady state value of the capacitor voltage is

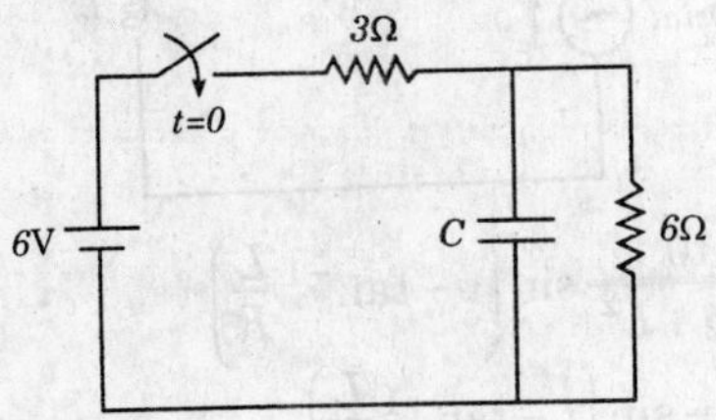


(*a*) 6 V (*b*) 3 V
(*c*) 9 V (*d*) 4 V

**45.** In the network, the value of the voltage $V$ is

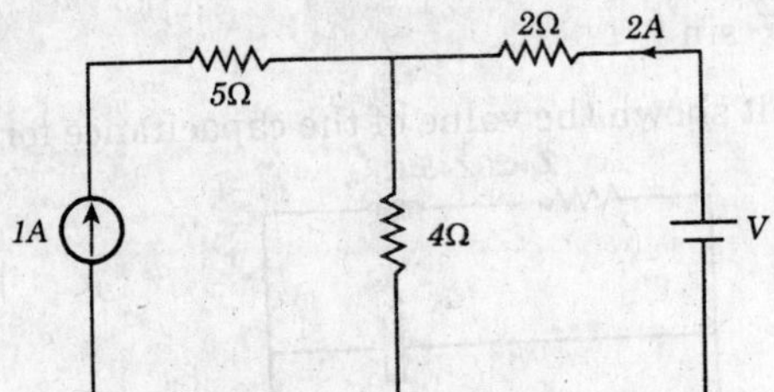


(*a*) 5 V (*b*) 16 V
(*c*) 4 V (*d*) 12 V

**46.** A series $RC$ circuit is connected to a d.c. supply voltage $V$. The rate of change voltage across the capacitor is

(a) $\frac{V}{RC}$ (b) $-\frac{V}{RC}$

(c) $V\,RC$ (d) $-V\,RC$

**47.** In a series *RLC* circuit shown below, the expression for the steady state current is given by

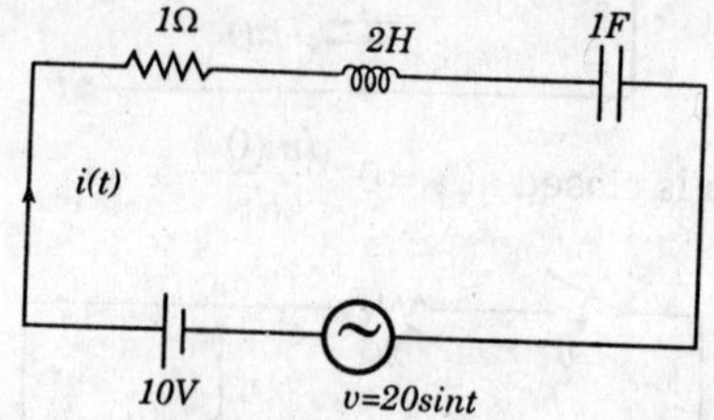


(a) $i(t) = 10\sin(t - 45°)$A. (b) $i(t) = 14.14\sin(t + 45°)$A.

(c) $i(t) = 14.14\sin(t + 45°)$A. (d) $i(t) = 14.14\sin(t - 45°)$A.

**48.** The switch is closed at $t = 0$. The expression for the steady state current is

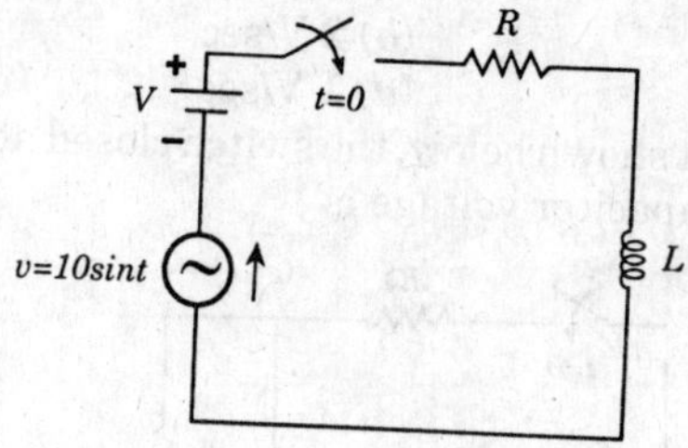


(a) $i(t) = \frac{V}{R} + \frac{10}{\sqrt{R2 + L^2}}\sin\left(t - \tan^{-1}\frac{L}{R}\right)$

(b) $i(t) = \frac{10\sqrt{2}}{\sqrt{R2 + L^2}}\sin\left(t - \tan^{-1}\frac{L}{R}\right)$

(c) $i(t) = \frac{V}{R}$

(d) $i(t) = \frac{10\sqrt{2}}{L}\sin t$

**49.** In the circuit shown the value of the capacitance for u.p.f. is

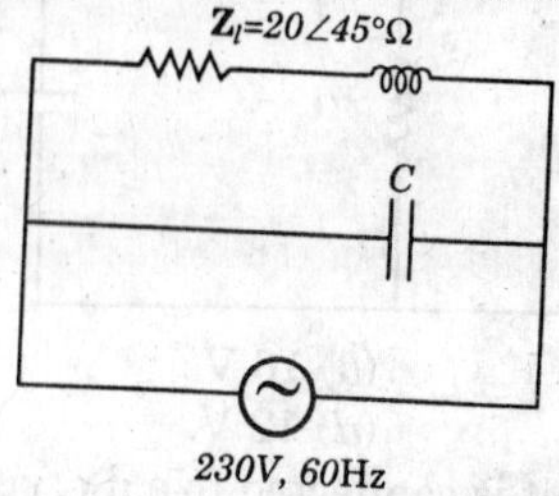

(*a*) 193 μF (*b*) 100 μF

(*c*) 53.8 μF (*d*) 93.8 μF

**50.** For the transient free response of the network given below, the switching time $t_0$ is

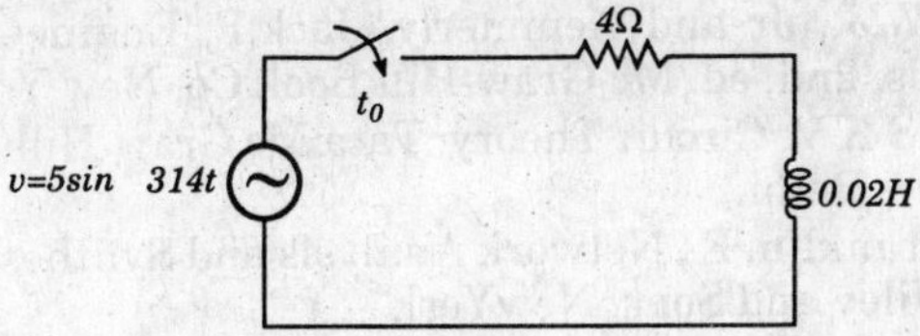


(*a*) 6.28 ms. (*b*) 5 ms.

(*c*) 3.19 ms. (*d*) 2 ms.

## ANSWERS

1. (*c*) 2. (*a*) 3. (*b*) 4. (*a*) 5. (*b*) 6. (*b*) 7. (*a*) 8. (*d*) 9. (*c*) 10. (*a*)
11. (*c*) 2. (*b*) 13. (*c*) 14. (*a*) 15. (*b*) 16. (*d*) 17. (*a*) 18. (*c*) 19. (*d*) 20. (*b*)
21. (*a*) 22. (*b*) 23. (*a*) 24. (*d*) 25. (*a*) 26. (*a*) 27. (*b*) 28. (*c*) 29. (*b*) 30. (*c*)
31. (*a*) 32. (*b*) 33. (*c*) 34. (*b*) 35. (*a*) 36. (*d*) 37. (*c*) 38. (*a*) 39. (*b*) 40. (*d*)
41. (*b*) 42. (*a*) 43. (*a*) 44. (*d*) 45. (*b*) 46. (*a*) 47. (*d*) 48. (*a*) 49. (*d*) 50. (*c*)

## REFERENCES


1. Cheng, David K., Analysis of Linear Systems, Addison - Wesley Publishing Co., Reading Mass.
2. Edminister, Joseph, A., Electrical Circuits, 1st.ed., Mc Graw-Hill. International Book Co., Singapore.
3. Hayt, W.J., Jr and Kemmerly, Jack.F, Engineering circuit Analysis, 2nd, ed. Mc Graw-Hill Book Co. New York.
4. Iyer, T S K V, Circuit Theory, Tata Mc Graw-Hill Publishing. Co., New Delhi.
5. K uo, Franklin. F., Network Analysis and Synthesis, 2nd. ed., John Wiley and Sons, NewYork
6. Reza, F.M. and Seeley, S. Modern Network Analysis, Mc Graw-Hill Book Co. , NewYork.
7. Roychowdhary, D.Roy, Networks and Systems, Wiley Eastern Ltd. , New Delhi.
8. Sudhakar, A and Shyammohan, S.P., Circuits and Networks, Tata Mc Graw-Hill, Publishing Co. New Delhi.
9. Van Valkendurg, M.E., Network Analysis, 3rd. ed. Prentice - Hall of India Ltd., New Delhi.

# INDEX

## U



## V



## Y



## Z